Discovering Computers

2006

A GATEWAY TO INFORMATION

Web Enhanced — INTRODUCTORY

Discovering Computers

2006

A GATEWAY TO INFORMATION

Web Enhanced — INTRODUCTORY

Gary B. Shelly
Thomas J. Cashman
Misty E. Vermaat

Contributing Authors

Jeffrey J. Quasney

Susan L. Sebok

Timothy J. Walker

Jeffrey J. Webb

Gary C. Kessler

THOMSON

COURSE TECHNOLOGY

COURSE TECHNOLOGY
25 THOMSON PLACE
BOSTON MA 02210

SHELLY
CASHMAN
SERIES.

Australia • Canada • Denmark • Japan • Mexico • New Zealand • Philippines • Puerto Rico • Singapore
South Africa • Spain • United Kingdom • United States

Discovering Computers 2006:
A Gateway to Information, Web Enhanced
Introductory

Gary B. Shelly

Thomas J. Cashman

Misty E. Vermaat

Managing Editor:
Alexandra Arnold

Series Consulting Editor:
Jim Quasney

Senior Acquisitions Editor:
Dana Merk

Product Manager:
Reed Cotter

Editorial Assistant:
Selena Coppock

Print Buyer:
Laura Burns

Production Editor:
Aimee Poirier

Researcher:
F. William Vermaat

Copy Editor:
Lyn Markowicz

Proofreader:
Nancy Lamm

Management Services:
Pre-Press Company, Inc.

Interior Designer:
Pre-Press Company, Inc.

Cover Image:
Pre-Press Company, Inc.

Illustrator:
Pre-Press Company, Inc.

Compositor:
Pre-Press Company, Inc.

Indexer:
Nancy Lamm

Printer:
Banta Menasha

Discovering Computers 2006

A GATEWAY TO INFORMATION

Web Enhanced — INTRODUCTORY

Contents

v

Special Feature
MAKING USE OF THE WEB 116

CHAPTER 3

Application Software 132

CHAPTER 4

The Components of the System Unit 182

CHAPTER 8

Operating Systems and Utility Programs 396

Special Feature
BUYER'S GUIDE 2006   **444**

CHAPTER 9

Communications and Networks 458

CHAPTER 10

Database Management

CHAPTER 11

Computer Security, Ethics, and Privacy

Special Feature

COMPUTER FORENSICS   **606**

Preface

The Shelly Cashman Series® offers the finest textbooks in computer education. We are proud of the fact that the previous ten editions of this textbook have been the most widely used in computer education. With each new edition of the book, we have implemented significant improvements based on current computer trends and comments made by instructors and students. *Discovering Computers 2006* continues with the innovation, quality, and reliability you have come to expect from the Shelly Cashman Series.

In *Discovering Computers 2006: A Gateway to Information*, you will find an educationally sound, highly visual, and easy-to-follow pedagogy that presents an in-depth treatment of introductory computer subjects. Students will finish the course with a solid understanding of computers, how to use computers, and how to access information on the World Wide Web.

OBJECTIVES OF THIS TEXTBOOK

Discovering Computers 2006: A Gateway to Information, Introductory is intended for use as a stand-alone textbook or in combination with an applications, Internet, or programming textbook in a one-quarter or one-semester introductory computer course. No experience with computers is assumed. The objectives of this book are to:

- Present the most-up-to-date technology in an ever-changing discipline
- Give students an in-depth understanding of why computers are essential components in business and society
- Teach the fundamentals of computers and computer nomenclature, particularly with respect to personal computer hardware and software, the World Wide Web, and enterprise computing
- Present the material in a visually appealing and exciting manner that motivates students to learn
- Assist students in planning a career and getting certified in the computer field
- Provide exercises and lab assignments that allow students to interact with a computer and learn by actually using the computer and the World Wide Web
- Present strategies for purchasing a desktop computer, a notebook computer, a Tablet PC, and a personal mobile device
- Offer alternative learning techniques and reinforcement via the Web
- Offer distance-education providers a textbook with a meaningful and exercise-rich companion Web site

DISTINGUISHING FEATURES

To date, more than six million students have learned about computers using a *Discovering Computers* textbook. With the additional World Wide Web integration and interactivity, streaming up-to-date audio and video, extraordinary step-by-step visual drawings and photographs, unparalleled currency, and the Shelly and Cashman touch, this book will make your computer concepts course exciting and dynamic. Distinguishing features of the Shelly Cashman Series *Discovering Computers* books include:

A Proven Pedagogy
Careful explanations of complex concepts, educationally-sound elements, and reinforcement highlight this proven method of presentation. A pictorial arrangement of the pedagogy can be found beginning on page xx.

A Visually Appealing Book that Maintains Student Interest
The latest technology, pictures, drawings, and text are combined artfully to produce a visually appealing and easy-to-understand book. Many of the figures include a step-by-step presentation

(see page 196), which simplifies the more complex computer concepts. Pictures and drawings reflect the latest trends in computer technology. Finally, the text is set in two columns, which instructors and reviewers say their students prefer. This combination of pictures, step-by-step drawings, and easy-to-read text layout sets a new standard for computer textbook design.

Latest Technologies and Terms

The technologies and terms your students see in this book are those they will encounter when they start using computers. Only the latest application software is shown throughout the book. New topics and terms include embedded computer, handtop computer, smart watch, fixed wireless, satellite modem, static Web page, dynamic Web page, hot spots, blog, moblogs, Internet telephony, Voice over IP, open source software, product activation, dual-core processor, liquid cooling technology, magnetic stripe card reader, magstripe reader, mouse gestures, picture messaging, native resolution, plasma monitor, satellite speakers, Blu-Ray disc, digital photo viewer, Hi-Speed USB, mini disc, pen drive, Serial Advanced Technology Attachment, anti-spam program, embedded Linux, file conversion utility, pop-up ad, pop-up blocker, scripts, spyware, spyware remover, Web filtering software, Windows Server System, WinFS, 802.11g, 802.11i, Centrino technology, hardware firewall, network standard, Wi-Fi mesh network, WiMAX, wireless Ethernet standard, wireless network card, 802.11i, back door, computer forensics, computer forensics specialist, cyberextortionist, cyberforensics, cyberterrorist, digital forensics, network forensics, phishing, script kiddie, spim, spoofing, war driving, war flying, Wi-Fi Protected Access, and wired equivalent privacy.

World Wide Web Enhanced

This book uses the World Wide Web as a major supplement. The purpose of integrating the World Wide Web into the book is to (1) offer students additional information and currency on important topics; (2) use its interactive capabilities to offer creative reinforcement and online quizzes; (3) make available alternative learning techniques with Web-based learning games, practice tests, and interactive labs; (4) underscore the relevance of the World Wide Web as a basic information tool that can be used in all facets of society; (5) introduce students to doing research on the Web; and (6) offer instructors the opportunity to organize and administer their traditional campus-based or distance-education-based courses on the Web using WebCT, Blackboard, or MyCourse 2.1. This textbook, however, does not depend on Web access to be used successfully. The Web access adds to the already complete treatment of topics within the book.

Extensive End-of-Chapter Materials

A notable strength of the *Discovering Computers* textbooks is the extensive student activities at the end of each chapter. Well-structured student activities can make the difference between students merely participating in a class and students retaining the information they learn. The activities in the *Discovering Computers 2006* books include: Chapter Review, Key Terms, Checkpoint, Learn It Online, Learn How To, Web Research, and Case Studies. A pictorial presentation of each end-of-chapter activities can be found beginning on page xx.

ORGANIZATION OF THIS TEXTBOOK

Discovering Computers 2006: A Gateway to Information, Introductory provides a thorough introduction to computers. The material is divided into eleven chapters, six special features, three appendices, and a glossary/index.

Chapter 1 – Introduction to Computers   In Chapter 1, students are introduced to basic computer concepts, such as what a computer is, how it works, and what makes it a powerful tool.

Special Feature – Timeline 2006 Milestones in Computer History   In this special feature, students learn about the major computer technology developments during the past 65 years.

Chapter 2 – The Internet and World Wide Web   In Chapter 2, students learn about the Internet, World Wide Web, browsers, e-mail, FTP, and instant messaging.

Special Feature – Making Use of the Web   In this special feature, more than 150 popular up-to-date Web sites are listed and described. Basic searching techniques also are introduced.

Chapter 3 – Application Software   In Chapter 3, students are introduced to a variety of business software, graphics and multimedia software, home/personal/educational software, and communications software.

Chapter 4 – The Components of the System Unit   In Chapter 4, students are introduced to the components of the system unit; how memory stores data, instructions, and information; and how the system unit executes an instruction.

Chapter 5 – Input   Chapter 5 describes the various techniques of input and commonly used input devices.

Special Feature – Personal Mobile Devices   In this special feature, students receive a detailed presentation of personal mobile device operating systems, built-in personal mobile device software, personal mobile device application software, and how to obtain and install personal mobile device software. Also included is a personal mobile device buyer's guide.

Chapter 6 – Output   Chapter 6 describes the various methods of output and commonly used output devices.

Special Feature – Digital Imaging and Video Technology   In this special feature, students are introduced to using a personal computer, digital camera, and video camera to manipulate photographs and video.

Chapter 7 – Storage   In Chapter 7, students learn about various storage media and storage devices.

Chapter 8 – Operating Systems and Utility Programs   In Chapter 8, students learn about a variety of stand-alone operating systems, network operating systems, and embedded operating systems.

Special Feature – Buyer's Guide 2006: How to Purchase a Personal Computer   In this special feature, students are introduced to purchasing a desktop computer, notebook computer, and Tablet PC.

Chapter 9 – Communications and Networks   Chapter 9 provides students with an overview of communications technology and applications.

Chapter 10 – Database Management   Chapter 10 presents students with the advantages of organizing data in a database and describes various types of data.

Chapter 11 – Computer Security, Ethics, and Privacy   In Chapter 11, students learn about computer and Internet risks, ethical issues surrounding information accuracy, intellectual property rights, codes of conduct, information privacy, and computer-related health issues.

Special Feature – Computer Forensics   This special feature introduces students to the scope of, process, and tools involved in computer forensics work. The feature underlines the importance of computer forensics in our increasingly digital world.

Appendix A – Coding Schemes and Number Systems   Appendix A presents the ASCII, EBCDIC, and Unicode coding schemes.

Appendix B – Quiz Yourself Answers   Appendix B provides the answers for the Quiz Yourself questions in the text.

Appendix C – Computer Acronyms   Appendix C summarizes the computer acronyms discussed in the book.

Glossary/Index   The Glossary/Index includes a definition and page references for every key term presented in the book.

SHELLY CASHMAN SERIES INSTRUCTOR RESOURCES

The Shelly Cashman Series is dedicated to providing you with all of the tools you need to make your class a success. Information on all supplementary materials is available through your Course Technology representative or by calling one of the following telephone numbers: Colleges and Universities, 1-800-648-7450; High Schools, 1-800-824-5179; Private Career Colleges, 1-800-347-7707; Canada, 1-800-268-2222; Corporations with IT Training Centers, 1-800-648-7450; and Government Agencies, Health-Care Organizations, and Correctional Facilities, 1-800-477-3692.

Instructor Resources CD-ROM

The Instructor Resources CD-ROM includes both teaching and testing aids. The contents of each item on the Instructor Resources CD-ROM (ISBN 0-619-25483-1) are described below.

Instructors Manual The Instructor's Manual is made up of Microsoft Word files, which include detailed lesson plans with page number references, lecture notes, classroom activities, discussion topics, and projects to assign.

Syllabus Sample syllabi, which can be customized easily to a course, are included. The syllabi cover policies, class and lab assignments and exams, and procedural information.

Figure Files Illustrations for every figure in the textbook are available in electronic form. Use this ancillary to present a slide show in lecture or to print transparencies for use in lecture with an overhead projector. If you have a personal computer and LCD device, this ancillary can be an effective tool for presenting lectures.

Solutions to Exercises Solutions are included for all end-of-chapter exercises.

Test Bank & Test Engine The ExamView test bank includes 220 questions for every chapter (50 multiple-choice, 100 true/false, and 70 completion) with page number references, and when appropriate, figure references. Each question also is identified by objective and type of term (primary or secondary). The test bank comes with a copy of the test engine, ExamView, the ultimate tool for your objective-based testing needs.

Printed Test Bank A Microsoft Word version of the test bank you can print also is included.

Test Out/Final Exam Use this objective-based test to test students out of your course, or use it as a final examination. A master answer sheet is included.

Pretest/Posttest Use these carefully prepared tests at the beginning and the end of the semester to measure student progress. A master answer sheet is included.

Data Files for Students All the files that are required by students to complete the exercises are included. You can distribute the files on the Instructor Resources CD-ROM to your students over a network, or you can have them follow the instructions on the inside back cover of this book to obtain a copy of the Data Disk.

Course Presenter

Course Presenter (ISBN 0-619-25484-X) is a one-click-per-slide presentation system on CD-ROM that provides PowerPoint slides for every subject in each chapter. Use this presentation system to give interesting, well-organized, and knowledge-based lectures. Several up-to-date G4TechTV computer-related video clips are available for optional presentation. Course Presenter provides consistent coverage for multiple lecturers.

Student Edition Labs

Thirty Web-based interactive labs will help your students master hundreds of computer concepts including input and output devices, file management and desktop applications, computer privacy, virus protection, and much more. Featuring up-to-the-minute content, eye-popping graphics, and rich animation, the highly interactive Student Edition Labs offer students an alternative way to learn through dynamic observation, step-by-step practice, and challenging review questions. Access the free Student Edition Labs from the *Discovering Computers 2006* Web site at scsite.com/dc2006 or see the Student Edition Lab exercises on the Learn It Online pages at the end of each chapter.

Online Content

Course Technology offers textbook-based content for Blackboard, WebCT, and MyCourse 2.1.

BlackBoard and WebCT As the leading provider of IT content for the Blackboard and WebCT platforms, Course Technology delivers rich content that enhances your textbook to give your students a unique learning experience.

MyCoure 2.1 MyCourse 2.1 is Course Technology's powerful online course management and content delivery system. MyCourse 2.1 allows nontechnical users to create, customize, and deliver Web-based courses; post content and assignments; manage student enrollment; administer exams; track results in the online grade book; and more.

SUPPLEMENTS

Two supplements can be used in combination with this textbook.

SAM Computer Concepts

Add the power of assessment and detailed reporting to your Student Edition Lab assignments with SAM Computer Concepts.

SAM (Skills Assessment Manager) Computer Concepts helps you energize your training assignments by allowing students to learn and quiz on important computer skills in an active, hands-on environment. By adding SAM Computer Concepts to your curriculum, you can:

- Reinforce your students' knowledge of key computer concepts with hands-on application exercises.
- Allow your students to "learn by listening," with rich audio in their computer concepts labs.
- Build computer concepts exams from a test bank of more than 50,000 objective-based questions or create your own test questions.
- Schedule your students' computer concepts training and testing assignments with powerful administrative tools.
- Track student exam grades and training progress using more than one dozen student and classroom reports.

Study Guide

This highly popular *Study Guide* (ISBN 0-619-25500-5) includes a variety of activities that help students recall, review, and master introductory computer concepts. The *Study Guide* complements the end-of-chapter material with a guided chapter outline; a self-test consisting of true/false, multiple-choice, short answer, fill-in, and matching questions; an entertaining puzzle; and other challenging exercises.

TO THE STUDENT...Getting the Most Out of Your Book

Welcome to *Discovering Computers 2006: A Gateway to Information, Web Enhanced*. You can save yourself a lot of time and gain a better understanding of the computer concepts presented in this book if you spend a few minutes reviewing this section.

1 Companion Web Site

Use the Companion Web site at scsite.com/dc2006, which includes additional information about important topics and provides unparalleled currency; and make use of online learning games, practice tests, and additional reinforcement. Gain access to this dynamic site with Course Technology's centralized login page, CoursePort.

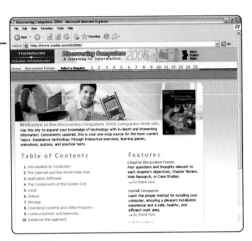

2 Picture Yourself

Picture yourself using the concepts presented in the chapter you are about to read. This section at the beginning of each chapter is intended to help you see how the specific material might apply to your everyday life using computers.

3 Chapter Objectives and Table of Contents

Before you read the chapter, carefully read through the Objectives and Contents so that you know what you should learn from the chapter.

4 Initial Chapter Figure

Carefully study the first figure in each chapter because it will give you an easy-to-follow overview of the major purpose of the chapter.

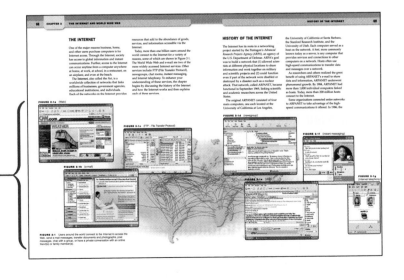

5 Web Link

Obtain current information
and a different perspective
about key terms and concepts
by visiting the Web addresses
in the Web Links found in the
margins throughout the book.

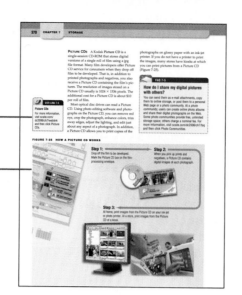

6 Step Figures

Each chapter includes numerous step figures that present
the more complex computer
concepts using a step-by-step
pedagogy.

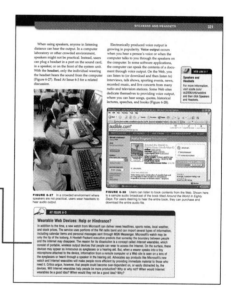

7 At Issue

At Issue boxes provide you
with computer-related controversial topics of the day and
stimulating questions that
offer insight into the general
concerns of computers in
society.

8 Looking Ahead

The Looking Ahead boxes offer you a
glimpse at the latest advances in computer technology that will be available,
usually within five years.

9 FAQ

FAQ (frequently asked questions) boxes offer common questions and answers about subjects related to the topic at hand.

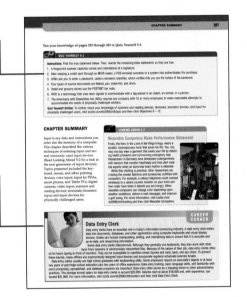

10 Quiz Yourself

Three Quiz Yourself boxes per chapter help ensure that you know the material you just read and are ready to move on in the chapter. Use the answers in Appendix B for a quick check of the answers, and take additional these quizzes on the Web for interactivity and easy use.

11 Career Corner

Each chapter ends with a Career Corner feature that introduces you to a computer-career opportunity relating to a topic covered in the chapter.

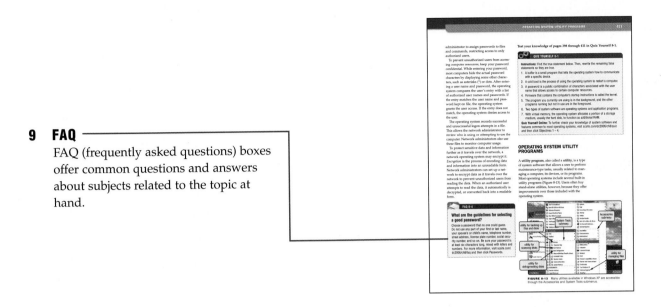

12 High-Tech Talk

If you are technically inclined, you will enjoy the High-Tech Talk article at the end of each chapter. These presentations expand on a topic covered in the chapter and present a more technical discussion.

13 Companies on the Cutting Edge

Each chapter includes a profile about two key computer-related companies of which you should be aware, especially if you plan to major in the computer field.

14 Technology Trailblazers

The Technology Trailblazers section in each chapter offers a glimpse into the life and times of the more famous leaders of the computer industry.

15 Chapter Review

Use the two-page Chapter Review before you take an examination to ensure that you are familiar with the computer concepts presented. This section includes each objective, followed by a one- or two-paragraph summary. Visit a Chapter Review page on the Web, and click the Audio button to listen to the Chapter Review.

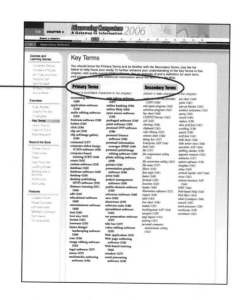

16 Primary and Secondary Key Terms

Before you take a test, use the Key Terms page as a checklist of terms you should know. In the text, primary key terms appear in bold font and secondary key terms appear in italic font. Ask your instructor whether you are responsible for knowing only the primary key terms or all the key terms. Visit a Key Terms page on the Web and click any term for additional information.

17 Checkpoint

Use these three pages of exercises to reinforce your understanding of the topics presented in the chapter.

18 Learn It Online

If you prefer online reinforcement, then the Learn It Online exercises are for you. The exercises include online videos, practice tests, interactive labs, learning games, and Web-based activities.

19 Learn How To

Apply what you learn in each chapter to your every day life with the Learn How To exercises. These hands-on activities solidify the concepts presented in the chapter with practical application.

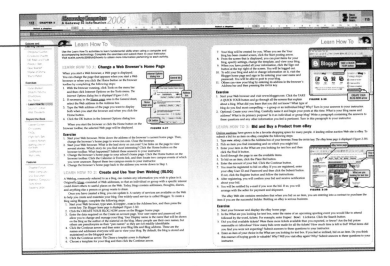

20 Web Research

If you enjoy doing research on the
Web, then you will like the Web
Research exercises. Each exercise in
this section references an element in
the book and suggests you write a
short article or do a class presentation
on your findings.

21 Case Studies

Exercise your mind and construct creative
solutions to the thought-provoking case
studies presented in each chapter. The
Case Study exercises are constructed to
discuss in class, research on your own, or
in a team environment.

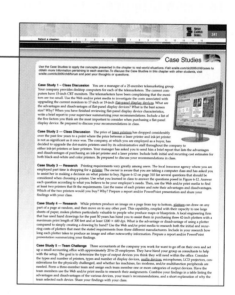

22 Special Features

Six special features following Chapters 1, 2, 5, 6, 8, and 11 encompass topics from the history of computers, to what's hot on the Web, to a buyer's guide, to the latest in new technology.

SHELLY CASHMAN SERIES – TRADITIONALLY BOUND TEXTBOOKS

The Shelly Cashman Series presents the following computer subjects in a variety of traditionally bound textbooks. For more information, see your Course Technology representative or call 1-800-648-7450. For Shelly Cashman Series information, visit Shelly Cashman Online at scseries.com

COMPUTERS	
Computers	Discovering Computers 2006: A Gateway to Information, Complete Discovering Computers 2006: A Gateway to Information, Introductory Discovering Computers 2006: A Gateway to Information, Brief Discovering Computers: Fundamentals, Second Edition Teachers Discovering Computers: Integrating Technology in the Classroom, Third Edition Essential Introduction to Computers, Sixth Edition (40-page)

WINDOWS APPLICATIONS	
Microsoft Office	Microsoft Office 2003: Essential Concepts and Techniques (5 projects) Microsoft Office 2003: Brief Concepts and Techniques (9 projects) Microsoft Office 2003: Introductory Concepts and Techniques, Second Edition (15 projects) Microsoft Office 2003: Advanced Concepts and Techniques (12 projects) Microsoft Office 2003: Post Advanced Concepts and Techniques (11 projects) Microsoft Office XP: Essential Concepts and Techniques (5 projects) Microsoft Office XP: Brief Concepts and Techniques (9 projects) Microsoft Office XP: Introductory Concepts and Techniques, Windows XP Edition (15 projects) Microsoft Office XP: Introductory Concepts and Techniques, Enhanced Edition (15 projects) Microsoft Office XP: Advanced Concepts and Techniques (11 projects) Microsoft Office XP: Post Advanced Concepts and Techniques (11 projects)
Integration	Teachers Discovering and Integrating Microsoft Office: Essential Concepts and Techniques, Second Edition Integrating Microsoft Office XP Applications and the World Wide Web: Essential Concepts and Techniques
PIM	Microsoft Outlook 2002: Essential Concepts and Techniques • Microsoft Office Outlook 2003: Introductory Concepts and Techniques
Microsoft Works	Microsoft Works 6: Complete Concepts and Techniques[1] • Microsoft Works 2000: Complete Concepts and Techniques[1]
Microsoft Windows	Microsoft Windows XP: Comprehensive Concepts and Techniques[2] Microsoft Windows XP: Brief Concepts and Techniques Microsoft Windows 2000: Comprehensive Concepts and Techniques[2] Microsoft Windows 2000: Brief Concepts and Techniques Microsoft Windows 98: Comprehensive Concepts and Techniques[2] Microsoft Windows 98: Essential Concepts and Techniques Introduction to Microsoft Windows NT Workstation 4
Notebook Organizer	Microsoft Office OneNote 2003: Introductory Concepts and Techniques
Word Processing	Microsoft Office Word 2003: Comprehensive Concepts and Techniques[2] • Microsoft Word 2002: Comprehensive Concepts and Techniques[2]
Spreadsheets	Microsoft Office Excel 2003: Comprehensive Concepts and Techniques[2] • Microsoft Excel 2002: Comprehensive Concepts and Techniques[2]
Database	Microsoft Office Access 2003: Comprehensive Concepts and Techniques[2] • Microsoft Access 2002: Comprehensive Concepts and Techniques[2]
Presentation Graphics	Microsoft Office PowerPoint 2003: Comprehensive Concepts and Techniques[2] • Microsoft PowerPoint 2002: Comprehensive Concepts and Techniques[2]
Desktop Publishing	Microsoft Office Publisher 2003: Comprehensive Concepts and Techniques[2] • Microsoft Publisher 2002: Comprehensive Concepts and Techniques[1]

PROGRAMMING	
Programming	Microsoft Visual Basic .NET: Comprehensive Concepts and Techniques[2] • Microsoft Visual Basic 6: Complete Concepts and Techniques[1] • Java Programming: Comprehensive Concepts and Techniques, Second Edition[2] • Structured COBOL Programming, Second Edition • Understanding and Troubleshooting Your PC • Programming Fundamentals Using Microsoft Visual Basic .NET

INTERNET	
Concepts	Discovering the Internet: Brief Concepts and Techniques • Discovering the Internet: Complete Concepts and Techniques
Browser	Microsoft Internet Explorer 6: Introductory Concepts and Techniques, Windows XP Edition • Microsoft Internet Explorer 5: An Introduction • Netscape Navigator 6: An Introduction
Web Page Creation	Web Design: Introductory Concepts and Techniques • HTML: Comprehensive Concepts and Techniques, Third Edition[2] • Microsoft Office FrontPage 2003: Comprehensive Concepts and Techniques[2] • Microsoft FrontPage 2002: Comprehensive Concepts and Techniques[2] • Microsoft FrontPage 2002: Essential Concepts and Techniques • JavaScript: Complete Concepts and Techniques, Second Edition[1] • Macromedia Dreamweaver MX: Comprehensive Concepts and Techniques[2]

SYSTEMS ANALYSIS	
Systems Analysis	Systems Analysis and Design, Sixth Edition

DATA COMMUNICATIONS	
Data Communications	Business Data Communications: Introductory Concepts and Techniques, Fourth Edition

[1]Also available as an Introductory Edition, which is a shortened version of the complete book, [2]Also available as an Introductory Edition and as a Complete Edition, which are shortened versions of the comprehensive book.

Discovering Computers
2006
A GATEWAY TO INFORMATION

CHAPTER ONE

Introduction to Computers

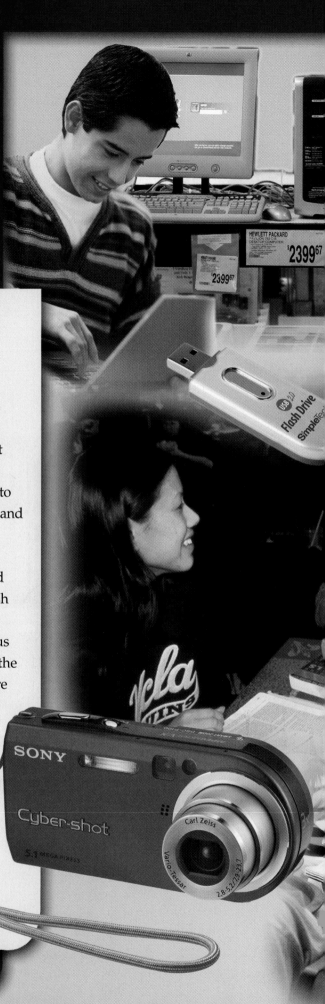

Picture Yourself in a Computer Class

While waiting for the instructor to begin her first lecture, you hear several classmates announce they will be meeting at the local coffee house to talk about homework and form study groups. Many of them sound nervous and anxious about this Introduction to Computers class. As they talk, you think about your experiences with computers. You had a beginning programming class in high school. You use the Internet regularly to chat with friends. With your digital camera, you take pictures and e-mail them to family members. No study groups for you.

During the lecture, the instructor reads several computer advertisements to the class. The ads use computer terms and acronyms you have never heard, like bus, SDRAM, USB flash drive, TFT, media player, SCSI, HT Technology, Bluetooth, Ethernet, firewall, NIC, and Wi-Fi. Now, *you* get a bit nervous and anxious. When she finishes reading, the instructor tells the class not to worry if some or most of the words in the ads are unfamiliar. "As we work through this course together," she says, "you will learn everything you need to know to buy a computer." While walking out the classroom door, you ask your friend, "What time is everyone meeting at the coffee house? I want to get in one of those study groups."

Read Chapter 1 to become familiar with some of the terms mentioned in the advertisement, discover practical uses of computers, and set a foundation for your further learning throughout this book.

A WORLD OF COMPUTERS

Computers are everywhere: at work, at school, and at home. Many daily activities either involve the use of or depend on information from a computer. As shown in Figure 1-1, people use all types and sizes of computers for a variety of reasons and in a range of places. Some computers sit on top of a desk or on the floor; others are small enough to carry.

Computers are a primary means of communication for billions of people. People use computers to correspond with businesses, employees with other employees and customers, students with teachers, and family members with friends and other family members. In addition to corresponding via text messages, people use computers to send each other pictures, diagrams, drawings, music, and videos.

Through computers, society has instant access to information from around the globe. Local and national news, weather reports, sports scores, airline schedules, telephone directories, maps and directions, job listings, credit reports, and countless forms of educational material always are accessible. From the computer, you can meet new friends, share photographs and videos, shop, fill prescriptions, file taxes, or take a course.

At home or while on the road, people use computers to manage schedules, balance checkbooks, pay bills, track personal income and expenses, transfer funds, and buy or sell stocks. Banks place automated teller machines (ATMs) all over the world, making it easy for customers to deposit or withdraw funds at anytime. At the grocery store, a computer tracks purchases, calculates the amount of money due, and often

FIGURE 1-1 People use computers in their daily activities.

generates coupons customized to buying patterns. Vehicles include onboard navigation systems that provide directions, call for emergency services, and track the vehicle if it is stolen.

In the workplace, employees use computers to create correspondence such as e-mail messages, memos, and letters; calculate payroll; track inventory; and generate invoices. Some applications such as automotive design and weather forecasting use computers to perform complex mathematical calculations. At school, teachers use computers to assist with classroom instruction. Students complete assignments and do research on computers in lab rooms and at home.

People also spend hours of leisure time on the computer. They play games, listen to music, watch videos and movies, read books and magazines, research genealogy, compose music and videos, retouch photographs, and plan vacations.

As technology continues to advance, computers are becoming more a part of everyday life. Thus, many people believe that computer literacy is vital to success in today's world. **Computer literacy** involves having a knowledge and understanding of computers and their uses.

This book presents the knowledge you need to be computer literate. As you read this first chapter, keep in mind it is an overview. Many of the terms and concepts introduced in this chapter will be discussed in more depth later in the book.

WHAT IS A COMPUTER?

A **computer** is an electronic device, operating under the control of instructions stored in its own memory, that can accept data, process the data according to specified rules, produce results, and store the results for future use.

Data and Information

Computers process data into information. **Data** is a collection of unprocessed items, which can include text, numbers, images, audio, and video. **Information** conveys meaning and is useful to people.

As shown in Figure 1-2, for example, computers process several data items to print information in the form of a payroll check.

FAQ 1-1

Is data a singular or plural word?

The word data is plural for datum. With respect to computers, however, it is accepted and common practice to use the word data in both the singular and plural context. For more information, visit scsite.com/dc2006/ch1/faq and then click Data.

An **FAQ** (frequently asked question) helps you find answers to commonly asked questions. Web sites often post an FAQ section, and each chapter in this book includes FAQ boxes related to topics in the text.

Information Processing Cycle

Computers process data (input) into information (output). A computer often holds data, information, and instructions in storage for future use. *Instructions* are the steps that tell the computer how to perform a particular task. Some people refer to the series of input, process, output, and storage activities as the *information processing cycle.*

Most computers today can communicate with other computers. As a result, communications also has become an essential element of the information processing cycle.

DATA

Kayla Robertson
1192 Reeder Road
Hammond, IN 46323
$12.50 per hour
28 hours

PROCESSES

- Multiplies hourly pay rate by hours to determine gross pay (350.00)
- Organizes data
- Computes payroll taxes (49.00)
- Subtracts payroll taxes from gross pay to determine net pay (301.00)

INFORMATION

FIGURE 1-2   A computer processes data into information. In this simplified example, the employee's name and address, hourly pay rate, and hours worked all represent data. The computer processes the data to produce the payroll check (information).

THE COMPONENTS OF A COMPUTER

A computer contains many electric, electronic, and mechanical components known as **hardware**. These components include input devices, output devices, a system unit, storage devices, and communications devices. Figure 1-3 shows some common computer hardware components.

Input Devices

An **input device** is any hardware component that allows you to enter data and instructions into a computer. Six widely used input devices are the keyboard, mouse, microphone, scanner, digital camera, and PC video camera (Figure 1-3).

A computer keyboard contains keys you press to enter data into the computer. A mouse is a small handheld device. With the mouse, you control movement of a small symbol on the screen, called the pointer, and you make selections from the screen.

A microphone allows a user to speak into the computer to enter data and instructions. A scanner converts printed material (such as text and pictures) into a form the computer can use.

With a digital camera, you take pictures and then transfer the photographed images to the computer or printer instead of storing the images on traditional film. A PC video camera is a digital video camera that allows users to create a movie or take still photographs electronically.

WEB LINK 1-1

Input Devices
For more information, visit scsite.com/dc2006/ch1/weblink and then click Input Devices.

FIGURE 1-3 Common computer hardware components include a keyboard, mouse, microphone, scanner, digital camera, PC video camera, printer, monitor, speakers, system unit, disk drives, USB flash drive, card reader/writer, and modem.

Output Devices

An **output device** is any hardware component that conveys information to one or more people. Three commonly used output devices are a printer, a monitor, and speakers (Figure 1-3 on the previous page).

A printer produces text and graphics on a physical medium such as paper. A monitor displays text, graphics, and videos on a screen. Speakers allow you to hear music, voice, and other audio (sounds).

System Unit

The **system unit** is a case that contains the electronic components of the computer that are used to process data (Figure 1-3). The circuitry of the system unit usually is part of or is connected to a circuit board called the motherboard.

Two main components on the motherboard are the processor and memory. The *processor* is the electronic component that interprets and carries out the basic instructions that operate the computer. *Memory* consists of electronic components that store instructions waiting to be executed and data needed by those instructions. Although some forms of memory are permanent, most memory keeps data and instructions temporarily, which means its contents are erased when the computer is shut off.

WEB LINK 1-2

Output Devices

For more information, visit scsite.com/dc2006/ch1/weblink and then click Output Devices.

FAQ 1-2

What is a CPU?

The processor. Most people in the computer industry use the terms *CPU* (*central processing unit*) and processor to mean the same. For more information, visit scsite.com/dc2006/ch1/faq and then click CPU.

Storage Devices

Storage holds data, instructions, and information for future use. For example, computers can store hundreds or millions of customer names and addresses. Storage holds these items permanently.

A computer keeps data, instructions, and information on **storage media**. Examples of storage media are floppy disks, Zip disks, USB flash drives, hard disks, CDs, DVDs,

---

and memory cards. A **storage device** records (writes) and/or retrieves (reads) items to and from storage media. Drives and readers/writers, which are types of storage devices (Figure 1-3), accept a specific kind of storage media. For example, a CD drive (storage device) accepts a CD (storage media). Storage devices often function as a source of input because they transfer items from storage to memory.

A floppy disk consists of a thin, circular, flexible disk enclosed in a square-shaped plastic shell that is inserted in and removed from a floppy disk drive. A typical floppy disk stores up to about 1.4 million characters. A Zip disk looks similar to a floppy disk but has much greater storage capabilities — up to about 750 million characters. You insert Zip disks in and remove them from Zip drives.

A USB flash drive is a portable storage device that has much more storage capacity than a floppy disk but is small and lightweight enough to be transported on a keychain or in a pocket (Figure 1-3). You plug a USB flash drive in a special, easily accessible opening on the computer.

A hard disk provides much greater storage capacity than a floppy disk, Zip disk, or USB flash drive. The average hard disk can hold more than 80 billion characters. Hard disks are enclosed in an airtight, sealed case. Although some are removable, most are housed inside the system unit (Figure 1-4).

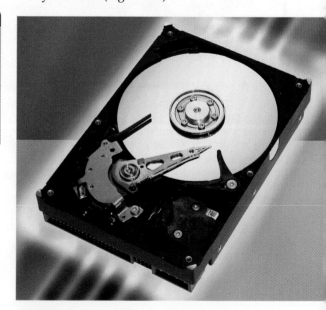

FIGURE 1-4 Hard disks are self-contained devices. The hard disk shown here must be installed in the system unit before it can be used.

A compact disc is a flat, round, portable metal disc with a plastic coating. One type of compact disc is a CD-ROM, which you can access using most CD and DVD drives (Figure 1-5). Another type of compact disc is a DVD-ROM, some of which have enough storage capacity to store two full-length movies. To use a DVD-ROM, you need a DVD drive.

Some portable devices, such as digital cameras, use memory cards as the storage media. You then can transfer the stored items, such as electronic photographs, from the memory card to a computer or printer using a card reader/writer (Figure 1-3 on page 7).

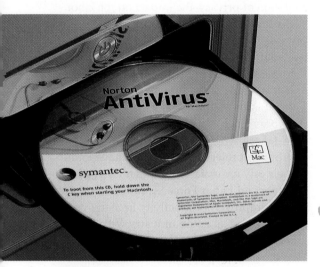

FIGURE 1-5 To use a CD or DVD, you need a CD or DVD drive.

Communications Devices

A **communications device** is a hardware component that enables a computer to send (transmit) and receive data, instructions, and information to and from one or more computers. A widely used communications device is a modem (Figure 1-3).

Communications occur over cables, telephone lines, cellular radio networks, satellites, and other transmission media. Some transmission media, such as satellites and cellular radio networks, are wireless, which means they have no physical lines or wires.

WEB LINK 1-3

Communications Devices

For more information, visit scsite.com/ dc2006/ch1/weblink and then click Communications Devices.

ADVANTAGES AND DISADVANTAGES OF USING COMPUTERS

Society has reaped many benefits from using computers. Both business and home users can make well-informed decisions because they have instant access to information from anywhere in the world. A **user** is anyone who communicates with a computer or utilizes the information it generates. Students, another type of user, have more tools to assist them in the learning process. Read Looking Ahead 1-1 for a look at the next generation of benefits from using computers.

LOOKING AHEAD 1-1

Bionic People Benefit from Processor Implants

Computers eventually will become an integral part of the human body. They already are used to help some hearing-impaired people hear by stimulating the nerves within the ear and to help the vision-impaired to see by converting light into electrical impulses.

The next step will involve implanting miniature computers or computer components in the body to help it perform basic functions. A processor, for example, could help release hormones. A brain computer interface may monitor and treat diseases, such as epilepsy and depression, that affect brain activity. A body-scanning machine will evaluate patients' pain when they cannot communicate.

In addition, robotic legs strapped to the body can assist people such as firefighters and soldiers who must bear heavy loads for extended periods of time. For more information, visit scsite.com/dc2006/ch1/looking and then click Processor Implants.

ADVANTAGES OF USING COMPUTERS Benefits of computers are possible because computers have the advantages of speed, reliability, consistency, storage, and communications.

- **Speed**: Computer operations occur through electronic circuits. When data, instructions, and information flow along these circuits, they travel at incredibly fast speeds. Many computers process billions or trillions of operations in a single second. Processing involves computing (adding, subtracting, multiplying, dividing), sorting (e.g., alphabetizing), organizing, formatting, checking spelling and grammar, charting, displaying pictures, recording audio clips, playing music, and showing a movie. For a more technical discussion about how computers process data, read the High-Tech Talk article on page 38.
- **Reliability**: The electronic components in modern computers are dependable and reliable because they rarely break or fail.
- **Consistency**: Given the same input and processes, a computer will produce the same results — consistently. Computers generate error-free results, provided the input is correct and the instructions work. A computing phrase — known as *garbage in, garbage out* — points out that the accuracy of a computer's output depends on the accuracy of the input. For example, if you do not use the flash on a digital camera when indoors, the resulting pictures that are displayed on the computer screen may be unusable because they are too dark.
- **Storage**: A computer can transfer data quickly from storage to memory, process it, and then store it again for future use. Many computers store enormous amounts of data and make this data available for processing anytime it is needed.
- **Communications**: Most computers today can communicate with other computers, often wirelessly. Computers with this capability can share any of the four information processing cycle operations — input, process, output, and storage — with another computer or a user.

DISADVANTAGES OF USING COMPUTERS Some disadvantages of computers relate to the violation of privacy, the impact on the labor force, health risks, and the impact on the environment.

- **Violation of Privacy**: Nearly every life event is stored in a computer somewhere…in medical records, credit reports, tax records, etc. It is crucial that personal and confidential records be protected properly. In many instances, where these records were not properly protected, individuals have found their privacy violated and identities stolen.
- **Impact on Labor Force**: Although computers have improved productivity in many ways and created an entire industry with hundreds of thousands of new jobs, the skills of millions of employees have been replaced by computers. Thus, it is crucial that workers keep their education up-to-date. A separate impact on the labor force is that some companies are outsourcing jobs to foreign countries instead of keeping their homeland labor force employed. Read At Issue 1-1 for a related discussion.

AT ISSUE 1-1

Is Job Outsourcing Inevitable?

To cut costs, some companies are replacing their homeland workers with workers in foreign countries. Many of these displaced workers are computer professionals. In an age of high-speed computer communications, companies believe that computer professionals in countries such as India, China, and Russia can be as effective as, and far less expensive than, their homeland counterparts. Corporate executives claim that outsourcing increases profits, thereby benefiting shareholders and supporting investment in other areas, which in turn creates new jobs. But disgruntled former employees insist that offshore outsourcing hinders technology development, forces customers to deal with workers who have a limited understanding of a country's native language and culture, and endangers national security. In the United States, legislation has been proposed to combat offshore outsourcing, including laws to deny federal funding for companies that outsource, provide tax breaks for companies that do not outsource, or force companies to make their outsourcing practices public, so that consumers can make informed choices. Should companies replace homeland workers with workers in foreign countries? Why or why not? What, if anything, should be done to counter the trend to outsource overseas? Why? Should workers simply accept that, to compete in today's global marketplace, they must develop more flexible skills or be willing to do more for less?

- **Health Risks**: Prolonged or improper computer use can lead to injuries or disorders of the hands, wrists, elbows, eyes, neck, and back. Computer users can protect themselves from these health risks through proper workplace design, good posture while at the computer, and appropriately spaced work breaks.

- **Impact on Environment**: Computer manufacturing processes and computer waste are depleting natural resources and polluting the environment. The amount of resources required to manufacture a personal computer equals that of a mid-sized car. When computers are discarded in landfills, they release toxic materials and potentially dangerous levels of lead, mercury, and flame retardants. Strategies that can help protect the environment include recycling, regulating manufacturing processes, extending the life of computers, and immediately donating replaced computers.

Test your knowledge of pages 4 through 11 in Quiz Yourself 1-1.

QUIZ YOURSELF 1-1

Instructions: Find the true statement below. Then, rewrite the remaining false statements so they are true.

1. A computer is a motorized device that processes output into input.

2. A storage device records (reads) and/or retrieves (writes) items to and from storage media.

3. An output device is any hardware component that allows you to enter data and instructions into a computer.

4. Computer literacy involves having a knowledge and understanding of computers and their uses.

5. Computers have the disadvantages of fast speeds, high failure rates, producing consistent results, storing small amounts of data, and communicating with others.

6. Three commonly used input devices are a printer, a monitor, and speakers.

Quiz Yourself Online: To further check your knowledge of computer literacy, computers and their components, and the advantages and disadvantages of computers, visit scsite.com/dc2006/ch1/quiz and then click Objectives 1 – 4.

NETWORKS AND THE INTERNET

A **network** is a collection of computers and devices connected together via communications devices and transmission media. When a computer connects to a network, it is **online**.

Networks allow computers to share *resources*, such as hardware, software, data, and information. Sharing resources saves time and money. In many networks, one or more computers act as a server. The *server* controls access to the resources on a network. The other computers on the network, each called a *client* or workstation, request resources from the server (Figure 1-6). The major differences between the server and client computers are that the server ordinarily has more power, more storage space, and expanded communications capabilities.

Many homes and most businesses and schools network their computers and devices. Home networks usually are small, existing within a single structure, and often are wireless. Business and school networks can be small, such as in a room or building, or widespread, connecting computers across a city, country, or the globe. The world's largest computer network is the Internet.

FIGURE 1-6 A server manages the resources on a network, and clients access the resources on the server. This network enables three separate computers to share the same printer, one wirelessly.

The Internet

The **Internet** is a worldwide collection of networks that connects millions of businesses, government agencies, educational institutions, and individuals (Figure 1-7).

More than one billion people around the world use the Internet daily for a variety of reasons, including the following purposes:

• Communicate with and meet other people
• Access a wealth of information, news, and research findings
• Shop for goods and services
• Bank and invest
• Take a class
• Access sources of entertainment and leisure, such as online games, music, videos, books, and magazines

WEB LINK 1-4

The Internet
For more information, visit scsite.com/dc2006/ch1/weblink and then click Internet.

Figure 1-8 shows examples in each of these areas.

People connect to the Internet to exchange information with others around the world. E-mail allows you to send messages to other users. With instant messaging, you can have a live conversation with another connected user. In a chat room, you can communicate with multiple users at the same time — much like a group discussion.

Businesses, called access providers, offer users and companies access to the Internet free or for a fee. By subscribing to an access provider, you can use your computer and a communications device, such as a modem, to connect to the many services of the Internet.

The Web, short for World Wide Web, is one of the more popular services on the Internet. Think of the Web as a global library of information available to anyone connected to the Internet. The **Web** contains billions of documents called Web pages. A **Web page** can contain text, graphics, audio, and video. The six screens shown in Figure 1-8 are examples of Web pages. Web pages often have built-in connections, or links, to other documents, graphics, other Web pages, or Web sites. A Web site is a collection of related Web pages.

FIGURE 1-7 The Internet is the largest computer network, connecting millions of computers around the world.

FIGURE 1-8b (access information)

FIGURE 1-8a (communicate)

FIGURE 1-8c (shop)

FIGURE 1-8f (access sources of entertainment)

FIGURE 1-8d (bank and invest)

FIGURE 1-8e (take a class)

FIGURE 1-8 Users access the Internet for a variety of reasons: to communicate with others, to access a wealth of information, to shop for goods and services, to bank and invest, to take a class, and for entertainment.

In addition to accessing and using information on the Web, many people use the Web as a means to share personal information, photographs, videos, or artwork with the world. Anyone can create a Web page and then make it available, or *publish* it, on the Internet for others to see (read At Issue 1-2 for a related discussion). A **photo sharing community**, for example, is a Web site that allows users to create an online photo album and store their electronic photographs (Figure 1-9). Some Web sites provide publishing services free.

FAQ 1-3

What do consumers buy on the Internet?

A recent survey found that online consumers spend the most on clothing, as shown in the chart to the right. For more information, visit scsite.com/dc2006/ch1/faq and then click Internet Purchases.

Online Spending Trends
(during a six-week period)

Clothing
Toys/Video Games
Electronics
Videos/DVDs
Books

0   0.5   1   1.5   2   2.5
Billions of Dollars

Source: Smart Computing

FIGURE 1-9 This proud dog owner posts pictures of her boxers to a photo sharing community.

AT ISSUE 1-2

Is Everything on the Web True?

Recently, a California city council considered banning foam cups when an official-looking Web page revealed that dihydrogen monoxide, which was characterized as a potentially dangerous chemical, was used to produce the cups. The council later was chagrined to discover that the information at the Web site was a hoax. That is, while dihydrogen monoxide is used in making foam cups, it hardly is dangerous — dihydrogen monoxide is the scientific name for water (H_2O). Many people think that anything in print is true, even what they read on the Web. Yet, authors with a wide range of expertise, authority, motives, and biases create Web pages. Web pages can be as accurate as the most scholarly journal, or no truer than the most disreputable supermarket tabloid. The Web makes it easy to obtain information, but Web page readers must make an extra effort to determine the quality of that information. In evaluating a Web page, experts suggest that you consider such factors as the purpose, scope, sponsor, timeliness, presentation, author, and permanence of the page. Ultimately, who is responsible for the accuracy of information on the Web? Why? What factors are most important in evaluating the accuracy of a Web page? Why?

COMPUTER SOFTWARE

Software, also called a **program**, consists of a series of instructions that tells the computer what to do and how to do it.

You interact with a program through its user interface. The user interface controls how you enter data and instructions and how information is displayed on the screen. Software today often has a graphical user interface. With a **graphical user interface (GUI** pronounced gooey), you interact with the software using text, graphics, and visual images such as icons (Figure 1-10). An *icon* is a miniature image that represents a program, an instruction, or some other object. You can use the mouse to select icons that perform operations such as starting a program.

The two categories of software are system software and application software. The following sections describe these categories of software.

System Software

System software consists of the programs that control or maintain the operations of the computer and its devices. System software serves as the interface between the user, the application software, and the computer's hardware. Two types of system software are the operating system and utility programs.

OPERATING SYSTEM   An *operating system* is a set of programs that coordinates all the activities among computer hardware devices. It provides a means for users to communicate with the computer and other software. Many of today's computers use Windows XP, which is one of Microsoft's operating systems (Figure 1-10).

When a user starts a computer, portions of the operating system load into memory from the computer's hard disk. It remains in memory while the computer is on.

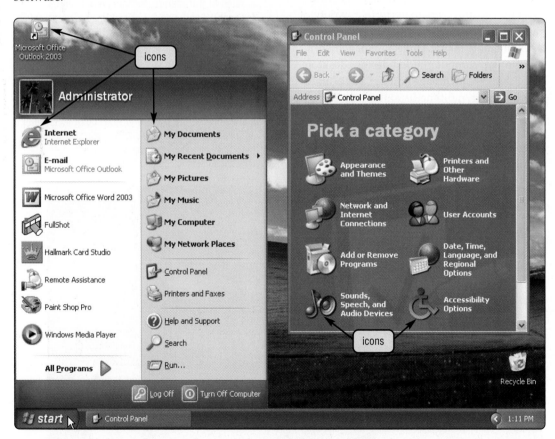

FIGURE 1-10   The graphical user interface of Windows XP.

WEB LINK 1-5

Computer Programs

For more information, visit scsite.com/ dc2006/ch1/weblink and then click Computer Programs.

UTILITY PROGRAM   A *utility program* allows a user to perform maintenance-type tasks usually related to managing a computer, its devices, or its programs. Most operating systems include several utility programs for managing disk drives, printers, and other devices. You also can buy utility programs that allow you to perform additional computer management functions.

Application Software

Application software consists of programs designed to make users more productive and/or assist them with personal tasks. A widely used type of application software related to communications is a Web browser, which allows users with an Internet connection to access and view Web pages. Other popular application software includes word processing software, spreadsheet software, database software, and presentation graphics software.

Many other types of application software exist that enable users to perform a variety of tasks. These include personal information management, note taking, project management, accounting, computer-aided design, desktop publishing, paint/image editing, audio and video editing, multimedia authoring, Web page authoring, personal finance, legal, tax preparation, home design/landscaping, education, reference, and entertainment (e.g., games or simulations, etc.). As shown in Figure 1-11,

you can purchase application software from a store that sells computer products. Read At Issue 1-3 for a related discussion.

AT ISSUE 1-3

Can Computers Provoke Violence?

Grand Theft Auto is one of today's most popular computer games. In the game, players advance through the mafia by conveying secret packages, following alleged snitches, and planting car bombs. Since its release, shoppers have bought millions of copies of Grand Theft Auto. Purchasers praise the game's vivid graphics, edgy characters, and wide range of allowable behaviors. Some parents and politicians, however, condemn the game's explicit violence and the rewards it gives players for participating in illegal acts. They fear that games like Grand Theft Auto eventually could corrupt players, perhaps leading to antisocial or criminal behavior. Grand Theft Auto is aimed at older gamers who grew up with Mario but now are looking for something more radical. The game is rated M (for Mature, meaning it is suitable for ages 17 and older), but children as young as 12 have purchased and played with it. Even worse, critics fear that the game's popularity may influence future developers of computer games aimed at younger children. What impact, if any, do violent computer games or games that promote unacceptable acts have on individual behavior? Do these games desensitize players to violence or increase aggression? Why or why not? Should restrictions be placed on sales of computer games?

FIGURE 1-11   Stores that sell computer products have shelves stocked with software for sale.

Installing and Running Programs

The instructions in a program are stored on storage media such as a hard disk or compact disc. When purchasing software from a computer store, you typically receive a box that includes a CD(s) or DVD(s) that contains the program. You also may receive a manual or printed instructions explaining how to install and use the software.

Installing is the process of setting up software to work with the computer, printer, and other hardware components. When you buy a computer, it usually has some software pre-installed on its hard disk. This enables you to use the computer the first time you turn it on. To begin installing additional software from a CD or DVD, insert the program disc in a CD or DVD drive. The computer then copies all or part of the program from the disc to the computer's hard disk.

Once software is installed, you can use, or **run**, it. When you instruct the computer to run an installed program, the computer *loads* it, which means the program is copied from storage to memory. Once in memory, the computer can carry out, or *execute*, the instructions in the program. Figure 1-12 illustrates the steps that occur when a user installs and runs a greeting card program.

FAQ 1-4

Which spelling is correct, disk or disc?

Both are correct, depending on usage. When referring to CD, DVD, and other *optical* (laser) storage, computer professionals typically use the term, disc. The term, disk, normally refers to floppy disks, Zip disks, hard disks, and other nonoptical storage media. For more information, visit scsite.com/dc2006/ch1/faq and then click Disk or Disc.

FIGURE 1-12   INSTALLING AND RUNNING A COMPUTER PROGRAM

Step 1: INSTALL
When you insert a greeting card program disc in the CD drive for the first time, the computer begins the procedure of installing the greeting card program on the hard disk.

CD-ROM

Step 2: RUN
Once installed, you can instruct the computer to run the greeting card program. The computer transfers instructions from the hard disk to memory.

instructions transfer to memory

Step 3: USE
The greeting card program executes. Using this program, you can create custom greeting cards.

Software Development

A *programmer* is someone who develops software or writes the instructions that direct the computer to process data into information. When writing instructions, a programmer must be sure the program works properly so the computer generates the desired results. Complex programs can require thousands to millions of instructions.

Programmers use a programming language or program development tool to create computer programs. Popular programming languages include C++, C#, Java, JavaScript, and Visual Basic .NET. Figure 1-13 shows some of the instructions a programmer may write to create a Web application.

FIGURE 1-13 The top figure illustrates some of the instructions a programmer writes in JavaScript to create the Web application shown in the bottom figure.

Test your knowledge of pages 11 through 18 in Quiz Yourself 1-2.

QUIZ YOURSELF 1-2

Instructions: Find the true statement below. Then, rewrite the remaining false statements so they are true.

1. A resource is a collection of computers and devices connected together via communications devices and transmission media.

2. Installing is the process of setting up software to work with the computer, printer, and other hardware components.

3. Popular system software includes Web browsers, word processing software, spreadsheet software, database software, and presentation graphics software.

4. The Internet is one of the more popular services on the Web.

5. Two types of application software are the operating system and utility programs.

Quiz Yourself Online: To further check your knowledge of networks, the Internet and Web, and system software versus application software, visit scsite.com/dc2006/ch1/quiz and then click Objectives 5 – 7.

CATEGORIES OF COMPUTERS

Industry experts typically classify computers in six categories: personal computers, mobile computers and mobile devices, midrange servers, mainframes, supercomputers, and embedded computers. A computer's size, speed, processing power, and price determine the category it best fits. Due to rapidly changing technology, however, the distinction among categories is not always clear-cut. Still, many people refer to these categories when discussing computers.

Figure 1-14 summarizes the six categories of computers. The following pages discuss computers and devices that fall in each category.

CATEGORIES OF COMPUTERS

Category	Physical Size	Number of Simultaneously Connected Users	General Price Range
Personal computers (desktop)	Fits on a desk	Usually one (can be more if networked)	Several hundred to several thousand dollars
Mobile computers and mobile devices	Fits on your lap or in your hand	Usually one	Less than a hundred dollars to several thousand dollars
Midrange servers	Small cabinet	Two to thousands	$1,000 to a million dollars
Mainframes	Partial room to a full room of equipment	Hundreds to thousands	$300,000 to several million dollars
Supercomputers	Full room of equipment	Hundreds to thousands	$500,000 to several billion dollars
Embedded computers	Miniature	Usually one	Embedded in the price of the product

FIGURE 1-14 This table summarizes some of the differences among the categories of computers. These should be considered general guidelines only because of rapid changes in technology.

PERSONAL COMPUTERS

A **personal computer** is a computer that can perform all of its input, processing, output, and storage activities by itself. A personal computer contains a processor, memory, and one or more input, output, and storage devices.

Two popular styles of personal computers are the PC (Figure 1-15) and the Apple (Figure 1-16). The term, *PC-compatible*, refers to any personal computer based on the original IBM personal computer design. Companies such as Dell, Gateway, Hewlett-Packard, and Toshiba sell PC-compatible computers. PC and PC-compatible computers have processors with different architectures than processors in Apple computers. These two types of computers also use different operating systems. PC and PC-compatible computers usually use a Windows operating system. Apple computers use a Macintosh operating system (Mac OS).

Two types of personal computers are desktop computers and notebook computers. The next section discusses desktop personal computers. Notebook computers are discussed in the mobile computers section.

WEB LINK 1-7

Personal Computers
For more information, visit scsite.com/dc2006/ch1/weblink and then click Personal Computers.

FIGURE 1-15 The PC and compatible computers usually use a Windows operating system.

FIGURE 1-16 Apple computers, such as the iMac, use a Macintosh operating system.

FAQ 1-5

How many PCs have been sold worldwide?

One billion PCs were sold during their first 25 years on the market. Experts predict that the next billion PCs will be sold between 2000 and 2008, a mere eight-year period. For more information, visit scsite.com/dc2006/ch1/faq and then click PC Sales.

Desktop Computers

A **desktop computer** is designed so the system unit, input devices, output devices, and any other devices fit entirely on or under a desk or table (Figures 1-15 and 1-16 on the previous page). In many models, the system unit is a tall and narrow *tower*, which can sit on the floor vertically — if desktop space is limited.

Some desktop computers are powerful enough to function as a server on a network. These high-end computers cost much more than the basic desktop computer.

Another expensive, powerful desktop computer is the workstation, which is geared for work that requires intense calculations and graphics capabilities. An architect uses a workstation to design buildings and homes. A graphic artist uses a workstation to create computer-animated special effects for full-length motion pictures and video games.

FAQ 1-6

Does the term, workstation, have two meanings?

Yes. In the computer industry, a *workstation* can be a high-powered computer or a client computer on a network. For more information, visit scsite.com/dc2006/ch1/faq and then click Workstation.

WEB LINK 1-8

Notebook Computers

For more information, visit scsite.com/dc2006/ch1/weblink and then click Notebook Computers.

MOBILE COMPUTERS AND MOBILE DEVICES

A **mobile computer** is a personal computer you can carry from place to place. Similarly, a **mobile device** is a computing device small enough to hold in your hand.

The most popular type of mobile computer is the notebook computer. The following sections discuss the notebook computer and widely used mobile devices.

Notebook Computers

A **notebook computer**, also called a **laptop computer**, is a portable, personal computer designed to fit on your lap. Notebook computers are thin and lightweight, yet they can be as powerful as the average desktop computer. Notebook computers are more expensive than desktop computers with equal capabilities.

On a typical notebook computer, the keyboard is on top of the system unit, and the monitor attaches to the system unit with hinges (Figure 1-17). These computers weigh on average between 2.5 and 9 pounds, which allows users easily to transport the computers from place to place. Most notebook computers can operate on batteries or a power supply or both.

display

CD or DVD drive

hinge

keyboard

FIGURE 1-17 On a typical notebook computer, the keyboard is on top of the system unit, and the display attaches to the system unit with hinges.

TABLET PC   Resembling a letter-sized slate, the **Tablet PC** is a special type of notebook computer that allows you to write or draw on the screen using a digital pen (Figure 1-18). With a *digital pen*, users write or draw by pressing the pen on the screen, and issue instructions to the Tablet PC by tapping on the screen. For users who prefer typing instead of handwriting, some Tablet PC designs have an attached keyboard; others allow you to connect a separate keyboard to the device. Tablet PCs also support voice input so users can enter text and issue instructions by speaking into the computer.

Tablet PCs are useful especially for taking notes in lectures, at meetings, conferences, and other forums where the standard notebook computer is not practical. With a cost of about $2,000, some users may find Tablet PCs more appropriate for their needs than traditional notebook computers.

Mobile Devices

Mobile devices, which are small enough to carry in a pocket, usually do not have disk drives. Instead, these devices store programs and data permanently on special memory inside the system unit or on small storage media such as memory cards. You often can connect a mobile device to a personal computer to exchange information between the computer and the mobile device.

Some mobile devices are **Internet-enabled**, meaning they can connect to the Internet wirelessly. With an Internet-enabled device, users can chat, send e-mail and instant messages, and access the Web.

Four popular types of mobile devices are handheld computers, PDAs, smart phones, and smart watches. Some combination mobile devices also are available, for example, a PDA/smart phone.

digital pen

FIGURE 1-18   A Tablet PC combines the features of a traditional notebook computer with the simplicity of pencil and paper.

HANDHELD COMPUTER   A **handheld computer**, sometimes called a *handtop computer*, is a computer small enough to fit in one hand (Figure 1-19). Because of their reduced size, the screens on handheld computers are small. Many handheld computers communicate wirelessly with other devices or computers and also include a digital pen or stylus for input. Similar to a digital pen, a *stylus* is a small metal or plastic device that looks like a ballpoint pen but uses pressure instead of ink to write, draw, or make selections.

Handheld computers often have specialized keyboards. Many handheld computers are industry-specific and serve the needs of mobile employees, such as meter readers and parcel delivery people, whose jobs require them to move from place to place.

FIGURE 1-19   This handheld computer fits in your hand.

PDA The PDA is one of the more popular lightweight mobile devices in use today. A **PDA** (*personal digital assistant*) provides personal organizer functions such as a calendar, appointment book, address book, calculator, and notepad (Figure 1-20). Most PDAs also offer a variety of other application software such as word processing, spreadsheet, personal finance, and games.

The primary input device of a PDA is a stylus. Some PDAs do have a built-in miniature keyboard. If you prefer to type on a PDA that does not have a keyboard, you can insert the PDA in a special separate keyboard. Some PDAs also support voice input.

Many PDAs are Internet-enabled so users can check e-mail and access the Web. Some also provide telephone capabilities. Because of all the added features, increasingly more people are replacing their pocket-sized appointment books with PDAs.

SMART PHONE Offering the convenience of one-handed operation, a **smart phone** is an Internet-enabled telephone that usually also provides PDA capabilities. In addition to basic telephone capabilities, a smart phone allows you to send and receive e-mail messages and access the Web. Higher-priced models have color screens, play music, and include built-in cameras so you can share photographs or videos with others as soon as you capture the image (Figure 1-21).

As smart phones and PDAs continue a trend of offering similar functions, it is becoming increasingly difficult to differentiate between the two devices. This trend, known as *convergence*, has led manufacturers to refer to PDAs and smart phones simply as *handhelds*. Some factors that affect a consumer's purchasing decision include the device's size, screen size, and capabilities of available software.

FIGURE 1-21 In addition to basic telephone functionality, smart phones allow you to check e-mail, access the Web, and share photos.

FAQ 1-7

Do PDAs have industry-specific applications?

Yes. Restaurant servers use PDAs to record customer orders and transmit them to the kitchen. Doctors use PDAs to access patients' records, view laboratory results, and transmit prescriptions to the pharmacy. Law enforcement officials use PDAs to log license plate numbers, run background checks, and issue tickets. For more information, visit scsite.com/dc2006/ch1/faq and then click PDAs.

SMART WATCH A **smart watch** is an Internet-enabled watch. In addition to basic timekeeping capabilities, a smart watch automatically adjusts to time zone changes, stores personal messages, reminds you of appointments, and wirelessly accesses news, weather, sports, and stocks (Figure 1-22).

stylus

FIGURE 1-20 PDAs provide personal information management functions as well as Internet access and telephone capabilities. Shown here are two different styles of PDAs.

FIGURE 1-22 A smart watch.

MIDRANGE SERVERS

A **midrange server** is more powerful and larger than a workstation computer (Figure 1-23). Midrange servers typically support several hundred and sometimes up to a few thousand connected computers at the same time.

Midrange servers store data and programs. In many cases, one server accesses data on another server. In other cases, people use personal computers or terminals to access programs on a server. A terminal is a device with a monitor, keyboard, and memory.

FIGURE 1-23
A midrange server is more powerful than a workstation, but less powerful than a mainframe.

MAINFRAMES

A **mainframe** is a large, expensive, powerful computer that can handle hundreds or thousands of connected users simultaneously (Figure 1-24). Mainframes store tremendous amounts of data, instructions, and information. Every major corporation uses mainframes for business activities. With mainframes, large businesses are able to bill millions of customers, prepare payroll for thousands of employees, and manage thousands of items in inventory. One study reported that mainframes process more than 83 percent of transactions around the world.

Mainframes also can act as servers in a network environment. Midrange servers and other mainframes can access data and information from a mainframe. People also can access programs on the mainframe using terminals or personal computers.

FIGURE 1-24
Mainframe computers can handle thousands of connected computers and process millions of instructions per second.

SUPERCOMPUTERS

A **supercomputer** is the fastest, most powerful computer — and the most expensive (Figure 1-25). The fastest supercomputers are capable of processing more than 100 trillion instructions in a single second. With weights that exceed 100 tons, these computers can store more than 20,000 times the data and information of an average desktop computer.

Applications requiring complex, sophisticated mathematical calculations use supercomputers. Large-scale simulations and applications in medicine, aerospace, automotive design, online banking, weather forecasting, nuclear energy research, and petroleum exploration use a supercomputer.

FIGURE 1-25 This supercomputer simulates various environmental occurrences such as global climate changes, pollution, and earthquakes.

EMBEDDED COMPUTERS

An **embedded computer** is a special-purpose computer that functions as a component in a larger product. Embedded computers are everywhere — at home, in your car, and at work. The list below identifies a variety of everyday products that contain embedded computers.

- Consumer Electronics: mobile and digital telephones, digital televisions, cameras, video recorders, game consoles, DVD players and recorders, answering machines
- Home Automation Devices and Appliances: thermostats, sprinkling systems, security monitoring systems, microwave ovens, washing machines
- Automobiles: antilock brakes, engine control modules, airbag controller, cruise control
- Process Controllers and Robotics: remote monitoring systems, power monitors, machine controllers, medical devices
- Computer Devices and Office Machines: keyboards, printers, faxes, copiers

Because embedded computers are components in larger products, they usually are small and have limited hardware. These computers perform various functions, depending on the requirements of the product in which they reside. Embedded computers in printers, for example, monitor the amount of paper in the tray, check the ink or toner level, signal if a paper jam has occurred, and so on. Figure 1-26 shows some of the many embedded computers in cars.

Adaptive cruise control systems detect if cars in front of you are too close and, if necessary, adjust the vehicle's throttle, may apply brakes, and/or sound an alarm.

Advanced airbag systems have crash-severity sensors that determine the appropriate level to inflate the airbag, reducing the chance of airbag injury in low-speed accidents.

Tire pressure monitoring systems send warning signals if tire pressure is insufficient.

Cars equipped with wireless communications capabilities, called *telematics*, include such features as navigation systems and Internet access.

Drive-by-wire systems sense pressure on the gas pedal and communicate electronically to the engine how much and how fast to accelerate.

FIGURE 1-26   Some of the embedded computers designed to improve your safety, security, and performance in today's automobiles.

ELEMENTS OF AN INFORMATION SYSTEM

To be valuable, information must be accurate, organized, timely, accessible, useful, and cost-effective to produce. Generating information from a computer requires the following five elements:

- Hardware
- Software
- Data
- People
- Procedures

Together, these elements (hardware, software, data, people, and procedures) comprise an *information system*. Figure 1-27 shows how each of the elements of an information system in a large business might interact.

The hardware must be reliable and capable of handling the expected workload. The software must be developed carefully and tested thoroughly. The data entered into the computer must be accurate.

Most companies with mid-sized and large computers have an IT (information technology) department. Staff in the IT department should be skilled and up-to-date on the latest technology. IT staff also should train users so they understand how to use the computer properly. Today's users also work closely with IT staff in the development of computer applications that relate to their areas of work.

Finally, all the IT applications should have readily available documented procedures that address operating the computer and using its applications.

FIGURE 1-27 HOW THE ELEMENTS OF AN INFORMATION SYSTEM IN A LARGE BUSINESS MIGHT INTERACT

Step 1: IT staff (people) develop procedures for processing time cards (data).

Step 2: Employees (people) in the payroll department use a program (software) to enter the time cards (data) in the computer.

Step 3: The computer (hardware) performs calculations required to process the payroll and stores the results on storage media such as a hard disk (hardware).

Step 4: Paychecks (information) print on a corporate printer (hardware).

WEB LINK 1-9

Women in Technology

For more information, visit scsite.com/dc2006/ch1/weblink and then click Women in Technology.

WEB LINK 1-10

Minorities in Technology

For more information, visit scsite.com/dc2006/ch1/weblink and then click Minorities in Technology.

EXAMPLES OF COMPUTER USAGE

Every day, people around the world rely on different types of computers for a variety of applications. To illustrate the range of uses for computers, this section takes you on a visual and narrative tour of five categories of users:

- Home user
- Small office/home office (SOHO) user
- Mobile user
- Power user
- Large business user

The following paragraphs discuss the types of hardware and software required by each category of user.

Home User

In an increasing number of homes, the computer no longer is a convenience. Instead, it is a basic necessity. Each family member, or **home user**, spends time on the computer for different reasons that include budgeting and personal financial management, Web access, communications, and entertainment (Figure 1-28).

FIGURE 1-28a (personal financial management)

FIGURE 1-28b (Web access)

FIGURE 1-28c (communications)

FIGURE 1-28d (entertainment)

FIGURE 1-28 The home user spends time on a computer for a variety of reasons.

On the Internet, home users access a huge amount of information, take college classes, pay bills, manage investments, shop, listen to the radio, watch movies, read books, play games, file taxes, and make airline reservations. They also communicate with others around the world through e-mail, instant messaging, and chat rooms using personal computers, PDAs, and smart phones. With a digital camera, home users take photographs and then send the electronic images to others (Figure 1-29). Using a PC video camera, which costs less than $100, home users easily have live video calls with friends, family members, and others. Read At Issue 1-4 for a related discussion.

Today's homes typically have one or more desktop computers. Many home users network multiple desktop computers throughout the house, often wirelessly. These small networks allow family members to share an Internet connection and a printer.

To meet their needs, home users have a variety of software. They type letters, homework assignments, and other documents with word processing software. Personal finance software helps the home user with personal finances, investments, and family budgets. Other software assists with preparing taxes, keeping a household inventory, and setting up maintenance schedules.

Reference software, such as encyclopedias, medical dictionaries, or a road atlas, provides valuable information for everyone in the family. With entertainment software, the home user can play games, compose music, research genealogy, or create greeting cards.

Educational software helps adults learn to speak a foreign language and youngsters to read, write, count, and spell.

FAQ 1-8

Can I listen to an audio CD on my computer?

Yes, in most cases. Simply insert the CD in the computer's CD or DVD drive. Within a few seconds, you should hear music from the computer's speakers or in your headset. If no music plays, it is possible you need to run a program that starts the audio CD. For more information, visit scsite.com/dc2006/ch1/faq and then click Audio CDs.

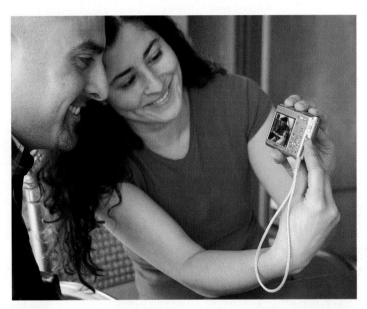

FIGURE 1-29 Home users take and view photographs on a digital camera.

AT ISSUE 1-4

Did You Meet Online?

Once, people met dates through family and friends, work, or community, religious, and recreational activities. These social networks sometimes resulted in a perfect match, but often time constraints, the limited pool of participants, and infrequent meetings made it difficult to find a potential partner. Today, many people are turning to another resource — online dating. Media experts forecast that 40 million people will use online dating services this year, and the market for these services has grown almost 40 percent in the past year. Online dating service members supply information about their interests and personalities and then search the service for people they might like to meet. The services are easy to use, have a large range of participants, allow relationships to develop at a comfortable pace, and usually offer advanced options such as live chat, voice mail, and computer matchmaking. On the other hand, in an online dating service it can be difficult to judge the appearance of members, obtain in-depth profiles, recognize false or exaggerated member claims, and avoid unwanted advertisements. Although introductory memberships often are free, many services require substantial fees for extended benefits. Are online dating services worth it? Why or why not? If you used an online dating service, what would you do to profit from its advantages and avoid its disadvantages?

Small Office/Home Office User

Computers assist small business and home office users in managing their resources effectively. **A small office/home office** (*SOHO*) includes any company with fewer than 50 employees, as well as the self-employed who work from home. Small offices include local law practices, accounting firms, travel agencies, and florists. SOHO users typically have a desktop computer to perform some or all of their duties. Many also have PDAs to manage appointments and contact information.

SOHO users access the Web — often wirelessly — to look up information such as addresses, directions (Figure 1-30a), postal codes, flights, and package shipping rates. Nearly all SOHO users communicate with others through e-mail. Many are entering the *e-commerce* arena and conduct business on the Web. Their Web sites advertise products and services and may provide a means for taking orders. Small business Web sites sometimes use a *Web cam*, which is a video camera that displays its output on a Web page. A Web cam allows SOHO users to show the world a live view of some aspect of their business.

To save money on hardware and software, small offices often network their computers. For example, the small office connects one printer to a network for all employees to share.

SOHO users often have basic business software such as word processing and spreadsheet software to assist with document preparation and finances (Figure 1-30b). They are likely to use other industry-specific types of software. A candy shop, for example, will have software that allows for taking orders and payments, updating inventory, and paying vendors.

FIGURE 1-30a   (Web access)

FIGURE 1-30b   (spreadsheet program)

FIGURE 1-30   People with a home office and employees in small offices typically use a desktop personal computer for some or all of their duties.

Mobile User

Today, businesses and schools are expanding to serve people across the country and around the world. Thus, increasingly more employees and students are **mobile users**, who work on a computer while away from a main office or school (Figure 1-31). Examples of mobile users are sales representatives, real estate agents, insurance agents, meter readers, package delivery people, journalists, consultants, and students.

Mobile users often have a notebook computer, Internet-enabled PDA, or smart phone. With these computers and devices, the mobile user connects to other computers — usually wirelessly — on a network or the Internet. Mobile users can transfer information between their mobile device and another computer, such as one at the main office or school.

The mobile user works with basic business software such as word processing and spreadsheet software. With presentation graphics software, the mobile user can create and deliver presentations to a large audience by connecting a mobile computer or device to a video projector that displays the presentation on a full screen. Many scaled-down programs are available for mobile devices such as PDAs and smart phones.

FIGURE 1-31 Mobile users have notebook computers, Tablet PCs, PDAs, and smart phones so they can work, do homework, send messages, or connect to the Internet while away from a wired connection.

Power User

Another category of user, called a **power user**, requires the capabilities of a workstation or other type of powerful computer (Figure 1-32). Examples of power users include engineers, scientists, architects, desktop publishers, and graphic artists. Power users often work with *multimedia*, combining text, graphics, audio, and video into one application. These users need computers with extremely fast processors because of the nature of their work.

The power user's workstation contains industry-specific software. For example, engineers and architects use software to draft and design floor plans, mechanical assemblies, or vehicles. A desktop publisher uses software to prepare marketing literature such as newsletters, brochures, and annual reports. A geologist uses software to study the earth's surface. This software usually is expensive because of its specialized design.

Power users exist in all types of businesses. Some also work at home. Their computers typically have network connections and Internet access.

FIGURE 1-32 This scientist uses a powerful computer to study blood cells for diabetes research.

Large Business User

A large business has hundreds or thousands of employees or customers that work in or do business with offices across a region, the country, or the world. Each employee or customer who uses a computer in the large business is a **large business user** (Figure 1-33).

Many large companies use the words, *enterprise computing,* to refer to the huge network of computers that meets their diverse computing needs. The network facilitates communications among employees at all locations. Users access the network of midrange servers or mainframes through desktop computers, mobile computers, PDAs, and smart phones.

Large businesses use computers and the computer network to process high volumes of transactions in a single day. Although they may differ in size and in the products or services offered, all generally use computers for basic business activities. For example, they bill millions of customers, prepare payroll for thousands of employees, and manage thousands of items in inventory.

Large businesses typically have e-commerce Web sites, allowing customers and vendors to conduct business online. The Web site also showcases products, services, and other company information. Customers, vendors, and other interested parties can access this information on the Web. Once an order is placed, computers update inventory records to reflect goods sold and goods purchased.

The marketing department in the large business uses desktop publishing software to prepare marketing literature. The accounting department uses software for accounts receivable, accounts payable, billing, general ledger, and payroll activities.

The employees in the *information technology (IT) department* keep the computers and the network running. They also determine when and if the company requires new hardware or software.

Large business users work with word processing, spreadsheet, database, and presentation graphics software. They also may use calendar programs to post their schedules on the network. And, they might use PDAs or smart phones to maintain contact information. E-mail and Web browsers enable communications among employees, vendors, and customers.

Some large businesses place kiosks in public locations. A *kiosk* is a freestanding computer, usually with a touch screen (Figure 1-34).

Many employees of large businesses telecommute. **Telecommuting** is a work arrangement in which employees work away from a company's standard workplace and often communicate with the office through the computer. Employees who telecommute have flexible work schedules so they can combine work and personal responsibilities, such as child care.

WEB LINK 1-11

Enterprise Computing

For more information, visit scsite.com/ dc2006/ch1/weblink and then click Enterprise Computing.

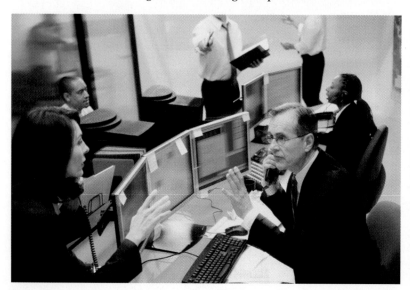

FIGURE 1-33 A large business can have hundreds or thousands of users in offices across a region, the country, or the world.

FIGURE 1-34 Airline travelers check in using this self-service kiosk.

Putting It All Together

The previous pages discussed the hardware and software requirements for the home user, small office/home office user, mobile user, power user, and large business user. The table in Figure 1-35 summarizes these requirements.

CATEGORIES OF USERS

User	Hardware	Software
HOME 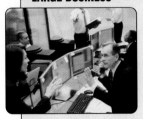	• Desktop computer • PDA or smart phone • Smart watch	• Business (e.g., word processing) • Personal information manager • Personal finance, online banking, tax preparation • Web browser • E-mail, instant messaging, and chat rooms • Photo editing • Reference (e.g., encyclopedias, medical dictionaries, road atlas) • Entertainment (e.g., games, music composition, greeting cards) • Educational (e.g., tutorials, children's math and reading software)
SMALL OFFICE/ HOME OFFICE	• Desktop computer • PDA or smart phone • Shared network printer	• Business (e.g., word processing, spreadsheet, database) • Personal information manager • Company specific (e.g., accounting, legal reference) • Network management • Web browser • E-mail
MOBILE	• Notebook computer equipped with a modem, or a Tablet PC • Video projector • PDA or smart phone	• Business (e.g., word processing, spreadsheet, note taking, presentation graphics) • Personal information manager • Web browser • E-mail
POWER	• Workstation or other powerful computer with multimedia capabilities • PDA or smart phone	• Desktop publishing • Multimedia authoring • Computer-aided design • Photo, audio, and video editing • Personal information manager • Web browser • E-mail
LARGE BUSINESS	• Midrange server or mainframe • Desktop or notebook computer • Industry-specific handheld computer • PDA or smart phone • Kiosk	• Business (e.g., word processing, spreadsheet, database, presentation graphics) • Personal information manager • Accounting • Network management • Web browser • E-mail

FIGURE 1-35   Today, computers are used by millions of people for work tasks, school assignments, and leisure activities. Different computer users require different kinds of hardware and software to meet their needs effectively.

COMPUTER APPLICATIONS IN SOCIETY

The computer has changed society today as much as the industrial revolution changed society in the eighteenth and nineteenth centuries.

People interact directly with computers in fields such as education, finance, government, health care, science, publishing, travel, and industry. In addition, they can reap the benefits from breakthroughs and advances in these fields. The following pages describe how computers have made a difference in people's interactions with these disciplines. Read Looking Ahead 1-2 for a look at the next generation of computer applications in society.

LOOKING AHEAD 1-2

Robots Add the Human Touch

Rosie, the robotic maid from "The Jetsons," delighted millions of television viewers with her household cleaning talents. Today's mobile, intelligent robots likewise perform tasks typically reserved for humans in a $5 billion global market.

Each day, the iRobot Roomba self-propelled vacuum cleans homes, and the da Vinci Surgical System's robotic hands drill through bones and make incisions. Sony's home robot, QRIO, responds to voices and faces, displays emotions, and walks and dances fluidly.

Tomorrow's practical and versatile robots will serve a variety of personal and industrial needs. By 2010, the expected $17 billion market should include products to care for senior citizens, transport people in major cities, and perform hundreds of thousands of mobile utility jobs, such as picking up and delivering items. For more information, visit scsite.com/dc2006/ch1/looking and then click Robots.

Education

Education is the process of acquiring knowledge. In the traditional model, people learn from other people such as parents, teachers, and employers. Many forms of printed material such as books and manuals are used as learning tools. Today, educators also are turning to computers to assist with education (Figure 1-36).

Many schools and companies equip labs and classrooms with computers. Some schools require students to have a notebook computer or PDA, along with textbooks and other supplies. To promote education by computer, many vendors offer substantial student discounts on software.

Sometimes, the delivery of education occurs at one place while the learning occurs at other locations. For example, students can take a class on the Web. Some classes are blended; that is, part of the learning occurs in a classroom and the other part occurs on the Web. More than 70 percent of colleges offer some type of distance learning classes. A few even offer entire degrees online.

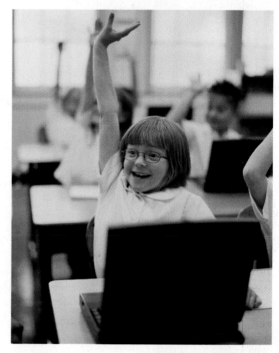

FIGURE 1-36 In some schools, students have notebook computers on their desks during classroom lectures.

Finance

Many people and companies use computers to help manage their finances. Some use finance software to balance checkbooks, pay bills, track personal income and expenses, manage investments, and evaluate financial plans. This software usually includes a variety of online services. For example, computer users can track investments and do online banking. With **online banking**, users access account balances, pay bills, and copy monthly transactions from the bank's computer right into their personal computers.

Many financial institutions' Web sites also offer online banking (Figure 1-37). When using a Web site instead of finance software on your computer, all your account information is stored on the bank's computer. The advantage is you can access your financial records from anywhere in the world.

FIGURE 1-37 Many financial institutions' Web sites offer online banking.

Investors often use **online investing** to buy and sell stocks and bonds — without using a broker. With online investing, the transaction fee for each trade usually is much less than when trading through a broker.

Government

A government provides society with direction by making and administering policies. To provide citizens with up-to-date information, most government offices have Web sites. People in the United States access government Web sites to file taxes, apply for permits and licenses, pay parking tickets, buy stamps, report crimes, apply for financial aid, and renew vehicle registrations and driver's licenses.

Employees of government agencies use computers as part of their daily routine. North American 911 call centers use computers to dispatch calls for fire, police, and medical assistance. Military and other agency officials use the U.S. Department of Homeland Security's network of information about domestic security threats to help protect against terrorist attacks. Law enforcement officers have online access to the FBI's National Crime Information Center (NCIC) in police cars that have rugged notebook computers and fingerprint scanners or through PDAs (Figure 1-38). The NCIC contains more than 52 million missing persons and criminal records, including names, fingerprints, parole/probation records, mug shots, and other information.

FIGURE 1-38 Law enforcement officials have in-vehicle computers and PDAs to access emergency, missing person, and criminal records in computer networks in local, state, and federal agencies.

Health Care

Nearly every area of health care uses computers. Whether you are visiting a family doctor for a regular checkup, having lab work or an outpatient test, or being rushed in for emergency surgery, the medical staff around you will be using computers for various purposes:

- Hospitals and doctors use computers to maintain patient records.
- Computers monitor patients' vital signs in hospital rooms and at home.
- Computers and computerized devices assist doctors, nurses, and technicians with medical tests (Figure 1-39).
- Doctors use the Web and medical software to assist with researching and diagnosing health conditions.
- Doctors use e-mail to correspond with patients.
- Pharmacists use computers to file insurance claims.
- Surgeons implant computerized devices, such as pacemakers, that allow patients to live longer.

- Surgeons use computer-controlled devices to provide them with greater precision during operations, such as for laser eye surgery and robot-assisted heart surgery.

Many Web sites provide up-to-date medical, fitness, nutrition, or exercise information. These Web sites also maintain lists of doctors and dentists to help you find the one that suits your needs. They have chat rooms, so you can talk to others diagnosed with similar conditions. Some Web sites even allow you to order prescriptions online.

An exciting development in health care is telemedicine, which is a form of long-distance health care. Through *telemedicine*, health-care professionals in separate locations conduct live conferences on the computer. For example, a doctor at one location can have a conference with a doctor at another location to discuss a bone X-ray. Live images of each doctor, along with the X-ray, are displayed on each doctor's computer.

Science

All branches of science, from biology to astronomy to meteorology, use computers to assist them with collecting, analyzing, and modeling data. Scientists also use the Internet to communicate with colleagues around the world.

Breakthroughs in surgery, medicine, and treatments often result from scientists' use of computers. Tiny computers now imitate functions of the central nervous system, retina of the eye, and cochlea of the ear. A cochlear implant allows a deaf person to listen. Electrodes implanted in the brain stop tremors associated with Parkinson's disease. Cameras small enough to swallow — sometimes called a camera pill — take pictures inside your body to detect polyps, cancer, and other abnormalities (Figure 1-40).

A *neural network* is a system that attempts to imitate the behavior of the human brain. Scientists create neural networks by connecting thousands of processors together much like the neurons in the brain are connected. The capability of a personal computer to recognize spoken words is a direct result of scientific experimentation with neural networks.

FIGURE 1-39 Doctors, nurses, technicians, and other medical staff use computers while performing tests on patients.

FIGURE 1-40 HOW A CAMERA PILL WORKS

Step 1:
A patient swallows a tiny capsule that contains a miniature disposable camera, lights, a transmitter, and batteries. The camera is positioned at the clear end of the capsule.

Step 2:
As the capsule moves through the inside of the patient's body, the camera snaps about 50,000 pictures, which are transmitted to a recording device worn as a belt on the patient's waist.

Step 3:
The doctor transfers the data on the recording device to a computer so it can be processed and analyzed.

Publishing

Publishing is the process of making works available to the public. These works include books, magazines, newspapers, music, film, and video. Special software assists graphic designers in developing pages that include text, graphics, and photographs; artists in composing and enhancing songs; filmmakers in creating and editing film; and journalists and mobile users in capturing and modifying video clips.

Many publishers make their works available online (Figure 1-41). Some Web sites allow you to copy the work, such as a book or music, to your desktop computer, handheld computer, PDA, or smart phone.

FIGURE 1-41 Many magazine and newspaper publishers make the content of their publications available online.

Travel

Whether traveling by car or airplane, your goal is to arrive safely at your destination. As you make the journey, you may interact with some of the latest technology.

Vehicles manufactured today often include some type of onboard navigation system. Many airlines now provide online access, allowing passengers to connect their mobile computer or device to the Internet (Figure 1-42). Some airlines even provide passengers with Internet-enabled devices during flights.

In preparing for a trip, you may need to reserve a car, hotel, or flight. Many Web sites offer these services to the public. For example, you can order airline tickets on the Web. If you plan to drive somewhere and are unsure of the road to take to your destination, you can print directions and a map from the Web.

Industry

Computer-aided manufacturing (*CAM*) refers to the use of computers to assist with manufacturing processes such as fabrication and assembly. Industries use CAM to reduce product development costs, shorten a product's time to market, and stay ahead of the competition.

Often, robots carry out processes in a CAM environment. CAM is used by a variety of industries, including oil drilling, power generation, food production, and automobile manufacturing. Automobile plants, for example, have an entire line of industrial robots that assemble a car (Figure 1-43).

Special computers on the shop floor record actual labor, material, machine, and computer time used to manufacture a particular product. The computers process this data and automatically update inventory, production, payroll, and accounting records on the company's network.

FAQ 1-9

Do home users book travel on the Web?

Yes, it is estimated that nearly 22 percent ($53 billion) of the travel industry's revenues stem from leisure travel bookings. As shown in the chart, computer users of all ages visit travel agency Web sites. For more information, visit scsite.com/dc2006/ch1/faq and then click Travel Bookings.

Online Travel Agency Use (by Age)

- 18–24: 11%
- 25–34: 19%
- 35–44: 25%
- 45–54: 23%
- 55+: 22%

Source: The ClickZ Network

FIGURE 1-43   Automotive factories use industrial robots to weld car bodies.

FIGURE 1-42   Airlines today offer inflight Internet connections to passengers.

Test your knowledge of pages 18 through 36 in Quiz Yourself 1-3.

QUIZ YOURSELF 1-3

Instructions: Find the true statement below. Then, rewrite the remaining false statements so they are true.

1. A desktop computer is a portable, personal computer designed to fit on your lap.

2. A personal computer contains a processor, memory, and one or more input, output, and storage devices.

3. Each large business user spends time on the computer for different reasons that include budgeting and personal financial management, Web access, communications, and entertainment.

4. A home user requires the capabilities of a workstation or other powerful computer.

5. Mainframes are the fastest, most powerful computers — and the most expensive.

6. The elements of an information system are hardware, e-mail, data, people, and the Internet.

7. With embedded computers, users access account balances, pay bills, and copy monthly transactions from the bank's computer right into their personal computers.

Quiz Yourself Online: To further check your knowledge of categories of computers, information system elements, computer users, and computer applications in society, visit scsite.com/dc2006/ch1/quiz and then click Objectives 8 – 11.

CHAPTER SUMMARY

Chapter 1 introduced you to basic computer concepts such as what a computer is, how it works, and its advantages and disadvantages. You learned about the components of a computer. Next, the chapter discussed networks, the Internet, and computer software. The many different categories of computers, computer users, and computer applications in society also were presented.

This chapter is an overview. Many of the terms and concepts introduced will be discussed further in later chapters. For a history of hardware and software developments, read the Timeline 2006 that follows this chapter.

Personal Computer Salesperson

When you decide to buy or upgrade a personal computer, the most important person with whom you interact probably will be a personal computer salesperson. This individual will be a valuable resource to you in providing the information and expertise you need to select a computer that meets your requirements.

Computer manufacturers and retailers that sell several types of personal computers need competent salespeople. A *personal computer salesperson* must be computer literate and have a specific knowledge of the computers he or she sells. In addition, a successful salesperson has a friendly, outgoing personality that helps customers feel comfortable. Through open-ended questions, the salesperson can determine a customer's needs and level of experience. With this information, the salesperson can choose the best computer for the customer and explain the features of the computer in language the customer will understand.

Most computer salespeople have at least a high school diploma. Before reaching the sales floor, however, salespeople usually complete extensive company training programs. These programs often consist of self-directed, self-paced Web-training classes. Most salespeople also participate in training updates, often on a monthly basis.

Personal computer salespeople generally earn a guaranteed amount plus a commission for each sale. A computer salesperson can earn about $40,000 a year. Top salespeople can be among a company's more highly compensated employees, earning in excess of $70,000. For more information, visit scsite.com/dc2006/ch1/careers and then click Personal Computer Salesperson.

High-Tech Talk

ANALOG VERSUS DIGITAL:
MAKING THE CONVERSION

Data is processed in one of two ways: analog or digital. People generally process *analog* data — that is, continuous wave patterns. The sight and sound of a traveling subway car transmits to your eyes and ears as light and sound waves, or smooth up-and-down patterns (Figure 1-44a). A computer, by contrast, is *digital*, which means computers process data in two discrete states: positive (on, or 1) and non-positive (off, or 0) as shown in Figure 1-44b. The 1 and 0 represent the two digits used by the binary number system. While this system is at the heart of digital computing, binary digital impulses appear as long strings of 1s and 0s.

If sound and light waves are analog and a computer is digital, how does a computer record audio clips, play music, or show a movie? How can a digital computer use an analog telephone line to dial up to access the Internet?

The key lies in analog-to-digital and digital-to-analog conversions. For example, the computer's sound card allows you to record sounds and playback sounds. The sound card performs these conversions to record a digital audio clip of your analog voice. The sound card connects to the microphone, which is an analog input source. The diaphragm in the microphone converts the analog sound waves into an analog electrical signal. This signal flows to the sound card's *analog-to-digital converter (ADC)*, which converts the signal into digital data. The digital data flows to the *digital signal processor (DSP)*, compressing the data to save space. Finally, the compressed data is stored in an audio file format.

To play a recorded sound, the computer reverses the process. The processor retrieves and sends the digital data to the DSP to be decompressed. The DSP sends the decompressed digital data to the sound card's *digital-to-analog converter (DAC)*, which converts the digital data back to an analog voltage for output via a speaker or headset. In other words, a DAC takes that long binary number string of 1s and 0s and turns it into an electronic signal that the sound output devices can decode and use.

Similarly, a video card allows you to record a video or play a movie on a DVD. A camera and microphone capture and send the analog picture and sound signals to a video card. The video card's ADC converts the signals into digital data. The digital data is compressed and saved in a file format such as AVI (audio/video interleave) or MPEG (Moving Picture Experts Group). When playing a movie, the computer decompresses and separates the video and audio data. It then sends the signals to the video card's DAC. The DAC translates the digital data into analog signals and sends them to the monitor and speakers, where they are displayed as your movie.

The modem in a computer also links the analog and digital worlds. When using a dial-up modem, the computer does not transmit digital data directly across analog telephone lines. Instead, the modem converts the computer's digital signals to analog signals (called *modulation*) to be sent over telephone lines. When the analog signal reaches its destination, another modem recreates the original digital signal (*demodulation*). This allows the receiving computer to process the data. The next time you dial up using a modem, pick up the telephone. The loud, screeching noise you hear is the sound of digital data after being converted to analog sound waves. For more information, visit scsite.com/dc2006/ch1/tech and then click Analog versus Digital.

FIGURE 1-44a (analog signal)

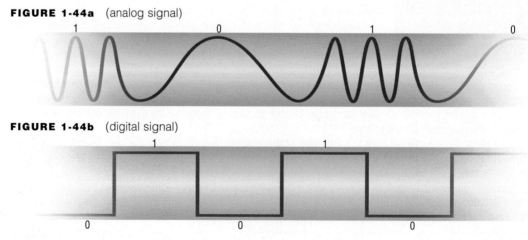

FIGURE 1-44b (digital signal)

FIGURE 1-44 Analog versus digital signals.

Companies on the Cutting Edge

DELL
COMPUTERS YOUR WAY

As a leading manufacturer of personal computers, *Dell* prides itself on its direct approach to computer sales. Founded by Michael Dell in 1984, the company deals openly with customers, one at a time. This direct approach eliminates retailers that add cost and time to the ordering process.

Dell uses the Internet to enhance the advantages of direct marketing and hosts one of the world's largest volume e-commerce Web sites. Customers can configure and price computers, order systems, and track their orders online.

In response to the U.S. Environmental Protection Agency's estimate that 250 million computers will be discarded from 2002 to 2007, Dell began an aggressive campaign to increase the amount of computer equipment it recycles by 50 percent. For more information, visit scsite.com/dc2006/ch1/companies and then click Dell.

APPLE COMPUTER
INTRODUCING INNOVATIVE TECHNOLOGIES

Millions of computer users in more than 120 countries loyally use *Apple Computer*'s hardware and software with a passion usually reserved for sports teams and musical groups.

Steven Jobs and Stephen Wozniak founded Apple in 1976 when they marketed the Apple I, a circuit board they had developed in Jobs's garage. In 1977, Apple Computer incorporated and introduced the Apple II, the first mass-marketed personal computer. Apple introduced the Macintosh product line in 1984, which featured a graphical user interface.

Under Jobs's direction as CEO, Apple introduced the iMac, the iBook, the Power Mac G5, the iPod digital music player, and Mac OS X. Strong demand for the iPod Mini helped boost the company's earnings. Product sales jumped after Apple introduced its pay-per-download iTunes online music store in 2003. For more information, visit scsite.com/dc2006/ch1/companies and then click Apple Computer.

Technology Trailblazers

BILL GATES
MICROSOFT'S FOUNDER

Bill Gates, the founder and chief software architect of Microsoft Corporation, suggests that college students should learn how to learn by getting the best education they can. Because he is considered by many as the most powerful person in the computing industry, it might be wise to listen to him.

Gates learned to program computers when he was 13. Early in his career, he developed the BASIC programming language for the MITS Altair, one of the first microcomputers. He founded Microsoft in 1975 with Paul Allen, and five years later, they provided the first operating system, called MS-DOS, for the IBM PC. Today, Microsoft's Windows and Office products dominate the software market.

Gates consistently has been placed at the top of *Forbes'* World's Richest People list, with assets of more than $46 billion. For more information, visit scsite.com/dc2006/ch1/people and then click Bill Gates.

CARLY FIORINA
TECHNOLOGY CORPORATE LEADER

Leadership, according to *Carly Fiorina*, involves influencing others and mastering change. As Hewlett-Packard's former chairman and CEO, she worked to return the company to its roots of innovation and invention.

Among the top names in Fortune magazine's list of the world's most powerful corporate women, Fiorina spent nearly 20 years at AT&T and Lucent Technologies, Inc., where she directed Lucent's initial public offering and subsequent spin-off. In 1999, she became CEO of Hewlett-Packard (HP), one of the oldest companies in Silicon Valley. Three years later, she led one of the largest high-tech corporate mergers in history when HP bought rival Compaq Computer.

The New York Stock Exchange named Fiorina to its newly formed board of executives in 2004, and in that year she was appointed as one of eight advisors to the U.S. President on future missions to the moon. For more information, visit scsite.com/dc2006/ch1/people and then click Carly Fiorina.

Chapter Review

The Chapter Review section summarizes the concepts presented in this chapter. To listen to the audio version of this Chapter Review, visit scsite.com/dc2006/ch1/review. To obtain help from other students regarding any subject in this chapter, visit scsite.com/dc2006/ch1/forum and post your thoughts or questions.

(1) Why Is Computer Literacy Important? **Computer literacy** involves having knowledge and understanding of computers and their uses. As computers become more a part of everyday life, many people believe that computer literacy is vital to success.

(2) What Is a Computer? A **computer** is an electronic device, operating under the control of instructions stored in its own memory, that can accept data, process the data according to specified rules, produce results, and store the results for future use.

(3) What Are the Components of a Computer? The electric, electronic, and mechanical components of a computer, or **hardware**, include input devices, output devices, a system unit, storage devices, and communications devices. An **input device** allows you to enter data or instructions into a computer. An **output device** conveys information to one or more people. The **system unit** is a case that contains the electronic components of a computer that are used to process data. A **storage device** records and/or retrieves items to and from **storage media**. A **communications device** enables a computer to send and receive data, instructions, and information to and from one or more computers.

(4) What Are the Advantages and Disadvantages of Using Computers? Computers have the advantages of speed, reliability, consistency, storage, and communications. They perform operations at incredibly fast speeds, are dependable and reliable, consistently generate error-free results, can store enormous amounts of data, and can share processing with other computers. Disadvantages of computers relate to the violation of privacy, the impact on the labor force, health risks, and the impact on the environment.

> Visit scsite.com/dc2006/ch1/quiz or click the Quiz Yourself button. Click Objectives 1 – 4.

(5) What Is the Purpose of a Network? A **network** is a collection of computers and devices connected together via communications devices and transmission media. Networks allow computers to share *resources*, such as hardware, software, data, and information.

(6) How Are the Internet and World Wide Web Used? The **Internet** is a worldwide collection of networks that connects millions of businesses, government agencies, educational institutions, and individuals. People use the Internet to communicate with and meet other people, access news and information, shop for goods and services, bank and invest, take classes, and access sources of entertainment and leisure. The **Web**, short for World Wide Web, is a global library of documents containing information that is available to anyone connected to the Internet.

(7) How Is System Software Different from Application Software? **Software**, also called a **program**, is a series of instructions that tells the computer what to do and how to do it. **System software** consists of the programs that control or maintain the operations of a computer and its devices. Two types of system software are the *operating system*, which coordinates activities among computer hardware devices, and *utility programs*, which perform maintenance-type tasks usually related to a computer, its devices, or its programs. **Application software** consists of programs that perform specific tasks for users. Popular application software includes Web browsers, word processing software, spreadsheet software, database software, and presentation graphics software.

> Visit scsite.com/dc2006/ch1/quiz or click the Quiz Yourself button. Click Objectives 5 – 7.

Chapter Review

⑧　What Are the Categories of Computers?　Industry experts typically classify computers in six categories: personal computers, mobile computers and mobile devices, midrange servers, mainframes, supercomputers, and embedded computers. A **personal computer** is a computer that can perform all of its input, processing, output, and storage activities by itself. A **mobile computer** is a personal computer that you can carry from place to place, and a **mobile device** is a computing device small enough to hold in your hand. A **midrange server** is a more powerful and larger computer that typically supports several hundred and sometimes up to a few thousand connected computers at the same time. A **mainframe** is a large, expensive, powerful computer that can handle hundreds or thousands of connected users simultaneously and can store tremendous amounts of data, instructions, and information. A **supercomputer** is the fastest, most powerful, and most expensive computer and is used for applications requiring complex, sophisticated mathematical calculations. An **embedded computer** is a special-purpose computer that functions as a computer in a larger product.

⑨　What Are the Elements of an Information System?　An *information system* combines hardware, software, data, people, and procedures to produce timely and useful information. People in an *information technology (IT) department* develop procedures for processing data. Following these procedures, people use hardware and software to enter the data into a computer. Software processes the data and directs the computer hardware to store changes on storage media and produce information in a desired form.

⑩　What Are the Types of Computer Users?　Computer users can be separated into five categories: home users, small office/home office users, mobile users, large business users, and power users. A **home user** is a family member who uses a computer for a variety of reasons, such as budgeting and personal financial management, Web access, communications, and entertainment. A **small office/home office** (*SOHO*) user is a small company or self-employed individual who works from home. SOHO users access the Web to look up information and use basic business software and sometimes industry-specific software. **Mobile users** are employees and students who work on a computer while away from a main office or school. A **power user** uses a workstation or other powerful computer to work with industry-specific software. Power users exist in all types of businesses. A **large business user** works in a company with many employees and uses a computer and computer network to process high volumes of transactions.

⑪　What Computer Applications Are Used in Society?　People interact directly with computers in fields such as education, finance, government, health care, science, publishing, travel, and industry. In education, students use computers and software to assist with learning or take distance learning classes. In finance, people use computers for **online banking** and **online investing**. Government offices have Web sites to provide citizens with up-to-date information, and government employees use computers as part of their daily routines. In health care, computers are used to maintain patient records, monitor patients, assist with medical tests and research, correspond with patients, file insurance claims, provide greater precision during operations, and as implants. All branches of science use computers to assist with collecting, analyzing, and modeling data and to communicate with colleagues around the world. Publishers use computers to assist in designing pages and make the content of their works available online.

Many vehicles use some type of online navigation system to help people travel more quickly and safely. Industries use **computer-aided manufacturing** (*CAM*) to assist with the manufacturing process.

> *connect*
> Visit scsite.com/dc2006/ch1/quiz or click the Quiz Yourself button. Click Objectives 8 – 11.

Quizzes and Learning Games

Computer Genius
Crossword Puzzle
DC Track and Field
Practice Test
Quiz Yourself
Wheel of Terms
You're Hired!

Exercises

Case Studies
Chapter Review
Checkpoint
▷ Key Terms
Learn How To
Learn It Online
Web Research

Beyond the Book

Career Corner
Companies
FAQs
High-Tech Talk
Looking Ahead
Making Use of the Web
Trailblazers
Web Links

Features

Chapter Forum
Install Computer
Lab Exercises
Maintain Computer
Tech News
Timeline 2006

Key Terms

You should know the Primary Terms and be familiar with the Secondary Terms. Use the list below to help focus your study. To further enhance your understanding of the Key Terms in this chapter, visit scsite.com/dc2006/ch1/terms. See an example of and a definition for each term, and access current and additional information about the term from the Web.

Primary Terms

(shown in bold-black characters in the chapter)

application software (16)
communications device (9)
computer (6)
computer literacy (5)
computer-aided manufacturing (36)
data (6)
desktop computer (20)
embedded computer (24)
FAQ (6)
graphical user interface (GUI) (15)
handheld computer (21)
hardware (7)
home user (26)
information (6)
input device (7)
installing (17)
Internet (12)
Internet-enabled (21)
laptop computer (20)
large business user (30)
mainframe (23)
midrange server (23)
mobile computer (20)
mobile device (20)
mobile users (29)
network (11)
notebook computer (20)
online (11)
online banking (32)
online investing (33)
output device (8)
PDA (22)
personal computer (19)
photo sharing community (14)
power user (29)
program (15)
run (17)
small office/home office (28)
smart phone (22)
smart watch (22)
software (15)
storage device (8)
storage media (8)
supercomputer (23)
system software (15)
system unit (8)
Tablet PC (21)
telecommuting (30)
user (9)
Web (12)
Web page (12)

Secondary Terms

(shown in italic characters in the chapter)

CAM (36)
client (11)
convergence (22)
digital pen (21)
e-commerce (28)
enterprise computing (30)
execute (17)
garbage in, garbage out (10)
handhelds (22)
handtop computer (21)
icon (15)
information processing cycle (6)
information system (25)
information technology (IT) department (30)
instructions (6)
kiosk (30)
loads (17)
memory (8)
multimedia (29)
neural network (34)
operating system (15)
PC-compatible (19)
personal digital assistant (22)
processor (8)
programmer (18)
publish (14)
resources (11)
server (11)
SOHO (28)
stylus (21)
telematics (24)
telemedicine (34)
tower (20)
utility program (16)
Web cam (28)

Checkpoint

Use the Checkpoint exercises to check your knowledge level of the chapter. The Beyond the Book exercises will help broaden your understanding of the concepts presented in this chapter. To complete the Checkpoint exercises interactively, visit scsite.com/dc2006/ch1/check.

 Label the Figure Identify these common computer hardware components.

a. card reader/writer (storage)
b. CD/DVD drive (storage)
c. digital camera (input)
d. floppy disk drive (storage)
e. hard disk drive (storage)
f. keyboard (input)
g. microphone (input)
h. modem (communications)
i. monitor (output)
j. mouse (input)
k. PC video camera (input)
l. printer (output)
m. scanner (input)
n. speaker (output)
o. system unit (processor, memory, storage)
p. USB flash drive (storage)

 True/False Mark T for True and F for False. (See page numbers in parentheses.)

_____ 1. Many people believe that computer literacy is vital to success in today's world. (5)

_____ 2. Computers process information into data. (6)

_____ 3. The circuitry of the system unit usually is part of or is connected to a circuit board called the motherboard. (8)

_____ 4. The computing phrase, garbage in, garbage out, points out that the accuracy of a computer's input depends on the accuracy of the output. (10)

_____ 5. When a computer connects to a network, it is offline. (11)

_____ 6. Businesses, called access providers, offer users and companies access to the Internet free or for a fee. (12)

_____ 7. System software serves as the interface between the user, the application software, and the computer's hardware. (15)

_____ 8. Mobile devices usually have disk drives. (21)

_____ 9. To be valuable, information should be accurate, organized, timely, accessible, useful, and cost-effective to produce. (25)

_____ 10. Home users type letters, homework assignments, and other documents with personal finance software. (27)

_____ 11. With online investing, the transaction fee for each trade usually is much more than when trading through a broker. (33)

Checkpoint

 Multiple Choice   Select the best answer. (See page numbers in parentheses.)

1. Computer literacy involves having a knowledge and understanding of _____. (5)
   a. computer programming
   b. computers and their uses
   c. computer repair
   d. all of the above

2. A computer can _____. (6)
   a. accept data
   b. process data according to specified rules
   c. produce and store results
   d. all of the above

3. The series of input, process, output, and storage sometimes is referred to as the _____ cycle. (6)
   a. information processing
   b. computer programming
   c. data entering
   d. Web browsing

4. Commonly used _____ devices are a printer, a monitor, and speakers. (8)
   a. input
   b. storage
   c. output
   d. communications

5. A disadvantage of computers is that _____. (10)
   a. computer operations occur at very slow speeds
   b. the components in computers are undependable
   c. prolonged computer use can lead to injuries
   d. most computers cannot communicate

6. A _____ controls access to the resources on a network. (11)
   a. server
   b. workstation
   c. client
   d. tower

7. _____ can be thought of as a library of information available to anyone connected to the Internet. (12)
   a. The Web
   b. E-mail
   c. Instant messaging
   d. A chat room

8. Popular _____ include(s) Web browsers, word processing software, and spreadsheet software. (16)
   a. system software
   b. operating systems
   c. application software
   d. utility programs

9. Two types of _____ are desktop computers and notebook computers. (19)
   a. embedded computers
   b. supercomputers
   c. midrange servers
   d. personal computers

10. A _____ is a special type of notebook computer that is useful for taking notes in lectures, at meetings, and other forums where the standard notebook computer is not practical. (21)
    a. smart phone
    b. Tablet PC
    c. smart watch
    d. PDA

11. An information system should have readily available documented _____ that address(es) operating the computer and using its applications. (25)
    a. hardware
    b. procedures
    c. software
    d. data

12. Examples of the _____ category of computer users include real estate agents, package delivery people, and meter readers. (29)
    a. mobile user
    b. home user
    c. power user
    d. small office/home office user

13. _____ is a system that attempts to imitate the behavior of the human brain. (34)
    a. Telemedicine
    b. A neural network
    c. E-commerce
    d. A kiosk

14. _____ refers to the use of computers to assist with processes such as fabrication and assembly. (36)
    a. Enterprise computing
    b. Telecommuting
    c. Information processing
    d. Computer-aided manufacturing (CAM)

Checkpoint

Matching

Match the terms with their definitions. (See page numbers in parentheses.)

_____ 1. processor (8)
_____ 2. memory (8)
_____ 3. publish (14)
_____ 4. icon (15)
_____ 5. install (17)
_____ 6. load (17)
_____ 7. execute (17)
_____ 8. stylus (21)
_____ 9. multimedia (29)
_____ 10. kiosk (30)

a. carry out the instructions in a computer program
b. stores instructions waiting to be executed and the data needed
c. set up software to work with a computer and other hardware components
d. collection of computers and devices connected together
e. miniature image that represents a program, an instruction, or some other object
f. combines text, graphics, audio, and video into one application
g. mobile device that can connect to the Internet wirelessly
h. interprets and carries out basic instructions that operate a computer
i. freestanding computer, usually with a touch screen
j. copy a program from storage to memory
k. metal or plastic device that uses pressure to write, draw, or make selections
l. make a Web page available on the Internet for others to see

Short Answer

Write a brief answer to each of the following questions.

1. How is data different from information? _____ What is the information processing cycle? _____
2. How is hardware different from software? _____ What is a programmer? _____
3. What is storage media? _____ What are examples of storage media? _____
4. Why do people use the Web? _____ What can be contained on a Web page? _____
5. What is telecommuting? _____ Why do people telecommute? _____

Beyond the Book

Read the following book elements, learn more about each using the Web, and then write a brief report.

1. At Issue — Is Job Outsourcing Inevitable? (10), Is Everything on the Web True? (14), Can Software Provoke Violence? (16), or Did You Meet Online? (27)
2. Career Corner — Personal Computer Salesperson (37)
3. Companies on the Cutting Edge — Dell or Apple Computer (39)
4. FAQs (6, 8, 14, 17, 20, 20, 22, 27)
5. High-Tech Talk — Analog versus Digital: Making the Conversion (38)
6. Looking Ahead — Bionic People Benefit from Processor Implants (9) or Robots Add the Human Touch (32)
7. Making Use of the Web — Fun and Entertainment (116)
8. Picture Yourself in a Computer Class (2)
9. Technology Trailblazers — Bill Gates or Carly Fiorina (39)
10. Timeline 2006 (52)
11. Web Links (7, 8, 9, 12, 15, 16, 19, 20, 26, 26, 30)

Learn It Online

Use the Learn It Online exercises to reinforce your understanding of the chapter concepts. To access the Learn It Online exercises, visit scsite.com/dc2006/ch1/learn.

 At the Movies — Walking the PC Pioneer Trail

To view the Walking the PC Pioneer Trail movie, click the number 1 button. Locate your video and click the corresponding High-Speed or Dial-Up link, depending on your Internet connection. Watch the movie and then complete the exercise by answering the question that follows. Many of the pioneers of the technology industry in the United States established their businesses in Silicon Valley. What explanation can you offer for why the founders of these companies all set up shop in this area?

 At the Movies — Black Viper's Windows XP Tips

To view the Black Viper's Windows XP Tips movie, click the number 2 button. Locate your video and click the corresponding High-Speed or Dial-Up link, depending on your Internet connection. Watch the movie and then complete the exercise by answering the question that follows. Windows XP is a large and powerful program that often runs many applications that you will never use. These programs require a lot of resources that can be used by other programs. Which of these programs would you turn off to make your computer run more efficiently and faster?

 Student Edition Labs — Using Input Devices

Click the number 3 button. When the Student Edition Labs menu appears (screen shown in the figure below), click *Using Input Devices* to begin. A new browser window will open. Follow the on-screen instructions to complete the Lab. When finished, click the Exit button. If required, submit your results to your instructor.

4 **Student Edition Labs — Using Windows**

Click the number 4 button. When the Student Edition Labs menu appears, click *Using Windows* to begin. A new browser window will open. Follow the on-screen instructions to complete the Lab. When finished, click the Exit button. If required, submit your results to your instructor.

5 **Practice Test**

Click the number 5 button. Answer each question. When completed, enter your name and click the Grade Test button to submit the quiz for grading. Make a note of any missed questions. If required, submit your score to your instructor.

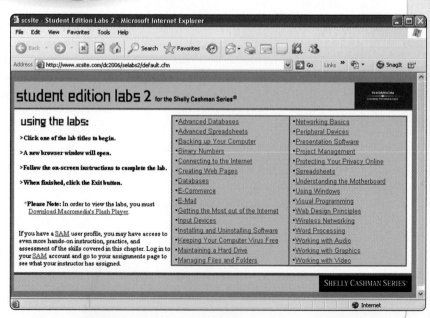

Learn It Online

⑥ Who Wants To Be a Computer Genius²?

Click the number 6 button to find out if you are a computer genius. Directions about how to play the game will be displayed. When you are ready to play, click the Play button. Submit your score to your instructor.

⑦ Wheel of Terms

Click the number 7 button to reinforce important terms you learned in this chapter by playing the Shelly Cashman Series version of this popular game. Directions about how to play the game will be displayed. When you are ready to play, click the Play button. Submit your score to your instructor.

⑧ DC Track and Field

Click the number 8 button to use what you have learned in this chapter to compete against other students in three track and field events. Directions about how to play the game will be displayed. When you are ready to play, click the start first event button. If required, submit your score to your instructor.

⑨ You're Hired!

Click the number 9 button to use what you have learned in this chapter to embark on the path to a career in computers. Directions about how to play the game will be displayed. When you are ready to play, click the begin game button. If required, submit your score to your instructor.

⑩ Crossword Puzzle Challenge

Click the number 10 button. Complete the puzzle to reinforce skills you learned in this chapter. Directions about how to play the game will be displayed. When you are ready to play, click the Play button. Submit the completed puzzle to your instructor.

⑪ Lab Exercises

Click the number 11 button. When the Lab Exercises menu appears, click the exercise assigned by your instructor. A new browser window will open. Follow the on-screen instructions to complete the exercise. When finished, click the Exit button. If required, submit your results to your instructor.

⑫ Learn the Web

No matter how much computer experience you have, navigating the Web for the first time can be intimidating. How do you get started? Click the number 12 button and click the links to discover how you can find out everything you want to know about the Internet.

⑬ Chapter Discussion Forum

Select an objective from this chapter on page 3 about which you would like more information. Click the number 13 button and post a short message listing a meaningful message title accompanied by one or more questions concerning the selected objective. In two days, return to the threaded discussion by clicking the number 13 button. Submit to your instructor your original message and at least one response to your message.

Learn How To

Use the Learn How To activities to learn fundamental skills when using a computer and accompanying technology. Complete the exercises and submit them to your instructor. Visit scsite.com/dc2006/ch1/howto to obtain more information pertaining to each activity.

LEARN HOW TO 1: Start and Close an Application

An application accomplishes tasks on a computer. You can start any application by using the Start button.

Complete these steps to start the Web browser application called Internet Explorer:

1. Click the Start button (**start**) at the left of the Windows taskbar on the bottom of the screen. *The Start menu is displayed.*
2. Point to All Programs on the Start menu. *The All Programs submenu appears (Figure 1-45).*
3. Click the program name, **Internet Explorer**, on the All Programs submenu. *The Internet Explorer browser window opens (Figure 1-46).*

An item on the All Programs submenu might have a small right arrow next to it. When this occurs, point to the item and another submenu will appear. Click the application name on this submenu to start the application. Some application names might appear on the Start menu itself. If so, click any of these names to start the corresponding application.

FIGURE 1-45

FIGURE 1-46

Below the line on the left side of the Start menu, Windows displays the names of the applications recently opened on the computer. You can start any of these applications by clicking the name of the application.

To close an application, click the Close button (⊠) in the upper-right corner of the window. If you have created but not saved a document, Windows will ask if you want to save the document. If you do not want to save it, click the No button in the displayed dialog box. If you want to save it, refer to Learn How To number 1 in Chapter 3 on page 178.

Exercise

1. Using the Start button, start the application named WordPad found on the Accessories submenu of the All Programs submenu. WordPad is a word processing application. Type the following: To start an application, click the application name on the All Programs submenu and then type your name. Click the Print button (🖨) on the toolbar. Submit the printout to your instructor.
2. Close the WordPad application. If you are asked if you want to save changes to the document, click the No button. Start the WordPad application again, type some new text, and then close the WordPad application. When the dialog box is displayed, click the Cancel button. What happened? Now, close the WordPad window without saving the document. Submit your answer to your instructor.

Learn How To

3. Using the Start button, start the e-mail program on the computer. What is the name of the e-mail program? In the program window, what menu names are displayed on the menu bar at the top of the window? Close the e-mail program. Submit your answers to your instructor.

LEARN HOW TO 2: Use the Discovering Computers 2006 Web Site (scsite.com/dc2006)

The Discovering Computers 2006 Web site provides a variety of activities and exercises. To use the site, you first must register and establish a user name and <u>password</u>. Perform the following steps to register:

1. Find your key code on the card at the front of this book.
2. Start the Web browser.
3. Type `scsite.com/dc2006` in the Address box of the Web browser. Press the ENTER key.
4. When the registration page is displayed, click the New User Registration link.
5. Enter the key code you found in Step 1.
6. Follow the on-screen instructions to complete registration.

When you first type a Web address to display a page from the dc2006 site, you must enter your user name and password to gain access to the site. When you are done using the site, close the browser so no one else can visit the site with your user name and password.

Exercise

1. Start the Web browser on your computer.
2. Type `scsite.com/dc2006/ch1/howto` in the Address box of the browser and then press the ENTER key.
3. If the registration page is displayed and you have not yet registered, complete the steps above. If you are registered, click Registered User, enter your user name and password, and then click the Submit button.
4. Navigate to the Chapter 1 home page.
5. Visit each of the Exercises Web pages (Chapter Review, Key Terms, Checkpoint, Learn It Online, Learn How To, Web Research, and Case Studies). Use the navigation bar on the left of the screen to display these pages.
6. Click the browser's Close button to close the application.
7. Write a report that describes the use of each of the Exercises pages you visited. Which page do you think will prove the most valuable to you when using the book and the Web site? Why? Which will be the least useful? Why? Submit your report to your instructor.

LEARN HOW TO 3: Find Out About Your Computer

By following these steps, you can find out about your computer:

1. Click the Start button on the Windows XP taskbar.
2. Point to All Programs on the Start menu, point to Accessories on the All Programs submenu, and then point to System Tools on the Accessories submenu.
3. Click <u>System Information</u> on the System Tools submenu. Windows displays a system summary in the right side of the window, and an index of categories in the left side of the window (Figure 1-47).

To determine more information about your computer, click any of the plus signs in the left side of the window. Then, click the item about which you want more information.

FIGURE 1-47

Exercise

1. Submit the answers to the following questions about your computer:
    a. What type of operating system (OS Name) is in use?
    b. What company manufactured the computer?
    c. How much RAM (physical memory) is on the computer?
    d. How much data can you store on the C: drive?
    e. What is the name of a CD or DVD drive found on the computer?

Web Research

Use the Internet-based Web Research exercises to broaden your understanding of the concepts presented in this chapter. Visit scsite.com/dc2006/ch1/research to obtain more information pertaining to each exercise. To discuss any of the Web Research exercises in this chapter with other students, post your thoughts or questions at scsite.com/dc2006/ch1/forum.

(1) Scavenger Hunt Use one of the <u>search engines</u> listed in Figure 2-10 in Chapter 2 on page 78 or your own favorite search engine to find the answers to the questions below. Copy and paste the Web address from the Web page where you found the answer. Some questions may have more than one answer. If required, submit your answers to your instructor. (1) What are three accredited online colleges or universities that offer a bachelor's degree in computer information technology? (2) Two National Science Foundation (NSF) programs were established in 1997 to interconnect 50 university and scientific computing sites. What colleges host these two sites? What were the locations of the five original NSF-financed supercomputer centers? (3) Personal finance software helps you balance your checkbook and manage your finances. What is the name of a popular personal finance software program? (4) What is the name of the first spreadsheet program? (5) A programming language developed by the U.S. Department of Defense was named to honor a famous woman mathematician. What is the name of this programming language? Click the Technology link on the left side of the page.

(2) Search Sleuth Visit the <u>Google Web site</u> (google.com) and then click the About Google link at the bottom of the page. Using your word processing program, answer the following questions and then, if required, submit your answers to your instructor. (1) Below Our Company, click Corporate Info. Who are the founders of Google? (2) Click the Technology link on the left side of the page. Provide a summary on how Google uses PageRank. (3) Click your browser's Back button or press the BACKSPACE key to return to the About Google page. Below Our Search, click the Google Web Search Features link. What is the purpose of the I'm Feeling Lucky button? What is the purpose of the Similar Pages link? What is Froogle? (4) Click your browser's Back button two times to return to the Google home page. In the Google Search text box, type HTML and click the Google Search button. Approximately how many hits resulted? Do any definitions appear? If so, list the definitions. How much time did it take to complete the search? (5) In the Google Search text box, type HTML Tutorial and click the Search button. Compare this to your earlier search. Are there more or fewer hits? How much time did it take to complete the second search? (6) Click one of the resulting HTML tutorial links and review the tutorial. Write a 50-word summary of the tutorial. Using the information contained within the tutorial, do you think you would be able to create your own Web site?

(3) Newsgroups One of the more popular topics for <u>newsgroups</u> is the Internet. Find three newsgroups, such as those listed in CyberFiber (cyberfiber.com/internet.htm) or Google Groups, that discuss an aspect of the Internet. Read the newsgroup postings and post a reply to one message. Summarize three topics under discussion and your reply to a message.

(4) Journaling Respond to your readings in this chapter by writing at least one page about your reactions, evaluations, and reflections about computer usage in your home. For example, how many appliances in your kitchen have a computer component? Has your <u>smart phone</u> replaced a camera or landline telephone? Have family members reduced their television viewing time with playing online games or surfing the Internet? You also can write about the new terms you learned by reading this chapter. If required, submit your journal to your instructor.

(5) Ethics in Action The Internet has increased the ease with which students can plagiarize material for research paper assignments. Teachers are using online services, such as Turnitin.com, to help detect plagiarized papers and to help students understand how to cite sources correctly. Visit the <u>Turnitin site</u> (turnitin.com) and then write a summary of how this service is used. How prevalent is plagiarism on your campus? What action should an instructor take when a student submits a plagiarized paper? If required, submit your summary to your instructor.

Case Studies

Use the Case Studies to apply the concepts presented in the chapter to real-world situations. Visit scsite.com/dc2006/ch1/cases to obtain more information pertaining to each exercise. To discuss the Case Studies in this chapter with other students, visit scsite.com/dc2006/ch1/forum and post your thoughts or questions.

CASE STUDY 1 — Class Discussion   You are a clerical worker for a small property management company. The company manages 30 industrial buildings. Currently, you serve as a receptionist, answer the telephone, file business documents, and perform other clerical tasks. Eventually, however, you would like to be promoted to an administrative position. Your supervisor has just purchased a new computer for the office. She has made it clear that, in order to be promoted, you must become proficient in the use of computers and **computer software**. Review the course offerings at your school. Prepare a list of courses you could take that would help you acquire the knowledge and skills you need to be promoted. Draft a memo to your supervisor detailing the courses you plan to take and explaining why each would be valuable. Be prepared to discuss your findings.

CASE STUDY 2 — Class Discussion   You are a member of your local school district's board of education. Over the past year, the number of computers purchased by the district increased by 85 percent, while the supply of library books declined by almost 10 percent. School officials claim that computers extend learning opportunities and develop the **computer literacy** needed in today's technological world. Yet, some parents are complaining that computer purchases represent frivolous, status-seeking spending. Notebook computers are purchased for teachers, while textbooks and library books are too old, too worn, and too scarce. Use the Web and/or print media to learn how computers are being used in schools. As a school board member, draft a proposal recommending the percentage of the instructional materials budget that should be spent on computers versus the percentage that should be spent on library books and textbooks. Note the factors that influenced your decision. Be prepared to discuss your recommendations.

CASE STUDY 3 — Research   Computers are everywhere. Watching television, driving a car, using a charge card, even ordering fast food all involve computers, not to mention browsing the Web on your personal computer. Your car computer is an **embedded computer** that can be described as special-purpose, because it only accepts specific input and performs limited functions. Your personal computer, on the other hand, is general-purpose, meaning it accepts a wide range of input and can perform a variety of tasks. For one day, make a list of each computer you encounter (be careful not to limit yourself just to the computers you see). How is the computer used? Is the computer special-purpose or general-purpose? Why? How was the task the computer performs accomplished before computers? Write a brief report or use PowerPoint to create a presentation and share your findings.

CASE STUDY 4 — Research   You are an assistant manager at a local computer store. Your manager suspects that for cultural, financial, or societal reasons, certain groups of people are more likely to buy computers than others. To increase the impact of the store's promotions, your manager has asked you to discover if computers are purchased by individuals from a broad spectrum, or if a certain type exists that represents most **computer buyers**. Use the Web and/or print media to learn more about the demographics of computer buyers. What gender are most buyers? In what age range do they fall? What seems to be the typical educational level? What is the approximate average income of a typical buyer? Do buyers tend to share any other characteristics? If you discover any trends, what reasons might be behind the results? Write a brief report or use PowerPoint to create a presentation and share your findings.

CASE STUDY 5 — Team Challenge   People use computers in a variety of fields, including education, finance, government, health care, science, publishing, travel, and industry. Although the way people use computers varies, each use of a computer involves **computer hardware**, computer software, and normally some type of communications capability over networks, such as the Internet. Form a three-member team and choose a field in which you all are interested. Using the Web and/or print media, assign one member of your team to investigate hardware used in the field, another member to investigate software used in the field, and the third member to investigate communications capabilities used in the field. After your investigation, characterize a hypothetical business or organization in the field. Based on your investigation, prepare a report that recommends specific hardware, software, and networking capabilities that would be best for the business or organization; explain your recommendations in the report.

Special Feature

Timeline 2006

MILESTONES IN COMPUTER HISTORY

Dr. John V. Atanasoff and Clifford Berry design and build the first electronic digital computer. Their machine, the Atanasoff-Berry-Computer, or ABC, provides the foundation for advances in electronic digital computers.

John von Neumann in front of the electronic computer built at the Institute for Advanced Study. This computer and its von Neumann architecture served as the prototype for subsequent stored program computers worldwide.

William Shockley, John Bardeen, and Walter Brattain invent the transfer resistance device, eventually called the transistor. The transistor would revolutionize computers, proving much more reliable than vacuum tubes.

1937 — **1943** — **1945** — **1946** — **1947** — **1951**

During World War II, British scientist Alan Turing designs the Colossus, an electronic computer created for the military to break German codes. The computer's existence is kept secret until the 1970s.

Dr. John W. Mauchly and J. Presper Eckert, Jr. complete work on the first large-scale electronic, general-purpose digital computer. The ENIAC (Electronic Numerical Integrator And Computer) weighs 30 tons, contains 18,000 vacuum tubes, occupies a 30-by-50-foot space, and consumes 160 kilowatts of power. The first time it is turned on, lights dim in an entire section of Philadelphia.

The first commercially available electronic digital computer, the UNIVAC I (UNIVersal Automatic Computer), is introduced by Remington Rand. Public awareness of computers increases when the UNIVAC I, after analyzing only five percent of the popular vote, correctly predicts that Dwight D. Eisenhower will win the presidential election.

Dr. Grace Hopper considers the concept of reusable software in her paper, "The Education of a Computer." The paper describes how to program a computer with symbolic notation instead of the detailed machine language that had been used.

The IBM 305 RAMAC system is the first to use magnetic disk for external storage. The system provides storage capacity similar to magnetic tape that previously was used, but offers the advantage of semi-random access capability.

More than 200 programming languages have been created.

IBM introduces two smaller, desk-sized computers: the IBM 1401 for business and the IBM 1620 for scientists. The IBM 1620 initially is called the CADET, but IBM drops the name when campus wags claim it is an acronym for, Can't Add, Doesn't Even Try.

Fortran (FORmula TRANslation), an efficient, easy-to-use programming language, is introduced by John Backus.

1952 1953 1957 1958 1959 1960

The IBM model 650 is one of the first widely used computers. Originally planning to produce only 50 machines, the system is so successful that eventually IBM manufactures more than 1,000. With the IBM 700 series of machines, the company will dominate the mainframe market for the next decade.

Core memory, developed in the early 1950s, provides much larger storage capacity than vacuum tube memory.

Jack Kilby of Texas Instruments invents the integrated circuit, which lays the foundation for high-speed computers and large-capacity memories. Computers built with transistors mark the beginning of the second generation of computer hardware.

COBOL, a high-level business application language, is developed by a committee headed by Dr. Grace Hopper. COBOL uses English-like phrases and runs on most business computers, making it one of the more widely used programming languages.

Computer Science Corporation becomes the first software company listed on the New York Stock Exchange.

Dr. John Kemeny of Dartmouth leads the development of the BASIC programming language. BASIC will be widely used on personal computers.

IBM

Under pressure from the industry, IBM announces that some of its software will be priced separately from the computer hardware. This unbundling allows software firms to emerge in the industry.

Digital Equipment Corporation (DEC) introduces the first minicomputer, the PDP-8. The machine is used extensively as an interface for time-sharing systems.

In a letter to the editor titled, "GO TO Statements Considered Harmful," Dr. Edsger Dijsktra introduces the concept of structured programming, developing standards for constructing computer programs.

ARPANET

The ARPANET network, a predecessor of the Internet, is established.

| **1964** | **1965** | **1968** | **1969** | **1970** |

The number of computers has grown to 18,000. Third-generation computers, with their controlling circuitry stored on chips, are introduced. The IBM System/360 computer is the first family of compatible machines, merging science and business lines.

Alan Shugart at IBM demonstrates the first regular use of an 8-inch floppy (magnetic storage) disk.

Fourth-generation computers, built with chips that use LSI (large-scale integration) arrive. While the chips used in 1965 contained as many as 1,000 circuits, the LSI chip contains as many as 15,000.

IBM introduces the term word processing for the first time with its Magnetic Tape/Selectric Typewriter (MT/ST). The MT/ST was the first reusable storage medium that allowed typed material to be edited without having to retype the document.

MITS, Inc. advertises one of the first microcomputers, the Altair. Named for the destination in an episode of *Star Trek*, the Altair is sold in kits for less than $400. Although initially it has no keyboard, no monitor, no permanent memory, and no software, 4,000 orders are taken within the first three months.

VisiCalc, a spreadsheet program written by Bob Frankston and Dan Bricklin, is introduced. Originally written to run on Apple II computers, VisiCalc will be seen as the most important reason for the acceptance of personal computers in the business world.

The IBM PC is introduced, signaling IBM's entrance into the personal computer marketplace. The IBM PC quickly garners the largest share of the personal computer market and becomes the personal computer of choice in business.

Ethernet, the first local area network (LAN), is developed at Xerox PARC (Palo Alto Research Center) by Robert Metcalf. The LAN allows computers to communicate and share software, data, and peripherals. Initially designed to link minicomputers, Ethernet will be extended to personal computers.

The first public online information services, CompuServe and the Source, are founded.

1971 — 1975 — 1976 — 1979 — 1980 — 1981

Dr. Ted Hoff of Intel Corporation develops a microprocessor, or microprogrammable computer chip, the Intel 4004.

IBM offers Microsoft Corporation cofounder, Bill Gates, the opportunity to develop the operating system for the soon-to-be announced IBM personal computer. With the development of MS-DOS, Microsoft achieves tremendous growth and success.

The first computer virus, Elk Cloner, is spread via Apple II floppy disks, which contained the operating system. A short rhyme would appear on the screen when the user pressed Reset after the 50th boot of an infected disk.

Steve Jobs and Steve Wozniak build the first Apple computer. A subsequent version, the Apple II, is an immediate success. Adopted by elementary schools, high schools, and colleges, for many students, the Apple II is their first contact with the world of computers.

Alan Shugart presents the Winchester hard drive, revolutionizing storage for personal computers.

Special Feature

scsite.com/dc2006/ch1/timeline

3.275 Million

3,275,000 personal computers are sold, almost 3,000,000 more than in 1981.

Apple introduces the Macintosh computer, which incorporates a unique, easy-to-learn, graphical user interface.

COMPAQ

Compaq, Inc. is founded to develop and market IBM-compatible PCs.

Hayes introduces the 300 bps smart modem. The modem is an immediate success.

Hewlett-Packard announces the first LaserJet printer for personal computers.

Microsoft

Microsoft has public stock offering and raises approximately $61 million. Within 20 years, Microsoft's stock is worth nearly $350 billion or 5,735 times the amount raised in the initial public stock offering.

1982   **1983**   **1984**   **1986**   **1988**

Instead of choosing a person for its annual award, *TIME* magazine names the computer Machine of the Year for 1982, acknowledging the impact of computers on society.

Lotus Development Corporation is founded. Its spreadsheet software, Lotus 1-2-3, which combines spreadsheet, graphics, and database programs in one package, becomes the best-selling program for IBM personal computers.

Microsoft surpasses Lotus Development Corporation to become the world's top software vendor.

While working at CERN, Switzerland, Tim Berners-Lee invents an Internet-based hypermedia enterprise for information sharing. Berners-Lee will call this innovation the World Wide Web.

World Wide Web Consortium releases standards that describe a framework for linking documents on different computers.

Several companies introduce computers using the Pentium processor from Intel. The Pentium chip is the successor to the Intel 486 processor. It contains 3.1 million transistors and is capable of performing 112,000,000 instructions per second.

Microsoft releases Microsoft Office 3 Professional, the first version of Microsoft Office.

1989　　1991　1992　　1993

The Intel 486 becomes the world's first 1,000,000 transistor microprocessor. It crams 1.2 million transistors on a .4" x .6" sliver of silicon and executes 15,000,000 instructions per second — four times as fast as its predecessor, the 80386 chip.

The White House launches its Web site, which includes an interactive citizens' handbook and White House history and tours.

Microsoft releases Windows 3.1, the latest version of its Windows operating system. Windows 3.1 offers improvements such as TrueType fonts, multimedia capability, and object linking and embedding (OLE). In two months, 3,000,000 copies of Windows 3.1 are sold.

U.S. Robotics introduces PalmPilot, a handheld personal organizer. The PalmPilot's user friendliness and low price make it a standout next to more expensive personal digital assistants (PDAs).

Jim Clark and Marc Andreessen found Netscape and launch Netscape Navigator 1.0, a browser for the World Wide Web.

Sun Microsystems launches Java, an object-oriented programming language that allows users to write one application for a variety of computer platforms. Java becomes one of the hotter Internet technologies.

Microsoft releases Windows NT 4.0, an operating system for client-server networks. Windows NT's management tools and wizards make it easier for developers to build and deploy business applications.

1994   1995   1996

Linus Torvalds creates the Linux kernel, a UNIX-like operating system that he releases free across the Internet for further enhancement by other programmers.

Microsoft releases Windows 95, a major upgrade to its Windows operating system. Windows 95 consists of more than 10,000,000 lines of computer instructions developed by 300 person-years of effort. More than 50,000 individuals and companies test the software before it is released.

Two out of three employees in the United States have access to a personal computer, and one out of every three homes has a personal computer. Fifty million personal computers are sold worldwide and more than 250,000,000 are in use.

Apple and Microsoft sign a joint technology development agreement. Microsoft buys $150,000,000 of Apple stock.

More than 10,000,000 people take up telecommuting, which is the capability of working at home and communicating with an office via computer. Increasingly more firms embrace telecommuting to help increase productivity, reduce absenteeism, and provide greater job satisfaction.

Apple Computer introduces the iMac, the next version of its popular Macintosh computer. The iMac abandons such conventional features as a floppy disk drive but wins customers with its futuristic design, see-through case, and easy setup. Consumer demand outstrips Apple's production capabilities, and some vendors are forced to begin waiting lists.

DVD, the next generation of optical disc storage technology, is introduced. DVD can store computer, audio, and video data in a single format, with the capability of producing near-studio quality. By year's end, 500,000 DVD players are shipped worldwide.

1997

1998

Intel introduces the Pentium II processor with 7.5 million transistors. The new processor, which incorporates MMX technology, processes video, audio, and graphics data more efficiently and supports applications such as movie editing, gaming, and more.

E-commerce, or electronic commerce — the marketing of goods and services over the Internet — booms. Companies such as Dell, E*TRADE, and Amazon.com spur online shopping, allowing buyers to obtain everything from hardware and software to financial and travel services, insurance, automobiles, books, and more.

Microsoft releases Internet Explorer 4.0 and seizes a key place in the Internet arena. This new Web browser is greeted with tremendous customer demand.

Microsoft ships Windows 98, an upgrade to Windows 95. Windows 98 offers improved Internet access, better system performance, and support for a new generation of hardware and software. In six months, more than 10,000,000 copies of Windows 98 are sold worldwide.

Fifty million users are connected to the Internet and World Wide Web.

Special Feature

Governments and businesses frantically work to make their computers Y2K (Year 2000) compliant, spending more than $500 billion worldwide. Y2K non-compliant computers cannot distinguish whether 01/01/00 refers to 1900 or 2000, and thus may operate using a wrong date. This Y2K bug can affect any application that relies on computer chips, such as ATMs, airplanes, energy companies, and the telephone system. In the end, the Y2K bug turned out not to be a problem.

U.S. District Judge Thomas Penfield Jackson rules in the antitrust lawsuit brought by the Department of Justice and 19 states that Microsoft used its monopoly power to stifle competition.

Shawn Fanning, 19, and his company, Napster, turn the music industry upside down by developing software that allows computer users to swap music files with one another without going through a centralized file server. The Recording Industry of America, on behalf of five media companies, sues Napster for copyright infringement and wins.

 1999

 2000

Microsoft introduces Office 2000, its premier productivity suite, offering new tools for users to create content and save it directly to a Web site without any file conversion or special steps.

E-commerce achieves mainstream acceptance. Annual e-commerce sales exceed $100 billion, and Internet advertising expenditures reach more than $5 billion.

Open Source Code software, such as the Linux operating system and the Apache Web server created by unpaid volunteers, begin to gain wide acceptance among computer users.

Dot-com companies (Internet based) go out of business at a record pace — nearly one per day — as financial investors withhold funding due to the companies' unprofitability.

Microsoft ships Windows 2000 and Windows Me. Windows 2000 offers improved behind-the-scene security and reliability. Windows Me is designed for home users and lets them edit home movies, share digital photos, index music, and create a home network.

Intel unveils its Pentium 4 chip with clock speeds starting at 1.4 GHz. The Pentium 4 includes 42 million transistors, nearly twice as many contained on its predecessor, the Pentium III.

Microsoft releases major operating system updates with Windows XP for the desktop and servers, and Pocket PC 2002 for handheld computers. Windows XP is significantly more reliable than previous versions, features a 32-bit computing architecture, and offers a new look and feel. Pocket PC 2002 offers the handheld computer user a familiar Windows interface and consistent functionality.

According to the U.S. Department of Commerce, Internet traffic is doubling every 100 days, resulting in an annual growth rate of more than 700 percent. It has taken radio and television 30 years and 15 years, respectively, to reach 60 million people. The Internet has achieved the same audience base in 3 years.

2000

2001

Microsoft introduces Office XP, the next version of the world's leading suite of productivity software. Features include speech and handwriting recognition, smart tags, and task panes.

Telemedicine uses satellite technology and videoconferencing to broadcast consultations and to perform distant surgeries. Robots are used for complex and precise tasks. Computer-aided surgery uses virtual reality to assist with training and planning procedures.

Avid readers enjoy e-books, which are digital texts read on compact computer screens. E-books can hold the equivalent of 10 traditional books containing text and graphics. Readers can search, highlight text, and add notes.

DVD writers begin to replace CD writers (CD-RW). DVDs can store up to eight times as much data as CDs. Uses include storing home movies, music, photos, and backups. Digital cameras and video editors help the average user develop quality video to store on DVDs.

Digital video cameras, DVD writers, easy-to-use video editing software, and improvements in storage capabilities allow the average computer user to create Hollywood-like videos with introductions, conclusions, scenes rearranged, music, and voice-over.

After several years of negligible sales, the Tablet PC is reintroduced as the next-generation mobile PC. The lightweight device, the size of a three-ring notebook, is ideal for people on the go. It runs Windows XP Tablet PC Edition, has wireless capabilities, and features natural input capabilities including pen and speech technologies.

2002

Microsoft launches its .NET strategy, which is a new environment for developing and running software applications featuring ease of development of Web-based services. Users of applications immediately see the benefit of .NET as instant access to data and services in the context of their current task.

Handspring begins shipping the Treo communicator, a handheld computer with cellular telephone, e-mail, text messaging, and wireless Web capabilities.

Intel ships its revamped Pentium 4 chip with the 0.13 micron processor and Hyper-Threading (HT) Technology, operating at speeds of 3.06 GHz. This new development eventually will enable processors with a billion transistors to operate at 20 GHz.

U.S. District Judge Colleen Kollar-Kotelly rules against the nine states appealing the antitrust settlement reached between Microsoft and the Justice Department. The nine states were seeking tougher sanctions against the software giant for abusing its monopoly power. Two of the nine states, Massachusetts and West Virginia, plan to appeal the latest ruling to the U.S. District Court of Appeals.

Computer manufacturers and software companies integrate high-end PCs and entertainment devices. The result is PCs with great entertainment functions that let you watch and record TV, burn CDs and DVDs, play games, and more.

IBM puts its weight behind On Demand computing. Its intention is to invest up to $10 billion in hardware and software, and then sell computing time and the use of applications to businesses in a manner similar to an electric utility company.

Wireless computers and devices, such as keyboards, mouse devices, home networks, and public Internet access points become commonplace. Latest operating systems include support for both the Wi-Fi (wireless fidelity) and Bluetooth standards. Wireless capabilities are standard on many PDAs and Tablet PCs.

2003

MSBlast worm and SoBig virus plague Microsoft Windows users. Microsoft Corporation responds by creating the Anti-Virus Reward Program, initially funded with $5 million, to help law enforcement agencies identify and bring to justice those who illegally release damaging worms, viruses and other types of malicious code on the Internet.

In an attempt to maintain their current business model of selling songs, the Recording Industry Association of American (RIAA) files over 250 lawsuits against individual computer users who offer copyrighted music over peer-to-peer networks.

Microsoft ships Office 2003, the latest version of its flagship Office suite. New features include a consistent user interface, an overhauled Outlook, increased emphasis on task panes, improved collaboration, enhanced XML functionality, and a new application called OneNote for organizing your notes.

Flat-panel LCD monitors overtake bulky CRT monitors as the popular choice of computer users. Although flat-panel LCD monitors cost more, they offer several advantages including physical size, weight, true display size, better power consumption, and no radiation emission.

Companies such as RealNetworks, Microsoft, Sony, and Wal-Mart stake out turf in the online music store business started by Apple Computer. In the previous year, Apple's iTunes Music Store Web site sold nearly 20 million songs for 99 cents each.

USB Flash Drives, which are small enough to fit on a key chain but can store up to 4 billion characters, become a cost-effective way to transport data and information from one computer to another.

2004

Linux, the open-source operating system, makes major inroads into the server market as a viable alternative to Microsoft Windows, Sun's Solaris, and the UNIX operating systems.

Major retailers begin requiring suppliers to include Radio Frequency Identification (RFID) tags or microchips with antennas, which can be as small as 1/3 of a millimeter across, in the goods they sell. When a transponder receives a certain radio query, it responds by transmitting its unique ID code. Besides carrying out the functions of the bar code, RFIDs may eventually eliminate long checkout lines.

Apple Computer introduces the sleek iMac G5. The new computer's display device contains the system unit.

106 million, or 53 percent, of the 200 million online population in America accesses the Internet via speedy broadband.

Linux

Microsoft
Windows^{XP}
Media Center Edition 2005

Spyware
Spam
Phishing
Spim Spit

The Mozilla Foundation, the creators of the free open source Firefox browser, predicts that by the end of 2005, it will have 10 percent of the browser market, primarily at the expense of Microsoft's Internet Explorer (IE) security-plagued browser.

Microsoft unveils Windows XP Media Center Edition 2005. This operating system allows users to access the routine capabilities of a Windows XP-based PC while focusing on delivering media content such as music, digital photography, movies, and television.

Spam, spyware, phishing, spim, and spit take center stage, along with viruses, as major nuisances to the 801 million computer users worldwide. Spam, which accounts for 45 percent of all e-mail, involves the sending of bulk e-mail that is unsolicited and masks its origin. Spyware is a program placed on the computer without the user's knowledge that secretly collects information about the user, often related to Web browsing habits. Phishing is the act of sending an e-mail to a user falsely claiming to be a legitimate enterprise in an attempt to trick the user into surrendering private information that will be used for identity theft. Spim is spam via instant messaging. Spit is spam via Internet telephony.

The OQO handheld computer is a fully-functional Windows XP computer with desktop capabilities. Just 4.9 inches long, 3.4 inches wide, .9 inch thick, and weighing only 14 ounces, the OQO fills the void between the bulk and awkwardness of a notebook computer and the limited capability of a smart phone or PDA.

2005

The smart phone overtakes the PDA as the personal mobile device of choice. A smart phone offers a cellular phone, full personal information management and e-mail functionality, a Web browser, instant message capabilities, and even the ability to listen to music, play video and games, and take pictures with its built-in camera.

To date, Microsoft has sold over 300 million copies of its Windows XP operating system. By early January, Microsoft automatically downloaded to its users' computers over 100 million copies of Service Pack 2 (SP2), its latest update to Windows XP. In addition to a new security center and firewall, SP2 adds a pop-up blocker in Internet Explorer and updated support for Wi-Fi and Bluetooth wireless technologies.

Microsoft introduces Visual Studio 2005. The product includes Visual Basic, Visual C#, Visual J#, Visual C++, and SQL Server. Microsoft also releases a Visual Studio 2005 Express Edition for hobbyists, students, and nonprofessionals.

Microsoft
Visual Studio 2005

CHAPTER TWO

The Internet and World Wide Web

Picture Yourself Instant Messaging

While eating popcorn and waiting for the movie to begin, you hear an alarm. Did you forget to turn off your smart phone? You look at the phone and notice that a friend is sending you an instant message from her home computer. With a few minutes until the lights dim in the theater, you open the message. At that moment, a chorus of your friends' voices singing "Happy Birthday" loudly plays through the phone while the same words appear on the phone's screen. Quickly, you turn off the phone's sound and look around — hoping no one heard. No such luck. Nearly everyone in the theater found it quite amusing.

With the phone's sound turned off, you press some buttons to reply to the instant message, thanking your musical friends for their greeting. Your friend replies that she just bought a PC video camera and wanted to try sending a video instant message over her high-speed Internet line. Everyone gathered at her house to sing and send you the message. After conversing for a few minutes, you punch in C U L8R on the phone and set your online status to Away — so everyone knows you will be unavailable. Then, you press another button to display the Cubs score and the weather report. Next, you decide to check e-mail messages. The movie is starting . . . time to disconnect from the Internet.

To learn how technology allows you access to your friends, sports scores, weather reports, and e-mail, read Chapter 2 and discover features of the Internet and World Wide Web.

OBJECTIVES

After completing this chapter, you will be able to:

1. Discuss the history of the Internet
2. Explain how to access and connect to the Internet
3. Analyze an IP address
4. Identify the components of a Web address
5. Explain the purpose of a Web browser
6. Search for information on the Web
7. Describe the types of Web sites
8. Recognize how Web pages use graphics, animation, audio, video, virtual reality, and plug-ins
9. Identify the steps required for Web publishing
10. Describe the types of e-commerce
11. Explain how e-mail, FTP, newsgroups and message boards, mailing lists, chat rooms, instant messaging, and Internet telephony work
12. Identify the rules of netiquette

CONTENTS

THE INTERNET

One of the major reasons business, home, and other users purchase computers is for Internet access. Through the Internet, society has access to global information and instant communications. Further, access to the Internet can occur anytime from a computer anywhere: at home, at work, at school, in a restaurant, on an airplane, and even at the beach.

The **Internet**, also called the *Net*, is a worldwide collection of networks that links millions of businesses, government agencies, educational institutions, and individuals. Each of the networks on the Internet provides resources that add to the abundance of goods, services, and information accessible via the Internet.

Today, more than one billion users around the world connect to the Internet for a variety of reasons, some of which are shown in Figure 2-1. The World Wide Web and e-mail are two of the more widely accessed Internet services. Other services include FTP (File Transfer Protocol), newsgroups, chat rooms, instant messaging, and Internet telephony. To enhance your understanding of these services, the chapter begins by discussing the history of the Internet and how the Internet works and then explains each of these services.

FIGURE 2-1a   (Web)

FIGURE 2-1c   (FTP – File Transfer Protocol)

FIGURE 2-1b   (e-mail)

FIGURE 2-1   Users around the world connect to the Internet to access the Web, send e-mail messages, transfer documents and photographs, post messages, chat with a group, or have a private conversation with an online friend(s) or family member(s).

HISTORY OF THE INTERNET

The Internet has its roots in a networking project started by the Pentagon's *Advanced Research Projects Agency (ARPA)*, an agency of the U.S. Department of Defense. ARPA's goal was to build a network that (1) allowed scientists at different physical locations to share information and work together on military and scientific projects and (2) could function even if part of the network were disabled or destroyed by a disaster such as a nuclear attack. That network, called *ARPANET*, became functional in September 1969, linking scientific and academic researchers across the United States.

The original ARPANET consisted of four main computers, one each located at the University of California at Los Angeles, the University of California at Santa Barbara, the Stanford Research Institute, and the University of Utah. Each computer served as a host on the network. A *host*, more commonly known today as a server, is any computer that provides services and connections to other computers on a network. Hosts often use high-speed communications to transfer data and messages over a network.

As researchers and others realized the great benefit of using ARPANET's e-mail to share data and information, ARPANET underwent phenomenal growth. By 1984, ARPANET had more than 1,000 individual computers linked as hosts. Today, more than 200 million hosts connect to the Internet.

Some organizations connected entire networks to ARPANET to take advantage of the high-speed communications it offered. In 1986, the

FIGURE 2-1d (newsgroup)

FIGURE 2-1f (instant messaging)

FIGURE 2-1e (chat)

FIGURE 2-1g (Internet telephony)

National Science Foundation (NSF) connected its huge network of five supercomputer centers, called *NSFnet*, to ARPANET. This configuration of complex networks and hosts became known as the Internet.

Until 1995, NSFnet handled the bulk of the communications activity, or **traffic**, on the Internet. In 1995, NSFnet terminated its network on the Internet and resumed its status as a research network.

Today, the Internet consists of many local, regional, national, and international networks. Numerous corporations, commercial firms, and other companies provide networks to handle the Internet traffic. Both public and private organizations own networks on the Internet. These networks, along with telephone companies, cable and satellite companies, and the government, all contribute toward the internal structure of the Internet. Read Looking Ahead 2-1 for a look at the next generation of the Internet.

Even as the Internet grows, it remains a public, cooperative, and independent network. Each organization on the Internet is responsible only for maintaining its own network. No single person, company, institution, or government agency controls or owns the Internet. The *World Wide Web Consortium* (W3C), however, oversees research and sets standards and guidelines for many areas of the Internet. The mission of the W3C is to contribute to the growth of the Web. About 350 organizations from around the world are members of the W3C. They advise, define standards, and address other issues.

HOW THE INTERNET WORKS

Data sent over the Internet travels via networks and communications media owned and operated by many companies. The following sections present various ways to connect to these networks on the Internet.

Connecting to the Internet

Employees and students often connect to the Internet through a business or school network. In this case, the computers usually are part of a network that connects to an Internet access provider through a high-speed connection line leased from a telephone company.

Many homes use dial-up access to connect to the Internet. **Dial-up access** takes place when the modem in your computer uses a standard telephone line to connect to the Internet. This type of access is an easy and inexpensive way for users to connect to the Internet. A dial-up connection, however, is slow-speed technology.

Some home and small business users are opting for higher-speed *broadband* Internet connections through DSL, cable television networks, radio signals, or satellite.

- **DSL** (*digital subscriber line*) is a technology that provides high-speed Internet connections using regular copper telephone lines.
- A **cable modem** allows access to high-speed Internet services through the cable television network.
- *Fixed wireless* high-speed Internet connections use an antenna on your house or business to communicate with a tower location via radio signals.
- A *satellite modem* communicates with a satellite dish to provide high-speed Internet connections via satellite.

In most cases, broadband Internet access is always on. That is, it is connected to the Internet the entire time the computer is running. With dial-up access, by contrast, you must establish the connection to the Internet. Usually a modem dials the telephone number to the Internet access provider.

Mobile users access the Internet using a variety of technologies. Most hotels and airports provide dial-up or broadband Internet connections. Wireless Internet access technologies, such as through radio networks, enable mobile users to connect easily to the Internet with notebook computers, Tablet PCs, PDAs, smart

LOOKING AHEAD 2-1

Internet Speeds into the Future

The Internet of the future will be much larger and faster. According to some Internet experts, in the next 20 years, Web surfers will be able to browse more than 250 million Web sites.

This increase in volume will be based, in part, on *Internet2*. This not-for-profit project develops and tests advanced Internet technologies for research, teaching, and learning. Internet2 members include more than 206 universities, 60 companies, and the U.S. government. Their goal is to change the current Internet's inefficiencies, such as relieving bottlenecks.

Recently, Internet2 researchers broke a speed record by sending data from Los Angeles to Geneva, Switzerland, at a speed that is nearly 10,000 times faster than the average home high-speed Internet connection. For more information, visit scsite.com/dc2006/ch2/looking and then click Internet2.

phones, and smart watches while away from a telephone, cable, or other wired connection. Many public locations, such as airports, hotels, schools, shopping malls, and coffee shops, are *hot spots* that provide wireless Internet connections to users with mobile computers or devices.

Access Providers

An **access provider** is a business that provides individuals and companies access to the Internet free or for a fee. The most common fee arrangement for an individual Internet account is a fixed amount, usually about $10 to $25 per month for dial-up, $40 to $55 for DSL and cable, $35 to $70 for fixed wireless, and $60 to $99 for satellite. For this fee, many providers offer unlimited Internet

access. Others specify a set number of access hours per month. With the latter arrangement, the provider charges extra for each hour of connection time that exceeds an allotted number of access hours. To attract more customers, some access providers also offer Web publishing services. Web publishing is discussed later in the chapter.

Users access the Internet through regional or national ISPs, online service providers, and wireless Internet service providers (Figure 2-2).

FAQ 2-1

What does bandwidth have to do with Internet access?

Bandwidth is a measure of how fast data and information travel over transmission media. Thus, higher-speed broadband Internet connections have a higher bandwidth than dial-up connections. For more information, visit scsite.com/dc2006/ch2/faq and then click Bandwidth.

FIGURE 2-2   Common ways to access the Internet are through a regional or national Internet service provider, an online service provider, or a wireless Internet service provider.

An **ISP** (**Internet service provider**) is a regional or national access provider. A *regional ISP* usually provides Internet access to a specific geographic area. A *national ISP* is a business that provides Internet access in cities and towns nationwide. For dial-up access, some national ISPs provide both local and toll-free telephone numbers. Due to their larger size, national ISPs usually offer more services and have a larger technical support staff than regional ISPs. Examples of national ISPs are AT&T Worldnet Service and EarthLink.

In addition to providing Internet access, an **online service provider** (**OSP**) also has many members-only features. These features include special content and services such as news, weather, legal information, financial data, hardware and software guides, games, travel guides, e-mail, photo communities, online calendars, and instant messaging. Some even have their own built-in Web browser. The fees for using an OSP sometimes are slightly higher than fees for an ISP. The two more popular OSPs are AOL (America Online) and MSN (Microsoft Network). AOL differs from many OSPs in that it provides gateway functionality to the Internet, meaning it regulates the Internet services to which members have access.

With dial-up Internet access, the telephone number you dial connects you to an access point on the Internet, called a *point of presence (POP)*. When selecting an ISP or OSP, ensure it provides at least one local POP telephone number. Otherwise, long-distance telephone charges will apply for the time you connect to the Internet.

A **wireless Internet service provider** (*WISP*) is a company that provides wireless Internet access to computers with wireless modems or access devices or to Internet-enabled mobile computers or devices. Internet-enabled mobile devices include PDAs, smart phones, and smart watches. An antenna on the computer or device typically sends signals through the airwaves to communicate with a wireless Internet service provider. Some examples of wireless Internet service providers include AT&T Wireless, GoAmerica, T-Mobile, and Verizon Wireless.

FAQ 2-2

How many people have broadband Internet access?

According to a recent study, 55 percent of adult Americans access the Internet using high-speed broadband connections at home or at work. Approximately 40 percent of home users have broadband Internet access. The main reason users switch to broadband access is they are frustrated with the slow speeds of dial-up access. For more information, visit scsite.com/dc2006/ch2/faq and then click Broadband.

How Data Travels the Internet

Computers connected to the Internet work together to transfer data and information around the world using servers and clients. On the Internet, your computer is a client that can access data, information, and services on a variety of servers.

The inner structure of the Internet works much like a transportation system. Just as interstate highways connect major cities and carry the bulk of the automotive traffic across the country, several main transmission media carry the heaviest amount of traffic on the Internet. These major carriers of network traffic are known collectively as the *Internet backbone*.

In the United States, the transmission media that make up the Internet backbone exchange data at several different major cities across the country. That is, they transfer data from one network to another until it reaches its final destination (Figure 2-3).

FAQ 2-3

How do I find the right access provider?

The Web provides many comprehensive lists of access providers. These lists often use the terms ISP and OSP interchangeably. One of the more popular lists on the Web is called The List. For more information, visit scsite.com/dc2006/ch2/faq and then click The List.

WEB LINK 2-1

Internet Backbone

For more information, visit scsite.com/dc2006/ch2/weblink and then click Internet Backbone.

FIGURE 2-3 HOW A HOME USER'S DATA MIGHT TRAVEL THE INTERNET USING A CABLE MODEM CONNECTION

Step 1: You initiate an action to request data from the Internet. For example, you request to display a Web page on your computer screen.

Step 2: A cable modem transfers the computer's digital signals to the cable television line in your house.

Step 3: Your request (digital signals) travels through cable television lines to a central cable system, which is shared by up to 500 homes in a neighborhood.

Step 4: The central cable system sends your request over high-speed fiberoptic lines to the cable operator, who often also is the ISP.

Step 5: The ISP routes your request through the Internet backbone to the destination server (in this example, the server that contains the requested Web site).

Step 6: The server retrieves the requested Web page and sends it back through the Internet backbone to your computer.

Internet Addresses

The Internet relies on an addressing system much like the postal service to send data to a computer at a specific destination. An **IP address**, short for *Internet Protocol address*, is a number that uniquely identifies each computer or device connected to the Internet. The IP address usually consists of four groups of numbers, each separated by a period. The number in each group is between 0 and 255. For example, the numbers 216.239.39.99 are an IP address. In general, the first portion of each IP address identifies the network and the last portion identifies the specific computer.

These all-numeric IP addresses are difficult to remember and use. Thus, the Internet supports the use of a text name that represents one or more IP addresses. A **domain name** is the text version of an IP address. Figure 2-4 shows an IP address and its associated domain name. As with an IP address, the components of a domain name are separated by periods.

In Figure 2-4, the com portion of the domain name is called the top-level domain. Every domain name contains a *top-level domain*, which identifies the type of organization associated with the domain. *Dot-com* is the term sometimes used to describe organizations with a top-level domain of com.

IP address ⟶ 216.239.39.99

Domain name ⟶ www.google.com

top-level domain

FIGURE 2-4 The IP address and domain name for the Google Web site.

The group that assigns and controls top-level domains is the *Internet Corporation for Assigned Names and Numbers (ICANN* pronounced EYE-can). Figure 2-5 lists current top-level domains. For international Web sites outside the United States, the domain name also includes a country code. In this case, the domain name ends with the country code, such as au for Australia or fr for France. For example, www.philips.com.au is the domain name for Philips Australia.

The *domain name system (DNS)* is the method that the Internet uses to store domain names and their corresponding IP addresses. When you specify a domain name, a **DNS server** translates the domain name to its associated IP address so data can be routed to the correct computer. A *DNS server* is an Internet server that usually is associated with an Internet access provider.

For a more technical discussion about Internet addresses, read the High-Tech Talk article on page 102.

TOP-LEVEL DOMAINS

Original Top-Level Domains	Type of Domain
com	Commercial organizations, businesses, and companies
edu	Educational institutions
gov	Goverment agencies
mil	Military organizations
net	Network provider
org	Nonprofit organizations
Newer Top-Level Domains	**Type of Domain**
museum	Accredited museums
biz	Businesses of all sizes
info	Businesses, organizations, or individuals providing general information
name	Individuals or families
pro	Certified professionals such as doctors, lawyers, and accountants
aero	Aviation community members
coop	Business cooperatives such as credit unions and rural electric co-ops
Proposed Top-Level Domains	**Type of Domain**
asia	Businesses that originate in Asian countries
cat	Catalan cultural community
jobs	Employment or human resource businesses
mail	Registries to control spam (Internet junk mail)
mobi	Delivery and management of mobile Internet services
post	Postal service
tel	Internet communications
travel	Travel industry
xxx	Adult content

FIGURE 2-5 With the dramatic growth of the Internet during the last few years, the Internet Corporation for Assigned Names and Numbers (ICANN) recently adopted seven new top-level domains and is evaluating nine additional TLDs.

FAQ 2-4

How does a person or company get a domain name?

For top-level domains of biz, com, info, name, net, and org, you register for a domain name from a *registrar*, which is an organization that maintains the master list of domain names. In addition to determining prices and policies for domain name registration, a registrar may offer additional services such as Web site hosting. For more information, visit scsite.com/dc2006/ch2/faq and then click Registrar.

Test your knowledge of pages 68 through 74 in Quiz Yourself 2-1.

QUIZ YOURSELF 2-1

Instructions: Find the true statement below. Then, rewrite the remaining false statements so they are true.

1. An access provider is a business that provides individuals and companies access to the Internet free or for a fee.

2. A WISP is a number that uniquely identifies each computer or device connected to the Internet.

3. An IP address, such as www.google.com, is the text version of a domain name.

4. Dial-up access takes place when the modem in your computer uses the cable television network to connect to the Internet.

5. The World Wide Web Consortium (W3C) oversees research and owns the Internet.

Quiz Yourself Online: To further check your knowledge of Internet history, accessing and connecting to the Internet, and Internet addresses, visit scsite.com/dc2006/ch2/quiz and then click Objectives 1 – 3.

THE WORLD WIDE WEB

Although many people use the terms World Wide Web and Internet interchangeably, the World Wide Web actually is a newer service of the Internet. While the Internet was developed in the late 1960s, the World Wide Web emerged nearly three decades later — in the early 1990s. Since then, however, it has grown phenomenally to become one of the more widely used services on the Internet.

The **World Wide Web** (*WWW*), or **Web**, consists of a worldwide collection of electronic documents. Each electronic document on the Web is called a **Web page**, which can contain text, graphics, audio (sound), and video. Additionally, Web pages usually have built-in connections to other documents.

Some Web pages are static (fixed); others are dynamic (changing). Visitors to a *static Web page* all see the same content. With a *dynamic Web page*, by contrast, visitors can customize some or all of the viewed content such as desired stock quotes, weather for a region, or ticket availability for flights.

A **Web site** is a collection of related Web pages and associated items, such as documents and pictures, stored on a Web server. A **Web server** is a computer that delivers requested Web pages to your computer. The same Web server can store multiple Web sites. For example, many access providers grant their subscribers free storage space on a Web server for personal or company Web sites.

The following pages discuss how to browse the Web, use a Web address, search for information on the Web, and recognize types of Web sites. Also discussed are multimedia on the Web and Web publishing.

Browsing the Web

A **Web browser**, or **browser**, is application software that allows users to access and view Web pages. To browse the Web, you need a computer that is connected to the Internet and that has a Web browser. The more widely used Web browsers for personal computers are Internet Explorer, Netscape, Mozilla, Opera, and Safari.

With an Internet connection established, you start a Web browser. The browser retrieves and displays a starting Web page, sometimes called the browser's home page. Figure 2-6 shows how a Web browser displays a home page. The initial home page that is displayed

FIGURE 2-6 HOW A WEB BROWSER DISPLAYS A HOME PAGE

Step 1:
Click the Web browser program name to start the Web browser software.

Step 2:
The Web browser looks up its home page setting, in this case, msn.com.

Step 3:
The Web browser communicates with a server maintained by your Internet access provider. The server translates the domain name of the home page to an IP address and then sends the IP address to your computer.

Step 4:
The Web browser uses the IP address to contact the Web server associated with the home page and then requests the home page from the server. The Web server sends the home page to the Web browser, which formats the page for display on your screen.

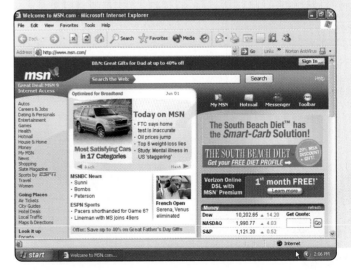

is one selected by your Web browser. You can change your browser's home page at anytime.

The more common usage of the term, **home page**, refers to the first page that a Web site displays. Similar to a book cover or a table of contents for a Web site, the home page provides information about the Web site's purpose and content. Often it provides connections to other documents, Web pages, or Web sites. Many Web sites allow you to personalize the home page so it contains areas of interest to you.

Internet-enabled mobile devices such as PDAs and smart phones use a special type of browser, called a *microbrowser*, which is designed for their small screens and limited computing power. Many Web sites design Web pages specifically for display on a microbrowser (Figure 2-7).

For a computer or mobile device to display a Web page, the page must be downloaded. **Downloading** is the process of a computer receiving information, such as a Web page, from a server on the Internet. While a browser downloads a Web page, it typically displays an animated logo or icon in the top-right corner of the browser window. The animation stops when the download is complete.

Depending on the speed of your Internet connection and the amount of graphics involved, a Web page download can take from a few seconds to several minutes. To speed up the display of Web pages, most Web browsers allow users to turn off the graphics and other multimedia elements.

FIGURE 2-7 Sample microbrowser screens.

Web Addresses

A Web page has a unique address, called a **URL** (*Uniform Resource Locator*) or **Web address**. For example, the home page for the San Diego Zoo Web site has http://www.sandiegozoo.org as its Web address. A Web browser retrieves a Web page, such as the zoo's home page, using its Web address.

If you know the Web address of a Web page, you can type it in the Address box at the top of the browser window. For example, if you type the Web address http://www.sandiegozoo.org/wap/condor/home.html in the Address box and then press the ENTER key, the browser downloads and displays a Web page about condors at the San Diego Zoo (Figure 2-8).

As shown in Figure 2-8, a Web address consists of a protocol, domain name, and sometimes the path to a specific Web page or location on a Web page. Many Web page addresses begin with http://. The *http*, which stands for *Hypertext Transfer Protocol*, is a set of rules that defines how pages transfer on the Internet.

To help minimize errors, most current browsers and Web sites do not require the http:// and www portions of the Web address. For example, typing sandiegozoo.org/wap/condor/home.html, instead of the entire address, still accesses the Web site. If you enter an incorrect Web address, a list of similar addresses from which you can select may be displayed in the browser window. Many Web sites also allow users to eliminate the .htm or .html from the Web page name.

When you enter the Web address, sandiegozoo.org/wap/condor/home.html in the Web browser, it sends a request to the Web server that contains the www.sandiegozoo.org Web site. The server then retrieves the Web page named home.html in the wap/condor/ path and delivers it to your browser, which then displays the Web page on the screen.

When you enter a Web address in a browser, you request, or *pull*, information from a Web server. Some Web servers also can *push* content to your computer at regular intervals or whenever updates are made to the site. For example, some Web servers provide the capability of displaying current sporting event scores or weather reports on your computer screen.

For information about useful Web sites and their associated Web addresses, read the Making Use of the Web feature that follows this chapter.

FIGURE 2-8 After entering the Web address http://www.sandiegozoo.org/wap/condor/home.html in the Address box, this Web page at the San Diego Zoo Web site is displayed. Notice the www portion of the domain name does not appear in the Address box after the Web page downloads.

Navigating Web Pages

Most Web pages contain links. A **link**, short for *hyperlink*, is a built-in connection to another related Web page or part of a Web page. Links allow you to obtain information in a nonlinear way. That is, instead of accessing topics in a specified order, you move directly to a topic of interest. Branching from one related topic to another in a nonlinear fashion is what makes links so powerful. Some people use the phrase, **surfing the Web**, to refer to the activity of using links to explore the Web.

On the Web, a link can be text or an image. Text links may be underlined and/or displayed in a color different from other text on the Web page. Pointing to, or positioning the pointer on, a link on the screen typically changes the shape of the pointer to a small hand with a pointing index finger. The Web page shown in Figure 2-9 contains a variety of link types, with the pointer on one of the links.

Each link on a Web page corresponds to another Web address. To activate a link, you *click* it, that is, point to the link and then press the left mouse button. Clicking a link causes the Web page associated with the link to be displayed on the screen. The linked object

might be on the same Web page, a different Web page at the same Web site, or a separate Web page at a different Web site in another city or country. To remind you visually that you have clicked a link, a text link often changes color after you click it.

FIGURE 2-9 This Web page contains various types of links: text that is underlined, text in a different color, and images.

Searching for Information on the Web

The Web is a global resource of information. One primary use of the Web is to search for specific information. The first step in successful searching is to identify the main idea or concept in the topic about which you are seeking information. Determine any synonyms, alternate spellings, or variant word forms for the topic. Then, use a search tool to locate the information.

The two most commonly used search tools are subject directories and search engines. A **subject directory** classifies Web pages in an organized set of categories, such as sports or shopping, and related subcategories. A **search engine** is a program that finds Web sites and Web pages.

Some Web sites offer the functionality of both a subject directory and a search engine. Yahoo! and Google, for example, are widely used search engines that also provide a subject directory. To use Yahoo! or Google, you enter the Web address (yahoo.com or google.com) in the Address box in a browser window. The table in Figure 2-10 lists the

Web addresses of several popular general-purpose subject directories and search engines.

SUBJECT DIRECTORIES　A subject directory provides categorized lists of links arranged by subject. Figure 2-11 shows how to use Yahoo!'s

WIDELY USED SEARCH TOOLS

Search Tool	Web Address	Subject Directory	Search Engine
A9.com	a9.com		X
AlltheWeb	alltheweb.com		X
Alta Vista	altavista.com	X	X
AOL Search	search.aol.com		X
AOMI	aomi.com		X
Ask Jeeves	askjeeves.com	X	X
Excite	excite.com	X	X
Gigablast	gigablast.com		X
Google	google.com	X	X
HotBot	hotbot.com		X
LookSmart	looksmart.com	X	X
Lycos	lycos.com	X	X
MSN Search	search.msn.com	X	X
Netscape Search	search.netscape.com	X	X
Open Directory Project	dmoz.org	X	X
Overture	overture.com		X
Teoma	teoma.com		X
WebCrawler	webcrawler.com		X
Yahoo!	yahoo.com	X	X

FIGURE 2-10　Many subject directories and search engines allow searching about any topic on the Web.

FIGURE 2-11　HOW TO USE A SUBJECT DIRECTORY

Step 1:
Type the subject directory's Web address (in this case, yahoo.com) in the Address box in the Web browser and then press the ENTER key.

Address box

Step 6:
Click the Comedians link to display the Comedians page. Scroll down to the SITE LISTINGS area, if necessary, and then point to Hope, Bob (1903–2003).

SITE LISTINGS area

Hope, Bob (1903–2003) link

Step 7:
Click the Hope, Bob (1903–2003) link to display the Hope, Bob (1903–2003) page. Scroll down to the SITE LISTINGS area, if necessary, and then point to the Bob Hope and American Variety link.

SITE LISTINGS area

Bob Hope and American Variety link

subject directory to search for information about Bob Hope. As shown in the figure, you locate a particular topic by clicking links through different levels, moving from the general to the specific. Each time you click a category link, the subject directory displays a list of subcategory links, from which you again choose. You continue in this fashion until the search tool displays a list of Web pages about the desired topic.

The major problem with a subject directory is deciding which categories to choose as you work through the menus of links presented.

Step 2:
When the Yahoo! home page is displayed, point to the scroll box on the right side of the screen.

Step 3:
Drag the scroll box downward to display the Web Site Directory area of the Web page. Point to the Entertainment link.

Step 5:
Click the Comedy link to display the Comedy page. In the CATEGORIES area, point to the Comedians link.

Step 4:
Click the Entertainment link to display the Entertainment page. Scroll down to the CATEGORIES area, if necessary, and then point to the Comedy link.

Step 8:
Click the Bob Hope and American Variety link to display the Bob Hope and American Variety Web page, which contains a variety of links to specific information about Bob Hope. After you click one of these links, click the Home button to display this home page.

SEARCH ENGINES A search engine is particularly helpful in locating Web pages about certain topics or in locating specific Web pages for which you do not know the exact Web address. Thousands of search engines are available. Some are general and perform searches on any topic; others are restricted to certain subjects, such as finding people, job hunting, or locating real estate.

Instead of clicking through links, search engines require that you enter a word or phrase, called **search text** or *keywords*, that define the item about which you want information. Search engines often respond with results that include thousands of links to Web pages, many of which may have little or no bearing on the information you are seeking. You can eliminate the superfluous pages by carefully crafting a keyword that limits the search.

Figure 2-12 shows how to use the Google search engine to search for the phrase, Bob Hope television career. The results of the search, called *hits*, shown in Step 3 include about 535,000 links to Web pages that reference Bob Hope's television career. Each hit in the list has a link that, when clicked, displays an associated Web site or Web page. Most search engines sequence the

FIGURE 2-12   HOW TO USE A SEARCH ENGINE

Step 1:
Type the search engine's Web address (in this case, google.com) in the Address box in the Web browser and then press the ENTER key.

Step 2:
When the Google home page is displayed, type Bob Hope television career as the search text and then point to the Google Search button.

Step 4:
Click the Bob Hope on TV link to display a Web page about Bob Hope's television career.

Step 3:
Click the Google Search button. When the results of the search are displayed, scroll through the links and read the descriptions. Point to the Bob Hope on TV link.

hits based on how close the words in the search text are to one another in the Web page titles and their descriptions. Thus, the first few links probably contain more relevant information.

If you enter a phrase with spaces between the words in the search text, most search engines display results (hits) that include all of the words, except for common words (e.g., to, the, and). The table in Figure 2-13 lists some common operators you can include in your search text to refine your search. Other techniques you can use to improve your Web searches include the following:

- Use specific nouns and put the most important terms first in the search text.
- List all possible spellings, for example, email, e-mail.
- Before using a search engine, read its Help information.

- If the search is unsuccessful with one search engine, try another.

Many search engines use a program called a *spider* to build and maintain lists of words found on Web sites. When you enter search text, the search engine scans this prebuilt list for hits. The more sophisticated the search engine combined with precise search criteria, the more rapid the response and effective the search.

In addition to searching for Web pages, many search engines allow you to search for images, news articles, and local businesses. Read Looking Ahead 2-2 for a look at the next generation of searching techniques.

FAQ 2-6

Who uses Google to search the Web?

People all around the world use Google to conduct more than 250 million searches per day. Google has been accessed in many languages including English, German, Japanese, Spanish, French, Chinese, and Dutch. For more information, visit scsite.com/dc2006/ch2/faq and then click Google Facts.

SEARCH ENGINE OPERATORS

Operator	Description	Examples	Explanation
Space or +	Use the space or plus operator (+) when you want search results to display hits that include specific words.	art + music art music	Results have both words art and music — in any order.
OR	Use OR operator when you want search results to display hits that include only one word from a list.	dog OR puppy	Results have either the word dog or puppy.
		dog OR puppy OR canine	Results have the word dog or puppy or canine.
-	Use minus operator (-) when you want to exclude a word from your search results.	automobile -convertible	Results include automobile but do not include convertible.
" "	Use quotation marks operator when you want to search for an exact phrase in a certain order.	"19th century literature"	Results include only hits that have the exact phrase, 19th century literature.
*	Use asterisk operator (*) when you want search results to substitute characters in place of the asterisk.	writer*	Results include any word that begins with writer (e.g., writer, writers, writer's).

FIGURE 2-13 Use search engine operators to help refine a search.

LOOKING AHEAD 2-2

3-D Search Engines Get the Picture

Conventional search engines, such as Google, use words to find information. But what happens when a computer user needs to locate a wing nut or camshaft based on a particular shape, not part number or model? The 3-D search engines being developed would help people who work with patterns and contours search for images. These search engines presently are being created to assist designers and engineers at large industrial companies with millions of inventoried parts, but university researchers predict image searches will be common on the Internet within 15 years.

Other search engines of the future will customize the results based on the researcher's background, include a voice interface, and use a thesaurus to keep a query in context. For more information, visit scsite.com/dc2006/ch2/looking and then click Search Engines.

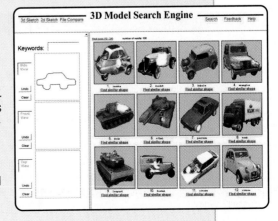

Types of Web Sites

Nine types of Web sites are portal, news, informational, business/marketing, educational, entertainment, advocacy, blog, and personal (Figure 2-14). Many Web sites fall in more than one of these categories. The following pages discuss each of these types of Web sites.

PORTAL A **portal** is a Web site that offers a variety of Internet services from a single, convenient location (Figure 2-14a). Most portals offer the following free services: search engine and/or subject directory; news; sports and weather; free Web publishing services; reference tools such as yellow pages, stock quotes, and maps; shopping malls and auctions; and e-mail and other forms of online communications. Companies often create their own portals for use by employees, vendors, and customers.

Many portals have Web communities. A **Web community** is a Web site that joins a specific group of people with similar interests or relationships. These communities may offer online photo albums, chat rooms, and other services to facilitate communications among members.

When you connect to the Internet, the first Web page that is displayed often is a portal. Popular portals include AltaVista, AOL, Excite, GO.com, HotBot, LookSmart, Lycos, MSN, NBCi, Netscape, and Yahoo!. You may notice that many of these portals are popular search engines or subject directories. Some also are Internet access providers.

A *wireless portal* is a portal designed for Internet-enabled mobile devices. Wireless portals attempt to provide all information a wireless user might require. These portals offer services geared to the mobile user such as search engines, news, stock quotes, weather, maps, e-mail, calendar, instant messaging, and shopping.

NEWS A news Web site contains newsworthy material including stories and articles relating to current events, life, money, sports, and the weather (Figure 2-14b). Many magazines and newspapers sponsor Web sites that provide summaries of printed articles, as well as articles not included in the printed versions. Newspapers and television and radio stations are some of the media that maintain news Web sites.

INFORMATIONAL An informational Web site contains factual information (Figure 2-14c). Many United States government agencies have informational Web sites providing information such as census data, tax codes, and the congressional budget. Other organizations provide information such as public transportation schedules and published research findings.

BUSINESS/MARKETING A business/marketing Web site contains content that promotes or sells products or services (Figure 2-14d). Nearly every business has a business/marketing Web site. Allstate Insurance Company, Dell Inc., General Motors Corporation, Kraft Foods Inc., and Walt Disney Company all have business/marketing Web sites. Many of these companies also allow you to purchase their products or services online.

EDUCATIONAL An educational Web site offers exciting, challenging avenues for formal and informal teaching and learning (Figure 2-14e). On the Web, you can learn how airplanes fly or how to cook a meal. For a more structured learning experience, companies provide online training to employees; and colleges offer online classes and degrees (read At Issue 2-1 for a related discussion). Instructors often use the Web to enhance classroom teaching by publishing course materials, grades, and other pertinent class information.

AT ISSUE 2-1

Diplomas Online?

College can be a rewarding experience, both personally and professionally. Some people, however, do not have the opportunity, time, or money needed to attend a traditional college. Many schools address this problem with online classes. Online classes allow students to learn whenever and wherever they can access a course's Web page, often for less cost than traditional tuitions. A student might be able to complete an entire degree program without ever physically attending a class. Many online classes present material using captivating simulations, real-life case studies, and interactive tools. And, online classes seem to work — one research report found that online students learn as well as or better than their classroom-based brethren. Yet, even the best online classes lack some of the most important features of the bricks-and-mortar campus experience, such as casual talks with professors, informal study groups in the dorm, or enthusiastic discussions in the campus coffee shop. What are the most important advantages and disadvantages of online classes? Why? Does a degree earned online have the same value as a traditional degree? Why? Does the answer depend more on the college or on the course of study? Why? What type of student is best, and least, suited for online classes? Why?

FIGURE 2-14b (news)

FIGURE 2-14a (portal)

FIGURE 2-14c (informational)

FIGURE 2-14e (educational)

FIGURE 2-14d (business/marketing)

FIGURE 2-14f (entertainment)

FIGURE 2-14h (blog)

FIGURE 2-14g (advocacy)

FIGURE 2-14i (personal)

FIGURE 2-14 Types of Web sites.

ENTERTAINMENT An entertainment Web site offers an interactive and engaging environment (Figure 2-14f on the previous page). Popular entertainment Web sites offer music, videos, sports, games, ongoing Web episodes, sweepstakes, chats, and more. Sophisticated entertainment Web sites often partner with other technologies. For example, you can cast your vote about a topic on a television show.

ADVOCACY An advocacy Web site contains content that describes a cause, opinion, or idea (Figure 2-14g on the previous page). The purpose of an advocacy Web site is to convince the reader of the validity of the cause, opinion, or idea. These Web sites usually present views of a particular group or association. Sponsors of advocacy Web sites include the Democratic National Committee, the Republican National Committee, the Society for the Prevention of Cruelty to Animals, and the Society to Protect Human Rights.

BLOG A **blog**, short for *Web log*, is a Web site that uses a regularly updated journal format to reflect the interests, opinions, and personalities of the author and sometimes site visitors (Figure 2-14h on the previous page). Blogs have an informal style that consists of a single individual's ideas (similar to a diary) or a collection of ideas and thoughts among visitors. Read At Issue 2-2 for a related discussion.

PERSONAL A private individual or family not usually associated with any organization may maintain a personal Web site or just a single Web page (Figure 2-14i on the previous page). People publish personal Web pages for a variety of reasons. Some are job hunting. Others simply want to share life experiences with the world.

Evaluating a Web Site

Do not assume that information presented on the Web is correct or accurate. Any person, company, or organization can publish a Web page on the Internet. No one oversees the content of these Web pages. Figure 2-15 lists guidelines for assessing the value of a Web site or Web page before relying on its content.

GUIDELINES FOR EVALUATING THE VALUE OF A WEB SITE

Evaluation Criteria	Reliable Web Sites
Affiliation	A reputable institution should support the Web site without bias in the information.
Audience	The Web site should be written at an appropriate level.
Authority	The Web site should list the author and the appropriate credentials.
Content	The Web site should be well organized and the links should work.
Currency	The information on the Web page should be current.
Design	The pages at the Web site should download quickly and be visually pleasing and easy to navigate.
Objectivity	The Web site should contain little advertising and be free of preconceptions.

FIGURE 2-15 Criteria for evaluating a Web site's content.

AT ISSUE 2-2

Mobile Web Logs with Photos — an Invasion of One's Privacy?

Camera-equipped smart phones are popular — almost 50 million were sold last year. A growing number of people use these phones to create online photo albums, called mobile Web blogs or *moblogs*, to share their visions of the world with thousands of people. Most moblogs are personal and, like family photo albums, interesting to a limited audience. To capture more exciting pictures, some moblog photographers use their smart phone cameras in private places. As a result, smart phone cameras have been banned from health club locker rooms, movie screenings, and corporate offices. Congress even is considering barring covert cameras from places where people should be able to expect some privacy. But, even in public, moblog paparazzi photograph unaware people at private, or embarrassing, times. The subjects of these moblog pictures often object to living in a fishbowl, where even personal moments can be captured and posted on the Web. Recognizing this, some Web sites that monitor moblogs refuse to show certain photos or encourage photographers to obtain permission from photo subjects. Yet, photographers insist they have the right to post any pictures they take. What, if anything, can be done to protect personal privacy? Should laws be enacted to regulate smart phone photographers, moblogs, or both? Why? Must we accept that, outside of our homes, private moments no longer exist?

Multimedia on the Web

Most Web pages include more than just formatted text and links. The more exciting Web pages use multimedia. **Multimedia** refers to any application that combines text with graphics, animation, audio, video, and/or virtual reality. Multimedia brings a Web page to life, increases the types of information available on the Web, expands the Web's potential uses, and makes the Internet a more entertaining place to explore. Multimedia Web pages often require proper hardware and software and take more time to download because they contain large graphics files and video or audio clips.

The sections that follow discuss how the Web uses graphics, animation, audio, video, and virtual reality.

GRAPHICS   A **graphic**, or *graphical image*, is a digital representation of nontext information such as a drawing, chart, or photograph. Today, many Web pages use colorful graphical designs and images to convey messages (Figure 2-16).

The Web contains countless images about a variety of subjects. You can download many of these images at no cost and use them for non-commercial purposes. Recall that downloading is the process of transferring an object from the Web to your computer. For example, you can insert images into greeting cards, announcements, and other documents.

Of the graphics formats that exist on the Web (Figure 2-17), the two more common are JPEG and GIF formats. *JPEG* (pronounced JAY-peg) is a format that compresses graphics to reduce their file size, which means the file takes up less storage space. Smaller file sizes result in faster downloading of Web pages because small files transmit faster than large files. The more compressed the file, the smaller the image and the lower the quality. The goal with JPEG graphics is to reach a balance between image quality and file size.

GIF (pronounced jiff) graphics also use compression techniques to reduce file sizes. The GIF format works best for images that have only a few distinct colors. The newer *PNG* (pronounced ping) graphics format improves upon the GIF format, and thus may eventually replace the GIF format.

The BMP and TIFF formats listed in Figure 2-17 may require special viewer software, and they have larger file sizes. Thus, these formats are not used on the Web as frequently as JPEG, GIF, and PNG formats.

FIGURE 2-16   This Web page uses colorful graphical designs and images to convey its messages.

GRAPHICS FORMATS USED ON THE WEB

Abbreviation	Name
BMP	Bit Map
GIF	Graphics Interchange Format
JPEG	Joint Photographic Experts Group
PNG	Portable Network Graphics
TIFF	Tagged Image File Format

FIGURE 2-17   The Web uses graphics file formats for images.

Some Web sites use thumbnails on their pages because graphics can be time-consuming to display. A *thumbnail* is a small version of a larger graphic. You usually can click a thumbnail to display a larger image (Figure 2-18).

thumbnail

FIGURE 2-18   Clicking the thumbnail in the top screen displays a larger image in a separate window.

ANIMATION   Many Web pages use **animation**, which is the appearance of motion created by displaying a series of still images in sequence. Animation can make Web pages more visually interesting or draw attention to important information or links. For example, text that animates by scrolling across the screen can serve as a ticker to display stock updates, news, sports scores, weather, or other information. Web-based games often use animation.

Web page developers add animation to Web pages using a variety of techniques. Web page authoring programs, such as Macromedia Flash, enable Web site developers to combine animation and interactivity in Web pages. Developers unfamiliar with Web page authoring programs can create an *animated GIF*, which combines several GIF images in a single GIF file.

AUDIO   On the Web, you can listen to audio clips and live audio. **Audio** includes music, speech, or any other sound.

Simple applications on the Web consist of individual audio files available for downloading to a computer. Once downloaded, you can play (listen to) the contents of these files. Some common Web audio file formats are listed in Figure 2-19. Audio files are compressed to reduce their file sizes. For example, the **MP3** format reduces an audio file to about one-tenth its original size, while preserving much of the original quality of the sound.

Some music publishers have Web sites that allow users to download sample tracks free to persuade them to buy the entire CD. Other Web sites allow a user to purchase and download an entire CD of music tracks to the hard disk (Figure 2-20). Keep in mind that it is legal to download copyrighted music only if the song's copyright holder has granted permission for users to download and play the song.

To listen to an audio file on your computer, you need special software called a **player**. Most current operating systems contain a player. Popular players include iTunes, RealOne Player, and Windows Media Player. If your player will not play a particular audio format, you can download the necessary player free from the Web.

Some applications on the Web use streaming audio. **Streaming** is the process of transferring data in a continuous and even flow. Streaming allows users to access and use a file while it is transmitting. For example, *streaming audio* enables you to listen to music as it downloads to your computer. Many radio and television stations use streaming audio to broadcast music, interviews, talk shows, sporting events, music videos, news, live concerts, and other segments.

FAQ 2-8

How long does it take to download a single song from a music Web site?

Depending on the speed of your Internet connection and the size of the file, a single song can take from one to twenty minutes to download. For more information, visit scsite.com/dc2006/ch2/faq and then click Downloading Audio Files.

AUDIO WEB FILE FORMATS

Audio File Format	Description
AA	Audible Audio (commonly used for downloadable e-books)
AAC	Advanced Audio Coding
AIFF	Audio Interchange File Format
ASF	Advanced Streaming (or Systems) Format (part of Windows Media framework)
MP3	Moving Pictures Experts Group Audio Layer 3 (MPEG-3)
WAV	Windows waveform
WMA	Windows Media Audio (part of Windows Media framework)
RA	RealAudio sound file (supported by RealOne Player)
QT	QuickTime audio, video, or 3-D animation (included with Mac OS, also available separately)

FIGURE 2-19 Popular Web audio file formats.

WEB LINK 2-3

Streaming Media
For more information, visit scsite.com/ dc2006/ch2/weblink and then click Streaming Media.

FIGURE 2-20 HOW TO PURCHASE AND DOWNLOAD MUSIC

Step 1:
Display the music Web site on the screen. Search for, select, and pay for the music you want to purchase from the music Web site.

Step 2:
Download the music from the Web site's server to your computer's hard disk.

Step 3:
Listen to the music from your computer's hard disk.

VIDEO Video consists of full-motion images that are played back at various speeds. Most video also has accompanying audio. Instead of turning on the television, you can use the Internet to watch live and/or prerecorded coverage of your favorite programs (Figure 2-21) or enjoy a live performance of your favorite vocalist.

Simple video applications on the Web consist of individual video files, such as movie or television clips, that you must download completely before you can play them on the computer. Video files often are compressed because they are quite large in size. These clips also are quite short in length, usually less than 10 minutes, because they can take a long time to download. The *Moving Pictures Experts Group (MPEG)* defines a popular video compression standard, a widely used one called *MPEG-4*.

As with streaming audio, *streaming video* allows you to view longer or live video

images as they download to your computer. Widely used standards supported by most Web browsers for transmitting streaming video data on the Internet are AVI (Audio Video Interleaved), QuickTime, Windows Media Format, and RealVideo. Like RealAudio, RealVideo is supported by RealOne Player.

VIRTUAL REALITY Virtual reality (**VR**) is the use of computers to simulate a real or imagined environment that appears as a three-dimensional (3-D) space. On the Web, VR involves the display of 3-D images that users explore and manipulate interactively (Figure 2-22).

Using special VR software, a Web developer creates an entire 3-D Web site that contains infinite space and depth, called a *VR world*. A VR world, for example, might show a room with furniture. Users walk through such a VR room by moving an input device forward, backward, or to the side.

Games often use VR. Many practical applications of VR also exist. Science educators create VR models of molecules, organisms, and other structures for students to examine. Companies use VR to showcase products or create advertisements. Architects create VR models of buildings and rooms so clients can see how a completed construction project will look before it is built.

FIGURE 2-21 A video of passengers having fun on a theme park ride.

mouse pointer

FIGURE 2-22 Web site visitors use VR to see the inside of Grand Central Station in New York. As you move the mouse pointer, you see different views inside the station.

PLUG-INS Most Web browsers have the capability of displaying basic multimedia elements on a Web page. Sometimes, a browser might need an additional program, called a plug-in. A **plug-in** is a program that extends the capability of a browser. You can download many plug-ins at no cost from various Web sites (Figure 2-23). Some plug-ins run on all sizes of personal computers and mobile devices. Others have special versions for mobile devices.

Web Publishing

Before the World Wide Web, the means to share opinions and ideas with others easily and inexpensively was limited to the media, classroom, work, or social environments. Generating an advertisement or publication that could reach a massive audience required much expense. Today, businesses and individuals convey information to millions of people by creating their own Web pages. The content of the Web pages ranges from new stories to product information to blogs.

POPULAR PLUG-IN APPLICATIONS

Plug-In Application	Description	Web Address
Acrobat Reader	View, navigate, and print Portable Document Format (PDF) files — documents formatted to look just as they look in print	adobe.com
Flash Player	View dazzling graphics and animation, hear outstanding sound and music, display Web pages across an entire screen	macromedia.com
QuickTime	View animation, music, audio, video, and VR panoramas and objects directly in a Web page	apple.com
RealOne Player	Listen to live and on-demand near-CD-quality audio and newscast-quality video; stream audio and video content for faster viewing; play MP3 files; create music CDs	real.com
Shockwave Player	Experience dynamic interactive multimedia, 3-D graphics, and streaming audio	macromedia.com
Windows Media Player	Listen to live and on-demand audio; play or edit WMA and MP3 files; burn CDs, watch DVD movies	microsoft.com

FIGURE 2-23 Most plug-ins can be downloaded free from the Web.

WEB LINK 2-4

Plug-Ins

For more information, visit scsite.com/dc2006/ch2/weblink and then click Plug-Ins.

Web publishing is the development and maintenance of Web pages. To develop a Web page, you do not have to be a computer programmer. For the small business or home user, Web publishing is fairly easy as long as you have the proper tools. The five major steps to Web publishing are as follows: (1) plan a Web site, (2) analyze and design a Web site, (3) create a Web site, (4) deploy a Web site, and (5) maintain a Web site. Figure 2-24 illustrates these steps with respect to a personal Web site.

FIGURE 2-24 HOW TO PUBLISH YOUR RESUME ON THE WEB

Step 1:
Plan a Web site.
Think about issues that could affect the design of the Web site.

Step 2:
Analyze and design a Web site. Design the layout of the elements of the Web site.

Step 3:
Create a Web site. Use word processing software or Web page authoring software to create the Web site.

Step 4:
Deploy a Web site. Save the Web site on a Web server.

Step 5:
Maintain a Web site. Visit your Web site regularly to be sure it is working and current.

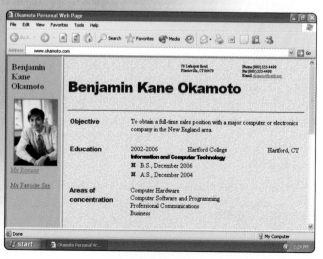

Test your knowledge of pages 75 through 91 in Quiz Yourself 2-2.

E-COMMERCE

E-commerce, short for *electronic commerce*, is a business transaction that occurs over an electronic network such as the Internet. Anyone with access to a computer, an Internet connection, and a means to pay for purchased goods or services can participate in e-commerce (Figure 2-25).

In the past, e-commerce transactions were conducted primarily using desktop computers. Today, many mobile computers and devices, such as PDAs and smart phones, also access the Web wirelessly. Some people use the term *m-commerce* (mobile commerce) to identify e-commerce that takes place using mobile devices.

Popular uses of e-commerce by consumers include shopping, investing, and banking. Users can purchase just about any product or service on the Web. Some examples include flowers, books, computers, prescription drugs, music, movies, cars, airline tickets, and concert tickets. Through online investing, individuals buy and sell stocks or bonds without using a broker.

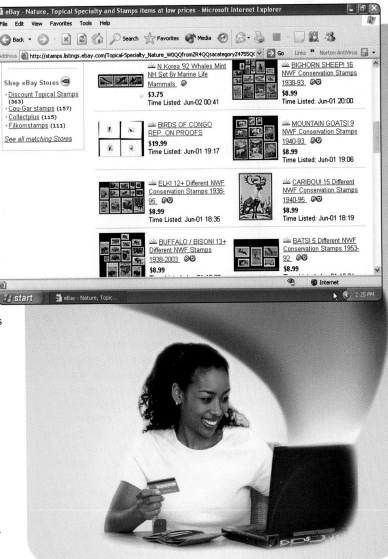

FIGURE 2-25 E-commerce activities include shopping for goods at an online auction. This user visits an eBay auction for specialty stamps.

Three different types of e-commerce are business-to-consumer, consumer-to-consumer, and business-to-business. *Business-to-consumer (B2C) e-commerce* consists of the sale of goods and services to the general public. For example, Dell has a B2C Web site. Instead of visiting a computer store to purchase a computer, customers can order one that meets their specifications directly from the Dell Web site.

A customer (consumer) visits an online business through an **electronic storefront**, which contains product descriptions, graphics, and a shopping cart. The **shopping cart** allows the customer to collect purchases. When ready to complete the sale, the customer enters personal data and the method of payment, preferably through a secure Internet connection (read At Issue 2-3 for a related discussion).

Instead of purchasing from a business, consumers can purchase from each other. For example, with an **online auction**, users bid on an item being sold by someone else. The highest bidder at the end of the bidding period purchases the item. *Consumer-to-consumer (C2C) e-commerce* occurs when one consumer sells directly to another, such as in an online auction. eBay is one of the more popular online auction Web sites.

Most e-commerce, though, actually takes place between businesses, which is called *business-to-business (B2B) e-commerce*. Businesses often provide goods and services to other businesses, such as online advertising, recruiting, credit, sales, market research, technical support, and training. For example, some MasterCard and Visa credit card companies provide corporations with Web-based purchasing, tracking, and transaction downloading capabilities.

FAQ 2-9

How popular is online shopping?

Researchers predict that e-commerce sales will grow at a steady rate of 19 percent per year until at least 2008. At that time, online shopping will account for approximately 10 percent of all retail sales in the United States, or 63 million households. For more information, visit scsite.com/ dc2006/ch2/faq and then click Online Shopping.

OTHER INTERNET SERVICES

The Web is only one of the many services on the Internet. The Web and other Internet services have changed the way we communicate. We can send e-mail messages to the president, have a discussion with experts about the stock market, chat with someone in another country about genealogy, and talk about homework assignments with classmates via instant messages. Many times, these communications take place completely in writing — without the parties ever meeting each other.

At home, work, and school, people use computers and Internet-enabled mobile devices so they always have instant access to e-mail, FTP (File Transfer Protocol), newsgroups and message boards, mailing lists, chat rooms, instant messaging, and Internet telephony. The following pages discuss each of these Internet services.

E-Mail

E-mail (short for *electronic mail*) is the transmission of messages and files via a computer network. E-mail was one of the original services on the Internet, enabling scientists and researchers working on government-sponsored projects to communicate with colleagues at

WEB LINK 2-5

E-Commerce

For more information, visit scsite.com/ dc2006/ch2/weblink and then click E-Commerce.

AT ISSUE 2-3

To Tax or Not to Tax Internet Sales?

The Supreme Court has ruled that merchants can charge state and local sales taxes only when they have a physical presence, such as a store or office building, where the purchase is made. Because Internet merchants often do not have a physical presence in a buyer's state, online purchases usually are sales tax free. One study predicts that by 2011 online sales will cost state and local governments more than $54 billion in sales tax revenues, forcing them either to raise taxes or cut services. In response, many states have enacted "use" taxes that require residents to report, and pay sales tax on, items purchased online but used at home. Even a use tax, though, does not address other problems. The sales-tax-free status of Internet purchases also may have a negative impact on local businesses that must charge sales tax and on lower-income families who are less likely to buy online. Yet, many feel any tax on e-commerce is unmanageable (forcing vendors to adjust to varying sales tax rates) and unjustified. Should a sales tax be applied to Internet purchases? Why? Is a use tax a viable alternative? Why or why not? How else can the problems of taxing, or not taxing, Internet purchases be addressed?

other locations. Today, e-mail is a primary communications method for both personal and business use.

You use an **e-mail program** to create, send, receive, forward, store, print, and delete e-mail messages. Outlook and Outlook Express are two popular e-mail programs. The steps in Figure 2-26 illustrate how to send an e-mail message using Outlook. The message can be simple text or can include an attachment such as a word processing document, a graphic, an audio clip, or a video clip.

FIGURE 2-26 HOW TO SEND AN E-MAIL MESSAGE

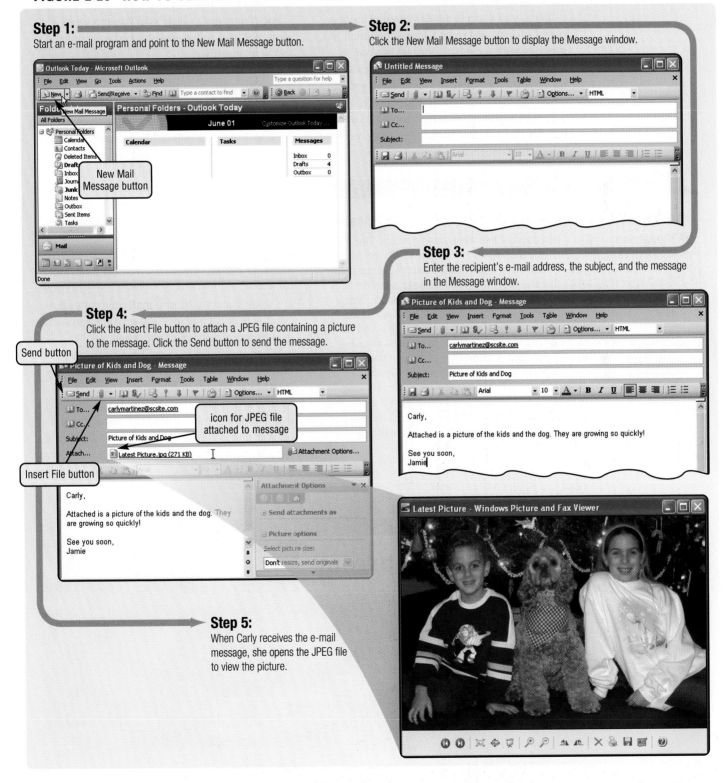

Step 1:
Start an e-mail program and point to the New Mail Message button.

New Mail Message button

Step 2:
Click the New Mail Message button to display the Message window.

Step 3:
Enter the recipient's e-mail address, the subject, and the message in the Message window.

Step 4:
Click the Insert File button to attach a JPEG file containing a picture to the message. Click the Send button to send the message.

Send button

icon for JPEG file attached to message

Insert File button

Step 5:
When Carly receives the e-mail message, she opens the JPEG file to view the picture.

Internet access providers typically supply an e-mail program as a standard part of their Internet access services. Some Web sites, such as MSN Hotmail and Yahoo!, provide free e-mail services. To use these Web-based e-mail programs, you connect to the Web site and set up an e-mail account, which typically includes an e-mail address and a password. Read At Issue 2-4 for a related discussion.

Just as you address a letter when using the postal system, you must address an e-mail message with the e-mail address of your intended recipient. Likewise, when someone sends you a message, they must have your e-mail address. An **e-mail address** is a combination of a user name and a domain name that identifies a user so he or she can receive Internet e-mail (Figure 2-27).

A **user name** is a unique combination of characters, such as letters of the alphabet and/or numbers, that identifies a specific user. Your user name must be different from the other user names in the same domain. For example, a user named Carly Martinez whose server has a domain name of scsite.com might want to select CMartinez as her user name. If scsite.com already has a CMartinez (for Carlos Martinez), Carly will have to select a different user name, such as carlymartinez or carly_martinez.

Sometimes, companies decide user names for employees. In many cases, however, users select their own user names, often selecting a nickname or any other combination of characters for their user name. Many users select a combination of their first and last names so others can remember it easily.

In an Internet e-mail address, an @ (pronounced at) symbol separates the user name from the domain name. Your service provider supplies the domain name. Using the example in Figure 2-27, a possible e-mail address for Carly Martinez would be carlymartinez@scsite.com, which would be read as follows: Carly Martinez at s c site dot com. Most e-mail programs allow you to create an **address book**, which contains a list of names and e-mail addresses.

When you send an e-mail message, an outgoing mail server that is operated by your Internet access provider determines how to route the message through the Internet and then sends the message. *SMTP (simple mail transfer protocol)* is a communications protocol used by some outgoing mail servers.

AT ISSUE 2-4

Are Free Web-Based E-Mail Services Worth the Price?

A popular search engine is introducing a free, Web-based e-mail service. The search technology built into the service allows users easily to find messages about a topic. Curious about reactions to a book being read in your literature course? Type in the book's title and see every e-mail message about the book that you have sent or received. But, you probably will see even more. Each message is scanned for key terms, and related advertisements are inserted in the message. So, a message about the book also may contain an advertisement from a book store. Some people feel that scanning personal messages and inserting unwanted advertisements is an invasion of privacy. One security expert also warns that investigators could subpoena the huge depository of messages and search it for evidence in criminal or civil cases. Privacy advocates believe Web-based e-mail services should be banned, even if people want them. Would you use a Web-based e-mail service? Why? Should these services be outlawed? Why or why not? What, if anything, should be done about privacy concerns related to Web-based e-mail services?

carlymartinez@scsite.com

FIGURE 2-27   An e-mail address is a combination of a user name and a domain name.

As you receive e-mail messages, an incoming mail server — also operated by your Internet access provider — holds the messages in your mailbox until you use your e-mail program to retrieve them. *POP3*, the latest version of POP (*Post Office Protocol*), is a communications protocol used by some incoming mail servers. Most e-mail programs have a mail notification alert that informs you via a message or sound when you receive new mail. Figure 2-28 illustrates how an e-mail message may travel from a sender to a receiver.

WEB LINK 2-6

E-Mail
For more information, visit scsite.com/ dc2006/ch2/weblink and then click E-Mail.

FAQ 2-10

Can my computer get a virus through e-mail?

Yes. A *virus* is a computer program that can damage files and the operating system. One way that virus authors attempt to spread a virus is by sending virus-infected e-mail attachments. If you receive an e-mail attachment, you should use an antivirus program to verify that it is virus free.

For more information, read the High-Tech Talk article on page 168, the section about viruses and antivirus programs in Chapter 8, and visit scsite.com/dc2006/ch2/faq and then click Viruses.

FIGURE 2-28 HOW AN E-MAIL MESSAGE MAY TRAVEL FROM A SENDER TO A RECEIVER

Step 1:
Using e-mail software, you create and send a message.

Internet service provider's outgoing mail server

Step 2:
Your software contacts software on your service provider's outgoing mail server.

outgoing mail server

Step 3:
Software on the outgoing mail server determines the best route for the data and sends the message, which travels along Internet routers to the recipient's incoming mail server.

Internet service provider's incoming mail server

Step 4:
When the recipient uses e-mail software to check for e-mail messages, the message transfers from the incoming mail server to the recipient's computer.

Internet router

Internet router

FTP

FTP (*File Transfer Protocol*) is an Internet standard that permits file uploading and downloading (transferring) with other computers on the Internet. Uploading is the opposite of downloading; that is, **uploading** is the process of transferring documents, graphics, and other objects from your computer to a server on the Internet. Web page authors, for example, often use FTP to upload their Web pages to a Web server.

Many operating systems include FTP capabilities (Figure 2-29). If yours does not, you can download FTP programs from the Web, usually for a small fee.

An *FTP server* is a computer that allows users to upload and/or download files using FTP. An FTP site is a collection of files including text, graphics, audio clips, video clips, and program files that reside on an FTP server. Many FTP sites have *anonymous FTP*, whereby anyone can transfer some, if not all, available

files. Some FTP sites restrict file transfers to those who have authorized accounts (user names and passwords) on the FTP server.

Large files on FTP sites often are compressed to reduce storage space and download time. Before you can use a compressed (zipped) file, you must uncompress (unzip) it. Chapter 8 discusses utilities that zip and unzip files.

Newsgroups and Message Boards

A **newsgroup** is an online area in which users have written discussions about a particular subject (Figure 2-30). To participate in a discussion, a user sends a message to the newsgroup, and other users in the newsgroup read and reply to the message. The entire collection of Internet newsgroups is called *Usenet*, which contains tens of thousands of newsgroups about a multitude of topics. Some major topic areas include news, recreation, society, business, science, and computers.

A computer that stores and distributes newsgroup messages is called a *news server*. Many universities, corporations, Internet access providers, and other large organizations have a news server. Some newsgroups require you to enter a user name and password to participate in the discussion. Only authorized members can use this type of newsgroup. For example, a newsgroup for students taking a college course may require a user name and password to access the newsgroup. This ensures that only students in the course participate in the discussion.

To participate in a newsgroup, typically you use a program called a *newsreader*. Outlook Express includes a newsreader. You also can download newsreaders free or for a fee on the Web. Instead of using your own newsreader, some Web sites that sponsor newsgroups have a built-in newsreader. A newsreader enables you to access a newsgroup to read previously entered messages, called *articles*. You can *post*, or add, articles of your own. The newsreader also keeps track of which articles you have and have not read.

Newsgroup members frequently post articles as a reply to another article — either to

FIGURE 2-29a   (FTP site being added to My Network Places folder)

FIGURE 2-29b   (FTP site link is displayed in My Network Places folder)

link to FTP site

FIGURE 2-29   Many operating systems, such as Windows XP, have built-in FTP capabilities.

FIGURE 2-30 Users in a newsgroup read and reply to other users' messages.

answer a question or to comment on material in the original article. These replies may cause the author of the original article, or others, to post additional articles related to the original article. A *thread* or *threaded discussion* consists of the original article and all subsequent related replies. A thread can be short-lived or continue for some time, depending on the nature of the topic and the interest of the participants.

Using a newsreader, you can search for newsgroups discussing a particular subject such as a type of musical instrument, brand of sports equipment, or employment opportunities. If you like the discussion in a particular newsgroup, you can *subscribe* to it, which means its location is saved in your newsreader for easy future access.

In some newsgroups, posted articles are sent to a moderator instead of immediately displaying on the newsgroup. The *moderator* reviews the contents of the article and then posts it, if appropriate. With a *moderated newsgroup*, the moderator decides if the article is relevant to the discussion. The moderator may choose to edit or discard inappropriate articles. For this reason, the content of a moderated newsgroup is considered more valuable.

A popular Web-based type of discussion group that does not require a newsreader is a **message board**. Many Web sites use message boards instead of newsgroups because they are easier to use.

Mailing Lists

A **mailing list** is a group of e-mail names and addresses given a single name. When a message is sent to a mailing list, every person on the list receives a copy of the message in his or her mailbox. To add your e-mail name and address to a mailing list, you **subscribe** to it (Figure 2-31). To remove your name, you **unsubscribe** from the mailing list. Some mailing lists are called *LISTSERVs*, named after a popular mailing list program.

FIGURE 2-31 When you join a mailing list, you and all others on the mailing list receive e-mail messages from the Web site.

WEB LINK 2-9

Mailing Lists

For more information, visit scsite.com/ dc2006/ch2/weblink and then click Mailing Lists.

Thousands of mailing lists exist about a variety of topics in areas of entertainment, business, computers, society, culture, health, recreation, and education. To locate a mailing list dealing with a particular topic, search for the keywords, mailing list or LISTSERV, in a search engine. Many vendors use mailing lists to communicate with their customer base.

Chat Rooms

A **chat** is a real-time typed conversation that takes place on a computer. **Real time** means that you and the people with whom you are conversing are online at the same time. A **chat room** is a location on an Internet server that permits users to chat with each other. Anyone in the chat room can participate in the conversation, which usually is specific to a particular topic.

As you type on your keyboard, a line of characters and symbols is displayed on the computer screen. Others connected to the same chat room server also see what you have typed (Figure 2-32). Some chat rooms support voice chats and video chats, in which people hear or see each other as they chat.

WEB LINK 2-10

Chat Rooms

For more information, visit scsite.com/ dc2006/ch2/weblink and then click Chat Rooms.

To start a chat session, you connect to a chat server through a program called a *chat client*. Today's browsers usually include a chat client. If yours does not, you can download a chat client from the Web.

Once you have installed a chat client, you can create or join a conversation on the chat server to which you are connected. The chat room should indicate the discussion topic. The person who creates a chat room acts as the operator and has responsibility for monitoring the conversation and disconnecting anyone who becomes disruptive. Operator status can be shared or transferred to someone else.

Instant Messaging

Instant messaging (**IM**) is a real-time Internet communications service that notifies you when one or more people are online and then allows you to exchange messages or files or join a private chat room with them. Some IM services support voice and video conversations (Figure 2-33). Many IM services also can alert you to information such as calendar appointments, stock quotes, weather, or sports scores. They also allow you to send pictures or other documents to a recipient. For IM to work, both parties must be online at the same time. Also, the receiver of a message must be willing to accept messages.

People use IM on all types of computers, including desktop computers and mobile computers and devices, such as smart phones. To use IM, you may have to install *instant messenger* software on the computer or device you plan to use. Some operating systems, such as Windows XP, include an instant messenger. No standards currently exist for IM. To ensure successful communications, all individuals on the notification list need to use the same or a compatible instant messenger.

FIGURE 2-32 As you type, the words and symbols you enter are displayed on the computer screens of other people in the same chat room.

FIGURE 2-33   AN EXAMPLE OF INSTANT MESSAGING

WEB LINK 2-11

Instant Messaging
For more information, visit scsite.com/dc2006/ch2/weblink and then click Instant Messaging.

Step 1:
Log in to the IM server.

Step 2:
The server determines if any of your established friends, family, or coworkers, called *buddies*, are online.

Step 3:
You send instant messages, voice, and/or video communications to an online buddy.

Step 4:
Your instant message, voice, and/or video travels through a messaging server and then to the online buddy's computer.

Step 5:
Your online buddy replies.

IM server

messaging server

Internet Telephony

Internet telephony, also called *Voice over IP* (Internet Protocol), enables users to speak to other users over the Internet using their desktop computer, mobile computer, or mobile device. That is, Internet telephony uses the Internet (instead of the public switched telephone network) to connect a calling party to one or more local or long-distance called parties.

To place an Internet telephone call, you need a high-speed Internet connection (e.g., via DSL or cable modem); Internet telephone service; a microphone or telephone, depending on the Internet telephone service; and Internet telephone software or a telephone adapter, depending on the Internet telephone service. Calls to other parties with the same Internet telephone service often are free, while calls that connect to the telephone network typically cost about $15 to $40 per month.

As you speak in a microphone or telephone connected to your computer, the Internet telephone software and the computer's sound card or the telephone adapter convert your spoken words (analog signals) to digital signals and then transmit the digitized audio over the Internet to the called parties. Software and equipment at the receiving end reverse the process so the receiving parties can hear what you have said. Figure 2-34 illustrates a user's equipment configuration for Internet telephony.

FAQ 2-11

How popular is Internet telephony?

One study predicts that by 2007, more than five million people will subscribe to Internet telephony services, which will account for 40 percent of all telephone calls. For more information, visit scsite.com/dc2006/ch2/faq and then click Internet Telephony.

FIGURE 2-34 Equipment configuration for a user making a call via Internet telephony.

NETIQUETTE

Netiquette, which is short for Internet etiquette, is the code of acceptable behaviors users should follow while on the Internet; that is, it is the conduct expected of individuals while online. Netiquette includes rules for all aspects of the Internet, including the World Wide Web, e-mail, FTP, newsgroups and message boards, chat rooms, and instant messaging. Figure 2-35 outlines some of the rules of netiquette.

NETIQUETTE

Golden Rule: Treat others as you would like them to treat you.

1. In e-mail, newsgroups, and chat rooms:
   - Keep messages brief. Use proper grammar, spelling, and punctuation.
   - Be careful when using sarcasm and humor, as it might be misinterpreted.
   - Be polite. Avoid offensive language.
   - Read the message before you send it.
   - Use meaningful subject lines.
   - Avoid sending or posting *flames,* which are abusive or insulting messages. Do not participate in *flame wars,* which are exchanges of flames.
   - Avoid sending spam, which is the Internet's version of junk mail. *Spam* is an unsolicited e-mail message or newsgroup posting sent to many recipients or newsgroups at once.
   - Do not use all capital letters, which is the equivalent of SHOUTING!
   - Use **emoticons** to express emotion. Popular emoticons include

:)	Smile	:\	Undecided
:(	Frown	:o	Surprised
:|	Indifference		

   - Use abbreviations and acronyms for phrases:

BTW	by the way
FYI	for your information
FWIW	for what it's worth
IMHO	in my humble opinion
TTFN	ta ta for now
TYVM	thank you very much

   - Clearly identify a *spoiler,* which is a message that reveals a solution to a game or ending to a movie or program.
2. Read the *FAQ* (frequently asked questions), if one exists. Many newsgroups and Web pages have an FAQ.
3. Do not assume material is accurate or up-to-date. Be forgiving of other's mistakes.
4. Never read someone's private e-mail.

FIGURE 2-35 Some of the rules of netiquette.

Test your knowledge of pages 91 through 100 in Quiz Yourself 2-3.

QUIZ YOURSELF 2-3

Instructions: Find the true statement below. Then, rewrite the remaining false statements so they are true.

1. A chat room is a location on an Internet server that permits users to chat with each other.

2. An e-mail address is a combination of a user name and an e-mail program that identifies a user so he or she can receive Internet e-mail.

3. Business-to-consumer e-commerce occurs when one consumer sells directly to another, such as in an online auction.

4. FTP is an Internet standard that permits file reading and writing with other computers on the Internet.

5. Spam uses the Internet (instead of the public switched telephone network) to connect a calling party to one or more called parties.

6. Netiquette is the code of unacceptable behaviors while on the Internet.

7. On a newsgroup, a subscription consists of the original article and all subsequent related replies.

Quiz Yourself Online: To further check your knowledge of e-commerce, e-mail, FTP, newsgroups and message boards, mailing lists, chat rooms, instant messaging, Internet telephony, and netiquette, visit scsite.com/dc2006/ch2/quiz and then click Objectives 10 – 12.

CHAPTER SUMMARY

This chapter presented the history and structure of the Internet. It discussed the World Wide Web at length, including topics such as browsing, navigating, searching, Web publishing, and e-commerce. It also introduced other services available on the Internet, such as e-mail (read At Issue 2-5 for a related discussion), FTP, newsgroups and message boards, chat rooms, instant messaging, and Internet telephony. Finally, the chapter listed rules of netiquette.

AT ISSUE 2-5

E-Mail: Irritant or Liberator?

E-mail is one of the more popular services on the Internet. Worldwide, more than 230 million people send and receive e-mail messages. E-mail makes business managers more productive by allowing them to share information, ideas, and opinions easily. But ironically, this easy sharing also can make managers less productive. Every day, managers wade through rivers of e-mail messages. Some of the messages are important, but many are copies of messages sent to others, notes on minor matters, or observations once shared in brief telephone calls or on walks to the water cooler. Most messages expect a quick reply, so hours can be spent dealing with e-mail. The constant flow of e-mail steals the time and interrupts the concentration needed for everyday work activities. Even worse, as managers become accustomed to the brief, rapid thinking demanded for e-mail, they can become unused to the creative, contemplative, persistent thought processes required for complex projects. Managers use a variety of measures to dam the flood of e-mail, including limiting the amount of time spent on messages, having colleagues telephone when they send important messages, and using filtering software to prioritize messages. What is the best way to deal with e-mail? Why? In terms of productivity, how can a company maximize the advantages of e-mail and minimize the disadvantages?

CAREER CORNER

Web Developer

If you are looking for a job working with the latest Internet technology, then Web developer could be the career for you. A *Web developer* analyzes, designs, develops, implements, and supports Web applications and functionality. Specialized programming skills required include HTML, JavaScript, Java, Perl, C++, and VBScript. Developers also may need multimedia knowledge, including Adobe Photoshop, Macromedia Flash, and Macromedia Director. Developers must be aware of emerging technologies and know how they can be used to enhance a Web presence.

A Web developer must be able to appreciate a client's needs, recognize the technologies involved to meet those needs, and explain those technologies to the client. For example, if the client is a large corporation seeking to set up an online store, a Web developer must understand e-commerce and be able to explain requirements, probable costs, and possible outcomes in a way the client can understand.

Educational requirements vary from company to company and can range from a high school education to a four-year degree. Many companies place heavy emphasis on certifications. Two of the more popular certifications are available through the International Webmasters Association (IWA) and the World Organization of Webmasters (WOW). A wide salary range exists — from $35,000 to $65,000 — depending on educational background and location. For more information, visit scsite.com/dc2006/ch2/careers and then click Web Developer.

High-Tech Talk

A COMPUTER'S INTERNET PROTOCOL (IP) ADDRESS

Every computer on the Internet has a unique address, called an IP address, that distinguishes it from other computers on the Internet. An IP address has two parts that identify a specific computer: one part to identify the network where that computer resides and a second part to pinpoint the specific computer or host within that network.

A typical IP address — such as 216.239.39.99 — has four groups of numbers that range from 0 through 255. This form of the IP address sometimes is called a *dotted decimal number* or *dotted quad*. The four groups of numbers in the dotted quad are called octets, because they each have 8 bits when viewed in binary form for a total of 32 bits in the IP address. For instance, the binary form of 216.239.39.99 is 11011000.11101111.00101001.01100011 (Figure 2-36). For more information about how the binary system works, see Appendix A.

FIGURE 2-36
Components of an IP address.

Because each of the 8 bits can be 1 or 0, the total possible combinations per octet are 2^8, or 256. Combining the four octets of an IP address provides a possible 2^{32} or 4,294,967,296 unique values. The actual number of available addresses is about 3 billion, because some values are reserved for special use and are, therefore, off limits.

To request data such as a Web page from a computer on the Internet, you need only an IP address. For instance, if you type the Web address, http://216.239.39.99, your browser will display the home page on the machine hosting the Google Web site. Of course, remembering one IP address out of billions is a little overwhelming — so you probably would just type the domain name, www.google.com, in your browser. Your browser then contacts a domain name server (DNS) to resolve the human-readable domain name into a machine-readable IP address. Each domain name server houses a simple database that maps domain names to IP addresses. The DNS would resolve the human-readable domain name, www.google.com, into a machine-readable IP address, 216.239.39.99.

Domain names are helpful because they are easier for people to remember than IP addresses. You can learn more about a domain using the whois form at the Network Solutions Web site (www.netsol.com and then click the whois link). If you type a domain name, such as google.com, the form displays the registration information for that domain, including its IP address.

Like all other computers, your computer must have an IP address to connect to the Internet or another computer that has an IP address. Servers generally have *static IP addresses*, because they usually are connected to the Internet and their IP addresses do not change often. When you connect to the Internet using your home computer, you most likely are using a temporary or *dynamic IP address*. Your access provider uses the *Dynamic Host Configuration Protocol (DHCP)* to assign your computer a temporary dynamic IP address from a pool of IP addresses. The dynamic IP address is unique only for that session. Once you disconnect, the DHCP server puts that IP address back in the IP address pool so it can assign it to the next requesting computer. Even if you immediately reconnect, the DHCP server might not assign you the same IP address. Using DHCP and dynamic IP addresses means an Internet service provider needs only one IP address for each modem it supports, rather than one for each of its millions of customers.

Billions of IP addresses sounds like a lot. But, because so many computers connected to the Internet need unique IP addresses, a growing shortage of IP addresses exists. A new IP addressing scheme, called *IPv6* or *IPng (IP Next Generation)* will lengthen IP addresses from 32 bits to 128 bits and increase the number of available IP addresses to a whopping 3.4×10^{38}, or 340,000,000,000,000,000,000,000,000,000,000,000,000.

Do you want to know the IP address currently assigned to your computer?

- With Windows 2000/XP, click the Start button on the taskbar and then click Run. Type `cmd` to open the MS-DOS window. Type `ipconfig` and then press the ENTER key.

- With Windows 98, click the Start button on the taskbar and then click Run. Type `winipcfg` and then press the ENTER key.

If you are using an older version of AOL, the IP address might read 0.0.0.0 because AOL uses a proprietary method to assign IP addresses. For more information, visit scsite.com/dc2006/ch2/tech and then click IP Addresses.

Companies on the Cutting Edge

GOOGLE
POPULAR SEARCH ENGINE

The founders of *Google*, the leading Internet search engine, state that their mission is to organize the world's information. Every day, their Web site handles hundreds of millions of queries for information. In seconds, it can locate specific phrases and terms on four billion Web pages by using more than 10,000 connected computers.

Sergey Brin and Larry Page launched Google in 1998 in a friend's garage. The name is derived from "googol," which is the name of the number 1 followed by 100 zeros. Nearly 2,000 Google employees work at Googleplex, the corporate headquarters in Mountain View, California. According to Initial Public Offering documents filed in 2004, the company is worth more than $2.7 billion. For more information, visit scsite.com/dc2006/ch2/companies and then click Google.

YAHOO!
POPULAR WEB PORTAL

Yahoo!, the first navigational portal to the Web, began as a hobby for Jerry Yang and David Filo when they were doctoral candidates in electrical engineering at Stanford University. They started creating and organizing lists of their favorite Web sites in 1994. The following year, they shared their creation, named Yahoo!, with fellow students and then released their product to the Internet community.

Yahoo! is an acronym for Yet Another Hierarchical Officious Oracle. What makes Yahoo! unique is that staff members build the directory by assuming the role of a typical Web researcher. In 2004 the site enhanced its Yahoo! Messenger service, with two-player games, expressive verbal animations, and the ability to listen to customized radio stations. For more information, visit scsite.com/dc2006/ch2/companies and then click Yahoo!.

Technology Trailblazers

TIM BERNERS-LEE
CREATOR OF THE WORLD WIDE WEB

The World Wide Web (WWW) has become one of the more widely used Internet services, and its roots are based on *Tim Berners-Lee's* work. Berners-Lee is credited with creating the first Web server, browser, and URL addresses.

He developed his ideas in 1989 while working at CERN, the European Particle Physics Laboratory in Geneva, Switzerland, and based his work on a program he had written for his own use to track random associations. Today, he works quietly in academia as director of the World Wide Web Consortium (W3C) at the Massachusetts Institute of Technology.

In 2004, Berners-Lee received the first Millennium Technology Prize, which is worth $1.2 million and recognizes technological developments that enhance the quality of life and encourage economic growth. For more information, visit scsite.com/dc2006/ch2/people and then click Tim Berners-Lee.

MEG WHITMAN
EBAY PRESIDENT AND CEO

Meg Whitman joined eBay in 1998 and has been instrumental in helping the company become the world's largest online marketplace. Before that time, she was an executive for the Keds Division of the Stride Rite Corporation and general manager of Hasbro Inc.'s Preschool Division. She then served as president and CEO of Florists Transworld Delivery (FTD).

She credits her success to listening to the loyal eBay community, and she occasionally answers their e-mails personally. She holds degrees in economics from Princeton University and management from the Harvard Business School.

Fortune magazine has named Whitman one of the most powerful women in business, and *Worth* magazine has ranked her at the top of its list of most powerful business managers. For more information, visit scsite.com/dc2006/ch2/people and then click Meg Whitman.

Chapter Review

The Chapter Review section summarizes the concepts presented in this chapter. To listen to the audio version of this Chapter Review, visit scsite.com/dc2006/ch2/review. To obtain help from other students regarding any subject in this chapter, visit scsite.com/dc2006/ch2/forum and post your thoughts or questions.

① What Is the History of the Internet?   The **Internet** is a worldwide collection of networks that links millions of businesses, government agencies, educational institutions, and individuals. The Internet has its roots in *ARPANET*, a network started in 1969 to link researchers across the United States. In 1986, the National Science Foundation connected its huge network, called *NSFnet*, to ARPANET, creating a configuration of complex networks and hosts that became known as the Internet.

② How Can You Access and Connect to the Internet?   Employees and students often connect to the Internet through a business or school network. The networks usually use a high-speed line leased from a telephone company. Many home and small businesses connect to the Internet with **dial-up access**, which uses a modem in the computer and a standard telephone line. Some home and small business users opt for higher-speed *broadband* connections, such as DSL, cable television networks, radio signals, or satellite. **DSL** provides Internet connections using regular copper telephone lines. A **cable modem** allows access to Internet services through the cable television network. *Fixed wireless* connections use an antenna to communicate via radio signals. A *satellite modem* communicates with a satellite dish. An **access provider** is a business that provides access to the Internet free or for a fee. An **ISP** (**Internet service provider**) is a regional or national access provider. An **online service provider** (**OSP**) provides Internet access in addition to members-only features. A **wireless Internet service provider** *(WISP)* provides wireless Internet access to users with wireless modems or Internet-enabled mobile devices.

③ What Is an IP Address?   An **IP address** (*Internet Protocol address*) is a number that uniquely identifies each computer or device connected to the Internet. The Internet relies on IP addresses to send data to computers at specific locations. A **domain name** is the text version of an IP address.

Visit scsite.com/dc2006/ch2/quiz or click the Quiz Yourself button. Click Objectives 1 – 3.

④ What Are the Components of a Web Address?   The **World Wide Web** (*WWW*), or **Web**, consists of a worldwide collection of electronic documents. Each electronic document is called a **Web page**. A **URL** (*Uniform Resource Locator*), or **Web address**, is a unique address for a Web page. A Web address consists of a protocol, a domain name, and sometimes the path to a specific Web page or location on a Web page.

⑤ What Is the Purpose of a Web Browser?   A **Web browser**, or **browser**, is application software that allows users to access and view Web pages. When you type a Web address in the Address box of a browser window, a computer called a **Web server** delivers the requested Web page to your computer. Most Web pages contain links. A **link** is a built-in connection that, when clicked, displays a related Web page or part of a Web page.

⑥ How Can You Search for Information on the Web?   Two commonly used search tools are subject directories and search engines. A **subject directory** classifies Web pages in an organized set of categories. By clicking links, you move through categories to display a list of Web pages about a desired topic. A **search engine** is a program that finds Web sites and Web pages. To use a search engine, you enter a word or phrase, called **search text**, that defines the item about which you want information. The search engine displays a list of *hits*. When clicked, each hit displays an associated Web site or Web page.

Chapter Review

(7) What Are the Types of Web Sites? A **portal** is a Web site that offers a variety of Internet services from a single location. A news Web site contains newsworthy material. An informational Web site contains factual information. A business/marketing Web site promotes or sells products or services. An educational Web site offers avenues for teaching and learning. An entertainment Web site provides an interactive and engaging environment. An advocacy Web site describes a cause, opinion, or idea. A **blog** is a Web site that uses a regularly updated journal format. A personal Web site is maintained by a private individual or family.

(8) How Do Web Pages Use Graphics, Animation, Audio, Video, Virtual Reality, and Plug-Ins? Some Web pages use **multimedia**, which combines text with graphics, animation, audio, video, and/or virtual reality. A **graphic** is a digital representation of nontext information such as a drawing or photograph. **Animation** is the appearance of motion created by displaying a series of still images. **Audio** includes music, speech, or any other sound. **Video** consists of full-motion images. **Virtual reality (VR)** is the use of computers to simulate an environment that appears as three-dimensional space. A **plug-in** is a program that extends a browser's capability to display multimedia elements.

(9) What Are the Steps Required for Web Publishing? **Web publishing** is the development and maintenance of Web pages. The five major steps to Web publishing are: (1) plan a Web site, (2) analyze and design a Web site, (3) create a Web site, (4) deploy a Web site, and (5) maintain a Web site.

> connect
> Visit scsite.com/dc2006/ch2/quiz or click the Quiz Yourself button. Click Objectives 4 – 9.

(10) What Are the Types of E-Commerce? **E-commerce**, short for *electronic commerce*, is a business transaction that occurs over an electronic network such as the Internet. *Business-to-consumer (B2C) e-commerce* consists of the sale of goods and services to the general public. *Consumer-to-consumer (C2C) e-commerce* occurs when one consumer sells directly to another, such as an **online auction**. *Business-to-business (B2B) e-commerce* takes place between businesses that exchange goods and services.

(11) How Do E-Mail, FTP, Newsgroups and Message Boards, Mailing Lists, Chat Rooms, Instant Messaging, and Internet Telephony Work? **E-mail** (short for *electronic mail*) is the transmission of messages and files via a computer network. **FTP** (*File Transfer Protocol*) is an Internet standard that permits file **uploading** and **downloading** with other computers. A **newsgroup** is an online area in which users have written discussions. A **message board** is a Web-based type of discussion group that is easier to use than a newsgroup. A **mailing list** is a group of e-mail names and addresses given a single name, so that everyone on the list receives a message sent to the list. A **chat room** is a location on an Internet server that permits users to conduct real-time typed conversations. **Instant messaging (IM)** is a real-time Internet communications service that notifies you when one or more people are online. **Internet telephony** enables users to speak over the Internet using a computer or mobile device.

(12) What Are the Rules of Netiquette? **Netiquette**, which is short for Internet etiquette, is the code of acceptable behaviors users should follow while on the Internet. Netiquette rules include: keep messages short, be polite, avoid sending *flames* or *spam*, use **emoticons** and acronyms, read the *FAQ*, do not assume material is accurate or up-to-date, and never read someone's private e-mail.

> connect
> Visit scsite.com/dc2006/ch2/quiz or click the Quiz Yourself button. Click Objectives 10 – 12.

Key Terms

You should know the Primary Terms and be familiar with the Secondary Terms. Use the list below to help focus your study. To further enhance your understanding of the Key Terms in this chapter, visit scsite.com/dc2006/ch2/terms. See an example of and a definition for each term, and access current and additional information about the term from the Web.

Primary Terms

(shown in bold-black characters in the chapter)

access provider (71)
address book (94)
animation (86)
audio (86)
blog (84)
browser (75)
cable modem (70)
chat (98)
chat room (98)
dial-up access (70)
DNS server (74)
domain name (73)
downloading (76)
DSL (70)
e-commerce (91)
electronic storefront (92)
e-mail (92)
e-mail address (94)
e-mail program (93)
emoticons (100)
FTP (96)
graphic (85)
home page (76)
instant messaging (IM)
  (98)
Internet (68)
Internet telephony (99)
IP address (73)
ISP (Internet service
  provider) (72)
link (77)
mailing list (97)
message board (97)
MP3 (86)
multimedia (85)
netiquette (100)

newsgroup (96)
online auction (92)
online service provider
  (OSP) (72)
player (86)
plug-in (89)
portal (82)
real time (98)
search engine (78)
search text (80)
shopping cart (92)
streaming (86)
subject directory (78)
subscribe (97)
surfing the Web (77)
traffic (70)
unsubscribe (97)
uploading (96)
URL (76)
user name (94)
video (88)
virtual reality (VR) (88)
Web (75)
Web address (76)
Web browser (75)
Web community (82)
Web page (75)
Web publishing (90)
Web server (75)
Web site (75)
wireless Internet service
  provider (72)
World Wide Web (75)

Secondary Terms

(shown in italic characters in the chapter)

*Advanced Research Projects
  Agency (ARPA) (69)*
animated GIF (86)
anonymous FTP (96)
ARPANET (69)
articles (96)
broadband (70)
*business-to-business (B2B)
  e-commerce (92)*
*business-to-consumer
  (B2C) e-commerce (92)*
chat client (98)
click (77)
*consumer-to-consumer
  (C2C) e-commerce (92)*
digital subscriber line (70)
DNS server (74)
*domain name system
  (DNS) (74)*
dot-com (73)
dynamic Web page (75)
electronic commerce (91)
electronic mail (92)
FAQ (100)
File Transfer Protocol (96)
fixed wireless (70)
flame wars (100)
flames (100)
FTP server (96)
GIF (85)
graphical image (85)
hits (80)
host (69)
hot spots (71)
http (76)
hyperlink (77)
*Hypertext Transfer
  Protocol (76)*
instant messenger (98)
Internet backbone (72)
*Internet Corporation for
  Assigned Names and
  Numbers (ICANN) (74)*
*Internet Protocol address
  (73)*
JPEG (85)
keywords (80)

LISTSERVs (97)
m-commerce (91)
microbrowser (76)
moderated newsgroup (97)
moderator (97)
*Moving Pictures Experts
  Group (MPEG) (88)*
MPEG-4 (88)
national ISP (72)
Net (68)
news server (96)
newsreader (96)
NSFnet (70)
PNG (85)
*point of presence (POP)
  (72)*
POP3 (95)
post (96)
Post Office Protocol (95)
pull (76)
push (76)
regional ISP (72)
satellite modem (70)
*SMTP (simple mail
  transfer protocol) (94)*
spam (100)
spider (81)
spoiler (100)
static Web page (75)
streaming audio (86)
streaming video (88)
subscribe (97)
thread (97)
threaded discussion (97)
thumbnail (86)
top-level domain (73)
*Uniform Resource Locator
  (76)*
Usenet (96)
Voice over IP (99)
VR world (88)
Web log (84)
wireless portal (82)
WISP (72)
*World Wide Web
  Consortium (W3C) (70)*
WWW (75)

Checkpoint

Use the Checkpoint exercises to check your knowledge level of the chapter. The Beyond the Book exercises will help broaden your understanding of the concepts presented in this chapter. To complete the Checkpoint exercises interactively, visit scsite.com/dc2006/ch2/check.

Label the Figure

Identify the types of Web sites.

a. advocacy
b. blog
c. business/marketing
d. educational
e. entertainment
f. informational
g. news
h. personal
i. portal

True/False

Mark T for True and F for False. (See page numbers in parentheses.)

_____ 1. A single government agency owns and controls the Internet. (70)

_____ 2. With dial-up Internet access, the telephone number you dial connects you to an access point on the Internet, called a point of presence (POP). (72)

_____ 3. In general, the first portion of each IP address identifies the specific computer and the last portion identifies the network. (73)

_____ 4. Most current browsers and Web sites require the http:// and www portions of a Web address. (76)

_____ 5. Pointing to, or positioning the pointer on, a link on a Web page typically changes the shape of the pointer to a small hand with a pointing index finger. (77)

_____ 6. A major problem with a subject directory is deciding which categories to choose as you work through the menus of links presented. (79)

_____ 7. The purpose of an informational Web site is to convince the reader of the validity of a cause, opinion, or idea. (84)

_____ 8. Developers unfamiliar with Web page authoring programs can create an animated GIF, which combines several GIF images in a single GIF file. (86)

_____ 9. To develop a Web page, you have to be a computer programmer. (90)

_____ 10. An online auction is an example of business-to-consumer (B2C) e-commerce. (92)

_____ 11. Universal standards currently exist for instant messaging (IM). (98)

_____ 12. Using all capital letters in e-mail, newsgroups, and chat rooms is the equivalent of SHOUTING! (100)

Checkpoint

 Multiple Choice   Select the best answer. (See page numbers in parentheses.)

1. The Internet has its roots in _____, which was a networking project started by an agency of the U.S. Department of Defense. (69)
   a. ICANN
   b. NSFnet
   c. WISP
   d. ARPANET

2. Many public locations are _____ that provide wireless Internet connections to users with mobile computers or devices. (71)
   a. plug-ins
   b. hot spots
   c. Web logs
   d. chat clients

3. As with an IP address, the components of a domain name are separated by _____. (73)
   a. commas
   b. periods
   c. colons
   d. semicolons

4. Many Web page addresses begin with _____, which stands for a set of rules that defines how pages transfer on the Internet. (76)
   a. http   b. W3C
   c. hits   d. pop

5. Some people use the phrase, _____, to refer to the activity of using links to explore the Web. (77)
   a. surfing the Web
   b. navigating the Net
   c. weaving the Web
   d. bringing in the Net

6. All of the following techniques can be used to improve Web searches except _____. (81)
   a. list all possible spellings
   b. read a search engine's Help information
   c. use general nouns and put the most important terms last
   d. if a search is unsuccessful, try another search engine

7. When you connect to the Internet, the first Web page displayed often is a(n) _____, such as AOL, Lycos, or MSN. (82)
   a. blog
   b. educational Web site
   c. portal
   d. news Web site

8. Some Web sites use _____ on their pages, which are smaller versions of larger graphics. (86)
   a. moderators
   b. threads
   c. players
   d. thumbnails

9. _____ is the process of transferring data in a continuous and even flow, allowing users to access and use a file while it is transmitting. (86)
   a. Streaming
   b. Linking
   c. Surfing
   d. Clicking

10. _____ is not a step in Web publishing. (90)
    a. Planning a Web site
    b. Deploying a Web site
    c. Creating a Web site
    d. Moderating a Web site

11. At a business-to-consumer (B2C) Web site, a _____ allows customers to collect purchases. (92)
    a. news server
    b. chat client
    c. wireless portal
    d. shopping cart

12. In an e-mail address, a _____ is a unique combination of characters that identifies a specific user. (94)
    a. domain name
    b. URL
    c. user name
    d. dot com

13. To add your e-mail name and address to a mailing list, you _____. (97)
    a. upload to it
    b. subscribe to it
    c. download from it
    d. unsubscribe from it

14. Use _____, such as :) for smile and :(for frown, to express emotions in e-mail, newsgroups, and chat rooms. (100)
    a. flames
    b. spam
    c. spoilers
    d. emoticons

Checkpoint

Matching

Match the terms with their definitions. (See page numbers in parentheses.)

_____ 1. traffic (70)
_____ 2. home page (76)
_____ 3. link (77)
_____ 4. spider (81)
_____ 5. Web community (82)
_____ 6. MP3 (86)
_____ 7. player (86)
_____ 8. m-commerce (91)
_____ 9. address book (94)
_____ 10. plug-in

a. software used to listen to an audio file on a computer
b. bulk of communications activity on the Internet
c. joins a specific group of people with similar interests or relationships
d. first page that a Web site displays
e. program that extends the capability of a browser
f. built-in connection to a related Web page or part of a Web page
g. browser designed for the small screens and limited power of PDAs and smart phones
h. term used to identify e-commerce that takes place using mobile devices
i. program used to build and maintain lists of words found on Web sites
j. copy a program from storage to memory
k. format that reduces an audio file to about one-tenth its original size
l. contains a list of names and e-mail addresses

Short Answer

Write a brief answer to each of the following questions.

1. How is a regional ISP different from a national ISP? _____ How is an OSP different from an ISP? _____
2. How is a static Web page different from a dynamic Web page? _____ What is a Web site? _____
3. What three graphics formats are used frequently on the Web? _____ How are they different? _____
4. What is a threaded discussion? _____ What is a moderated newsgroup? _____
5. What are flame wars? _____ How is spam different from a spoiler? ____

Beyond the Book

Read the following book elements, learn more about each using the Web, and then write a brief report.

1. At Issue — Diplomas Online? (82), Mobile Web Logs with Photos — an Invasion of One's Privacy? (84), To Tax or Not to Tax Internet Sales? (92), Are Free Web-Based E-Mail Services Worth the Price? (94), or E-Mail: Irritant or Liberator? (101)
2. Career Corner — Web Developer (101)
3. Companies on the Cutting Edge — Google or Yahoo! (103)
4. FAQs (71, 72, 72, 74, 77, 81, 85, 86, 92, 95, 100)
5. High-Tech Talk — A Computer's Internet Protocol (IP) Address (102)
6. Looking Ahead — Internet Speeds into the Future (70) or 3-D Search Engines Get the Picture (81)
7. Making Use of the Web — Travel (118)
8. Picture Yourself Instant Messaging (66)
9. Technology Trailblazers — Tim Berners-Lee or Meg Whitman (103)
10. Web Links (72, 77, 86, 89, 92, 95, 96, 97, 98, 98, 99)

Learn It Online

Use the Learn It Online exercises to reinforce your understanding of the chapter concepts. To access the Learn It Online exercises, visit scsite.com/dc2006/ch2/learn.

① At the Movies — Google Search Secrets

To view the Google Search Secrets movie, click the number 1 button. Locate your video and click the corresponding High-Speed or Dial-Up link, depending on your Internet connection. Watch the movie and then complete the exercise by answering the question that follows. Using the Internet to gather information can seem daunting. The introduction of powerful search engines has enhanced the Internet research experience. Properly utilizing a search engine can benefit almost any project. How might you go about using Google to search for information for a research paper?

② At the Movies — Instant Message from Anywhere

To view the Instant Message from Anywhere movie, click the number 2 button. Locate your video and click the corresponding High-Speed or Dial-Up link, depending on your Internet connection. Watch the movie, and then complete the exercise by answering the question that follows. Instant messaging (IM) is a fun way to stay in touch with your friends, but until now it has been limited to use on the computer. New technology developments have cut the wires, and now you can take IM on the road. What are some of the limitations of wireless instant messaging?

③ Student Edition Labs — Connecting to the Internet

Click the number 3 button. When the Student Edition Labs menu appears, click *Connecting to the Internet* to begin. A new browser window will open. Follow the on-screen instructions to complete the Lab. When finished, click the Exit button. If required, submit your results to your instructor.

④ Student Edition Labs — Getting the Most out of the Internet

Click the number 4 button. When the Student Edition Labs menu appears, click *Getting the Most out of the Internet* to begin. A new browser window will open. Follow the on-screen instructions to complete the Lab. When finished, click the Exit button. If required, submit your results to your instructor.

⑤ Student Edition Labs — E-mail

Click the number 5 button. When the Student Edition Labs menu appears, click *E-mail* to begin. A new browser window will open. Follow the on-screen instructions to complete the Lab. When finished, click the Exit button. If required, submit your results to your instructor.

⑥ Practice Test

Click the number 6 button. Answer each question. When completed, enter your name and click the Grade Test button to submit the quiz for grading. Make a note of any missed questions. If required, submit your score to your instructor.

⑦ Who Wants To Be a Computer Genius²?

Click the number 7 button to find out if you are a computer genius. Directions about how to play the game will be displayed. When you are ready to play, click the Play button. Submit your score to your instructor.

Learn It Online

 8 Wheel of Terms

Click the number 8 button to reinforce important terms you learned in this chapter by playing the Shelly Cashman Series version of this popular game. Directions about how to play the game will be displayed. When you are ready to play, click the Play button. Submit your score to your instructor.

 9 DC Track and Field

Click the number 9 button to use what you have learned in this chapter to compete against other students in three track and field events. Directions about how to play the game will be displayed. When you are ready to play, click the start first event button. If required, submit your score to your instructor.

10 You're Hired!

Click the number 10 button to use what you have learned in this chapter to embark on the path to a career in computers. Directions about how to play the game will be displayed. When you are ready to play, click the begin game button. If required, submit your score to your instructor.

 11 Crossword Puzzle Challenge

Click the number 11 button. Complete the puzzle to reinforce skills you learned in this chapter. Directions about how to play the game will be displayed. When you are ready to play, click the Play button. Submit the completed puzzle to your instructor.

12 Lab Exercises

Click the number 12 button. When the Lab Exercises menu appears, click the exercise assigned by your instructor. A new browser window will open. Follow the on-screen instructions to complete the exercise. When finished, click the Exit button. If required, submit your results to your instructor.

 13 In the News

In her book, *Caught in the Net*, Kimberly S. Young contends that the Internet can be addictive. Young's methodology and conclusions have been questioned by several critics, but Young remains resolute. She points out that at one time, no one admitted to the existence of alcoholism. Click the number 13 button and read a news article about the impact of Internet use on human behavior. What effect did the Internet have? Why? In your opinion, is the Internet's influence positive or negative? Why?

14 Chapter Discussion Forum

Select an objective from this chapter on page 67 about which you would like more information. Click the number 14 button and post a short message listing a meaningful message title accompanied by one or more questions concerning the selected objective. In two days, return to the threaded discussion by clicking the number 14 button. Submit to your instructor your original message and at least one response to your message.

Learn How To

Use the Learn How To activities to learn fundamental skills when using a computer and accompanying technology. Complete the exercises and submit them to your instructor. Visit scsite.com/dc2006/ch2/howto to obtain more information pertaining to each activity.

LEARN HOW TO 1: Change a Web Browser's Home Page

When you start a Web browser, a Web page is displayed. You can change the page that appears when you start a Web browser or when you click the Home button on the browser toolbar by completing the following steps:

1. With the browser running, click Tools on the menu bar and then click Internet Options on the Tools menu. *The Internet Options dialog box is displayed (Figure 2-37).*
2. If necessary, in the **Home page** area in the General sheet, select the Web address in the Address box.
3. Type the Web address of the page you want to display both when you start the browser and when you click the Home button.
4. Click the OK button in the Internet Options dialog box.

When you start the browser or click the Home button on the browser toolbar, the selected Web page will be displayed.

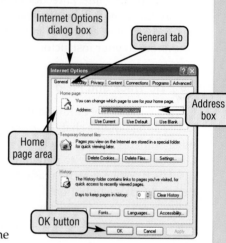

FIGURE 2-37

Exercise

1. Start your Web browser. Write down the address of the browser's current home page. Then, change the browser's home page to www.cnn.com. Close the browser.
2. Start your Web browser. What is the lead story on cnn.com? Use links on the page to view several stories. Which story do you find most interesting? Click the Home button on the browser toolbar. What happened? Submit these answers to your instructor.
3. Change the browser's home page to your school's home page. Click the Home button on the browser toolbar. Click the Calendar or Events link, and then locate two campus events of which you were unaware. Report these two campus events to your instructor.
4. Change the browser's home page back to the address you wrote down in Step 1.

LEARN HOW TO 2: Create and Use Your Own Web Log (Blog)

A Web log, commonly referred to as a blog, can contain any information you wish to place in it. Originally, **blogs** consisted of Web addresses, so that an individual or group with a specific interest could direct others to useful places on the Web. Today, blogs contain addresses, thoughts, diaries, and anything else a person or group wants to share.

Once you have created a blog, you can update it. A variety of services are available on the Web to help you create and maintain your blog. One widely used service is called Blogger. To create a blog using Blogger, complete the following steps:

1. Start your Web browser, type `www.blogger.com` in the Address box, and then press the ENTER key. *The Blogger home page is displayed (Figure 2-38).*
2. Click the CREATE YOUR BLOG NOW arrow on the Blogger home page.
3. Enter the data required on the Create an account page. Your user name and password will allow you to change and manage your blog. Your Display name is the name that will be shown on the blog as the author of the material on the blog. Many people use their own names, but others use pseudonyms as their "pen names" so they are not readily identifiable.
4. Click the Continue arrow and then enter your Blog title and Blog address. These are the names and addresses everyone will use to view your blog. By default, the blog is stored and maintained on the blogspot server.
5. Click the Continue arrow. *The Choose a template screen is displayed.*
6. Choose a template for your blog and then click the Continue arrow.

Learn How To

7. Your blog will be created for you. When you see the Your blog has been created screen, click the Start posting arrow.
8. From the screen that is displayed, you can post items for your blog, specify settings, change the template, and view your blog.
9. When you have posted all your information, click the Sign out button at the top right of the screen. You will be logged out.
10. To edit your blog and add or change information on it, visit the Blogger home page and sign in by entering your user name and password. You will be able to post to your blog.
11. Others can view your blog by entering its address in the browser's Address bar and then pressing the ENTER key.

FIGURE 2-38

Exercise

1. Start your Web browser and visit www.blogger.com. Click the TAKE A QUICK TOUR button and go through all the screens that explain about a blog. What did you learn that you did not know? What type of blog do you find most compelling — a group or an individual blog? Why? Turn in your answers to your instructor.
2. Optional: Create your own blog. Carefully name it and begin your posts at this time. What is your blog name and address? What is its primary purpose? Is it an individual or group blog? Write a paragraph containing the answers to these questions and any other information you feel is pertinent. Turn in this paragraph to your instructor.

LEARN HOW TO 3: Bid and Buy a Product from eBay

<u>Online auctions</u> have grown to be a favorite shopping space for many people. A leading online auction Web site is eBay. To submit a bid for an item on eBay, complete the following steps:

1. Type www.ebay.com in the Address box of your browser. Press the ENTER key. *The eBay home page is displayed (Figure 2-39).*
2. Pick an item you find interesting and on which you might bid.
3. Enter your item in the What are you looking for text box and then click the Find It button.
4. Scroll through the page to see the available items.
5. To bid on an item, click the Place Bid button.
6. Enter the amount of your bid. Click the Continue button.
7. You must be registered to bid on eBay. If you are registered, enter your eBay User ID and Password and then click the Submit button. If not, click the Register button and follow the instructions.
8. After registering, you will confirm your bid and receive notification about your bid.
9. You will be notified by e-mail if you won the bid. If so, you will arrange with the seller for payment and shipment.

FIGURE 2-39

The eBay Web site contains reminders that when you bid on an item, you are entering into a contract to purchase the item if you are the successful bidder. Bidding on eBay is serious business.

Exercise

1. Start your browser and display the eBay home page.
2. In the What are you looking for text box, enter the name of an upcoming sporting event you would like to attend followed by the word, tickets. For example, enter Super Bowl tickets. Click the Search button.
3. Did you find available tickets? Were there more tickets available than you expected, or fewer? Are the bid prices reasonable or ridiculous? How many bids were made for all the tickets? How much time is left to bid? What items did you find you were not expecting? Submit answers to these questions to your instructor.
4. Enter an item of your choice in the What are you looking for text box. If you feel so inclined, bid on an item. Do you think this manner of buying goods is valuable? Why? Will you visit eBay again? Why? Submit answers to these questions to your instructor.

Web Research

Use the Internet-based Web Research exercises to broaden your understanding of the concepts presented in this chapter. Visit scsite.com/dc2006/ch2/research to obtain more information pertaining to each exercise. To discuss any of the Web Research exercises in this chapter with other students, post your thoughts or questions at scsite.com/dc2006/ch2/forum.

① Scavenger Hunt   Use one of the <u>search engines</u> listed in Figure 2-10 in Chapter 2 on page 78 or your own favorite search engine to find the answers to the questions below. Copy and paste the Web address from the Web page where you found the answer. Some questions may have more than one answer. If required, submit your answers to your instructor. (1) Microsoft Internet Explorer and Netscape Navigator are the two more popular Web browsers. What is the name of the first graphical Web browser? (2) What cable company was established in 1858 to carry instantaneous communications across the ocean that would eventually be used for Internet communications? (3) What American president in 1957 created both the interstate highway system and the Advanced Research Projects Agency (ARPA)? (4) Where is the location of Microsoft's headquarters? (5) How many Web pages is Google currently searching?

② Search Sleuth   The Internet has provided the opportunity to access encyclopedias online. One of the more comprehensive encyclopedia research sites is **Encyclopedia.com**. Visit this Web site and then use your word processing program to answer the following questions. Then, if required, submit your answers to your instructor. (1) The site's home page provides information about who was born and died and what significant events occurred on this date. What are these facts for today? (2) Type `computer` as the keyword in the Search text box. How many articles discussing computers are found on the Encyclopedia.com Web site? (3) Click your browser's Back button or press the BACKSPACE key to return to the home page. Type `modem` as the keyword in the Search text box. How many articles discussing modems are found on this Web site? (4) In the search results list, click the modem link. What are wireless and a fax modems? (5) Click your browser's Back button or press the BACKSPACE key to return to the home page. Type `Bill Gates` as the keyword in the Search text box and then click the Bill Gates link and read the article. According to this source, why did the Justice Department sue Microsoft in 1997? (6) Click your browser's Back button or press the BACKSPACE key to return to the home page. Click one of the Top Searches links and review the material. Summarize the information you read and then write a 50-word summary.

③ Newsgroups   One of the more popular topics for <u>newsgroups</u> is netiquette. Read the information Borland Software Corporation (info.borland.com/newsgroups/netiquette.html) provides on general newsgroup conduct. Then find three newsgroups, such as those listed in CyberFiber (cyberfiber.com/internet.htm) or Google Groups, that discuss this topic. Read the information and then summarize the advice provided.

④ Journaling   Respond to your readings in this chapter by writing at least one page about your reactions, evaluations, and reflections about the first time you used the <u>Internet</u>. For example, to whom did you send your first e-mail message? Have you used chat rooms? Have you bought or sold any items through an online auction Web site? Have you shopped online? Have your instructors required you to access the Internet for class projects? You also can write about the new terms you learned by reading this chapter. If required, submit your journal to your instructor.

⑤ Ethics in Action   <u>Web cams</u> are video cameras that display their output on a Web page. The feasibility of installing Web cams in 47,000 locations susceptible to terrorist threats, such as nuclear and chemical plants, national airports, and gas storage facilities, is being explored. Citizens would monitor the cameras and report suspicious activity. Critics of this proposal state that the constant surveillance is an invasion of privacy. Visit the USHomeGuard Web site (ushomeguard.org) and then write a summary of the citizen corps' roles in this project. Then locate other Web sites that oppose this plan and summarize their views. If required, submit your summary to your instructor.

Case Studies

Use the Case Studies to apply the concepts presented in the chapter to real-world situations. Visit scsite.com/dc2006/ch2/cases to obtain more information pertaining to each exercise. To discuss the Case Studies in this chapter with other students, visit scsite.com/dc2006/ch2/forum and post your thoughts or questions.

CASE STUDY 1 — Class Discussion   The owner of Deuce Investments, where you are employed part-time as a stock-research analyst, recently attended a one-day continuing education course for small businesses at the local community college. The title of the course was *Ten Reasons Why Your Company Needs the Internet to Compete in Today's Business Environment*. She now feels that the Internet might be useful as an investment-research tool, and she has asked you to investigate the costs associated with making the Internet available for use in the company during business hours. Examine the types of **access providers** available in your community, the monthly cost, and other significant factors that might influence her decision. Draft a memo to the owner summarizing your recommendations. Be prepared to discuss your recommendations in class.

CASE STUDY 2 — Class Discussion   Many retailers, such as Best Buy, Kohl's, and Circuit City, are **brick-and-click businesses**. That is, they allow customers to conduct complete transactions at a physical location as well as online at a Web site. Choose a local brick-and-click business in which you have shopped at the physical location and visit the Web site of the business. Compare the type, availability, and cost (include tax and shipping) of products or services available. Prepare a report that summarizes the advantages and disadvantages of dealing with the physical location versus the Web site of a brick-and-click business. Would you rather shop at the physical location or at the Web site? Why? Does the answer depend on the business, the product, or some other factor? Be prepared to share your findings in class.

CASE STUDY 3 — Research   This chapter lists nine types of Web sites: **portal**, news, informational, business/marketing, educational, entertainment, advocacy, blog, and personal. Use the Internet to find at least one example of each type of Web site. For each Web site, identify the Web address, the multimedia elements used, the purpose of the Web site, and the type of Web site. Explain why you classified each site as you did. Then, keeping in mind the purpose of each Web site, rank the sites in terms of their effectiveness. Write a brief report or use PowerPoint to create a presentation and share your findings with your class.

CASE STUDY 4 — Research   **The Internet** has had a tremendous impact on business. For some businesses, that influence has not been positive. For example, surveys suggest that as a growing number of people order products online, traditional brick-and-mortar businesses are seeing fewer customers. Use the Web and/or print media to learn more about businesses that that have been affected negatively by the Internet. What effect has the Internet had? How can the business compete with the Internet? How has the Internet changed business in positive ways? Write a brief report or use PowerPoint to create a presentation and share your findings with your class.

CASE STUDY 5 — Team Challenge   Recently, Captain Jack Stone, a senior pilot with a major airline, and three of his associates received financial approval to start a new discount airline called Stones Throw. Their plan includes leasing three Boeing 737-200s jetliners and one gate and ticket counter each at LaGuardia airport in New York and LAX airport in Los Angeles. Initially, Stones Throw will offer six daily round-trip flights between New York and Los Angeles. Besides selling tickets at the ticket counter in the airports and through travel agents, they want to develop a compelling Web site that will allow the discount airline to sell seats at declining prices as flight time approaches. Form a three-member team and assist Captain Stone in evaluating current major airline Web sites by listing the advantages and disadvantages of each. Assign each team member the task of evaluating three of the following airlines: American Airlines, AirTran, ATA, Continental, Delta, JetBlue, Southwest, United, and US Airways. Make sure every airline listed is assigned to at least one team member. Have each member print out the **home page** of the airlines they are assigned. In evaluating the Web sites, each team member should pay particular attention to the following areas: (1) design of Web site, (2) ease of use, (3) reservations, (4) online check-in, (5) flight status, (6) award miles, (7) specials, (8) online Help, (9) about the airline, and (10) contact the airline. Meet with your team to share each member's findings and then write a final report or create a PowerPoint presentation that summarizes the team's conclusions and ranks the sites in terms of their effectiveness.

Special Feature

Making Use of the Web

A wealth of information is available on the World Wide Web. The riches are yours if you know where to find this material. Locating useful Web sites may be profitable for your educational and professional careers, as the resources may help you research class assignments and make your life more fulfilling and manageable.

Because the World Wide Web does not have an organizational structure to assist you in locating reliable material, you need additional resources to guide you in searching. To help you find useful Web sites, this Special Feature describes specific information about a variety of Web pages, and it includes tables of Web addresses, so you can get started. The material is organized in several areas of interest.

AREAS OF INTEREST	
Fun and Entertainment	Learning
Travel	Science
Finance	Environment
Resources	Health
Auctions	Research
Government	Careers
Shopping	Arts and Literature
Weather, Sports, and News	

Web Exercises at the end of each category will reinforce the material and help you discover Web sites that may add a treasure trove of knowledge to your life.

Fun and Entertainment
THAT'S ENTERTAINMENT

Rock 'n' Roll on the Web

Consumers place great significance on buying entertainment products for fun and recreation. Nearly 10 percent of the United States's economy is spent on attending concerts and buying DVDs, CDs, reading materials, sporting goods, and toys.

Many Web sites supplement our cravings for fun and entertainment. For example, you can see and hear the musicians inducted into the Rock and Roll Hall of Fame and Museum (Figure 1). If you need an update on your favorite reality-based television program or a preview of an upcoming movie, E! Online and Entertainment Tonight provide the latest features on television and movie stars. The Internet Movie Database contains credits and reviews of more than 400,000 titles.

Watch the surfers riding the waves in Hawaii and romp with pandas at the San Diego Zoo. Web cams, which are video cameras that display their output on Web pages, take armchair travelers across the world for views of natural attractions, historical monuments, colleges, and cities. Many Web sites featuring Web cams are listed in the table in Figure 2.

FIGURE 1 Visitors exploring the Rock and Roll Hall of Fame and Museum Web site will find history, exhibitions, programs, and the names and particulars of the latest inductees.

FUN AND ENTERTAINMENT WEB SITES

Web Cams	URL
AfriCam Virtual Game Reserve	africam.com
Discovery Channel Cams	dsc.discovery.com/cams/cams.html
EarthCam — Webcam Network	earthcam.com
Iowa State Insect Zoo Live Camera	zoocam.ent.iastate.edu
Panda Cam San Diego Zoo	sandiegozoo.org/pandas/pandacam/index.html
The Automated Astrophysical Site-Testing Observatory (AASTO) (South Pole)	www.phys.unsw.edu.au/southpolediaries/webcam.html
Weather and Webcams from OnlineWeather.com and CamVista	onlineweather.com/v4/webcams/index.html
Wild Birds Unlimited Bird FeederCam	wbu.com/feedercam_home.htm
World Surf Cameras	surfrock.com.br/surfcam.htm
WorldLIVE	worldlive.cz/en/webcams

Entertainment	URL
AMG All Music Guide	allmusic.com
E! Online	eonline.com
Entertainment Tonight	etonline.com
Entertainment Weekly's EW.com	ew.com/ew
MSN Entertainment	entertainment.msn.com
Old Time Radio (OTR) — Radio Days: A Soundbite History	otr.com
Rock and Roll Hall of Fame and Museum	rockhall.com
The Internet Movie Database (IMDb)	imdb.com
World Radio Network (WRN)	wrn.org

For more information on fun and entertainment Web sites, visit scsite.com/dc2006/ch2/web.

FIGURE 2 When you visit Web sites offering fun and entertainment resources, you can be both amused and informed.

FUN AND ENTERTAINMENT WEB EXERCISES

1 Visit the WorldLIVE site listed in Figure 2. View two of the Web cams closest to your hometown, and describe the scenes. Then, visit the Discovery Channel Cams Web site and view two of the animal cams in the Featured Cams. What do you observe? Visit another Web site listed in Figure 2 and describe the view. What are the benefits of having Web cams at these locations throughout the world?

2 What are your favorite movies? Use The Internet Movie Database Web site listed in Figure 2 to search for information about two of these films, and write a brief description of the biographies of the major stars and director for each movie. Then, visit one of the entertainment Web sites and describe three of the featured stories. At the Rock and Roll Hall of Fame and Museum Web site, view the information on Elvis and one of your favorite musicians. Write a paragraph describing the information available about these rock stars.

Travel
GET PACKING!

Explore the World without Leaving Home

When you are ready to arrange your next travel adventure or just want to explore destination possibilities, the Internet provides ample resources to set your plans in motion.

To discover exactly where your destination is on this planet, cartography Web sites, including MapQuest (Figure 3), Maps.com, and Rand McNally, allow you to pinpoint your destination. These Web pages generally are divided into geographical areas, such as North America and Europe.

Some good starting places are general travel Web sites such as Expedia Travel, Cheap Tickets, and Travelocity, which is owned by the electronic booking service travel agents use. These all-encompassing Web sites, including those in Figure 4, have tools to help you find the lowest prices and details on flights, car rentals, cruises, and hotels.

FIGURE 3 MapQuest provides directions, traffic reports, maps, and more.

TRAVEL WEB SITES

General Travel	URL
Cheap Tickets	cheaptickets.com
Expedia.com	expedia.com
Orbitz	orbitz.com
Travelocity.com	travelocity.com
Yahoo! Travel	travel.yahoo.com
Cartography	**URL**
MapQuest	mapquest.com
Maps.com	maps.com
Rand McNally	randmcnally.com
Travel and City Guides	**URL**
All the Largest Cities of the World	greatestcities.com
Frommers.com	frommers.com
U.S.-Parks.com — US National Parks Adventure Travel Guide	us-parks.com

For more information on travel Web sites, visit scsite.com/dc2006/ch2/web.

FIGURE 4 These travel resources Web sites offer travel information to exciting destinations throughout the world.

TRAVEL WEB EXERCISES

1 Visit one of the cartography Web sites listed in Figure 4 and obtain the directions from your campus to one of these destinations: the White House in Washington, D.C.; Elvis's home in Memphis, Tennessee; Walt Disney World in Orlando, Florida; or the Grand Old Opry in Nashville, Tennessee. How many miles is it to your destination? What is the estimated driving time? Then, visit one of the general travel Web sites listed in the table and plan a flight from the nearest major airport to one of the four destinations for the week after finals and a return trip one week later. What is the lowest economy coach fare for this round-trip flight? What airline, flight numbers, and departure and arrival times did you select? Finally, explore car rental rates for a subcompact car for this one-week vacation. What rental agency and rate did you choose?

2 Visit one of the travel and city guides Web sites listed in Figure 4, and choose a destination for a getaway this coming weekend. Write a one-page paper giving details about this location, such as popular hotels and lodging, expected weather, population, local colleges and universities, parks and recreation, ancient and modern history, and tours. Include a map of this place. Why did you select this destination? How would you travel there and back? What is the breakdown of expected costs for this weekend, including travel expenditures, meals, lodging, and tickets to events and activities? What URLs did you use to complete this exercise?

Finance
MONEY MATTERS

Cashing In on Financial Advice

You can manage your money with advice from financial Web sites that offer online banking, tax help, personal finance, and small business and commercial services.

If you do not have a personal banker or a financial planner, consider a Web adviser to guide your investment decisions. The Motley Fool (Figure 5) provides commentary and education on investing strategies, financial news, and taxes.

If you are ready to ride the ups and downs of the NASDAQ and the Dow, an abundance of Web sites listed in Figure 6, including FreeEDGAR and Morningstar.com, can help you pick companies that fit your interests and financial needs.

Claiming to be the fastest, easiest tax publication on the planet, the Internal Revenue Service Web site contains procedures for filing tax appeals and contains IRS forms, publications, and legal regulations.

FIGURE 5 The Motley Fool Web site contains strategies and news stories related to personal financing and investing.

FINANCE WEB SITES

Advice and Education	URL
Bankrate.com	bankrate.com
LendingTree	lendingtree.com
Loan.com	loan.com
MSN Money	money.msn.com
The Motley Fool	fool.com
Wells Fargo	wellsfargo.com
Yahoo! Finance	finance.yahoo.com
Stock Market	**URL**
E*TRADE Financial	us.etrade.com
Financial Engines	financialengines.com
FreeEDGAR®	www.freeedgar.com
Harris*direct*	harrisdirect.com
Merrill Lynch Direct	mldirect.ml.com
Morningstar.com	www.morningstar.com
The Vanguard Group	vanguard.com
Taxes	**URL**
H&R Block	hrblock.com
Internal Revenue Service	www.irs.gov

For more information on finance Web sites, visit scsite.com/dc2006/ch2/web.

FIGURE 6 Financial resources Web sites offer general information, stock market analyses, and tax advice, as well as guidance and money-saving tips.

FINANCE WEB EXERCISES

1) Visit three advice and education Web sites listed in Figure 6 and read their top business world reports. Write a paragraph about each, summarizing these stories. Which stocks or mutual funds do these Web sites predict as being sound investments today? What are the current market indexes for the DJIA (Dow Jones Industrial Average), S&P 500, and NASDAQ, and how do these figures compare with the previous day's numbers?

2) Using two of the stock market Web sites listed in Figure 6, search for information about Microsoft, Adobe Systems, and one other software vendor. Write a paragraph about each of these stocks describing the revenues, net incomes, total assets for the previous year, current stock price per share, highest and lowest prices of each stock during the past year, and other relevant investment information.

Resources
LOOK IT UP

Web Resources Ease Computer Concerns

From dictionaries and encyclopedias to online technical support, the Web is filled with a plethora of resources to answer your computer questions.

Keep up with the latest developments by viewing online dictionaries and encyclopedias that add to their collections of computer and product terms on a regular basis. Shopping for a new computer can be a daunting experience, but many online guides, including PCWorld.com (Figure 7), can help you select the components that best fit your needs and budget.

If you are not confident in your ability to solve a problem alone, turn to online technical support. Web sites, such as those shown in Figure 8, often provide streaming how-to video lessons, tutorials, and real-time chats with experienced technicians. Hardware and software reviews, price comparisons, shareware, technical questions and answers, and breaking technology news are found on comprehensive portals.

FIGURE 7 Buying and upgrading a computer is simplified with helpful Web sites such as PCWorld.com.

RESOURCES WEB SITES

Dictionaries and Encyclopedias	URL
CDT's Guide to Online Privacy	cdt.org/privacy/guide/terms
ComputerUser High-Tech Dictionary	computeruser.com/resources/dictionary
TechWeb: The Business Technology Network	www.techweb.com/encyclopedia
Webopedia: Online Computer Dictionary for Computer and Internet Terms	webopedia.com
whatis?com	whatis.com

Computer Shopping Guides	URL
A Computer Guide: Reviews on Software and Hardware, Software, Review and More	acomputerguide.com
The CPU Scorecard	cpuscorecard.com
The Online Computer Buying Guide™	grohol.com/computers
Viewz Desktop Computer Buying Guide	viewz.com/shoppingguide/compbuy.shtml
ZDNet	shopper-zdnet.com.com
A Computer Guide: Reviews on Software and Hardware	acomputerguide.com/www/
Online Computer Buying Guide™	grohol.com/computers
Viewz Desktop Computer Buying Guide	viewz.com/shoppingguide/compbuy.shtml
The CPU Scorecard	cpuscorecard.com
ZDNet Shopper	shopper-zdnet.com.com

Upgrading Guides	URL
CNET Shopper.com	shopper.cnet.com
eHow™	ehow.com
Focus on Macs	macs.about.com
PCWorld.com	pcworld.com/howto
Upgrade Source	upgradesource.com

Online Technical Support	URL
Dux Computer Digest	duxcw.com
MSN Tech & Gadgets	computingcentral.msn.com
PC911	pcnineoneone.com
PC Pitstop	pcpitstop.com

Technical and Consumer Information	URL
CNET.com	cnet.com
CompInfo — The Computer Information Center	www.compinfo-center.com
NewsHub	newshub.com/tech
Wired News	wirednews.com
ZDNet	zdnet.com

For more information on resources Web sites, visit scsite.com/dc2006/ch2/web.

FIGURE 8 A variety of Web resources can provide information about buying, repairing, and upgrading computers.

RESOURCES WEB EXERCISES

1 Visit the dictionaries and encyclopedias Web sites listed in Figure 8. Search these resources for five terms. Create a table with two columns: one for the cyberterm and one for the Web definition. Then, create a second table listing five recently added or updated words and their definitions on these Web sites. Next, visit two of the listed computer shopping guides Web sites to choose the components you would buy if you were building a customized desktop computer and notebook computer. Create a table for both computers, listing the computer manufacturer, processor model name or number and manufacturer, clock speed, RAM, cache, number of expansion slots, and number of bays.

2 Visit three upgrading guides Web sites listed in Figure 8. Write a paragraph describing available advice for buying a motherboard. Describe the strengths and weaknesses of these Web sites, focusing on such criteria as clarity of instructions, thoroughness, and ease of navigation. Would you use these Web sites as a resource to troubleshoot computer problems? Then, view two technical and consumer information Web sites listed in the table and write a paragraph about each one, describing the top two news stories of the day.

Auctions
GOING ONCE, GOING TWICE

Rare, Common Items Flood Web Sites

Online auction Web sites can offer unusual items, including *Star Wars* props and memorabilia and a round of golf with Tiger Woods. eBay (Figure 9) is one of thousands of Internet auction Web sites and is the world's largest personal online trading community.

Traditional auction powerhouses, such as Christie's in London and Sotheby's on Manhattan's Upper East Side, are known for their big-ticket items, including a Tyrannosaurus rex fossil that sold for $8.4 million.

If those prices are a bit out of your league, you can turn to a wealth of other auction Web sites, including those listed in Figure 10, to find just the items you need, and maybe some you really do not need, for as little as $1. Categories include antiques and collectibles, automotive, computers, electronics, music, sports, sports cards and memorabilia, and toys.

AUCTION WEB SITES

	URL
Christie's	christies.com
eBay®	ebay.com
Dargate Auction Galleries	dargate.com
musichotbid	musichotbid.com
Penbid.com	penbid.com
Sotheby's	sothebys.com
uBid™	ubid.com
Yahoo! Shopping Auctions	auctions.yahoo.com
For more information on auction Web sites, visit scsite.com/dc2006/ch2/web.	

FIGURE 10 These auction Web sites feature a wide variety of items.

AUCTIONS WEB EXERCISES

1 Visit the Christie's and Sotheby's Web sites and read about the items that have been sold recently. Find two unusual objects and write a paragraph about each one, summarizing your discoveries. What were the opening and final bids on these objects? Then, review two of the upcoming auctions. When are the auctions' dates? What items are available? What are some of the opening bids? What are the advantages and disadvantages of bidding online?

2 Using one of the auction Web sites listed in Figure 10, search for two objects pertaining to your hobbies or interests. For example, if you are a baseball fan, you can search for a complete set of Topps cards. If you are a car buff, search for your dream car. Describe these two items. How many people have bid on these items? Who are the sellers? What are the opening and current bids?

FIGURE 9 eBay is one of the world's more popular auction Web sites.

Government
STAMP OF APPROVAL

Making a Federal Case for Useful Information

When it is time to buy stamps to mail your correspondence, you no longer need to wait in long lines at your local post office. The U.S. Postal Service has authorized several corporations to sell stamps online.

You can recognize U.S. Government Web sites on the Internet by their .gov top-level domain abbreviation. For example, The Library of Congress Web site is lcweb.loc.gov, as shown in Figure 11. Government and military Web sites offer a wide range of information, and some of the more popular sites are listed in Figure 12. The Time Service Department Web site will provide you with the correct time. If you are looking for a federal document, FedWorld lists thousands of documents distributed by the government on its Web site. For access to the names of your congressional representatives, visit the extensive Hieros Gamos Web site.

GOVERNMENT RESOURCES WEB SITES

Postage	URL
Endicia	endicia.com
Pitney Bowes	pb.com
Stamps.com	stamps.com

Government	URL
FedWorld	www.fedworld.gov
Hieros Gamos — Law and Legal Research Center	hg.org
NARA — United States National Archives and Records Administration	archives.gov
National Agricultural Library	www.nal.usda.gov
The Library of Congress	lcweb.loc.gov
THOMAS Legislative Information	thomas.loc.gov
Time Service Department	tycho.usno.navy.mil
United States Department of Education	ed.gov
United States Department of the Treasury	www.treas.gov
United States Government Printing Office	www.access.gpo.gov
United States National Library of Medicine	www.nlm.nih.gov
United States Patent and Trademark Office	www.uspto.gov
USAJOBS	www.usajobs.opm.gov
White House	whitehouse.gov

For more information on government Web sites, visit scsite.com/dc2006/ch2/web.

FIGURE 12 These Web sites offer information about buying U.S.-approved postage online and researching federal agencies.

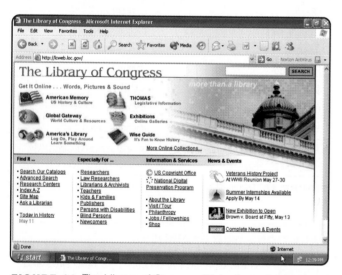

FIGURE 11 The Library of Congress Web site contains more than 119 million items written in 470 languages.

GOVERNMENT WEB EXERCISES

1 View the three postage Web sites listed in Figure 12. Compare and contrast the available services on each one. Consider postage cost, necessary equipment, shipping services, security techniques, and tracking capability. Explain why you would or would not like to use this service.

2 Visit the Hieros Gamos Web site listed in Figure 12. What are the names, addresses, and telephone numbers of your two state senators and your local congressional representative? On what committees do they serve? Who is the chief justice of the Supreme Court, and what has been this justice's opinion on two recently decided cases? Who are the members of the president's cabinet? Then, visit two other Web sites listed in Figure 12. Write a paragraph about each Web site describing its content and features.

Shopping
CYBERMALL MANIA

Let Your Mouse Do Your Shopping

From groceries to clothing to computers, you can buy just about everything you need with just a few clicks of your mouse. Electronic retailers (e-tailers) are cashing in on cybershoppers' purchases. Books, computer software and hardware, and music are the hottest commodities.

Holiday sales account for a large portion of Internet purchases with more than nine million households doing some of their holiday shopping online. During this season, millions of shoppers visit Web sites such as BestBuy.com (Figure 13) daily. Macy's, Bloomingdale's and other e-tailers ship more than 300,000 boxes daily out of warehouses the size of 20 football fields and stocked with five million items.

The two categories of Internet shopping Web sites are those with physical counterparts, such as Eddie Bauer, Wal-Mart, and Tower Records, and those with only a Web presence, such as Amazon.com. Popular Web shopping sites are listed in Figure 14.

SHOPPING WEB SITES

Apparel	URL
Eddie Bauer Since 1920	eddiebauer.com
J.Crew	jcrew.com
Lands' End	landsend.com
Books and Music	**URL**
Amazon.com	amazon.com
Barnes & Noble.com	bn.com
Tower Records	towerrecords.com
Computers and Electronics	**URL**
Crutchfield.com	crutchfield.com
BestBuy.com	bestbuy.com
buy.com	buy.com
Miscellaneous	**URL**
1-800-flowers.com	1800flowers.com
drugstore.com	drugstore.com
Froogle	froogle.com
The Sharper Image	sharperimage.com
Walmart.com	walmart.com
For more information on shopping Web sites, visit scsite.com/dc2006/ch2/web.	

FIGURE 13 Shopping for popular computer equipment online eliminates waiting in lines in stores.

FIGURE 14 Making online purchases can help ease the strain of driving to and fighting the crowds in local malls.

SHOPPING WEB EXERCISES

1 Visit two of the three apparel Web sites listed in the table in Figure 14 and select a specific pair of jeans and a shirt from each one. Create a table with these headings: e-tailer, style, fabric, features, price, tax, and shipping fee. Enter details about your selections in the table. Then, visit two of the books and music Web sites and search for a CD you would consider purchasing. Create another table with the names of the Web site, artist, and CD, as well as the price, tax, and shipping fee.

2 Visit two of the computers and electronics and two of the miscellaneous Web sites listed in Figure 14. Write a paragraph describing the features these Web sites offer compared with the same offerings from stores. In another paragraph, describe any disadvantages of shopping at these Web sites instead of actually seeing the merchandise. Then, describe their policies for returning unwanted merchandise and for handling complaints.

Weather, Sports, and News
WHAT'S NEWS?

Weather, Sports, and News Web Sites Score Big Hits

Rain or sun? Hot or cold? Weather is the leading online news item, with at least 10,000 Web sites devoted to this field. The Weather Channel (Figure 15) receives more than 10 million hits each day.

Baseball may be the national pastime, but sports aficionados yearn for everything from auto racing to cricket. The Internet has more than one million pages of multimedia sports news, entertainment, and merchandise.

The Internet has emerged as a major source for news, with one-third of Americans going online at least once a week and 15 percent going online daily for reports of major news events. These viewers, who tend to be under the age of 50 and college graduates, are attracted to the Internet's flashy headline format, immediacy, and in-depth reports. Popular weather, sports, and news Web sites are listed in Figure 16.

FIGURE 15 Local, national, and international weather conditions and details about breaking weather stories are available on The Weather Channel Web pages.

WEATHER, SPORTS, AND NEWS WEB SITES

Weather	URL
Infoplease Weather	infoplease.com/weather.html
Intellicast.com	intellicast.com
STORMFAX®	stormfax.com
The Weather Channel	weather.com
WX.com	wx.com

Sports	URL
CBS SportsLine.com	cbs.sportsline.com
ESPN.com	espn.com
NCAAsports.com	ncaasports.com
OFFICIAL WEBSITE OF THE OLYMPIC MOVEMENT	olympic.org
SIRC — A World of Sport Information	sirc.ca
Sporting News Radio	radio.sportingnews.com

News	URL
MSNBC	msnbc.com
NYPOST.COM	nypost.com
onlinenewspapers.com	onlinenewspapers.com
Privacy.org	privacy.org
SiliconValley.com	siliconvalley.com
Starting Page Best News Sites	startingpage.com/html/news.html
USATODAY.com	usatoday.com
washingtonpost.com	washingtonpost.com

For more information on weather, sports, and news Web sites, visit scsite.com/dc2006/ch2/web.

FIGURE 16 Keep informed about the latest weather, sports, and news events with these Web sites.

WEATHER, SPORTS, AND NEWS EXERCISES

1 Visit two of the weather Web sites listed in the table in Figure 16. Do they contain the same local and five-day forecasts for your city? What similarities and differences do they have in coverage of a national weather story? Next, visit two of the sports Web sites in the table and write a paragraph describing the content these Web sites provide concerning your favorite sport.

2 Visit the onlinenewspapers.com and Starting Page Best News Sites Web sites listed in Figure 16 and select two newspapers from each site. Write a paragraph describing the top national news story featured in each of these four Web pages. Then, write another paragraph describing the top international news story displayed at each Web site. In the third paragraph, discuss which of the four Web sites is the most interesting in terms of story selection, photographs, and Web page design.

Learning
YEARN TO LEARN

Discover New Worlds Online

While you may believe your education ends when you finally graduate from college, learning is a lifelong process. For example, enhancing your culinary skills can be a rewarding endeavor. No matter if you are a gourmet chef or a weekend cook, you will be cooking in style with the help of online resources, including those listed in Figure 17.

LEARNING WEB SITES

Cooking	URL
Betty Crocker	bettycrocker.com
recipecenter.com	recipecenter.com
Internet	**URL**
Learn the Net	learnthenet.com
Search Engine Watch	searchenginewatch.com
Wiredguide™	wiredguide.com
Technology and Science	**URL**
HowStuffWorks	howstuffworks.com
ScienceMaster	sciencemaster.com
General Learning	**URL**
Bartleby.com: Great Books Online	bartleby.com
Blue Web'n	www.kn.pacbell.com/wired/bluewebn
MSN Encarta	encarta.msn.com

For more information on learning Web sites, visit scsite.com/dc2006/ch2/web.

FIGURE 17 The information gleaned from these Web sites can help you learn about many aspects of our existence.

If you would rather sit in front of the computer than stand in front of the stove, you can increase your technological knowledge by visiting several Web sites with tutorials on building your own Web sites, the latest news about the Internet, and resources for visually impaired users.

Have you ever wondered how the Global Positioning System (GPS) works? Take a look at the ScienceMaster site to find details. You might be interested in finding out about how your car's catalytic converter reduces pollution or how the Electoral College functions. Marshall Brain's HowStuffWorks Web site (Figure 18) is filled with articles and animations.

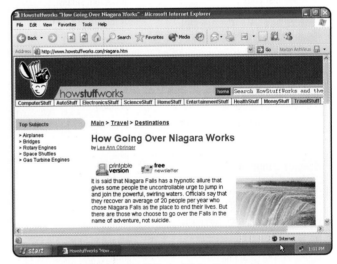

FIGURE 18 The HowStuffWorks Web site provides easy-to-understand information about technology and other facets of our lives.

LEARNING WEB EXERCISES

1 Visit one of the cooking Web sites listed in Figure 17 and find two recipes or cooking tips that you can use when preparing your next meal. Write a paragraph about each one, summarizing your discoveries. What are the advantages and disadvantages of accessing these Web sites on the new Web appliances that might someday be in your kitchen?

2 Using one of the technology and science Web sites and one of the other Web sites listed in Figure 17, search for information about communications and networks. Write a paragraph about your findings. Then, review the material in the general learning Web sites listed in Figure 18, and write a paragraph describing the content on each Web site that is pertinent to your major.

Science
E = MC²

Rocket Science on the Web

For some people, space exploration is a hobby. Building and launching model rockets allow these scientists to participate in exploring the great frontier of space. For others, space exploration is their life. Numerous Web sites, including those in Figure 19, provide in-depth information about the universe.

The NASA Liftoff Web site contains information about rockets, the space shuttle, the International Space Station, space transportation, and communications. Other science resources explore space-related questions about astronomy, physics, the earth sciences, microgravity, and robotics.

Rockets and space are not the only areas to explore in the world of science. Where can you find the latest pictures taken with the Hubble Space Telescope? Do you know which cities experienced an earthquake today? Have you ever wondered what a 3-D model of the amino acid glutamine looks like? You can find the answer to these questions and many others through the Librarians' Index to the Internet (lii.org) shown in Figure 20.

SCIENCE WEB SITES

Periodicals	URL
Astronomy.com	astronomy.com
Archaeology Magazine	archaeology.org
NewScientist.com	newscientist.com
OceanLink	oceanlink.island.net
Science Magazine	sciencemag.org
SCIENTIFIC AMERICAN.com	sciam.com
Resources	**URL**
National Science Foundation (NSF)	nsf.gov
Science.gov: FirstGov for Science	science.gov
SOFWeb	www.sofweb.vic.edu.au
Science Community	**URL**
American Scientist, The Magazine of Sigma Xi, The Scientific Research Society	amsci.org
Federation of American Scientists	fas.org
NASA	www.nasa.gov
Sigma Xi, The Scientific Research Society	sigmaxi.org
For more information on science Web sites, visit scsite.com/dc2006/ch2/web.	

FIGURE 19 Resources available on the Internet offer a wide range of subjects for enthusiasts who want to delve into familiar and unknown territories in the world of science.

FIGURE 20 Numerous science resources are organized clearly in the Librarians' Index to the Internet.

SCIENCE WEB EXERCISES

1 Visit the Liftoff to Space Exploration Web site listed in the table in Figure 19. View the links about spacecraft, the universe, or tracking satellites and spacecraft, and then write a summary of your findings.

2 Visit the Librarians' Index to the Internet shown in Figure 20. Click the Science, Computers, & Technology link and then click the Inventions topic. View the Web site for the Greatest Engineering Achievements of the Twentieth Century. Pick two achievements, read their history, and write a paragraph summarizing each of these accomplishments. Then, view two of the science Web sites listed in Figure 19 and write a paragraph about each of these Web sites describing the information each contains.

Arts and Literature
FIND SOME CULTURE

Get Ready to Read, Paint, and Dance

Brush up your knowledge of Shakespeare, grab a canvas, and put on your dancing shoes. Visual arts and literature Web sites, including those in Figure 29, are about to sweep you off your cyberfeet.

ARTS AND LITERATURE WEB SITES

Arts	URL
Access Place Arts	accessplace.com/arts.htm
Art News — absolutearts.com	absolutearts.com
GalleryGuide.org	galleryguide.org
Louvre Museum	www.louvre.fr
Montreal Museum of Fine Arts	www.mmfa.qc.ca
The Children's Museum of Indianapolis	childrensmuseum.org
The Getty	getty.edu
The New York Times: Arts	nytimes.com/pages/arts/index.html
Virtual Library museums pages (VLmp)	vlmp.museophile.com
Literature	**URL**
Bartleby.com	bartleby.com
Bibliomania	bibliomania.com
Electronic Literature Directory	directory.wordcircuits.com
Fantastic Fiction Bibliographies	fantasticfiction.co.uk
Project Gutenberg	promo.net/pg
shakespeare.com	shakespeare.com
The Modern Library eBook List	randomhouse.com/modernlibrary/ebookslist.html

For more information on arts and literature Web sites, visit scsite.com/dc2006/ch2/web.

FIGURE 29 Discover culture throughout the world by visiting these arts and literature Web sites.

The full text of hundreds of books is available online from the Bibliomania and Project Gutenberg Web sites. Shakespeare.com provides in-depth reviews and news of the world's most famous playwright and his works. The Bartleby.com Web site features biographies, definitions, quotations, dictionaries, and indexes.

When you are ready to absorb more culture, you can turn to various art Web sites. Many museums have images of their collections online. Among them are the Getty Museum in Los Angeles (Figure 30), the Montreal Museum of Fine Arts, and the Louvre Museum in Paris.

Access Place Arts and The New York Times Web sites focus on the arts and humanities and provide fascinating glimpses into the worlds of dance, music, performance, cinema, and other topics pertaining to creative expression.

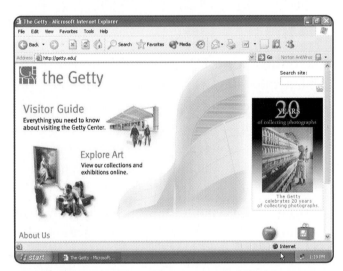

FIGURE 30 Permanent and temporary exhibitions, educational activities, and a bookstore are featured on the Getty Museum Web site.

ARTS AND LITERATURE WEB EXERCISES

1 Visit The Modern Library eBook List Web site listed in Figure 29 and view one book in the 20th CENTURY NOVELS, 19th CENTURY NOVELS, BRITISH LITERATURE, and HISTORY sections. Create a table with columns for the book name, author, cost, online store, local store, and description. Then, read the excerpt from each of the four books and write a paragraph describing which of these four books is the most interesting to you. What are the advantages and disadvantages of reading classic literature electronically?

2 Using the arts Web sites listed in Figure 29, search for three temporary exhibitions in galleries throughout the world. Describe the venues, the artists, and the works. What permanent collections are found in these museums? Some people shop for gifts in the museums' stores. View and describe three items for sale.

CHAPTER THREE

Application Software

Picture Yourself Using Software

As your biology instructor reviews for the upcoming test, you use note taking software and a digital pen to highlight important points in your electronic notes. Then, you circle the animal cell structure diagram and write "Memorize this for test." At the end of class, you start the appointment calendar software in your PDA and record the date of the test.

Later that day, when you open your e-mail program to check messages, you see a message from a friend asking what he missed in biology class. You type a reply to his message, attach a copy of your electronic lecture notes to the message, and then click the Send button.

Time to start composing your philosophy paper about Socrates. You use the research feature of your word processing program to learn about this ancient Greek philosopher and then write the paper — being sure to cite all sources. While writing the paper, your personal finance software alerts you that it is time to download transaction information from the bank's computer to your computer. With this service, your computerized checkbook balance always is up-to-date. Ready for a break, you fire up the flight simulator program and experience the thrill of piloting an airplane.

Read Chapter 3 to learn more about note taking software, PDA application software, e-mail programs, word processing software, personal finance software, and entertainment software, and discover many other types of application software.

Environment
THE FATE OF THE ENVIRONMENT

Protecting the Planet's Ecosystem

From the rain forests of Africa to the marine life in the Pacific Ocean, the fragile ecosystem is under extreme stress. Many environmental groups have developed Internet sites, including those listed in Figure 21, in attempts to educate worldwide populations and to increase resource conservation.

ENVIRONMENT WEB SITES

	URL
Central African Regional Program for the Environment (CARPE)	carpe.umd.edu
Earthjustice	www.earthjustice.org
EarthTrends: The Environmental Information Portal	earthtrends.wri.org
Environmental Defense	edf.org
Environmental Sites on the Internet	www.ima.kth.se/im/envsite/envsite.htm
EPA AirData — Access to Air Pollution Data	epa.gov/air/data
Green Solitaire.org	greensolitaire.bizland.com
GreenNet	www.gn.apc.org
The Center for a New American Dream	newdream.org
The Virtual Library of Ecology & Biodiversity	conbio.org/vl
USGS Acid rain data and reports	bqs.usgs.gov/acidrain
UWM Environmental Health, Safety & Risk Management	www.uwm.edu/Dept/EHSRM/EHSLINKS
For more information on environment Web sites, visit scsite.com/dc2006/ch2/web.	

FIGURE 21 Environment Web sites provide vast resources for ecological data and action groups.

On an international scale, the Environmental Sites on the Internet Web page developed by the Royal Institute of Technology in Stockholm, Sweden, has been rated as one of the better ecological Web sites. Its comprehensive listing of environmental concerns range from aquatic ecology to wetlands.

The U.S. federal government has a number of Web sites devoted to specific environmental concerns. For example, the U.S. Environmental Protection Agency (EPA) provides pollution data, including ozone levels and air pollutants, for specific areas. Its AirData Web site, shown in Figure 22, displays air pollution emissions and monitoring data from the entire United States and is the world's most extensive collection of air pollution data.

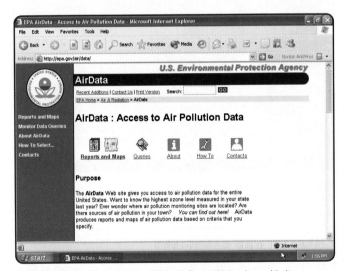

FIGURE 22 A visit to the EPA AirData Web site, with its extensive database, can assist you in checking your community's ozone and air pollutant levels.

ENVIRONMENT WEB EXERCISES

1 The Center for a New American Dream Web site encourages consumers to reduce the amount of junk mail sent to their homes. Using the table in Figure 21, visit the Web site and write a paragraph stating how many trees are leveled each year to provide paper for these mailings, how many garbage trucks are needed to haul this waste, and other statistics. Read the letters that you can use to eliminate your name from bulk mail lists. To whom would you mail these letters? How long does it take to stop these unsolicited letters?

2 Visit the EPA AirData Web site. What is the highest ozone level recorded in your state this past year? Where are the nearest air pollution monitoring Web sites, and what are their levels? Where are the nearest sources of air pollution? Read two reports about two different topics, such as acid rain and air quality, and summarize their findings. Include information on who sponsored the research, who conducted the studies, when the data was collected, and the impact of this pollution on the atmosphere, water, forests, and human health. Whom would you contact for further information regarding the data and studies?

Health
NO PAIN, ALL GAIN

Store Personal Health Records Online

More than 70 million consumers use the Internet yearly to search for health information, so using the Web to store personal medical data is a natural extension of the Internet's capabilities. Internet health services and portals are available online to store your personal health history, including prescriptions, lab test results, doctor visits, allergies, and immunizations. Web sites such as WellMed (Figure 23) are free to consumers.

In minutes, you can register with a health Web site by choosing a user name and password. Then, you create a record to enter your medical history. You also can store data for your emergency contacts, primary care physicians, specialists, blood type, cholesterol levels, blood pressure, and insurance plan. No matter where you are in the world, you and medical personnel can obtain records via the Internet or fax machine. Some popular online health database management systems are shown in Figure 24.

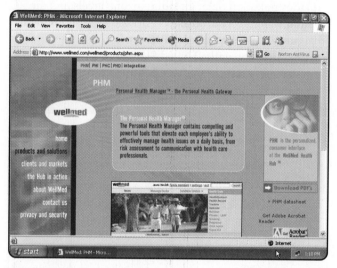

FIGURE 23 You can store health records for you and your family in the WellMed database.

HEALTH WEB SITES

	URL
AboutMyHealth	aboutmyhealth.com
Aetna InteliHealth	intelihealth.com
GlobalMedic	globalmedic.com
PersonalMD	personalmd.com
WebMD®	my.webmd.com/ my_health_record
WellMed	wellmed.com
For more information on health Web sites, visit scsite.com/dc2006/ ch2/web.	

FIGURE 24 These Internet-based health database management systems Web sites allow you to organize your medical information and store it in an online database.

HEALTH WEB EXERCISES

1. Access one of the health Web sites listed in Figure 24. Register yourself or a family member, and then enter the full health history. Create an emergency medical card if the Web site provides the card option. Submit this record and emergency card to your instructor.

2. Visit three of the health Web sites listed in Figure 24. Describe the features of each. Which of the three is the most user-friendly? Why? Describe the privacy policies of these three Web sites. Submit your analysis of these Web sites to your instructor.

Research
SEARCH AND YE SHALL FIND

Info on the Web

A 2004 Web Usability survey conducted by the Nielsen Norman Group found that 88 percent of people log onto a computer and then use a search engine as their first action. Search engines require users to type words and phrases that characterize the information being sought. Yahoo! (Figure 25), Google, and AltaVista are some of the more popular search engines. The key to effective searching on the Web is composing search queries that narrow the search results and place the most relevant Web sites at the top of the results list.

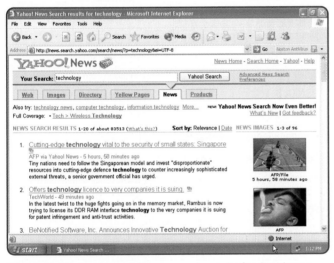

FIGURE 25 The Yahoo! News search results for the phrase, technology, lists more than 83,000 stories.

Subject directories are collections of related Web sites. Yahoo! and LookSmart have two of the more comprehensive subject directories on the Web. Their organized lists often are called trees because a few main categories, such as Entertainment, Computing, Lifestyle, and Work, branch out to more specific subtopics. Popular subject directories and search engines are listed in Figure 26.

RESEARCH WEB SITES

Search Engines	URL
AltaVista	altavista.com
Excite	excite.com
Fast Search & Transfer (FAST)	fastsearch.com
GO.com	go.com
Google	google.com
Northern Light®	northernlight.com
Yahoo!	yahoo.com

Subject Directories	URL
About	about.com
Librarians' Index to the Internet	lii.org
LookSmart	looksmart.com
The Internet Public Library	ipl.org
The WWW Virtual Library	vlib.org
Yahoo!	yahoo.com

For more information on research Web sites, visit scsite.com/dc2006/ch2/web.

FIGURE 26 Web users can find information by using search engines and subject directories.

RESEARCH WEB EXERCISES

1 Use two of the search engines listed in Figure 26 to find three Web sites that review the latest digital cameras from Sony and Kodak. Make a table listing the search engines, Web site names, and the cameras' model numbers, suggested retail price, megapixels, memory, and features.

2 If money were no object, virtually everyone would have an exquisite car. On the other hand, drivers need a practical vehicle to drive around town daily. Use one of the subject directories listed in Figure 26 to research your dream car and another directory to research your practical car. Write a paragraph about each car describing the particular subject directory tree you used, the manufacturer's suggested retail price (MSRP) of the car, standard and optional equipment, engine size, miles per gallon, and safety features.

Careers
IN SEARCH OF THE PERFECT JOB

Web Helps Career Hunt

While your teachers give you valuable training to prepare you for a career, they rarely teach you how to begin that career. You can broaden your horizons by searching the Internet for career information and job openings.

First, examine some of the job search Web sites. These resources list thousands of openings in hundreds of fields, companies, and locations. For example, the Monster Web site, shown in Figure 27, allows you to choose a broad job area, narrow your search to specific fields within that area, and then search for specific salary ranges, locations, and job functions.

When a company contacts you for an interview, learn as much about it and the industry as possible before the interview. Many of the Web sites listed in Figure 28 include detailed company profiles and links to their corporate Web sites.

CAREER WEB SITES

Job Search	URL
BestJobsUSA.com	ultimatecareerfair.com
CareerBuilder	careerbuilder.com
CareerExchange.com	careerexchange.com
CareerNet	careernet.com
College Grad Job Hunter	collegegrad.com
EmploymentGuide.com	employmentguide.com
HotJobs.com	hotjobs.com
JobBankUSA.com	jobbankusa.com
JobWeb.com	www.jobweb.com
Monster	monster.com
MonsterTRAK	www.jobtrak.com
Spherion	spherion.com
USAJOBS	usajobs.opm.gov
VolunteerMatch	volunteermatch.org

Company/Industry Information	URL
Career ResourceCenter.com	www.resourcecenter.com
Forbes.com	www.forbes.com/2003/03/26/500sland.html
FORTUNE	fortune.com
Hoover's Online	hoovers.com
Occupational Outlook Handbook	stats.bls.gov/oco

For more information on career Web sites, visit scsite.com/dc2006/ch2/web.

FIGURE 28 Career Web sites provide a variety of job openings and information about major companies worldwide.

FIGURE 27 Monster's global online network connects companies with career-minded individuals.

CAREERS WEB EXERCISES

1 Use two of the job search Web sites listed in Figure 28 to find three companies with job openings in your field. Make a table listing the Web site name, position available, description, salary, location, desired education, and desired experience.

2 It is a good idea to acquire information before graduation about the industry in which you would like to work. Are you interested in the automotive manufacturing industry, the restaurant service industry, or the financial industry? Use two of the company/industry information Web sites listed in Figure 28 to research a particular career related to your major. Write a paragraph naming the Web sites and the specific information you found, such as the nature of the work, recommended training and qualifications, employment outlook, and earnings. Then, use two other Web sites to profile three companies with positions available in this field. Write a paragraph about each of these companies, describing the headquarters' location, sales and earnings for the previous year, total number of employees, working conditions, perks, and competitors.

- **Custom software** performs functions specific to a business or industry. Sometimes a company cannot find packaged software that meets its unique requirements. In this case, the company may use programmers to develop tailor-made custom software, which usually costs more than packaged software.
- **Open source software** is software provided for use, modification, and redistribution. This software has no restrictions from the copyright holder regarding modification of the software's internal instructions and redistribution of the software. If redistributed, changes made to the software's internal instructions must be noted and the original copyright notice must remain intact. Open source software usually can be downloaded from the Web at no cost.
- **Shareware** is copyrighted software that is distributed at no cost for a trial period. To use a shareware program beyond that period, you send payment to the program developer. Shareware developers trust users to send payment if software use extends beyond the stated trial period. In some cases, a scaled-down version of the software is distributed free, and payment entitles the user to the fully functional product.
- **Freeware** is copyrighted software provided at no cost by an individual or a company that retains all rights to the software. Thus, programmers typically cannot incorporate freeware in applications they intend to sell. The word, free, in freeware indicates the software has no charge.
- **Public-domain software** has been donated for public use and has no copyright restrictions. Anyone can copy or distribute public-domain software to others at no cost.

Thousands of shareware, freeware, and public-domain programs are available on the Web for users to download. Examples include communications programs, graphics programs, and games. These programs usually have fewer capabilities than retail programs.

After you purchase or download software, you install it. During installation, the program may ask you to register and/or activate the software. Registering the software is optional and usually involves submitting your name and other personal information to the software manufacturer or developer. Registering the

software often entitles you to product support. *Product activation* is a technique that some software manufacturers use to ensure the software is not installed on more computers than legally licensed. Usually, the software does not function or has limited functionality until you activate it via the Internet or telephone. Thus, activation is a required process for programs requesting it.

The Role of System Software

System software serves as the interface between the user, the application software, and the computer's hardware (Figure 3-2). To use application software, such as a word processing program, your computer must be running system software — specifically, an operating system. Three popular personal computer operating systems are Windows XP, Linux, and Mac OS X.

Each time you start a computer, the operating system is *loaded* (copied) from the computer's hard disk into memory. Once the operating system is loaded, it coordinates all the activities of the computer. This includes starting application software and transferring data among input and output devices and memory. While the computer is running, the operating system remains in memory.

Application Software

System Software

FIGURE 3-2 A user does not communicate directly with the computer hardware. Instead, system software is the interface between the user, the application software, and the hardware. For example, when a user instructs the application software to print, the application software sends the print instruction to the system software, which in turn sends the print instruction to the hardware.

Working with Application Software

To use application software, you must instruct the operating system to start the program. The steps in Figure 3-3 illustrate how to start and interact with the Paint program. The following paragraphs explain the steps in Figure 3-3.

Personal computer operating systems often use the concept of a desktop to make the computer easier to use. The **desktop** is an on-screen work area that has a graphical user interface (Read Looking Ahead 3-1 for a look at the next generation of user interfaces). Step 1 of Figure 3-3 shows icons, a button, and a pointer on the Windows XP desktop. An **icon** is a small image

displayed on the screen that represents a program, a document, or some other object. A **button** is a graphical element that you activate to cause a specific action to take place. One way to activate a button is to click it. To **click** a button on the screen requires moving the pointer to the button and then pressing and releasing a button on the mouse (usually the left mouse button). The **pointer** is a small symbol displayed on the screen that moves as you move the mouse. Common pointer shapes are an I-beam (I); a block arrow ( ); and a pointing hand ( ).

The Windows XP desktop contains a Start button on the lower-left corner of the taskbar.

FIGURE 3-3 HOW TO START AN APPLICATION

Step 1:
When you turn on a PC-compatible computer, Windows XP loads into memory and displays the desktop on the screen.

icon

desktop

button

pointer

taskbar

Start menu

Accessories command

Accessories submenu

All Programs command

Paint program

Start button

All Programs submenu

Step 2:
Click the Start button on the Windows taskbar, point to All Programs on the Start menu, point to Accessories on the All Programs submenu, and then point to Paint on the Accessories submenu.

Step 5:
Instruct the Paint program to print the picture. When the Print dialog box is displayed, click the Print button.

Print dialog box

option button

check box

command button

text box

document file name

file contains picture stored on disk

Paint window

title bar

Step 3:
Click Paint. The Paint window is displayed on the desktop.

Step 4:
Instruct the Paint program to open a file that is stored on the hard disk.

When you click the Start button, the Start menu is displayed on the desktop. A **menu** contains a list of commands from which you make selections. A **command** is an instruction that causes a program to perform a specific action.

The arrowhead symbol at the right edge of some menu commands indicates a submenu of additional commands is available. A *submenu* is a menu that is displayed when you point to a command on a previous menu. As illustrated in Step 2 of Figure 3-3, when you click the Start button and point to the All Programs command on the Start menu, the All Programs submenu is displayed. Pointing to the Accessories command on the All Programs submenu displays the Accessories submenu.

To start a program, you can click its program name on a menu or submenu. This action instructs the operating system to start the application, which means the program's instructions load from a storage medium (such as a hard disk) into memory. For example, when you click Paint on the Accessories submenu, Windows loads the Paint program instructions from the computer's hard disk into memory.

Once loaded into memory, the program is displayed in a window on the desktop (Step 3 of Figure 3-3). A **window** is a rectangular area of the screen that displays data and information. The top of a window has a **title bar**, which is a horizontal space that contains the window's name.

With the program loaded, you can create a new file or open an existing one. A *file* is a named collection of stored data, instructions, or information. A file can contain text, images, audio, and video. To distinguish among various files, each file has a file name. A *file name* is a unique combination of letters of the alphabet, numbers, and

other characters that identifies a file. The title bar of the document window usually displays a document's file name. Step 4 of Figure 3-3 shows the contents of the file, Castle, displaying in the Paint window. The file contains an image photographed with a digital camera.

In some cases, when you instruct a program to perform an activity such as printing, the program displays a dialog box. A *dialog box* is a special window that provides information, presents available options, or requests a response. Dialog boxes, such as the one shown in Step 5 of Figure 3-3, often contain option buttons, text boxes, check boxes, and command buttons. Clicking the Print button in the dialog box instructs the computer to print the picture.

Test your knowledge of pages 134 through 137 in Quiz Yourself 3-1.

FAQ 3-1

Will a document print like it looks on a screen?

Yes, because most application software is *WYSIWYG* (*what you see is what you get*). The software embeds invisible codes around the text and graphics, which instructs the computer how to present the information. For more information, visit scsite.com/dc2006/ch3/faq and then click WYSIWYG.

QUIZ YOURSELF 3-1

Instructions: Find the true statement below. Then, rewrite the remaining false statements so they are true.

1. Application software is used to make business activities more efficient; assist with graphics and multimedia projects; support home, personal, and educational tasks; and facilitate communications.

2. Public-domain software is mass-produced, copyrighted retail software that meets the needs of a wide variety of users, not just a single user or company.

3. To use system software, your computer must be running application software.

4. When an application is started, the program's instructions load from memory into a storage medium.

Quiz Yourself Online: To further check your knowledge of application software categories, ways software is distributed, and working with application software, visit scsite.com/dc2006/ch3/quiz and then click Objectives 1 – 3.

LOOKING AHEAD 3-1

User Interfaces of the Future

Most computers today use a graphical user interface. Next-generation user interfaces will be more natural and human-centric, meaning they will enable people to interact with a computer using human-like communication methods. Three developments in this area are gesture recognition, 3-D interfaces, and BrainGate.

With gesture recognition, the computer will detect human motions. Computers with this type of user interface will have the capability of recognizing sign language, reading lips, tracking facial movements, and following eye gazes.

Imagine rotating a window or object to read its flipside, switching from a desktop view to a panoramic view, or tacking sticky notes right on a Web screen. All these scenarios will be possible with the upcoming 3-D user interfaces.

The BrainGate neural interface may help quadriplegic people gain independence with everyday activities, such as maneuvering wheelchairs and typing. The system includes a tiny chip with 100 sensors implanted on the brain and external computers that convert brainwaves into output signals the person can control. For more information, visit scsite.com/dc2006/ch3/looking and then click User Interfaces.

BUSINESS SOFTWARE

Business software is application software that assists people in becoming more effective and efficient while performing their daily business activities. Business software includes programs such as word processing, spreadsheet, database, presentation graphics, note taking, personal information manager software, PDA business software, software suites, project management, accounting, and enterprise computing software. Figure 3-4 lists popular programs for each of these categories.

The following sections discuss the features and functions of business software. Word processing and spreadsheet software have a heavier emphasis because of their predominant use.

Word Processing Software

Word processing software is one of the more widely used types of application software. **Word processing software**, sometimes called a *word processor*, allows users to create and manipulate documents containing mostly text and sometimes graphics (Figure 3-5). Millions of people use word processing software every day to develop documents such as letters, memos, reports, fax cover sheets, mailing labels, newsletters, and Web pages.

Word processing software has many features to make documents look professional and visually appealing. Some of these features include the capability of changing the shape and size of characters, changing the color of characters, and organizing text in newspaper-style columns. When using colors for characters, however, they will print as black or gray unless you have a color printer.

Most word processing software allows users to incorporate many types of graphical images in documents. One popular type of graphical image is clip art. **Clip art** is a collection of

POPULAR BUSINESS PROGRAMS

Application Software	Manufacturer	Program Name
Word Processing	Microsoft	Word
	Sun	StarOffice Writer
	Corel	WordPerfect
Spreadsheet	Microsoft	Excel
	Sun	StarOffice Calc
	Corel	Quattro Pro
Database	Microsoft	Access
	Sun	StarOffice Base
	Corel	Paradox
	Microsoft	Visual FoxPro
	Oracle	Oracle
	MySQL AB	MySQL
Presentation Graphics	Microsoft	PowerPoint
	Sun	StarOffice Impress
	Corel	Presentations
Note Taking	Microsoft	OneNote
	Agilix	GoBinder
	Corel	Grafigo
Personal Information Manager (PIM)	Microsoft	Outlook
	IBM	Lotus Organizer
	Palm	Desktop
PDA Business Software	CNetX	Pocket SlideShow
	Microsoft	Pocket Word
	Microsoft	Pocket Excel
	Microsoft	Pocket Outlook
	PalmOne	VersaMail
	Ultrasoft	Money Pocket Edition

Application Software	Manufacturer	Program Name
Software Suite (for the Professional)	Microsoft	Office
		Office for Mac
	Sun	StarOffice Office Suite
	Corel	WordPerfect Office
	IBM	Lotus SmartSuite
Project Management	Microsoft	Project
	Primavera	SureTrak Project Manager
Accounting	Intuit	QuickBooks
	Peachtree	Complete Accounting
Enterprise Computing Software	PeopleSoft	Enterprise Human Resources
	Best Software	MAS 500 Engineering
	MSC Software	MSC.SimManager Manufacturing
	Oracle	Oracle Manufacturing
	SmartPath	SmartPath MMS Sales
	SAP	mySAP Customer Relationship Management Distribution
	NetSuite	NetERP
	Apropos Technology	Apropos Enterprise Edition

FIGURE 3-4   Popular business software.

drawings, diagrams, maps, and photographs that you can insert in documents. In Figure 3-5, a user inserted a clip art image of a race car in the document. Word processing software usually includes public-domain clip art. You can find additional public-domain and proprietary images on the Web or purchase them on CD or DVD.

All word processing software provides at least some basic capabilities to help users create and modify documents. Defining the size of the paper on which to print and specifying the *margins* — that is, the portion of the page outside the main body of text, including the top, the bottom, and both sides of the paper — are examples of some of these capabilities. If you type text that extends beyond the right page margin, the word processing software automatically positions text at the beginning of the next line. This feature, called *wordwrap*, allows users to type words in a paragraph continually without pressing the ENTER key at the end of each line. When you modify paper size or margins, the word processing software automatically rewraps text so it fits in the adjusted paper size and margins.

As you type more lines of text than can be displayed on the screen, the top portion of the document moves upward, or scrolls, off the screen. *Scrolling* is the process of moving different portions of the document on the screen into view.

A major advantage of using word processing software is that users easily can change what

they have written. For example, a user can insert, delete, or rearrange words, sentences, paragraphs, or entire sections. The find, or *search*, feature allows you to locate all occurrences of a certain character, word, or phrase. This feature, in combination with the *replace* feature, allows you to substitute existing characters or words with new ones.

Word processing software includes a *spelling checker*, which reviews the spelling of individual words, sections of a document, or the entire document. The spelling checker compares the words in the document with an electronic dictionary that is part of the word processing software. You can customize the

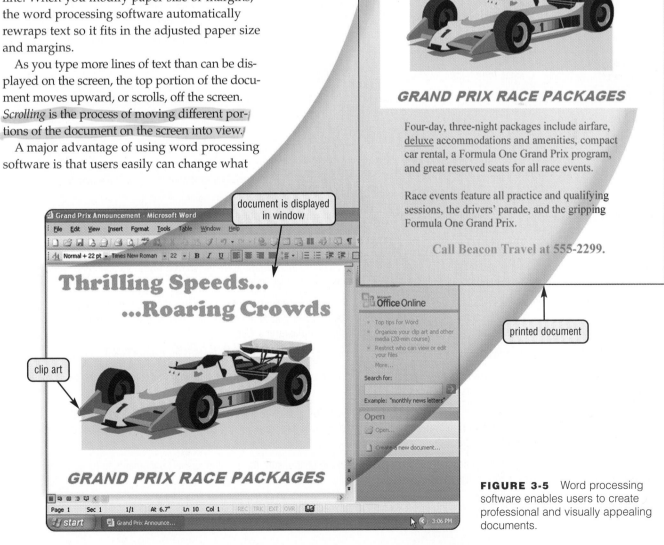

FIGURE 3-5 Word processing software enables users to create professional and visually appealing documents.

electronic dictionary by adding words such as companies, streets, cities, and personal names, so the software can check the spelling of those words too.

Another benefit of word processing software is the capability to insert headers and footers in a document. A *header* is text that appears at the top of each page, and a *footer* is text that appears at the bottom of each page. Page numbers, company names, report titles, and dates are examples of items often included in headers and footers.

In addition to these basic capabilities, most current word processing programs provide numerous additional features, which are listed in the table in Figure 3-6.

ADDITIONAL WORD PROCESSING FEATURES

AutoCorrect	As you type words, the AutoCorrect feature corrects common spelling errors. AutoCorrect also corrects capitalization mistakes.
AutoFormat	As you type, the AutoFormat feature automatically applies formatting to the text. For example, it automatically numbers a list or converts a Web address to a hyperlink.
Collaboration	Collaboration includes discussions and online meetings. Discussions allow multiple users to enter comments in a document and read and reply to each other's comments. Through an online meeting, users share documents with others in real time and view changes as they are being made.
Columns	Most word processing software can arrange text in two or more columns to look like a newspaper or magazine. The text from the bottom of one column automatically flows to the top of the next column.
Grammar Checker	The grammar checker proofreads documents for grammar, writing style, sentence structure errors, and reading statistics.
Ink Input	Supports input from a digital pen. Word processing software that supports ink input incorporates user's handwritten text and drawings in a word processing document. Ink input is popular on Tablet PCs.
Macros	A *macro* is a sequence of keystrokes and instructions that a user records and saves. When you want to execute the same series of instructions, execute the macro instead.
Mail Merge	Creates form letters, mailing labels, and envelopes.
Reading Layout	For those users who prefer reading on the screen, reading layout increases the readability and legibility of an on-screen document by hiding unnecessary toolbars, increasing the size of displayed characters, and providing navigation tools.
Research	Some word processing software allows you to search through various forms of online and Internet reference information — based on selected text in a document. Research services available include a thesaurus, English and bilingual dictionaries, encyclopedias, and Web sites that provide information such as stock quotes, news articles, and company profiles.
Smart Tags	*Smart tags* automatically appear on the screen when you perform a certain action. For example, typing an address causes a smart tag to appear. Clicking this smart tag provides options to display a map of the address or driving directions to or from the address.
Tables	Tables organize information into rows and columns. In addition to evenly spaced rows and columns, some word processing programs allow you to draw tables of any size or shape.
Templates	A *template* is a document that contains the formatting necessary for a specific document type. Templates usually exist for memos, fax cover sheets, and letters. In addition to templates provided with the software, users have access to many online templates through the manufacturer's Web site.
Thesaurus	With a thesaurus, a user looks up a synonym (word with the same meaning) for a word in a document.
Tracking Changes	If multiple users work with a document, the word processing software highlights or color-codes changes made by various users.
Voice Recognition	With some word processing programs, users can speak into the computer's microphone and watch the spoken words appear on the screen as they talk. With these programs, users edit and format the document by speaking or spelling an instruction.
Web Page Development	Most word processing software allows users to create, edit, format, and convert documents to be displayed on the World Wide Web.

FIGURE 3-6   Many additional features are included with word processing software.

Developing a Document

With application software, such as word processing, users create, edit, format, save, and print documents. During the process of developing a document, users likely will switch back and forth among all of these activities.

When you **create** a document, you enter text or numbers, insert graphical images, and perform other tasks using an input device such as a keyboard, mouse, microphone, or digital pen. If you are using Microsoft Office Word to design an announcement, for example, you are creating a document.

To **edit** a document means to make changes to its existing content. Common editing tasks include inserting, deleting, cutting, copying, and pasting. Inserting text involves adding text to a document. Deleting text means that you are removing text or other content. Cutting is the process of removing a portion of the document and storing it in a temporary storage location, sometimes called a *clipboard*. A clipboard also contains items that you copy (duplicate) in a document. *Pasting* is the process of transferring an item from a clipboard to a specific location in a document. Read At Issue 3-1 for a related discussion.

When users **format** a document, they change its appearance. Formatting is important because the overall look of a document significantly can affect its ability to communicate clearly. Examples of formatting tasks are changing the font, font size, or font style of text.

A **font** is a name assigned to a specific design of characters. Two basic types of fonts are serif and sans serif. A *serif font* has short decorative lines at the upper and lower ends of the characters. Sans means without. Thus, a *sans serif font* does not have the short decorative lines at the upper and lower ends of the characters. Times New Roman is an example of a serif font. Arial is an example of a sans serif font.

Font size indicates the size of the characters in a particular font. Font size is gauged by a measurement system called points. A single *point* is about 1/72 of an inch in height. The text you are reading in this book is about 10 point. Thus, each character is about 5/36 (10/72) of a inch in height. A *font style* adds emphasis to a font. Bold, italic, and underline are examples of font styles. Figure 3-7 illustrates fonts, font sizes, and font styles.

AT ISSUE 3-1

How Should Schools Deal with Internet Plagiarism?

A high school teacher failed 28 students for plagiarizing, or copying, material from the Internet. When parents complained, the school board passed the students, and the teacher resigned. Plagiarism is not new, but word processing software and the Internet make it easier than ever. With the click of a couple buttons, students can copy parts of Web pages and paste the text into their term papers. Students also can use term paper Web sites to copy complete papers on a variety of topics. According to one study, more than 35 percent of college students had copied material from Internet sources. Students who plagiarize blame peer pressure, classroom competition, the "busy work" nature of some assignments, and the permissive attitude that pervades the Internet. Teachers have several tools to catch plagiarists, including a variety of Web sites that compare suspected papers to papers found on the Internet and produce an originality report highlighting text that may have been copied. Some instructors, however, are reluctant to investigate the integrity of a student's work and possibly ruin an academic career. How should educators deal with plagiarism? Why? Should a school's response to plagiarism depend on such factors as the material copied, the assignment for which it was copied, or the reason it was copied? Why or why not?

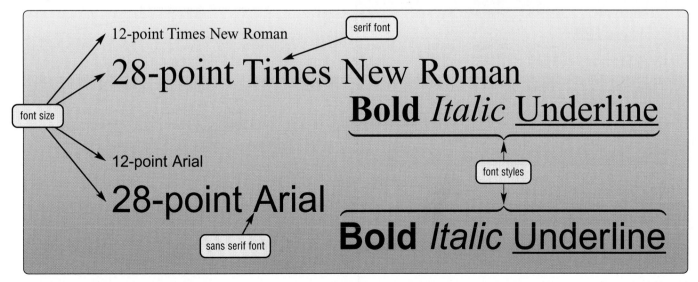

FIGURE 3-7   The Times New Roman and Arial fonts are shown in two font sizes and a variety of font styles.

FAQ 3-2

How often should I save a document?

Saving at regular intervals ensures that the majority of your work will not be lost in the event of a power loss or system failure. Many programs have an AutoSave feature that automatically saves open documents at specified time intervals, such as every 10 minutes. For more information, visit scsite.com/dc2006/ch3/faq and then click Saving Documents.

During the process of creating, editing, and formatting a document, the computer holds it in memory. To keep the document for future use requires that you save it. When you **save** a document, the computer transfers the document from memory to a storage medium such as a floppy disk, USB flash drive, hard disk, or CD. Once saved, a document is stored permanently as a file on the storage medium.

When you **print** a document, the computer places the contents of the document on paper or some other medium. One of the benefits of word processing software is the ability to print the same document many times, with each copy looking just like the first. Instead of printing a document and physically distributing it, some users e-mail the document to others on a network such as the Internet.

Spreadsheet Software

Spreadsheet software is another widely used type of application software. **Spreadsheet software** allows users to organize data in rows and columns and perform calculations on the data. These rows and columns collectively are called a *worksheet*. For years, people used paper to organize data and perform calculations by hand. In an electronic worksheet, you organize data in the same manner, and the computer performs the calculations more quickly and accurately (Figure 3-8). Because of spreadsheet software's logical approach to organizing data, many people use this software to organize and present nonfinancial data, as well as financial data.

As with word processing software, most spreadsheet software has basic features to help users create, edit, and format worksheets. Spreadsheet software also incorporates many of the features found in word processing software such as macros, checking spelling, changing fonts and font sizes, adding colors, tracking changes, recognizing voice input, inserting audio and video clips, providing research capabilities, recognizing handwritten text and drawings, and creating Web pages from existing spreadsheet documents.

The following sections describe the features of most spreadsheet programs.

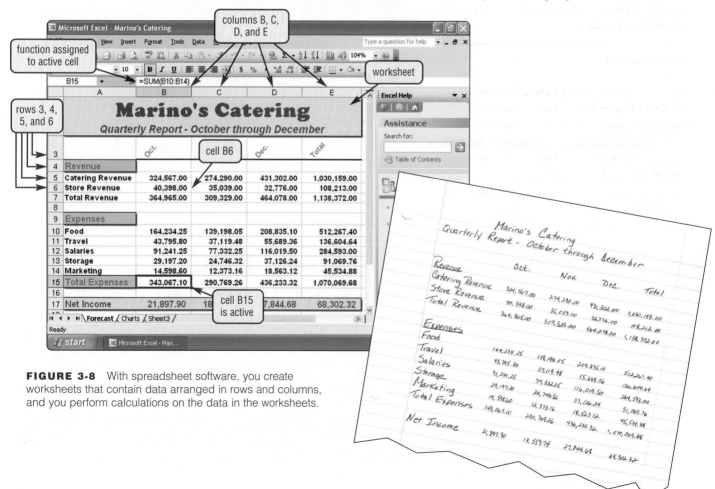

FIGURE 3-8 With spreadsheet software, you create worksheets that contain data arranged in rows and columns, and you perform calculations on the data in the worksheets.

SPREADSHEET ORGANIZATION A spreadsheet file is similar to a notebook with up to 255 related individual worksheets. Data is organized vertically in columns and horizontally in rows on each worksheet (Figure 3-8). Each worksheet typically has 256 columns and 65,536 rows. One or more letters identify each column, and a number identifies each row. The column letters begin with A and end with IV. The row numbers begin with 1 and end with 65,536. Only a small fraction of these columns and rows are displayed on the screen at one time. Scrolling through the worksheet displays different parts of it on the screen.

A *cell* is the intersection of a column and row. Each worksheet has more than 16 million (256 × 65,536) cells in which you can enter data. The spreadsheet software identifies cells by the column and row in which they are located. For example, the intersection of column B and row 6 is referred to as cell B6. As shown in Figure 3-8, cell B6 contains the number, 40,398.00, which represents the store revenue for October.

Cells may contain three types of data: labels, values, and formulas. The text, or *label*, entered in a cell identifies the worksheet data and helps organize the worksheet. Using descriptive labels, such as Total Revenue and Total Expenses, helps make a worksheet more meaningful.

CALCULATIONS Many of the worksheet cells shown in Figure 3-8 contain a number, called a *value*, that can be used in a calculation. Other cells, however, contain formulas that generate values. A *formula* performs calculations on the data in the worksheet and displays the resulting value in a cell, usually the cell containing the formula. When creating a worksheet, you can enter your own formulas.

In many spreadsheet programs, you begin a formula with an equal sign, a plus sign, or a minus sign. Next, you enter the formula, separating cell references (e.g., B10) with operators. Common operators are + for addition, − for subtraction, * for multiplication, and / for division. In Figure 3-8, for example, cell B15 could contain the formula =B10+B11+B12+B13+B14, which would add together (sum) the contents of cells B10, B11, B12, B13, and B14. That is, this formula calculates the total expenses for October. A more efficient way to sum the contents of cells, however, is to use special type of formula, called a function.

A *function* is a predefined formula that performs common calculations such as adding the values in a group of cells or generating a value such as the time or date. For example, instead of using the formula =B10+B11+B12+B13+B14 to calculate the total expenses for October, you could use the SUM function. This function requires you to identify the starting cell and the ending cell in a group to be summed, separating these two cell references with a colon. For example, the function =SUM(B10:B14) instructs the spreadsheet program to add all of the numbers in cells B10 through B14. Figure 3-9 lists functions commonly included in spreadsheet programs.

Rather than

SPREADSHEET FUNCTIONS

Financial	
FV (rate, number of periods, payment)	Calculates the future value of an investment
NPV (rate, range)	Calculates the net present value of an investment
PMT (rate, number of periods, present value)	Calculates the periodic payment for an annuity
PV (rate, number of periods, payment)	Calculates the present value of an investment
RATE (number of periods, payment, present value)	Calculates the periodic interest rate of an annuity
Date and Time	
DATE	Returns the current date
NOW	Returns the current date and time
TIME	Returns the current time
Mathematical	
ABS (number)	Returns the absolute value of a number
INT (number)	Rounds a number down to the nearest integer
LN (number)	Calculates the natural logarithm of a number
LOG (number, base)	Calculates the logarithm of a number to a specified base
ROUND (number, number of digits)	Rounds a number to a specified number of digits
SQRT (number)	Calculates the square root of a number
SUM (range)	Calculates the total of a range of numbers
Statistical	
AVERAGE (range)	Calculates the average value of a range of numbers
COUNT (range)	Counts how many cells in the range have numeric entries
MAX (range)	Returns the maximum value in a range
MIN (range)	Returns the minimum value in a range
STDEV (range)	Calculates the standard deviation of a range of numbers
Logical	
IF (logical test, value if true, value if false)	Performs a test and returns one value if the result of the test is true and another value if the result is false

FIGURE 3-9 Functions typically found in spreadsheet software.

RECALCULATION One of the more powerful features of spreadsheet software is its capability of recalculating the rest of the worksheet when data in a worksheet changes. When you enter a new value to change data in a cell, any value affected by the change is updated automatically and instantaneously. In Figure 3-8 on page 142, for example, if you change the store revenue for October from 40,398.00 to 45,398.00, the total revenue in cell B7 automatically changes from 364,965.00 to 369,965.00.

Spreadsheet software's capability of recalculating data also makes it a valuable budgeting, forecasting, and decision making tool. Most spreadsheet software includes a *what-if analysis* feature, where you change certain values in a spreadsheet to reveal the effects of those changes.

CHARTING Another standard feature of spreadsheet software is *charting*, which depicts the data in graphical form. A visual representation of data through charts often makes it easier for users to see at a glance the relationship among the numbers.

Three popular chart types are line charts, column charts, and pie charts. Figure 3-10 shows examples of these charts that were plotted from the data in Figure 3-8. A *line chart* shows a trend during a period of time, as indicated by a rising or falling line. For example, a line chart could show the total expenses for the three months. A *column chart*, also called a *bar chart*, displays bars of various lengths to show the relationship of data. The bars can be horizontal, vertical, or stacked on top of one another. For example, a column chart might show the total monthly expenses, with each bar representing a different category of expense. A *pie chart*, which has the shape of a round pie cut into slices, shows the relationship of parts to a whole. For example, you might use a pie chart to show the percentage each expense category contributed to the total expenses.

Charts, as well as any other part of a workbook, can be linked to or embedded in a word processing document.

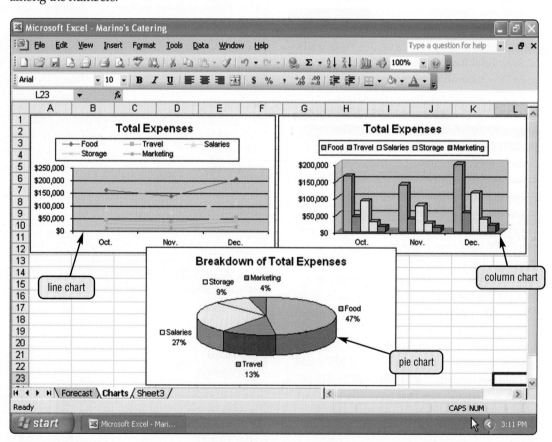

FIGURE 3-10 Three basic types of charts provided with spreadsheet software are line charts, column charts, and pie charts. The charts shown here were created from the data in the worksheet in Figure 3-8.

Database Software

A **database** is a collection of data organized in a manner that allows access, retrieval, and use of that data. In a manual database, you might record data on paper and store it in a filing cabinet. With a computerized database, such as the one shown in Figure 3-11, the computer stores the data in an electronic format on a storage medium such as a hard disk.

Database software is application software that allows users to create, access, and manage a database. Using database software, you can add, change, and delete data in a database; sort and retrieve data from the database; and create forms and reports using the data in the database.

With most popular personal computer database programs, a database consists of a collection of tables, organized in rows and columns. Each row, called a *record*, contains data about a given person, product, object, or event. Each column, called a *field*, contains a specific category of data within a record.

The Store database shown in Figure 3-11 consists of two tables: a Product table and a Supplier table. The Product table contains ten records (rows), each storing data about one item. The product data is grouped into six fields (columns): Product ID, Description, On Hand, Cost, Selling Price, and Supplier Code. The On Hand field, for instance, contains the quantity on hand in inventory. The Product and Supplier tables relate to one another through a common field, Supplier Code.

Users run queries to retrieve data. A *query* is a request for specific data from the database. For example, a query might request products that are low on hand. Database software can take the results of a query and present it in a window on the screen or send it to the printer.

FAQ 3-3

How big is the largest database?

According to a recent survey, the world's largest database holds 29 trillion characters. In the next few years, the size of the largest database is expected to exceed 5 quadrillion characters. For more information, visit scsite.com/dc2006/ch3/faq and then click Enterprise Databases.

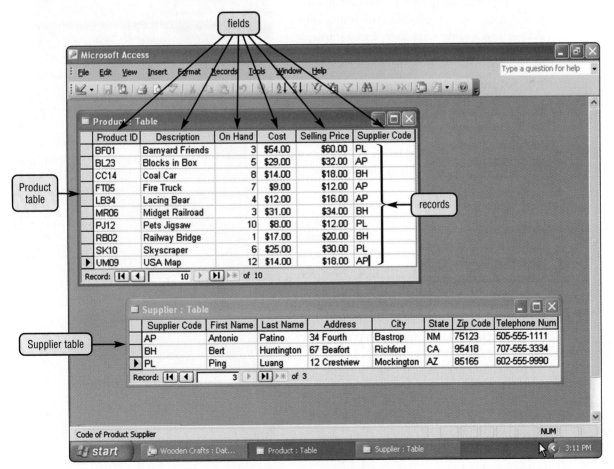

FIGURE 3-11 This database contains two tables: one for the products and one for the suppliers. The Product table has 10 records and 6 fields; the Supplier table has 3 records and 8 fields.

Presentation Graphics Software

Presentation graphics software is application software that allows users to create visual aids for presentations to communicate ideas, messages, and other information to a group. The presentations can be viewed as slides, sometimes called a *slide show*, that are displayed on a large monitor or on a projection screen (Figure 3-12).

Presentation graphics software typically provides a variety of predefined presentation formats that define complementary colors for backgrounds, text, and graphical accents on the slides. This software also provides a variety of layouts for each individual slide such as a title slide, a two-column slide, and a slide with clip art, a picture (Figure 3-13), a chart, a table, or animation. In addition, you can enhance any text, charts, and graphical images on a slide with 3-D and other special effects such as shading, shadows, and textures.

When building a presentation, users can set the slide timing so the presentation automatically displays the next slide after a preset delay. Presentation graphics software allows you to apply special effects to the transition between each slide. One slide, for example, might fade away slowly as the next slide is displayed.

To help organize the presentation, you can view thumbnail versions of all the slides in slide sorter view. *Slide sorter view* presents a screen view similar to how 35mm slides look on a photographer's light table. The slide sorter allows users to arrange the slides in any order.

Presentation graphics software typically includes a clip gallery that provides images, pictures, video clips, and audio clips to enhance multimedia presentations. Users with an artistic ability can create their own graphics using paint/image editing software (discussed later in the chapter) and then *import* (bring in) the graphics into the slide. Users also can insert their own video, music, and audio commentary in a presentation.

Presentation graphics software incorporates some of the features found in word processing software such as checking spelling, formatting, recognizing voice input, providing research capabilities, recognizing handwritten text and drawings, and creating Web pages from existing slide shows.

WEB LINK 3-3

Presentation Graphics Software

For more information, visit scsite.com/dc2006/ch3/weblink and then click Presentation Graphics Software.

FIGURE 3-12 This presentation created with presentation graphics software consists of five slides.

FIGURE 3-13 In presentation graphics software, users can change the design and layout of any slide in a presentation.

Note Taking Software

Note taking software is application software that enables users to enter typed text, handwritten comments, drawings, or sketches anywhere on a page and then save the page as part of a notebook (Figure 3-14). The software can convert handwritten comments to typed text or store the notes in handwritten form. Users also can include audio recordings as part of their notes.

Once the notes are captured (entered and saved), users easily can organize them, reuse them, and share them. This software allows users to search through saved notes for specific text. It even can search through an entire notebook. Users also can flag important notes with color, highlights, and shapes.

On a desktop or notebook computer, users enter notes primarily via the keyboard or microphone. On a Tablet PC, however, the primary input device is a digital pen. Users find note taking software convenient during meetings, class lectures, conferences, in libraries, and other settings that previously required a pencil and tablet of paper for recording thoughts and discussions.

Note taking software incorporates many of the features found in word processing software such as checking spelling, changing fonts and font sizes, adding colors, recognizing voice input, inserting audio and video clips, and providing research capabilities.

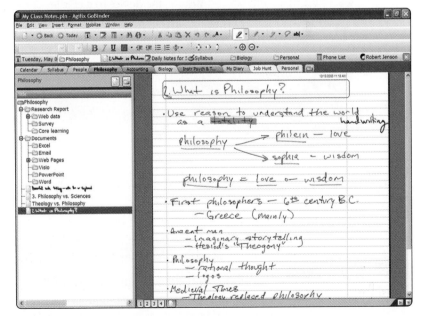

FIGURE 3-14 With note taking software, students and other mobile users can handwrite notes, draw sketches, and type text.

Personal Information Manager Software

A **personal information manager (PIM)** is application software that includes an appointment calendar, address book, notepad, and other features to help users organize personal information. With a PIM, you can take information previously tracked in a weekly or daily calendar, and organize and store it on your computer. The appointment calendar allows you to schedule activities for a particular day and time. With the address book, you can enter and maintain names, addresses, telephone numbers, and e-mail addresses of customers, coworkers, family members, and friends. You can use the notepad to record ideas, reminders, and other important information.

Most PDAs and many smart phones today include, among many other features, PIM functionality. Using a PDA or smart phone, you can synchronize, or coordinate, information so that both the PDA or smart phone and the computer have the latest version of the information.

Some PDAs and smart phones synchronize with the computer wirelessly. With others, you connect the PDA or smart phone to the computer with a cable, or you insert the device in a cradle, which has a cable that plugs in the computer (Figure 3-15).

PDA Business Software

In addition to PIM software, a huge variety of business software is available for PDAs. Although some PDAs have software built in, most have the capability of accessing software on miniature storage media such as memory cards. Business software for PDAs allows users to create documents and worksheets, manage databases and lists, create slide shows, take notes, manage budgets and finances, view and edit photographs, read electronic books, plan travel routes, compose and read e-mail messages, send instant messages, and browse the Web. For additional information about software for PDAs, read the Smart Phones and PDAs feature that follows Chapter 5.

Software Suite

A **software suite** is a collection of individual programs sold as a single package. Business software suites typically include, at a minimum, the following programs: word processing, spreadsheet, e-mail, and presentation graphics. Two of the more widely used software suites are Microsoft Office and Sun StarOffice.

Software suites offer two major advantages: lower cost and ease of use. Buying a collection of programs in a software suite usually costs significantly less than purchasing them individually. Software suites provide ease of use because the programs in a software suite normally use a similar interface and share features such as clip art and spelling checker. For example, once you learn how to print using the software suite's word processing program, you can apply the same skill to the spreadsheet and presentation graphics programs in the software suite.

FIGURE 3-15   With most PDAs and smart phones, you can synchronize or transfer information from the device to a desktop computer, so the updated important information always is available.

FAQ 3-4

What is the difference between Microsoft Office and Microsoft Office System?

Microsoft Office is a suite of core desktop business programs. Office is available in a variety of editions, each of which includes at least Word, Excel, and Outlook. *Microsoft Office System* is a portfolio of programs and services that are tightly integrated yet available for purchase as separate entities. In addition to Microsoft Office, other products in the Microsoft Office System include OneNote, InfoPath, Visio, FrontPage, and Project. For more information, visit scsite.com/dc2006/ch3/faq and then click Microsoft Office System.

Project Management Software

Project management software allows a user to plan, schedule, track, and analyze the events, resources, and costs of a project (Figure 3-16). Project management software helps users manage project variables, allowing them to complete a project on time and within budget. An engineer, for example, might use project management software to manage new product development to schedule product screening, market evaluation, technical product evaluation, and manufacturing processes.

Accounting Software

Accounting software helps companies record and report their financial transactions (Figure 3-17). With accounting software, business users perform accounting activities related to the general ledger, accounts receivable, accounts payable, purchasing, invoicing, and payroll functions. Accounting software also enables users to write and print checks, track checking account activity, and update and reconcile balances on demand.

Newer accounting software supports online credit checks, billing, direct deposit, and payroll services. Some accounting software offers more complex features such as job costing and estimating, time tracking, multiple company reporting, foreign currency reporting, and forecasting the amount of raw materials needed for products. The cost of accounting software for small businesses ranges from less than one hundred to several thousand dollars. Accounting software for large businesses can cost several hundred thousand dollars.

FIGURE 3-16 Project management software allows you to track, control, and manage the events, resources, and costs of a project.

FIGURE 3-17 Accounting software helps companies record and report their financial transactions.

Enterprise Computing Software

A large organization, commonly referred to as an enterprise, requires special computing solutions because of its size and large geographic distribution. A typical enterprise consists of a wide variety of departments, centers, and divisions — collectively known as functional units. Nearly every enterprise has the following functional units: human resources, accounting and finance, engineering or product development, manufacturing, marketing, sales, distribution, customer service, and information technology. Each of these functional units has specialized software requirements, as outlined below.

- Human resources software manages employee information such as benefits, personal information, performance evaluations, training, and vacation time.
- Accounting software manages everyday transactions, such as sales and payments to suppliers. Financial software helps managers budget, forecast, and analyze.
- Engineering or product development software allows engineers to develop plans for new products and test their product designs.
- Manufacturing software assists in the assembly process, as well as in scheduling and managing the inventory of parts and products.
- Marketing software allows marketing personnel to create marketing campaigns and track their effectiveness.
- Sales software enables the sales force to manage contacts, schedule meetings, log customer interactions, manage product information, and take customer orders.
- Distribution software analyzes and tracks inventory and manages product shipping status.
- Customer service software manages the day-to-day interactions with customers, such as telephone calls, e-mail messages, Web interactions, and instant messaging sessions.
- Information technology staff use a variety of software to maintain and secure the hardware and software in an enterprise.

GRAPHICS AND MULTIMEDIA SOFTWARE

In addition to business software, many people work with software designed specifically for their field of work. Power users such as engineers, architects, desktop publishers, and graphic artists often use sophisticated software that allows them to work with graphics and multimedia. This software includes computer-aided design, desktop publishing, paint/image editing, video and audio editing, multimedia authoring, and Web page authoring. Figure 3-18 lists some popular programs in each of these categories. Many of these programs incorporate user-friendly interfaces and/or have scaled-down versions, making it possible for the home and small business users to create documents using these programs. The following sections discuss the features and functions of graphics and multimedia software.

Computer-Aided Design

Computer-aided design (CAD) software is a sophisticated type of application software that assists a professional user in creating engineering, architectural, and scientific designs. For example, engineers create design plans for airplanes and security systems. Architects design building structures and floor plans (Figure 3-19). Scientists design drawings of molecular structures.

CAD software eliminates the laborious manual drafting that design processes can require. Three-dimensional CAD programs allow designers to rotate designs of 3-D objects to view them from any angle. Some CAD software even can generate material lists for building designs.

POPULAR GRAPHICS AND MULTIMEDIA SOFTWARE

Application Software	Manufacturer	Program Name
Computer-Aided Design (CAD)	Autodesk	AutoCAD
	Quality Plans	Chief Architect
	Microsoft	Visio
Desktop Publishing (for the Professional)	Adobe	InDesign
	Corel	Ventura
	Quark	QuarkXPress
Paint/Image Editing (for the Professional)	Adobe	Illustrator
		Photoshop
	Corel	Painter
	Macromedia	FreeHand
Video and Audio Editing (for the Professional)	Adobe	Audition
		Encore DVD
		Premiere Pro
	Cakewalk	SONAR
	Macromedia	SoundEdit
	Sony	ACID Pro
	Ulead	MediaStudio Pro
		DVD Workshop
Multimedia Authoring	SumTotal Systems	ToolBook Instructor
	Macromedia	Authorware
		Director
Web Page Authoring	Adobe	GoLive
	Lotus	FastSite
	Macromedia	Dreamweaver
		Fireworks
		Flash
	Microsoft	FrontPage

FIGURE 3-18 Popular graphics and multimedia programs — for the professional.

FIGURE 3-19 CAD software is sophisticated software that assists engineers, architects, and scientists in creating designs.

Desktop Publishing Software (for the Professional)

Desktop publishing (DTP) software enables professional designers to create sophisticated documents that contain text, graphics, and many colors. Professional DTP software is ideal for the production of high-quality color documents such as textbooks, corporate newsletters, marketing literature (Figure 3-20), product catalogs, and annual reports. Today's DTP software allows designers to convert a color document into a format for use on the World Wide Web.

Although many word processing programs have some of the capabilities of DTP software, professional designers and graphic artists use DTP software because it supports page layout. *Page layout* is the process of arranging text and graphics in a document on a page-by-page basis. DTP software includes color libraries to assist in color selections for text and graphics. A *color library* is a standard set of colors used by designers and printers to ensure that colors will print exactly as specified. Designers and graphic artists can print finished publications on a color printer, take them to a professional printer, or post them on the Web.

FAQ 3-5

Why am I not able to view some files on the Web that contain company brochures?

In many cases, you need Adobe *Acrobat Reader* software because some companies save documents on the Web, such as brochures, using the Adobe PDF format. To view and print a PDF file, simply download the free Adobe Acrobat Reader software from Adobe's Web site. For more information, visit scsite.com/dc2006/ch3/faq and then click Adobe Acrobat Reader.

Paint/Image Editing Software (for the Professional)

Graphic artists, multimedia professionals, technical illustrators, and desktop publishers use paint software and image editing software to create and modify graphical images such as those used in DTP documents and Web pages. **Paint software**, also called *illustration software*, allows users to draw pictures, shapes, and other graphical images with various on-screen tools such as a pen, brush, eyedropper, and paint bucket. **Image editing software** provides the capabilities of paint software and also includes the capability to enhance and modify existing images and pictures (Figure 3-21). Modifications can include adjusting or enhancing image colors, and adding special effects such as shadows and glows. Read At Issue 3-2 for a related discussion.

FIGURE 3-20 Professional designers and graphic artists use DTP software to produce sophisticated publications such as marketing literature.

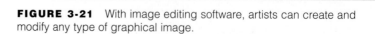

FIGURE 3-21 With image editing software, artists can create and modify any type of graphical image.

Altering Digital Photographs — Art or Fraud?

A *Los Angeles Times* photographer combined two digital photographs of the Iraq war, taken minutes apart, to create a single picture that appeared on the newspaper's front page. The photographer merged the photos to improve the composition, but when the source of the picture became known, the newspaper fired the photographer, citing a policy that forbids altering the content of news photos. Many commercial artists, photojournalists, and creators of cartoons, book covers, and billboards use paint and image editing software to alter photographs. With this software, an artist can convert photographs to a digital form that can be colorized, stretched, squeezed, texturized, or otherwise altered. The National Press Photographers Association, however, has expressed reservations about digital altering and endorses the following: "As [photo] journalists we believe the guiding principle of our profession is accuracy; therefore, we believe it is wrong to alter the content of a photograph in any way…that deceives the public." Yet, some insist that the extent to which a photo "deceives the public" is in the eye of the beholder. Is it ethical to alter digital photographs? Why or why not? Does the answer depend on the reason for the alteration, the extent of the alteration, or some other factor? If some alteration is accepted, can photographic integrity still be guaranteed? Why or why not?

Video and Audio Editing Software (for the Professional)

Video editing software (Figure 3-22) allows professionals to modify a segment of a video, called a clip. For example, users can reduce the length of a video clip, reorder a series of clips, or add special effects such as words that move horizontally across the screen.

Video editing software typically includes audio editing capabilities. **Audio editing software** lets users modify audio clips and produce studio-quality soundtracks. Audio editing software usually includes *filters*, which are designed to enhance audio quality. For example, a filter might remove a distracting background noise from the audio clip. Read At Issue 3-3 for a related discussion.

FIGURE 3-22 With video editing software, users modify video images.

What Should Be Done to Prevent Music or Video File Sharing?

It is illegal to use networks to share copyrighted music or video files. Despite this, a number of file-sharing networks exist, and an estimated 60 million Americans use file-sharing software to locate and download copyrighted music and videos without paying. Much of this illegal activity takes place at colleges and universities, where high-speed network connections make file sharing almost instantaneous. To combat illegal file sharing, some schools have turned to new programs that intentionally slow the performance of file-sharing software. The Recording Industry Association of America (RIAA) has gone even further, filing law suits against people suspected of downloading copyrighted music. Individuals found guilty can be liable for fines up to $150,000 for every stolen song. The RIAA maintains that downloading copyrighted music steals from both the recording artist and the recording industry. Yet, many people feel that the response to sharing copyrighted music and video files is excessive. They argue that copying music from the radio to an audio cassette is legal and insist that downloading copyrighted music is no different. Besides, someone who downloads a copyrighted song later may be inspired to purchase an artist's CD or attend a concert. Should it be illegal to share copyrighted music or video files over a network? Why or why not? Are slowing file-sharing software and filing thousand-dollar lawsuits unwarranted reactions to what some people consider a victimless violation? Why?

Multimedia Authoring Software

Multimedia authoring software allows users to combine text, graphics, audio, video, and animation in an interactive application (Figure 3-23). With this software, users control the placement of text and images and the duration of sounds, video, and animation. Once created, multimedia presentations often take the form of interactive computer-based presentations or Web-based presentations designed to facilitate learning, demonstrate product functionality, and elicit direct-user participation. Training centers, educational institutions, and online magazine publishers all use multimedia authoring software to develop interactive applications. These applications may be available on a CD or DVD, over a local area network, or via the Internet.

FAQ 3-6

How do I know which program to buy?

Many companies offer downloadable *trial versions* of their software that allow you to use the software free for a limited time. Try a few. Read computer magazines and Web sites for reviews of various products. For more information, visit scsite.com/dc2006/ch3/faq and then click Trial Versions.

Web Page Authoring Software

Web page authoring software helps users of all skill levels create Web pages that include graphical images, video, audio, animation, and other special effects with interactive content (Figure 3-24). In addition, many Web page authoring programs allow users to organize, manage, and maintain Web sites.

Application software, such as Word and Excel, often includes Web page authoring features. This allows home users to create basic Web pages using application software they already own. For more sophisticated Web pages, users work with Web page authoring software. Many Web page developers also use multimedia authoring software along with, or instead of, Web page authoring software for Web page development.

FIGURE 3-23 Multimedia authoring software allows you to create dynamic presentations that include text, graphics, video, sound, and animation.

FIGURE 3-24 With Web page authoring software, users create sophisticated Web pages.

Test your knowledge of pages 138 through 154 in Quiz Yourself 3-2.

QUIZ YOURSELF 3-2

Instructions: Find the true statement below. Then, rewrite the remaining false statements so they are true.

1. Audio editing software typically includes video editing capabilities.
2. Enterprise computing software provides the capabilities of paint software and also includes the capability to modify existing images.
3. Millions of people use spreadsheet software every day to develop documents such as letters, memos, reports, fax cover sheets, mailing labels, newsletters, and Web pages.
4. Professional accounting software is ideal for the production of high-quality color documents such as textbooks, corporate newsletters, marketing literature, product catalogs, and annual reports.
5. Spreadsheet software is application software that allows users to create visual aids for presentations to communicate ideas, messages, and other information to a group.
6. Two of the more widely used CAD programs are Microsoft Office and Sun StarOffice.
7. Web page authoring software helps users of all skill levels create Web pages.

Quiz Yourself Online: To further check your knowledge of types and features of business programs and graphics/multimedia programs, visit scsite.com/dc2006/ch3/quiz and then click Objectives 4 – 5.

SOFTWARE FOR HOME, PERSONAL, AND EDUCATIONAL USE

A large amount of application software is designed specifically for home, personal, and educational use. Most of the programs in this category are relatively inexpensive, often priced less than $100 and sometimes free. Figure 3-25 lists popular programs for many of these categories. The following sections discuss the features and functions of this application software.

POPULAR SOFTWARE PROGRAMS FOR HOME/PERSONAL/EDUCATIONAL USE

Application Software	Manufacturer	Program Name
Software Suite (for Personal Use)	Microsoft	Works
	Sun	OpenOffice.org
Personal Finance	Intuit	Quicken
	Microsoft	Money
Legal	Broderbund	Family Lawyer
	Cosmi	Perfect Attorney
	H&R Block Kiplinger	Home & Business Attorney WILLPower
	Nolo	Quicken Legal Business Quicken WillMaker
Tax Preparation	2nd Story Software	TaxACT
	H&R Block Kiplinger	TaxCut
	Intuit	Quicken TurboTax
Desktop Publishing (for Personal Use)	Broderbund	The Print Shop PrintMaster
	Microsoft	Publisher
Paint/Image Editing (for Personal Use)	Corel	CorelDRAW
	Jasc	Paint Shop Pro
	Sun	StarOffice Draw
	The GIMP Team (open source software)	The Gimp

Application Software	Manufacturer	Program Name
Photo Editing	Adobe	Photoshop Elements
	Corel	Photobook
	Dell	Image Expert
	Microsoft	Picture It! Photo Picture Manager
	Roxio	PhotoSuite
	Ulead	PhotoImpact Photo Express
Clip Art/Image Gallery	Broderbund	ClickArt
	Nova Development	Art Explosion
Video and Audio Editing (for Personal Use)	Microsoft	Movie Maker
	Pinnacle Systems	Studio Moviebox
	Roxio	VideoWave
	Ulead	VideoStudio
Home Design/ Landscaping	ART	Home Designer Suite
	Broderbund	3D Home Architect Design Suite
	Quality Plans	Home Designer Suite
	ValuSoft	Custom LandDesigner
Reference	American Heritage	Talking Dictionary Classic
	Microsoft	Encarta Streets & Trips
	Rand McNally	StreetFinder TripMaker

FIGURE 3-25 Many popular software programs are available for home, personal, and educational use.

Software Suite (for Personal Use)

A software suite (for personal use) combines application software such as word processing, spreadsheet, database, and other programs in a single, easy-to-use package. Many computer vendors install a software suite for personal use, such as Microsoft Works, on new computers sold to home users.

As mentioned earlier, the programs in a software suite use a similar interface and share some common features. The programs in software suites for personal use typically are available only through the software suite; that is, you cannot purchase them individually. These programs may not have all the capabilities of business application software. For many home users, however, the capabilities of software suites for personal use more than meet their needs.

Personal Finance Software

Personal finance software is a simplified accounting program that helps home users and small office/home office users balance their checkbooks (Figure 3-26), pay bills, track personal income and expenses, set up budgets, manage home inventory, track investments, and evaluate financial plans. Personal finance software helps determine where, and for what purpose, you are spending money so you can manage your finances. Reports can summarize transactions by category (such as dining), by payee (such as the electric company), or by time (such as the last two months). Financial planning features include analyzing home and personal loans, preparing income taxes, and managing retirement savings.

Most of these personal finance programs also offer a variety of online services, which require access to the Internet. For example, users can track investments online, compare insurance rates from leading insurance companies, and bank online. **Online banking** offers access to account balances, provides bill paying services, and allows you to download monthly transactions and statements from the Web directly to your computer.

WEB LINK 3-5

Personal Finance Software

For more information, visit scsite.com/ dc2006/ch3/weblink and then click Personal Finance Software.

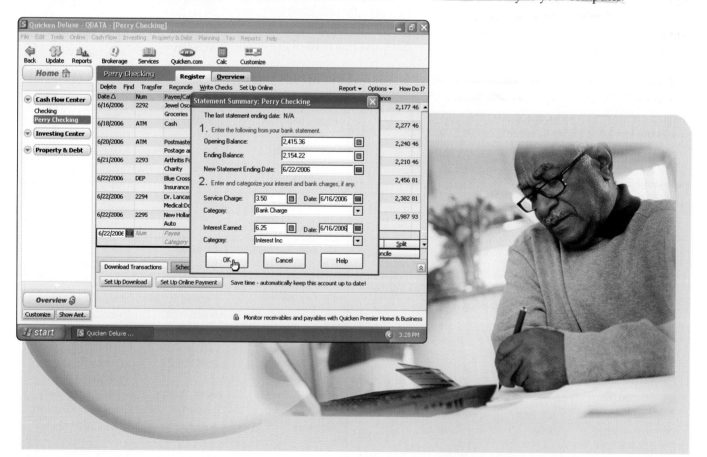

FIGURE 3-26   Personal finance software assists home users with balancing their checkbooks and paying bills.

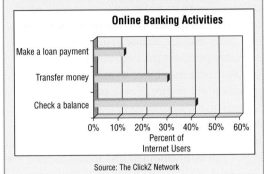
Legal Software

Legal software assists in the preparation of legal documents and provides legal information to individuals, families, and small businesses (Figure 3-27). Legal software provides standard contracts and documents associated with buying, selling, and renting property; estate planning; marriage and divorce; and preparing a will or living trust. By answering a series of questions or completing a form, the legal software tailors the legal document to specific needs.

Once the legal document is created, you can file the paperwork with the appropriate agency, court, or office; or take the document to your attorney for his or her review and signature. Before using one of these software programs to create a document, you may want to check with your local bar association for its legality.

Tax Preparation Software

Tax preparation software is used to guide individuals, families, or small businesses through the process of filing federal taxes (Figure 3-28). These programs forecast tax liability and offer money-saving tax tips, designed to lower your tax bill. After you answer a series of questions and complete basic forms, the software creates and analyzes your tax forms to search for potential errors and deduction opportunities. Once the forms are complete, you can print any necessary paperwork, and then they are ready for filing.

FIGURE 3-27 Legal software provides legal information to individuals, families, and small businesses and assists in record keeping and the preparation of legal documents.

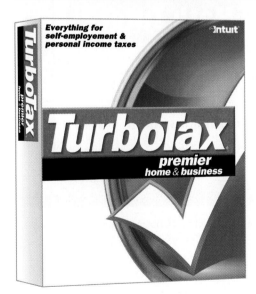

FIGURE 3-28 Tax preparation software guides individuals, families, or small businesses through the process of filing federal taxes.

Desktop Publishing Software (for Personal Use)

Instead of using professional DTP software (as discussed earlier in this chapter), many home and small business users work with simpler, easy-to-understand DTP software designed for smaller-scale desktop publishing projects (Figure 3-29). **Personal DTP software** helps home and small business users create newsletters, brochures, advertisements, postcards, greeting cards, letterhead, business cards, banners, calendars, logos, and Web pages.

Personal DTP programs provide hundreds of thousands of graphical images. You also can import (bring in) your own digital photographs into the documents. These programs typically guide you through the development of a document by asking a series of questions, offering numerous predefined layouts, and providing standard text you can add to documents. Then, you can print a finished publication on a color printer or post it on the Web.

Many personal DTP programs also include paint/image editing software and photo editing software.

Paint/Image Editing Software (for Personal Use)

Personal paint/image editing software provides an easy-to-use interface, usually with more simplified capabilities than its professional counterpart, including functions tailored to meet the needs of the home and small business user.

As with the professional versions, personal paint software includes various simplified tools that allow you to draw pictures, shapes, and other images. Personal image editing software provides the capabilities of paint software and the ability to modify existing graphics and photos. These products also include many templates to assist you in adding an image to documents such as greeting cards (Figure 3-30), banners, calendars, signs, labels, business cards, and letterhead.

FAQ 3-9

How do pictures get in the computer from a digital camera?

Most digital cameras save pictures on miniature storage media, such as a memory card. By inserting the memory card in a card reader/writer in or attached to the computer, users can access images the same way they access files on a disk drive. With some cameras, pictures also can transfer along a cable that connects the camera to the computer. For more information, visit scsite.com/dc2006/ch3/faq and then click Digital Imaging.

FIGURE 3-29   With Publisher, home and small business users can create professional looking publications such as this flyer with tear-offs.

FIGURE 3-30   Home users can purchase affordable paint/image editing programs that enable them to include personal pictures and graphics in many different types of documents.

Photo Editing Software

Photo editing software is a popular type of image editing software that allows users to edit digital photographs by removing red-eye, erasing blemishes, restoring aged photos, adding special effects (Figure 3-31), or creating electronic photo albums. When you purchase a digital camera, it usually includes photo editing software. You can print edited photographs on labels, calendars, business cards, and banners; or post them on a Web page. Some photo editing software allows users to send digital photographs to an online print service, which will deliver high-resolution printed images through the postal service. Many online print services have a photo community where users can post photographs on the Web for others to view.

FIGURE 3-31 Photo editing software enables home users to edit digital photographs.

Clip Art/Image Gallery

Application software often includes a **clip art/image gallery,** which is a collection of clip art and photographs. Some applications have links to additional clips available on the Web. You also can purchase clip art/image gallery software that contains hundreds of thousands of images (Figure 3-32).

In addition to clip art, many clip art/image galleries provide fonts, animations, sounds, video clips, and audio clips. You can use the images, fonts, and other items from the clip art/image gallery in all types of documents, including word processing, desktop publishing, spreadsheet, and presentation graphics.

FIGURE 3-32 Clip art/image gallery software contains hundreds of thousands of images.

WEB LINK 3-7

Microsoft Office Clip Art

For more information, visit scsite.com/ dc2006/ch3/weblink and then click Microsoft Office Clip Art.

Video and Audio Editing Software (for Personal Use)

Many home users work with easy-to-use video and audio editing software, which is much simpler to use than its professional counterpart, for small-scale movie making projects (Figure 3-33). With these programs, home users can edit home movies, add music or other sounds to the video, and share their movies on the Web. Some operating systems include video editing and audio editing software.

FIGURE 3-33 Operating systems, such as Windows XP, include video and audio editing software so home users can create their own movies.

Home Design/Landscaping Software

Homeowners or potential homeowners can use **home design/landscaping software** to assist them with the design, remodeling, or improvement of a home, deck, or landscape (Figure 3-34). Home design/landscaping software includes hundreds of pre-drawn plans that you can customize to meet your needs. Once designed, many home design/landscaping programs print a materials list outlining costs and quantities for the entire project.

FIGURE 3-34 Home design/landscaping software can help you design or remodel a home, deck, or landscape.

Reference and Educational Software

Reference software provides valuable and thorough information for all individuals (Figure 3-35). Popular reference software includes encyclopedias, dictionaries, health/medical guides, and travel directories.

FIGURE 3-35 This reference software shows text you can read about butterflies and moths and includes a variety of pictures, videos, and links to the Web.

WEB LINK 3-8

Entertainment Software

For more information, visit scsite.com/dc2006/ch3/weblink and then click Entertainment Software.

Educational software is software that teaches a particular skill. Educational software exists for just about any subject, from learning how to type to learning how to cook. Preschool to high school learners use educational software to assist them with subjects such as reading and math or to prepare them for class or college entry exams. Educational software often includes games and other content to make the learning experience more fun.

Many educational programs use a computer-based training approach. **Computer-based training** (CBT), also called computer-aided instruction (CAI), is a type of education in which students learn by using and completing exercises with instructional software. CBT typically consists of self-directed, self-paced instruction about a topic. Beginning athletes, for example, use CBT programs to learn the intricacies of baseball, football, soccer, tennis, and golf. The military and airlines use CBT simulations to train pilots to fly in various conditions and environments. Schools use CBT to teach students math, language, and software skills.

Entertainment Software

Entertainment software for personal computers includes interactive games, videos, and other programs designed to support a hobby or provide amusement and enjoyment. For example, you might use entertainment software to play games (Figure 3-36), make a family tree, listen to music, or fly an aircraft.

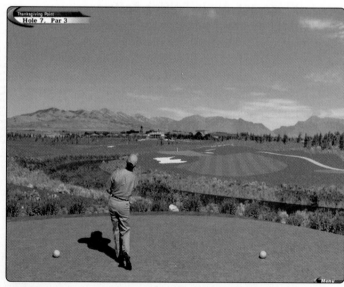

FIGURE 3-36 Entertainment software can provide hours of recreation.

APPLICATION SOFTWARE FOR COMMUNICATIONS

One of the main reasons people use computers is to communicate and share information with others. Some communications software is considered system software because it works with hardware and transmission media.

Other communications software makes users more productive and/or assists them with personal tasks, and thus, is considered application software. Chapter 2 presented a variety of application software for communications, which are summarized in the table in Figure 3-37. Read At Issue 3-4 for a related discussion.

APPLICATION SOFTWARE FOR COMMUNICATIONS

E-Mail
- Messages and files sent via a network such as the Internet
- Requires an e-mail program
  - Integrated in many software suites and operating systems
  - Available free at portals on the Web
  - Included with paid Internet access service
  - Can be purchased separately from retailers

FTP
- Method of uploading and downloading files with other computers on the Internet
- Download may require an FTP program; upload usually requires an FTP program
  - Integrated in some operating systems
  - Available for download on the Web for a small fee
  - Can be purchased separately from retailers

Web Browser
- Allows users to access and view Web pages on the Internet
- Requires a Web browser program
  - Integrated in some operating systems
  - Available for download on the Web free or for a fee
  - Included with paid Internet access service

Video Conferencing/Telephone Calls
- Meeting/conversation between geographically separated people who use a network such as the Internet to transmit video/audio
- Requires a microphone, speakers, and sometimes a video camera attached to your computer
- Requires video conferencing software

Newsgroup/Message Board
- Online area where users have written discussions
- Newsgroup may require a newsreader program
  - Integrated in some operating systems, e-mail programs, and Web browsers
  - Available for download on the Web, usually at no cost
  - Included with some paid Internet access services
  - Built into some Web sites

Chat Room
- Real-time, online typed conversation
- Requires chat client software
  - Integrated in some operating systems, e-mail programs, and Web browsers
  - Available for download on the Web, usually at no cost
  - Included with some paid Internet access services
  - Built into some Web sites

Instant Messaging
- Real-time exchange of messages, files, audio, and/or video with another online user
- Requires instant messenger software
  - Integrated in some operating systems
  - Available for download on the Web, usually at no cost
  - Included with some paid Internet access services

FIGURE 3-37 A summary of application software for home and business communications.

AT ISSUE 3-4

Should Companies Monitor Employees' E-Mail and Web Browsing?

According to one survey, more than 75 percent of Fortune 500 companies routinely monitor employees' computer use. Employers can use software to see what is on the screen or stored on hard disks, scrutinize e-mail and Web browsing habits, and even supervise keyboard activity. About one company in four has fired an employee based on its discoveries. Companies monitor computer use to improve productivity, increase security, reduce misconduct, and control liability risks. Few laws regulate employee monitoring, and courts have given employers a great deal of leeway in watching work on company-owned computers. In one case, an employee's termination for using her office e-mail system to complain about her boss was upheld, even though the company allowed e-mail use for personal communications. The court decreed that the employee's messages were inappropriate for workplace communications. Many employees believe that monitoring software violates their privacy rights. To reduce employee anxiety about monitoring computer use, one expert suggests that companies publish written policies and accept employee feedback, provide clear descriptions of acceptable and unacceptable behavior, respect employee needs and time, and establish a balance between security and privacy. Should companies monitor how their employees use computers at work? Why or why not? How can a company balance workplace security and productivity with employee privacy? If a company monitors computer use, what guidelines should be followed to maintain worker morale? Why?

POPULAR STAND-ALONE UTILITY PROGRAMS

Utility programs are considered system software because they assist a user with controlling or maintaining the operation of a computer, its devices, or its software. Some utility programs are included with the operating system, and others are available as stand-alone programs.

Stand-alone utility programs typically offer features that provide an environment conducive to successful use of application software. One of the more important utility programs protects a computer against viruses. A computer *virus* is a potentially damaging computer program that affects, or infects, a computer negatively by altering the way the computer works without the user's knowledge or permission. For a technical discussion about viruses, read the High-Tech Talk article on page 168.

Other features of stand-alone utility programs include removing spyware from a computer; filtering e-mail messages, Web content, and advertisements; compressing files; converting files; burning (recording on) a CD or DVD; and maintaining a personal computer. The table in Figure 3-38 briefly describes several stand-alone utility programs. Chapter 8 discusses them in more depth.

FAQ 3-10

How much does a computer virus attack cost a company?

A recent survey found that it typically costs an enterprise about $10,000 to recover from a computer virus attack. When the virus attacks multiple servers, however, the costs can exceed $100,000. For more information, visit scsite.com/dc2006/ch3/faq and then click Computer Virus Attacks.

WEB LINK 3-9

Antivirus Programs

For more information, visit scsite.com/dc2006/ch3/weblink and then click Antivirus Programs.

WIDELY USED STAND-ALONE UTILITY PROGRAMS

Utility Program	Description
Antivirus Program	An *antivirus program* protects a computer against viruses by identifying and removing any computer viruses found in memory, on storage media, or in incoming files.
Spyware Remover	A *spyware remover* detects and deletes spyware on your computer.
Internet Filters	
• Anti-Spam Program	An *anti-spam program* attempts to remove spam (Internet junk mail) before it reaches your e-mail inbox.
• Web Filter	A *Web filter* restricts access to specified Web sites.
• Pop-up Blocker	A *pop-up blocker* stops advertisements from displaying on Web pages and disables pop-up windows.
File Compression	A *file compression utility* shrinks the size of a file(s), so the file takes up less storage space than the original file.
File Conversion	A *file conversion utility* transforms a file from one format to another, eliminating the need to reenter data in a new program.
CD/DVD Burning	A *CD/DVD burner* writes text, graphics, audio, and video files on a recordable or rewritable CD or DVD.
Personal Computer Maintenance	A *personal computer maintenance utility* identifies and fixes operating system problems, detects and repairs disk problems, and includes the capability of improving a computer's performance.

FIGURE 3-38 A summary of widely used stand-alone utility programs.

APPLICATION SOFTWARE ON THE WEB

As discussed earlier in this chapter, users can purchase application software from a software vendor, retail store, or Web-based business. Users typically install purchased application software on a computer before they run it. Installed software has two disadvantages: (1) it requires disk space on your computer, and (2) it can be costly to upgrade as vendors release new versions. As an alternative, some users opt to access Web applications.

A **Web application** is application software that exists on a Web site. Users access Web applications anywhere from any computer or device, as long as it has an Internet connection (read Looking Ahead 3-2 for a look at the next generation of Web access). Web applications usually store users' data and information on their servers. For this reason, users concerned with data security may shy away from this option.

Some Web sites provide free access to the application. For example, one site creates a map and driving directions when a user enters a starting and destination point (Figure 3-39). Other Web sites allow you to use the program free and pay a fee when a certain action occurs. For example, you can prepare your tax return free using TurboTax for the Web, but if you elect to print it or file it electronically, you pay a minimal fee.

LOOKING AHEAD 3-2

Driving Down the Web Highway

Analysts predict you will access the Internet from practically everywhere: home, office, airport, grocery store, and the local coffee shop. Why not from your car?

As it sits in your garage, your car's computer could connect to your home computer and then relay information about fluid levels and the amount of gas in the tank. It could notify you when the oil needs to be changed and when the tires should be rotated. You even could start the car remotely on chilly days by pressing a button on your notebook computer as you eat your breakfast cereal at the kitchen table.

Automobile manufacturers are touting their cyber cars of the future equipped with Internet access. They are planning in-dash screens with continuous information about traffic, weather forecasts, and restaurant guides. Their plans also call for having the Internet access disconnect when the vehicle is in motion so that drivers do not attempt to drive and surf the Web simultaneously. For more information, visit scsite.com/dc2006/ch3/looking and then click Cyber Cars.

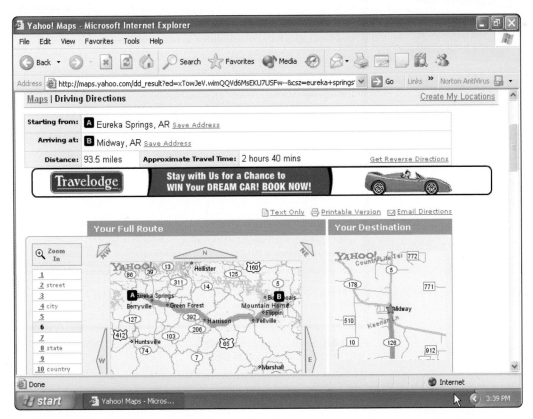

FIGURE 3-39 This Web site creates a map and provides directions when you enter a starting and destination point.

Application Service Providers

Storing and maintaining programs can be a costly investment for businesses. Thus, some have elected to outsource one or more facets of their information technology (IT) needs to an application service provider. An *application service provider* (*ASP*) is a third-party organization that manages and distributes software and services on the Web. That is, instead of installing the software on your computer, you run the programs from the Internet.

The five categories of ASPs are:

1. *Enterprise ASP*: customizes and delivers high-end business applications, such as finance and database
2. *Local/Regional ASP*: offers a variety of software applications to a specific geographic region
3. *Specialist ASP*: delivers applications to meet a specific business need, such as human resources or project management
4. *Vertical Market ASP*: provides applications for a particular industry, such as construction, health care, or retail
5. *Volume Business ASP*: supplies prepackaged applications, such as accounting, to businesses

A variety of payment schemes are available. Some rent use of the application on a monthly basis or charge based on the number of user accesses. Others charge a one-time fee.

LEARNING AIDS AND SUPPORT TOOLS FOR APPLICATION SOFTWARE

Learning how to use application software effectively involves time and practice. To assist in the learning process, many programs provide online Help, Web-based Help, wizards, and templates.

Online Help is the electronic equivalent of a user manual (Figure 3-40a). It usually is integrated in a program. In most programs, a function key or a button on the screen starts the Help feature. When using a program, you can use the Help feature to ask a question or access the Help topics in subject or alphabetical order.

Most online Help also links to Web sites that offer *Web-based Help*, which provides updates and more comprehensive resources to respond to technical issues about software (Figure 3-40b). Some Web sites contain chat rooms, in which a user can talk directly with a technical support

FIGURE 3-40a (online Help)

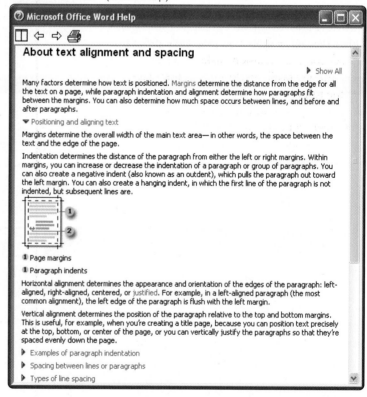

FIGURE 3-40 Many programs include online Help, Web-based Help, and templates. *(continued)*

FIGURE 3-40b   (Web-based Help)

FIGURE 3-40c   (template)

FIGURE 3-40   Many programs include online Help, Web-based Help, and templates. *(continued)*

person or join a conversation with other users who may be able to answer questions or solve problems.

A *wizard* is an automated assistant that helps a user complete a task by asking questions and then automatically performing actions based on the responses. A *template* is a document that contains the formatting necessary for a specific document type (Figure 3-40c). Many software applications include wizards and templates. For example, word processing software uses wizards for creating charts and documents and contains templates for memorandums, meeting agendas, fax cover sheets, flyers, letters, and resumes. Spreadsheet software includes wizards for creating charts and building functions and templates for invoices and purchase orders.

If you want to learn more about a particular program from a printed manual, many books are available to help you learn to use the features of personal computer programs. These books typically are available in bookstores and software stores (Figure 3-41).

Many colleges and schools provide training on several of the applications discussed in this chapter. For more information, contact your local school for a list of class offerings.

FIGURE 3-41
Bookstores often sell trade books to help you learn to use the features of personal computer application software.

Web-Based Training

Web-based training (*WBT*) is a type of CBT (computer-based training) that uses Internet technology and consists of application software on the Web. Similar to CBT, WBT typically consists of self-directed, self-paced instruction about a topic. WBT is popular in business, industry, and schools for teaching new skills or enhancing existing skills of employees, teachers, or students. When using a WBT product, students actively become involved in the learning process instead of remaining passive recipients of information.

Many Web sites offer WBT to the general public (Figure 3-42). Such training covers a wide range of topics, from how to change a flat tire to creating documents in Word. Many of these Web sites are free. Others require registration and payment to take the complete Web-based course.

WBT often is combined with other materials for distance learning courses. **Distance learning** (**DL**) is the delivery of education at one location while the learning takes place at other locations. DL courses provide time, distance, and place advantages for students who live far from a college campus or work full time. These courses enable students to attend class from anywhere in the world and at times that fit their schedules. Many national and international companies offer DL training. These training courses eliminate the costs of airfare, hotels, and meals for centralized training sessions.

WBT companies often specialize in providing instructors with the tools for preparation, distribution, and management of DL courses. These tools enable instructors to create rich, educational Web-based training sites and allow the students to interact with a powerful Web learning environment. Through the training site, students can check their progress, take practice tests, search for topics, send e-mail, and participate in discussions and chats.

WEB LINK 3-10

Web-Based Training

For more information, visit scsite.com/ dc2006/ch3/weblink and then click Web-Based Training.

FIGURE 3-42   At the HowStuffWorks Web-based training site, you can learn how computers, autos, electronics, and many other products work.

Test your knowledge of pages 155 through 166 in Quiz Yourself 3-3.

QUIZ YOURSELF 3-3

Instructions: Find the true statement below. Then, rewrite the remaining false statements so they are true.

1. An anti-spam program protects a computer against viruses by identifying and removing any computer viruses found in memory, on storage media, or in incoming files.

2. Computer-based training is a type of Web-based training that uses Internet technology and consists of application software on the Web.

3. E-mail and Web browsers are examples of communications software that are considered application software.

4. Legal software is a simplified accounting program that helps home users and small office/home office users balance their checkbooks, pay bills, track investments, and evaluate financial plans.

5. Personal DTP software is a popular type of image editing software that allows users to edit digital photographs.

Quiz Yourself Online: To further check your knowledge of types and features of home, personal, educational, and communications programs, stand-alone utility programs, Web applications, and software learning aids, visit scsite.com/dc2006/ch3/quiz and then click Objectives 6 – 10.

CHAPTER SUMMARY

This chapter illustrated how to start and use application software. It then presented an overview of a variety of business software, graphics and multimedia software, home/personal/educational software, and communications software (read At Issue 3-5 for a related discussion).

The chapter also described widely used stand-alone utility programs and identified various Web applications. Finally, learning aids and support tools for application software were presented.

AT ISSUE 3-5

Copying Software — A Computer Crime!

Usually, when you buy software, you legally can make one copy of the software for backup purposes. Despite the law, many people make multiple copies, either to share or to sell. In one survey, more than 50 percent of respondents admitted that they had illegally copied, or would illegally copy, software. Microsoft, a leading software manufacturer, estimates that almost 25 percent of software in the United States has been copied illegally. Among small businesses, the rate may be even higher. The Business Software Alliance, an industry trade association, believes that 40 percent of small U.S. businesses use illegally copied software. Illegally copied software costs the software industry more than $13 billion a year in lost revenues. People and companies copy software illegally for a variety of reasons, insisting that software prices are too high, software manufacturers make enough money, software often is copied for educational or other altruistic purposes, copied software makes people more productive, no restrictions should be placed on the use of software after it is purchased, and everyone copies software. What should be the penalty for copying software? Why? Can you counter the reasons people give for copying software illegally? How? Would you copy software illegally? Why or why not?

Help Desk Specialist

A Help Desk specialist position is an entryway into the information technology (IT) field. A *Help Desk specialist* deals with problems in hardware, software, or communications systems. Job requirements may include the following: solve procedural and software questions both in person and over the telephone, develop and maintain Help Desk operations manuals, and assist in training new Help Desk personnel

Usually, a Help Desk specialist must be knowledgeable about the major programs in use. Entry-level positions primarily involve answering calls from people with questions. Other positions provide additional assistance and assume further responsibilities, often demanding greater knowledge and problem-solving skills that can lead to more advanced IT positions. This job is ideal for people who must work irregular hours, because many companies need support people to work evenings, weekends, or part-time.

Educational requirements are less stringent than they are for other jobs in the computer field. In some cases, a high school diploma is sufficient. Advancement requires a minimum of a two-year degree, while management generally requires a bachelor's degree in IT or a related field. Certification is another way Help Desk specialists can increase their attractiveness in the marketplace. Entry-level salaries range from $27,500 to $56,500 per year. Managers range from $49,000 to $72,500. For more information, visit scsite.com/dc2006/ch3/careers and then click Help Desk Specialist.

High-Tech Talk

COMPUTER VIRUSES:
DELIVERY, INFECTION, AND AVOIDANCE

Sasser. Netsky. Lovgate. Nachi. Like the common cold, virtually countless variations of computer viruses exist. Unlike the biological viruses that cause the common cold, people create computer viruses. To create a virus, an unscrupulous programmer must code and then test the virus code to ensure the virus can replicate itself, conceal itself, monitor for certain events, and then deliver its *payload* — the destructive event or prank the virus was created to deliver. Despite the many variations of viruses, most have two phases to their execution: infection and delivery.

To start the infection phase, the virus must be activated. Today, the most common way viruses spread is by people running infected programs disguised as e-mail attachments. During the infection phase, viruses typically perform three actions:

1. First, a virus replicates by attaching itself to program files. A *macro virus* hides in the macro language of an application, such as Word. A *boot sector virus* targets the master boot record and executes when the computer boots up. A *file virus* attaches itself to program files. The file virus, Win32.Hatred, for example, replicates by first infecting Windows executable files for the Calculator, Notepad, Help, and other programs on the hard disk. The virus then scans the computer to locate .exe files on other drives and stores this information in the system registry. The next time an infected file is run, the virus reads the registry and continues infecting another drive.

2. Viruses also conceal themselves to avoid detection. A *stealth virus* disguises itself by hiding in fake code sections, which it inserts within working code in a file. A *polymorphic virus* actually changes its code as it infects computers. Win32.Hatred uses both concealment techniques. The virus writes itself to the last file section, while modifying the file header to hide the increased file size. It also scrambles and encrypts the virus code as it infects files.

3. Finally, viruses watch for a certain condition or event and activate when that condition or event occurs. The event might be booting up the computer or hitting a date on the system clock. A *logic bomb* activates when it detects a specific condition (say, a name deleted from the employee list). A *time bomb* is a logic bomb that activates on a particular date or time. Win32.Hatred, for instance, unleashes its destruction when the computer clock hits the seventh day of any month. If the triggering condition does not exist, the virus simply replicates.

During the delivery phase, the virus unleashes its payload, which might be a harmless prank that displays a silly message — or it might be destructive, corrupting or deleting data and files. When Win32.Hatred triggers, it displays the author's message and then covers the screen with black dots. The virus also deletes several antivirus files as it infects the system. The most dangerous viruses do not have an obvious payload, instead they quietly modify files. A virus, for example, could randomly change numbers in an inventory program or introduce delays to slow a computer.

Other kinds of electronic annoyances exist in addition to viruses. While often called viruses, worms and Trojan horse applications actually are part of a broader category called *malicious-logic programs*.

- A *worm*, such as the CodeRed or Sircam worm, resides in active memory and replicates itself over a network to infect machines, using up the system resources and possibly shutting the system down.

- A *Trojan horse* is a destructive program disguised as a real application, such as a screen saver. When a user runs a seemingly innocent program, a Trojan horse hiding inside can capture information, such as user names and passwords, from your system or open up a backdoor that allows a hacker remotely to control your computer. Unlike viruses, Trojan horses do not replicate themselves.

As with the common cold, every computer user is susceptible to a computer virus. In 1995, the chance that a virus would infect your computer was 1 in 1,000; by 2004, the odds were only 1 in 7. Even with better antivirus software, viruses are tough to avoid, as deceitful programmers craft new electronic maladies to infect your computer. Figure 3-43 lists steps you can follow to protect your computer from a virus infection. For more information, visit scsite.com/dc2006/ch3/tech and then click Computer Viruses.

STEPS TO VIRUS PROTECTION

1. Install the latest Windows updates.
2. Purchase a good antivirus program.
3. After installing an antivirus program, scan your entire computer to be sure your system is clean.
4. Update your antivirus definitions regularly.
5. Be suspicious of any and all unsolicited e-mail attachments.
6. Stay informed about viruses and virus hoaxes.
7. Install a personal firewall program.
8. Download software only if you are sure the Web site is legitimate.
9. Avoid as best you can visiting unscrupulous Web sites.

FIGURE 3-43   Guidelines to keep your computer virus free.

Companies on the Cutting Edge

ADOBE SYSTEMS
DIGITAL IMAGING LEADER

Practically every image seen on a computer and in print has been shaped by software developed by *Adobe Systems, Inc.* The company, based in San Jose, California, is one of the world's largest application software corporations and is committed to helping people communicate effectively.

Adobe Photoshop and Photoshop Album have set the industry standard for digital imaging and digital video software, while Creative Suite is used for design and publishing. The company's Portable Document Format (PDF) and Adobe Reader are used to share documents among users electronically. More than 600 million copies of the free Adobe Reader have been downloaded.

Fortune magazine named Adobe as the best high-tech company to work for in America in 2004. For more information, visit scsite.com/dc2006/ch3/companies and then click Adobe.

MICROSOFT
REALIZING POTENTIAL WITH BUSINESS SOFTWARE

Microsoft's mission is "to enable people and businesses throughout the world to realize their potential." As the largest software company in the world, *Microsoft* has indeed helped computer users in every field reach their goals.

When Microsoft was incorporated in 1975, the company had three programmers, one product, and revenues of $16,000. Thirty years later, the company employs more than 56,000 people, produces scores of software titles with Office and Windows leading the industry, and has annual revenue of more than $32 billion.

The company's recent efforts have focused on developing the next version of its operating system, which is named Longhorn, and the Smart Personal Objects Technology (SPOT), which brings computing power into everyday objects, such as wristwatches. For more information, visit scsite.com/dc2006/ch3/companies and then click Microsoft.

Technology Trailblazers

DAN BRICKLIN
VISICALC DEVELOPER

When *Dan Bricklin* was enrolled at the Harvard Business School in the 1970s, he often used his calculator to determine the effect of changing one value on a balance sheet. He recognized the need to develop a program that would perform a series of calculations automatically when the first number was entered.

He named his creation VisiCalc, short for Visible Calculator. He and a friend formed a company called Software Arts and programmed the VisiCalc prototype using Apple Basic on an Apple II computer. The small program was the first piece of application software that provided a reason for businesses to buy Apple computers. It laid the foundation for the development of other spreadsheets and included many of the features found in today's spreadsheet software.

His current venture is Trellix, which lets people turn everyday documents into Web pages with colors, graphics, and links. For more information, visit scsite.com/dc2006/ch3/people and then click Dan Bricklin.

MASAYOSHI SON
SOFTBANK PRESIDENT AND CEO

Many students carry photographs of family and friends in their wallets and book bags. As a 16-year-old student in the 1970s, *Masayoshi Son* carried a picture of a microchip. He predicted that the microchip was going to change people's lives, and he wanted to be part of that trend.

While majoring in economics at the University of California, Berkeley, he earned his first million dollars by importing arcade games from Japan to the campus, developing new computer games, and selling a patent for a multilingual pocket translator to Sharp Corporation.

At age 23 he founded Softbank, which is Japan's foremost software distributor and publisher and the country's largest broadband Internet service provider. Today, he is one of the world's wealthiest entrepreneurs. For more information, visit scsite.com/dc2006/ch3/people and then click Masayoshi Son.

Chapter Review

The Chapter Review section summarizes the concepts presented in this chapter. To listen to the audio version of this Chapter Review, visit scsite.com/dc2006/ch3/review. To obtain help from other students regarding any subject in this chapter, visit scsite.com/dc2006/ch3/forum and post your thoughts or questions.

(1) What Are the Categories of Application Software? **Application software** consists of programs designed to make users more productive and/or assist them with personal tasks. The major categories of application software are business software; graphics and multimedia software; home, personal, and educational software; and communications software.

(2) How Is Software Distributed? Application software is available in a variety of forms. **Packaged software** is mass-produced, copyrighted retail software that meets the needs of a variety of users. **Custom software** performs functions specific to a business or industry. **Open source software** is provided for use, modification, and redistribution. **Shareware** is copyrighted software that is distributed free for a trial period. **Freeware** is copyrighted software provided at no cost by an individual or a company that retains all rights to the software. **Public-domain software** is free software donated for public use and has no copyright restrictions.

(3) How Do You Work with Application Software? Personal computer operating systems often use the concept of a **desktop**, which is an on-screen work area that has a graphical user interface. To start an application in Windows XP, move the **pointer** to the Start **button** in the corner of the desktop and **click** the Start button by pressing and releasing a button on the mouse. Then, click the program name on the Start **menu** or on the *submenu* that displays when you point to a **command**. Once loaded into memory, the program is displayed in a **window** on the desktop.

> Visit scsite.com/dc2006/ch3/quiz or click the Quiz Yourself button. Click Objectives 1 – 3.

(4) What Are the Key Features of Widely Used Business Programs? **Business software** assists people in becoming more effective and efficient while performing daily business activities. Business software includes the following programs. **Word processing software** allows users to **create** a document by entering text and inserting graphical images, **edit** the document by making changes, and **format** the document by altering its appearance. **Spreadsheet software** allows users to organize data in rows and columns, perform calculations, recalculate when data changes, and chart the data. **Database software** allows users to create a **database**, which is a collection of data organized to allow access, retrieval, and use of that data. **Presentation graphics software** allows users to create a *slide show* that is displayed on a monitor or projection screen. **Note taking software** enables users to enter typed text, handwritten comments, drawings, or sketches on a page and then save the page as part of a notebook. A **personal information manager (PIM)** is software that includes features to help users organize personal information. A **software suite** is a collection of individual programs sold as a single package. **Project management software** allows users to plan, schedule, track, and analyze a project. **Accounting software** helps companies record and report their financial transactions.

(5) What Are the Key Features of Widely Used Graphics and Multimedia Programs? Graphics and multimedia software includes the following programs. **Computer-aided design (CAD) software** assists in creating engineering, architectural, and scientific designs. **Desktop publishing (DTP) software** enables professional designers to create sophisticated documents that contain text, graphics, and colors. **Paint software** lets users draw graphical images with various on-screen tools. **Image editing software** provides the capabilities of paint software and includes the capability to modify existing images. **Video editing software** allows professionals to modify segments of a video.

> Visit scsite.com/dc2006/ch3/quiz or click the Quiz Yourself button. Click Objectives 4 – 5.

Chapter Review

Audio editing software lets users modify audio clips and produce studio-quality soundtracks. **Multimedia authoring software** allows users to combine text, graphics, audio, video, and animation into an interactive application. **Web page authoring software** helps users create Web pages that include graphical images, video, audio, animation, and other special effects.

(6) What Are the Key Features of Widely Used Home, Personal, and Educational Programs?
Software for home, personal, and educational use includes the following applications. A software suite (for personal use) combines application software such as word processing, spreadsheet, and database into a single package. **Personal finance software** is an accounting program that helps users balance their checkbooks, pay bills, track income and expenses, track investments, and evaluate financial plans. **Legal software** assists in the preparation of legal documents. **Tax preparation software** guides users through filing federal taxes. **Personal DTP software** helps users create newsletters, brochures, advertisements, greeting and business cards, logos, and Web pages. **Personal paint/image editing software** provides an easy-to-use interface with functions tailored to meet the needs of home and small business users. **Photo editing software** is a type of image editing software used to edit digital photographs. Application software often includes a **clip art/image gallery**, which is a collection of clip art and photographs. **Home design/landscaping software** assists with the design, remodeling, or improvement of a home or landscape. **Educational software** teaches a particular skill. **Reference software** provides valuable and thorough information for all individuals. **Entertainment software** includes interactive games, videos, and other programs to support hobbies or provide amusement.

(7) What Are the Types of Application Software Used in Communications? Application software for communications includes e-mail programs to transmit messages via a network; FTP programs to upload and download files on the Internet; Web browsers to access and view Web pages; video conferencing/telephone call software for meetings or conversations on a network; newsreader/message board programs that allow online written discussions; chat room software to have real-time, online typed conversations; and instant messaging software for real-time exchange of messages or files.

(8) What Are the Functions of Stand-Alone Utility Programs? Stand-alone utility programs support the successful use of application software. An *antivirus program* protects a computer against a computer *virus*, which is a potentially damaging computer program. A *spyware remover* detects and deletes spyware. An *anti-spam program* removes spam (Internet junk-mail). A *Web filter* restricts access to specified Web sites. A *pop-up blocker* disables pop-up windows. A *file compression utility* shrinks the size of a file. A *file conversion utility* transforms a file from one format to another. A *CD/DVD burner* writes files to a recordable CD or DVD. A *personal computer maintenance utility* fixes operating system and disk problems.

(9) What Are the Advantages of Using Application Software on the Web? A **Web application** is application software that exists on a Web site. Web applications require less disk space on a computer than installed software and are less costly to upgrade. An *application service provider (ASP)* is a third-party organization that manages and distributes software and services on the Web.

(10) What Learning Aids Are Available for Application Software? To assist in the learning process, many programs offer Help features. **Online Help** is the electronic equivalent of a user manual. Most online Help links to *Web-based help*, which provides updates and more comprehensive resources. A *wizard* is an automated assistant that helps users complete a task by asking questions and then performing actions based on the responses. A *template* is a document that contains the formatting necessary for a specific document type.

connect
Visit scsite.com/dc2006/ch3/quiz or click the Quiz Yourself button. Click Objectives 6 – 10.

Discovering Computers 2006
A Gateway to Information

3   Application Software

Quizzes and Learning Games

Computer Genius
Crossword Puzzle
DC Track and Field
Practice Test
Quiz Yourself
Wheel of Terms
You're Hired!

Exercises

Case Studies
Chapter Review
Checkpoint
▶ Key Terms
Learn How To
Learn It Online
Web Research

Beyond the Book

Career Corner
Companies
FAQs
High-Tech Talk
Looking Ahead
Making Use of the Web
Trailblazers
Web Links

Features

Chapter Forum
Install Computer
Lab Exercises
Maintain Computer
Tech News
Timeline 2006

Key Terms

You should know the Primary Terms and be familiar with the Secondary Terms. Use the list below to help focus your study. To further enhance your understanding of the Key Terms in this chapter, visit scsite.com/dc2006/ch3/terms. See an example of and a definition for each term, and access current and additional information about the term from the Web.

Primary Terms

(shown in bold-black characters in the chapter)

accounting software (149)
application software (134)
audio editing software (153)
business software (138)
button (136)
click (136)
clip art (139)
clip art/image gallery (159)
command (137)
computer-aided design (CAD) software (150)
computer-based training (CBT) (160)
create (141)
custom software (135)
database (145)
database software (145)
desktop (136)
desktop publishing (DTP) software (152)
distance learning (DL) (166)
edit (141)
educational software (160)
entertainment software (160)
font (141)
font size (141)
format (141)
freeware (135)
home design/ landscaping software (160)
icon (136)
image editing software (152)
legal software (157)
menu (137)
multimedia authoring software (154)

note taking software (147)
online banking (156)
online Help (164)
open source software (135)
packaged software (134)
paint software (152)
personal DTP software (158)
personal finance software (156)
personal information manager (PIM) (148)
personal paint/image editing software (158)
photo editing software (159)
pointer (136)
presentation graphics software (146)
print (142)
project management software (149)
public-domain software (135)
reference software (160)
save (142)
shareware (135)
software suite (148)
spreadsheet software (142)
tax preparation software (157)
title bar (137)
video editing software (153)
Web application (163)
Web page authoring software (154)
Web-based training (166)
window (137)
word processing software (138)

Secondary Terms

(shown in italic characters in the chapter)

application service provider (ASP) (164)
anti-spam program (162)
antivirus program (162)
bar chart (144)
CD/DVD burner (162)
cell (143)
charting (144)
clipboard (141)
color library (152)
column chart (144)
dialog box (137)
Enterprise ASP (164)
field (145)
file (137)
file compression utility (162)
file conversion utility (162)
file name (137)
filters (153)
font style (141)
footer (140)
formula (143)
function (143)
header (140)
illustration software (152)
import (146)
label (143)
line chart (144)
loaded (135)
local/regional ASP (164)
margins (139)
page layout (152)
pasting (141)
personal computer maintenance utility (162)

pie chart (144)
point (141)
pop-up blocker (162)
product activation (135)
query (145)
record (145)
replace (139)
sans serif font (141)
scrolling (139)
search (139)
serif font (141)
slide show (146)
slide sorter view (146)
specialist ASP (164)
spelling checker (139)
spyware remover (162)
submenu (137)
system software (135)
template (165)
value (143)
vertical market ASP (164)
virus (162)
volume business ASP (164)
WBT (166)
Web-based Help (164)
Web filter (162)
what-if analysis (144)
wizard (165)
word processor (138)
wordwrap (139)
worksheet (142)

Checkpoint

Use the Checkpoint exercises to check your knowledge level of the chapter. The Beyond the Book exercises will help broaden your understanding of the concepts presented in this chapter. To complete the Checkpoint exercises interactively, visit scsite.com/dc2006/ch3/check.

Label the Figure

Identify these elements in the Windows XP graphical user interface.

a. Accessories command
b. Accessories submenu
c. All Programs command
d. All Programs submenu
e. Start button
f. Start menu
g. Paint command

True/False

Mark T for True and F for False. (See page numbers in parentheses.)

_____   1. The four categories of application software are mutually exclusive. (134)

_____   2. Programmers typically can incorporate freeware in applications they intend to sell. (135)

_____   3. To click a button on the screen requires moving the pointer away from the button and then pressing and holding down a button on the mouse (usually the right mouse button). (136)

_____   4. The wordwrap feature allows users of word processing software to type words in a paragraph continually without pressing the ENTER key. (139)

_____   5. In many spreadsheet programs, you begin a formula with an equal sign, a plus sign, or a minus sign. (143)

_____   6. Many graphics and multimedia programs have user-friendly interfaces and scaled-down versions, making it possible for the home and small business user to create documents using these programs. (150)

_____   7. Most of the programs for home, personal, and educational use are priced at more than $100. (155)

_____   8. Personal DTP programs never include paint/image editing software or photo editing software. (158)

_____   9. Some communications software is considered system software because it works with hardware and transmission media. (161)

_____ 10. Utility programs are considered application software because they make users more productive or assist with personal tasks. (162)

_____ 11. Web applications store users' data and information on their servers, so users concerned with data security may shy away from this option. (163)

_____ 12. Few software applications include wizards or templates. (164)

Checkpoint

 Multiple Choice   Select the best answer. (See page numbers in parentheses.)

1. Presentation graphics software, project management software, accounting software, and enterprise computing software are examples of _____ software. (134)
   a. business
   b. graphics and multimedia
   c. communications
   d. home/personal/educational

2. _____ has no restrictions from the copyright holder regarding modification of the software's internal instructions and redistribution of the software. (135)
   a. Packaged software
   b. Custom software
   c. Open source software
   d. Shareware

3. In a document window, the _____ usually displays a document's file name. (137)
   a. status bar   b. submenu
   c. title bar   d. dialog box

4. In word processing, pasting is the process of _____. (141)
   a. moving different portions of the document on the screen into view
   b. transferring an item from the clipboard to a specific location in a document
   c. locating all occurrences of a certain character, word, or phrase
   d. removing a portion of a document and storing it in a temporary storage location

5. Most spreadsheet software includes a what-if analysis feature, where you _____. (144)
   a. depict the data in a spreadsheet in graphical form
   b. enter labels to identify worksheet data and organize the worksheet
   c. review the spelling of individual words and sections of a worksheet
   d. change values in a spreadsheet to identify the effects of those changes

6. With database software, users can run a _____, which is a request for specific data from the database. (145)
   a. query   b. function
   c. record   d. field

7. Users find _____ software convenient during meetings, class lectures, and other settings that previously required a pencil and paper for recording thoughts and discussions. (147)
   a. word processing   b. database
   c. note taking   d. accounting

8. DTP software supports page layout, which is the process of _____. (152)
   a. creating engineering, architectural, and scientific designs
   b. arranging text and graphics in a document on a page-by-page basis
   c. enhancing and modifying existing images and pictures
   d. standardizing the colors on a page used by designers and printers

9. _____ helps home users determine where, and for what purpose, they are spending money. (156)
   a. Legal software
   b. Personal DTP software
   c. Tax preparation software
   d. Personal finance software

10. Many educational programs use a _____ approach, in which students learn by using and completing exercises with instructional software. (160)
    a. computer-aided design (CAD)
    b. desktop teaching program (DTP)
    c. computer-based training (CBT)
    d. personal information manager (PIM)

11. A(n) _____, which can be used to upload and download files with other computers and on the Internet, is integrated in some operating systems. (161)
    a. FTP program   b. Web browser
    c. e-mail program   d. chat client

12. A(n) _____ is a stand-alone utility program that attempts to remove Internet junk mail before it reaches your e-mail inbox. (162)
    a. anti-spam program b. Web filter
    c. spyware remover   d. antivirus program

13. Vertical market ASP _____. (164)
    a. supplies packaged applications
    b. provides applications for a particular industry
    c. customizes and delivers high-end business applications
    d. offers a variety of software applications to specific regions

14. _____ is the delivery of education at one location while the learning takes place at other locations. (166)
    a. Online Help (OH)
    b. Software wizards (SW)
    c. Online banking (OB)
    d. Distance learning (DL)

Checkpoint

Matching

Match the terms with their definitions. (See page numbers in parentheses.)

_____ 1. icon (136)

_____ 2. button (136)

_____ 3. menu (137)

_____ 4. clip art (139)

_____ 5. cell (143)

_____ 6. slide sorter view (146)

_____ 7. color library (152)

_____ 8. online banking (156)

_____ 9. volume business ASP (164)

_____ 10. wizard (165)

a. list of commands from which you make a selection

b. small symbol on the screen that moves as you move the mouse

c. intersection of a row and column in a spreadsheet

d. small image that represents a program, document, or some other object

e. offers access to account balances and provides bill paying services

f. automated assistant that helps users complete a task

g. standard set of colors used by designers and printers

h. text that appears at the bottom of every page

i. graphical image activated to cause a specific action to take place

j. screen view similar to how 35mm slides look on a light table

k. provides prepackaged applications, such as accounting, to businesses

l. collection of drawings, diagrams, maps, and photographs that can be inserted

Short Answer

Write a brief answer to each of the following questions.

1. When using spreadsheet software, what is charting? _____ How are line charts, column charts, and pie charts different? _____

2. What is a software suite? _____ What are the major advantages of using a software suite? _____

3. Why do professional designers use DTP software instead of word processing programs? _____ What is a color library? _____

4. What are disadvantages of installed software? _____ How can you access a Web application? _____

5. In most programs, how do you start the online Help feature? _____ How is a wizard different from a template? _____

Beyond the Book

Read the following book elements, learn more about each using the Web, and then write a brief report.

1. At Issue — How Should Schools Deal with Internet Plagiarism? (141), Altering Digital Photographs — Art or Fraud? (153), What Should Be Done to Prevent Music or Video File Sharing? (153), or Should Companies Monitor Employees' E-Mail and Web Browsing? (161), or Copying Software — A Computer Crime! (167)

2. Career Corner — Help Desk Specialist (167)

3. Companies on the Cutting Edge — Adobe Systems or Microsoft (169)

4. FAQs (137, 142, 145, 148, 152, 154, 157, 158, 162)

5. High-Tech Talk — Computer Viruses: Delivery, Infection, and Avoidance (168)

6. Looking Ahead — User Interfaces of the Future (137) or Driving Down the Web Highway (163)

7. Making Use of the Web — Finance (119)

8. Picture Yourself Using Software (132)

9. Technology Trailblazers — Dan Bricklin or Masayoshi Son (169)

10. Web Links (140, 144, 146, 148, 156, 158, 159, 160, 162, 166)

Learn It Online

Use the Learn It Online exercises to reinforce your understanding of the chapter concepts. To access the Learn It Online exercises, visit scsite.com/dc2006/ch3/learn.

(1) At the Movies — Detect Spyware on Your Computer

To view the Detect Spyware on Your Computer movie, click the number 1 button. Locate your video and click the corresponding High-Speed or Dial-Up link, depending on your Internet connection. Watch the movie and then complete the exercise by answering the question that follows. Many of the programs installed on your computer also installed spyware along with the program you loaded. Several different types of spyware exist, two of which are keystroke recorders and advertising spyware. Spyware either collects information and sends it over the Internet to whoever installed it or stores it for later retrieval. Why might you want to detect and delete a keystroke recorder from your computer?

(2) At the Movies — History of Adobe

To view the History of Adobe movie, click the number 2 button. Locate your video and click the corresponding High-Speed or Dial-Up link, depending on your Internet connection. Watch the movie and then complete the exercise by answering the question that follows. At the dawn of the computer age, computers were used mostly by scientists, and printers were large, cumbersome machines. The advent of desktop publishing gave average people access to the power of computing. Users finally were able to publish documents and images easily, and the computer became a tool for creative expression for everyone. Compare how you complete your homework assignments now to how homework was

done in the 1950s. How has desktop publishing changed the way students research and write reports?

(3) Student Edition Labs — Word Processing

Click the number 3 button. When the Student Edition Labs menu appears, click *Word Processing* to begin. A new browser window will open. Follow the on-screen instructions to complete the Lab. When finished, click the Exit button. If required, submit your results to your instructor.

(4) Student Edition Labs — Spreadsheets

Click the number 4 button. When the Student Edition Labs menu appears, click *Spreadsheets* to begin. A new browser window will open. Follow the on-screen instructions to complete the Lab. When finished, click the Exit button. If required, submit your results to your instructor.

(5) Student Edition Labs — Databases

Click the number 5 button. When the Student Edition Labs menu appears, click *Databases* to begin. A new browser window will open. Follow the on-screen instructions to complete the Lab. When finished, click the Exit button. If required, submit your results to your instructor.

(6) Student Edition Labs — Presentation Software

Click the number 6 button. When the Student Edition Labs menu appears, click *Presentation Software* to begin. A new browser window will open. Follow the on-screen instructions to complete the Lab. When finished, click the Exit button. If required, submit your results to your instructor.

(7) Practice Test

Click the number 7 button. Answer each question. When completed, enter your name and click the Grade Test button to submit the

Learn It Online

quiz for grading. Make a note of any missed questions. If required, submit your score to your instructor.

⑧ Who Wants To Be a Computer Genius²?

Click the number 8 button to find out if you are a computer genius. Directions about how to play the game will be displayed. When you are ready to play, click the Play button. Submit your score to your instructor.

⑨ Wheel of Terms

Click the number 9 button to reinforce important terms you learned in this chapter by playing the Shelly Cashman Series version of this popular game. Directions about how to play the game will be displayed. When you are ready to play, click the Play button. Submit your score to your instructor.

⑩ DC Track and Field

Click the number 10 button to use what you have learned in this chapter to compete against other students in three track and field events. Directions about how to play the game will be displayed. When you are ready to play, click the start first event button. If required, submit your score to your instructor.

⑪ You're Hired!

Click the number 11 button to use what you have learned in this chapter to embark on the path to a career in computers. Directions about how to play the game will be displayed. When you are ready to play, click the begin game button. If required, submit your score to your instructor.

⑫ Crossword Puzzle Challenge

Click the number 12 button. Complete the puzzle to reinforce skills you learned in this chapter. Directions about how to play the game will be displayed. When you are ready to play, click the Play button. Submit the completed puzzle to your instructor.

⑬ Lab Exercises

Click the number 13 button. When the Lab Exercises menu appears, click the exercise assigned by your instructor. A new browser window will open. Follow the on-screen instructions to complete the exercise. When finished, click the Exit button. If required, submit your results to your instructor.

⑭ In the News

It is a computer user's worst fear — he or she opens an unfamiliar e-mail message or uses a disk of unknown origin and a computer virus is released that damages and/or deletes files. Fortunately, specialized software prevents such things from happening to your computer. Click the number 14 button and read a news article about antivirus programs. Which program does the article recommend? What does it do? Who will benefit from using this software? Why? Where can the software be obtained? Would you be interested in this software? Why or why not?

⑮ Chapter Discussion Forum

Select an objective from this chapter on page 133 about which you would like more information. Click the number 15 button and post a short message listing a meaningful message title accompanied by one or more questions concerning the selected objective. In two days, return to the threaded discussion by clicking the number 15 button. Submit to your instructor your original message and at least one response to your message.

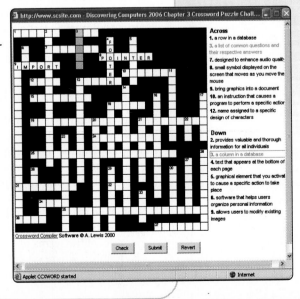

Learn How To

Use the Learn How To activities to learn fundamental skills when using a computer and accompanying technology. Complete the exercises and submit them to your instructor. Visit scsite.com/dc2006/ch3/howto to obtain more information pertaining to each activity.

LEARN HOW TO 1: Save a File in Application Software

When you use application software, usually you either will create a new file or modify an existing file. If you turn off your computer or lose electrical power while working on the file, the file will not be retained. In order to retain the file, you must save it.

To save a new file, you must complete several tasks:
1. Initiate an action indicating you want to save the file, such as clicking the Save button.
2. Designate where the file should be stored. This includes identifying both the device (such as drive C) and the folder (such as My Documents).
3. Specify the name of the file.
4. Click the Save button to save the file.

Tasks 2 through 4 normally can be completed using a dialog box such as shown in Figure 3-44.

If you close a program prior to saving a new or modified file, the program will display a dialog box asking if you want to save the file. If you click the Yes button, a modified file will be saved using the same file name in the same location. Saving a new file requires that you complete tasks 2 through 4.

Exercise
1. Start the <u>WordPad program</u> from the Accessories submenu on the All Programs submenu.
2. Type `Saving a file is the best insurance against losing work.`
3. Click the Save button on the WordPad toolbar. What dialog box is displayed? Where will the file be saved? What is the default file name? If you wanted to save the file on the desktop, what would you do? Click the Cancel button in the dialog box. Submit your answers to your instructor.
4. Click the Close button in the WordPad window. What happened? Click the Yes button in the WordPad dialog box. What happened? Place either a floppy disk in drive A or a USB drive in a USB port. Select either the floppy disk or the USB drive as the location for saving the file. Name the file, Chapter 3 How To 1. Save the file. What happened? Submit your answers to your instructor.

FIGURE 3-44

LEARN HOW TO 2: Install and Uninstall Application Software

When you purchase application software, you must install the software on the computer where you want to run it. The exact installation process varies with each program, but generally you must complete the following steps:
1. Insert the CD-ROM containing the application software into a drive.
2. The opening window will appear. If the CD-ROM contains more than one program, choose the program you want to install. Click the Continue or Next button.
3. Some file extractions will occur and then an Install Wizard will begin. You normally must accomplish the following steps by completing the directions within the wizard:
   a. Accept the terms of the license agreement.
   b. Identify where on your computer the software will be stored. The software usually selects a default location on drive C, and you normally will accept the default location.

Learn How To

c. Select any default options for the software.

d. Click a button to install the software.

4. A Welcome/Help screen often will be displayed. Click a button to finish the installation process.

At some point, you may want to remove software. Most software includes uninstall programming that will remove the program and all its software components. To uninstall a program, complete the following steps:

1. Click the Start button on the Windows taskbar.
2. Click Control Panel on the Start menu.
3. Click or double-click **Add or Remove Programs**. *The Add or Remove Programs window will open (Figure 3-45).*
4. Select the program you wish to remove. *In Figure 3-45, Macromedia Dreamweaver is selected as the program to remove.*
5. Click the Change/Remove button.
6. A dialog box will be displayed informing you that the software is being prepared for uninstall. You then will be informed that the process you are following will remove the program. You will be asked if you want to continue. To uninstall the program, click the Yes button.

The program will be removed from the computer.

FIGURE 3-45

Exercise

1. Optional: Insert the CD-ROM containing the software you want to install into a drive and follow the instructions for installing the software. **Warning: If you are using a computer other than your own, particularly in a school laboratory, do not perform this exercise unless you have specific permission from your instructor.**
2. Optional: Follow the steps above to uninstall software you want to remove. Be aware that if you uninstall software, the software will not be available for use until you reinstall it. **Warning: If you are using a computer other than your own, particularly in a school laboratory, do not perform this exercise unless you have specific permission from your instructor.**

LEARN HOW TO 3: Check Application Software Version

Most application software will be modified from time to time by its developer. Each time the software is changed, it acquires a **new version number** and sometimes an entirely new name. To determine what version of software you have, perform the following steps:

1. Start the application program.
2. Click Help on the menu bar and then click About on the Help menu (the program name often follows the word, About). *The program displays the About window (Figure 3-46).*
3. To close the About window, click the OK button.

Depending on the software, in the About window you also might be able to determine further information.

FIGURE 3-46

Exercise

1. Start your Web browser and display the About window for the browser. What is the name of the browser? What version of the browser are you using? What is the product ID? What does the copyright notice say? Submit your answers to your instructor.
2. Start any other application software. Display the About window. What is the name of the program? What is the version number? What information do you find that you did not see in Exercise 1? Which window do you find more useful? Why? Submit your answers to your instructor.

Web Research

Use the Internet-based Web Research exercises to broaden your understanding of the concepts presented in this chapter. Visit scsite.com/dc2006/ch3/research to obtain more information pertaining to each exercise. To discuss any of the Web Research exercises in this chapter with other students, post your thoughts or questions at scsite.com/dc2006/ch3/forum.

① Scavenger Hunt Use one of the <u>search engines</u> listed in Figure 2-10 in Chapter 2 on page 78 or your own favorite search engine to find the answers to the questions below. Copy and paste the Web address from the Web page where you found the answer. Some questions may have more than one answer. If required, submit your answers to your instructor. (1) What is the name of the curves Adobe Systems used to define shapes in its PostScript programming language? (2) Microsoft developed what popular entertainment software in 1983 in cooperation with Bruce Artwick of SubLogic? (3) What application software company did Microsoft acquire in 1987 that developed and marketed PowerPoint? (4) What is the name of the first successful spreadsheet program?

② Search Sleuth A <u>virus</u> is a potentially damaging computer program that can harm files and the operating system. The National Institute of Standards and Technology Computer Security Resource Center (csrc.nist.gov/virus/) is one of the more comprehensive Web sites discussing viruses. Visit this Web site and then use your word processing program to answer the following questions. Then, if required, submit your answers to your instructor. (1) The Virus Information page provides general information about viruses and links to various resources that provide more specific details. What two steps does the National Institute recommend to detect and prevent viruses from spreading? (2) Click the Symantec link in the Virus Resources & Other Areas of Interest section. What viruses are the latest threats, and when were they discovered? (3) Click Search at the top of the page and then type "Sasser worm" as the keyword in the Search text box. How many articles discuss the Sasser worm on the Symantec Web site? What three functions does the Sasser Removal Tool perform? (4) Click one of the Latest News links and review the material. Review the information you read and then write a 50-word summary.

③ Journaling Respond to your readings in this chapter by writing at least one page about your reactions, evaluations, and reflections about the first time you used <u>word processing software</u>. For example, what word processing software did you use? What was the first document you created? Have your instructors required you to use word processing software for class projects? How did you edit and format your document? Did you back up your file? You also can write about the new terms you learned by reading this chapter. If required, submit your journal to your instructor.

④ Expanding Your Understanding Microsoft seeks to help customers use its products by maintaining the <u>Microsoft Help and Support</u> Web site (support.microsoft.com). This Web site has a link to the Knowledge Base, which contains more than 250,000 articles written by Microsoft employees who support the company's products. Also included are software downloads and updates, public newsgroups, methods of getting online or telephone assistance, and the Security Support Center. View this site and then search the Knowledge Base for information on Microsoft Word. Also view the common issues, updates, security issues, and visitors' top links listed on the Web site. Write a report summarizing your findings. If required, submit your report to your instructor.

⑤ Ethics in Action A hacker is someone who tries to access a computer or network illegally. Although the activity sometimes is a harmless prank, it sometimes causes extensive damage. Some hackers say their activities give them a sense of excitement and test their skills. Others say their activities are a form of civil disobedience that allows them to challenge authority and force companies to make their products more secure. View online sites such as <u>Hackers: Outlaws & Angels</u> (tlc.discovery.com/convergence/hackers/hackers.html) that provide information about whether hackers provide some benefit to the Internet society. Write a report summarizing your findings and include a table of links to Web sites that provide additional details. If required, submit your report to your instructor.

Case Studies

Use the Case Studies to apply the concepts presented in the chapter to real-world situations. Visit scsite.com/dc2006/ch3/cases to obtain more information pertaining to each exercise. To discuss the Case Studies in this chapter with other students, visit scsite.com/dc2006/ch3/forum and post your thoughts or questions.

CASE STUDY 1 – Class Discussion   The owner of Mel's Hair Salon for Men and Women has decided to obtain a personal desktop computer for use in his business. In addition to using the computer for writing letters, developing advertising pieces, performing basic accounting, and maintaining lists of customers, the owner would like his employees to use a <u>digital camera</u> to take pictures of customers after they have had their hair done and create a file of printed full-color pictures of customers for marketing purposes. The owner has asked you to recommend the type of camera, software, and computer he should buy. Prepare a brief report detailing your findings and recommendations. Be prepared to discuss your recommendations in class.

CASE STUDY 2 – Class Discussion   Your manager at Jane's Discount Furniture Warehouse intends to choose a word processing program that the entire company will use. She prefers to learn about software using trade books — written texts that explain the features of a program and how to use it — rather than using online Help or tutorials. She has asked you to evaluate the <u>word processing</u> trade books available in bookstores on the Web. Visit a bookstore Web site and other Web sites that sell books to survey the word processing trade books available for Microsoft Word, StarOffice Writer, DisplayWrite, and WordPerfect. Which word processing program has the most books available? How difficult would it be to learn each program using the trade books at hand? Which trade book do you think is the best? Why? If you were going to purchase software solely on the basis of the related trade books, which program would you buy? Why? Be prepared to discuss your recommendations in class.

CASE STUDY 3 – Research   After attending a seminar on Web applications, the chief financial officer of Eastern Steel, Inc. has asked you to investigate the feasibility of using the Web to collect data from company offices and customers throughout the world. Recall that a <u>Web application</u> is application software that exists on a Web site. Users access the Web application through their browser. Use the Web and/or print media to create a brief report describing at least two Web applications and how Eastern Steel could use similar applications effectively. Include in your report a description of each application, a short overview of any online Help, and the Web address for each application. Write a brief report and share your findings with your class.

CASE STUDY 4 – Research   Frank's Custom Design frequently enhances its work with scanned photographs or graphics obtained with <u>illustration software</u>. The owner recently read that the Internet is providing a new resource for desktop publishers. Companies such as Corbis, Picture Network International, Muse, and Liaison International are offering archives of artwork and photographs. You have been asked to investigate the feasibility of using this new resource. Information about all four companies can be found on the World Wide Web. Pick two companies that provide digital images and find out more about their product. Prepare a brief report that answers the following questions. What kinds of illustrations are available? How are pictures on a specific subject located? How are the illustrations provided? What fees are involved? Would the cost be different for a high school student creating one paper than for an organization newsletter with a state-wide distribution? Which company do you prefer? Why?

CASE STUDY 5 – Team Challenge   The new superintendent of Lisle Elementary School District 205 has recommended that <u>educational software</u> play a major role in the learning process at every grade level. In her presentation to the school board, she claimed that educational software is available for a wide variety of skills and subjects. She also indicated that educational software lets students learn at their own pace, shows infinite patience, and usually offers an entertaining approach. The president of the school board is not so sure. Unlike human instructors, educational software often does not recognize unique problems, fails to address individual goals, and provides limited feedback. Form a three-member team and investigate the use of educational software. Have each member of your team visit a software vendor's Web site, or an educational cooperative's Web site and list the advantages and disadvantages of using educational software. Select a program on the Web or from your school's education department library and use it. Note the subject being taught, the audience to which the software is directed, the approach used, and any special features. Then, meet with your team, discuss your findings, prepare a team report or PowerPoint presentation, and share it with your class.

CHAPTER FOUR

The Components of the System Unit

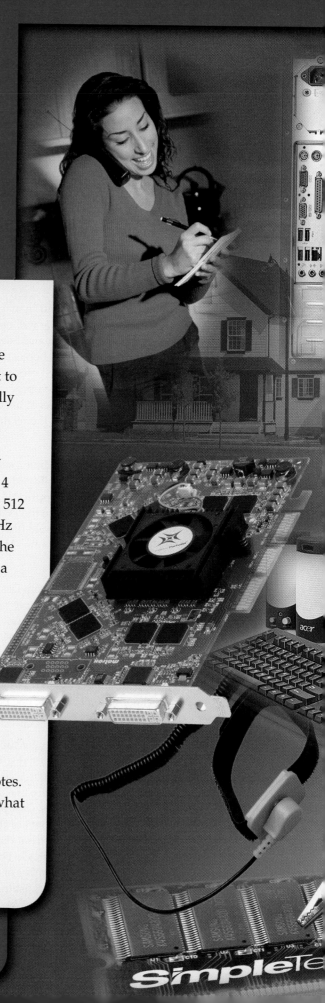

Picture Yourself Buying a Computer

Your neighbor, who is a computer guru and always has the latest computers and devices, just called to see if you want to buy one of his *old* computers. What he considers old actually still is state of the art. He says it would include the system unit, monitor, speakers, keyboard, and mouse.

He starts rattling off all the features while you frantically make quick notes. The system unit has a 3.0 GHz Pentium 4 processor with HT Technology and 256 KB L2 cache. It has 512 MB of dual channel SDRAM expandable to 2 GB, a 533 MHz bus, and integrated modem and networking capabilities. The back of the system unit has ports for a keyboard, a mouse, a monitor, speakers, a network, and a modem. It also has a serial port, a parallel port, six USB ports (two in front and four in back), and a FireWire port. It is not Bluetooth-enabled, but you can buy a wireless port adapter if you need that capability. He says he will set up the computer for you, clean it for you once a year, and be available for personal support anytime. "Five hundred bucks," he says, "and it's yours." Sold!

After hanging up the telephone, you glance at all your notes. You know he gave you a great deal, but you have no idea what all these terms and numbers mean. To find out, you plan to read Chapter 4 to learn about processor chips, RAM, cache, adapter cards, and ports, and discover the many other components of the system unit.

CONTENTS

THE SYSTEM UNIT

Whether you are a home user or a business user, you most likely will make the decision to purchase a new computer or upgrade an existing computer within the next several years. Thus, you should understand the purpose of each component in a computer. As Chapter 1 discussed, a computer includes devices used for input, processing, output, storage, and communications. Many of these components are part of the system unit.

The **system unit** is a case that contains electronic components of the computer used to process data. System units are available in a variety of shapes and sizes. The case of the system unit, sometimes called the *chassis*, is made of metal or plastic and protects the internal electronic components from damage. All computers have a system unit (Figure 4-1).

On desktop personal computers, the electronic components and most storage devices are part of the system unit. Other devices, such as the keyboard, mouse, microphone, monitor, printer, scanner, PC video camera, and speakers, normally occupy space outside the system unit. The trend is toward a smaller form factor, or size and shape, of the desktop personal computer system unit.

FIGURE 4-1 All sizes of computers have a system unit.

On notebook computers, the keyboard and pointing device often occupy the area on the top of the system unit, and the display attaches to the system unit by hinges. The location of the system unit on a Tablet PC varies, depending on the design of the Tablet PC. Some models position the system unit below the keyboard, while others build the system unit behind the display. The system unit on a PDA and smart phone usually consumes the entire device. On these mobile devices, the display often is built into the system unit.

At some point, you might have to open the system unit on a desktop personal computer to replace or install a new electronic component. For this reason, you should be familiar with the electronic components of a system unit. Figure 4-2 identifies some of these components, which include the processor, memory, adapter cards, ports, drive bays, and the power supply.

The processor interprets and carries out the basic instructions that operate a computer. Memory typically holds data waiting to be processed and instructions waiting to be executed. The electronic components and circuitry of the system unit, such as the processor and memory, usually are part of or are connected to a circuit board called the motherboard. Many current motherboards also integrate modem and networking capabilities.

FIGURE 4-2 The system unit on a typical personal computer consists of numerous electronic components, some of which are shown in this figure. The sound card and video card are two types of adapter cards.

Adapter cards are circuit boards that provide connections and functions not built into the motherboard. Two adapter cards found in some desktop personal computers today are a sound card and a video card. Devices outside the system unit often attach to ports on the system unit by a connector on a cable. These devices may include a keyboard, mouse, microphone, monitor, printer, scanner, card reader/writer, digital camera, PC video camera, and speakers. A drive bay holds one or more disk drives. The power supply converts electricity from a power cord plugged in a wall outlet into a form that can be used by the computer.

The Motherboard

The **motherboard**, sometimes called a *system board*, is the main circuit board of the system unit. Many electronic components attach to the motherboard; others are built into it. Figure 4-3 shows a photograph of a current desktop personal computer motherboard and identifies components that attach to it, including adapter cards, a processor chip, and a memory module. Memory chips are installed on memory cards (modules) that fit in a slot on the motherboard.

A computer **chip** is a small piece of semi-conducting material, usually silicon, on which integrated circuits are etched. An *integrated circuit* contains many microscopic pathways capable of carrying electrical current. Each integrated circuit can contain millions of elements such as resistors, capacitors, and transistors. A *transistor*, for example, can act as an electronic switch that opens or closes the circuit for electrical charges. Most chips are no bigger than one-half-inch square. Manufacturers package chips so the chips can be attached to a circuit board, such as a motherboard or an adapter card.

FIGURE 4-3 Many electronic components attach to the motherboard in a desktop personal computer, including a processor chip, memory module, and adapter cards.

PROCESSOR

The **processor**, also called the **central processing unit (CPU)**, interprets and carries out the basic instructions that operate a computer. The processor significantly impacts overall computing power and manages most of a computer's operations. On larger computers, such as mainframes and supercomputers, the various functions performed by the processor extend over many separate chips and often multiple circuit boards. On a personal computer, all functions of the processor usually are on a single chip. Some computer and chip manufacturers use the term *microprocessor* to refer to a personal computer processor chip.

Processors contain a control unit and an arithmetic logic unit (ALU). These two components work together to perform processing operations. Figure 4-4 illustrates how other devices connected to the computer communicate with the processor to carry out a task.

The Control Unit

The **control unit** is the component of the processor that directs and coordinates most of the operations in the computer. The control unit has a role much like a traffic cop: it interprets each instruction issued by a program and then initiates the appropriate action to carry out the instruction. Read At Issue 4-1 for a related discussion.

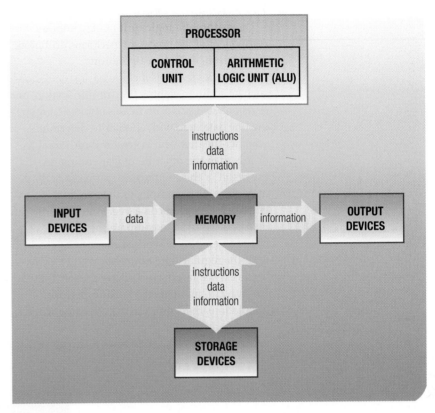

FIGURE 4-4 Most devices connected to the computer communicate with the processor to carry out a task. When a user starts a program, for example, its instructions transfer from a storage device to memory. Data needed by programs enters memory from either an input device or a storage device. The control unit interprets and executes instructions in memory, and the ALU performs calculations on the data in memory. Resulting information is stored in memory, from which it can be sent to an output device or a storage device for future access, as needed.

AT ISSUE 4-1

Can Computers Think?

Ever since a computer defeated world chess champion Gary Kasparov in a chess match, people have wondered, can computers think? As computer processors become more powerful, the question is more hotly debated. People who believe computers can think argue that, if a question was submitted to a person and a computer, it would be impossible to tell the person's response from the computer's response. Therefore, computers can think. Opponents counter this argument by saying that, if a question written in a foreign language was submitted to a person who can read and write the language and a person who cannot read or write the language but has a list of questions and appropriate answers, it might be impossible to tell the response of one person from the other. But, the person who cannot read or write the language really does not understand it, any more than a computer really can think. Besides, computers lack an essential component of human thinking — common sense. Computers can consider millions of chess moves a second, but humans have the common sense to recognize that some moves are not worthy of consideration. Can computers think? Why or why not? If computers cannot think now, might they be able to think in the future? Why?

The Arithmetic Logic Unit

The **arithmetic logic unit** (*ALU*), another component of the processor, performs arithmetic, comparison, and other operations.

Arithmetic operations include basic calculations such as addition, subtraction, multiplication, and division. *Comparison operations* involve comparing one data item with another to determine whether the first item is greater than, equal to, or less than the other item. Depending on the result of the comparison, different actions may occur. For example, to determine if an employee should receive overtime pay, software instructs the ALU to compare the number of hours an employee worked during the week with the regular time hours allowed (e.g., 40 hours). If the hours worked are greater than 40, software instructs the ALU to perform calculations that compute the overtime wage.

Machine Cycle

For every instruction, a processor repeats a set of four basic operations, which comprise a *machine cycle* (Figure 4-5): (1) fetching, (2) decoding, (3) executing, and, if necessary, (4) storing. *Fetching* is the process of obtaining a program instruction or data item from memory. The term *decoding* refers to the process of translating the instruction into signals the computer can execute. *Executing* is the process of carrying out the commands. *Storing*, in this context, means writing the result to memory (not to a storage medium).

In some computers, the processor fetches, decodes, executes, and stores only one instruction at a time. In these computers, the processor waits until an instruction completes all four stages of the machine cycle (fetch, decode, execute, and store) before beginning work on the next instruction.

FIGURE 4-5 THE STEPS IN A MACHINE CYCLE

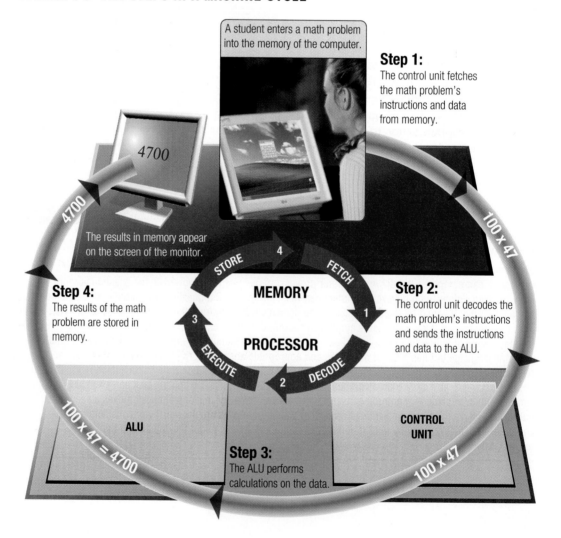

A student enters a math problem into the memory of the computer.

Step 1:
The control unit fetches the math problem's instructions and data from memory.

The results in memory appear on the screen of the monitor.

Step 4:
The results of the math problem are stored in memory.

Step 2:
The control unit decodes the math problem's instructions and sends the instructions and data to the ALU.

Step 3:
The ALU performs calculations on the data.

STORE 4 FETCH
MEMORY
1
3
EXECUTE PROCESSOR
2 DECODE

ALU

CONTROL UNIT

4700
100 × 47
100 × 47 = 4700
100 × 47

Most of today's personal computers support a concept called pipelining. With *pipelining*, the processor begins fetching a second instruction before it completes the machine cycle for the first instruction. Processors that use pipelining are faster because they do not have to wait for one instruction to complete the machine cycle before fetching the next. Think of a pipeline as an assembly line. By the time the first instruction is in the last stage of the machine cycle, three other instructions could have been fetched and started through the machine cycle (Figure 4-6).

MACHINE CYCLE (without pipelining):

| FETCH | DECODE | EXECUTE | STORE | FETCH | DECODE | EXECUTE | STORE |

INSTRUCTION 1 → INSTRUCTION 2

MACHINE CYCLE (with pipelining):

| FETCH | DECODE | EXECUTE | STORE |

INSTRUCTION 1
INSTRUCTION 2
INSTRUCTION 3
INSTRUCTION 4

FIGURE 4-6 Most modern personal computers support pipelining. With pipelining, the processor fetches a second instruction before the first instruction is completed. The result is faster processing.

Registers

A processor contains small, high-speed storage locations, called *registers*, that temporarily hold data and instructions. Registers are part of the processor, not part of memory or a permanent storage device. Processors have many different types of registers, each with a specific storage function. Register functions include storing the location from where an instruction was fetched, storing an instruction while the control unit decodes it, storing data while the ALU computes it, and storing the results of a calculation.

The System Clock

The processor relies on a small quartz crystal circuit called the **system clock** to control the timing of all computer operations. Just as your heart beats at a regular rate to keep your body functioning, the system clock generates regular electronic pulses, or ticks, that set the operating pace of components of the system unit.

Each tick equates to a *clock cycle*. In the past, processors used one or more clock cycles to execute each instruction. Processors today often are *superscalar*, which means they can execute more than one instruction per clock cycle.

The pace of the system clock, called the **clock speed**, is measured by the number of ticks per second. Current personal computer processors have clock speeds in the gigahertz range. Giga is a prefix that stands for billion, and a *hertz* is one cycle per second. Thus, one **gigahertz (GHz)** equals one billion ticks of the system clock per second. A computer that operates at 3.2 GHz has 3.2 billion (giga) clock cycles in one second (hertz).

The system clock is one of the factors that influence a computer's speed. The faster the clock speed, the more instructions the processor can execute per second. The speed of the system clock has no effect on devices such as a printer or disk drive.

FAQ 4-1

Does the system clock also keep track of the current date and time?

No, a separate battery-backed chip, called the *real-time clock*, keeps track of the date and time in a computer. The battery continues to run the real-time clock even when the computer is off. For more information, visit scsite.com/dc2006/ch4/faq and then click Computer Clock.

WEB LINK 4-2

Clock Speed
For more information, visit scsite.com/dc2006/ch4/weblink and then click Clock Speed.

Some computer professionals measure a processor's speed according to the number of *MIPS* (*millions of instructions per second*) it can process. Current desktop personal computers can process more than 7,000 MIPS. No real standard for measuring MIPS exists, however, because different instructions require varying amounts of processing time. Read Looking Ahead 4-1 for a look at the next generation of processing speeds.

LOOKING AHEAD 4-1

U.S. Plans World's Fastest Computer

Nine of the world's ten fastest computers are located in the United States. The fastest computer is located in Japan, according to the Top500 Project, a group that monitors supercomputers throughout the world.

The U.S. Department of Energy is planning to have the United States regain the record as having the world's fastest civilian computer. It is helping to fund a new supercomputer at a research laboratory in Oak Ridge, Tennessee, with $50 million in federal grants and assistance from Cray Corp., IBM Corp., and Silicon Graphics Inc.

Oak Ridge scientists predict the new computer will be able to perform 50 trillion calculations per second or about 500 trillion (500,000,000,000,000) calculations in the time it takes to blink your eye. The Japanese computer sustains 36 trillion calculations per second. For more information, visit scsite.com/dc2006/ch4/looking and then click Fastest Computer.

Comparison of Personal Computer Processors

The leading processor chip manufacturers for personal computers are Intel, AMD (Advanced Micro Devices), IBM, Motorola, and Transmeta. These manufacturers often identify their processor chips by a model name or model number. Figure 4-7 categorizes the historical development of the personal computer processor and documents the increases in clock speed and number of transistors in chips since 1982. The greater the number of transistors, the more complex and powerful the chip.

With its earlier processors, Intel used a model number to identify the various chips. After learning that processor model numbers could not be trademarked and protected from use by competitors, Intel began identifying its processors with names — thus emerged the series of processors known as the Pentium. Most high-performance PCs use some type of **Pentium** processor. Notebook computers and Tablet PCs use a **Pentium M**

processor. Less expensive, basic PCs use a brand of Intel processor called the **Celeron**. Two more brands, called the **Xeon** and **Itanium** processors, are ideal for workstations and low-end servers.

AMD is the leading manufacturer of *Intel-compatible processors*, which have an internal design similar to Intel processors, perform the same functions, and can be as powerful, but often are less expensive. Transmeta, also a manufacturer of Intel-compatible processors, specializes in processors for mobile computers and devices. Intel and Intel-compatible processors are used in PCs.

In the past, chip manufacturers listed a processor's clock speed in marketing literature and advertisements. Today, however, clock speed is only one factor that impacts processing speed. Other factors include cache and bus speed, each of which is discussed later in this chapter. To help consumers evaluate various processors, manufacturers such as Intel and AMD now use a numbering scheme that more accurately reflects the processing speed of their chips.

Apple computers use an *IBM processor* or a *Motorola processor*, which has a design different from the Intel-style processor. The PowerPC processor has a new architecture that increased the speed of the latest Apple computers.

Processor chips include technologies to improve processing performance. Intel's latest processor chips contain *Hyper-Threading* (*HT*) *Technology*, which improves processing power and time by allowing the processor chip to mimic the power of two processors. For even higher levels of performance with lower levels of power consumption, several processor chip manufacturers now offer a *dual-core processor*, which is a chip that has two separate processors. Most processors have built-in instructions to improve the performance of multimedia and 3-D graphics. Processors for notebook computers include technology to integrate wireless capabilities and optimize and extend battery life.

A new type of processor, called *system on a chip*, integrates the functions of a processor, memory, and a video card on a single chip. Lower-priced personal computers, Tablet PCs, networking devices, and consumer electronics such as music players and game consoles sometimes have a system-on-a-chip processor. The goal of system-on-a-chip manufacturers is to create processors that have faster clock speeds, consume less power, are small, and are cost effective.

COMPARISON OF WIDELY USED PERSONAL COMPUTER PROCESSORS

	NAME	DATE INTRODUCED/ UPDATED	MANUFACTURER	CLOCK SPEED	NUMBER OF TRANSISTORS
SERVER PROCESSORS	Xeon MP	2002/2004	Intel	1.4–3 GHz	108–169 million
	Itanium 2	2003/2004	Intel	1.3–1.6 GHz	220–410 million
	Xeon	2001/2003	Intel	1.4–3.6 GHz	42–108 million
	Itanium	2001	Intel	733–800 MHz	25.4–60 million
	Pentium III Xeon	1999/2000	Intel	500–900 MHz	9.5–28 million
	Pentium II Xeon	1998/1999	Intel	400–450 MHz	7.5–27 million
	Opteron	2003	AMD	1.4–2.4 GHz	100 million
	Athlon MP	2002	AMD	1.53–2.25 GHz	54.3 million
DESKTOP PERSONAL COMPUTER PROCESSORS	Pentium 4 with HT Technology	2002/2004	Intel	2.4–3.6 GHz	55–178 million
	Pentium 4	2000/2004	Intel	1.3–3.2 GHz	42–55 million
	Pentium III	1999/2003	Intel	450 MHz–1.4 GHz	9.5–44 million
	Celeron D	2004	Intel	2.4–2.8 GHz	26.2 million
	Celeron	1998/2003	Intel	266 MHz–3.06 GHz	7.5–44 million
	Pentium II	1997/1998	Intel	233–450 MHz	7.5 million
	Pentium with MMX technology	1997	Intel	166–233 MHz	4.5 million
	Pentium Pro	1995/1999	Intel	150–200 MHz	5.5 million
	Pentium	1993/1997	Intel	75–200 MHz	3.3 million
	80486DX	1989/1994	Intel	25–100 MHz	1.6 million
	80386	1985/1990	Intel	16–33 MHz	275,000
	80286	1982	Intel	6–12 MHz	134,000
	Sempron	2004	AMD	1.5–2 GHz	68.5 million
	Athlon 64	2003	AMD	2–2.4 GHz	105.9 million
	Athlon	1999/2002	AMD	500 MHz–1.4 GHz	22–38 million
	Duron	1999/2001	AMD	600 MHz–1.3 GHz	25 million
	AMD–K6 III	1999	AMD	400–450 MHz	21.3 million
	AMD–K6-2	1998	AMD	366–550 MHz	9.3 million
	AMD–K6	1997	AMD	300 MHz	8.8 million
	PowerPC G5	2003/2004	Motorola/IBM	1.4–2.0 GHz	58 million
	PowerPC G4	1999/2004	Motorola/IBM	350 MHz–1.5 GHz	33 million
	PowerPC G3	1997	Motorola/IBM	233 MHz–1.1 GHz	6.35–29 million
	PowerPC G2	1995	Motorola/IBM	75–350 MHz	1.6–5.1 million
	PowerPC G1	1994	Motorola/IBM	60–110 MHz	2.8 million
	68040	1989	Motorola	25–40 MHz	1.2 million
	68030	1987	Motorola	16–50 MHz	270,000
	68020	1984	Motorola	16–33 MHz	190,000
MOBILE PROCESSORS	Celeron M	2004	Intel	900 MHz–1.5 GHz	55 million
	Pentium M	2003/2004	Intel	1–2 GHz	77–140 million
	Mobile Celeron	1999/2003	Intel	266 MHz–2.8 GHz	18.9 million
	Mobile Pentium	1997/2002	Intel	200 MHz–3.2 GHz	55 million
	Mobile Sempron	2004	AMD	1.6–1.8 GHz	37.5 million
	Mobile Athlon	2001/2002	AMD	1.4–2.2 GHz	37.5–105.9 million
	Mobile Duron	2000/2001	AMD	1.3 GHz	25 million
	Efficeon	2003	Transmeta	1–1.2 GHz	79 million
	Crusoe	2000	Transmeta	500 MHz–1 GHz	6.7 million

FIGURE 4-7 A comparison of some of the more widely used processors.

Buying a Personal Computer

If you are ready to buy a new computer, the processor you select should depend on how you plan to use the computer. If you purchase an IBM-compatible PC, you will choose an Intel processor or an Intel-compatible processor (Figure 4-8). Apple Macintosh and Power Macintosh computers have a Motorola or IBM processor. Current Apple processors include the PowerPC G4 and PowerPC G5.

Your intended use also will determine the clock speed you need. A home user surfing the Web, for example, may need only a 2 GHz processor, while an artist working with graphics or applications requiring multimedia capabilities such as full-motion video may require at least a 3 GHz processor. The higher the clock speed, the faster the processor, and the more expensive the computer.

Instead of buying an entirely new computer, you might be able to upgrade your processor to increase the computer's performance. Be certain the processor you buy is compatible with your computer's motherboard; otherwise, you will have to replace the motherboard, too. Replacing a processor is a fairly simple process, whereas replacing a motherboard is much more complicated.

For detailed computer purchasing guidelines, read the Buyer's Guide 2006 feature that follows Chapter 8. Read At Issue 4-2 for a related discussion.

GUIDELINES FOR SELECTING AN INTEL OR INTEL-COMPATIBLE PROCESSOR

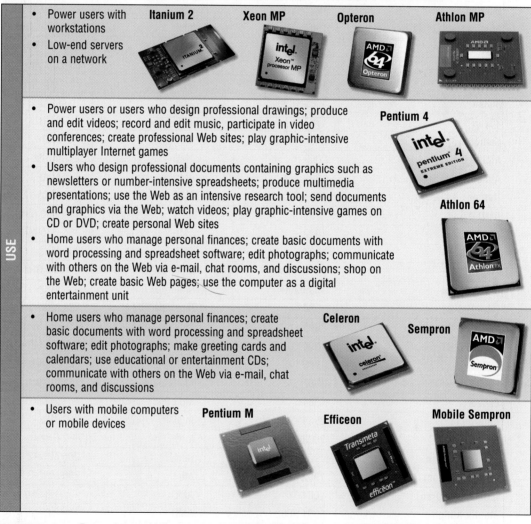

USE

- Power users with workstations
- Low-end servers on a network

Itanium 2   **Xeon MP**   **Opteron**   **Athlon MP**

- Power users or users who design professional drawings; produce and edit videos; record and edit music, participate in video conferences; create professional Web sites; play graphic-intensive multiplayer Internet games
- Users who design professional documents containing graphics such as newsletters or number-intensive spreadsheets; produce multimedia presentations; use the Web as an intensive research tool; send documents and graphics via the Web; watch videos; play graphic-intensive games on CD or DVD; create personal Web sites
- Home users who manage personal finances; create basic documents with word processing and spreadsheet software; edit photographs; communicate with others on the Web via e-mail, chat rooms, and discussions; shop on the Web; create basic Web pages; use the computer as a digital entertainment unit

Pentium 4   **Athlon 64**

- Home users who manage personal finances; create basic documents with word processing and spreadsheet software; edit photographs; make greeting cards and calendars; use educational or entertainment CDs; communicate with others on the Web via e-mail, chat rooms, and discussions

Celeron   **Sempron**

- Users with mobile computers or mobile devices

Pentium M   **Efficeon**   **Mobile Sempron**

FIGURE 4-8   Determining which processor to obtain when you purchase a computer depends on computer usage.

FAQ 4-2

What is Moore's Law?

Moore's Law is a prediction made by one of the founders of Intel, Gordon Moore, that the number of transistors and resistors placed on computer chips would double every year, with a proportional increase in computing power and decrease in cost. The chart below shows the growth of Intel processors. For more information, read the Technology Trailblazer article on page 219 and visit scsite.com/dc2006/ch4/faq and then click Moore's Law.

Intel Processor Chip Complexity

AT ISSUE 4-2

Computer Waste and the Environment: Whose Problem Is It?

Experts estimate that about 1 billion computers will be discarded by 2010. As technology advances and prices fall, many people think of computers as disposable items. But, disposing of old system units, monitors, and other computer components is a major problem. Computers contain several toxic elements, including lead, mercury, and barium. Computers thrown into landfills or burned in incinerators can pollute the ground and the air. One solution is to recycle old computers. Computers for Schools refurbishes donated computers and makes them available to schools and students at very low prices, and donors earn tax breaks. Some lawmakers prefer a more aggressive approach, such as setting up a recycling program that would be paid for by adding a $10 fee to a computer's purchase price, or forcing computer makers to be responsible for collecting and recycling their products. Manufacturers already have taken steps. Several have reduced the amount of toxic material in their products, and some have set up their own recycling programs, for which users pay a fee. One manufacturer admits, however, that only seven percent of the computers it has sold have been recycled. What can be done to ensure that computers are disposed of safely? Should government, manufacturers, or users be responsible for safe disposal? Why? How can computer users be motivated to recycle obsolete equipment?

Heat Sinks, Heat Pipes, and Liquid Cooling

Processor chips generate quite a bit of heat, which could cause the chip to burn up. Although the computer's main fan generates airflow, today's processors require additional cooling. A *heat sink* is a small ceramic or metal component with fins on its surface that absorbs and disperses heat produced by electrical components such as a processor (Figure 4-9). Some heat sinks are packaged as part of a processor chip. Others are installed on the top or the side of the chip. Because a heat sink consumes extra space, a smaller device called a *heat pipe* cools processors in notebook computers.

Some computers use liquid cooling technology to reduce the temperature of a processor. *Liquid cooling technology* uses a continuous flow of fluid(s), such as water and glycol, in a process that transfers the heated fluid away from the processor to a radiator-type grill, which cools the liquid, and then returns the cooled fluid to the processor.

FIGURE 4-9 A heat sink, which is attached to the top of a processor, prevents the chip from overheating. The heat sink fan, which attaches to the top of the heat sink, helps distribute air dissipated by the heat sink.

Parallel Processing

Some computers use more than one processor to speed processing times. Known as *parallel processing*, this method uses multiple processors simultaneously to execute a program (Figure 4-10). Parallel processing divides a problem into portions so that multiple processors work on their assigned portion of the problem at the same time. Parallel processing requires special software that recognizes how to divide the problem and then bring the results back together again.

Some personal computers implement parallel processing with dual-core processors or multi-core processors (more than two processors on a single chip). Others have two or more separate processor chips, respectively called dual processor or multiprocessor computers.

Supercomputers use parallel processing for applications such as weather forecasting. Some applications draw on the idle time of home users' personal computers to achieve parallel processing.

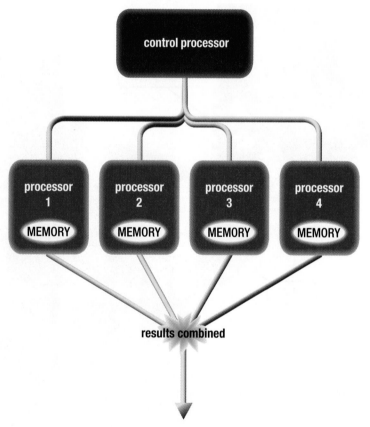

FIGURE 4-10   Parallel processing divides a problem into portions so that multiple processors work on their assigned portion of a problem at the same time. In this illustration, one processor, called the control processor, is managing the operations of four other processors.

Test your knowledge of pages 184 through 194 in Quiz Yourself 4-1.

QUIZ YOURSELF 4-1

Instructions: Find the true statement below. Then, rewrite the remaining false statements so they are true.

1. A computer chip is a small piece of semiconducting material, usually silicon, on which integrated circuits are etched.

2. Four basic operations in a machine cycle are: (1) comparing, (2) decoding, (3) executing, and, if necessary, (4) pipelining.

3. Processors contain a motherboard and an arithmetic logic unit (ALU).

4. The central processing unit, sometimes called a system board, is the main circuit board of the system unit.

5. The leading processor chip manufacturers for personal computers are Microsoft, AMD, IBM, Motorola, and Transmeta.

6. The pace of the system clock, called the clock speed, is measured by the number of ticks per minute.

7. The system unit is a case that contains mechanical components of the computer used to process data.

Quiz Yourself Online: To further check your knowledge of system unit styles, motherboards, processor components and machine cycles, and characteristics of personal computer processors, visit scsite.com/dc2006/ch4/quiz and then click Objectives 1 – 4.

DATA REPRESENTATION

To understand fully the way a computer processes data, you should know how a computer represents data. People communicate through speech by combining words into sentences. Human speech is **analog** because it uses continuous (wave form) signals that vary in strength and quality. Most computers are **digital**. They recognize only two discrete states: on and off. This is because computers are electronic devices powered by electricity, which also has only two states: on and off.

The two digits, 0 and 1, easily can represent these two states (Figure 4-11). The digit 0 represents the electronic state of off (absence of an electronic charge). The digit 1 represents the electronic state of on (presence of an electronic charge).

BINARY DIGIT (BIT)	ELECTRONIC CHARGE	ELECTRONIC STATE
1		ON
0		OFF

FIGURE 4-11 A computer circuit represents the 0 or the 1 electronically by the presence or absence of an electronic charge.

When people count, they use the digits in the decimal system (0 through 9). The computer, by contrast, uses a binary system because it recognizes only two states. The **binary system** is a number system that has just two unique digits, 0 and 1, called bits. A **bit** (short for *binary digit*) is the smallest unit of data the computer can process. By itself, a bit is not very informative.

When 8 bits are grouped together as a unit, they form a **byte**. A byte provides enough different combinations of 0s and 1s to represent 256 individual characters. These characters include numbers, uppercase and lowercase letters of the alphabet, punctuation marks, and others, such as the letters of the Greek alphabet.

The combinations of 0s and 1s that represent characters are defined by patterns called a coding scheme. In one coding scheme, the number 4 is represented as 00110100, the number 6 as 00110110, and the capital letter E as 01000101 (Figure 4-12). Two popular coding schemes are ASCII and EBCDIC (Figure 4-13). The *American Standard Code for Information Interchange* (*ASCII* pronounced ASK-ee) scheme is the most widely used coding system to represent data. Most personal computers and midrange servers use the ASCII coding scheme. The *Extended Binary Coded Decimal Interchange Code* (*EBCDIC* pronounced EB-see-dik) scheme is used primarily on mainframe computers and high-end servers.

The ASCII and EBCDIC coding schemes are sufficient for English and Western European languages but are not large enough for Asian and other languages that use different alphabets. *Unicode* is a 16-bit coding scheme that has the capacity of representing more than 65,000 characters and symbols. The Unicode coding scheme is capable of representing almost all the world's current written languages, as well as classic and historical languages. To allow for expansion, Unicode reserves 30,000 codes for future use and 6,000 codes for private use. Unicode is implemented in several operating systems, including Windows XP, Mac OS X, and Linux. Unicode-enabled programming languages and software products include Java, XML, Microsoft Office, and Oracle.

Appendix A at the back of this book discusses the ASCII, EBCDIC, and Unicode schemes in more depth, along with the parity bit and number systems.

Coding schemes such as ASCII make it possible for humans to interact with a digital computer that processes only bits. When you press a key on a keyboard, a chip

ASCII	SYMBOL	EBCDIC
00110000	0	11110000
00110001	1	11110001
00110010	2	11110010
00110011	3	11110011
00110100	4	11110100
00110101	5	11110101
00110110	6	11110110
00110111	7	11110111
00111000	8	11111000
00111001	9	11111001
01000001	A	11000001
01000010	B	11000010
01000011	C	11000011
01000100	D	11000100
01000101	E	11000101
01000110	F	11000110
01000111	G	11000111
01001000	H	11001000
01001001	I	11001001
01001010	J	11010001
01001011	K	11010010
01001100	L	11010011
01001101	M	11010100
01001110	N	11010101
01001111	O	11010110
01010000	P	11010111
01010001	Q	11011000
01010010	R	11011001
01010011	S	11100010
01010100	T	11100011
01010101	U	11100100
01010110	V	11100101
01010111	W	11100110
01011000	X	11100111
01011001	Y	11101000
01011010	Z	11101001
00100001	!	01011010
00100010	"	01111111
00100011	#	01111011
00100100	$	01011011
00100101	%	01101100
00100110	&	01010000
00101000	(	01001101
00101001	)	01011101
00101010	*	01011100
00101011	+	01001110

8-BIT BYTE FOR THE NUMBER 4

0	0	1	1	0	1	0	0

8-BIT BYTE FOR THE NUMBER 6

0	0	1	1	0	1	1	0

8-BIT BYTE FOR THE LETTER E

0	1	0	0	0	1	0	1

FIGURE 4-12 Eight bits grouped together as a unit are called a byte. A byte represents a single character in the computer.

FIGURE 4-13 Two popular coding schemes are ASCII and EBCDIC.

in the keyboard converts the key's electronic signal into a special code that is sent to the system unit. Then, the system unit converts the code into a binary form the computer can process and stores it in memory. Every character is converted to its corresponding byte. The computer then processes the data as bytes, which actually is a series of on/off electrical states. When processing is finished, software converts the byte into a human-recognizable number, letter of the alphabet, or special character that is displayed on a screen or is printed (Figure 4-14). All of these conversions take place so quickly that you do not realize they are occurring.

Standards, such as those defined by ASCII, EBCDIC, and Unicode, also make it possible for components in computers to communicate with each other successfully. By following these and other standards, manufacturers can produce a component and be assured that it will operate correctly in a computer.

MEMORY

Memory consists of electronic components that store instructions waiting to be executed by the processor, data needed by those instructions, and the results of processed data (information). Memory usually consists of one or more chips on the motherboard or some other circuit board in the computer.

Memory stores three basic categories of items: (1) the operating system and other system software that control or maintain the computer and its devices; (2) application programs that carry out a specific task such as word processing; and (3) the data being processed by the application programs and resulting information. This role of memory to store both data and programs is known as the *stored program concept*.

Bytes and Addressable Memory

A byte (character) is the basic storage unit in memory. When application program instructions and data are transferred to memory from storage devices, the instructions and data exist as bytes. Each byte resides temporarily in a location in memory that has an *address*. An address simply is a unique number that identifies the location of a byte in memory. The illustration in Figure 4-15 shows how seats in a concert hall are similar to addresses in memory: (1) a seat, which is identified by a unique seat number, holds one person at a time, and a location in memory, which is identified by a unique address, holds a single byte; and (2) both a seat, identified by a seat number, and a byte, identified by an address, can be empty. To access data or instructions in memory, the computer references the addresses that contain bytes of data.

FIGURE 4-14   HOW A LETTER IS CONVERTED TO BINARY FORM AND BACK

Step 1:
The user presses the capital letter **T** (SHIFT+T keys) on the keyboard, which in turn creates a special code for the capital letter **T**.

Step 2:
The scan code for the capital letter **T** is sent to the system unit.

Step 3:
The system unit converts the scan code for the capital letter **T** to its ASCII binary code (01010100) and stores it in memory for processing.

Step 4:
After processing, the binary code for the capital letter **T** is converted to an image and displayed on the output device.

FIGURE 4-15 Seats in a concert hall are similar to addresses in memory: a seat holds one person at a time, and a location in memory holds a single byte; and both a seat and a byte can be empty.

Memory Sizes

Manufacturers state the size of memory chips and storage devices in terms of the number of bytes the chip or device has available for storage (Figure 4-16). Recall that storage devices hold data, instructions, and information for future use, while most memory holds these items temporarily. A **kilobyte** (**KB** or **K**) is equal to exactly 1,024 bytes. To simplify memory and storage definitions, computer users often round a kilobyte down to 1,000 bytes. For example, if a memory chip can store 100 KB, it can hold approximately 100,000 bytes (characters). A **megabyte** (**MB**) is equal to approximately 1 million bytes. A **gigabyte** (**GB**) equals approximately 1 billion bytes. A **terabyte** (**TB**) is equal to approximately 1 trillion bytes.

Types of Memory

The system unit contains two types of memory: volatile and nonvolatile. When the computer's power is turned off, *volatile memory* loses its contents. *Nonvolatile memory*, by contrast, does not lose its contents when power is removed from the computer. Thus, volatile memory is temporary and nonvolatile memory is permanent. RAM is the most common type of volatile memory. Examples of nonvolatile memory include ROM, flash memory, and CMOS. The following sections discuss these types of memory. Read At Issue 4-3 for a related discussion.

AT ISSUE 4-3

Ready for RFID?

Move over bar codes, make way for RFID. *RFID* (*radio frequency identification*) uses a tiny computer memory chip that is mounted on a tag attached to a product or sewn into an article of clothing. An RFID reader reads identifying information on the memory chip via radio waves. Unlike bar codes, RFID does not require line-of-sight transmission and can identify unique items, not just a category. For merchants, RFID can help to locate items in a warehouse, identify items that need to be replenished, and track items that have been removed from store shelves. For consumers, RFID can supply detailed product information, reduce costs associated with inventory management, and someday let buyers bypass check-out lines and take purchases directly from the store, with the item's cost charged to their card. Privacy advocates worry, however, that RFID could obliterate a buyer's anonymity. They fear that with an RFID reader, any individual or organization could track a purchaser's movements and make that information available to marketers or government agencies. To protect privacy, privacy advocates insist that merchants should be forced to disable RFID transmitters as soon as buyers leave a store. Would you be comfortable purchasing a product using RFID? Why or why not? Should buyers be allowed to request that RFID transmitters be disabled after they make a purchase, or should merchants be required to render transmitters inoperable when the product leaves the store? Why?

MEMORY AND STORAGE SIZES

Term	Abbreviation	Approximate Number of Bytes	Exact Amount of Bytes	Approximate Number of Pages of Text
Kilobyte	KB or K	1 thousand	1,024	1/2
Megabyte	MB	1 million	1,048,576	500
Gigabyte	GB	1 billion	1,073,741,824	500,000
Terabyte	TB	1 trillion	1,099,511,627,776	500,000,000

FIGURE 4-16 Terms commonly used to define memory and storage sizes.

RAM

Users typically are referring to RAM when discussing computer memory. **RAM** (*random access memory*), also called *main memory*, consists of memory chips that can be read from and written to by the processor and other devices. When you turn on power to a computer, certain operating system files (such as the files that determine how the Windows XP desktop appears) load into RAM from a storage device such as a hard disk. These files remain in RAM as long as the computer has continuous power. As additional programs and data are requested, they also load into RAM from storage.

The processor interprets and executes a program's instructions while the program is in RAM. During this time, the contents of RAM may change (Figure 4-17). RAM can accommodate multiple programs simultaneously.

Most RAM is volatile, which means it loses its contents when the power is removed from the computer. For this reason, you must save any data, instructions, and information you

FIGURE 4-17   HOW PROGRAM INSTRUCTIONS TRANSFER IN AND OUT OF RAM

Step 1:
When you start the computer, certain operating system files are loaded into RAM from the hard disk. The operating system displays the user interface on the screen.

Step 2:
When you start a Web browser, the program's instructions are loaded into RAM from the hard disk. The Web browser and certain operating system instructions are in RAM. The Web browser window is displayed on the screen.

Step 3:
When you start a word processing program, the program's instructions are loaded into RAM from the hard disk. The word processing program, along with the Web browser and certain operating system instructions, are in RAM. The word processing program window is displayed on the screen.

Step 4:
When you quit a program, such as the Web browser, its program instructions are removed from RAM. The Web browser no longer is displayed on the screen.

may need in the future. Saving is the process of copying data, instructions, and information from RAM to a storage device such as a hard disk.

Three basic types of RAM chips exist: dynamic RAM, static RAM, and magnetoresistive RAM.

- *Dynamic RAM* (*DRAM* pronounced DEE-ram) chips must be re-energized constantly or they lose their contents. Many variations of DRAM chips exist, most of which are faster than the basic DRAM. *Synchronous DRAM* (*SDRAM*) chips are much faster than DRAM chips because they are synchronized to the system clock. *Double Data Rate SDRAM* (*DDR SDRAM*) chips are even faster than SDRAM chips because they transfer data twice for each clock cycle, instead of just once, and DDR 2 is even faster than DDR. Dual channel SDRAM is faster than single channel SDRAM because it delivers twice the amount of data to the processor. *Rambus DRAM* (*RDRAM*) is yet another type of DRAM that is much faster than SDRAM because it uses pipelining techniques. Most personal computers today use some form of SDRAM chips or RDRAM chips.
- *Static RAM* (*SRAM* pronounced ESS-ram) chips are faster and more reliable than any variation of DRAM chips. These chips do not have to be re-energized as often as DRAM chips, thus, the term static. SRAM chips, however, are much more expensive than DRAM chips. Special applications such as cache use SRAM chips. A later section in this chapter discusses cache.
- A newer type of RAM, called *magnetoresistive RAM* (*MRAM* pronounced EM-ram), stores data using magnetic charges instead of electrical charges. Manufacturers claim that MRAM has greater storage capacity, consumes less power, and has faster access times than electronic RAM. Also, MRAM retains its contents after power is removed from the computer, which could prevent loss of data for users. As the cost of MRAM declines, experts predict MRAM could replace both DRAM and SRAM.

RAM chips usually reside on a **memory module**, which is a small circuit board. **Memory slots** on the motherboard hold memory modules (Figure 4-18). Three types of memory modules are SIMMs, DIMMs, and

RIMMs. A *SIMM* (*single inline memory module*) has pins on opposite sides of the circuit board that connect together to form a single set of contacts. With a *DIMM* (*dual inline memory module*), by contrast, the pins on opposite sides of the circuit board do not connect and thus form two sets of contacts. SIMMs and DIMMs typically hold SDRAM chips. A *RIMM* (*Rambus inline memory module*) houses RDRAM chips. For a more technical discussion about RAM, read the High-Tech Talk article on page 218 at the end of this chapter.

FIGURE 4-18 This photo shows a memory module being inserted in a motherboard.

RAM CONFIGURATIONS The amount of RAM necessary in a computer often depends on the types of software you plan to use. A computer executes programs that are in RAM. Think of RAM as the workspace on the top of your desk. Just as the top of your desk needs a certain amount of space to hold papers, a computer needs a certain amount of memory to store programs, data, and information. The more RAM a computer has, the faster the computer will respond.

A software package typically indicates the minimum amount of RAM it requires. If you want the application to perform optimally, usually you need more than the minimum specifications on the software package. Some programs, such as operating systems, also have specified maximums.

Generally, home users running Windows XP and using basic application software such as word processing should have at least 256 MB of RAM. Most business users who work with accounting, financial, or spreadsheet programs, voice recognition, and programs requiring multimedia capabilities should have a minimum of 512 MB of RAM. Users creating professional Web sites or using graphics-intensive applications will want at least 2 GB of RAM.

Figure 4-19a lists guidelines for the amount of RAM for various types of users. Figure 4-19b shows advertisements that match to each user requirement. Advertisements normally list the type of processor, the clock speed of the processor, and the amount of RAM in the computer.

The amount of RAM in computers purchased today ranges from 256 MB to 16 GB. In an advertisement, manufacturers specify the maximum amount of RAM a computer can hold, for example, 512 GB expandable to 2 GB. Read At Issue 4-4 for a related discussion.

FAQ 4-3

Can I add more RAM to my computer?

Check your computer documentation to see how much RAM you can add. RAM modules are relatively inexpensive and usually include easy-to-follow installation instructions. Be sure to purchase RAM compatible with your brand and model of computer. For more information, visit scsite.com/dc2006/ch4/faq and then click Upgrading RAM.

AT ISSUE 4-4

Do Lower Computer Prices Mean Less Value?

Today, you can buy a personal computer for less than $1,000 that can do more than one sold at nearly twice its cost three years ago. Some manufacturers even are offering basic computers for less than $500. Part of the plunge in prices is lower-cost components, but another factor is a growing demand for cheaper machines. One computer maker estimates that it sells almost 3,500 sub-$500 computers a month. Many of the new buyers are from families earning less than $40,000, far below the $50,000 average that once characterized typical computer buyers. These consumers are looking for inexpensive computers that are adequate for the most popular tasks, such as word processing, spreadsheets, and Internet access. They feel that spending higher prices for faster processors, more memory, 3-D graphics cards, higher-quality sound cards, more hard disk space, and other extras is an unnecessary, frivolous expense. As one industry analyst asks, "Why buy a Porsche when you are going to drive only 55 miles per hour?" How might a greater availability of lower costing personal computers change the way people, schools, and businesses buy and use them? With respect to computers, does a higher price always mean greater usefulness? Why or why not? Who might be satisfied with less than the latest and greatest computer technology? Why?

FIGURE 4-19a (RAM guidelines)

RAM	256 MB to 1 GB	512 MB to 2 GB	2 GB and up
Use	Home and business users managing personal finances; using standard application software such as word processing; using educational or entertainment CD-ROMs; communicating with others on the Web	Users requiring more advanced multimedia capabilities; running number-intensive accounting, financial, or spreadsheet programs; using voice recognition; working with videos, music, and digital imaging; creating Web sites; participating in video conferences; playing Internet games	Power users creating professional Web sites; running sophisticated CAD, 3-D design, or other graphics-intensive software

FIGURE 4-19b (computers for sale)

Model	A220	P240	A240	P300	X300	A225
Processor	2.20 GHz Athlon XP processor	2.40 GHz Celeron processor	2.40 GHz Athlon 64 processor	3.0 GHz Pentium 4 processor	3.0 GHz Xeon MP processor	2.25 GHz Opteron processor
Memory	256 MB SDRAM	512 MB SDRAM	512 MB SDRAM	1 GB SDRAM	2 GB RDRAM	4 GB SDRAM

FIGURE 4-19 Determining how much RAM you need depends on the applications you intend to run on your computer. Advertisements for computers normally list the type of processor, the speed of the processor, and the amount of RAM installed.

Cache

Most of today's computers improve processing times with **cache** (pronounced cash). Two types of cache are memory cache and disk cache. This chapter discusses memory cache. Chapter 7 discusses disk cache.

Memory cache helps speed the processes of the computer because it stores frequently used instructions and data. Most personal computers today have two types of memory cache: L1 cache and L2 cache. Some also have L3 cache.

- *L1 cache* is built directly in the processor chip. L1 cache usually has a very small capacity, ranging from 8 KB to 128 KB. The more common sizes for personal computers are 8 KB or 16 KB.
- *L2 cache* is slightly slower than L1 cache but has a much larger capacity, ranging from 64 KB to 16 MB. When discussing cache, most users are referring to L2 cache. Current processors include *advanced transfer cache (ATC)*, a type of L2 cache built directly on the processor chip. Processors that use ATC perform at much faster rates than those that do not use it.

  Personal computers today typically have from 512 KB to 2 MB of advanced transfer cache. Servers and workstations have from 2 MB to 6 MB of advanced transfer cache.

- *L3 cache* is a cache on the motherboard that is separate from the processor chip. L3 cache exists only on computers that use L2 advanced transfer cache. Personal computers often have up to 2 MB of L3 cache; servers and workstations have from 2 MB to 6 MB of L3 cache.

Cache speeds up processing time because it stores frequently used instructions and data. When the processor needs an instruction or data, it searches memory in this order: L1 cache, then L2 cache, then L3 cache (if it exists), then RAM — with a greater delay in processing for each level of memory it must search (Figure 4-20). If the instruction or data is not found in memory, then it must search a slower speed storage medium such as a hard disk, CD, or DVD.

ROM

Read-only memory (**ROM** pronounced rahm) refers to memory chips storing permanent data and instructions. The data on most ROM chips cannot be modified — hence, the name read-only. ROM is nonvolatile, which means its contents are not lost when power is removed from the computer. In addition to computers, many devices contain ROM chips. For example, ROM chips in printers contain data for fonts.

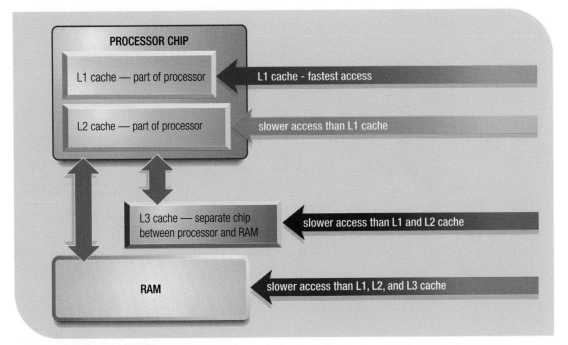

FIGURE 4-20 Cache helps speed processing times when the processor requests data, instructions, or information.

Manufacturers of ROM chips often record data, instructions, or information on the chips when they manufacture the chips. These ROM chips, called **firmware**, contain permanently written data, instructions, or information.

A *PROM* (*programmable read-only memory*) *chip* is a blank ROM chip on which a programmer can write permanently. Programmers use *microcode* instructions to program a PROM chip. Once a programmer writes the microcode on the PROM chip, it functions like a regular ROM chip and cannot be erased or changed.

A variation of the PROM chip, called an *EEPROM* (*electrically erasable programmable read-only memory*) *chip*, allows a programmer to erase the microcode with an electric signal.

Flash Memory

Flash memory is a type of nonvolatile memory that can be erased electronically and rewritten, similar to EEPROM. Most computers use flash memory to hold their startup instructions because it allows the computer easily to update its contents. For example, when the computer changes from standard time to daylight savings time, the contents of a flash memory chip (and the real-time clock chip) change to reflect the new time.

Flash memory chips also store data and programs on many mobile computers and devices, such as PDAs, smart phones, printers, digital cameras, automotive devices, music players, digital voice recorders, and pagers. When you enter names and addresses in a PDA or smart phone, a flash memory chip stores the data. Some MP3 players store music on flash memory chips (Figure 4-21); others store music on tiny hard disks or flash memory cards. A later section in this chapter discusses flash memory cards, which contain flash memory on a removable device instead of a chip.

WEB LINK 4-5

Flash Memory

For more information, visit scsite.com/ dc2006/ch4/weblink and then click Flash Memory.

FAQ 4-4

How much music can I store on an MP3 player?

MP3 players that store music on flash memory chips can hold up to 8 or 9 hours of music, which is about 120 songs in the WMA format or 60 songs in the MP3 format. MP3 players with tiny hard disks have a much greater storage capacity — from 1,000 to 10,000 songs. For more information, visit scsite.com/ dc2006/ch4/faq and then click MP3 Players.

FIGURE 4-21   HOW AN MP3 MUSIC PLAYER MIGHT STORE MUSIC ON FLASH MEMORY

Step 1: Purchase and download MP3 music tracks from a Web site. With one end of a special cable connected to the system unit, connect the other end to the USB port in the MP3 player.

Step 2: Instruct the computer to copy the MP3 music tracks to a flash memory chip in the MP3 player.

Step 3: Plug the headphones in the MP3 player, push a button on the MP3 player, and listen to the music through the headphones.

USB port

flash memory chips

from the computer

MP3 player

headphones cable

CMOS

Some RAM chips, flash memory chips, and other types of memory chips use **complementary metal-oxide semiconductor** (**CMOS** pronounced SEE-moss) technology because it provides high speeds and consumes little power. CMOS technology uses battery power to retain information even when the power to the computer is off. Battery-backed CMOS memory chips, for example, can keep the calendar, date, and time current even when the computer is off. The flash memory chips that store a computer's startup information often use CMOS technology.

FAQ 4-5

What should I do if my computer's date and time are wrong?

First, try resetting the date and time. To do this in Windows XP, double-click the time at the right edge of the taskbar. If the computer continues to lose time or display an incorrect date, you may need to replace the CMOS battery on the motherboard that powers the system clock. For more information, visit scsite.com/dc2006/ch4/faq and then click CMOS Battery.

Memory Access Times

Access time is the amount of time it takes the processor to read data, instructions, and information from memory. A computer's access time directly affects how fast the computer processes data. Accessing data in memory can be more than 200,000 times faster than accessing data on a hard disk because of the mechanical motion of the hard disk.

Today's manufacturers use a variety of terminology to state access times (Figure 4-22). Some use fractions of a second, which for memory occurs in nanoseconds. A **nanosecond** (abbreviated *ns*) is one billionth of a second. A nanosecond is extremely fast (Figure 4-23). In fact, electricity travels about one foot in a nanosecond.

Other manufacturers state access times in MHz; for example, 133 MHz SDRAM. If a manufacturer states access time in megahertz, you can convert it to nanoseconds by dividing the megahertz number into 1 billion ns. For example, 133 MHz equals approximately 7.5 ns (1,000,000,000/133,000,000).

The access time (speed) of memory contributes to the overall performance of the computer. Standard SDRAM chips can have access times up to 133 MHz (about 7.5 ns), and access times of the DDR SDRAM chips reach 533 MHz (about 1.9 ns). The higher the megahertz, the faster the access time; conversely, the lower the nanoseconds, the faster the access time. The faster RDRAM chips can have access times up to 1600 MHz (about 0.625 ns). ROM access times range from 25 to 250 ns.

While access times of memory greatly affect overall computer performance, manufacturers and retailers usually list a computer's memory in terms of its size, not its access time. Thus, an advertisement might describe a computer as having 512 MB of SDRAM upgradeable to 2 GB.

ACCESS TIME TERMINOLOGY

Term	Abbreviation	Speed
Millisecond	ms	One-thousandth of a second
Microsecond	μs	One-millionth of a second
Nanosecond	ns	One-billionth of a second
Picosecond	ps	One-trillionth of a second

FIGURE 4-22 Access times are measured in fractions of a second. This table lists the terms used to define access times.

10 million operations = 1 blink

FIGURE 4-23 It takes about one-tenth of a second to blink your eye, which is the equivalent of 100 million nanoseconds. In the time it takes to blink your eye, a computer can perform some operations 10 million times.

Test your knowledge of pages 194 through 203 in Quiz Yourself 4-2.

QUIZ YOURSELF 4-2

Instructions: Find the true statement below. Then, rewrite the remaining false statements so they are true.

1. A computer's memory access time directly affects how fast the computer processes data.

2. A gigabyte (GB) equals approximately 1 trillion bytes.

3. Memory cache helps speed the processes of the computer because it stores seldom used instructions and data.

4. Most computers are analog, which means they recognize only two discrete states: on and off.

5. Most RAM retains its contents when the power is removed from the computer.

6. Read-only memory (ROM) refers to memory chips storing temporary data and instructions.

Quiz Yourself Online: To further check your knowledge of bits, bytes, data representation, and types of memory, visit scsite.com/dc2006/ch4/quiz and then click Objectives 5 – 7.

EXPANSION SLOTS AND ADAPTER CARDS

An **expansion slot** is a socket on the motherboard that can hold an adapter card. An **adapter card**, sometimes called an *expansion card*, is a circuit board that enhances functions of a component of the system unit and/or provides connections to peripherals. A **peripheral** is a device that connects to the system unit and is controlled by the processor in the computer. Examples of peripherals are modems, disk drives, printers, scanners, and keyboards.

Figure 4-24 lists currently used types of adapter cards. Sometimes, all functionality is built in the adapter card. With others, a cable connects the adapter card to a peripheral, such as a scanner, outside the system unit. Figure 4-25 shows an adapter card being inserted in an expansion slot on a personal computer motherboard.

Some motherboards include all necessary capabilities and do not require adapter cards. Other motherboards may require adapter cards to provide capabilities such as sound and video. A **sound card** enhances the sound-generating capabilities of a personal computer by allowing sound to be input through a microphone and output through external speakers or headset. A **video card**, also called a *graphics card*, converts computer output into a video signal that travels through a cable to the monitor, which displays an image on the screen.

WEB LINK 4-6

Adapter Cards

For more information, visit scsite.com/dc2006/ch4/weblink and then click Adapter Cards.

TYPES OF ADAPTER CARDS

Adapter Card	Purpose
Disk controller	Connects disk drives
FireWire	Connects to FireWire devices
Graphics accelerator	Increases the speed at which graphics are displayed
MIDI	Connects musical instruments
Modem	Connects other computers through telephone or cable television lines
Network	Connects other computers and peripherals
PC-to-TV converter	Connects a television
Sound	Connects speakers or a microphone
TV tuner	Allows viewing of television channels on the monitor
USB 2.0	Connects to USB 2.0 devices
Video	Connects a monitor
Video capture	Connects a camcorder

FIGURE 4-24 Currently used adapter cards and their functions.

FIGURE 4-25 An adapter card being inserted in an expansion slot on the motherboard of a personal computer.

In the past, installing a card was not easy and required you to set switches and other elements on the motherboard. Many of today's computers support **Plug and Play**, which means the computer automatically can configure adapter cards and other peripherals as you install them. Having Plug and Play support means you can plug in a device, turn on the computer, and then immediately begin using the device.

PC Cards, Flash Memory Cards, and USB Flash Drives

Notebook and other mobile computers have at least one **PC Card slot**, which is a special type of expansion slot that holds a PC Card. A **PC Card** is a thin, credit card-sized device that adds memory, storage, sound, fax/modem, network, and other capabilities to mobile computers (Figure 4-26). Because of their small size and versatility, some consumer electronics products such as digital cameras use PC Cards.

All PC Cards conform to standards developed by the *Personal Computer Memory Card International Association* (these cards originally were called *PCMCIA cards*). These standards help to ensure the interchangeability of PC Cards among mobile computers. Although some PC cards contain tiny hard disks, many PC Cards are a type of flash memory card.

A **flash memory card** is a removable flash memory device that allows users to transfer data and information conveniently from mobile devices to their desktop computers (Figure 4-27). Many mobile and consumer devices, such as PDAs, smart phones, digital cameras, and digital music players, use these memory cards. Some printers and computers have built-in card readers/writers or slots that read flash memory cards. In addition, you can purchase an external card reader/writer that attaches to any computer. Flash memory cards are available in a variety of shapes and sizes. The type of flash memory card you have will determine the type of card reader/writer you need. Storage capacities of flash memory cards range from 64 MB to 5 GB.

Another widely used type of removable flash memory is the USB flash drive (Figure 4-27). A *USB flash drive* is a flash memory storage device that plugs in a USB port on a computer or portable device. (The next section discusses USB ports.) Storage capacities of USB flash drives range from 64 MB to 1 GB.

Unlike adapter cards that require you to open the system unit and install the card on the motherboard, you can change a removable flash memory device without having to open the system unit or restart the computer. This feature, called *hot plugging*, allows you to insert and remove the removable flash memory and other devices while the computer is running.

WEB LINK 4-7

Removable Flash Memory Devices

For more information, visit scsite.com/ dc2006/ch4/weblink and then click Removable Flash Memory Devices.

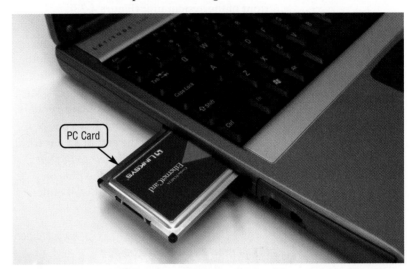

FIGURE 4-26 A PC card slides in a PC Card slot on a notebook computer.

FIGURE 4-27 Removable flash memory devices are available in a range of sizes.

PORTS AND CONNECTORS

A **port** is the point at which a peripheral attaches to a system unit so the peripheral can send data to or receive information from the computer. An external device, such as a keyboard, monitor, printer, mouse, and microphone, often attaches by a cable to a port on the system unit. Instead of port, the term **jack** sometimes is used to identify audio and video ports. The back of the system unit contains many ports; some newer personal computers also have ports on the front of the system unit (Figure 4-28).

Ports have different types of connectors. A **connector** joins a cable to a peripheral. One end of a cable attaches to the connector on the system unit, and the other end of the cable attaches to a connector on the peripheral. Most connectors are available in one of two genders: male or female. *Male connectors* have one or more exposed pins, like the end of an electrical cord you plug in the wall. *Female connectors* have matching holes to accept the pins on a male connector, like an electrical wall outlet.

Sometimes, attaching a new peripheral to the computer is not possible because the connector on the system unit is the same gender as the connector on the cable. In this case, purchasing a gender changer solves this problem. A *gender changer* is a device that enables you to join two connectors that are both female or both male.

Manufacturers often identify the cables by their connector types to assist you with purchasing a cable to connect a computer to a peripheral. Figure 4-29 shows the different types of connectors on a system unit. Some system units include these connectors when you buy the computer. You add other connectors by inserting adapter cards on the motherboard. Certain adapter cards have ports that allow you to attach a peripheral to the adapter card.

Most desktop personal computers have at least one serial port, one parallel port, several USB ports, and a FireWire port. The next section discusses these and other ports.

WEB LINK 4-8

Ports and Connectors

For more information, visit scsite.com/ dc2006/ch4/weblink and then click Ports and Connectors.

FIGURE 4-28 The back of a system unit has many ports. Most computers have ports on the front of the system unit, also.

CONNECTOR TYPES

Connector Type	Picture	Connector Type	Picture
Audio in		Mouse	
Cable TV		Network	
Composite video in		Printer	
FireWire		Serial	
FM reception		Speaker	
Headphone		S-video in	
Keyboard		S-video out	
Microphone		Telephone line in	
Monitor		USB	

FIGURE 4-29 Examples of different types of connectors on a system unit.

Serial Ports

A **serial port** is a type of interface that connects a device to the system unit by transmitting data one bit at a time (Figure 4-30). Serial ports usually connect devices that do not require fast data transmission rates, such as a mouse, keyboard, or modem. The *COM port* (short for communications port) on the system unit is one type of serial port.

Some modems that connect the system unit to a telephone line use a serial port because the telephone line expects the data in a specific frequency. Serial ports conform to either the RS-232 or RS-422 standard, which specifies the number of pins used on the port's connector.

serial transmission of data

byte representation for number 1 (00110001)

byte representation for number 3 (00110011)

byte representation for number 5 (00110101)

connector

port

FIGURE 4-30
A serial port transmits data one bit at a time. One wire sends data, another receives data, and the remaining wires are used for other communications operations.

Parallel Ports

Unlike a serial port, a **parallel port** is an interface that connects devices by transferring more than one bit at a time (Figure 4-31). Originally, parallel ports were developed as an alternative to the slower speed serial ports.

Many printers connect to the system unit using a parallel port. This parallel port can transfer eight bits of data (one byte) simultaneously through eight separate lines in a single cable.

byte representation for number 1 ➔ **00110001**
byte representation for number 3 ➔ **00110011**
byte representation for number 5 ➔ **00110101**

connector

port

FIGURE 4-31 A parallel port is capable of transmitting more than one bit at a time. The port shown in this figure has eight wires that transmit data; the remaining wires are used for other communications operations.

USB Ports

A **USB port**, short for *universal serial bus port*, can connect up to 127 different peripherals together with a single connector type. Devices that connect to a USB port include the following: mouse, printer, digital camera, scanner, speakers, MP3 music player, CD, DVD, and removable hard disk. Personal computers typically have six to eight USB ports either on the front or back of the system unit (Figure 4-28 on page 206). The latest version of USB, called *USB 2.0*, is a more advanced and faster USB, with speeds 40 times higher than that of its predecessor.

To attach multiple peripherals using a single USB port, you can daisy chain the devices together outside the system unit. *Daisy chain* means the first USB device connects to the USB port on the computer, the second USB device connects to the first USB device, the third USB device connects to the second USB device, and so on. An alternative to daisy chaining is to use a USB hub. A **USB hub** is a device that plugs in a USB port on the system unit and contains multiple USB ports in which you plug cables from USB devices.

USB also supports hot plugging and Plug and Play, which means you can attach peripherals while the computer is running. With serial and parallel port connections, by contrast, you often must restart the computer after attaching the peripheral.

Some newer peripherals may attach only to a USB port. Others attach to either a serial or parallel port, as well as a USB port.

FAQ 4-6

Can older USB devices plug in a USB 2.0 port?

Yes. USB 2.0 is *backward compatible*, which means that it supports older USB devices as well as new USB 2.0 devices. Keep in mind, though, that older USB devices do not run any faster in a USB 2.0 port. For more information, visit scsite.com/dc2006/ch4/faq and then click USB 2.0.

FireWire Ports

Previously called an *IEEE 1394 port*, a **FireWire port** is similar to a USB port in that it can connect multiple types of devices that require faster data transmission speeds, such as digital video cameras, digital VCRs, color printers, scanners, digital cameras, and DVD drives, to a single connector. A FireWire port allows you to connect up to 63 devices together. The FireWire port supports Plug and Play.

Some newer peripherals may attach only to a FireWire port. Having standard ports and connectors, such as FireWire and USB, greatly simplify the process of attaching devices to a personal computer. For newer computers that do not have a parallel port, users plug the device in a USB or FireWire port — as specified by the device's manufacturer. In general, FireWire has replaced parallel and SCSI ports, which are discussed in the next section. USB ports have replaced mouse, keyboard, serial, audio, and parallel ports. Figure 4-32 shows how FireWire and USB ports are replacing other ports completely.

Special-Purpose Ports

Four special-purpose ports are MIDI, SCSI, IrDA, and Bluetooth. These ports are not included in typical computers. For a computer to have these ports, you must customize the computer purchase order. The following sections discuss MIDI, SCSI, IrDA, and Bluetooth ports.

MIDI PORT A special type of serial port that connects the system unit to a musical instrument, such as an electronic keyboard, is called a **MIDI port**. Short for *Musical Instrument Digital Interface*, MIDI (pronounced MID-dee) is the electronic music industry's standard that defines how devices, such as sound cards and synthesizers, represent sounds electronically. A *synthesizer*, which can be a peripheral or a chip, creates sound from digital instructions.

A system unit with a MIDI port has the capability of recording sounds that have been created by a synthesizer and then processing the sounds (the data) to create new sounds. Nearly every sound card supports the MIDI standard, so you can play and manipulate on one computer sounds that originally were created on another computer.

TRADITIONAL PORTS

NEW PORTS

FIGURE 4-32 USB and FireWire ports are replacing traditional ports completely.

SCSI PORT   A special high-speed parallel port, called a **SCSI port**, allows you to attach SCSI (pronounced skuzzy) peripherals such as disk drives and printers. Depending on the type of *SCSI*, which stands for *small computer system interface*, you can daisy chain up to either 7 or 15 devices together. Some computers include a SCSI port. Others have a slot that supports a SCSI card.

IrDA PORT   Some devices can transmit data via infrared light waves. For these wireless devices to transmit signals to a computer, both the computer and the device must have an **IrDA port** (Figure 4-33). These ports conform to standards developed by the *IrDA (Infrared Data Association)*.

To ensure nothing obstructs the path of the infrared light wave, you must align the IrDA port on the device with the IrDA port on the computer, similarly to the way you operate a television remote control. Devices that use IrDA ports include a PDA, smart phone, keyboard, mouse, printer, and pager. Several of these devices use a high-speed IrDA port, sometimes called a *fast infrared port*.

BLUETOOTH PORT   An alternative to IrDA, **Bluetooth** technology uses radio waves to transmit data between two devices (Figure 4-34). Unlike IrDA, the Bluetooth devices do not have to be aligned with each other. Many computers, peripherals, PDAs, smart phones, cars, and other consumer electronics are Bluetooth-enabled, which means they contain a small chip that allows them to communicate with other Bluetooth-enabled computers and devices. The latest version of Bluetooth, called Bluetooth 2.0, supports higher connection speeds and is backward compatible with its predecessors.

If you have a computer that is not Bluetooth enabled, you can purchase a Bluetooth wireless port adapter that will convert an existing USB port or serial port into a Bluetooth port. Also available are Bluetooth PC Cards for notebook computers and Bluetooth cards for PDAs and smart phones.

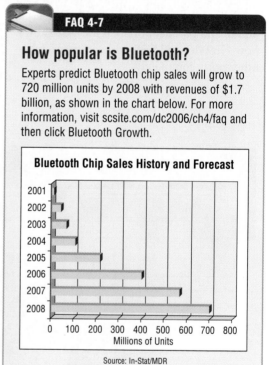

FAQ 4-7

How popular is Bluetooth?

Experts predict Bluetooth chip sales will grow to 720 million units by 2008 with revenues of $1.7 billion, as shown in the chart below. For more information, visit scsite.com/dc2006/ch4/faq and then click Bluetooth Growth.

Bluetooth Chip Sales History and Forecast

(Years: 2001, 2002, 2003, 2004, 2005, 2006, 2007, 2008. Horizontal axis: 0, 100, 200, 300, 400, 500, 600, 700, 800 Millions of Units)

Source: In-Stat/MDR

FIGURE 4-33   Many devices communicate wirelessly with desktop or notebook computers through IrDA ports.

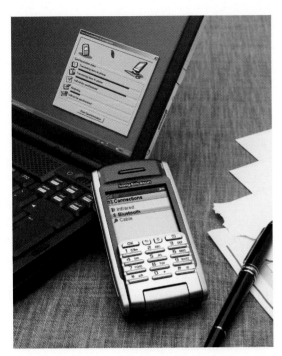

FIGURE 4-34 This smart phone wirelessly communicates with a Bluetooth-enabled notebook computer.

BUSES

As explained earlier in this chapter, a computer processes and stores data as a series of electronic bits. These bits transfer internally within the circuitry of the computer along electrical channels. Each channel, called a **bus**, allows the various devices both inside and attached to the system unit to communicate with each other. Just as vehicles travel on a highway to move from one destination to another, bits travel on a bus (Figure 4-35).

Buses transfer bits from input devices to memory, from memory to the processor, from the processor to memory, and from memory to output or storage devices. Buses consist of two parts: a data bus and an address bus. The *data bus* transfers actual data and the *address bus* transfers information about where the data should reside in memory.

The size of a bus, called the *bus width*, determines the number of bits that the computer can transmit at one time. For example, a 32-bit bus can transmit 32 bits (4 bytes) at a time. On a 64-bit bus, bits transmit from one location to another 64 bits (8 bytes) at a time. The larger the number of bits handled by the bus, the faster the computer transfers data. Using the highway analogy again, assume that one lane

on a highway can carry one bit. A 32-bit bus is like a 32-lane highway. A 64-bit bus is like a 64-lane highway.

If a number in memory occupies 8 bytes, or 64 bits, the computer must transmit it in two separate steps when using a 32-bit bus: once for the first 32 bits and once for the second 32 bits. Using a 64-bit bus, the computer can transmit the number in a single step, transferring all 64 bits at once. The wider the bus, the fewer number of transfer steps required and the faster the transfer of data. Most personal computers today use a 64-bit bus.

In conjunction with the bus width, many computer professionals refer to a computer's word size. **Word size** is the number of bits the processor can interpret and execute at a given time. That is, a 64-bit processor can manipulate 64 bits at a time. Computers with a larger word size can process more data in the same amount of time than computers with a smaller word size. In most computers, the word size is the same as the bus width.

FIGURE 4-35 Just as vehicles travel on a highway, bits travel on a bus. Buses transfer bits from input devices to memory, from memory to the processor, from the processor to memory, and from memory to output or storage devices.

Every bus also has a clock speed. Just like the processor, manufacturers state the clock speed for a bus in hertz. Recall that one megahertz (MHz) is equal to one million ticks per second. Most of today's processors have a bus clock speed of 400, 533, or 800 MHz. The higher the bus clock speed, the faster the transmission of data, which results in applications running faster.

A computer has two basic types of buses: a system bus and an expansion bus. A *system bus* is part of the motherboard and connects the processor to main memory. An *expansion bus* allows the processor to communicate with peripherals. When computer professionals use the term bus by itself, they usually are referring to the system bus.

Expansion Bus

Some peripherals outside the system unit connect to a port on an adapter card, which is inserted in an expansion slot on the motherboard. This expansion slot connects to the expansion bus, which allows the processor to communicate with the peripheral attached to the adapter card. Data transmitted to memory or the processor travels from the expansion slot via the expansion bus and the system bus.

The types of expansion buses on a motherboard determine the types of cards you can add to the computer. Thus, you should understand these expansion buses commonly found in today's personal computers: PCI bus, AGP bus, USB, FireWire bus, and PC Card bus.

- The *PCI bus* (*Peripheral Component Interconnect bus*) is a high-speed expansion bus that connects higher speed devices. Types of cards you can insert in a PCI bus expansion slot include video cards, sound cards, SCSI cards, and high-speed network cards.
- The *Accelerated Graphics Port* (*AGP*) is a bus designed by Intel to improve the speed with which 3-D graphics and video transmit. With an AGP video card in an AGP bus slot, the AGP bus provides a faster, dedicated interface between the video card and memory. Newer processors support AGP technology.
- The USB (*universal serial bus*) and *FireWire bus* are buses that eliminate the need to install cards in expansion slots. In a computer with a USB, for example, USB devices connect to each other

outside the system unit, and then a single cable attaches to the USB port. The USB port then connects to the USB, which connects to the PCI bus on the motherboard. The FireWire bus works in a similar fashion. With these buses, expansion slots are available for devices not compatible with USB or FireWire.

- The expansion bus for a PC Card is the *PC Card bus*. With a PC Card inserted in a PC Card slot, data travels on the PC Card bus to the PCI bus.

BAYS

After you purchase a computer, you may want to install an additional storage device, such as a disk drive, in the system unit. A **bay** is an opening inside the system unit in which you can install additional equipment. A bay is different from a slot, which is used for the installation of adapter cards. Rectangular openings, called **drive bays**, typically hold disk drives.

Two types of drive bays exist: external and internal. An *external drive bay* allows a user to access the drive from outside the system unit (Figure 4-36). Floppy disk drives, CD drives, DVD drives, Zip drives, and tape drives are examples of devices installed in external drive bays. An *internal drive bay* is concealed entirely within the system unit. Hard disk drives are installed in internal bays.

WEB LINK 4-9

Buses

For more information, visit scsite.com/dc2006/ch4/weblink and then click Buses.

CD drive

DVD drive

floppy disk drive

FIGURE 4-36 External drive bays usually are located beside or on top of one another.

POWER SUPPLY

Many personal computers plug in standard wall outlets, which supply an alternating current (AC) of 115 to 120 volts. This type of power is unsuitable for use with a computer, which requires a direct current (DC) ranging from 5 to 12 volts. The **power supply** is the component of the system unit that converts the wall outlet AC power into DC power. Different motherboards and computers require different wattages on the power supply. If a power supply is not providing the necessary power, the computer will not function properly.

Near the power supply is a fan that keeps the power supply and other components of the system unit cool. This fan dissipates heat generated by the processor and other components of the system unit. Many newer computers have additional fans near certain components in the system unit such as the processor, hard disk, and ports.

Some external peripherals such as an external modem, speakers, or a tape drive have an **AC adapter**, which is an external power supply. One end of the AC adapter plugs in the wall outlet and the other end attaches to the peripheral. The AC adapter converts the AC power into DC power that the peripheral requires.

FAQ 4-8

How many fans are in a system unit?

Most systems units have at least three fans: one in the power supply, one on the case, and one on the processor heat sink. Some computers allow you to turn off noisy fans until they are needed. You also can purchase utility programs that slow or stop the fan until the temperature reaches a certain level. For more information, visit scsite.com/dc2006/ch4/faq and then click Computer Fan.

MOBILE COMPUTERS AND DEVICES

As businesses and schools expand to serve people across the country and around the world, increasingly more people need to use a computer while traveling to and from a main office or school to conduct business, communicate, or do homework. As Chapter 1 discussed, users with such mobile computing needs — known as mobile users — often have a mobile computer, such as a notebook computer or Tablet PC, or a mobile device such as a smart phone or PDA (Figure 4-37).

FIGURE 4-37 Users with mobile computing needs often have a notebook computer, PDA, and/or smart phone.

Weighing on average between 2.5 and 8 pounds, notebook computers can run either using batteries or using a standard power supply. Smaller PDAs and smart phones run strictly on batteries. Like their desktop counterparts, mobile computers and devices have a motherboard that contains electronic components that process data. Read At Issue 4-5 for a related discussion.

A notebook computer usually is more expensive than a desktop computer with the same capabilities because it is more costly to miniaturize the components. The typical notebook computer often has video, serial, parallel,

modem, network, FireWire, USB, headphones, and microphone ports (Figure 4-38).

Two basic designs of Tablet PC are available: slate and convertible. With the slate Tablet PC (shown in Figure 4-1 on page 184), all the hardware is behind the display — much like a PDA. Users can attach a removable keyboard to the slate Tablet PC. The display on the convertible Tablet PC, which is attached to a keyboard, can be rotated 180 degrees and folded down over the keyboard. Thus, the convertible Tablet PC can be repositioned to look like either a notebook computer or a slate Tablet PC. Tablet PCs usually include several slots and ports (Figure 4-39).

video port   serial port   parallel port   network port   USB ports   microphone port

FIGURE 4-38 Ports on a typical notebook computer.   modem port   FireWire port   headphones port

AT ISSUE 4-5

Should Smart Shoes Be Banned from Competitive Events?

Titanium golf clubs. Graphite tennis rackets. Aluminum baseball bats. Advances in technology have impacted many sports. Now, Adidas is changing the sport of running with the introduction of a computerized running shoe. The lightweight, battery-powered shoe, sometimes called a "smart shoe," contains a sensor and a 20 MHz microprocessor. Every second, the sensor sends thousands of readings to the tiny mobile computer, which uses a motorized screw and cable system to adjust the heel cushion based on the conditions and the runner's style. The goal is to ensure ideal cushioning for the runner and the situation. The smart shoe is innovative, but is it fair? To maintain competitive balance, the governing bodies of golf and tennis place restrictions on the composition of equipment. Some racers would like similar limitations placed on running shoes. At a cost of about $250, the smart shoe could provide an unfair advantage to wealthier runners. The advantage would be evident at high school, college, and amateur races, where not all competitors could afford the shoe. Should smart shoes be banned from races? Why or why not? Baseball banned aluminum bats at the professional level; should smart shoes be banned at the high school, college, and amateur levels, where they would be most apt to upset competitive balance? Why?

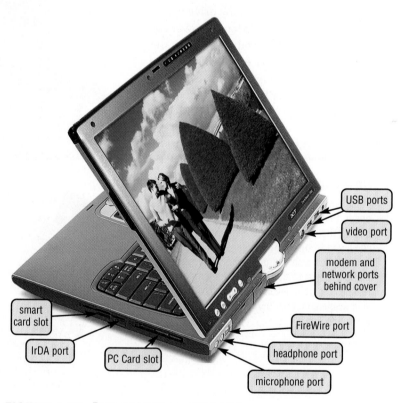

USB ports

video port

modem and network ports behind cover

FireWire port

headphone port

microphone port

smart card slot

IrDA port

PC Card slot

FIGURE 4-39 Ports and slots on a Tablet PC.

PDAs and smart phones are quite affordable, usually priced at a few hundred dollars or less. These mobile devices often have an IrDA port or are Bluetooth enabled so users can communicate wirelessly with other computers or devices such as a printer. Read Looking Ahead 4-2 for a look at the next generation of mobile computer.

LOOKING AHEAD 4-2

DNA Computer Works to Fight Cancer

One of the newest computers is so tiny that one trillion of them can fit inside a drop of water. The hardware of this biological invention is composed of enzymes that manipulate DNA, and the software is composed of actual DNA.

The concept for this computer had been proposed in 1936, but the actual computer was developed at the Weizmann Institute in Israel in 2001. Today, researchers at the Weizmann Institute are developing applications that process biological information. Their most current success is being able to program the computer to diagnose and treat cancer.

The researchers are hopeful they will be able to have the medical computer function inside a human cell. For more information, visit scsite.com/dc2006/ch4/looking and then click DNA Computer.

PUTTING IT ALL TOGETHER

When you purchase a computer, it is important to understand how the components of the system unit work. Many components of the system unit influence the speed and power of a computer. These include the type of processor, the clock speed of the processor, the amount of RAM, bus width, and the clock speed of the bus. The configuration you require depends on your intended use.

The table in Figure 4-40 lists the suggested minimum processor, clock speed, and RAM requirements based on the needs of various types of computer users.

SUGGESTED MINIMUM CONFIGURATIONS BY USER

User	Processor, Clock Speed, and RAM
HOME	Celeron (3 GHz or higher) or Sempron (2 GHz or higher) or Pentium 4 (2.8 GHz or higher) or Sempron (2 GHz or higher) Minimum RAM: 256 MB
SMALL OFFICE/ HOME OFFICE 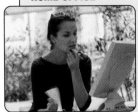	Pentium 4 (3 GHz or higher) or Athlon 64 (2.4 GHz or higher) Minimum RAM: 512 MB
MOBILE	Celeron M (1.5 GHz or higher) or Pentium M (2 GHz or higher) or Mobile Sempron (1.8 GHz or higher) Minimum RAM: 512 MB
POWER	Itanium 2 (1.6 GHz or higher) or Opteron (2.4 GHz or higher) or Xeon MP (3 GHz or higher) or Athlon MP (2.25 GHz or higher) Minimum RAM: 2 GB
LARGE BUSINESS	Pentium 4 (3.4 GHz or higher) or Athlon 64 (2.4 GHz or higher) Minimum RAM: 1 GB

FIGURE 4-40 Suggested processor, clock speed, and RAM configurations by user.

KEEPING YOUR COMPUTER CLEAN

Over time, the system unit collects dust — even in a clean environment. Built up dust can block airflow in the computer, which can cause it to overheat, corrode, or even stop working. By cleaning your computer once or twice a year, you can help extend its life. This preventive maintenance task requires a few basic products (Figure 4-41):

- can of compressed air — removes dust and lint from difficult-to-reach areas
- lint-free antistatic wipes and swabs
- bottle of rubbing alcohol
- small computer vacuum (or small attachments on your house vacuum)
- antistatic wristband — to avoid damaging internal components with static electricity
- small screwdriver (may be required to open the case or remove adapter cards)

Before cleaning the computer, turn it off, unplug it from the electrical outlet, and unplug all cables from the ports. Blow away any dust from all openings on the computer case, such as drives, slots, and ports. Vacuum the power supply fan on the back of the computer case to remove any dust that has accumulated on it. Next, release short blasts of compressed air on the power supply fan. Then, use an antistatic wipe to clean the exterior of the case.

If you need assistance opening the computer case, refer to the instructions that came with the computer. Once the case is open, put the antistatic wristband on your wrist and attach its clip to the case of the computer. Use the antistatic wipes to clean dust and grime inside the walls of the computer case. Vacuum as much dust as possible from the interior of the case, including the wires, chips, adapter cards, and fan blades. Next, release short blasts of compressed air in areas the vacuum cannot reach. If the motherboard and adapter cards still look dirty, gently clean them with lint-free wipes or swabs lightly dampened with alcohol.

When finished, be sure all adapter cards are tightly in their expansion slots. Then close the case, plug in all cables, and attach the power cord. Write down the date you cleaned the computer so you have a record for your next cleaning.

If you do not feel comfortable cleaning the system unit yourself, have a local computer company clean it for you.

FIGURE 4-41 With a few products, this computer user keeps his computer clean.

FAQ 4-9

How do I clean components in the system unit?

Never pour or spray any form of liquid on the motherboard — or on any hardware. Always apply the liquid to a cloth or swab, and then use the cloth or swab to clean the hardware. If you can squeeze liquid out of the cloth or swab, then it is too moist. For more information, visit scsite.com/dc2006/ch4/faq and then click PC Hygiene.

Test your knowledge of pages 204 through 216 in Quiz Yourself 4-3.

QUIZ YOURSELF 4-3

Instructions: Find the true statement below. Then, rewrite the remaining false statements so they are true.

1. A bus is the point at which a peripheral attaches to a system unit so the peripheral can send data to or receive information from the computer.
2. An AC adapter is a socket on the motherboard that can hold an adapter card.
3. Near the power supply is a heater that keeps components of the system unit warm.
4. Serial ports can connect up to 127 different peripherals together with a single connector type.
5. The higher the bus clock speed, the slower the transmission of data.
6. When cleaning the inside of the system unit, wear an antistatic wristband to avoid damaging internal components with static electricity.

Quiz Yourself Online: To further check your knowledge of expansion slots, adapter cards, ports, buses, components of mobile computers and devices, and cleaning a computer, visit scsite.com/dc2006/ch4/quiz and then click Objectives 8 – 12.

CHAPTER SUMMARY

Chapter 4 presented the components of the system unit; described how memory stores data, instructions, and information; and discussed the sequence of operations that occur when a computer executes an instruction. The chapter included a comparison of various personal computer processors on the market today. It also discussed how to clean a system unit.

CAREER CORNER

Computer Engineer

A *computer engineer* designs and develops the electronic components found in computers and peripheral devices. They also can work as researchers, theorists, and inventors. Companies may hire computer engineers for permanent positions or as consultants, with jobs that extend from a few months to a few years, depending on the project. Engineers in research and development often work on projects that will not be released to the general public for two years.

Responsibilities vary from company to company. All computer engineering work, however, demands problem-solving skills and the ability to create and use new technologies. The ability to handle multiple tasks and concentrate on detail is a key component. Assignments often are taken on as part of a team. Therefore, computer engineers must be able to communicate clearly with both computer personnel and computer users, who may have little technical knowledge.

Before taking in-depth computer engineering design and development classes, students usually take mathematics, physics, and basic engineering. Computer engineering degrees include B.S., M.S., and Ph.D. Because computer engineers employed in private industry often advance into managerial positions, many computer engineering graduates obtain a master's degree in business administration (M.B.A.). Most computer engineers earn between $56,000 and $92,000 annually, depending on their experience and employer, but salaries can exceed $115,000. For more information, visit scsite.com/dc2006/ch4/careers and then click Computer Engineer.

High-Tech Talk

RANDOM ACCESS MEMORY (RAM): THE GENIUS OF MEMORY

Inside your computer, RAM takes the form of separate microchip modules that plug in slots on the computer's motherboard. These slots connect through a line (bus) or set of electrical paths to the computer's processor. Before you turn on a computer, its RAM is a blank slate. As you start and use your computer, the operating system files, applications, and any data currently being used by the processor are written to and stored in RAM so the processor can access them quickly.

How is this data written to and stored in RAM? In the most common form of RAM, dynamic random access memory (DRAM), *transistors* (in this case, acting as switches) and a *capacitor* (as a data storage element) create a *memory cell*, which represents a single bit of data.

Memory cells are etched onto a silicon wafer in a series of columns (bitlines) and rows (wordlines), known as an *array*. The intersection of a column and row constitutes the *address* of the memory cell (Figure 4-42). Each memory cell has a unique address that can be found by counting across columns and then counting down by row. The address of a character consists of a series of memory cell addresses put together.

To write data to RAM, the processor sends the memory controller the address of a memory cell in which to store data. The *memory controller* organizes the request and sends the column and row address in an electrical charge along the appropriate address lines, which are very thin electrical lines etched into the RAM chip. This causes the transistors along those address lines to close.

These transistors act as a switch to control the flow of electrical current in an either closed or open circuit. While the transistors are closed, the software sends bursts of electricity along selected data lines. When the electrical charge traveling down the data line reaches an address line where a transistor is closed, the charge flows through the closed transistor and charges the capacitor.

A capacitor works as electronic storage that holds an electrical charge. Each charged capacitor along the address line represents a 1 bit. An uncharged capacitor represents a 0 bit. The combination of 1s and 0s from eight data lines forms a single byte of data.

The capacitors used in dynamic RAM, however, lose their electrical charge. The processor or memory controller continuously has to recharge all of the capacitors holding a charge (a 1 bit) before the capacitor discharges. During this *refresh operation*, which happens automatically thousands of times per second, the memory controller reads

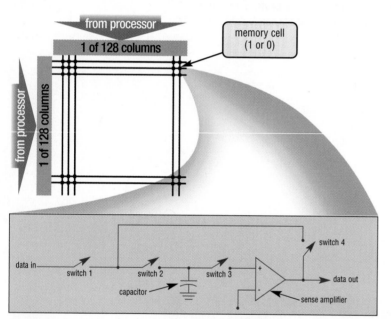

FIGURE 4-42 An illustration of one type of DRAM. When writing data, switches 1 and 2 in the circuit are closed and switches 3 and 4 are open. When reading data, switches 2, 3, and 4 in the circuit are closed and switch 1 is open. Most DRAM chips actually have arrays of memory cells (upper-left corner of figure) that are 16 rows deep.

memory and then immediately rewrites it. This refresh operation is what gives dynamic RAM its name. Dynamic RAM has to be refreshed continually, or it loses the charges that represent bits of data. A specialized circuit called a counter tracks the refresh sequence to ensure that all of the rows are refreshed.

The process of reading data from RAM uses a similar, but reverse, series of steps. When the processor gets the next instruction it is to perform, the instruction may contain the address of a memory cell from which to read data. This address is sent to the memory controller. To locate the memory cell, the memory controller sends the column and row address in an electrical charge down the appropriate address lines.

This electrical charge causes the transistors along the address line to close. At every point along the address line where a capacitor is holding a charge, the capacitor discharges through the circuit created by the closed transistors, sending electrical charges along the data lines.

A specialized circuit called a *sense amplifier* determines and amplifies the level of charge in the capacitor. A capacitor charge over a certain voltage level represents the binary value 1; a capacitor charge below that level represents a 0. The sensed and amplified value is sent back down the address line to the processor.

As long as a computer is running, data continuously is being written to and read from RAM. As soon as you shut down a computer, RAM loses its data. The next time you turn on a computer, operating system files and other data are again loaded into RAM and the read/write process starts all over. For more information, visit scsite.com/dc2006/ch4/tech and then click Memory.

Companies on the Cutting Edge

AMD
PC PROCESSOR SUPPLIER

Customer needs influence the integrated circuits *Advanced Micro Devices* (*AMD*) develops for the computing, communications, and consumer electronics industries. AMD calls this philosophy "customer-centric innovation."

As a global supplier of PC processors, AMD engineers its technologies at its Submicron Development Center (SDC) in Sunnyvale, California. The technologies are put into production at manufacturing facilities in the United States, Europe, Asia, and Japan.

Among the company's most recent products are the AMD Athlon 64 processor for desktop and personal computers and the AMD Opteron processor for servers and workstations. The company also is working with personal computer manufacturers to develop media-center computers based on its Athlon 64 chips for playing and distributing music and video throughout a home. For more information, visit scsite.com/dc2006/ch4/companies and then click AMD.

INTEL
CHIP MAKER DOMINATES THE COMPUTER MARKET

When Gordon Moore and Robert Noyce started Intel in 1968, their goal was to replace magnetic core memory with semiconductor memory. Noyce and Moore, together with Andy Grove, refined the process of placing thousands of tiny electronic devices on a silicon chip. In 1971, the company introduced the Intel 4004, the first single-chip microprocessor.

When IBM chose the Intel 8008 chip for its new personal computer in 1980, Intel chips became standard for all IBM-compatible personal computers. Today, Intel's microprocessors are the building blocks in countless personal computers, servers, networks, and communications devices. In 2003, Intel developed its Centrino mobile technology, which integrates wireless capabilities in notebook computers and Tablet PCs. For more information, visit scsite.com/dc2006/ch4/companies and then click Intel.

Technology Trailblazers

JACK KILBY
INTEGRATED CIRCUIT INVENTOR

Jack Kilby holds more than 60 patents, but one has changed the world. His integrated circuit, or microchip, invention made microprocessors possible.

Kilby started his work with miniature electrical components at Centralab, where he developed transistors for hearing aids. He then took a research position with Texas Instruments and developed a working model of the first integrated circuit, which was patented in 1959. Kilby applied this invention to various industrial, military, and commercial applications, including the first pocket calculator, called the Pocketronic.

Kilby is retired from Texas Instruments and works as a consultant and teacher. He was awarded the Nobel Prize in physics in 2000 for his invention of the integrated circuit, an invention he believes will continue to change the world. For more information, visit scsite.com/dc2006/ch4/people and then click Jack Kilby.

GORDON MOORE
INTEL COFOUNDER

More than 40 years ago, *Gordon Moore* predicted that the number of transistors and resistors placed on computer chips would double every year, with a proportional increase in computing power and decrease in cost. This bold forecast, now known as Moore's Law, proved amazingly accurate for 10 years. Then, Moore revised the estimate to doubling every two years.

Convinced of the future of silicon chips, Moore founded Intel in 1968. Moore's lifelong interest in technology was kindled at an early age when he experimented with a neighbor's chemistry set. Even then, he displayed the passion for practical outcomes that has typified his work as a scientist and engineer.

Moore says that the semiconductor industry's progress will far surpass that of nearly all other industries. For more information, visit scsite.com/dc2006/ch4/people and then click Gordon Moore.

Chapter Review

The Chapter Review section summarizes the concepts presented in this chapter. To listen to the audio version of this Chapter Review, visit scsite.com/dc2006/ch4/review. To obtain help from other students regarding any subject in this chapter, visit scsite.com/dc2006/ch4/forum and post your thoughts or questions.

(1) How Are Various Styles of System Units Different?   The **system unit** is a case that contains electronic components of the computer used to process data. On desktop personal computers, most storage devices also are part of the system unit. On notebook computers, the keyboard and pointing device often occupy the area on top of the system unit, and the display attaches to the system unit by hinges. On mobile devices, the display often is built into the system unit.

(2) What Are Chips, Adapter Cards, and Other Components of the Motherboard?   The **motherboard** is the main circuit board of the system unit. The motherboard contains many electronic components including a processor chip, memory chips, expansion slots, and adapter cards. A **chip** is a small piece of semiconducting material, usually silicon, on which integrated circuits are etched. Expansion slots hold adapter cards that provide connections and functions not built into the motherboard.

(3) What Are the Components of a Processor, and How Do They Complete a Machine Cycle?   The **processor** interprets and carries out the basic instructions that operate a computer. Processors contain a **control unit** that directs and coordinates most of the operations in the computer and an **arithmetic logic unit** (*ALU*) that performs arithmetic, comparison, and other operations. The *machine cycle* is a set of four basic operations — *fetching, decoding, executing,* and *storing* — that the processor repeats for every instruction. The control unit fetches program instructions and data from memory and decodes the instructions into commands the computer can execute.

(4) What Are the Characteristics of Various Personal Computer Processors?   Intel produces the **Pentium** processor for high-performance PCs, the **Celeron** processor for basic PCs, and the **Xeon** and **Itanium** processors for workstations and low-end servers. AMD manufactures *Intel-compatible processors*, which have an internal design similar to Intel processors. Motorola produces the *Motorola processor*, with a design different from the Intel-style processor, for Apple computers. Some devices have a *system on a chip* processor that integrates the functions of a processor, memory, and a video card on a single chip.

Connect
Visit scsite.com/dc2006/ch4/quiz or click the Quiz Yourself button. Click Objectives 1 – 4.

(5) What Is a Bit, and How Does a Series of Bits Represent Data?   Most computers are **digital** and recognize only two discrete states: off and on. To represent these states, computers use the **binary system**, which is a number system that has just two unique digits — 0 (for off) and 1 (for on) — called bits. A **bit** is the smallest unit of data a computer can process. Grouped together as a unit, 8 bits form a **byte**, which provides enough different combinations of 0s and 1s to represent 256 individual characters. The combinations are defined by patterns, called coding schemes, such as *ASCII, EBCDIC,* and *Unicode*.

(6) How Do Programs Transfer In and Out of Memory?   When an application program starts, the program's instructions load into memory from the hard disk. The program and operating system instructions are in memory, and the program's window is displayed on the screen. When you quit the program, the program instructions are removed from memory, and the program no longer is displayed on the screen.

Chapter Review

(7) What Are the Various Types of Memory? The system unit contains volatile and nonvolatile memory. *Volatile memory* loses its contents when the computer's power is turned off. *Nonvolatile memory* does not lose its contents when the computer's power is turned off. RAM is the most common type of volatile memory. ROM, flash memory, and CMOS are examples of nonvolatile memory. **RAM** consists of memory chips that can be read from and written to by the processor and other devices. **ROM** refers to memory chips storing permanent data and instructions that usually cannot be modified. **Flash memory** can be erased electronically and rewritten. **CMOS** technology uses battery power to retain information even when the power to the computer is turned off.

> *connect*
> Visit scsite.com/dc2006/ch4/quiz or click the Quiz Yourself button. Click Objectives 5 – 7.

(8) What Are the Types of Expansion Slots and Adapter Cards? An **expansion slot** is a socket on the motherboard that can hold an adapter card. An **adapter card** is a circuit board that enhances functions of a component of the system unit and/or provides a connection to a **peripheral** such as a modem, disk drive, printer, scanner, or keyboard. Several types of adapter cards exist. A **sound card** enhances the sound-generating capabilities of a personal computer. A **video card** converts computer output into a video signal that displays an image on the screen. Many computers today support **Plug and Play**, which enables the computer to configure adapter cards and peripherals automatically.

(9) How Are a Serial Port, a Parallel Port, a USB Port, a FireWire port, and Other Ports Different? A **port** is the point at which a peripheral attaches to a system unit so it can send data to or receive information from the computer. A **serial port**, which transmits data one bit at a time, usually connects devices that do not require fast data transmission, such as a mouse, keyboard, or modem. A **parallel port**, which transfers more than one bit at a time, often connects a printer to the system unit. A **USB port** can connect up to 127 different peripherals together with a single connector type. A **FireWire port** can connect multiple types of devices that require faster data transmission speeds. Four special-purpose ports are MIDI, SCSI, IrDA, and Bluetooth. A **MIDI port** connects the system unit to a musical instrument. A **SCSI port** attaches the system unit to SCSI peripherals, such as disk drives. An **IrDA port** and **Bluetooth** technology allow wireless devices to transmit signals to a computer via infrared light waves or radio waves.

(10) How Do Buses Contribute to a Computer's Processing Speed? A **bus** is an electrical channel along which bits transfer within the circuitry of a computer, allowing devices both inside and attached to the system unit to communicate. The size of a bus, called the *bus width*, determines the number of bits that the computer can transmit at one time. The larger the bus width, the faster the computer transfers data.

(11) What Are the Components in Mobile Computers and Mobile Devices? In addition to the motherboard, processor, memory, sound card, PC Card slot, and **drive bay**, a mobile computer's system unit also houses devices such as the keyboard, pointing device, speakers, and display. The system unit for a typical notebook computer often has video, serial, parallel, modem, network, FireWire, USB, headphone, and microphone ports. Tablet PCs usually include several slots and ports. PDAs often have an IrDA port or are Bluetooth enabled so users can communicate wirelessly.

(12) How Do You Clean a System Unit? Before cleaning a system unit, turn off the computer and unplug it from the wall. Use a small vacuum and a can of compressed air to remove external dust. After opening the case, wear an antistatic wristband and vacuum the interior. Wipe away dust and grime using lint-free antistatic wipes and rubbing alcohol.

> *connect*
> Visit scsite.com/dc2006/ch4/quiz or click the Quiz Yourself button. Click Objectives 8 – 12.

Quizzes and
Learning Games

Computer Genius
Crossword Puzzle
DC Track and Field
Practice Test
Quiz Yourself
Wheel of Terms
You're Hired!

Exercises

Case Studies
Chapter Review
Checkpoint
▸ Key Terms
Learn How To
Learn It Online
Web Research

Beyond the Book

Career Corner
Companies
FAQs
High-Tech Talk
Looking Ahead
Making Use of
the Web
Trailblazers
Web Links

Features

Chapter Forum
Install Computer
Lab Exercises
Maintain Computer
Tech News
Timeline 2006

Key Terms

You should know the Primary Terms and be familiar with the Secondary Terms. Use the list below to help focus your study. To further enhance your understanding of the Key Terms in this chapter, visit scsite.com/dc2006/ch4/terms. See an example of and a definition for each term, and access current and additional information about the term from the Web.

Primary Terms

(shown in bold-black characters in the chapter)

AC adapter (213)
access time (203)
adapter card (204)
analog (194)
arithmetic logic unit (188)
bay (212)
binary system (195)
bit (195)
Bluetooth (210)
bus (211)
byte (195)
cache (201)
Celeron (190)
central processing unit (CPU) (187)
chip (186)
clock speed (189)
complementary metal-oxide semiconductor (CMOS) (203)
connector (206)
control unit (187)
digital (194)
drive bays (212)
expansion slot (204)
FireWire port (209)
firmware (202)
flash memory (202)
flash memory card (205)
gigabyte (GB) (197)
gigahertz (GHz) (189)
IrDA port (210)
Itanium (190)
jack (206)

kilobyte (KB or K) (197)
megabyte (MB) (197)
memory (196)
memory cache (201)
memory module (199)
memory slots (199)
MIDI port (209)
motherboard (186)
nanosecond (203)
parallel port (207)
PC Card (205)
PC Card slot (205)
Pentium (190)
Pentium M (190)
peripheral (204)
Plug and Play (205)
port (206)
power supply (213)
processor (187)
RAM (198)
read-only memory (ROM) (201)
SCSI port (210)
serial port (207)
sound card (204)
system clock (189)
system unit (184)
terabyte (TB) (197)
USB hub (208)
USB port (207)
video card (204)
word size (211)
Xeon (190)

Secondary Terms

(shown in italic characters in the chapter)

Accelerated Graphics Port (AGP) (212)
address (196)
address bus (211)
advanced transfer cache (ATC) (201)
ALU (188)
American Standard Code for Information Interchange (ASCII) (195)
arithmetic operations (188)
binary digit (195)
bus width (211)
chassis (184)
clock cycle (189)
COM port (207)
comparison operations (188)
daisy chain (208)
data bus (211)
decoding (188)
DIMM (dual inline memory module) (199)
Double Data Rate SDRAM (DDR SDRAM) (199)
dual-core processor (190)
dynamic RAM (DRAM) (199)
EEPROM (electrically erasable programmable read-only memory) chip (202)
executing (188)
expansion bus (212)
expansion card (204)
Extended Binary Coded Decimal Interchange Code (EBCDIC) (195)
external drive bay (212)
fast infrared port (210)
female connectors (206)
fetching (188)
FireWire bus (212)
gender changer (206)
graphics card (204)
heat pipe (193)
heat sink (193)
hertz (189)
hot plugging (205)
Hyper-Threading (HT) Technology (190)
IBM processor (190)
IEEE 1394 port (209)
integrated circuit (186)
Intel-compatible processors (190)
internal drive bay (212)
IrDA (Infrared Data Association) (210)

L1 cache (201)
L2 cache (201)
L3 cache (201)
liquid cooling technology (193)
machine cycle (188)
magnetoresistive RAM (MRAM) (199)
main memory (198)
male connectors (206)
microcode (202)
microprocessor (187)
MIPS (millions of instructions per second) (190)
Motorola processor (190)
Musical Instrument Digital Interface (209)
nonvolatile memory (197)
ns (203)
parallel processing (194)
PC Card bus (212)
PCI bus (Peripheral Component Interconnect bus) (212)
Personal Computer Memory Card International Association (PCMCIA) cards (205)
pipelining (189)
PROM (programmable read-only memory) chip (202)
Rambus DRAM (RDRAM) (199)
random access memory (198)
registers (189)
RIMM (Rambus inline memory module) (199)
SCSI (small computer system interface) (210)
SIMM (single inline memory module) (199)
static RAM (SRAM) (199)
stored program concept (196)
storing (188)
superscalar (189)
synchronous DRAM (SDRAM) (199)
synthesizer (209)
system board (186)
system bus (212)
system on a chip (190)
transistor (186)
Unicode (195)
universal serial bus (212)
universal serial bus port (208)
USB 2.0 (208)
USB flash drive (205)
volatile memory (197)

Checkpoint

Use the Checkpoint exercises to check your knowledge level of the chapter. The Beyond the Book exercises will help broaden your understanding of the concepts presented in this chapter. To complete the Checkpoint exercises interactively, visit scsite.com/dc2006/ch4/check.

Label the Figure
Identify these components.

a. processor chip in a processor slot

b. motherboard

c. memory module

d. expansion slots

e. adapter cards

1.

2.

3.

4.

5.

True/False
Mark T for True and F for False. (See page numbers in parentheses.)

_____ 1. On notebook computers, the keyboard and pointing device attach to the system unit by hinges. (185)

_____ 2. The processor interprets and carries out the basic instructions that operate a computer. (185)

_____ 3. The greater the number of transistors, the more complex and powerful the processor chip. (190)

_____ 4. A Pentium M processor typically is used for workstations and low-end servers. (192)

_____ 5. Replacing a motherboard is a fairly simple process, whereas replacing a processor is much more complicated. (192)

_____ 6. Computers can use only one processor at a time. (194)

_____ 7. A byte is the smallest unit of data the computer can process. (195)

_____ 8. Coding schemes make it possible for humans to interact with a digital computer that processes only bits. (195)

_____ 9. Magnetoresistive RAM stores data using magnetic charges instead of electrical charges. (199)

_____ 10. Two types of cache are memory cache and disk cache. (201)

_____ 11. Serial ports usually connect devices that require fast data transmission rates. (207)

_____ 12. Serial ports transfer more than one bit at a time. (207)

Checkpoint

 Multiple Choice   Select the best answer. (See page numbers in parentheses.)

1. On _____, the display often is built into the system unit. (185)
   a. desktop personal computers
   b. notebook computers
   c. mobile devices
   d. all of the above

2. The processor also is called the _____. (187)
   a. chip
   b. adapter card
   c. motherboard
   d. central processing unit (CPU)

3. Processors contain _____. (187)
   a. a chip and an adapter
   b. a motherboard and a port
   c. a control unit and an arithmetic logic unit
   d. adapter cards

4. _____ is the process of obtaining a program instruction or data item from memory. (188)
   a. Fetching   b. Decoding
   c. Executing   d. Storing

5. A processor contains small, high-speed storage locations, called _____, that temporarily hold data and instructions. (189)
   a. flash drives   b. registers
   c. jacks   d. heat sinks

6. Processors that can execute more than one instruction per clock cycle are said to be _____. (189)
   a. superscalar
   b. dual-core processors
   c. system on a chip
   d. flash drives

7. _____ is a 16-bit coding scheme that is capable of representing more than 65,000 characters and symbols, enough for almost all the world's current written languages. (195)
   a. Unicode   b. ASCII
   c. Microcode   d. EBCDIC

8. Memory stores _____. (196)
   a. the operating system and other system software
   b. application programs that carry out specific tasks
   c. the data being processed by the application program
   d. all of the above

9. A _____ of memory is equal to exactly 1,024 bytes, but often is rounded down to 1,000 bytes. (197)
   a. kilobyte (KB or K)
   b. megabyte (MB)
   c. gigabyte (GB)
   d. terabyte (TB)

10. A _____ is a type of memory module with pins on opposite sides of the circuit board that do not connect, and thus form two sets of contacts. (199)
    a. RIMM (Rambus inline memory module)
    b. DIMM (dual inline memory module)
    c. ROMM (Rambus online memory module)
    d. SIMM (single inline memory module)

11. Many of today's computers support _____, which means the computer automatically can configure adapter cards and other peripherals as you install them. (205)
    a. Pack and Go
    b. Park and Ride
    c. Pick and Choose
    d. Plug and Play

12. Personal computers typically have six to eight _____ either on the front or back of the system unit. (208)
    a. MIDI ports
    b. serial ports
    c. USB ports
    d. parallel ports

13. Word size is the _____. (211)
    a. pace of the system clock
    b. size of the bus
    c. amount of time it takes the processor to read instructions from memory
    d. number of bits the processor can interpret and execute at a given time.

14. _____ usually are installed in internal bays. (212)
    a. Floppy disk drives
    b. DVD drives
    c. Zip drives
    d. Hard disk drives

Checkpoint

Matching

Match the terms with their definitions. (See page numbers in parentheses.)

_____ 1. motherboard (186)

_____ 2. chip (186)

_____ 3. ALU (188)

_____ 4. byte (195)

_____ 5. memory (196)

_____ 6. RAM (198)

_____ 7. flash memory (202)

_____ 8. expansion slot (204)

_____ 9. PC Card (205)

_____ 10. FireWire port (209)

a. electronic components that store instructions, data, and results of processed data

b. eight bits formed together as a unit

c. thin, credit card-sized device that adds memory, storage, sound, fax/modem, network, and other capabilities to mobile computers

d. memory chips that can be read from and written to by the processor and other devices

e. performs arithmetic, comparison, and other operations

f. amount of time it takes the processor to read data, instructions, and information from memory

g. socket on the motherboard that can hold an adapter card

h. connects multiple types of devices that require faster data transmission speeds

i. main circuit board of the system unit

j. number of bits the processor can interpret and execute at a given time

k. nonvolatile memory that can be erased electronically and rewritten

l. small piece of semiconducting material on which integrated circuits are etched

Short Answer

Write a brief answer to each of the following questions.

1. What are the two parts of a processor? _____ What does each do? _____

2. What are the four basic operations in a machine cycle? _____ What is pipelining, and how does it affect processing speed? _____

3. What is the system clock? _____ How does clock speed affect a computer's speed? _____

4. What is a system on a chip? _____ What types of devices typically have them? _____

5. What is the difference between volatile and nonvolatile memory? _____ How does dynamic RAM differ from RAM? _____

Beyond the Book

Read the following book elements, learn more about each using the Web, and then write a brief report.

1. At Issue — Can Computers Think? (187), Computer Waste and the Environment: Whose Problem Is It? (193), Ready for RFID? (197), Do Lower Computer Prices Mean Less Value? (200), or Should Smart Shoes Be Banned from Competitive Events? (214)

2. Career Corner — Computer Engineer (217)

3. Companies on the Cutting Edge — AMD or Intel (219)

4. FAQs (189, 193, 200, 202, 203, 208, 210, 213, 216)

5. High-Tech Talk — Random Access Memory (RAM): The Genius of Memory (218)

6. Looking Ahead — U.S. Plans World's Fastest Computer (190) or DNA Computer Works to Fight Cancer (215)

7. Making Use of the Web — Resources (xx)

8. Picture Yourself Buying a Computer (182)

9. Technology Trailblazers — Jack Kilby or Gordon Moore (219)

10. Web Links (186, 189, 199, 201, 202, 204, 205, 206, 212)

Learn It Online

Use the Learn It Online exercises to reinforce your understanding of the chapter concepts. To access the Learn It Online exercises, visit scsite.com/dc2006/ch4/learn.

 At the Movies — Computing Clusters

To view the Computing Clusters movie, click the number 1 button. Locate your video and click the corresponding High-Speed or Dial-Up link, depending on your Internet connection. Watch the movie and then complete the exercise by answering the questions below. Many graphics and animation programs have heavy data loads. When using a processing cluster, these difficult, memory-intensive tasks can be divided over several different computers linked through a network. Using multiple computers to perform a big job means it gets done faster. What types of tasks are best accomplished by a cluster? How would you handle a large, time-consuming project?

 At the Movies — USB Basics

To view the USB Basics movie, click the number 2 button. Locate your video and click the corresponding High-Speed or Dial-Up link, depending on your Internet connection. Watch the movie and then complete the exercise by answering the questions below. A universal serial bus (USB) is a peripheral bus standard developed by Intel which allows you to connect external equipment such as digital cameras and MP3 players to your computer. The USB enables the external equipment to communicate with your computer and share information and power. How can you tell if your USB port is working? What are some ways you can troubleshoot your USB ports?

 Student Edition Labs — Understanding the Motherboard

Click the number 3 button. When the Student Edition Labs menu appears, click *Understanding the Motherboard* to begin. A new browser window will open. Follow the on-screen instructions to complete the Lab. When finished, click the Exit button. If required, submit your results to your instructor.

④ **Student Edition Labs — Binary Numbers**

Click the number 4 button. When the Student Edition Labs menu appears, click *Binary Numbers* to begin. A new browser window will open. Follow the on-screen instructions to complete the Lab. When finished, click the Exit button. If required, submit your results to your instructor.

⑤ **Practice Test**

Click the number 5 button. Answer each question. When completed, enter your name and click the Grade Test button to submit the quiz for grading. Make a note of any missed questions. If required, submit your score to your instructor.

 Who Wants To Be a Computer Genius²?

Click the number 6 button to find out if you are a computer genius. Directions about how to play the game will be displayed. When you are ready to play, click the Play button. Submit your score to your instructor.

 Wheel of Terms

Click the number 7 button to reinforce important terms you learned in this chapter by playing the Shelly Cashman Series version of this popular game. Directions about how to play the game will be displayed. When you are ready to play, click the Play button. Submit your score to your instructor.

Learn It Online

 DC Track and Field

Click the number 8 button to use what you have learned in this chapter to compete against other students in three track and field events. Directions about how to play the game will be displayed. When you are ready to play, click the start first event button. If required, submit your score to your instructor.

 You're Hired!

Click the number 9 button to use what you have learned in this chapter to embark on the path to a career in computers. Directions about how to play the game will be displayed. When you are ready to play, click the begin game button. If required, submit your score to your instructor.

 Crossword Puzzle Challenge

Click the number 10 button. Complete the puzzle to reinforce skills you learned in this chapter. Directions about how to play the game will be displayed. When you are ready to play, click the Play button. Submit the completed puzzle to your instructor.

 Lab Exercises

Click the number 11 button. When the Lab Exercises menu appears, click the exercise assigned by your instructor. A new browser window will open. Follow the on-screen instructions to complete the exercise. When finished, click the Exit button. If required, submit your results to your instructor.

 In the News

In February 2006, the forerunner of the modern computer will have its 60th anniversary. By today's standards for electronic computers, the ENIAC (Electronic Numerical Integrator And Computer) was a grotesque monster. With 30 separate units, plus a power supply and forced-air cooling, it weighed more than 30 tons. Its 19,000 vacuum tubes, 1,500 relays, and hundreds of thousands of resistors, capacitors,

and inductors consumed almost 200 kilowatts of electrical power. The ENIAC performed fewer than 1,000 calculations per minute; today, personal computers can process more than 300 million instructions per second. The rapid development of computing power and capabilities is astonishing, and the rate of that development is accelerating. Click the number 12 button and read a news article about the introduction of a new or improved computer component. What is the component? Who is introducing it? Will the component change the way people use computers? If so, how?

Chapter Discussion Forum

Select an objective from this chapter on page 183 about which you would like more information. Click the number 13 button, and post a short message listing a meaningful message title accompanied by one or more questions concerning the selected objective. In two days, return to the threaded discussion by clicking the number 13 button. Submit to your instructor your original message and at least one response to your message.

Learn How To

Use the Learn How To activities to learn fundamental skills when using a computer and accompanying technology. Complete the exercises and submit them to your instructor. Visit scsite.com/dc2006/ch4/howto to obtain more information pertaining to each activity.

LEARN HOW TO 1: Purchase and Install Memory in a Computer

One of the less expensive and more effective ways to speed up a computer, make it capable of processing more programs at the same time, and enable it to handle graphics, gaming, and other high-level programs is to increase the amount of memory. The process of increasing memory is accomplished in two phases — purchasing the memory and installing the memory. To purchase memory for a computer, complete the following steps:

1. Determine the amount of memory currently in the computer. For a method to do this, see Learn How To number 3 in Chapter 1.
2. Determine the maximum amount of memory your computer can contain. This value can change for different computers, based primarily on the number of slots on the motherboard available for memory and the size of the **memory modules** you can place in each slot. On most computers, different size memory modules can be inserted in slots. A computer, therefore, might allow a 128 MB, 256 MB, or 512 MB memory module to be inserted in each slot. To determine the maximum memory for a computer, multiply the number of memory slots on the computer by the maximum size memory module that can be inserted in each slot.

   For example, if a computer contains four memory slots and is able to accept memory modules of 128 MB, 256 MB, or 512 MB in each of its memory slots, the maximum amount of memory the computer can contain is 2 GB (4 x 512 MB).

   You can find the number of slots and the allowable sizes of each memory module by contacting the computer manufacturer, looking in the computer's documentation, or contacting sellers of memory such as Kingston (www.kingston.com) or Crucial (www.crucial.com) on the Web. These sellers have documentation for most computers, and even programs you can download to run on your computer that will specify how much memory your computer currently has and how much you can add.
3. Determine how much memory you want to add, which will be somewhere between the current memory and the maximum memory allowed on the computer.
4. Determine the current configuration of memory on the computer. For example, if a computer with four memory slots contains 512 MB of memory, it could be using one memory module of 512 MB in a single slot and the other three slots would be empty; two memory modules of 256 MB each in two slots with two slots empty; one memory module of 256 MB and two memory modules of 128 MB each in three slots with one slot empty; or four memory modules of 128 MB each in four slots with no slots empty. You may be required to look inside the system unit to make this determination. The current memory configuration on a computer will determine what new memory modules you should buy to increase the memory to the amount determined in Step 3.

   You also should be aware that a few computers require memory to be installed in matching pairs. This means a computer with four slots could obtain 512 MB of memory with two memory modules of 256 MB in two slots, or four memory modules of 128 MB in four slots.
5. Determine the number of available memory slots on your computer and the number and size memory modules you must buy to fulfill your requirement. Several scenarios can occur (in the following examples, assume you can install memory one module at a time).
   a. Scenario 1: The computer has one or more open slots. In this case, you might be able to purchase a memory module that matches the amount of memory increase you desire. For example, if you want to increase memory by 256 MB, you should purchase a 256 MB memory module for insertion in the open slot. Generally, you should buy the maximum size module you can for an open slot. So, if you find two empty slots and wish to increase memory by 256 MB, it is smarter to buy one 256 MB module and leave one empty slot rather than buy two 128 MB memory modules and use both slots. This allows you to increase memory again without removing currently used modules.

Learn How To

b. Scenario 2: The computer has no open slots. For example, a computer containing 512 MB of memory could have four slots each containing 128 MB memory modules. If you want to increase the memory on the computer to 1 GB, you will have to remove some of the 128 MB memory modules and replace them with the new memory modules you purchase. In this example, you want to increase the memory by 512 MB. You would have several options: (1) You could replace all four 128 MB memory modules with 256 MB memory modules; (2) You could replace all four 128 MB memory modules with two 512 MB memory modules; (3) You could replace one 128 MB memory module with a 512 MB memory module, and replace a second 128 MB module with a 256 MB memory module. Each of these options results in a total memory of 1 GB. The best option will depend on the price of memory and whether you anticipate increasing the memory size at a later time. The least expensive option probably would be number 3.

c. Scenario 3: Many combinations can occur. You may have to perform calculations to decide the combination of modules that will work for the number of slots on the computer and the desired additional memory.

6. Determine the type of memory to buy for the computer. Computer memory has many types and configurations, and it is critical that you buy the kind of memory for which the computer was designed. It is preferable to buy the same type of memory that currently is found in the computer. That is, if the memory is DDR SDRAM with a certain clock speed, then that is the type of additional memory you should place in the computer. The documentation for the computer should specify the memory type. In addition, the Web sites cited above, and others as well, will present a list of memory modules that will work with your computer. Enough emphasis cannot be placed on the fact that the memory you buy must be compatible with the type of memory usable on your computer. Because there are so many types and configurations, you must be especially diligent to ensure you purchase the proper memory for your computer.

7. Once you have determined the type and size of memory to purchase, buy it from a reputable dealer. Buying poor or mismatched memory is a major reason for a computer's erratic performance and is a difficult problem to troubleshoot.

After purchasing the memory, you must install it on your computer. Complete the following steps to install memory:

1. Unplug the computer, and remove all electrical cords and device cables from the ports on the computer. Open the case of the system unit. You may want to consult the computer's documentation to determine the exact procedure.

2. Ground yourself so you do not generate static electricity that can cause memory or other components within the system unit to be damaged. To do this, wear an antistatic wristband you can purchase inexpensively in a computer or electronics store; or, before you touch any component within the system unit, touch an unpainted metal surface. If you are not wearing an antistatic wristband, periodically touch an unpainted metal surface to dissipate any static electricity.

3. Within the system unit, find the memory slots on the motherboard. The easiest way to do this is look for memory modules that are similar to those you purchased. The memory slots often are located near the processor. If you cannot find the slots, consult the documentation. A diagram often is available to help you spot the memory slots.

4. Insert the memory module in the next empty slot. Orient the memory module in the slot to match the modules currently installed. A notch or notches on the memory module will ensure you do not install the module backwards. If your memory module is a DIMM, insert the module straight down into grooves on the clips and then apply gentle pressure. If your memory is SIMM, insert the module at a 45 degree angle and then rotate it to a vertical position until the module snaps into place.

5. If you must remove one or more memory modules before inserting the new memory, carefully release the clips before lifting the memory module out of the memory slot.

6. Plug in the machine and replace all the device cables without replacing the cover.

7. Start the computer. In most cases, the new memory will be recognized and the computer will run normally. If an error message appears, determine the cause of the error.

8. Replace the computer cover.

Exercise

1. Assume you have a computer that contains 256 MB of memory. It contains four memory slots. Each slot can contain 128 MB or 256 MB memory modules. Two of the slots contain 128 MB memory modules. What memory chip(s) would you buy to increase the memory on the computer to 512 MB? What is the maximum memory on the computer? Submit your answers to your instructor.

2. Assume you have a computer that contains 1 GB of memory. It contains four memory slots. Each slot can contain 128 MB, 256 MB, 512 MB, or 1 GB memory modules. Currently, each slot contains a 256 MB memory module. What combinations of memory modules will satisfy your memory upgrade to 2 GB? Visit a Web site to determine which of these combinations is the least expensive. Submit your answers and recommendations to your instructor.

Web Research

Use the Internet-based Web Research exercises to broaden your understanding of the concepts presented in this chapter. Visit scsite.com/dc2006/ch4/research to obtain more information pertaining to each exercise. To discuss any of the Web Research exercises in this chapter with other students, post your thoughts or questions at scsite.com/dc2006/ch4/forum.

(1) Scavenger Hunt   Use one of the <u>search engines</u> listed in Figure 2-8 in Chapter 2 on page 78 or your own favorite search engine to find the answers to the questions below. Copy and paste the Web address from the Web page where you found the answer. Some questions may have more than one answer. If required, submit your answers to your instructor. (1) Which Microsoft Windows operating systems support USB? (2) The USB port supports hot plugging or hot swapping. What is "hot plugging"? (3) What is the name of the suit that people wear when they work in chip manufacturing clean rooms? (4) What is the name of the group of integrated circuits designed to orchestrate the flow of data to and from key components of a personal computer? (5) What is the name of the type of memory that retains its contents until it is exposed to ultraviolet light?

(2) Search Sleuth   <u>Ask Jeeves</u> (ask.com) is one of the faster growing research Web sites. The search engine uses natural language, which allows researchers to type millions of questions each day using words a human would use rather than words a computer understands. Visit this Web site and then use your word processing program to answer the following questions. Then, if required, submit your answers to your instructor. (1) Click the P.G. Wodehouse link at the bottom of the home page. Who are P.G. Wodehouse and Bertie Wooster? (2) Click your browser's Back button or press the BACKSPACE key to return to the Ask Jeeves home page. Click the Search text box and then type `What were the top grossing films this weekend?` as the keywords in the Search text box. (3) Scroll through the links Ask Jeeves returns and then click one that provides the information requested. What three films grossed the most money this weekend? How much did the top film gross? (4) Click your browser's Back button or press the BACKSPACE key to return to the Ask Jeeves home page. Click the News Search link at the bottom of the page. (5) Click one of the Top Stories links and review the material. Summarize the information you read and then write a 50-word summary.

(3) Journaling   Respond to your readings in this chapter by writing at least one page containing your reactions, evaluations, and reflections about when you have considered <u>buying a computer</u>. For example, did you shop online, at a local computer dealer, at a local large retail store, or your school bookstore? What type of processor? How much memory? Desktop or mobile? Apple or PC? What type of ports did the computer have? How many bays? You also can write about the new terms you learned by reading this chapter. If required, submit your journal to your instructor.

(4) Expanding Your Understanding   A <u>brick-and-click</u> business allows customers to conduct transactions at a physical location as well as online. Many banks and retailers, such as Citibank and Best Buy, are brick-and-click businesses. Choose a brick-and-click business and then visit the physical location and its Web site. Compare the type, availability, and cost of products or services. Write a report summarizing your findings, focusing on the advantages and disadvantages of conducting business at a physical location and online. If required, submit your report to your instructor.

(5) Ethics in Action   More than 50 law enforcement agencies use handheld wireless devices to access commercial databases. For example, Massachusetts state police stationed at Logan International Airport use the <u>LocatePLUS Holdings Corporation</u>'s database, which has information on 98 percent of Americans. The data is composed of motor vehicle records, credit bureau reports, property tax payments, and telephone directories. Police say accessing this information helps them perform their jobs more efficiently. Privacy experts, in contrast, say that information collected for one purpose should not be available in other contexts. View online sites that provide information about commercial databases for sale. Write a report summarizing your findings, and include a table of links to Web sites that provide additional details. If required, submit your report to your instructor.

Case Studies

Use the Case Studies to apply the concepts presented in the chapter to real-world situations. Visit scsite.com/dc2006/ch4/cases to obtain more information pertaining to each exercise. To discuss the Case Studies in this chapter with other students, visit scsite.com/dc2006/ch4/forum and post your thoughts or questions.

CASE STUDY 1 — Class Discussion   You are the office manager at SportsGraphics, a company that designs and produces apparel for local school and recreational sports teams. The company has 25 nonnetworked computers that are used by various departments for common business applications. The computers are four years old, and you would like to replace them. The director of information technology agrees, but he has reservations. He has asked you to complete a study on the cost of new computers, comparing the major features found on <u>system units</u> at three different price levels: less than $800; $800 to $1,500; and greater than $1,500. Prepare a brief summary report on the major features of system units at the various price levels. Include recommendations on which system units would meet the company's needs most economically. Be prepared to discuss your recommendations in class.

CASE STUDY 2 — Class Discussion   On Demand Computing, Inc. has decided to upgrade several hundred PCs used in their offices nationwide. The Information Technology Department has recommended that the company again purchase PCs for approximately $1,200 each. The system units would include Pentium 4 processors with speeds of 3.0 GHz with 512 MB of RAM. From her days in college, the CFO has preferred Apple computers and currently uses an <u>Apple iMac</u> at home. She has hired you as a consultant to determine if the company would be better off purchasing iMacs in the same price range and with similar capabilities. Use the Web and/or print media to select a comparable iMac. Which one starts faster? Which one opens files faster? Which one loads Web pages faster? Is the iMac in the same price range as the PC? List any other advantages and disadvantages of each. Prepare a brief summary report and be prepared to discuss your findings in class.

CASE STUDY 3 — Research   Your family has decided to purchase a computer for use at home. Because you are enrolled in a computer course, you have been asked to make recommendations. Your instructor has pushed the premise "software drives hardware." List the application programs you and your family members plan to use. Visit the Web sites of the manufacturers of each application program, and note the capabilities required of the system unit (type of processor, amount of <u>RAM</u>, and so on). On the basis of your findings, what are the minimum system requirements you and your family would require in a personal computer? What system requirements would be sufficient to provide a "cushion" so that you could be sure the system also could run other, or new, application packages? Write a brief report and share your findings with your class.

CASE STUDY 4 — Research   Many system unit manufacturers provide a toll-free telephone number that customers can call with technical problems or questions. If the <u>service technician</u> determines a difficulty is a hardware problem that the customer can fix, the technician might ask the customer to open the system unit and make some adjustments. For this reason, every computer user can benefit by being familiar with the inside of the system unit. If you own a personal computer or have access to a personal computer, unplug the power supply and take the cover off the system unit. Be careful not to touch any of the system unit components. Make a sketch of the system unit and try to identify each part. By referring to the computer's *User Guide*, list some of the computer's specifications (clock speed, memory size, and so on). Compare your sketch and list with a classmate who has done this exercise with a different computer. How are the computers similar? How are they different?

CASE STUDY 5 — Team Challenge   The chief financial officer of SkateJam, Inc. has asked her Information Technology Department to look into replacing the company's desktop computers with <u>notebook computers</u>. The director of information technology has hired your team as consultants to examine the advantages and disadvantages of notebook computers. Form a three-member team and assign each team member one of the following companies — Dell, HP, and Apple. Have each member of your team use the Web and/or print media to find a notebook computer and a desktop computer with comparable middle-of-the-road system units sold by the company assigned to them. What is the price of each computer? How are the processors and RAM similar? How are they different? Meet with the members of your team to discuss results of your investigations. Is the notebook computer the better buy? If so, why? Write a summary report or use PowerPoint to create a group presentation and share your findings with the class.

CHAPTER FIVE

Input

Picture Yourself Going Digital

Your daughter claims you have been stuck in the last decade — still connected by cords, still writing appointments in a daily planner, still using the house telephone as your main method of communication, and still visiting photo labs to process 35 mm film. To get up to speed with digital technology, you have been using gift cards that you have received for birthdays and other occasions to purchase new devices for your computer.

First, you bought a wireless keyboard and mouse, which the sales clerk explained communicates via radio waves. More importantly to you, these two devices give you the freedom to work without the clutter of cords. You now can position the keyboard and mouse anywhere on your desk and not worry about whether the cord is long enough.

You then bought a smart phone that has PDA capabilities. First, you learned how to enter contact information and appointments and how to use the digital pen. Next, you learned how to send picture messages and post them to a Web site. You plan to send or post regular photo updates to keep friends and family up-to-date of all your activities.

Most recently, you purchased a digital camera. You have become quite adept at transferring the digital images to your computer, editing them with your photo editing software, printing the images in a variety of sizes, and, of course, e-mailing the pictures.

To learn more about keyboards, mouse devices, input for PDAs and smart phones, and digital cameras, read Chapter 5 and discover features of many other types of input devices.

OBJECTIVES

After completing this chapter, you will be able to:

1. Define input
2. List the characteristics of a keyboard
3. Describe different mouse types and how they work
4. Summarize how various pointing devices work
5. Explain how voice recognition works
6. Describe various input devices for PDAs, smart phones, and Tablet PCs
7. Explain how a digital camera works
8. Describe the uses of PC video cameras, Web cams, and video conferencing
9. Discuss various scanners and reading devices and how they work
10. Explain the types of terminals
11. Summarize the various biometric devices
12. Identify alternative input devices for physically challenged users

CONTENTS

WHAT IS INPUT?

Input is any data and instructions entered into the memory of a computer. As shown in Figure 5-1, people have a variety of options for entering data or instructions into a computer.

Input to a computer consists of either data or instructions. As discussed in Chapter 1, *data* is a collection of unprocessed text, numbers, images, audio, and video. Once data is in memory, the computer interprets and executes instructions to process the data into information. Instructions entered into the computer can be in the form of programs, commands, and user responses.

• A *program* is a series of instructions that tells a computer what to do and how to do it. When a programmer writes a program, he or she enters the program into the computer by using a keyboard, mouse, or other input device. The programmer then stores the program in a file that a user can execute

keyboard

mouse

joystick

wheel

touch screen

biometric input

data collection device

input

MICR

magnetic stripe card reader

RFID reader

bar code reader

FIGURE 5-1 Users can enter data and instructions into a computer in a variety of ways.

(run). When a user runs a program, the computer loads the program from a storage medium into memory. Thus, a program is entered into a computer's memory.

- Programs respond to commands that a user issues. A *command* is an instruction that causes a program to perform a specific action. Users issue commands by typing or pressing keys on the keyboard, clicking a mouse button, speaking into a microphone, or touching an area on a screen.

- A *user response* is an instruction a user issues by replying to a question displayed by a program. A response to the question instructs the program to perform certain actions. Assume the program asks the question, Is the time card correct? If you answer Yes, the program processes the time card. If you answer No, the program gives you the opportunity to modify the time card entries.

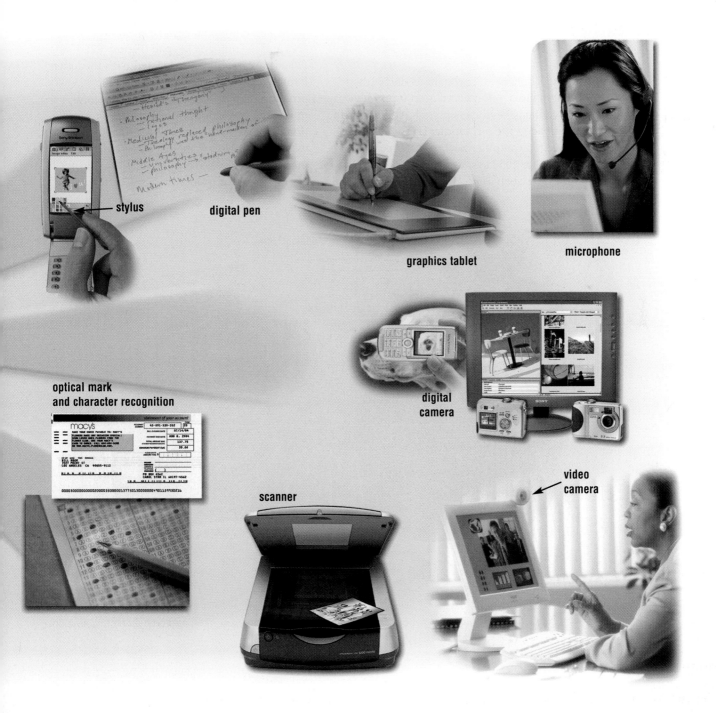

stylus

digital pen

graphics tablet

microphone

optical mark and character recognition

digital camera

video camera

scanner

WHAT ARE INPUT DEVICES?

An **input device** is any hardware component that allows users to enter data and instructions (programs, commands, and user responses) into a computer. Depending on the application and your particular requirements, the input device selected may vary. The following pages discuss a variety of input devices.

Storage devices, such as disk drives, serve as both input and output devices. Chapter 7 discusses storage devices.

THE KEYBOARD

Many people use a keyboard as one of their input devices. A **keyboard** is an input device that contains keys users press to enter data and instructions into a computer (Figure 5-2).

Desktop computer keyboards typically have from 101 to 105 keys. Keyboards for smaller computers such as notebook computers contain fewer keys. All computer keyboards have a typing area that includes the letters of the alphabet, numbers, punctuation marks, and other basic keys. Many desktop computer keyboards also have a numeric keypad on the right side of the keyboard. A keyboard also contains other keys that allow users to enter data and instructions into the computer. Read At Issue 5-1 for a related discussion.

Most of today's desktop computer keyboards are enhanced keyboards. An *enhanced keyboard* has twelve function keys along the top; it also has two CTRL keys, two ALT keys, and a set of arrow and additional keys between the typing area and the numeric keypad (Figure 5-2). *Function keys*, which are labeled with the letter F followed by a number, are special keys programmed to issue commands to a computer. The command associated with a function key may vary, depending on the program with which you are interacting. For example, the F3 key may issue one command to an operating system and an entirely different

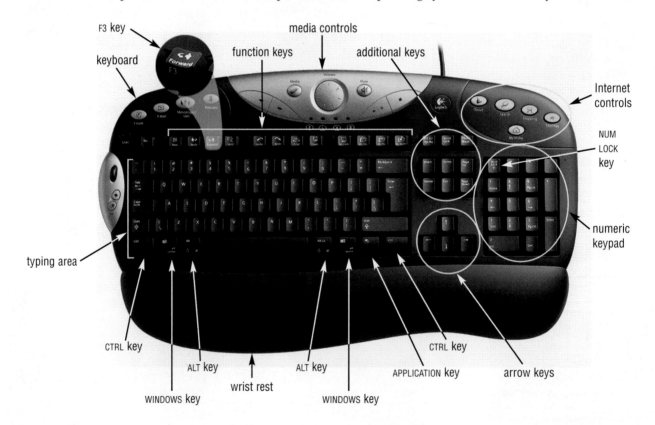

FIGURE 5-2   On a desktop computer keyboard, you type using keys in the typing area and on the numeric keypad.

AT ISSUE 5-1

Keyboard Monitoring — Privacy Risk?

Are you nervous about your employees' work on company computers? Are you curious about your spouse's long e-mail messages to a mutual friend? Are you concerned about your teenager's conversations in Internet chat rooms? Keyboard monitoring software can dispel your doubts. When installed on a computer, *keyboard monitoring software* records every keystroke in a hidden file, which later can be accessed by supplying the correct password. With keyboard monitoring software, you can see everything that was typed on the computer keyboard, including documents, e-mail, and other messages. In an office, keyboard monitoring software can be used to measure employee productivity by counting the number of keystrokes per hour. Some programs also store a record of software used, Web sites visited, user logons, and periodic screen shots. The software can run completely undetected. With keyboard monitoring software, you can catch a disgruntled employee preparing a resume on company time, discover that your spouse is e-mailing gardening tips, or recognize that your teenager has made a potentially dangerous contact in a chat room. Many maintain, however, that keyboard monitoring software is an invasion of privacy. Should keyboard monitoring software ever be used? If so, when? Some marketers of keyboard monitoring software recommend computer users be informed that the software is installed. Is this a good idea? Why or why not?

command to a word processing program. To issue commands, users often can press a function key in combination with other special keys (SHIFT, CTRL, ALT, and others).

Nearly all keyboards have toggle keys. A *toggle key* is a key that switches between two states each time a user presses the key. When you press the NUM LOCK key, for example, it locks the numeric keypad so you can use the keypad to type numbers. When you press the NUM LOCK key again, the numeric keypad unlocks so the same keys can serve to move the insertion point. Many keyboards have status lights that light up when you activate a toggle key.

Keyboards also often have a WINDOWS key(s) and an APPLICATION key. When pressed, the WINDOWS key displays the Start menu, and the APPLICATION key displays an item's shortcut menu.

Keyboards also contain keys that allow you to position the insertion point, also known as a *cursor* in some programs. The **insertion point** is a symbol on the screen, usually a blinking vertical bar, that indicates where the next character you type will be displayed (Figure 5-3). Users can move the insertion point left, right, up, or down by pressing the arrow keys and other keys on the keyboard.

Newer keyboards include media control buttons that allow you to access the computer's CD/DVD drive and adjust speaker volume, and Internet control buttons that allow you to open an e-mail program, start a Web browser, and search the Internet. Some keyboards also have USB ports so a user can plug a USB device directly in the keyboard instead of in the system unit.

FAQ 5-1

What is the rationale for the arrangement of keys in the typing area?

The keys originally were arranged to reduce the frequency of key jams on old mechanical typewriters. Called a *QWERTY keyboard*, the first letters on the top alphabetic line spell QWERTY. A *Dvorak keyboard*, by contrast, places frequently typed letters in the middle of the typing area. Despite the Dvorak keyboard's logical design, most people and computers use a QWERTY keyboard. For more information, visit scsite.com/dc2006/ch5/faq and then click Keyboards.

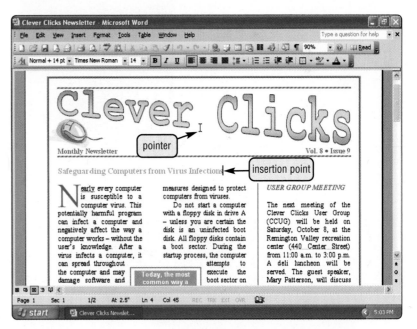

FIGURE 5-3 In most programs, such as Word, the insertion point is a blinking vertical bar. You use the keyboard or other input device to move the insertion point. The pointer, another symbol that is displayed on the screen, is controlled using a pointing device such as a mouse.

Keyboard Connections

Desktop computer keyboards often attach via a cable to a serial port, a keyboard port, or a USB port on the system unit. Some keyboards, however, do not use wires at all. A *wireless keyboard*, or *cordless keyboard*, is a battery-powered device that transmits data using wireless technology, such as radio waves or infrared light waves. Wireless keyboards often communicate with a receiver attached to a port on the system unit. The port type varies depending on the type of wireless technology. For example, a Bluetooth-enabled keyboard communicates via radio waves with a Bluetooth receiver plugged in a serial, parallel, or USB port (Figure 5-4).

On notebook computers and some handheld computers, PDAs, and smart phones, the keyboard is built in the top of the system unit. To fit in these mobile computers and devices, the keyboards usually are smaller and have fewer keys. A typical notebook computer keyboard usually has only about 85 keys. To provide all of the functionality of a desktop computer keyboard, manufacturers design many of the keys to serve two or three purposes.

Keyboard Ergonomics

Regardless of size, many keyboards have a rectangular shape with the keys aligned in straight, horizontal rows. Users who spend a lot of time typing on these keyboards sometimes experience repetitive strain injuries (RSI) of their wrists and hands. For this reason, some manufacturers offer ergonomic keyboards. An *ergonomic keyboard* has a design that reduces the chance of wrist and hand injuries. Even keyboards that are not ergonomically designed attempt to offer a user more comfort by including a wrist rest or palm rest (Figure 5-2 on page 236).

The goal of **ergonomics** is to incorporate comfort, efficiency, and safety in the design of the workplace. Employees can be injured or develop disorders of the muscles, nerves, tendons, ligaments, and joints from working in an area that is not ergonomically designed.

receiver plugged in USB port

up to 30 feet

transmitter in keyboard

FIGURE 5-4 Some personal computers have built-in Bluetooth technology. On computers that are not Bluetooth-enabled, you plug a Bluetooth receiver in a USB port or serial port on the system unit. A transmitter inside the keyboard communicates with the receiver, which should be within 30 feet from each other.

FAQ 5-2

What can I do to reduce chances of experiencing repetitive strain injuries?

Do not rest your wrist on the edge of a desk; use a wrist rest. Keep your forearm and wrist level so your wrist does not bend. Do hand exercises every 15 minutes. Keep your shoulders, arms, hands, and wrists relaxed while you work. Maintain good posture. Keep feet flat on the floor, with one foot slightly in front of the other. For more information, visit scsite.com/dc2006/ch5/faq and then click Repetitive Strain Injuries.

POINTING DEVICES

A **pointing device** is an input device that allows a user to control a pointer on the screen. In a graphical user interface, a **pointer** is a small symbol on the screen (Figure 5-3 on page 237) whose location and shape change as a user moves a pointing device. A pointing device can be used to move the insertion point; select text, graphics, and other objects; and click buttons, icons, links, and menu commands. The following sections discuss the mouse and other pointing devices.

MOUSE

A **mouse** is a pointing device that fits under the palm of your hand comfortably. The mouse is the most widely used pointing device on desktop computers.

With a mouse, users control the movement of the pointer, often called a *mouse pointer* in this case. As you move a mouse, the pointer on the screen also moves. Generally, you use the mouse to move the pointer on the screen to an object such as a button, a menu, an icon, a link, or text. Then, you press a mouse button to perform a certain action associated with that object. The top and sides of a mouse have one to four buttons; some also have a small wheel. The bottom of a mouse is flat and contains a mechanism that detects movement of the mouse.

Mouse Types

A *mechanical mouse* has a rubber or metal ball on its underside (Figure 5-5). When the ball rolls in a certain direction, electronic circuits in the mouse translate the movement of the mouse into signals the computer can process. You should place a mechanical mouse on a mouse pad. A **mouse pad** is a rectangular rubber or foam pad that provides better traction than the top of a desk. The mouse pad also protects the ball in the mouse from a build-up of dust and dirt, which could cause it to malfunction.

An optical mouse, by contrast, has no moving mechanical parts inside. Instead, an *optical mouse* uses devices that emit and sense light to detect the mouse's movement. Some use optical sensors, others use a laser (Figure 5-6). You can place an optical mouse on nearly all types of surfaces, eliminating the need for a mouse pad. An optical mouse is more precise than a

mechanical mouse and does not require cleaning as does a mechanical mouse, but it also is more expensive.

A mouse connects to a computer in several ways. Many types connect with a cable that attaches to a serial port, mouse port, or USB port on the system unit. A *wireless mouse*, or *cordless mouse*, is a battery-powered device that transmits data using wireless technology, such as radio waves or infrared light waves. The technology used for a wireless mouse is similar to that of a wireless keyboard discussed earlier. Some users prefer a wireless mouse because it frees up desk space and eliminates the clutter of a cord.

FIGURE 5-5 A mechanical mouse contains a small ball.

FIGURE 5-6a (optical mouse that uses optical sensor)

FIGURE 5-6b (optical mouse that uses laser)

FIGURE 5-6 An optical mouse uses an optical sensor or a laser. Many also include buttons you push with your thumb that enable forward and backward navigation through Web pages.

Using a Mouse

Windows users work with a mouse that has at least two buttons. For a right-handed user, the left button usually is the primary mouse button, and the right mouse button is the secondary mouse button. Left-handed people, however, can reverse the function of these buttons.

Operations you can perform with the mouse include point, click, right-click, double-click, triple-click, drag, right-drag, rotate wheel, press wheel button, and tilt wheel. The table in Figure 5-7 explains how to perform these mouse operations. Some programs also use keys in combination with the mouse to perform certain actions. The function of the mouse buttons and the wheel varies depending on the program. Read At Issue 5-2 for a related discussion.

Some programs support *mouse gestures*, where the user performs certain operations by holding a mouse button while moving the

mouse in a particular pattern. For example, moving the mouse down and to the left may close all open windows. Mouse gestures minimize the amount of time users spend navigating through menus or toolbars because users can perform these tasks by simply moving (gesturing) the mouse.

FAQ 5-3

How do I use a wheel on a mouse?

Roll it forward or backward to scroll up or down. Tilt it to the right or left to scroll horizontally. Hold down the CTRL key while rolling the wheel to make the text on the screen bigger or smaller. These scrolling and zooming functions work with most software and also on the Web. For more information, visit scsite.com/dc2006/ch5/faq and then click Using a Mouse.

MOUSE OPERATIONS

Operation	Mouse Action	Example
Point	Move the mouse across a flat surface until the pointer on the desktop is positioned on the item of choice.	Position the pointer on the screen.
Click	Press and release the primary mouse button, which usually is the left mouse button.	Select or deselect items on the screen or start a program or program feature.
Right-click	Press and release the secondary mouse button, which usually is the right mouse button.	Display a shortcut menu.
Double-click	Quickly press and release the left mouse button twice without moving the mouse.	Start a program or program feature.
Triple-click	Quickly press and release the left mouse button three times without moving the mouse.	Select a paragraph.
Drag	Point to an item, hold down the left mouse button, move the item to the desired location on the screen, and then release the left mouse button.	Move an object from one location to another or draw pictures.
Right-drag	Point to an item, hold down the right mouse button, move the item to the desired location on the screen, and then release the right mouse button.	Display a shortcut menu after moving an object from one location to another.
Rotate wheel	Roll the wheel forward or backward.	Scroll vertically.
Press wheel button	Press the wheel button while moving the mouse on the desktop.	Scroll continuously.
Tilt wheel	Press the wheel toward the right or left.	Scroll horizontally.

FIGURE 5-7 The more common mouse operations.

OTHER POINTING DEVICES

The mouse is the most widely used pointing device today. Some users, however, work with other pointing devices. These include the track-ball, touchpad, pointing stick, joystick, wheel, light pen, touch screen, stylus, and pens. The following sections discuss each of these pointing devices.

Trackball

Similar to a mechanical mouse that has a ball on the bottom, a **trackball** is a stationary pointing device with a ball on its top or side (Figure 5-8). The ball in most trackballs is about the size of a Ping-Pong ball.

To move the pointer using a trackball, you rotate the ball with your thumb, fingers, or the palm of your hand. In addition to the ball, a trackball usually has one or more buttons that work just like mouse buttons.

A trackball requires frequent cleaning because it picks up oils from fingers and dust from the environment. For users who have limited desk space, however, a trackball is a good alternative to a mouse because the device is stationary.

Touchpad

A **touchpad** is a small, flat, rectangular pointing device that is sensitive to pressure and motion (Figure 5-9). To move the pointer using a touchpad, slide your fingertip across the surface of the pad. Some touchpads have one or more buttons around the edge of the pad that work like mouse buttons. On most touchpads, you also can tap the pad's surface to imitate mouse operations such as clicking. Touchpads are found most often on notebook computers.

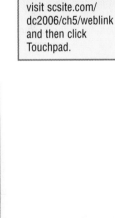

WEB LINK 5-2

Touchpad

For more information, visit scsite.com/dc2006/ch5/weblink and then click Touchpad.

FIGURE 5-8 You rotate the ball on a trackball to move the pointer on the screen.

touchpad

FIGURE 5-9 Most notebook computers have a touchpad that allows users to control the movement of the pointer.

Pointing Stick

A **pointing stick** is a pressure-sensitive pointing device shaped like a pencil eraser that is positioned between keys on a keyboard (Figure 5-10). To move the pointer using a pointing stick, you push the pointing stick with a finger. The pointer on the screen moves in the direction you push the pointing stick. By pressing buttons below the keyboard, users can click and perform other mouse-type operations with a pointing stick.

A pointing stick does not require any additional desk space. In addition, it does not require cleaning like a mechanical mouse or trackball. IBM developed the pointing stick for its notebook computers.

WEB LINK 5-3

Pointing Stick

For more information, visit scsite.com/dc2006/ch5/weblink and then click Pointing Stick.

pointing stick

FIGURE 5-10
Some notebook computers include a pointing stick to allow a user to control the movement of the pointer.

Joystick and Wheel

Users running game software or flight and driving simulation software often use a joystick or wheel as a pointing device (Figure 5-11). A **joystick** is a vertical lever mounted on a base.

joystick

wheel

pedal

FIGURE 5-11   Joysticks and wheels help a user control the actions of players and vehicles in game and simulation software.

You move the lever in different directions to control the actions of the simulated vehicle or player. The lever usually includes buttons called triggers that you press to activate certain events. Some joysticks also have additional buttons you set to perform other actions.

A **wheel** is a steering-wheel-type input device. Users turn the wheel to simulate driving a car, truck, or other vehicle. Most wheels also include foot pedals for acceleration and braking actions. A joystick and wheel typically attach via a cable to a USB port.

Light Pen

A **light pen** is a handheld input device that can detect the presence of light. Some light pens require a specially designed monitor, while others work with a standard monitor (Figure 5-12). To select objects on the screen, a user presses the light pen against the surface of the screen or points the light pen at the screen and then presses a button on the pen.

Light pens also are ideal for areas where employees' hands might contain food, dirt, grease, or other chemicals that could damage the computer. Health-care professionals, such as doctors, use light pens because they can slide a protective sleeve over the pen — keeping their fingers free of contaminants.

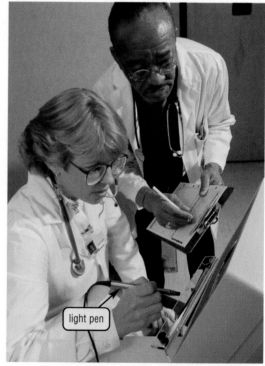

light pen

FIGURE 5-12   To use a light pen, you press the pen against the screen or press a button on the pen while pointing the pen toward an object on the screen.

Touch Screen

A **touch screen** is a touch-sensitive display device. Users can interact with these devices by touching areas of the screen. Because touch screens require a lot of arm movements, you do not enter large amounts of data using a touch screen. Instead, you touch words, pictures, numbers, letters, or locations identified on the screen.

Kiosks, which are freestanding computers, often have touch screens (Figure 5-13). Travelers use kiosks in airports to print tickets ordered online and in hotels for easy check in and check out. Museum kiosks give visitors information. To allow easy access of your bank account from a car, many ATM machines have touch screens.

FIGURE 5-13 A voter uses a kiosk touch screen to cast ballots in an election.

Pen Input

Mobile users often enter data and instructions with a pen-type device. With **pen input**, users write, draw, and tap on a flat surface to enter input. The surface may be a monitor, a screen, or a special type of paper. Two devices used for pen input are the stylus and digital pen. A **stylus** is a small metal or plastic device that looks like a tiny ink pen but uses

pressure instead of ink (Figure 5-14). A **digital pen**, which is slightly larger than a stylus, is available in two forms: some are pressure-sensitive; others have built-in digital cameras.

Some mobile computers and nearly all mobile devices have touch screens. Instead of using a finger to enter data and instructions, most of these devices include a pressure-sensitive digital pen or stylus. You write, draw, or make selections on the computer screen by touching the screen with the pen or stylus. For example, Tablet PCs use a pressure-sensitive digital pen (Figure 5-15) and PDAs use a stylus. Pressure-sensitive digital pens, often simply called pens, typically provide more functionality than a stylus, featuring electronic erasers and programmable buttons.

Computers and mobile devices often use *handwriting recognition software* that translates the handwritten letters and symbols into characters that the computer or device can process.

FIGURE 5-14 PDAs and smart phones use a stylus.

stylus

digital pen

pressure sensitive capacitor

coil circuit

cover and protective glass

LCD display

sensor board

FIGURE 5-15 Tablet PCs use a pressure-sensitive digital pen.

If you want to use pen input on a computer that does not have a touch screen, you can attach a graphics tablet to the computer. A **graphics tablet** is a flat, rectangular, electronic, plastic board. Architects, mapmakers, designers, artists, and home users create drawings and sketches by using a pressure-sensitive pen or a cursor on a graphics tablet (Figure 5-16). A *cursor* looks similar to a mouse, except it has a window with cross hairs, so the user can see through to the tablet. Each location on the graphics tablet corresponds to a specific location on the screen. When drawing on the tablet with a pen or cursor, the tablet detects and converts the movements into digital signals that are sent in the computer. Large-scale applications sometimes refer to the graphics tablet as a *digitizer*.

Digital pens that have built-in digital cameras work differently from pressure-sensitive digital pens. These pens look much like a ballpoint pen and typically do not contain any additional buttons. In addition to the tiny digital camera, these pens contain a processor, memory, and an ink cartridge. As you write or draw on special digital paper with the pen, it captures every handwritten mark by taking more than 100 pictures per second and then stores the images in the pen's memory. You transfer the images from the pen to a computer (Figure 5-17) or mobile device, such as a smart phone. Some pens have a cradle for transferring images; others communicate wirelessly using Bluetooth.

WEB LINK 5-5

Pen Input

For more information, visit scsite.com/dc2006/ch5/weblink and then click Pen Input.

FIGURE 5-16a (artist using a pen)

FIGURE 5-16b
(civil engineer using a cursor)

FIGURE 5-16 Graphics tablets use digital pens or cursors.

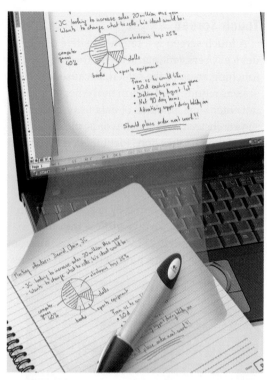

FIGURE 5-17 Some digital pens have built-in digital cameras that store handwritten marks and allow you to transfer your handwriting to a computer.

Test your knowledge of pages 234 through 244 in Quiz Yourself 5-1.

QUIZ YOURSELF 5-1

Instructions: Find the true statement below. Then, rewrite the remaining false statements so they are true.

1. A keyboard is an output device that contains keys users press to enter data in a computer.

2. A light pen is a flat, rectangular, electronic, plastic board.

3. A trackball is a small, flat, rectangular pointing device commonly found on notebook computers.

4. Input is any data or instructions entered into the memory of a computer.

5. Operations you can perform with a wheel include point, click, right-click, double-click, triple-click, drag, right-drag, rotate wheel, press wheel button, and tilt wheel.

6. PDAs use a pressure-sensitive digital pen, and Tablet PCs use a stylus.

Quiz Yourself Online: To further check your knowledge of input techniques, the keyboard, the mouse, and other pointing devices, visit scsite.com/dc2006/ch5/quiz and then click Objectives 1 – 4.

VOICE INPUT

As an alternative to using a keyboard to enter data and instructions, some users talk to their computers and watch the spoken words appear on the screen as they talk. **Voice input** is the process of entering input by speaking into a microphone. The microphone may be a stand-alone peripheral that sits on top of a desk, or built in the computer or device, or in a headset. Some external microphones have a cable that attaches to a port on the sound card on the computer. Others communicate using wireless technology such as Bluetooth.

Voice recognition, also called *speech recognition*, is the computer's capability of distinguishing spoken words. Popular voice recognition programs include IBM ViaVoice and Dragon NaturallySpeaking. Many programs, such as Microsoft Office, support voice recognition. Figure 5-18 illustrates how Word recognizes dictated words and voice commands.

FIGURE 5-18 HOW TO DICTATE WORDS AND COMMANDS

Step 1:
Say, "dictation" to instruct the program you will be dictating and then say, "garage sale."

Step 2:
Say, "voice command" to instruct the program you will be issuing commands and then say, "center."

Step 3:
Say, "select line." Say, "all caps" and then say, "font."

Step 4:
Say, "Stencil" and then say, "font size."

Step 5:
Say, "forty eight" and then say, "font color."

Step 6:
Say, "blue" and then say, "end."

Voice recognition programs recognize a vocabulary of preprogrammed words. The vocabulary of voice recognition programs can range from two words to millions of words. The automated telephone system at your bank may ask you to answer questions by speaking the words Yes or No into the telephone. A voice recognition program on your computer, by contrast, may recognize up to two million words.

Most voice recognition programs are a combination of speaker dependent and speaker independent. With *speaker-dependent software*, the computer makes a profile of your voice, which means you have to train the computer to recognize your voice. To train the computer, you must speak words and phrases into the computer repeatedly. *Speaker-independent software* has a built-in set of word patterns so you do not have to train a computer to recognize your voice. Many products today include a built-in set of words that grows as the software learns your words.

Some voice recognition software requires *discrete speech*, which means you have to speak slowly and separate each word with a short pause. Most of today's products, however, allow you to speak in a flowing conversational tone, called *continuous speech*.

Keep in mind that the best voice recognition programs are 90 to 95 percent accurate, which means the software may interpret as many as one in ten words incorrectly.

Audio Input

Voice input is part of a larger category of input called audio input. **Audio input** is the process of entering any sound into the computer such as speech, music, and sound effects. To enter high-quality sound into a personal computer, the computer must have a sound card. Users enter sound into a computer via devices such as microphones, tape players, CD/DVD players, or radios, each of which plugs in a port on the sound card.

Some users also enter music and other sound effects into a computer using external MIDI devices such as an electronic piano keyboard (Figure 5-19). As discussed in the previous chapter, in addition to being a port, *MIDI (musical instrument digital interface)* is the electronic music industry's standard that defines how digital musical devices represent sounds electronically. These devices connect to the sound card on a computer. Software that conforms to the MIDI standard allows users to compose and edit music and many other sounds. For example, you can change the speed, add notes, or rearrange the score to produce an entirely new sound.

FAQ 5-4

Which type of microphone is best?

For voice recognition software, headsets that have a microphone provide the highest quality because they typically do not pick up background noises. For group discussions, however, where multiple people will use the same microphone at the same time, you need a stand-alone or built-in microphone. For more information, visit scsite.com/dc2006/ch5/faq and then click Microphones.

FIGURE 5-19 An electronic piano keyboard is an external MIDI device that allows users to record music, which can be stored in the computer.

INPUT FOR PDAs, SMART PHONES, AND TABLET PCs

Mobile devices, such as the PDA and smart phone, and mobile computers, such as the Tablet PC, offer convenience for the mobile user. A variety of alternatives for entering data and instructions is available for these devices and computers.

PDAs

A user enters data and instructions into a PDA in many ways (Figure 5-20). PDAs ship with a basic stylus, which is the primary input device. Users often purchase a more elaborate stylus that has a ballpoint pen at one end and a stylus at the other. With the stylus, you enter data in two ways: using an on-screen keyboard or using handwriting recognition software that

FIGURE 5-20 Users enter data and instructions into a PDA using a variety of techniques.

is built in the PDA. For example, drawing a straight vertical line in a downward motion displays the number 1 on the PDA. With a specialized pen and data reader, you can transfer notes as you write them on a pad of paper.

For users who prefer typing to handwriting, some PDAs have a built-in mini keyboard. Other users type on a desktop computer or notebook computer keyboard and transfer the data to the PDA. Some users prefer to enter data into a PDA using a portable keyboard. A *portable keyboard* is a full-sized keyboard you conveniently use with a PDA or other mobile device. Some portable keyboards physically attach to and remove from a PDA; others are wireless. Figure 5-21 shows a pocket-sized portable wireless keyboard that unfolds into a full-sized keyboard.

As an alternative to typing, some PDAs allow users to speak data and instructions into the device. Some PDAs also have cameras built in so you can take photographs and view them on a PDA. On other models, you simply attach a digital camera directly to the PDA. You also can use a PDA to scan small documents, such as business cards and product labels, by attaching a scanner to the PDA. For more information about PDAs, read the Personal Mobile Devices feature that follows this chapter.

Smart Phones

Voice is the traditional method of input for smart phones. That is, a user speaks into the phone. Today, however, text messaging, instant messaging, and picture messaging have become popular methods of entering data and instructions into a smart phone.

TEXT MESSAGING   Instead of calling someone's smart phone or cellular telephone, users can enter and send typed messages using *text messaging*. To send a text message, you type a short message, typically less than 160 characters, to another smart phone by pressing buttons on the telephone's keypad. As with chat rooms and instant messaging, text messaging uses abbreviations and emoticons to minimize the amount of typing required. For example, instead of typing the text, I am surprised, a user can type the emoticon, :-O.

INSTANT MESSAGING   Recall that instant messaging (IM) is a real-time communications service that allows you to exchange messages with other online users. Some wireless Internet services providers (WISPs) partner with IM services so you can use your smart phone to communicate with computer users of the same IM service. For example, with AT&T Wireless service, users can send and receive instant messages with AOL Instant Messenger, Yahoo! Messenger, and MSN Messenger.

FIGURE 5-21   This convenient portable wireless keyboard unfolds into a full-sized keyboard, to which you can attach a PDA.

PICTURE MESSAGING   With *picture messaging*, users can send graphics, pictures, video clips, and sound files, as well as short text messages to another smart phone with a compatible picture messaging service. Many smart phones today have a built-in or attachable camera so users easily can take pictures and videos and even incorporate short voice recordings in their picture messages (Figure 5-22).

As an alternative to text messaging, some users write a message with a digital pen, transfer the message from the pen to the smart phone, and then use picture messaging to send the handwritten message. Read At Issue 5-3 for a related discussion.

Most smart phones include PDA capabilities. Thus, input devices used with PDAs typically also are available for smart phones.

AT ISSUE 5-3

Should Driving While Using Smart Phones Be Illegal?

Smart phone sales are soaring. In addition to providing a cellular telephone's capability to communicate wirelessly, smart phones allow users to send and receive text messages, instant messages, picture messages, and e-mail, and to access and view Web pages. For drivers, however, smart phones may be a liability. Estimates vary widely, but news accounts link up to 8,000 fatalities on U.S. highways to cell phone use. Because of their additional capabilities, some experts believe smart phones pose an even greater risk. Many countries have placed bans or restrictions on the use of mobile phones while driving. In the United States, several states have considered or enacted similar legislation. New York, for example, permits vehicle operators to use only hands-free mobile phones. Yet, some studies report that just talking on a portable phone can cause enough driver inattention to trigger an accident. Supporters of a mobile phone ban cite a British study that found drivers talking on cell phones had reaction times 50 percent slower than when not talking on a phone, and 30 percent slower than drivers who were intoxicated. Opponents of a ban note, however, that other driver activities, like tuning a radio or having a conversation, can be equally distracting. Should the use of cell phones and/or smart phones be banned while driving? Why? What other measures, if any, could be taken to prevent drivers from endangering themselves and others while using cell phones or smart phones?

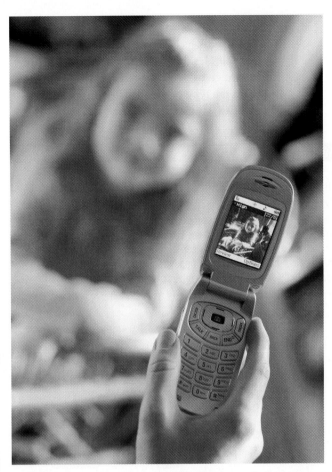

FIGURE 5-22   Many smart phones include a digital camera so users can send pictures and videos to others.

Tablet PCs

The primary input device for a Tablet PC is a pressure-sensitive digital pen, which allows users to write on the device's screen. A Tablet PC's handwriting recognition software works similarly to that of a PDA. The computer converts the handwriting into characters it can process.

Both the slate and convertible designs of Tablet PC provide a means for keyboard input for those users who prefer typing to handwriting. You can attach a removable keyboard to the slate Tablet PC. The convertible Tablet PC has an attached keyboard that can be rotated 180 degrees so the computer resembles a notebook computer.

To access peripherals at their home or office, users can slide their Tablet PC in a docking station. A *docking station*, which is an external device that attaches to a mobile computer or device, contains a power connection and provides connections to peripherals. In the docking station, Tablet PC users can work with a full-sized keyboard, mouse, CD/DVD drives, and other desktop peripherals (Figure 5-23). The design of docking stations varies, depending on the type of mobile computer or the device to which they are attached.

FAQ 5-5

Can a mobile computer or device get a virus?

Yes. Mobile computers and devices can get a virus from a downloaded Web page. A virus can transfer from a desktop computer to a mobile device when users connect the two to synchronize data. Viruses also can transmit via wireless data transfer when two wireless devices communicate with one another, such as when receiving a text or picture message. For more information, visit scsite.com/dc2006/ch5/faq and then click Viruses and Mobile Devices.

Tablet PC

docking station

FIGURE 5-23   To use a slate Tablet PC while working at a desk, insert the Tablet PC in a docking station. Devices such as a keyboard and CD drive can be plugged in the docking station.

DIGITAL CAMERAS

A **digital camera** allows users to take pictures and store the photographed images digitally, instead of on traditional film (Figure 5-24). While many digital cameras look like a traditional camera, some models attach to or are built in PDAs and smart phones. Mobile users such as real estate agents, insurance agents, general contractors, and photojournalists use digital cameras so they immediately can view photographed images on the camera. Home and business users have digital cameras to save the expense of film developing, duplication, and postage.

Some digital cameras use internal flash memory to store images. Others store images on mobile storage media, such as a flash memory card, memory stick, and mini-disc. Chapter 7 discusses these and other storage media in depth. Generally, higher-capacity storage devices can hold more pictures.

Digital cameras typically allow users to review, and sometimes edit, images while they are in the camera. Some digital cameras can connect to or communicate wirelessly with a printer or television, allowing users to print or view images directly from the camera.

FIGURE 5-24   With a digital camera, users can view photographed images immediately through a small screen on the camera to see if the picture is worth keeping.

Often users prefer to *download*, or transfer a copy of, the images from the digital camera to the computer's hard disk. With some digital cameras, images download through a cable that connects between the digital camera (or the camera's docking station) and a USB port or a FireWire port on the system unit. For cameras that store images on miniature mobile storage media, simply insert the media in a reading/writing device that communicates wirelessly or attaches to a port on the system unit. Copying images from the miniature media to the computer's hard disk is just like copying files from any other disk drive. Some cameras store images on a mini CD/DVD. In this case, insert the disc in the computer's disc drive and then copy the pictures to the computer's hard disk (or you can view the contents of the disc by inserting it in a CD or DVD player).

When you copy images to the hard disk in a computer, the images are available for editing with photo editing software, printing, faxing, sending via e-mail, including in another document, or posting to a Web site or photo community for everyone to see. Many users add pictures to greeting cards, a computerized photo album, a family newsletter, certificates, and awards.

The three basic types of digital cameras are studio cameras, field cameras, and point-and-shoot cameras. The most expensive and highest quality of the three is a *studio camera*, which is a stationary camera used for professional studio work. Often used by photojournalists, a *field camera* is a portable camera that has many lenses and other attachments. As with the studio camera, a field camera can be quite expensive. A *point-and-shoot camera* is much more affordable and lightweight and provides acceptable quality photographic images for the home or small business user. Figure 5-25 illustrates how one make of point-and-shoot digital camera works.

A point-and-shoot camera often features flash, zoom, automatic focus, and special effects. Some allow users to record short audio narrations for photographed images. Others even record short video clips in addition to still images. Point-and-shoot digital cameras often have a built-in TV out port, allowing users to

FIGURE 5-25 HOW A DIGITAL CAMERA MIGHT WORK

Step 1:
Point to the image to photograph and take the picture. Light passes into the lens of the camera.

Step 2:
The image is focused on a chip called a *charge-coupled device* (*CCD*).

Step 3:
The CCD generates an analog signal that represents the image.

Step 4:
The analog signal is converted to a digital signal by an analog-to-digital converter (ADC).

Step 5:
A processor in the camera adjusts the quality of the image and usually stores the digital image on miniature mobile storage media inserted in the camera.

display photographed images or play recorded video clips directly on a television.

For additional information about digital cameras, read the Digital Imaging and Video Technology feature that follows Chapter 6.

Digital Camera Quality

One factor that affects the quality of a digital camera is its resolution. **Resolution** is the number of horizontal and vertical pixels in a display device. A *pixel* (short for picture element) is the smallest element in an electronic image (Figure 5-26). The greater the number of pixels the camera uses to capture an image, the better the quality of the image. Thus, the higher the resolution, the better the image quality, but the more expensive the camera.

Digital camera resolutions range from approximately 1 million to more than 8 million pixels (*MP*). A camera with a 5.1-megapixel (5,100,000 pixels) resolution will provide a better quality than one with a 3.2-megapixel resolution. As a general rule, a 1-megapixel camera is fine for pictures sent via e-mail or posted on the Web. For good quality printed photographs, users should have a 2-megapixel camera for 4×6 inch photographs, a 3-megapixel camera for 8×10 photographs, and 5-megapixel or greater camera for larger size prints.

Manufacturers often use pixels per inch to represent a digital camera's resolution. *Pixels per inch (ppi)* is the number of pixels in one inch of screen display. For example, a 2304 ×

1728 (pronounced 2304 by 1728) ppi camera has 2,304 pixels per vertical inch and 1,728 pixels per horizontal inch. Multiplying these two numbers together gives an approximate total number of megapixels. For example, 2304 times 1728 equals approximately 4 million, or 4 megapixels. If just one number is stated, such as 1600 ppi, then both the vertical and horizontal numbers are the same.

Many digital cameras provide a means to adjust the ppi to the desired resolution. With a lower ppi, you can capture and store more images in the camera. For example, a camera set at 800×600 ppi might capture and store 61 images, if it has sufficient storage capacity. The number of images may reduce to 24 on the same camera set at 1600×1200 ppi, because each image consumes more storage space.

The actual photographed resolution is known as the *optical resolution*. Some manufacturers state *enhanced resolution*, instead of, or in addition to, optical resolution. Optical resolution is different from enhanced resolution. The enhanced resolution usually is higher because it uses a special formula to add pixels between those generated by the optical resolution. Be aware that some manufacturers compute a digital camera's megapixels from the enhanced resolution, instead of optical resolution.

Another measure of a digital camera's quality is the number of bits it stores in a pixel. Each pixel consists of one or more bits of data. The more bits used to represent a pixel, the more colors and shades of gray that can be represented. One bit per pixel is enough for simple one-color images. For multiple colors and shades of gray, each pixel requires more than one bit of data. A point-and-shoot camera should be at least 24 bit.

FIGURE 5-26 A pixel is a single point in an electronic image.

FAQ 5-7

What is dpi?

Some advertisements incorrectly use dpi to mean the same as ppi. The acronym *dpi*, which stands for *dots per inch*, is a measure of a print resolution. For screen resolution, the proper measurement term is ppi (pixels per inch). For more information, visit scsite.com/dc2006/ch5/faq and then click Resolution.

VIDEO INPUT

Video input is the process of capturing full-motion images and storing them on a computer's storage medium such as a hard disk or DVD.

Some video devices record video using analog signals. Computers, by contrast, use digital signals. To enter video from an analog device into a personal computer, the analog signal must be converted to a digital signal. To do this, plug a video camera, VCR, or other analog video device in a video capture port on the system unit. One type of adapter card that has a video capture port is a *video capture card*, which converts an analog video signal into a digital signal that a computer can process. Most new computers are not equipped with a video capture card because not all users have the need for this type of adapter card.

A **digital video (DV) camera**, by contrast, records video as digital signals instead of analog signals. Many DV cameras can capture still frames, as well as motion. To transfer recorded images to a hard disk or CD or DVD, users connect DV cameras directly to a USB port or a FireWire port on the system unit. Thus, the computer does not need a video capture card. Simply connect the video device to the computer and begin transferring images. After saving the video on a storage medium, such as a hard disk or DVD, you can play it or edit it using video editing software on a computer (Figure 5-27).

PC Video Cameras

A **PC video camera**, or **PC camera**, is a type of digital video camera that enables a home or small business user to capture video and still images, send e-mail messages with video attachments, add live images to instant messages, broadcast live images over the Internet, and make video telephone calls. During a *video telephone call*, both parties see each other as they communicate over the Internet (Figure 5-28). The cost of PC video cameras usually is less than $100.

Attached to the computer's USB port or FireWire port, a PC video camera usually sits on top of the monitor. For more flexibility, some PC video cameras are portable. That is, you can detach them from the base and use them as a stand-alone digital camera.

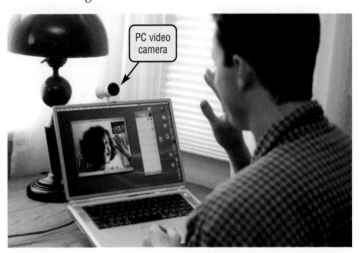

FIGURE 5-28 Using a PC video camera, home users can see each other as they communicate over the Internet.

video camera

video is displayed on computer screen

FIGURE 5-27 Home users can transfer videos to their computers and then use video editing software to edit the video.

WEB LINK 5-7

PC Video Cameras

For more information, visit scsite.com/ dc2006/ch5/weblink and then click PC Video Cameras.

Web Cams

A **Web cam** is any video camera that displays its output on a Web page. A Web cam attracts Web site visitors by showing images that change regularly. Home or small business users might use Web cams to show a work in progress, weather and traffic information, employees at work, photographs of a vacation, and countless other images. Read At Issue 5-4 for a related discussion.

Some Web sites have live Web cams that display still pictures and update the displayed image at a specified time or time intervals, such as 15 seconds. Another type of Web cam, called a *streaming cam*, has the illusion of moving images because it sends a continual stream of still images.

AT ISSUE 5-4

Should Cameras Be Able to Monitor Your Every Move?

Imagine if while driving to school you could use your cell phone or an Internet-enabled device to find out which campus parking lot had the most spaces available. Far-fetched? Maybe not. IrisNet (Internet-scale Resource-Intensive Sensor Network Services), a project under development by Intel and Carnegie Mellon University, someday may be able to give you just this sort of information. IrisNet's goal is to provide current information about the outside world. IrisNet relies on a sensor network made up of Internet-connected personal computers equipped with sensing devices such as Web cams. Project planners envision a worldwide sensor network storing real-time and historical data from thousands, or even millions, of widely distributed sensors. IrisNet would provide the software infrastructure for the network, allowing users to query the collected data. Users could ask what the weather conditions are in a distant city, when a child arrived safely at school, or where spaces are available in campus parking lots. IrisNet raises, however, certain privacy concerns. Should every action captured by one of IrisNet's sensors be available to anyone who creates a query? Should queries be prioritized or even rejected? Why or why not? Can IrisNet's potential benefits be balanced with its possible pitfalls? How?

Video Conferencing

A **video conference** is a meeting between two or more geographically separated people who use a network or the Internet to transmit audio and video data (Figure 5-29). To participate in a video conference, you need video conferencing software along with a microphone, speakers, and a video camera attached to a computer.

As you speak, members of the meeting hear your voice on their speakers. Any image in front of the video camera, such as a person's face, appears in a window on each participant's screen. A *whiteboard* is another window on the screen that displays notes and drawings simultaneously on all participants' screens. This window provides multiple users with an area on which they can write or draw.

As the costs of video conferencing hardware and software decrease, increasingly more business meetings, corporate training, and educational classes will be conducted as video conferences.

FAQ 5-8

How popular is video conferencing?

A recent survey found that 40 percent of computer users participate in video conferences with desktop equipment. Annual expenditures exceed $7.7 billion on voice and video conferencing equipment. For more information, visit scsite.com/dc2006/ch5/faq and then click Video Conferencing.

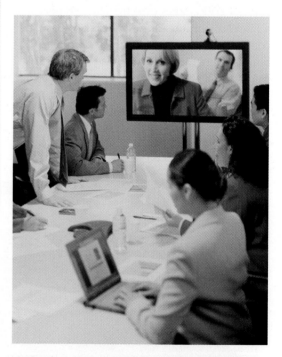

FIGURE 5-29 To save on travel expenses, many large businesses are turning to video conferencing.

Test your knowledge of pages 245 through 254 in Quiz Yourself 5-2.

QUIZ YOURSELF 5-2

Instructions: Find the true statement below. Then, rewrite the remaining false statements so they are true.

1. A digital camera allows users to take pictures and store the photographed images digitally, instead of on traditional film.

2. DV cameras record video as analog signals.

3. Instant messaging is the computer's capability of distinguishing spoken words.

4. Many smart phones today have a built-in or attachable camera so users easily can send text messages.

5. The lower the resolution of a digital camera, the better the image quality, but the more expensive the camera.

Quiz Yourself Online: To further check your knowledge of voice input; input for PDAs, smart phones, and Tablet PCs; digital cameras; and video input, visit scsite.com/dc2006/ch5/quiz and then click Objectives 5 – 8.

SCANNERS AND READING DEVICES

Some input devices save users time by eliminating manual data entry. With these devices, users do not type, speak, or write into the computer. Instead, these devices capture data from a *source document*, which is the original form of the data. Examples of source documents include time cards, order forms, invoices, paychecks, advertisements, brochures, photographs, inventory tags, or any other document that contains data to be processed.

Devices that can capture data directly from a source document include optical scanners, optical readers, bar code readers, RFID readers, magnetic stripe card readers, and magnetic-ink character recognition readers. The following pages discuss each of these devices.

Optical Scanners

An *optical scanner*, usually called a **scanner**, is a light-sensing input device that reads printed text and graphics and then translates the results into a form the computer can process. Four types of scanners are flatbed, pen, sheet-fed, and drum (Figure 5-30).

TYPES OF SCANNERS

Scanner	Method of Scanning and Use	Scannable Items
Flatbed	• Similar to a copy machine • Scanning mechanism passes under the item to be scanned, which is placed on a glass surface	• Single-sheet documents • Bound material • Photographs • Some models include trays for slides, transparencies, and negatives
Pen or Handheld 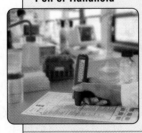	• Move pen over text to be scanned, then transfer data to computer • Ideal for mobile users, students, and researchers • Some connect to a PDA or smart phone	• Any printed text
Sheet-fed	• Item to be scanned is pulled into a stationary scanning mechanism • Smaller than a flatbed scanner • A model designed specifically for photographs is called a *photo scanner*	• Single-sheet documents • Photographs • Slides (with an adapter) • Negatives
Drum	• Item to be scanned rotates around stationary scanning mechanism • Very expensive • Used in publishing industry	• Single-sheet documents • Photographs • Slides • Negatives

FIGURE 5-30 This table describes the various types of scanners.

A **flatbed scanner** works in a manner similar to a copy machine except it creates a file of the document in memory instead of a paper copy (Figure 5-31). Once you scan a document or picture, you can display the scanned object on the screen, store it on a storage medium, print it, fax it, attach it to an e-mail message, include it in another document, or post it to a Web site or photo community for everyone to see.

As with a digital camera, the quality of a scanner is measured by the number of bits it stores in a pixel and the number of pixels per inch, or resolution. The higher each number, the better the quality, but the more expensive the scanner. Most of today's affordable color desktop scanners for the home or small business range from 30 to 48 bits and have an optical resolution ranging from 600 to 4800 ppi. Commercial scanners designed for power users range from 4800 to 14,000 ppi.

Many scanners include *OCR (optical character recognition) software*, which can read and convert text documents into electronic files. OCR software is useful if you need to modify a document but do not have the original word processing file. For example, if you scan a business report with a flatbed scanner and do not use OCR software, you cannot edit the report because the scanner saves the report as an image. This is because the scanner does not differentiate between text and graphics. OCR

software, however, would convert the scanned image into a text file that you could edit, for example, with a word processing program. Current OCR software has a high success rate and usually can identify more than 99 percent of scanned material.

Businesses often use scanners for *image processing*, which consists of capturing, storing, analyzing, displaying, printing, and manipulating images. Image processing allows users to convert paper documents such as reports, memos, and procedure manuals into electronic images. Users distribute and publish these electronic documents on networks and the Internet.

Business users typically store and index electronic documents with an image processing system. An *image processing system* is similar to an electronic filing cabinet that provides access to exact reproductions of the original documents. Local governments, for example, use image processing systems to store property deeds and titles to provide the public and professionals, such as lawyers and loan officers, quick access to electronic documents.

WEB LINK 5-8

Scanners

For more information, visit scsite.com/dc2006/ch5/weblink and then click Scanners.

FAQ 5-9

How can I improve the quality of scanned documents?

Place a blank sheet of paper behind translucent papers, newspapers, and other see-through types of paper. If the original image is crooked, draw a line on the back at the bottom of the image. Use that mark to align the original on the scanner. Use photo editing software to fix imperfections in images. For more information, visit scsite.com/dc2006/ch5/faq and then click Scanning.

FIGURE 5-31   HOW A FLATBED SCANNER WORKS

Step 1: Place the document to be scanned face down on the glass window. Using buttons on the scanner or the scanner program, start the scanning process.

Step 2: The scanner converts the document content to digital information, which is transmitted through the cable to the memory of the computer.

Step 3: Once in the memory of the computer, users can display the image, print it, e-mail it, include it in a document, or place it on a Web page.

Optical Readers

An *optical reader* is a device that uses a light source to read characters, marks, and codes and then converts them into digital data that a computer can process. Two technologies used by optical readers are optical character recognition and optical mark recognition.

OPTICAL CHARACTER RECOGNITION Optical **character recognition** (**OCR**) is a technology that involves reading typewritten, computer-printed, or hand-printed characters from ordinary documents and translating the images into a form that the computer can process. Most **OCR devices** include a small optical scanner for reading characters and sophisticated software to analyze what is read.

OCR devices range from large machines that can read thousands of documents per minute to handheld wands that read one document at a time. OCR devices read printed characters in an OCR font. A widely used OCR font is called OCR-A (Figure 5-32). During the scan of a document, an OCR device determines the shapes of characters by detecting patterns of light and dark. OCR software then compares these shapes with predefined shapes stored in memory and converts the shapes into characters the computer can process.

```
ABCDEFGHIJKLM
NOPQRSTUVWXYZ
1234567890
-=█;',.·/
```

FIGURE 5-32 A portion of the characters in the OCR-A font. Notice how characters such as the number 0 and the letter O are shaped differently so the reading device easily can distinguish between them.

Many companies use OCR characters on turnaround documents. A **turnaround document** is a document that you return (turn around) to the company that creates and sends it. For example, when consumers receive a bill, they often tear off a portion of the bill and send it back to the company with their payment (Figure 5-33). The portion of the bill they return usually has their payment amount, account number, and other information printed in OCR characters.

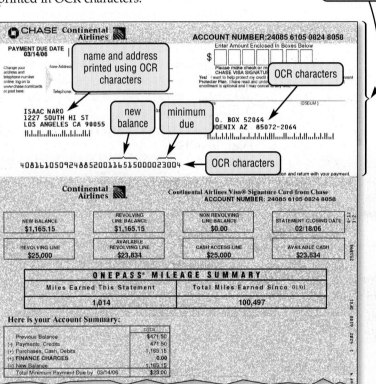

FIGURE 5-33 OCR characters frequently are used with turnaround documents. With this bill, you tear off the top portion and return it with a payment.

OPTICAL MARK RECOGNITION Optical **mark recognition** (**OMR**) is a technology that reads hand-drawn marks such as small circles or rectangles. A person places these marks on a form, such as a test, survey, or questionnaire answer sheet. With a test, the OMR device first scans the answer key sheet to record correct answers based on patterns of light. The OMR device then scans the remaining documents and matches their patterns of light against the answer key sheet.

Bar Code Readers

A **bar code reader**, also called a **bar code scanner**, is an optical reader that uses laser beams to read bar codes by using light patterns that pass through the bar code lines (Figure 5-34). A **bar code** is an identification code that consists of a set of vertical lines and spaces of different widths. The bar code represents data that identifies the manufacturer and the item.

Manufacturers print a bar code either on a product's package or on a label that is affixed to a product. A variety of products such as groceries, books, clothing, vehicles, mail, and packages have bar codes. Each industry uses its own type of bar code. The United States Postal Service (USPS) uses a POSTNET bar code. Retail and grocery stores use the *UPC* (*Universal Product Code*) bar code (Figure 5-35). Read At Issue 5-5 for a related discussion.

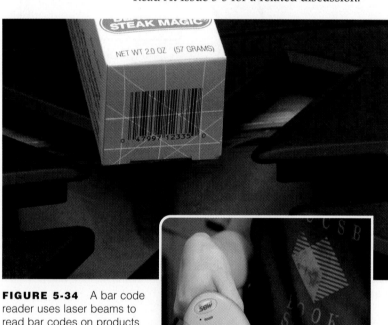

FIGURE 5-34 A bar code reader uses laser beams to read bar codes on products such as groceries and books.

AT ISSUE 5-5

Scanner Errors at the Checkout Counter?

Have you ever taken an item to a store's check-out and discovered that the price displayed when the item's bar code was scanned was different from the price shown on a shelf tag, sign, or advertisement? If you have, you are not alone. A government survey found that eight percent of the time, an item's scanned price is different from the price presented elsewhere. When an item is scanned at a store's checkout counter, a computer finds the item's price in the store's database. Store owners claim that discrepancies between the scanned price and a listed price are the result of human error — either failure to update the store's price database or incorrect shelf tags, signs, or advertisements. Yet, some consumer advocates claim that the discrepancy is intentional. They accuse stores of *scanner fraud*, insisting that some stores advertise one price and then charge another, hoping buyers will not recognize the difference. Even if consumers identify a pricing error, they may not bring the mistake to the store's attention, especially if the discrepancy is detected after the item is purchased or if the amount at issue is small. Who do you think is responsible for differences between scanned prices and posted costs? Why? Should stores be responsible for pricing errors? Why or why not?

FIGURE 5-35 This UPC identifies a carton of skim milk.

RFID Readers

RFID (*radio frequency identification*) is a technology that uses radio signals to communicate with a tag placed in or attached to an object, an animal, or a person. RFID tags, which contain a memory chip and an antenna, are available in many shapes and sizes and sometimes are embedded in glass, labels, or cards. Some RFID tags are as small as a grain of sand; others are the size of a luggage tag. An **RFID reader** reads information on the tag via radio waves. RFID readers can be handheld devices or mounted in a stationary object such as a doorway.

Many retailers see RFID as an alternative to bar code identification because it does not require direct contact or line-of-site transmission. Each product in a store would contain a tag that identifies the product (Figure 5-36). As consumers remove products from the store shelves and walk through a checkout area, an RFID reader reads the tag(s) and communicates with a computer that calculates the amount due, eliminating the need for checking out each item.

Other uses of RFID include tracking times of runners in a marathon; tracking location of soldiers, employee wardrobes, and airline baggage; checking lift tickets of skiers; gauging pressure and temperature of tires on a vehicle; checking out library books; and tracking payment as vehicles pass through booths on tollway systems. Read Looking Ahead 5-1 for a look at the next generation of tracking devices.

RFID tag embedded in label attached to garment

memory chip

FIGURE 5-36 RFID readers read information stored on an RFID tag and then communicate this information to computers, which instantaneously compute payments and update inventory records. In this example, the RFID tag is embedded in a label attached to the garment.

Magnetic Stripe Card Readers

A **magnetic stripe card reader**, often called a *magstripe reader*, reads the magnetic stripe on the back of credit cards, entertainment cards, bank cards, and other similar cards. The stripe, which is divided in three horizontal tracks, contains information identifying you and the card issuer (Figure 5-37). Some information stored in the stripe includes your name, account number, the card's expiration date, and a country code.

When a consumer swipes a credit card through the magstripe reader, it reads the information stored on the magnetic stripe on the card. If the magstripe reader rejects your card, it is possible that the magnetic stripe on the card is scratched, dirty, or erased. Exposure to a magnet or magnetic field can erase the contents of a card's magnetic stripe.

In many cases, a magstripe reader is part of a point-of-sale terminal. The function of point-of-sale terminals is discussed later in this chapter.

MICR Readers

MICR (*magnetic-ink character recognition*) devices read text printed with magnetized ink. An **MICR reader** converts MICR characters into a form the computer can process. The banking industry almost exclusively uses MICR for check processing. Each check in your checkbook has precoded MICR characters beginning at the lower-left edge (Figure 5-38). The MICR characters represent the bank number, the customer account number, and the check number. These numbers may appear in a different order than the ones shown in the sample in Figure 5-38.

When a bank receives a check for payment, it uses an MICR inscriber to print the amount of the check in MICR characters in the lower-right corner. The check then is sorted or routed to the customer's bank, along with thousands of others. Each check is inserted in an MICR reader, which sends the check information — including the amount of the check — to a computer for processing. When you balance your checkbook, verify that the amount printed in the lower-right corner is the same as the amount written on the check; otherwise, your statement will not balance.

The banking industry has established an international standard not only for bank numbers, but also for the font of the MICR characters. This standardization makes it possible for people to write checks in other countries.

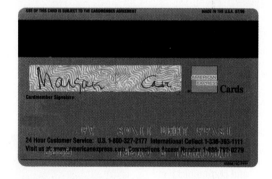

FIGURE 5-37 A magnetic stripe card reader reads information encoded on the stripe on the back of your credit card.

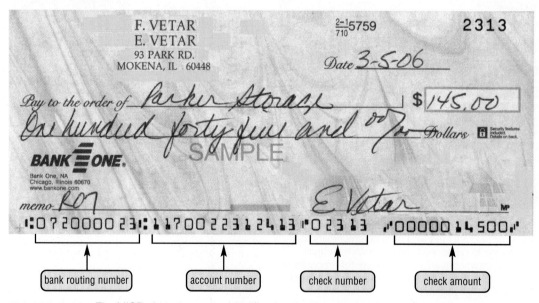

bank routing number   account number   check number   check amount

FIGURE 5-38 The MICR characters preprinted on the check represent the bank routing number, the customer account number, and the check number. The amount of the check in the lower-right corner is added after the check is cashed.

Data Collection Devices

Instead of reading or scanning data from a source document, a *data collection device* obtains data directly at the location where the transaction or event takes place. For example, employees use bar code readers, PDAs, handheld computers, or other mobile devices to collect data wirelessly (Figure 5-39). These types of data collection devices are used in restaurants, factories, warehouses, the outdoors, or other locations where heat, humidity, and cleanliness are not easy to control.

Data collection devices and many mobile computers and devices have the capability of wirelessly transmitting data over a network or the Internet. Increasingly more users today send data wirelessly to central office computers using these devices.

FIGURE 5-39   A chef uses this rugged handheld computer, which includes a bar code reader, that wirelessly transmits information about the scanned produce to the restaurant's inventory system.

TERMINALS

A *terminal* consists of a keyboard, a monitor, a video card, and memory. Often, these components are housed in a single unit.

Terminals fall into three basic categories: dumb terminals, smart terminals, and special-purpose terminals. A *dumb terminal* has no processing power; thus, it cannot function as an independent device. Users enter data and instructions in a dumb terminal and then transmit the data to a host computer over a network. The host computer processes the input and then, if necessary, sends information (output) back to the dumb terminal. The host computer usually is a midrange server or mainframe. A *smart terminal* has a processor, giving it the capability of performing some functions independent of the host computer. In recent years, personal computers have replaced most smart terminals.

Special-purpose terminals perform specific tasks and contain features uniquely designed for use in a particular industry. Two widely used special-purpose terminals are point-of-sale (POS) terminals and automated teller machines.

Point-of-Sale Terminals

The location in a retail or grocery store where a consumer pays for goods or services is the *point of sale (POS)*. Most retail stores use a **POS terminal** to record purchases, process credit or debit cards, and update inventory.

In a grocery store, the POS terminal is a combination of an electronic cash register, bar code reader, and printer. When the checkout clerk scans the bar code on the food product, the computer uses the manufacturer and item numbers to look up the price of the item and the complete product name in a database. Then, the price of the item in the database shows on the display device, the name of the item and its price print on a receipt, and the item being sold is recorded so the inventory can be updated. Thus, the output from a POS terminal serves as input to other computers to maintain sales records, update inventory, verify credit, and perform other activities associated with the sales transactions that are critical to running the business. Some POS terminals are Web-enabled, which allows updates to inventory at geographically separate locations.

Many POS terminals handle credit card or debit card payments and thus also include a magstripe reader. After swiping your card through the reader, the POS terminal connects to a system that authenticates the purchase. Once the transaction is approved, the terminal prints a receipt for the customer.

A self-service POS terminal allows consumers to perform all checkout-related activities (Figure 5-40). That is, they scan the items, bag the items, and pay for the items themselves. Consumers with small orders find the new self-service POS terminals convenient because these terminals often eliminate the hassle of waiting in long lines.

FIGURE 5-40 Some grocery stores offer self-serve checkouts, where the consumers themselves use the POS terminals to scan purchases, scan their store saver card and coupons, and then pay for the goods. This POS terminal prints a receipt for the customer.

Automated Teller Machines

An **automated teller machine** (**ATM**) is a self-service banking machine that connects to a host computer through a network (Figure 5-41). Banks place ATMs in convenient locations, including grocery stores, convenience stores, retail outlets, shopping malls, and gas stations, so customers conveniently can access their bank accounts.

Using an ATM, people withdraw cash, deposit money, transfer funds, or inquire about an account balance. Some ATMs have a touch screen; others have special buttons or keypads for entering input. To access a bank account, you insert a plastic bankcard in the ATM's magstripe reader. The ATM asks you to enter a password, called a *personal identification number* (*PIN*),

which verifies that you are the holder of the bankcard. When your transaction is complete, the ATM prints a receipt for your records.

FIGURE 5-41 An ATM is a self-service banking terminal that allows customers to access their bank accounts.

BIOMETRIC INPUT

Biometrics is the technology of authenticating a person's identity by verifying a personal characteristic. Biometric devices grant users access to programs, systems, or rooms by analyzing some biometric identifier. A *biometric identifier* is a physiological (related to physical or chemical activities in the body) or behavioral characteristic. Examples include fingerprints, hand geometry, facial features, voice, signatures, and eye patterns.

A *biometric device* translates a personal characteristic (the input) into a digital code that is compared with a digital code stored in the computer. If the digital code in the computer does not match the personal characteristic's code, the computer denies access to the individual.

The most widely used biometric device today is a fingerprint scanner. A **fingerprint scanner** captures curves and indentations of a fingerprint. With the cost of fingerprint scanners less than $100, home and small business users install fingerprint scanners to authenticate users before they can access a personal computer. Instead of lunch money, grade schools use fingerprint scanners to identify students in the cafeteria and adjust account balances for each lunch purchased (Figure 5-42).

External fingerprint scanners usually plug into a parallel or USB port. To save on desk space, some newer keyboards and notebook computers have a fingerprint scanner built into them. For a technical discussion about fingerprint scanners, read the High-Tech Talk article on page 268.

A *face recognition system* captures a live face image and compares it with a stored image to determine if the person is a legitimate user. Some buildings use face recognition systems to secure access to rooms. Law enforcement, surveillance systems, and airports use face recognition to protect the public. Some notebook computers use this security technique to safeguard a computer. The computer will not start unless the user is legitimate. These programs are becoming more sophisticated and can recognize people with or without glasses, makeup, or jewelry, and with new hairstyles.

Biometric devices measure the shape and size of a person's hand using a *hand geometry system* (Figure 5-43). Because their cost is more than $1,000, larger companies use these systems as time and attendance devices or as security devices. Colleges use hand geometry systems to verify students' identities. Day-care centers and hospital nurseries use them to verify parents who pick up their children.

A *voice verification system* compares a person's live speech with their stored voice pattern. Larger organizations sometimes use voice verification systems as time and attendance devices. Many companies also use this technology for access to sensitive files and networks. Some financial services use voice verification systems to secure telephone banking transactions. These systems use speaker-dependent voice recognition software. That is, users train the computer to recognize their inflection patterns.

A *signature verification system* recognizes the shape of your handwritten signature, as well as measures the pressure exerted and the motion used to write the signature. Signature verification systems use a specialized pen and tablet.

FIGURE 5-42 This elementary school student pays for lunch by placing his finger on a fingerprint scanner.

FIGURE 5-43 A hand geometry system verifies this student's identity before he is allowed access to the school library.

High security areas use iris recognition systems. The camera in an *iris recognition system* uses iris recognition technology to read patterns in the iris of the eye (Figure 5-44). These patterns are as unique as a fingerprint. Iris recognition systems are quite expensive and are used by government security organizations, the military, and financial institutions that deal with highly sensitive data.

Sometimes, fingerprint, iris, and other biometric data are stored on a smart card. A **smart card**, which is comparable in size to a credit card or ATM card, stores the personal data on a thin microprocessor embedded in the card (Figure 5-45). Smart cards add an extra layer of protection. For example, when a user places a smart card through a smart card reader, the computer compares a fingerprint stored on the card with the one read by the fingerprint scanner. Some credit cards are smart cards; that is, the microprocessor contains the card holder's information instead of a magnetic stripe.

FIGURE 5-44 An iris recognition system.

FAQ 5-11

How popular is biometrics technology?

One study estimates that revenue from biometric solutions has and will continue to grow by about 35 percent annually for the next several years, as shown in the chart below. For more information, visit scsite.com/dc2006/ch5/faq and then click Biometrics.

Source: International Biometric Group

FIGURE 5-45 A smart card reader reads data stored on a smart card's microprocessor.

PUTTING IT ALL TOGETHER

When you purchase a computer, you should have an understanding of the input devices included with the computer, as well as those you may need that are not included. Many factors influence the type of input devices you may use: the type of input desired, the hardware and software in use, and the desired cost. The type of input devices you require depends on your intended use. Figure 5-46 outlines several suggested input devices for specific computer users.

SUGGESTED INPUT DEVICES BY USER

User	Input Device
HOME	• Enhanced keyboard or ergonomic keyboard • Mouse • Stylus for PDA or smart phone • Joystick or wheel • 30-bit 600 x 1200 ppi color scanner • 2-megapixel digital camera • Headset that includes a microphone • PC video camera
SMALL OFFICE/ HOME OFFICE	• Enhanced keyboard or ergonomic keyboard • Mouse • Stylus and portable keyboard for PDA or smart phone, or digital pen for Tablet PC • 36-bit 600 x 1200 ppi color scanner • 2-megapixel digital camera • Headset that includes a microphone • PC video camera
MOBILE	• Wireless mouse for notebook computer • Trackball, touchpad, or pointing stick on notebook computer • Stylus and portable keyboard for PDA or smart phone, or digital pen for Tablet PC • 2- or 3-megapixel digital camera • Headset that includes a microphone • Fingerprint scanner for notebook computer
POWER	• Enhanced keyboard or ergonomic keyboard • Mouse • Stylus and portable keyboard for PDA or smart phone • Pen for graphics tablet • 48-bit 1200 x 1200 ppi color scanner • 5- or 6-megapixel digital camera • Headset that includes a microphone • PC video camera
LARGE BUSINESS	• Enhanced keyboard or ergonomic keyboard • Mouse • Stylus and portable keyboard for PDA or smart phone, or digital pen for Tablet PC • Touch screen • Light pen • 42-bit 1200 x 1200 ppi color scanner • OCR/OMR readers, bar code readers, MICR reader, or data collection devices • Microphone • Video camera for video conferences • Fingerprint scanner or other biometric device

FIGURE 5-46   This table recommends suggested input devices.

INPUT DEVICES FOR PHYSICALLY CHALLENGED USERS

The ever-increasing presence of computers in everyone's lives has generated an awareness of the need to address computing requirements for those who have or may develop physical limitations. The **Americans with Disabilities Act (ADA)** requires any company with 15 or more employees to make reasonable attempts to accommodate the needs of physically challenged workers.

Besides voice recognition, which is ideal for blind or visually impaired users, several other input devices are available. A *keyguard* is a metal or plastic plate placed over the keyboard that allows users to rest their hands on the keyboard without accidentally pressing any keys (Figure 5-47). A keyguard also guides a finger or pointing device so a user presses only one key at a time.

Keyboards with larger keys also are available. Still another option is the *on-screen keyboard*, in which a graphic of a standard keyboard is displayed on the user's screen (Figure 5-48).

Various pointing devices are available for users with motor disabilities. Small trackballs that the user controls with a thumb or one finger can be attached to a table, mounted to a wheelchair, or held in the user's hand. Another option for people with limited hand movement is a *head-mounted pointer* to control the pointer or insertion point (Figure 5-49). To simulate the functions of a mouse button, a user works with switches that control the pointer. The switch might be a hand pad, a foot pedal, a receptor that detects facial motions, or a pneumatic instrument controlled by puffs of air.

Two exciting developments in this area are gesture recognition and computerized implant devices. Both in the prototype stage, they attempt to provide users with a natural computer interface.

With *gesture recognition*, the computer will detect human motions. Computers with gesture recognition capability have the potential to recognize sign language, read lips, track facial movements, or follow eye gazes. For paralyzed or speech impaired individuals, a doctor will implant a computerized device into the brain. This device will contain a transmitter. As the user thinks thoughts, the transmitter will send signals to the computer.

FIGURE 5-47 A keyguard.

FIGURE 5-48 As you click letters on the on-screen keyboard, they appear in the document at the location of the insertion point.

FIGURE 5-49 A camera/receiver mounted on the monitor tracks the position of the head-mounted pointer, which is reflective material that this user is wearing on the brim of her hat. As the user moves her head, the pointer on the screen also moves.

Test your knowledge of pages 255 through 266 in Quiz Yourself 5-3.

QUIZ YOURSELF 5-3

Instructions: Find the true statement below. Then, rewrite the remaining false statements so they are true.

1. A fingerprint scanner captures curves and indentations of a signature.

2. After swiping a credit card through an MICR reader, a POS terminal connects to a system that authenticates the purchase.

3. ATMs ask you to enter a password, called a biometric identifier, which verifies that you are the holder of the bankcard.

4. Four types of source documents are flatbed, pen, sheet-fed, and drum.

5. Retail and grocery stores use the POSTNET bar code.

6. RFID is a technology that uses laser signals to communicate with a tag placed in an object, an animal, or a person.

7. The Americans with Disabilities Act (ADA) requires any company with 15 or more employees to make reasonable attempts to accommodate the needs of physically challenged workers.

Quiz Yourself Online: To further check your knowledge of scanners and reading devices, terminals, biometric devices, and input for physically challenged users, visit scsite.com/dc2006/ch5/quiz and then click Objectives 9 – 12.

CHAPTER SUMMARY

Input is any data and instructions you enter into the memory of a computer. This chapter described the various techniques of entering input and several commonly used input devices (Read Looking Ahead 5-2 for a look at the next generation of input devices). Topics presented included the keyboard, mouse, and other pointing devices; voice input; input for PDAs, smart phones, and Tablet PCs; digital cameras; video input; scanners and reading devices; terminals; biometric input; and input devices for physically challenged users.

LOOKING AHEAD 5-2

Wearable Computers Make Performance Statement

Frodo, the hero in the *Lord of the Rings* trilogy, wears a durable, inconspicuous tunic that saves his life. You, too, may one day wear a garment that saves your life by detecting health problems and summoning emergency help. Researchers in Germany have developed undergarments with sensors that monitor heartbeats and then alert medical experts when an abnormal heart rhythm is detected.

While this clothing is practical, other researchers are creating the newest fashions and accessories outfitted with computers. For example, a cellular telephone could connect wirelessly to a calorie counter monitor on your wrist and then order food when it detects you are hungry. Other wearable computers can change color depending upon weather conditions, deliver e-mail messages, and improve a golf swing. For more information, visit scsite.com/dc2006/ch5/looking and then click Wearable Computers.

Data Entry Clerk

Data entry clerks have an essential role in today's information-producing industry. A *data entry clerk* enters data into documents, databases, and other applications using computer keyboards and visual display devices. Duties can include manipulating, editing, and maintaining data to ensure that it is accurate and up-to-date, and researching information.

Some data entry clerks telecommute. Although they generally use keyboards, they also work with other input from scanners or electronically transmitted files. Because of the nature of their job, data entry clerks often sit for hours typing in front of monitors. They can be susceptible to repetitive stress injuries and neck, back, and eye strain. To prevent these injuries, many offices use ergonomically designed input devices and incorporate regularly scheduled exercise breaks.

Data entry clerks usually are high school graduates with keyboarding skills. Some employers require an associate's degree or at least two years of post-high-school education plus two years of office experience. Data entry training, basic language skills, and familiarity with word processing, spreadsheet, and database programs are important. Data entry often serves as a stepping-stone to other administrative positions. The average annual salary for data entry clerks is around $23,000. Salaries start at about $18,000 and, with experience, can exceed $31,000. For more information, visit scsite.com/dc2006/ch5/careers and then click Data Entry Clerk.

High-Tech Talk

BIOMETRICS: PERSONALIZED SECURITY

Biometric authentication is based on the measurement of an individual's unique physiological and behavioral characteristics. The most common measurements, described earlier in this chapter, such as fingerprints, hand geometry, facial features, and eye patterns are physiological biometrics. Some of the more novel measurements, such as body odor, brain wave patterns, DNA, ear shape, sweat pores, and vein patterns also fall into the category of physiological biometrics. Voice scan and signature scan are examples of behavioral biometrics.

Any biometric technology process involves two basic steps — enrollment and matching. To illustrate these steps, this High-Tech Talk uses the most common biometric technology, finger-scan technology.

ENROLLMENT Enrollment is the process in which a user presents the fingerprint data to be stored in a template for future use, as shown in the top of Figure 5-50. This initial template is called the *enrollment template*. Creating the enrollment template involves four basic steps: (1) acquire fingerprint, (2) extract fingerprint feature, (3) create enrollment template, and (4) store enrollment template. The enrollment template usually is created only after the user has submitted several samples of the same fingerprint. Most fingerprint images will have false details, usually caused by cuts, scars, or even dirt, which must be filtered out.

The first step, acquire fingerprint, presents a major challenge to finger-scan technology. The quality of a fingerprint may vary substantially from person to person and even finger to finger. The two main methods of acquiring images are optical and silicon. With optical technology, a camera is used to register the fingerprint image against a plastic or glass platen (scanner). Silicon technology uses a silicon chip as a platen, which usually produces a higher quality fingerprint image than optical devices.

The second step, extract fingerprint feature, involves thinning the ridges of the raw image to a minuscule size and then converting the characteristics to binary format. Fingerprints are comprised of ridges and valleys that have unique patterns, such as arches, loops, and swirls. Irregularities and discontinuities in these ridges and valleys are known as *minutiae*. Minutiae are the distinctive characteristics upon which most finger-scan technology is based. The fingerprint-feature extraction process used is highly sophisticated, patented, and a closely-held vendor secret.

In the third step, the binary format is used to create the enrollment template. The fourth and final step involves storing the template on a storage device, such as a hard disk or smart card for future use when the same person attempts to be authenticated.

MATCHING Matching is the process of comparing a match template to an enrollment template. A *match template* is created when the user attempts to gain access through a fingerprint scanner. Most computer and network systems are set up so that the person also must claim an identity, such as a user name, along with the fingerprint. In this case, the match template is compared directly to the enrollment template for that user name. Other systems, such as those used for criminal investigations, will search the entire enrollment template database for a match.

The match template is created in the same fashion as the enrollment template described earlier. Rather than storing the match template on disk, however, it is compared to the user's stored enrollment template, as shown in the bottom of Figure 5-50. The result of the matching process is a score. The score is compared against a threshold. The threshold is a predefined number that can be adjusted depending on the desired level of security.

The scoring process leads to the decision process. The decision process will produce one of three actions: (1) the threshold has been exceeded, thereby resulting in a match; (2) the threshold has not been met, thereby resulting in a nonmatch; or (3) the data may have been insufficient, resulting in the system requesting a new sample from the user to begin a new comparison.

Finger-scan technology is likely to continue to grow as the centerpiece of the biometric industry. For more information, visit scsite.com/dc2006/ch5/tech and then click Biometrics.

FIGURE 5-50 The two steps in biometric technology.

Companies on the Cutting Edge

LOGITECH
PERSONAL INTERFACE PRODUCTS LEADER

The average Internet user has more than 40 inches of cords on his desktop, according to a *Logitech* survey. This company is working to reduce desktop clutter with a variety of cordless peripherals, including mouse devices, keyboards, mobile headsets, and game controllers.

A market leader, Logitech has sold more than 45 million wireless devices. It also designs, manufactures, and markets corded devices. The company's retail sales account for more than 80 percent of its revenue.

Two engineering students from Stanford University, Italian-born Pierluigi Zappacosta and Swiss-born Daniel Borel, launched Logitech in 1981. Today, the corporation is the world's largest manufacturer of the mouse, having sold more than 500 million since the company's founding. For more information, visit scsite.com/dc2006/ch5/companies and then click Logitech.

palmOne
HANDHELD COMPUTING DEVICES MANUFACTURER

The PalmPilot holds the distinction of being the most rapidly adopted new computing product ever manufactured. More than two million units of this PDA were sold since Palm Computing introduced the product in 1996.

Palm Computing was founded in 1992 and became a subsidiary of 3Com Corp. in 1997. In 2000, the Palm subsidiary became an independent, publicly traded company. In 2003, shareholders voted to spin off PalmSource, Inc., maker of the Palm operating system, as an independent company and acquire Handspring, Inc. The combined company is known as *palmOne, Inc.*

The palmOne product family includes the Zire and Tungsten handheld devices and the Treo smart phones. For more information, visit scsite.com/dc2006/ch5/companies and then click palmOne.

Technology Trailblazers

HIDEKI KOMIYAMA
SONY ELECTRONICS PRESIDENT AND CEO

Sony introduced its first U.S. product more than 30 years ago much to the credit of *Hideki Komiyama*. The Trinitron color television was the start of Sony's dominance in the consumer electronics field.

Under Komiyama's leadership, Sony has introduced a music download service and engineered new products, including liquid crystal display televisions and DVD recorders. Popular consumer electronics products include the VAIO personal computer and the Mavica and Cyber-shot digital cameras. Komiyama's goal is to make new consumer products extremely user friendly. He believes that the consumer electronics industry gradually will shift from audio and video technologies to information technology.

Komiyama was promoted to president and CEO in 2003. He joined Sony in 1967, and his other executive-level positions in the United States have included senior vice president of consumer video products and president of the Consumer Television Company. For more information, visit scsite.com/dc2006/ch5/people and then click Hideki Komiyama.

DOUGLAS ENGELBART
CREATOR OF THE MOUSE

The phrase "point and click" might not be part of every computer user's vocabulary if *Douglas Engelbart* had not pursued his engineering dreams. In 1964, he developed the first prototype computer mouse with the goal of making it easier to move a cursor around a computer screen.

Ten years later, engineers at Xerox refined Engelbart's prototype and showed the redesigned product to Apple's Steve Jobs, who applied the concept to his graphical Macintosh computer. The mouse was mass produced in the mid-1980s, and today it is the most widely used pointing device.

Engelbart currently serves as director of the Bootstrap Institute, a company he founded with his daughter to form strategic alliances and consequently improve corporations' performances. For more information, visit scsite.com/dc2006/ch5/people and then click Douglas Engelbart.

Chapter Review

The Chapter Review section summarizes the concepts presented in this chapter. To listen to the audio version of this Chapter Review, visit scsite.com/dc2006/ch5/review. To obtain help from other students regarding any subject in this chapter, visit scsite.com/dc2006/ch5/forum and post your thoughts or questions.

① **What Is Input?** Input is any *data* or instructions entered into the memory of a computer. An **input device** is any hardware component that allows users to enter data and instructions.

② **What Are the Characteristics of a Keyboard?** A **keyboard** is an input device that contains keys users press to enter data into a computer. Computer keyboards have a typing area that includes letters of the alphabet, numbers, punctuation marks, and other basic keys. Most keyboards also have *function keys* programmed to issue commands; keys used to move the **insertion point**, usually a blinking vertical bar, on the screen; and *toggle keys* that switch between two states when pressed.

③ **What Are Different Mouse Types, and How Do They Work?** A **pointing device** is an input device that allows users to control a small graphical symbol, called a **pointer**, on the computer screen. A **mouse** is a pointing device that fits under the palm of your hand. As you move a mouse, the pointer on the screen also moves. A *mechanical mouse* translates the movement of a ball on its underside into signals the computer can process. An *optical mouse* uses devices that emit and sense light to detect the mouse's movement. A *cordless mouse* transmits data using wireless technology.

④ **How Do Pointing Devices Work?** A **trackball** is a stationary pointing device with a ball that you rotate to move the pointer. A **touchpad** is a flat, pressure-sensitive device that you slide your finger across to move the pointer. A **pointing stick** is a device positioned on the keyboard that you push to move the pointer. A **joystick** is a vertical lever that you move to control a simulated vehicle or player. A **wheel** is a steering-wheel-type device that you turn to simulate driving a vehicle. A **light pen** is a light-sensitive device that you press against or point at the screen to select objects. A **touch screen** is a touch-sensitive display device that you interact with by touching areas of the screen. A **stylus** and a **digital pen** use pressure to write or draw.

> *connect!* Visit scsite.com/dc2006/ch5/quiz or click the Quiz Yourself button. Click Objectives 1 – 4.

⑤ **How Does Voice Recognition Work?** **Voice recognition** is the computer's capability of distinguishing spoken words. Voice recognition programs recognize a vocabulary of preprogrammed words. Most voice recognition programs are a combination of *speaker-dependent software*, which makes a profile of your voice, and *speaker-independent software*, which has a built-in set of word patterns.

⑥ **What Are Input Devices for PDAs, Smart Phones, and Tablet PCs?** A primary input device for a PDA is a basic stylus. Some PDAs have a built-in keyboard or support voice input. You can attach a full-sized *portable keyboard* to a PDA. Voice is the traditional input method for smart phones. Users can send typed messages using *text messaging*. Some smart phones can use IM to communicate over the Internet, and many have a camera so that users can use *picture messaging*. The primary input device for a Tablet PC is a digital pen, with which you can write on the device's screen. If you slide a Tablet PC into a *docking station*, you can use a full-sized keyboard and mouse.

⑦ **How Does a Digital Camera Work?** A **digital camera** allows users to take pictures and store the photographed images digitally. When you take a picture, light passes into the camera lens, which focuses the image on a *charge-coupled device (CCD)*. The CCD generates an analog signal that represents the image. An analog-to-digital converter (ADC) converts the analog signal to a digital signal. A processor in the camera stores the digital image on the camera's storage media. The image is downloaded to a computer's hard disk via cable or copied from the camera's storage media.

Chapter Review

⑧ How Are PC Video Cameras, Web Cams, and Video Conferencing Used? A **PC video camera** is a digital video camera that enables users to capture video and still images and then send or broadcast the images over the Internet. A **Web cam** is any video camera that displays its output on a Web page. A **video conference** is a meeting between geographically separated people who use a network or the Internet to transmit audio and video data.

> Visit scsite.com/dc2006/ch5/quiz or click the Quiz Yourself button. Click Objectives 5 – 8.

⑨ What Are Various Types of Scanners and Reading Devices, and How Do They Work? A **scanner** is a light-sensing input device that reads printed text and graphics and translates the results into a form the computer can process. A **flatbed scanner** works in a manner similar to a copy machine except it creates a file of the document. An optical reader uses a light source to read characters, marks, and codes and converts them into digital data. **Optical character recognition (OCR)** reads characters from ordinary documents. **Optical mark recognition (OMR)** reads hand-drawn marks such as small circles. A **bar code reader** is an optical reader that uses laser beams to read a **bar code**, or identification code. **RFID** (*radio frequency identification*) uses radio signals to communicate with an embedded tag. **MICR** (*magnetic-ink character recognition*) reads text printed with magnetized ink.

⑩ What Are Types of Terminals? A *terminal* consists of a keyboard, a monitor, a video card, and memory. A *dumb terminal* has no processing power and relies on a host computer for processing. A *smart terminal* has a processor and can perform some functions independent of the host computer. POS terminals and ATMs are special-purpose terminals. A **POS (point-of-sale) terminal** records purchases, processes credit or debit cards, and updates inventory. An **automated teller machine (ATM)** is a self-service banking machine that connects to a host computer. To access a bank account, you insert a bankcard into the ATM's card reader and enter a *personal identification number (PIN)*.

⑪ What Are Various Biometric Devices? A *biometric device* translates a personal characteristic into digital code that is compared with a digital code stored in the computer to identify an individual. A **fingerprint scanner** captures curves and indentations of a fingerprint. A *face recognition system* captures a live face image. A *hand geometry system* measures the shape and size of a hand. A *voice verification system* compares live speech with a stored voice pattern. A *signature verification system* recognizes the shape of a signature. An *iris recognition system* reads patterns in the iris of the eye.

⑫ What Are Alternative Input Devices for Physically Challenged Users? Voice recognition is ideal for visually impaired users. A *keyguard* is a plate placed over the keyboard that allows users with limited hand mobility to rest their hands and press only one key at a time. Keyboards with larger keys or an *on-screen keyboard* displayed on a user's screen also are available. A small trackball or a *head-mounted pointer* helps users with limited hand movement to control the pointer. Two developments in the prototype stage are *gesture recognition* and computerized implant devices.

> Visit scsite.com/dc2006/ch5/quiz or click the Quiz Yourself button. Click Objectives 9 – 12.

Key Terms

You should know the Primary Terms and be familiar with the Secondary Terms. Use the list below to help focus your study. To further enhance your understanding of the Key Terms in this chapter, visit scsite.com/dc2006/ch5/terms. See an example of and a definition for each term, and access current and additional information about the term from the Web.

Primary Terms

(shown in bold-black characters in the chapter)

Americans with Disabilities Act (ADA) (266)
audio input (246)
automated teller machine (ATM) (262)
bar code (258)
bar code reader (258)
bar code scanner (258)
digital camera (250)
digital pen (243)
digital video (DV) camera (253)
ergonomics (238)
fingerprint scanner (262)
flatbed scanner (256)
graphics tablet (244)
input (234)
input device (236)
insertion point (237)
joystick (242)
keyboard (236)
light pen (242)
magnetic stripe card reader (260)
MICR (260)
MICR reader (260)
mouse (239)
mouse pad (239)
OCR devices (257)

optical character recognition (OCR) (257)
optical mark recognition (OMR) (257)
PC camera (253)
PC video camera (253)
pen input (243)
pointer (239)
pointing device (239)
pointing stick (241)
POS terminal (261)
resolution (252)
RFID (259)
RFID reader (259)
scanner (255)
smart card (264)
stylus (243)
touch screen (242)
touchpad (241)
trackball (241)
turnaround document (257)
video conference (254)
video input (253)
voice input (245)
voice recognition (245)
Web cam (254)
wheel (242)

Secondary Terms

(shown in italic characters in the chapter)

biometric device (262)
biometric identifier (262)
biometrics (262)
charge-coupled device (CCD) (251)
command (235)
continuous speech (246)
cordless keyboard (238)
cordless mouse (239)
cursor (application program) (237)
cursor (graphics tablet) (244)
data (234)
data collection device (261)
digitizer (244)
discrete speech (246)
docking station (249)
download (251)
dumb terminal (261)
enhanced keyboard (237)
enhanced resolution (252)
ergonomic keyboard (238)
face recognition system (263)
field camera (251)
function keys (236)
gesture recognition (266)
hand geometry system (263)
handwriting recognition software (243)
head-mounted pointer (266)
image processing (256)
image processing system (256)
iris recognition system (264)
keyguard (266)
magnetic-ink character recognition (260)
magstripe reader (260)
mechanical mouse (239)
MIDI (musical instrument digital interface) (246)
mouse gestures (240)
mouse pointer (239)

MP (252)
OCR (optical character recognition) software (256)
on-screen keyboard (266)
optical mouse (239)
optical reader (257)
optical resolution (252)
optical scanner (255)
personal identification number (PIN) (262)
picture messaging (249)
pixel (252)
pixels per inch (ppi) (252)
point-and-shoot camera (251)
point of sale (POS) (261)
portable keyboard (248)
program (234)
radio frequency identification (259)
signature verification system (263)
smart terminal (261)
source document (255)
speaker-dependent software (246)
speaker-independent software (246)
speech recognition (245)
streaming cam (254)
studio camera (251)
terminal (261)
text messaging (248)
toggle key (237)
UPC (Universal Product Code) (258)
user response (235)
video capture card (253)
video telephone call (253)
voice verification system (263)
whiteboard (254)
wireless keyboard (238)
wireless mouse (239)

Checkpoint

Use the Checkpoint exercises to check your knowledge level of the chapter. The Beyond the Book exercises will help broaden your understanding of the concepts presented in this chapter. To complete the Checkpoint exercises interactively, visit scsite.com/dc2006/ch5/check.

Label the Figure   Identify these areas and keys on a desktop computer keyboard.

a. function keys
b. media controls
c. numeric keypad
d. additional keys
e. APPLICATION key
f. arrow keys
g. typing area
h. WINDOWS key

True/False   Mark T for True and F for False. (See page numbers in parentheses.)

_____ 1. Once data is in memory, the computer interprets and executes instructions to process the data into information. (234)

_____ 2. An input device is any hardware component that allows users to enter data and instructions into a computer. (236)

_____ 3. The command associated with a function key will remain the same from program to program. (236)

_____ 4. An optical mouse has a rubber or metal ball on its underside. (239)

_____ 5. The trackball is the most widely used pointing device today. (241)

_____ 6. A pointing stick requires special cleaning, just like a mechanical mouse or trackball. (241)

_____ 7. Pressure-sensitive digital pens typically provide more functionality than a stylus. (243)

_____ 8. A stylus is the primary input device for a PDA. (247)

_____ 9. The primary input device for a Tablet PC is a pressure-sensitive digital pen. (249)

_____ 10. Digital cameras typically allow users to review, and sometimes edit, images while they are in the camera. (250)

_____ 11. A scanner is a light-sensing input device that reads printed text and graphics and then translates the results into a form the computer can process. (255)

_____ 12. Many companies use optical mark recognition (OMR) to read hand-printed characters on turnaround documents. (257)

Checkpoint

 Multiple Choice

Select the best answer. (See page numbers in parentheses.)

1. _____ is a series of instructions that tells a computer what to do and how to do it. (234)
   a. Data
   b. A program
   c. A command
   d. A user response

2. _____ keys are special keys programmed to issue commands to a computer. (236)
   a. Toggle
   b. Arrow
   c. Function
   d. Numeric

3. A(n) _____ is a key that switches between two states each time the user presses the key. (237)
   a. arrow
   b. insertion point
   c. toggle
   d. function key

4. _____ is a common mouse operation in which you press and release the primary mouse button. (240)
   a. Point
   b. Click
   c. Drag
   d. Right-click

5. A _____ is a small, flat, rectangular pointing device that is sensitive to pressure and motion. (241)
   a. stylus
   b. pointing stick
   c. trackball
   d. touchpad

6. Architects, mapmakers, designers, artists, and home users create drawings and sketches on a _____. (244)
   a. trackball
   b. touch screen
   c. graphics tablet
   d. touchpad

7. A portable keyboard _____. (248)
   a. is an infrared image of a keyboard projected on a flat surface
   b. is built into the top of a handheld computer
   c. has a design that reduces the chance of wrist and hand injuries
   d. is a full-sized keyboard you use with a PDA or other mobile device

8. The most expensive and highest quality digital camera is a _____, which is a stationary camera used for professional work. (251)
   a. PC camera
   b. point-and-shoot camera
   c. studio camera
   d. field camera

9. A digital video (DV) camera _____. (253)
   a. records video as analog signals instead of digital signals
   b. is a stationary camera used for professional studio work
   c. records video as digital signals instead of analog signals
   d. is a mobile camera used for amateur studio work

10. Scanners capture data from a _____, which is the original form of the data. (255)
    a. duplicate document
    b. secondary document
    c. derivative document
    d. source document

11. The UPC (Universal Product Code) bar code is used by _____. (258)
    a. retail and grocery stores
    b. libraries, blood banks, and air parcel carriers
    c. the United States Postal Service (USPS)
    d. nonretail applications such as game tickets

12. Point-of-sale terminals and automated teller machines are types of _____ that perform specific tasks and contain features uniquely designed for use in a particular industry. (261)
    a. smart terminals
    b. dumb terminals
    c. general-purpose terminals
    d. special-purpose terminals

13. The most widely used biometric device is the _____. (262)
    a. face recognition system
    b. fingerprint scanner
    c. hand geometry system
    d. iris recognition system

14. A(n) _____ is a metal or plastic plate that allows users to rest their hands on the keyboard without accidentally pressing any keys. (266)
    a. on-screen keyboard
    b. keyguard
    c. head-mounted pointer
    d. computerized implant

Checkpoint

Matching

Match the terms with their definitions. (See page numbers in parentheses.)

_____ 1. insertion point (237)

_____ 2. ergonomic keyboard (238)

_____ 3. pointer (239)

_____ 4. mouse pad (239)

_____ 5. graphics tablet (244)

_____ 6. docking station (249)

_____ 7. video capture card (253)

_____ 8. bar code (258)

_____ 9. RFID (259)

_____ 10. smart card (264)

a. designed to reduce the chance of wrist and hand injuries

b. symbol on the screen that indicates where the next character typed will be displayed

c. stores personal data on a thin, embedded computer

d. technology that uses radio signals to communicate with a tag placed in an item

e. graphical symbol whose location and shape change with the movement of a pointing device

f. identification code that consists of vertical lines and spaces of different widths

g. rectangular pad that provides better traction than the top of a desk

h. external device that attaches to a mobile computer or device that contains a power connection and provides connections to peripherals

i. flat, rectangular, electronic plastic board sometimes called a digitizer

j. self-service banking machine that connects to a host computer

k. converts an analog video signal to a digital signal that a computer can use

l. projects an infrared image of a keyboard on any flat surface

Short Answer

Write a brief answer to each of the following questions.

1. How does voice recognition work? _____ How is discrete speech different from continuous speech? _____

2. What is a video capture card? _____ Why is a video capture card not needed with a digital video (DV) camera? _____

3. What is OCR (optical character recognition) software? _____ What is an image processing system? _____

4. What is a bar code reader? _____ Define RFID, and list some of its uses. _____

5. What is the Americans with Disabilities Act (ADA)? _____ How might gesture recognition and computerized implant devices help physically challenged users in the future? _____

Beyond the Book

Read the following book elements, learn more about each using the Web, and then write a brief report.

1. At Issue — Keyboard Monitoring — Privacy Risk? (237), Should the Government Set Computer Use Standards? (240), Should Driving While Using Smart Phones Be Illegal? (249), Should Cameras Be Able to Monitor Your Every Move? (254), or Scanner Errors at the Checkout Counter? (258)

2. Career Corner — Data Entry Clerk (267)

3. Companies on the Cutting Edge — Logitech or palmOne (269)

4. FAQs (237, 238, 240, 246, 250, 251, 252, 254, 256, 259, 264)

5. High-Tech Talk — Biometrics: Personalized Security (268)

6. Looking Ahead — Smart Dust Monitors the Environment (259) or Wearable Computers Make Performance Statement (267)

7. Making Use of the Web — Auctions (121)

8. Picture Yourself Going Digital (232)

9. Technology Trailblazers — Hideki Komiyama and Douglas Engelbart (269)

10. Web Links (240, 241, 242, 244, 246, 253, 256, 264)

Learn It Online

Use the Learn It Online exercises to reinforce your understanding of the chapter concepts. To access the Learn It Online exercises, visit scsite.com/dc2006/ch5/learn.

1 At the Movies — Get the Best of Both Worlds with a Convertible Tablet PC

To view the Get the Best of Both Worlds with a Convertible Tablet PC movie, click the number 1 button. Locate your video and click the corresponding High-Speed or Dial-Up link, depending on your Internet connection. Watch the movie, and then complete the exercise by answering the questions that follow. Taking classroom notes with pen and paper may be a thing of the past if the Tablet PC continues its rise in popularity. Switching to a Tablet PC can offer you some options that are not available on a regular notebook or desktop computer. What are some of the drawbacks to using a Tablet PC? What are some of the benefits?

2 At the Movies — Buy the Right Digital Camera

To view the Buy the Right Digital Camera movie, click the number 2 button. Locate your video and click the corresponding High-Speed or Dial-Up link, depending on your Internet connection. Watch the movie and then complete the exercise by answering the questions that follow. A single digital camera that is perfect for every user simply does not exist. When making the decision about which model to purchase, you must consider how and where you will use the camera and what results you will expect. If you wanted to purchase a digital camera, what options would be important to you? Which options would not be important to you? How important would portability be? What about picture quality?

3 Student Edition Labs — Working with Audio

Click the number 3 button. When the Student Edition Labs menu appears, click *Working with Audio* to begin. A new browser window will open. Follow the on-screen instructions to complete the Lab. When finished, click the Exit button. If required, submit your results to your instructor.

4 Student Edition Labs — Working with Video

Click the number 4 button. When the Student Edition Labs menu appears, click *Working with Video* to begin. A new browser window will open. Follow the on-screen instructions to complete the Lab. When finished, click the Exit button. If required, submit your results to your instructor.

5 Practice Test

Click the number 5 button. Answer each question. When completed, enter your name and click the Grade Test button to submit the quiz for grading. Make a note of any missed questions. If required, submit your results to your instructor.

6 Who Wants To Be a Computer Genius[2]?

Click the number 6 button to find out if you are a computer genius. Directions about how to play the game will be displayed. When you are ready to play, click the Play button. Submit your score to your instructor.

7 Wheel of Terms

Click the number 7 button to reinforce important terms you learned in this chapter by playing the Shelly Cashman Series version of this popular game. Directions about how to play the game will be displayed. When you are ready to play, click the Play button. Submit your score to your instructor.

Learn It Online

 DC Track and Field

Click the number 8 button to use what you have learned in this chapter to compete against other students in three track and field events. Directions about how to play the game will be displayed. When you are ready to play, click the start first event button. If required, submit your score to your instructor.

 You're Hired!

Click the number 9 button to use what you have learned in this chapter to embark on the path to a career in computers. Directions about how to play the game will be displayed. When you are ready to play, click the begin game button. If required, submit your score to your instructor.

10 **Crossword Puzzle Challenge**

Click the number 10 button. Complete the puzzle to reinforce skills you learned in this chapter. Directions about how to play the game will be displayed. When you are ready to play, click the Submit button. Submit the completed puzzle to your instructor.

11 **Lab Exercises**

Click the number 11 button. When the Lab Exercises menu appears, click the exercise assigned by your instructor. A new browser window will open. Follow the on-screen instructions to complete the exercise. When finished, click the Exit button. If required, submit your results to your instructor.

 In the News

Many people spend a great deal of time jotting notes on scratch pads, napkins, or self-stick notes. This may be fine for the occasional thought; however, in a situation where you would rather concentrate on the substance of the ideas being expressed, you may need a more sophisticated method for taking notes. Tape recorders have long been the mainstay for recording lectures, interviews, or one's thoughts, but they are restricted by the fact that the tapes last only so long before they

have to be flipped over or switched altogether. One new development is the voice pen, which is a flash-memory-based recording device. It records digitally, which offers higher quality over standard tapes, easy indexing, and instant erasure. It is approximately the size of a small cellular telephone or remote control unit and can record up to 500 minutes on long play settings. Click the number 12 button and read a news article about a new or improved input device, an input device being used in a new way, or an input device being made more available. What is the device? Who is promoting it? How will it be used? Will the input device change the number, or effectiveness, of potential users? If so, why?

13 **Chapter Discussion Forum**

Select an objective from this chapter on page 233 about which you would like more information. Click the number 13 button and post a short message listing a meaningful message title accompanied by one or more questions concerning the selected objective. In two days, return to the threaded discussion by clicking the number 13 button. Submit to your instructor your original message and at least one response to your message.

Learn How To

Use the Learn How To activities to learn fundamental skills when using a computer and accompanying technology. Complete the exercises and submit them to your instructor. Visit scsite.com/dc2006/ch5/howto to obtain more information pertaining to each activity.

LEARN HOW TO 1: Install and Use a PC Video Camera

A **PC video camera**, sometimes called a Web cam, is a digital video camera that allows you to capture video and still images. The videos can be used in live instant messages or for live images over the Internet. Recordings of the videos can be included on Web pages or in e-mail messages as attachments. In addition, some cameras include software that enables you to establish a visual security environment where the camera can be used to detect and record movement in its general vicinity.

Using a PC video camera requires two phases: 1) purchasing and installing the PC video camera, and 2) using the video camera to transmit live video or to record video or digital images. To purchase and install a PC video camera, complete the following steps:

1. Determine how you want to use the video camera in order to decide the quality of camera you require and the camera software you need. PC video cameras range in price from about $25 to more than $125, and vary in picture quality, features, and accompanying software. If you are not sure of all features and prices, search the Web to determine the best camera for your use.
2. After making your purchase, you will find that most cameras are accompanied by a CD-ROM containing the software that enables the camera to communicate and work with the computer. Often, the instructions with the device will specify that you should place the CD-ROM in a CD or DVD drive and follow the on-screen instructions to install the software on the computer.
3. After the software is installed, you likely will be told to connect the camera to the computer. You do so by connecting the USB cable first to the camera and then to a USB port on your computer. When the camera is connected, you will be able to start the camera software from either the All Programs submenu or the Windows taskbar.

Once you have started the camera software, you will be able to use the camera for any of the tasks you require. Each camera and its accompanying software will allow you to create a video, use instant messaging to send live video to your IM contacts, and other uses as well. In addition, you often will be able to control the quality of your video output by modifying brightness, contrast, and clarity. With many cameras, you will be able to zoom in and out, and, from your keyboard, enter commands to move the camera lens left, right, up, and down.

On some cameras, you even can use a feature called face tracking, where the camera will remain focused on your face even when you move. This feature allows you to be more natural and not be concerned with always making sure you are placed exactly right for the camera.

As you can see, once you have purchased and installed a PC video camera, you will open an entirely new world of communication right from your computer.

Exercise

1. Assume you have decided to purchase a PC video camera to use for instant messaging. Search the Web to find the highest rated cameras available for purchase that can be used for your purposes. What is the most expensive camera you found? The least expensive? What features distinguish the two? Based on your use of the camera for instant messaging, what camera would you choose to buy? Why? Submit your answers to your instructor.
2. Optional: Purchase a PC video camera or borrow one from a friend. Install the camera software on a computer. Warning: If you are using a computer that is not your own, complete this exercise only with the owner's permission. Connect the camera to the computer. Practice with the camera and the accompanying software. What features does the software provide? Which feature do you find the most compelling? What features could you do without? Record a video of yourself answering these questions. Submit the video to your instructor.

Learn How To

LEARN HOW TO 2: Use the On-Screen Keyboard for Physically Challenged Users

Everyone who uses a computer must enter data and instructions into the computer. For people with limited hand and arm mobility, this can prove a daunting task. Windows XP and a variety of other applications provide a number of aids that can be useful. One of these is the on-screen keyboard.

The **on-screen keyboard** allows a user to view the keyboard on the screen and select characters to enter by using several different methods. To display and use the on-screen keyboard, complete the following steps:

1. Click the Start button on the Windows taskbar, point to All Programs on the Start menu, point to Accessories on the All Programs submenu, point to Accessibility on the Accessories submenu, and then click On-Screen Keyboard on the Accessibility submenu. *The On-Screen Keyboard window opens. In addition, an On-Screen Keyboard dialog box might appear that indicates the on-screen keyboard provides a minimum level of functionality and that a more robust product might be needed for daily use.* If this dialog box is displayed, click the OK button to close it.
2. In the On-Screen Keyboard window, click Settings on the menu bar. Ensure a check mark is next to Always on Top.
3. If necessary, click Settings on the menu bar again. Click Typing Mode on the Settings menu. *The Typing Mode dialog box is displayed (Figure 5-51).*
4. Ensure the Click to select button is selected and then click the OK button in the Typing Mode dialog box.
5. Start your Web browser and click the Address bar.
6. Using the on-screen keyboard, enter the characters www.cnn.com and then click the ent key.
7. When the cnn.com Web page appears, click the enter symbol box in the Stock/Fund Quotes section of the page. Using the on-screen keyboard, enter ibm and then click the ent key.
8. After finding the stock price for IBM, close the browser window.
9. Start the WordPad program (see Learn How To number 1 on page 48).
10. In the On-Screen Keyboard window, click Settings on menu bar and then click Typing Mode on the Settings menu.
11. Ensure the Hover to select button is selected in the Typing Mode dialog box. Click the Minimum time to hover box arrow and select 1.00 seconds in the list. Click the OK button.
12. Click in the WordPad window to position the insertion point.
13. You can cause a character to be entered in the WordPad window by placing the mouse pointer over the desired key (hovering) for one second. Type the following using the on-screen keyboard: Accessibility tools are vital for computer users.
14. Close the WordPad window and then close the On-Screen Keyboard window.

FIGURE 5-51

You have seen how one of the Accessibility tools within Windows XP functions. You are encouraged to explore all of the tools and discover how these tools can be useful to those people for whom they were designed.

Exercise

1. Start WordPad and then display the on-screen keyboard. In the On-Screen Keyboard window, click Settings on the menu bar and then click Typing Mode. In the Typing Mode dialog box, select Joystick or key to select. Click the Advanced button. Ensure the Keyboard key box contains a checkmark and then click Space in the list. Click the OK buttons to close the dialog boxes. Then, on the Keyboard menu, select Block Layout. Click in the WordPad window and then press the SPACEBAR. What happened? Keep pressing the SPACEBAR until you cause a character to be entered in the WordPad window. Use the bksp key on the on-screen keyboard to backspace and erase the character, and then use the on-screen keyboard to type On-Screen Keyboard usage in the WordPad window. When you are done, close the WordPad window and the On-Screen Keyboard window. Which means of using the on-screen keyboard (click a key, hover, or the SPACEBAR) did you find easiest to use? Why? Why would a physically challenged person prefer one method over another? Prepare your answers using the on-screen keyboard and then submit your answers to your instructor.

Web Research

Use the Internet-based Web Research exercises to broaden your understanding of the concepts presented in this chapter. Visit scsite.com/dc2006/ch5/research to obtain more information pertaining to each exercise. To discuss any of the Web Research exercises in this chapter with other students, post your thoughts or questions at scsite.com/dc2006/ch5/forum.

(1) Scavenger Hunt   Use one of the search engines listed in Figure 2-10 in Chapter 2 on page 78 or your own favorite search engine to find the answers to the questions below. Copy and paste the Web address from the Web page where you found the answer. Some questions may have more than one answer. If required, submit your answers to your instructor. (1) The primary inventor of the first commercial typewriter wanted to persuade people to buy and use the device, so he ordered the keys to allow users to type as quickly as possible. Who was the QWERTY keyboard's primary inventor? (2) Many of the new handheld devices allow you to input data through the use of handwriting software. What are the three more popular handwriting/input programs? (3) Find two Web sites that sell these programs, and create a table listing the cost of each of these programs.

(2) Search Sleuth   MetaCrawler (metacrawler.com) is a different type of search Web site because it returns combined results from leading search engines. Visit this Web site and then use your word processing program to answer the following questions. Then, if required, submit your answers to your instructor. (1) Click the Tools and Tips link at the top of the page. Browse and then explore some of the tools, such as MiniCrawler and MetaSpy. (2) Scroll down and then read some of the information contained in the Basic Searching section. Makes notes of two new things you learned. (3) Click your browser's Back button or press the BACKSPACE key to return to the MetaCrawler home page. What are the six most popular searches today? Click a link for one of these popular searches and scroll through the results MetaCrawler returns. (4) Click your browser's Back button or press the BACKSPACE key to return to the MetaCrawler home page. Click the Search text box and then type What is the top selling SUV? as the keywords in the Search text box. (5) Scroll through the links MetaCrawler returns and then click one that provides the information requested. What are the three most popular SUVs? Read the information and then write a 50-word summary.

(3) Journaling   Respond to your readings in this chapter by writing at least one page about your reactions, evaluations, and reflections about using input devices. For example, do you recall the first time you used a mouse? What experiences have you had with voice recognition? Do you own a PDA or Tablet PC, digital camera, or smart phone? Have you ever suffered from repetitive strain injuries from using a mouse or keyboard? What do you do to reduce the chances of experiencing repetitive strain injuries? You also can write about the new terms you learned by reading this chapter. If required, submit your journal to your instructor.

(4) Expanding Your Understanding   Journalists, attorneys, law enforcement officials, and students consider tape recorders and notepads essential components of their daily activities. An alternate means of capturing information is a voice pen, which is a flash-memory-based recording device approximately the size of a small smart phone. Visit a local electronics store or view electronics Web sites to learn more about voice pens. Compare their features, cost, recording time, and warranty. Write a report summarizing your findings, focusing on comparing and contrasting the voice pens. If required, submit your report to your instructor.

(5) Ethics in Action   Some reports suggest that a global surveillance system is monitoring e-mail messages, telephone calls, and faxes. This organization known as Echelon attempts to intercept more than three billion satellite, microwave, cellular, and fiber-optic messages per day, according to the reports. The National Security Agency is forbidden to monitor U.S. citizens, but privacy experts contend that at least 90 percent of U.S. communication is gathered and reviewed. View online sites that provide information about Echelon, including Echelon Watch (www.echelonwatch.org). Write a report summarizing your findings, and include a table of links to Web sites that provide additional details. If required, submit your report to your instructor.

Case Studies

Use the Case Studies to apply the concepts presented in the chapter to real-world situations. Visit scsite.com/dc2006/ch5/cases to obtain more information pertaining to each exercise. To discuss the Case Studies in this chapter with other students, visit scsite.com/dc2006/ch5/forum and post your thoughts or questions.

CASE STUDY 1 — Class Discussion   You work in the Efficiency Analysis department of one of the largest retail companies in the world, with multiple stores in every state and many other countries. For the past 25 years, the company has used optical scanners at checkout counters that read the UPC bar code on products to determine from a database the price to charge customers. The company is considering replacing the optical scanners with __radio frequency identification__, or RFID. The reader receives the code identifying the product via a chip with an antenna that is part of the box or label on the outside of the product. Your manager has asked you to draft a memo outlining the impact such a change would have on the company, its suppliers, and its customers. Be prepared to discuss your findings in class.

CASE STUDY 2 — Class Discussion   You have been asked to serve on your company's Voice Recognition Committee. The committee has been charged with investigating the feasibility of using voice recognition as a primary method for entering data and instructions into the company's computers. The chairperson of the committee has asked for your opinion on the use of __voice recognition__. When would voice recognition be an advantage over the keyboard and mouse? Might it ever be a disadvantage? Why? Prepare a brief report and be prepared to discuss your recommendations in class.

CASE STUDY 3 — Research   While attending college part-time for the past two years, you have worked as a data entry clerk for Salmon Mirror. Recently, you began to feel an unusual pain in your right wrist. Your doctor diagnosed the problem as __carpal tunnel syndrome__, which is the most well-known of a series of musculoskeletal disorders that fall under the umbrella of repetitive strain injuries (RSIs). Your doctor made several recommendations to relieve the pain, one of which was to find a new job. Before you begin job hunting, however, you want to learn more about this debilitating injury. Use the Web and/or print media to investigate carpal tunnel syndrome. Prepare a report and/or PowerPoint presentation on your findings. Include information about carpal tunnel syndrome warning signs, risk factors, suggestions about proper workstation ergonomics, and procedures for healing the injury. Share your report or presentation with your class.

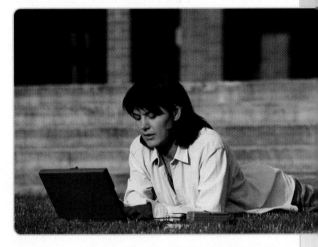

CASE STUDY 4 — Research   An electronics company where you are employed as an analyst spends hundreds of thousands of dollars each year on travel to the multiple locations where they operate around the country. In an effort to curb the ever-increasing costs of travel, the CFO has asked you to look into the feasibility of adopting __video conferencing__ at all of its major locations. Use the Web and/or print media to determine the advantages and disadvantages of video conferencing. Can the technology replace all or most face-to-face meetings? What are the costs of common video conferencing systems and the recurring costs their use incurs? Compare those costs to the cost of travel for a team of three people making six trips per year between New York and Los Angeles, including hotel, airline, and food expenses. Write a brief report or use PowerPoint to create a presentation and share your findings with your class.

CASE STUDY 5 — Team Challenge   The Transportation Security Administration (TSA) is looking into ways to expedite the airport screening experience of frequent flyers without compromising security. The TSA has hired your team as consultants to investigate __biometric technology__. In particular, they want your team to review three biometric devices for screening frequent flyers — fingerprint scanner, face recognition system, and iris recognition system. Form a three-member team and have each team member choose a different biometric device. Using the Web and/or print media, have each team member determine the advantages and disadvantages of their chosen biometric device. Include in each report how frequent flyer applicants would apply, accuracy rates of the device, and whether the device would indeed enhance security or open a loophole for terrorists. As a team, merge your findings into a team report and/or PowerPoint presentation and share your recommendations with your class.

Special Feature

Personal Mobile Devices

Mobile devices that usually can fit in your pocket, such as PDAs, smart phones, and smart pagers, are referred to as personal mobile devices (Figure 1). Page 22 in Chapter 1 discusses PDAs and smart phones. A **PDA** provides personal organizer functions, such as calendar, appointment book, address book, calculator, and notepad. A **smart phone** is an Internet-enabled telephone that usually provides PDA functionality. A **smart pager** is a wireless mobile device that provides data services, such as e-mail alerts, news alerts, and Internet access. Smart pagers usually provide PDA functionality, such as an address book and calendar. Additionally, some smart pagers include telephone capabilities.

Because the various types of personal mobile devices often offer similar capabilities, they typically are categorized by their form factor. A device's **form factor** refers to its size, shape, and configuration. For example, Figure 1 shows a smart phone that has a PDA form factor and a smart phone that has a phone form factor. While the device with the phone form factor may include PDA functionality, its main purpose is to be used as a phone. Its smaller size may make using it as a PDA more cumbersome than the smart phone with a PDA form factor. The PDA form factor, while larger, provides a better interface for accessing the PDA functionality.

Most personal mobile devices allow you to enhance their functionality through the use of accessories — such as headsets, cameras, and memory cards — and software. Not long ago, PDA (personal digital assistant) software consisted of a few programs, such as a to-do list and an address book. PDAs previously contained embedded software, meaning that a user could not change the software or add programs to the PDA. Today's PDAs, smart phones, and smart pagers allow for as much choice and versatility in their software as a typical personal computer. Most personal mobile devices come equipped with a rich set of programs. In some cases, a user may want to use enhanced versions of the included software, such as an enhanced calculator program, or install additional software, such as a game.

This special feature provides an overview of accessories and software available for personal mobile devices. The final section of the feature lists the criteria you should consider when deciding which personal mobile device is right for you.

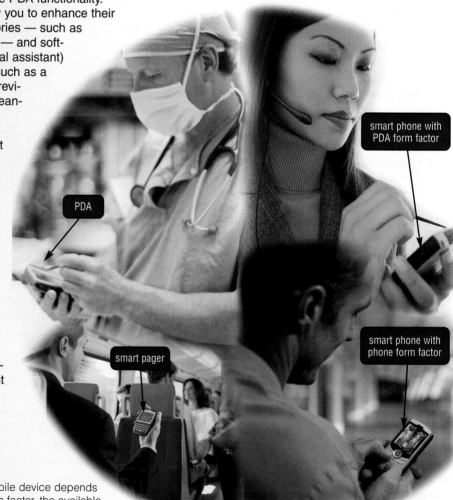

PDA

smart pager

smart phone with PDA form factor

smart phone with phone form factor

FIGURE 1 Your choice of a personal mobile device depends on the features you require, the desired form factor, the available accessories, and the available software for the device.

PERSONAL MOBILE DEVICE OPERATING SYSTEMS

As with personal computers, personal mobile devices run an operating system. A personal mobile device runs software made only for the operating system of the device. Personal mobile devices can be categorized by the operating system that each runs. Figure 2 lists the common personal mobile device operating systems, the manufacturer, and a brief description of the operating system.

PERSONAL MOBILE DEVICE OPERATING SYSTEMS

Operating System	Manufacturer	Device Types	Description
Palm OS (versions 5 and later)	PalmSource	PDA Smart phone	The latest version of the operating system for Palm OS-based PDAs supports faster processors, multimedia, and more memory.
Palm OS (earlier versions)	PalmSource	PDA Smart phone	Several PDA manufacturers continue to use earlier versions of the Palm OS operating system because of the simplicity and lower power requirements, resulting in longer usage between recharges.
Windows Mobile for Pocket PC	Microsoft	PDA	The Windows Mobile operating system tightly integrates with Microsoft's Windows operating systems and includes scaled-down versions of many of Microsoft's popular programs, including Word, Outlook, Excel, and MSN Messenger.
Windows Mobile for Pocket PC Phone Edition	Microsoft	Smart phone with PDA form factor	The Pocket PC Phone Edition includes enhancements for the Windows Mobile operating system geared for phone use, such as enhancing the contact manager with the ability to dial a telephone number. This edition includes all of the Windows Mobile PDA functionality.
Windows Mobile for Smartphone	Microsoft	Smart phone with phone form factor	The Smartphone edition of the Windows Mobile operating system is designed for smaller screens and devices with less functionality than a typical PDA.
Blackberry	Research in Motion (RIM)	Smart pager Smart phone with PDA form factor	The Blackberry operating system runs on devices supplied by RIM. The devices include enhanced messaging and e-mail features when compared to smart phones.
Symbian OS	Symbian	Smart phone	Symbian OS is a popular PDA operating system commonly used on cellular telephones. Symbian OS is more popular in Europe and with business users.
Embedded Linux	Open source	PDA Smart phone	Some PDAs use a scaled down version of the free Linux operating system.

FIGURE 2   Personal mobile device capabilities depend on the operating system that they run.

Special Feature

ACCESSORIES FOR PERSONAL MOBILE DEVICE SOFTWARE

Most personal mobile devices have the capability to take advantage of add-on accessories. For example, using an external keyboard with a device greatly enhances the ability to enter data or notes quickly. Figure 3 lists the more common accessories available for a personal mobile device.

ACCESSORIES FOR PERSONAL MOBILE DEVICES

Accessory	Description
Keyboard	External keyboards provide much faster input when taking notes as opposed to using a small, built-in keyboard on a device. Keyboards may be wireless or attached to the device using a special cable.
Memory card	Memory cards provide additional storage space for a device. Some memory cards may include hardware enhancements such as wireless capability, a camera, or Bluetooth capability. Some cards come with preinstalled software or vast amount of data, such as a dictionary, on them.
Car kit	Car kits allow you to integrate a device with your car by providing mounting and/or hands-free operation of a device.
Chargers	Special chargers allow you to recharge a device's battery almost anywhere, such as an airplane, hotel, or foreign country. Some chargers provide emergency battery backup in case the device's batteries start running low when no electrical outlet is nearby.
Camera	Add-on cameras provide picture and video taking capability to devices with no such built-in functionality.
Case	Most mobile devices can be placed in a case or holster for protection while the device is not in use. Some devices include built-in flip screens to protect the device. You may want a case that fits comfortably in your shirt pocket, or one that includes a belt clip. A good case protects the device when it is dropped from a height of 3 or 4 feet.
Headset/earphones	Headsets allow you to wear a combined earpiece and microphone while keeping the device in your hand, pocket, or next to you. Some headsets use Bluetooth to communicate wirelessly with the device. Earphones are used when you want to listen to sound on your device, such as when listening to music or an e-book, or when watching a video.
GPS receiver	A GPS receiver contains an antenna, radio receiver, and processor and receives signals from GPS satellites to determine a location and/or speed. GPS receivers turn a personal mobile device into a complete GPS unit. The receivers typically include software that you must install on the device.

FIGURE 3 Some accessories for personal mobile devices are common to most devices, while others are specialized.

BUILT-IN PERSONAL MOBILE DEVICE SOFTWARE

Most personal mobile devices include several programs that provide basic functionality, such as an **address book** and **date book**. Figure 4 lists the types of software that usually are preinstalled on a personal mobile device.

BUILT-IN PERSONAL MOBILE DEVICE SOFTWARE

Application	Description
Address book and contacts	Maintains a list of acquaintances, including names, addresses, telephone numbers, e-mail addresses, and notes.
To-do list	Maintains a list of tasks. Tasks can be categorized and assigned a priority.
Calculator	Offers functionality of standard desktop calculators.
Datebook and calendar	Maintains appointments and important dates, such as birthdays and holidays. A user also sets audio or visual alarms to trigger when an appointment time arrives.
Memos and notepad	Keeps track of notes.
Launcher	The interface that allows a user to execute, or launch, programs, shown on the PDA screen in Figure 4.
Dialer	Smart phones typically include dialer software that assists you in using the telephone capabilities of a device. Some dialer software is integrated into the operating system so that you use dialing capabilities in other applications. For example, you can select a telephone number in the word processing program and request that the number be dialed.

FIGURE 4   Personal mobile devices typically contain this preinstalled software.

SYNCHRONIZATION SOFTWARE

Most personal mobile devices allow a user to share data and information between his or her personal computer and the device. The software that enables the sharing is called **synchronization software**. A personal mobile device may synchronize, or sync (pronounced sink), with a personal computer or a server on a network. Corporations often standardize their synchronization software so that employees share data across the corporate network, and so the data is backed up properly on a server. Figure 5 lists popular synchronization software for personal mobile devices.

SYNCHRONIZATION SOFTWARE FOR PERSONAL MOBILE DEVICES

Application	Description	Samples
Built-in	Most devices include software that the user loads on a personal computer that allows the computer to communicate with the device and share data and information.	• The Palm OS includes HotSync software • Pocket PC PDAs include ActiveSync software • Blackberry devices use the Blackberry Desktop Software
Synching many sources	Some device users have data and information stored in many places. For example, users may want to have their address books on the Web, on their personal computers, on their cellular telephones, and on their PDAs. Special synchronization software allows users to keep all of the address books up-to-date.	• Starfish TrueSync • PocketMirror • XTNDConnect Server
SyncML	**SyncML** is a standard that is being adopted by many companies that create personal mobile devices. SyncML allows for common information stored on a device to be shared among many devices, such as cellular telephones, other personal mobile devices, and personal computers.	• IBM WebSphere Everyplace Access • Pumatech Intellisync • Starfish TrueSync • fusionOne MightyPhone • Symbian based devices use SyncML
iSync	Apple's iSync software allows a user to keep a calendar and contact information synchronized up to the minute between a smart phone, an Apple iPod, a Palm OS device, or multiple Macs.	• Apple iSync

FIGURE 5   Personal mobile devices use synchronization software to share data and information with a personal computer or server.

BUSINESS SOFTWARE

Most programs used on a personal mobile device have some counterpart program on a desktop computer. For example, both a personal computer and a PDA or smart phone may include a word processing program. Many business programs have counterparts on personal mobile devices. The personal mobile device versions of these programs generally have fewer features and options. For example, a word processing program on a PDA may not have a spelling checker, and a spreadsheet program may not include all of the built-in calculations of its desktop computer counterpart. A smart phone with a phone form factor may allow you only to view documents, rather than edit documents. Figure 6 lists business software for personal mobile devices.

BUSINESS SOFTWARE FOR PERSONAL MOBILE DEVICES

Application	Description	Samples
Word processing	Allows for simple creation, editing, and viewing of documents.	• Documents To Go • WordSmith • PocketWord
Spreadsheet	Allows a user to create, edit, and view worksheets on a personal mobile device.	• Pocket Excel • TinySheet • Quickoffice • SmartSheet
Readers	Allows read-only (view only) access to word processing documents, spreadsheets, or databases that a user downloads to a personal mobile device from a personal computer. Readers are useful for taking large documents on the road to read them without the ability to modify them. Some readers allow the user to view all of these types of documents, while others are targeted to specific desktop program counterparts, such as presentation viewers or word processing document viewers.	• Pocket SlideShow • TealDoc • iSilo • Microsoft Reader
Database and list management	Allows creation, editing, and viewing of databases or lists. List management is a popular use of personal mobile devices. Some examples of lists that are handy to store on a device include shopping lists, to-do lists, exercise logs, and automobile maintenance logs.	• HanDBase • thinkDB • SmartList To Go • JFile • ListPro • Mobile Data Viewer
Financial	Financial software includes programs to manage a bank account, track expenses during a trip, manage a budget, or track an investment portfolio. Many personal computer financial programs include personal mobile device companion software that keeps the information on a device synchronized with the financial information on a personal computer or the Web.	• Microsoft Money for Pocket PC • Pocket Quicken • BankBook • Ultrasoft Money • Handy Expense

FIGURE 6   Business software provides scaled-down versions of common desktop programs.

SOFTWARE FOR WIRELESS DEVICES

Most of the software used to interact with the Internet using a personal computer has a counterpart on wireless mobile devices. Some devices come equipped with e-mail software or a Web browser. Often, special servers allow the device to communicate securely with corporate databases or Web sites. For personal mobile devices that do not include wireless Internet connectivity, a special modem connects the device to the Internet. Often, a device without built-in wireless capability can be connected to a mobile phone that can connect the device to the Internet. Web content and e-mail also synchronize to the device from a personal computer, and the information may be browsed offline while using the device. Figure 7 provides a list of popular communications software for personal mobile devices.

COMMUNICATIONS SOFTWARE FOR PERSONAL MOBILE DEVICES

Application	Description	Samples
E-mail	Used for composing and reading e-mail.	• Pocket Outlook • riteMail • Mail+ • SnapperMail
Web browsers	Allows Web browsing. Some browsers use an **intermediate server** to make the pages smaller by stripping out images or making images smaller. Others attempt to display the full Web page on the personal mobile device.	• Pocket Internet Explorer • Blazer • AvantGo • Opera browser
Clipping	**Web clippings** are programs that gather and display only the critical elements, or clips, of a Web page.	• Travelocity.com • The Weather Channel • Moviefone.com
Instant messaging	Instant messaging programs usually allow the user to use the same instant messaging ID as that used on a personal computer.	• MSN Messenger • AIM for Palm OS • Agile Messenger

FIGURE 7 Communications software allows a mobile device to access the Internet and other data sources while the user is away from the classroom or office.

CORPORATE/GOVERNMENT SOFTWARE

Large organizations, such as corporations and government agencies, take advantage of personal mobile devices' capability of keeping current information in the hands of their personnel. The organization's central employee telephone book is kept up-to-date and synchronized to each employee's device on a regular basis. Executives synchronize key corporate information. Traveling sales personnel and field technicians synchronize appointments, e-mail, notes about contact with customers, product lists, and sales information. Corporate/government software for personal mobile devices is listed in Figure 8.

CORPORATE/GOVERNMENT SOFTWARE FOR PERSONAL MOBILE DEVICES

Application	Description	Samples
Executive	Executives keep up-to-date corporate information on their personal mobile devices. Executives may keep current sales information, financial information, and inventory information available to make informed decisions.	• mySAP.com • Siebel 7 Mobile Solutions
Sales	Sales people working out of the office are perhaps the largest group of personal mobile device users. The devices are useful for keeping product information handy, keeping scheduled appointments, and maintaining customer information.	• Siebel 7 Mobile Sales • Salesforce.com • ActionNames
Field technicians and mobile workers	Field technicians visit customer locations to troubleshoot problems. Personal mobile devices help technicians keep track of customer information, maintain up-to-date information on replacement parts, and log troubleshooting information.	• UPS and FedEx use specialized devices and software for their drivers to track package pickups and drop offs.
Military and law enforcement	The military and law enforcement agencies deploy personal mobile devices to manage the special needs of the military and law enforcement.	• Most software of this nature is custom made for the needs of particular agencies. Such programs help track cases or serve as legal references.
Connecting and synchronizing with corporate data sources	Several solutions exist for synchronizing corporate data with personal mobile devices. Special software keeps track of user permissions and makes certain that the right people get the data they require on a day-to-day basis.	• Pumatech Intellisync • Starfish TrueSync Server • MessageWireless
Large organization management issues	In organizations with thousands of personal mobile device users, the support of those devices becomes tedious, especially when users install unsupported software on the devices that may interfere with the corporate software and data for which the device was intended. Server software may detect these conflicts when the user synchronizes with the corporate server and deletes or reports the offending software.	• Much of the software of this nature is custom built for each enterprise, as needs and infrastructure of each organization are different.

FIGURE 8 Large organizations utilize special software to keep their employees synchronized.

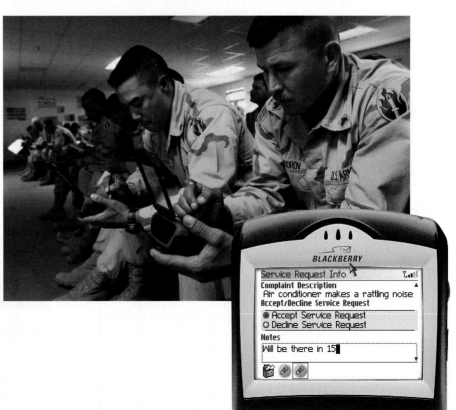

MEDICAL SOFTWARE

One of the largest communities to adopt personal mobile device software in significant numbers is the medical community. Physicians and other medical workers routinely use specialized software to track patient charts, check information on drugs, and browse electronic versions of large reference books. The end result is a savings in time and money, and an increase in the level of care for the patient. Figure 9 lists some popular medical software for personal mobile devices.

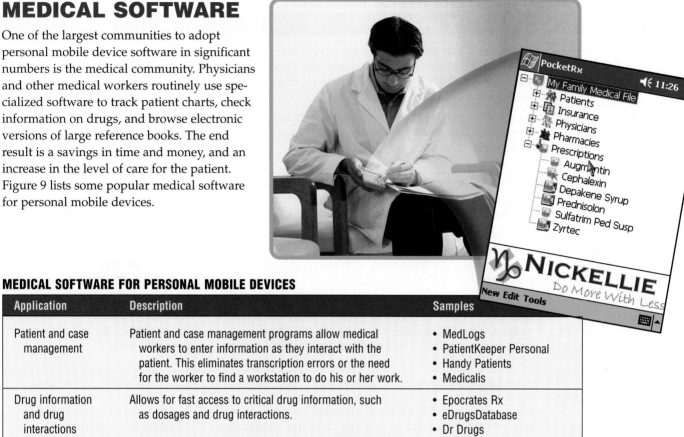

MEDICAL SOFTWARE FOR PERSONAL MOBILE DEVICES

Application	Description	Samples
Patient and case management	Patient and case management programs allow medical workers to enter information as they interact with the patient. This eliminates transcription errors or the need for the worker to find a workstation to do his or her work.	• MedLogs • PatientKeeper Personal • Handy Patients • Medicalis
Drug information and drug interactions	Allows for fast access to critical drug information, such as dosages and drug interactions.	• Epocrates Rx • eDrugsDatabase • Dr Drugs
Reference books	Medical workers often rely on a large collection of references to do their jobs. Electronic versions of many popular references, such as the *Physicians' Desk Reference*, are available in electronic format and are kept up-to-date easily through regular downloads.	• PDRDrugs • eDrugs Database • DiagnosisPro for Pocket PC • MedRules
Prescriptions	With electronic prescribing, physicians write prescriptions electronically. Physicians print legible prescriptions and hand the prescriptions to the patient. If the personal mobile device is connected to the Internet or hospital network, the physician checks the patient's medication or medical history.	• iScribe • PocketRx • Medicalis
Medical calculations	Medical workers often make quick calculations for medication dosages or patient status. Programs assist many of these calculations and target the worker's specialty.	• MedMath • MedCalc • Medical MathPad

FIGURE 9 The medical community quickly has become one of the larger users of specialized PDA software.

SCIENTIFIC SOFTWARE

The mobility of personal mobile devices makes them valuable tools for scientific use. Researchers use these devices to gather and record data in the field and later download the data to a personal computer or server. Scientists also use specialized software targeted to their specific field, such as astronomy or meteorology, as a replacement for bulky reference manuals or observation notes (Figure 10).

SCIENTIFIC SOFTWARE FOR PERSONAL MOBILE DEVICES

Application	Description	Samples
Data gathering	Scientists can enter observations quickly into a personal mobile device. These programs often are used in the field for gathering research statistics.	• iCollect
Calculations and conversions	Users can perform specialized calculations or data conversions. Many fields of science, such as astronomy, require special calculations that are useful to have available on a personal mobile device.	• ME Tools • CoolCalc for the Pocket PC • Convert It! • APCalc Converter
Reference	Scientists can look up information quickly, rather than using cumbersome manuals or textbooks.	• ChemRef Basic • PTE (Periodic Table of the Elements) • Gene • ABC's of Science
Astronomy	Observers can follow the stars. With the large number of amateur astronomers in the world, programs specific to astronomy are some of the more popular scientific titles.	• Pocket Universe • Planetarium • Star Pilot • Pocket Stars
Weather	Meteorologists' specific needs are addressed because these programs allow quick calculations or data gathering in a changing environment. Some programs are linked to add-on hardware that measure temperature, humidity, and other meteorological data.	• Weather Manager • WorldMate • Weather Calculator for Palm OS • Weather.com

FIGURE 10 Scientific programs help scientists manage complex information.

TRAVEL SOFTWARE

The portable nature of personal mobile devices makes them ideal for the business or leisure traveler. Even a night on the town can be enhanced by a list of popular hot spots. The user keeps his or her itinerary handy along with maps and directions while traveling to new places. A GPS-enabled mobile device tracks a user's route and keeps the user on course. Wireless connectivity allows the user to book flights and hotels from the back of a taxi cab. Figure 11 lists travel software for personal mobile devices.

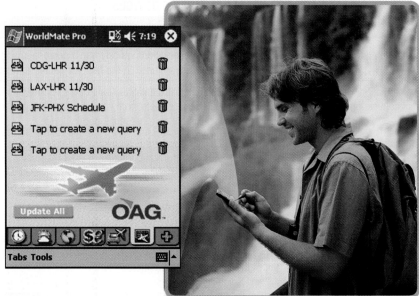

TRAVEL SOFTWARE FOR PERSONAL MOBILE DEVICES

Application	Description	Samples
Itinerary consolidation	Manages travel itineraries, including flights, hotels, and car rentals. The software may keep track of travel preferences and make suggestions about travel and accommodations when planning a new trip.	• Traveler (Pocket PC edition) • Time Traveler • Travel Pal
Mapping	Mapping software may download maps from the Web or a personal computer. Or, the software may include maps. The software may suggest travel routes from point to point, or simply serve as a reference.	• Vindigo for Palm OS or Pocket PC • Pocket Streets • HandMap
City guides	City guides are one of the more popular personal mobile device programs. The user installs city guides for specific cities or an entire country. Guides include restaurant listings and ratings, hotels, directions, popular attractions, and local customs.	• Weissmann City Profiles • Vindigo for Palm OS or Pocket PC • WorldMate • Frommer's Port@ble Guide • iFodor's
Hotel and flight	Users can view current hotel and flight information while planning a trip. Some of these programs require the device to connect to the Internet. Others occasionally allow downloading the information to a device from a personal computer. Some programs link to booking systems on the Internet, so the user makes reservations directly from a personal mobile device.	• OAG Club • SkyGuide
GPS	Usually requires additional GPS hardware connected to the device. Some software includes mapping data or only displays and saves GPS information, such as location and speed.	• GPS Port@ble Navigator — Travelers Edition • GPS Wireless Navigation System • GPS Atlas

FIGURE 11 Travel software acts as a personal concierge for the business or leisure traveler.

EDUCATIONAL SOFTWARE

With so much to organize, students and instructors greatly benefit from mobile software geared for educational uses (Figure 12). Students load textbook chapters or entire textbooks onto expansion cards and use special software to read the books and highlight key material. Instructors distribute electronic versions of the class syllabus, automatically updating each student's calendar on the students' devices. Some schools even acquire PDAs for the entire student body and require their use in the classroom.

EDUCATIONAL SOFTWARE FOR PERSONAL MOBILE DEVICES

Application	Description	Samples
E-books and references	E-books are electronic versions of books. E-books are specially formatted files that may be viewed using Reader software, as noted in Figure 6 on page 287. Many e-books are available at no cost, and many authors and publishing companies make e-books available to those who have purchased a hard copy of a particular book.	• TomeRaider • PocketLingo Pro • Formulas for Palm OS • Speed Reader Plus • The collected works of William Shakespeare for Microsoft Reader • eWord for Blackberry • Mobipocket Reader Pro for Symbian OS
Class schedules and course management	Helps instructors and students manage their respective schedules. The information may include syllabus details distributed in electronic format by an instructor. The software also may link to a central data repository of a school. The software helps track grading, assignments, to-do lists, instructor office hours, and notes.	• 4.0Student by Handmark course management • Pocket ClassPro for Pocket PC • MyClasses
Roster	Manages grading, rosters, attendance, and contact information for students.	• Teachers PET • Head Start • Teach File
Review	Includes programs for quizzing students and reviewing coursework. Students often train the application to help them review troublesome material.	• Math Classic • Mental Arithmetic • Quizzler

FIGURE 12 Educational software benefits both students and instructors.

MULTIMEDIA SOFTWARE

Most personal mobile devices include the capability of viewing images, and some are powerful enough to view short video clips. Some devices also double as audio players, allowing the user to take his or her favorite music anywhere. Devices that are more recent contain, or allow the user to attach, a camera or recording device to capture video or audio and then download the captured media to a personal computer. Some image viewers allow the user to use a personal mobile device as an electronic picture frame while the device rests in its cradle on the user's desk. Popular multimedia software for personal mobile devices is listed in Figure 13.

MULTIMEDIA SOFTWARE FOR PERSONAL MOBILE DEVICES

Application	Description	Samples
Picture viewer	Allows a user to view images uploaded to a personal mobile device using software on a personal computer or camera. Some viewers have a slide show mode that rotates through a list of images automatically.	• SplashPhoto • PocketPhoto • Palbum Picture Viewer • Resco Photo Viewer for Smartphone • FireViewer
Video player	Allows the user to watch video clips on a personal mobile device.	• Windows Media Player for Pocket PC • PocketTV for Pocket PC • ActiveSky Media Player
Audio player	Permits a user to listen to his or her favorite music or record and playback voice recordings for meetings or personal audio notes. Some devices are equipped with additional hardware such as microphones, headphones, or audio controls to enhance the audio experience.	• AudioPlus • Windows Media Player for Pocket PC • Replay Radio

FIGURE 13 Multimedia software gives personal mobile device users the ability to view images, watch video, and listen to audio.

ENTERTAINMENT SOFTWARE

While on the train ride to work or waiting at the airport, a personal mobile device user can enjoy his or her favorite games. The infrared port or wireless connectivity of a device allows a user to play some games against other players. Most devices include buttons to control games. Figure 14 lists popular entertainment software for personal mobile devices.

ENTERTAINMENT SOFTWARE FOR PERSONAL MOBILE DEVICES

Application	Description	Samples
Strategy	Includes classic board games such as chess, backgammon, and Monopoly.	• PocketChess • ChessGenius • Handmark Monopoly • SimCity
Card	Includes casino games, solitaire games, and other card games.	• AcidSolitaire • BlackJack++ • Pocket Cribbage
Action	Games that require quick reflexes, including many arcade-style games.	• Tomb Raider • Bejeweled • Breakfast • Vexed for Symbian
Puzzle	Thought-provoking puzzles to pass time and sharpen the mind, such as crossword puzzles, mazes, and word games.	• Handmark SCRABBLE • Crossword • ChessPuzzles

FIGURE 14 Entertainment software allows a user to relax with a personal mobile device and enjoy his or her favorite games.

OBTAINING AND INSTALLING PERSONAL MOBILE DEVICE SOFTWARE

Software often is available at computer or electronics stores. A significant number of programs are available as shareware, freeware, or trial editions at various Web sites. Most of the software listed in the previous figures is accessible on the Web sites listed in Figure 15. Because software for personal mobile devices usually is smaller than the personal computer counterparts, downloading the software from the Web to your personal computer and then uploading it to your device often is the best alternative when you want to try something new. Software downloaded from the Web to a personal computer requires that the software be installed using the device's synchronization software. Additionally, some personal computer application software includes accompanying mobile device software that corresponds with the personal computer software. Wireless devices, such as smart phones and smart pagers, may allow you to download new software over the wireless connection.

Software for personal mobile devices sold in a retail location often is supplied on a CD-ROM. The CD-ROM first installs the software on a personal computer. The device's synchronization software then is used to load the software onto the device while the device is connected to the personal computer. Depending on the type of software installed, this process may be automatic. Some software is packaged as an add-on card that the user inserts into the device's expansion slot. Some Web sites allow the user to browse a software catalog from a wireless device's Web browser and download the software directly to the device. When synchronizing a personal mobile device on a corporate network, some companies automatically install software to the employees' devices with no interaction required from the employee.

WHERE TO OBTAIN PERSONAL MOBILE DEVICE SOFTWARE

Application	Description	Samples
Web sites	Software publishers make their products available at their Web sites. Several Web sites also exist specifically to distribute mobile device software. Tens of thousands of titles are available, and most can be downloaded on a trial basis.	www.palmgear.com www.handandgo.com www.pdamd.com www.tucows.com
Retail	Many popular software titles can be purchased at electronic and computer stores. The most popular titles at these locations include productivity and entertainment software.	www.bestbuy.com www.compusa.com
Develop in-house	Many corporations develop their own personal mobile device software to use internally to meet specific needs. These programs usually tap into existing corporate databases of product and customer information. The companies that produce mobile device operating systems often make the development tools for such software available at no cost or a minimal cost.	www.palmsource.com www.microsoft.com/mobile/developer http://www.blackberry.net/developers/index.shtml http://www.symbian.com/developer/index.html

For an updated list of where to obtain PDA software, visit scsite.com/dc2006/ch5/pda.

FIGURE 15   Personal mobile device software is available from a number of sources.

HOW TO PURCHASE A PERSONAL MOBILE DEVICE

Whether you choose a PDA, smart phone, or smart pager depends on where, when, and how you will use the device. If you need to stay organized when you are on the go, then a PDA may be the right choice. PDAs typically are categorized by the operating system they run (Figure 2 on page 283). If you need to stay organized and in touch when on the go, then a smart phone or smart pager may be the right choice. Just as with PDAs, smart phones, and smart pagers are categorized by the operating system they run. The six primary operating systems for these devices are the Palm OS, Windows Mobile for Pocket PC, Windows Mobile for Smartphone, Symbian OS, Blackberry, and Embedded Linux.

This section lists guidelines you should consider when purchasing a PDA, smart phone, or smart pager. You also should visit the Web sites listed in Figure 16 to gather more information about the type of personal mobile device that best suits your computing needs.

 DETERMINE THE PROGRAMS YOU PLAN TO RUN ON YOUR DEVICE.

All PDAs and most smart phones and smart pagers can handle basic organizer-type software such as a calendar, address book, and notepad. The availability of other software depends on the operating system you choose. The depth and breadth of software for the Palm OS is significant, with more than 20,000 basic programs and over 600 wireless programs. Devices that run Windows-based operating systems, such as Windows Mobile or Windows Smartphone, may have fewer programs available, but the operating system and application software are similar to those with which you are familiar, such as Word and Excel. Some Symbian-based smart phones also include the capability to read and/or edit Microsoft Office documents.

 CONSIDER HOW MUCH YOU WANT TO PAY.

The price of a personal mobile device can range from $100 to $800, depending on its capabilities. Some Palm OS devices are at the lower end of the cost spectrum, and Windows-based devices often are at the higher end. For the latest prices, capabilities, and accessories, visit the Web sites listed in Figure 16.

 DETERMINE WHETHER YOU NEED WIRELESS ACCESS TO THE INTERNET AND E-MAIL OR MOBILE TELEPHONE CAPABILITIES WITH YOUR DEVICE.

Smart pagers give you access to e-mail and other data and Internet services. Smart phones typically include these features, but also include the ability to make and receive phone calls on cellular networks. Some PDAs and smart phones include wireless networking capability to allow you to connect to the Internet wirelessly. These wireless features and services allow personal mobile device users to access real-time information from anywhere to help make decisions while on the go.

 FOR WIRELESS DEVICES, DETERMINE HOW AND WHERE YOU WILL USE THE SERVICE.

When purchasing a wireless device, you must subscribe to a wireless service. Determine if the wireless network (carrier) you choose has service in the area where you plan to use the device. Some networks have high-speed data networks only in certain areas, such as large cities or business districts. Also, a few carriers allow you to use your device in other countries.

When purchasing a smart phone, determine if you plan to use the device more as a phone, PDA, or wireless data device. Some smart phones, such as those based on the Pocket PC Phone edition or the Palm OS, are geared more for use as a PDA and have a PDA form factor. Other smart phones, such as those based on Microsoft Smartphone or Symbian operating systems, mainly are phone devices that include robust PDA functionality. RIM Blackberry-based smart phones include robust data features that are oriented to accessing e-mail and wireless data services.

 MAKE SURE YOUR DEVICE HAS ENOUGH MEMORY.

Memory (RAM) is not a major issue with low-end devices with monochrome displays and basic organizer functions. Memory is a major issue, however, for high-end devices that have color displays and wireless features. Without enough memory, the performance level of your device will drop dramatically. If you plan to purchase a high-end device running the Palm OS operating system, the device should have at least 16 MB of RAM. If you plan to purchase a high-end device running the Windows Mobile operating system, the PDA should have at least 48 MB of RAM.

6 PRACTICE WITH THE TOUCH SCREEN, HANDWRITING RECOGNITION, AND BUILT-IN KEYBOARD BEFORE DECIDING ON A MODEL.

To enter data into a PDA or smart phone, you use a pen-like stylus to handwrite on the screen or a keyboard. The keyboard either slides out or is mounted on the front of the device. With handwriting recognition, the device translates the handwriting into a computerized font. You also can use the stylus as a pointing device to select items on the screen and enter data by tapping on an on-screen keyboard. By practicing data entry before buying a device, you can learn if one device may be easier for you to use than another. You also can buy third-party software to improve a device's handwriting recognition.

 7 DECIDE WHETHER YOU WANT A COLOR DISPLAY.

Pocket PC devices usually come with a color display that supports as many as 65,536 colors. Palm OS devices also have a color display, but the less expensive models display in 4 to 16 shades of gray. Symbian- and Blackberry-based devices also have the option for color displays. Having a color display does result in greater on-screen detail, but it also requires more memory and uses more power. Resolution also influences the quality of the display.

 8 COMPARE BATTERY LIFE.

Any mobile device is good only if it has the power required to run. For example, Palm OS devices with monochrome screens typically have a much longer battery life than Pocket PC devices with color screens. The use of wireless networking will shorten battery time considerably. To help alleviate this problem, most devices have incorporated rechargeable batteries that can be recharged by placing the device in a cradle or connecting it to a charger.

 9 SERIOUSLY CONSIDER THE IMPORTANCE OF ERGONOMICS.

Will you put the device in your pocket, a carrying case, or wear it on your belt? How does it feel in your hand? Will you use it indoors or outdoors? Many screens are unreadable outdoors. Do you need extra ruggedness, such as would be required in construction, in a plant, or in a warehouse?

 10 CHECK OUT THE ACCESSORIES.

Determine which accessories you want for your personal mobile device. Accessories include carrying cases, portable mini- and full-sized keyboards, removable storage, modems, synchronization cradles and cables, car chargers, wireless communications, global positioning system modules, digital camera modules, expansion cards, dashboard mounts, replacement styli, hands-free headsets, and more.

 11 DECIDE WHETHER YOU WANT ADDITIONAL FUNCTIONALITY.

In general, off-the-shelf Microsoft operating system-based devices have broader functionality than devices with other operating systems. For example, voice-recording capability, e-book players, MP3 players, and video players are standard on most Pocket PC devices. If you are leaning towards a Palm OS device and want these additional functions, you may need to purchase additional software or expansion modules to add them later. Determine whether your employer permits devices with cameras on the premises, and if not, do not consider devices with cameras.

 12 DETERMINE WHETHER SYNCHRONIZATION OF DATA WITH OTHER DEVICES OR PERSONAL COMPUTERS IS IMPORTANT.

Most devices come with a cradle that connects to the USB or serial port on your computer so you can synchronize data on your device with your desktop or notebook computer. Increasingly more devices are Bluetooth and/or wireless networking enabled, which gives them the capability of synchronizing wirelessly. Many devices today also have an infrared port that allows you to synchronize data with any device that has a similar infrared port, including desktop and notebook computers or other personal mobile devices.

Web Site	Web Address
Hewlett-Packard	hp.com
CNET Shopper	shopper.cnet.com
palmOne	palmone.com
Microsoft	windowsmobile.com pocketpc.com microsoft.com/smartphone
PDA Buyers Guide	pdabuyersguide.com
Research in Motion	rim.com
Danger	danger.com
Symbian	symbian.com
Wireless Developer Network	wirelessdevnet.com
Sharp	myzaurus.com

For an updated list of reviews and information about personal mobile devices and their Web addresses, visit scsite.com/dc2006/ch5/pda.

FIGURE 16 Web site reviews and information about personal mobile devices.

CHAPTER SIX

Output

Picture Yourself Saving Money Using a Computer

While eating lunch with some friends, your conversation centers around rising prices and the cost of hotels, postage stamps, greeting cards, gasoline, and services such as banking and film developing. After the discussion, each of you decides to take measures to reduce some of these costs by using your computers.

Instead of paying for personal checks and postage, you decide to use online banking to pay your bills and balance your statements while viewing them on a computer monitor. For those items that still must be mailed through the postal service, you will print the postage stamps on your printer. You also will print addresses directly on the envelopes or print mailing labels. You soon discover that not only do you save on costs but also the amount of time it takes to complete these activities. No more time spent driving to the post office!

With greeting card software, you will design your own greeting cards on the computer screen, personalizing them with pictures and special notes, and then print them in color on card stock paper. You also will make personalized T-shirts as gifts by printing pictures on T-shirt transfer paper and then ironing the transfer on a plain T-shirt.

The next time photo paper is on sale, you plan to stock up. With the photo paper in the printer, you will print copies of your digital pictures in a variety of sizes — wallet, 4 × 6, 5 × 7, and 8 × 10.

Read Chapter 6 to learn about various types of monitors, printers, and paper and to discover many other forms of output.

After completing this chapter, you will be able to:

1. Describe the four categories of output

2. Summarize the characteristics of LCD monitors, LCD screens, plasma monitors, and HDTVs

3. Describe the characteristics of a CRT monitor and factors that affect its quality

4. Explain the relationship between graphics chips and monitors

5. Describe various ways to print

6. Differentiate between a nonimpact printer and an impact printer

7. Summarize the characteristics of ink-jet printers, photo printers, laser printers, thermal printers, mobile printers, label and postage printers, and plotters and large-format printers

8. Describe the uses of speakers and headsets

9. Identify the output characteristics of fax machines and fax modems, multifunction peripherals, data projectors, joysticks, and wheels

10. Identify output options for physically challenged users

CONTENTS

WHAT IS OUTPUT?

Output is data that has been processed into a useful form. That is, computers process data (input) into information (output). A computer generates several types of output, depending on the hardware and software being used and the requirements of the user.

Users view output on a screen, print it, or hear it through speakers or headsets. Monitors, notebook computers, Tablet PCs, PDAs, and smart phones have screens that allow users to view documents, Web sites, e-mail messages, and other types of output. Some printers produce black-and-white documents, and others produce brilliant colors, enabling users to print color documents, photographs, and transparencies. Through the computer's speakers or a headset, users listen to sounds, music, and voice messages.

While working with a computer, a user encounters four basic categories of output: text, graphics, audio, and video (Figure 6-1). Very often, a single form of output, such as a Web page, includes more than one of these categories.

- Text — Examples of text-based output are memos, letters, announcements, press releases, reports, advertisements, newsletters, envelopes, mailing labels, and e-mail messages. On the Web, users view and print many other types of text-based output. These include newspapers, magazines, books, play or television show transcripts, stock quotes, famous speeches, and historical lectures.
- Graphics — Output often includes graphics to enhance its visual appeal and convey information. Business letters have logos. Reports include charts. Newsletters use drawings, clip art, and photographs. Users print high-quality photographs taken with a

FIGURE 6-1   Four categories of output are text, graphics, audio, and video.

digital camera, eliminating the need for film or film developers. Many Web sites use animated graphics, such as blinking icons, scrolling messages, or simulations.

- Audio — Users insert their favorite music CD in a CD or DVD drive and listen to the music while working on the computer. Software such as games, encyclopedias, and simulations often have musical accompaniments for entertainment and audio clips, such as narrations and speeches, to enhance understanding. On the Web, users tune into radio and television stations and listen to audio clips or live broadcasts of interviews, talk shows, sporting events, news, music, and concerts. They also use the Internet to conduct real-time conversations with friends, coworkers, or family members, just as if they were speaking on the telephone.
- Video — As with audio, software and Web sites often include video clips to enhance understanding. Users watch a live or prerecorded news report, view a movie, see a doctor perform a life-saving surgery, observe a hurricane in action, or enjoy a live performance of their favorite musician or musical group on the computer.

Attaching a video camera to the computer allows users to watch home movies on the computer. They also can attach a television's antenna or cable to the computer and watch a television program on the computer screen.

An **output device** is any type of hardware component that conveys information to one or more people. Commonly used output devices include display devices, printers, speakers and headsets, fax machines and fax modems, multifunction peripherals, data projectors, and force-feedback joysticks and wheels. This chapter discusses each of these output devices.

DISPLAY DEVICES

A **display device**, or simply *display*, is an output device that visually conveys text, graphics, and video information. Information on a display device, sometimes called *soft copy*, exists electronically and appears for a temporary period.

Display devices consist of a screen and the components that produce the information on the screen. Desktop computers typically use a monitor as their display device. A **monitor** is a display device that is packaged as a separate peripheral. Most monitors have a tilt-and-swivel base that allows users to adjust the angle of the screen to minimize neck strain and reduce glare from overhead lighting. Monitor controls permit users to adjust the brightness, contrast, positioning, height, and width of images.

Most mobile computers and devices integrate the display and other components into the same physical case. For example, the display on a notebook computer attaches with hinges. Some PDA and smart phone displays also attach with a hinge to the device; with others, the display is built into the PDA or smart phone case.

Most display devices show text, graphics, and video information in color. Some, however, are monochrome. *Monochrome* means the information appears in one color (such as white, amber, green, black, blue, or gray) on a different color background (such as black or grayish-white). Some PDAs and other mobile devices use monochrome displays to save battery power.

Two types of display devices are flat-panel displays and CRT monitors. The following sections discuss each of these display devices.

FAQ 6-1

What can I do to ease eyestrain while using my computer?

Blink your eyes every five seconds. Adjust the room lighting. Use larger fonts or zoom a display. Take an eye break every 30 minutes: look into the distance and focus on an object for 20 to 30 seconds, roll your eyes in a complete circle, and then close your eyes for at least 30 seconds. If you wear glasses, ask your doctor about computer glasses. For more information, visit scsite.com/dc2006/ch6/faq and then click Eye Strain.

FLAT-PANEL DISPLAYS

A *flat-panel display* is a lightweight display device with a shallow depth and flat screen that typically uses LCD (liquid crystal display) or gas plasma technology. Types of flat-panel displays include LCD monitors, LCD screens, plasma monitors, and many HDTVs.

LCD Monitors and Screens

An **LCD monitor**, also called a *flat panel monitor*, is a desktop monitor that uses a liquid crystal display to produce images (Figure 6-2). These monitors produce sharp, flicker-free images.

LCD monitors have a small *footprint*; that is, they do not take up much desk space. For additional space savings, some LCD monitors are wall mountable. LCD monitors are available in a variety of sizes, with the more common being 15, 17, 18, 19, 20, 21, and 23 inches — some are 30 or 40 inches. You measure a monitor the same way you measure a television, that is, diagonally from one corner to the other.

Determining what size monitor to purchase depends on your intended use. A large monitor allows you to view more information on the screen at once, but usually is more expensive. You may want to invest in a 19-inch monitor if you use multiple applications at one time or do a lot of research on the Web. Users working with intense graphics applications, such as desktop publishing and engineering, typically have larger monitors.

FIGURE 6-2   An LCD monitor is thin and lightweight.

For an even wider screen area, some users position two or more monitors side by side or stacked (Figure 6-3). For example, one monitor can show the left side of a document, game, graphic design, or other item, with the other monitor showing the right side. This arrangement also is convenient if you want to run multiple applications simultaneously. Users of side-by-side or stacked monitors include music editors, video editors, network administrators, gamers, researchers, Web developers, graphic designers, and engineers.

Mobile computers, such as notebook computers and Tablet PCs, and mobile devices, such as PDAs and smart phones, often have built-in LCD screens (Figure 6-4). Notebook computer screens are available in a variety of sizes, with the more common being 14.1, 15.4, and 17.1 inches. Tablet PC screens range from 10.4 inches to 15 inches. PDA screens average 3.5 inches. On smart phones, screen sizes range from 2.5 to 3.5 inches.

FIGURE 6-3 Users sometimes have multiple LCD monitors stacked or side by side to increase their viewing area.

FAQ 6-2

Can I read a book on a PDA or smart phone screen?

Yes, you can download an electronic book, called an *e-book*, to a mobile device or computer. To read an e-book, your mobile device or computer requires a reader program such as *Microsoft Reader* or *Adobe Reader*. Both of these programs can be downloaded free on the Web. For more information, visit scsite.com/dc2006/ch6/faq and then click E-Books.

FIGURE 6-4 Notebook computers and Tablet PCs have color LCD screens. Many PDAs and smart phones also have color displays.

LCD Technology

A **liquid crystal display (LCD)** uses a liquid compound to present information on a display device. Computer LCDs typically contain fluorescent tubes that emit light waves toward the liquid-crystal cells, which are sandwiched between two sheets of material. When an electrical charge passes through the cells, the cells twist. This twisting causes some light waves to be blocked and allows others to pass through, creating images on the display.

LCD monitors and LCD screens produce color using either passive-matrix or active-matrix technology. An *active-matrix display*, also known as a *TFT (thin-film transistor) display*, uses a separate transistor to apply charges to each liquid crystal cell and thus displays high-quality color that is viewable from all angles. A newer type of TFT technology, called *organic LED (OLED)*, uses organic molecules that produce an even brighter, easier-to-read display than standard TFT displays. OLEDs are less expensive to produce, consume less power, and can be fabricated on flexible surfaces. Read Looking Ahead 6-1 for a look at the next generation of OLEDs.

A *passive-matrix display* uses fewer transistors, requires less power, and is less expensive than an active-matrix display. The color on a passive-matrix display often is not as bright as an active-matrix display. Users view images on a passive-matrix display best when working directly in front of it.

WEB LINK 6-1

LCD Technology

For more information, visit scsite.com/dc2006/ch6/weblink and then click LCD Technology.

LOOKING AHEAD 6-1

Flexible Screens Lock and Roll

Your newspaper arrives each morning at your front door rolled up and secured with a rubber band or in a plastic bag. Your computer monitor soon may arrive rolled up so you can transport it easily in your book bag or luggage.

Flexible screens are being developed to curve against your car's dashboard and bend around corners. Unlike today's flat-panel displays manufactured from rigid, weighty glass, the flexible screens are made from pliable organic light-emitting diodes (OLEDs). These screens are based on layers of carbon that are sealed perfectly to prevent any exposure to moisture or air. They could be mass produced using a low-cost, high-efficiency method.

The OLED technology also could be used for televisions, cellular telephones, and PDAs. For more information, visit scsite.com/dc2006/ch6/looking and then click Flexible Screens.

LCD Quality

The quality of an LCD monitor or LCD screen depends primarily on its resolution, response time, brightness, and pixel pitch.

- As mentioned in Chapter 5, **resolution** is the number of horizontal and vertical pixels in a display device. For example, a monitor that has a 1600 × 1200 resolution displays up to 1600 pixels per horizontal row and 1200 pixels per vertical row, for a total of 1,920,000 pixels to create a screen image. Recall that a *pixel* (short for picture element) is a single point in an electronic image. A higher resolution uses a greater number of pixels and thus provides a smoother, sharper, and clearer image. As you increase the resolution, however, some items on the screen appear smaller, such as menu bars, toolbars, and rulers (Figure 6-5).

  With LCD monitors and screens, resolution generally is proportional to the size of the device. That is, the resolution increases for larger monitors and screens. For example, a 17-inch LCD monitor typically has a resolution of 1280 × 1024, while a 20-inch LCD monitor has a resolution of 1600 × 1200. LCDs are geared for a specific resolution, called the *native resolution*. When set at other resolutions, the quality may not be as good as the native resolution.

- *Response time* of an LCD monitor or screen is the time in milliseconds (ms) that it takes to turn a pixel on or off. LCD monitors' and screens' response times range from 16 to 25 ms. The lower the number, the faster the response time.

- Brightness of an LCD monitor or LCD screen is measured in nits. A *nit* is a unit of visible light intensity equal to one candela (formerly called candlepower) per square meter. The *candela* is the standard unit of luminous intensity. LCD monitors and screens today range from 200 to 350 nits. The higher the nits, the brighter the images.

- *Pixel pitch*, sometimes called *dot pitch*, is the distance in millimeters between pixels on a display device. Text created with a smaller dot pitch is easier to read. Advertisements normally specify a monitor's pixel pitch or dot pitch. Average pixel pitch on LCD monitors and screens should be .28 mm or lower. The lower the number, the sharper the image.

FIGURE 6-5a (screen resolution at 800 × 600)

FIGURE 6-5b (screen resolution at 1600 × 1200)

FIGURE 6-5 A higher screen resolution displays smaller images on the screen. This comparison illustrates that all elements on the screen become smaller when the resolution is increased from 800 × 600 to 1600 × 1200. The higher resolution also displays more text on the screen.

Graphics Chips, Ports, and LCD Monitors

A cable on a monitor plugs in a port on the system unit, which enables communications from a graphics chip. This chip, called the *graphics processing unit*, controls the manipulation and display of graphics on a display device. The graphics processing unit either is integrated on the motherboard or resides on a video card in a slot in the motherboard. Video cards usually contain a fan or heat sink to keep this and other chips from overheating.

LCD monitors use a digital signal to produce a picture. To display the highest quality images, an LCD monitor should plug in a *DVI* (*Digital Video Interface*) *port*, which enables digital signals to transmit directly to the LCD monitor. Current models of system units either have an integrated DVI chip or contain a video card that has a DVI port. They usually also have a standard monitor port and an *S-video port*, allowing users to connect external devices such as a television, DVD player, or video recorder, to the computer (Figure 6-6).

Over the years, several video standards have been developed to define the resolution, number of colors, and other display properties.

Current video standards include *SVGA* (Super Video Graphics Array), which has a resolution of 800 × 600; *XGA* (eXtended Graphics Array), a resolution of 1024 × 768; *SXGA* (Super XGA), a resolution of 1280 × 1024; and *UGA* (Ultra XGA), a resolution of 1600 × 1200. Many display devices have resolutions beyond UGA, such as 2048 × 1536. Some display devices support all of these standards; others support only a subset of them. For a display device to show images as defined by a video standard, both the display device and graphics processing unit must support the same video standard.

standard monitor port

S-video port

DVI port

FIGURE 6-6 Ports on current video cards.

The number of colors a graphics processing unit displays is determined by bit depth. The *bit depth*, also called *color depth*, is the number of bits used to store information about each pixel. For example, a video card with a 24-bit depth uses 24 bits to store information about each pixel. Thus, this video card can display 2^{24} or 16.7 million colors. The greater the number of bits, the better the resulting image. Today's video cards typically have a 24-bit depth or a 32-bit depth.

A video card or motherboard, in the case of integrated video, must have enough video memory to generate the resolution and number of colors you want to display. This memory, which often is 128 MB or 256 MB on current video cards, stores information about each pixel.

WEB LINK 6-2

Video Memory

For more information, visit scsite.com/dc2006/ch6/weblink and then click Video Memory.

FAQ 6-3

How much do video cards cost?

Although video cards for the home user cost less than $100, professional artists and designers use video cards that can cost up to $1,500. These cards have more than 384 MB of memory and support resolutions of 2048 × 1536. For more information, visit scsite.com/dc2006/ch6/faq and then click Video Cards.

Plasma Monitors

Large business or power users sometimes have plasma monitors, which often measure more than 60 inches wide (Figure 6-7). A **plasma monitor** is a display device that uses gas plasma technology, which sandwiches a layer of gas between two glass plates. When voltage is applied, the gas releases ultraviolet (UV) light. This UV light causes the pixels on the screen to glow and form an image.

Plasma monitors offer larger screen sizes and higher display quality than LCD monitors but are more expensive. These monitors also can hang directly on a wall.

FAQ 6-4

What is the largest monitor to date?

The Sydney Olympics had a monitor wall that contained more than 400 screens, measuring about 150 feet wide and 7½ feet tall. For more information, visit scsite.com/dc2006/ch6/faq and then click Monitor Wall.

Televisions and HDTVs

Home users sometimes use their television as a display device (Figure 6-8). Connecting a computer to an analog television requires a converter that translates the digital signal from the computer into an analog signal that the television can display. The best analog televisions have a resolution of only 520 × 400 pixels. Thus, users are turning to *digital television* (*DTV*) for crisper, higher-quality output.

Digital television signals provide two major advantages over analog signals. First, digital signals produce a higher-quality picture. Second, many programs can be broadcast on a single digital channel, whereas only one program can be broadcast on an analog channel. By 2006, all broadcast stations must be transmitting digital signals, as mandated by the FCC.

HDTV (*high-definition television*) is the most advanced form of digital television, working with digital broadcast signals, transmitting digital sound, supporting wide screens, and providing resolutions up to 1920 × 1080 pixels. With HDTV, the broadcast signals are digitized when they are sent via over-the-air (OTA) broadcasts from local television networks, satellite, or cable. To receive the HDTV signals via OTA broadcasts, you need a VHF/UHF antenna; via satellite, you need an HDTV-compatible satellite receiver/tuner; and via cable, you need an HDTV-compatible cable box.

FIGURE 6-7 Large plasma monitors can measure more than 60 inches wide.

As HDTV becomes more affordable, home users may begin to use it as their computer's display device. HDTV also is ideal for presenting material to a large group. HDTV technology makes the use of interactive TV more widespread because HDTV works directly with interactive TV.

Interactive TV is a two-way communications technology in which users interact with television programming. Although interactive TV can be set up to work with analog televisions, it has much higher levels of performance when used with digital televisions. Uses of interactive TV include selecting a movie from a central library of movies, voting or responding to network questionnaires, banking and shopping, playing games, pausing or recording live television programs, and video conferencing.

FAQ 6-5

Can I watch digital television broadcasts on my analog television?

Yes, if you buy a device that converts the digital signal to an analog signal. The image on your analog television, however, will not have HDTV resolution. For more information, visit scsite.com/dc2006/ch6/faq and then click HDTV.

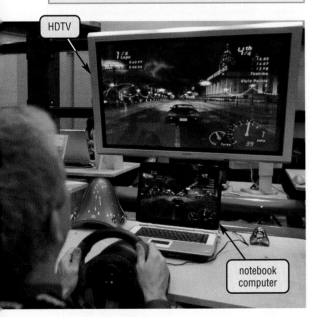

FIGURE 6-8 This user tests HDTV as a display device. Notice how much bigger the screen area is compared to the notebook computer.

CRT MONITORS

A **CRT monitor** is a desktop monitor that contains a cathode-ray tube (Figure 6-9). A *cathode-ray tube* (*CRT*) is a large, sealed glass tube. The front of the tube is the screen. Tiny dots of phosphor material coat the screen on a CRT. Each dot consists of a red, a green, and a blue phosphor. The three dots combine to make up each pixel. Inside the CRT, an electron beam moves back and forth across the back of the screen. This causes the dots on the front of the screen to glow, which produces an image on the screen.

CRT monitors have a much larger footprint than do LCD monitors; that is, they take up more desk space. CRT monitors for desktop computers are available in various sizes, with the more common being 15, 17, 19, 21, and 22 inches. In addition to monitor size, advertisements also list a CRT monitor's viewable size. The *viewable size* is the diagonal measurement of the actual viewing area provided by the screen in the CRT monitor. A 21-inch monitor, for example, may have a viewable size of 20 inches.

In the past, CRT monitor screens were curved slightly. Today's models have flat screens. A flat screen reduces glare, reflection, and distortion of images. With a flat screen, users do not notice as much eyestrain and fatigue.

A CRT monitor costs less than an LCD monitor, but it also generates more heat and uses more power than an LCD monitor. To help reduce the amount of electricity used by monitors and other computer components, the United States Department of Energy (DOE) and the United States Environmental Protection Agency (EPA) developed the **ENERGY STAR program**. This program encourages manufacturers to create energy-efficient devices that require little power when they are not in use. Monitors and devices that meet ENERGY STAR guidelines display an ENERGY STAR label.

FIGURE 6-9 The core of a CRT monitor is a cathode-ray tube.

CRT monitors produce a small amount of electromagnetic radiation. *Electromagnetic radiation (EMR)* is a magnetic field that travels at the speed of light. Excessive amounts of EMR can pose a health risk. To be safe, all high-quality CRT monitors comply with MPR II standards. *MPR II* is a set of standards that defines acceptable levels of EMR for a monitor. To protect yourself even further, sit at arm's length from the CRT monitor because EMR travels only a short distance. In addition, EMR is greatest on the sides and back of the CRT monitor.

FAQ 6-6

Is a flat display the same as a flat-panel display?

No. A *flat display* refers to a CRT monitor that has a flat screen. A flat-panel display, by contrast, has a shallow depth and uses LCD, gas plasma, or some technology other than CRT. For more information, visit scsite.com/dc2006/ch6/faq and then click Flat-Panel Displays.

Quality of a CRT Monitor

The quality of a CRT monitor depends largely on its resolution, dot pitch, and refresh rate.

• Most CRT monitors support a variety of screen resolutions. Standard CRT monitors today usually display up to a maximum of 1800×1440 pixels, with 1280×1024 often the norm. High-end CRT monitors (for the power user) can display 2048×1536 pixels or more. The display resolution you choose is a matter of preference. Larger monitors typically look best at a higher resolution, and smaller monitors look best at a lower resolution.

• As with LCD monitors, text created with a smaller dot pitch, or pixel pitch, is easier to read. To minimize eye fatigue, use a CRT monitor with a dot pitch of .27 millimeters or lower.

• Electron beams inside a CRT monitor "draw" an image on the entire screen many times per second so the phosphor dots, and therefore the image, do not fade. The number of times the image is drawn per second is called the *refresh rate*, or *scan rate*. A CRT monitor's refresh rate, which is expressed in hertz (Hz), should be fast enough to maintain a constant,

flicker-free image. A slower refresh rate causes the image to fade and then flicker as it is redrawn. This flicker can lead to eye fatigue and cause headaches for some users.

A high-quality CRT monitor will provide a vertical refresh rate of at least 68 Hz. This means the image on the screen redraws itself vertically 68 times in a second.

Graphics Chips and CRT Monitors

Many CRT monitors use an analog signal to produce an image. As with an LCD monitor, a cable on the CRT monitor plugs in a port on the system unit, which enables communications from a graphics chip. If the graphics chip resides on a video card, for example, the video card converts digital output from the computer into an analog video signal and sends the signal through the cable to the monitor, which displays output on the screen (Figure 6-10).

As with LCD monitors, the greater the video card's bit depth, the better the resulting image. Both the video card and the monitor must support the video standard to generate the desired resolution and number of colors, and the video card must have enough memory to generate the resolution and number of colors you want to display.

FAQ 6-7

What type of video content do users view on display devices?

Music videos and newscasts are the most widely viewed video content on display devices, as shown in the chart below. For more information, visit scsite.com/dc2006/ch6/faq and then click Video Output Content.

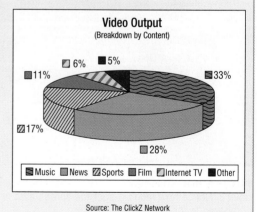

Video Output
(Breakdown by Content)

6% 5%
11%
33%
17%
28%

Music News Sports Film Internet TV Other

Source: The ClickZ Network

FIGURE 6-10 HOW VIDEO TRAVELS FROM THE PROCESSOR TO A CRT MONITOR VIA A VIDEO CARD

video card

Step 1:
The processor sends digital video data to the video card.

00100110110101101

processor

Step 2:
The video card's digital-to-analog converter (DAC) converts the digital video data to an analog signal.

Step 3:
The analog signal is sent through a cable to the CRT monitor.

Step 4:
The CRT monitor separates the analog signal into red, green, and blue signals.

Step 5:
Electron guns fire the three color signals to the front of the CRT.

Step 6:
An image is displayed on the screen when the electrons hit phosphor dots on the back of the screen.

Test your knowledge of pages 300 through 309 in Quiz Yourself 6-1.

 QUIZ YOURSELF 6-1

Instructions: Find the true statement below. Then, rewrite the remaining false statements so they are true.

1. A lower resolution uses a greater number of pixels and thus provides a smoother image.

2. An output device is any type of software component that conveys information to one or more people.

3. Documents often include text to enhance their visual appeal and convey information.

4. LCD monitors have a larger footprint than CRT monitors.

5. Types of CRTs include LCD monitors, LCD screens, plasma monitors, and many HDTVs.

6. You measure a monitor diagonally from one corner to the other.

Quiz Yourself Online: To further check your knowledge of output, flat-panel displays, and CRT monitors, visit scsite.com/dc2006/ch6/quiz and then click Objectives 1 – 4.

PRINTERS

A **printer** is an output device that produces text and graphics on a physical medium such as paper or transparency film. Printed information, called *hard copy*, exists physically and is a more permanent form of output than that presented on a display device (soft copy).

A hard copy, also called a *printout*, is either in portrait or landscape orientation (Figure 6-11). A printout in *portrait orientation* is taller than it is wide, with information printed across the shorter width of the paper. A printout in *landscape orientation* is wider than it is tall, with information printed across the widest part of the paper. Letters, reports, and books typically use portrait orientation. Spreadsheets, slide shows, and graphics often use landscape orientation.

Home computer users might print less than a hundred pages a week. Small business computer users might print several hundred pages a day. Users of mainframe computers, such as large utility companies that send printed statements to hundreds of thousands of customers each month, require printers that are capable of printing thousands of pages per hour.

To meet this range of printing needs, many different printers exist with varying speeds, capabilities, and printing methods. Figure 6-12 presents a list of questions to help you decide on the printer best suited to your needs.

The following pages discuss various ways of producing printed output, as well as many different types of printers.

FIGURE 6-11a (portrait orientation)

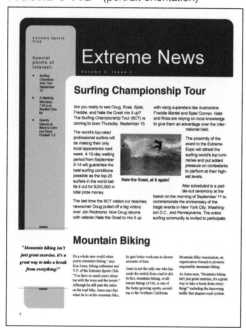

FIGURE 6-11b (landscape orientation)

Fitness Progress Chart for Men

Date	Weight (pounds)	Chest (inches)	Waist (inches)	Hips (inches)	Estimated Lean Body Weight	Estimated Body Fat Weight	Estimated Body Fat Percentage	Estimated Body Mass Index (BMI)
10-Jun	200	42	36	34	161 3/7	38 4/7	19 2/7	26.84
17-Jun	200	42	36	34	161 3/7	38 4/7	19 2/7	26.84
24-Jun	199	42	35.5	33.6	162 2/5	36 3/5	18 2/5	26.71
1-Jul	199	42	35	33	164 1/2	34 1/2	17 1/3	26.71
8-Jul	198	42.5	35	33	163 2/5	34 3/5	17 1/2	26.57
15-Jul	197	42.5	35	33	162 1/3	34 2/3	17 3/5	26.44
22-Jul	197	42.5	35	33	162 1/3	34 2/3	17 3/5	26.44
29-Jul	196	42.5	34.5	33	163 1/3	32 2/3	16 2/3	26.30
5-Aug	196	42.5	34.5	33	163 1/3	32 2/3	16 2/3	26.30
12-Aug	195	42.5	34.5	33	162 1/4	32 3/4	16 4/5	26.17
19-Aug	193	42.5	34.5	33	160	33	17	25.90
26-Aug	191	42.5	34.5	33	158	33	17 1/3	25.63
2-Sep	190	42.5	34.5	33	156 5/6	33 1/6	17 1/2	25.50
9-Sep	190	43	34.5	33	156 5/6	33 1/6	17 1/2	25.50
16-Sep	190	43	34.5	33	156 5/6	33 1/6	17 1/2	25.50
23-Sep	189	43	34	32	157 4/5	31 1/5	16 1/2	25.37
30-Sep	189	43	34	32	157 4/5	31 1/5	16 1/2	25.37
7-Oct	190	43	34	33	158 8/9	31 1/9	16 3/8	25.50
14-Oct	192	43	34	33	161	31	16 1/9	25.77
21-Oct	191	43	34	32	160	31	16 1/4	25.63
28-Oct	191	43	34	32	160	31	16 1/4	25.63
4-Nov	192	43	34	33	161	31	16 1/9	25.77
11-Nov	192	43	34	33	161	31	16 1/9	25.77
18-Nov	193	43	34	33	162 1/7	30 6/7	16	25.90
25-Nov	193	43	34	33	162 1/7	30 6/7	16	25.90
2-Dec	192	43	34	33	161	31	16 1/9	25.77
9-Dec	193	43	34	33	162 1/7	30 6/7	16	25.90

FIGURE 6-11 Portrait orientation is taller than it is wide. Landscape orientation is wider than it is tall.

1. What is my budget?
2. How fast must my printer print?
3. Do I need a color printer?
4. What is the cost per page for printing?
5. Do I need multiple copies of documents?
6. Will I print graphics?
7. Do I want to print photographs?
8. Do I want to print directly from a memory card or other type of miniature storage media?
9. What types of paper does the printer use?
10. What sizes of paper does the printer accept?
11. Do I want to print on both sides of the paper?
12. How much paper can the printer tray hold?
13. Will the printer work with my computer and software?
14. How much do supplies such as ink and paper cost?
15. Can the printer print on envelopes and transparencies?
16. How many envelopes can the printer print at a time?
17. How much do I print now, and how much will I be printing in a year or two?
18. Will the printer be connected to a network?
19. Do I want wireless printing capability?

FIGURE 6-12 Questions to ask when purchasing a printer.

Producing Printed Output

Until a few years ago, printing a document required connecting a computer to a printer with a cable via the USB or parallel port on the computer. Although many users today continue to print using this method, a variety of printing options are available, as shown in Figure 6-13.

Today, wireless printing technology makes the task of printing from a notebook computer, Tablet PC, PDA, or smart phone much easier. As discussed in Chapter 4, two wireless technologies for printing are Bluetooth and infrared. With *Bluetooth printing*, a device transmits output to a printer via radio waves. The computer and devices do not have to be aligned with each other; rather, they need to be within an approximate 30-foot range. With *infrared printing*, a printer communicates with a device using infrared light waves. To print from a smart phone, for example, a user lines up the IrDA port on the smart phone with the IrDA port on the printer.

Users can print images taken with a digital camera without downloading the images to the computer using a variety of techniques. Some cameras connect directly to a printer via a cable. Others store images on media cards that can be removed and inserted in the printer. Some printers have a docking station, into which the user inserts the camera to print pictures stored in the camera.

Printer cable connects to computer via USB or parallel port.

printer cable

Smart phone communicates with printer via IrDA port.

Smart phone communicates with printer via Bluetooth.

wireless printers

Various Ways Users Print Documents and Pictures

Printer connected to network receives print jobs from many computers.

Printer connects to camera via cable.

cable

Printer prints images in camera when camera sits in docking station.

docking station

media card

Printer prints images on media card removed from camera and inserted in printer.

FIGURE 6-13 Users print documents and pictures using a variety of printing methods.

Finally, many home and business users print to a central printer on a network. Their computer may communicate with the network printer via cables or wirelessly.

Nonimpact Printers

A **nonimpact printer** forms characters and graphics on a piece of paper without actually striking the paper. Some spray ink, while others use heat or pressure to create images.

Commonly used nonimpact printers are ink-jet printers, photo printers, laser printers, thermal printers, mobile printers, label and postage printers, plotters, and large-format printers.

Ink-Jet Printers

An **ink-jet printer** is a type of nonimpact printer that forms characters and graphics by spraying tiny drops of liquid ink onto a piece of paper. Ink-jet printers have become a popular type of color printer for use in the home. A reasonable quality ink-jet printer costs less than $100.

Ink-jet printers produce text and graphics in both black-and-white and color on a variety of paper types (Figure 6-14). These printers normally use individual sheets of paper stored in one or two removable or stationary trays. Ink-jet printers accept papers in many sizes, ranging from 3 × 5 inches to 8½ × 14 inches. Available paper types include plain paper, ink-jet paper, photo paper, glossy paper, and banner paper. Most ink-jet

FIGURE 6-14 Ink-jet printers are a popular type of color printer used in the home.

printers can print photographic-quality images on any of these types of paper.

Ink-jet printers also print on other materials such as envelopes, labels, index cards, greeting card paper (card stock), transparencies, and iron-on T-shirt transfers. Many ink-jet printers include software for creating greeting cards, banners, business cards, letterheads, and transparencies.

As with many other input and output devices, one factor that determines the quality of an ink-jet printer is its resolution. Printer resolution is measured by the number of *dots per inch* (*dpi*) a printer can print. With an ink-jet printer, a dot is a drop of ink. A higher dpi means the drops of ink are smaller. Most ink-jet printers can print from 600 to 4800 dpi.

As shown in Figure 6-15, the higher the dpi, the better the print quality. The difference in quality becomes noticeable when the size of the printed image increases. That is, a wallet-sized image printed at 600 dpi may look similar in quality to one printed at 1200 dpi. When you increase the size of the image, to 8 × 10 for example, the printout of the 600 dpi resolution

may look grainier than the one printed using a 1200 dpi resolution.

The speed of an ink-jet printer is measured by the number of pages per minute (ppm) it can print. Most ink-jet printers print from 3 to 26 ppm. Graphics and colors print at a slower rate. For example, an ink-jet printer may print 20 ppm for black text and only 15 ppm for color and/or graphics.

FIGURE 6-15 You will notice a higher quality output with printers that can print at a higher dpi.

The print head mechanism in an ink-jet printer contains ink-filled print cartridges. Each cartridge has fifty to several hundred small ink holes, or nozzles. The steps in Figure 6-16 illustrate how a drop of ink appears on a page. The ink propels through any combination of the nozzles to form a character or image on the paper.

FIGURE 6-16 HOW AN INK-JET PRINTER WORKS

Step 1:
A small resistor heats the ink, causing the ink to boil and form a vapor bubble.

Step 2:
The vapor bubble forces the ink through the nozzle.

Step 3:
Ink drops onto the paper.

Step 4:
As the vapor bubble collapses, fresh ink is drawn into the firing chamber.

When the print cartridge runs out of ink, you simply replace the cartridge. Most ink-jet printers have at least two print cartridges: one containing black ink and the other(s) containing colors. Cartridges with black ink cost $15 to $30 each. Color ink cartridge prices range from $20 to $35 each. The number of pages a single cartridge can print varies by manufacturer and the type of documents you print. For example, black ink cartridges typically print from 200 to 800 pages, and color ink cartridges from 125 to 450 pages. Read At Issue 6-1 for a related discussion.

WEB LINK 6-4

Ink-Jet Printers

For more information, visit scsite.com/ dc2006/ch6/weblink and then click Ink-Jet Printers.

AT ISSUE 6-1

Ink-Jet Ink Wars?

In 1903, King Camp Gillette introduced an innovative product — a safety razor with disposable blades. Gillette accompanied his product with an even more innovative idea — sell the razor, which was purchased once, at or below cost, and rely on sales of the razor blades, which were purchased repeatedly, for profit. The idea made Gillette a millionaire. Manufacturers of ink-jet printers use a similar approach. The printers are inexpensive, often less than $200. The ink cartridges the printers use, however, can cost from $30 to $50 each time they are replaced. To avoid the high cost of cartridges, some people use ink refill kits. These kits, which are far less expensive than a new cartridge, typically include several vials of ink and a syringe-like tool used to inject the ink into existing ink cartridges. To counter the kits, some printer manufacturers have inserted special chips that keep a cartridge from being refilled and, some claim, shut down a cartridge before it really is out of ink. Ink refill kits cost much less than a new cartridge, but the kits can be messy, contain low-quality ink, and even damage a print head if used improperly. Should manufacturers be allowed to prevent people from refilling ink cartridges? Why? Would you use an ink refill kit? Why or why not?

Photo Printers

A **photo printer** is a color printer that produces photo-lab-quality pictures (Figure 6-17). Some photo printers print just one or two sizes of images, for example, 3 × 5 inches and 4 × 6 inches. Others print up to letter size, legal size, or even larger. Some even print panoramic photographs. Generally, the more sizes the printer prints, the more expensive the printer.

Many photo printers use ink-jet technology. With models that can print letter-sized documents, users connect the photo printer to their computer and use it for all their printing needs. For a few hundred dollars, this type of photo printer is ideal for the home or small business user. Other photo printer technologies are discussed later in the chapter. Read At Issue 6-2 for a related discussion.

WEB LINK 6-5

Photo Printers

For more information, visit scsite.com/ dc2006/ch6/weblink and then click Photo Printers.

prints only 4 × 6 size

prints 4 × 6, 5 × 7, 8 × 10, 8½ × 11, and panoramic sizes

prints 4 × 6, 5 × 7, 8 × 10, 8½ × 11, 11 × 14, 13 × 19, and panoramic sizes

FIGURE 6-17 Photo printers print in a range of sizes.

AT ISSUE 6-2

Who Is Responsible for Stopping Counterfeiting?

Some college students found a solution to their money problems: they made their own. With a scanner, personal computer, and color printer, they produced bogus bills and passed more than $1,000 in counterfeit currency before they were caught. As printer quality continues to improve, it is estimated that more than $1 million in fraudulent funds is produced every week. Police have arrested counterfeiters ranging from high school students to senior citizens. As one federal agent points out, counterfeiting has gone from a high-skill, low-tech job to a high-tech, low-skill job. While counterfeiters used to specialize in higher-domination bills ($20, $50, and $100), today phony $10, $5, and even $1 bills are circulated. Spotting fake money is not that difficult, but most people never look that closely. Counterfeiting does not stop with money. With templates for diplomas, degrees, transcripts, social security cards, driver's licenses, birth certificates, deeds, certified checks, and green cards available on the Web, almost any document can be produced. Should the manufacturers of high-quality printers take responsibility for this problem? Why or why not? What, if anything, could printer manufacturers do? It is illegal to pass counterfeit currency knowingly. Should it be illegal to offer templates knowingly online that could be used to produce counterfeit documents? Can you offer any other possible solutions?

Many photo printers have a built-in card slot so the printer can print digital photographs directly from a media card. Simply remove the media card from the digital camera and insert it in the printer's card slot. Then, push buttons on the printer to select the desired photo, specify the number of copies, and indicate the size of the printed image. Some photo printers have built-in LCD color screens, allowing users to view and enhance the pictures before printing them.

FAQ 6-9

What type of paper is available for a photo printer?

Many photo papers are available in various surface finishes, brightness, and weights. Surface finishes include high gloss, soft gloss, satin, or matte. The higher the brightness rating, the more brilliant the whiteness. The greater the paper weight, which is measured in pounds, the thicker the paper. In the United States, the weight of paper is stated in pounds per 500 sheets of 17" × 22" paper, each sheet of which equals four letter-sized sheets. For more information, visit scsite.com/dc2006/ch6/faq and then click Photo Paper.

Laser Printers

A **laser printer** is a high-speed, high-quality nonimpact printer (Figure 6-18). Laser printers are available in both black-and-white and color models. A laser printer for personal computers ordinarily uses individual 8½ × 11-inch sheets of paper stored in one or more removable trays that slide in the printer case. Some laser printers have built-in trays that accommodate different sizes of paper, while others require separate trays for letter- and legal-sized paper. Most laser printers have a manual feed slot where you can insert individual sheets and envelopes. You also can print transparencies on a laser printer.

Laser printers print text and graphics in high-quality resolutions, usually 1200 dpi for black-and-white printers and up to 2400 dpi for color printers. While laser printers usually cost more than ink-jet printers, they also are much faster. A laser printer for the home and small office user typically prints black-and-white text at speeds of 15 to 50 ppm. Color laser printers print 4 to 24 ppm. Laser printers for large business users print more than 150 ppm.

black-and-white laser printer

color laser printer

FIGURE 6-18 Laser printers are available in both black-and-white and color models.

Depending on the quality, speed, and type of laser printer, the cost ranges from a few hundred to several thousand dollars for the home and small office user, and several hundred thousand dollars for the large business user. Color laser printers are slightly higher priced than otherwise equivalent black-and-white laser printers.

When printing a document, laser printers process and store the entire page before they actually print it. For this reason, laser printers sometimes are called page printers. Storing a page before printing requires that the laser printer has a certain amount of memory in the device.

Depending on the amount of graphics you intend to print, a laser printer for the home or small business user can have up to 416 MB of memory and a 20 GB hard disk. To print a full-page 1200-dpi picture, for instance, you might need 32 MB of memory in the printer. If the printer does not have enough memory to print the picture, either it will print as much of the picture as its memory will allow, or it will display an error message and not print any of the picture.

Laser printers use software that enables them to interpret a *page description language (PDL)*, which tells the printer how to lay out the contents of a printed page. When you purchase a laser printer, it comes with at least one of two common page description languages: PCL or PostScript. Developed by Hewlett-Packard, a leading printer manufacturer, *PCL (Printer Control Language)* is a standard printer language

that supports the fonts and layout used in standard office documents. Professionals in the desktop publishing and graphic art fields commonly use *PostScript* because it is designed for complex documents with intense graphics and colors.

Operating in a manner similar to a copy machine, a laser printer creates images using a laser beam and powdered ink, called *toner*. The laser beam produces an image on a special drum inside the printer. The light of the laser alters the electrical charge on the drum wherever it hits. When this occurs, the toner sticks to the drum and then transfers to the paper through a combination of pressure and heat (Figure 6-19).

When the toner runs out, you replace the toner cartridge. Toner cartridge prices range from $50 to $100 for about 5,000 printed pages.

WEB LINK 6-6

Laser Printers

For more information, visit scsite.com/dc2006/ch6/weblink and then click Laser Printers.

FAQ 6-10

How do I dispose of toner cartridges?

Do not throw them in the garbage. The housing contains iron, metal, and aluminum that is not biodegradable. The ink toner inside the cartridges contains toxic chemicals that pollute water and soil if discarded in dumps. Instead, recycle empty toner cartridges. Contact your printer manufacturer to see if it has a recycling program. For more information, visit scsite.com/dc2006/ch6/faq and then click Recycling Toner Cartridges.

FIGURE 6-19   HOW A BLACK-AND-WHITE LASER PRINTER WORKS

Step 1:
After the user sends an instruction to print a document, the drum rotates as gears and rollers feed a sheet of paper into the printer.

Step 2:
A rotating mirror deflects a low-powered laser beam across the surface of a drum.

Step 3:
The laser beam creates a charge that causes toner to stick to the drum.

Step 4:
As the drum continues to rotate and press against the paper, the toner transfers from the drum to the paper.

Step 5:
A set of rollers uses heat and pressure to fuse the toner permanently to the paper.

Thermal Printers

A **thermal printer** generates images by pushing electrically heated pins against heat-sensitive paper. Basic thermal printers are inexpensive, but the print quality is low and the images tend to fade over time. Self-service gas pumps often print gas receipts using a built-in lower-quality thermal printer.

Two special types of thermal printers have high print quality. A *thermal wax-transfer printer* generates rich, nonsmearing images by using heat to melt colored wax onto heat-sensitive paper. Thermal wax-transfer printers are more expensive than ink-jet printers, but less expensive than many color laser printers.

A *dye-sublimation printer*, sometimes called a *digital photo printer*, uses heat to transfer colored dye to specially coated paper. Most dye-sublimation printers create images that are of photographic quality (Figure 6-20). Professional applications requiring high image quality, such as photography studios, medical labs, and security identification systems, use dye-sublimation printers. These high-end printers cost thousands of dollars and print images in a wide range of sizes. Most dye-sublimation printers for the home or small business user, by contrast, typically print images in only one or two sizes and are much slower than their professional counterparts. These lower-end dye-sublimation printers are comparable in cost to a photo printer based on ink-jet technology. Some are small enough for the mobile user to carry the printer in a briefcase.

Mobile Printers

A **mobile printer** is a small, lightweight, battery-powered printer that allows a mobile user to print from a notebook computer, Tablet PC, PDA, or smart phone while traveling (Figure 6-21). Barely wider than the paper on which they print, mobile printers fit easily in a briefcase alongside a notebook computer.

Mobile printers mainly use ink-jet, thermal, thermal wax-transfer, or dye-sublimation technology. Many of these printers connect to a parallel port or USB port. Others have a built-in wireless port through which they communicate with the computer wirelessly.

FIGURE 6-20a (dye-sublimation printer for the professional)

FIGURE 6-20b (dye-sublimation printer for the home or small office user)

FIGURE 6-20 The printers shown in this figure use dye-sublimation technology to create photographic-quality output.

FIGURE 6-21 A mobile printer is a compact printer that allows the mobile user to print from a notebook computer or mobile device.

Label and Postage Printers

A **label printer** is a small printer that prints on an adhesive-type material (Figure 6-22) that can be placed on a variety of items such as envelopes, packages, floppy disks, CDs, DVDs, audio-cassettes, photographs, file folders, and toys. Most label printers also print bar codes. Label printers typically use thermal technology.

A *postage printer* is a special type of label printer that has a built-in digital scale and prints postage stamps. Postage printers allow users to buy and print digital postage, called *Internet postage*, right from their computer. That is, you purchase an amount of postage from an authorized postal service Web site. As you need a stamp, you print it on the postage printer. Each time a postage stamp prints, your postage account is updated.

FIGURE 6-22
A label printer.

Plotters and Large-Format Printers

Plotters are sophisticated printers used to produce high-quality drawings such as blue-prints, maps, and circuit diagrams. These printers are used in specialized fields such as engineering and drafting and usually are very costly. Current plotters use a row of charged wires (called styli) to draw an electrostatic pattern on specially coated paper and then fuse toner to the pattern. The printed image consists of a series of very small dots, which provides high-quality output.

Using ink-jet printer technology, but on a much larger scale, a **large-format printer** creates photo-realistic-quality color prints. Graphic artists use these high-cost, high-performance printers for signs, posters, and other professional quality displays (Figure 6-23).

Plotters and large-format printers can accommodate paper with widths up to 60 inches because blueprints, maps, signs, posters and other such drawings and displays can be quite large. Some plotters and large-format printers use individual sheets of paper, while others take large rolls.

Impact Printers

An **impact printer** forms characters and graphics on a piece of paper by striking a mechanism against an inked ribbon that physically contacts the paper. Impact printers characteristically are noisy because of this striking activity. These printers commonly produce *near letter quality* (NLQ) output, which is print quality slightly less clear than what is acceptable for business letters. Companies may use impact printers for routine jobs such as printing mailing labels, envelopes, and invoices. Impact printers also are ideal for printing multipart forms because they easily print through many layers of paper. Factories and retail counters use impact printers because these printers withstand dusty environments, vibrations, and extreme temperatures.

Two commonly used types of impact printers are dot-matrix printers and line printers.

FIGURE 6-23 Graphic artists use large-format printers to print signs, posters, and other professional quality displays.

DOT-MATRIX PRINTERS   A **dot-matrix printer** is an impact printer that produces printed images when tiny wire pins on a print head mechanism strike an inked ribbon (Figure 6-24). When the ribbon presses against the paper, it creates dots that form characters and graphics.

Most dot-matrix printers use *continuous-form paper*, in which thousands of sheets of paper are connected together end to end. The pages have holes along the sides to help feed the paper through the printer.

The print head mechanism on a dot-matrix printer contains 9 to 24 pins, depending on the manufacturer and the printer model. A higher number of pins means the printer prints more dots per character, which results in higher print quality.

The speed of a dot-matrix printer is measured by the number of characters per second (cps) it can print. The speed of most dot-matrix printers ranges from 400 to 1100 characters per second (cps), depending on the desired print quality.

LINE PRINTERS   A **line printer** is a high-speed impact printer that prints an entire line at a time (Figure 6-25). The speed of a line printer is measured by the number of lines per minute (lpm) it can print. Some line printers print as many as 3,000 lpm. Mainframes, midrange servers, or networked applications, such as manufacturing, distribution, or shipping, often use line printers. These printers typically use 11-by-17-inch continuous-form paper.

Two popular types of line printers used for high-volume output are band and shuttle-matrix. A *band printer* prints fully formed characters when hammers strike a horizontal, rotating band that contains shapes of numbers, letters of the alphabet, and other characters. A *shuttle-matrix printer* functions more like a dot-matrix printer. The difference is the shuttle-matrix printer moves a series of print hammers back and forth horizontally at incredibly high speeds, as compared with standard line printers. Unlike a band printer, a shuttle-matrix printer prints characters in various fonts and font sizes.

FIGURE 6-25   A line printer is a high-speed printer often connected to a mainframe, midrange server, or network.

continuous-form paper

FIGURE 6-24   A dot-matrix printer produces printed images when tiny pins strike an inked ribbon.

Test your knowledge of pages 310 through 319 in Quiz Yourself 6-2.

QUIZ YOURSELF 6-2

Instructions: Find the true statement below. Then, rewrite the remaining false statements so they are true.

1. A laser printer generates images by pushing electrically heated pins against heat-sensitive paper.
2. A photo printer creates images using a laser beam and powdered ink, called toner.
3. An ink-jet printer is a type of impact printer that forms characters and graphics by spraying tiny drops of liquid nitrogen onto a piece of paper.
4. Printed information is called soft copy.
5. Two commonly used types of impact printers are ink-jet printers and line printers.
6. With Bluetooth printing, a device transmits output to a printer via radio waves.

Quiz Yourself Online: To further check your knowledge of ways to print and various type of printers, visit scsite.com/dc2006/ch6/quiz and then click Objectives 5 – 7.

SPEAKERS AND HEADSETS

An **audio output device** is a component of a computer that produces music, speech, or other sounds, such as beeps. Two commonly used audio output devices are speakers and headsets.

Most personal computers have a small internal speaker that usually emits only low-quality sound. Thus, many personal computer users add surround sound **speakers** to their computers to generate a higher-quality sound for playing games, interacting with multimedia presentations, listening to music CDs, and viewing DVDs (Figure 6-26).

Most surround sound computer speaker systems include one or two center speakers and two or more *satellite speakers* that are positioned so sound emits from all directions. Speakers typically have tone and volume controls, allowing users to adjust settings. To boost the low bass sounds, surround sound speaker systems also include a *subwoofer*.

Surround sound systems are available in a variety of configurations. For example, a 2.1 speaker system contains two speakers and a subwoofer. A 5.1 speaker system has four satellite speakers, a center speaker, and a subwoofer. A 6.1 speaker system has four satellite speakers, a front center speaker, a rear center speaker, and a subwoofer.

Users connect the speakers and subwoofer to ports on the sound card. To take full advantage of high-end surround sound speaker systems, be sure the sound card in the computer is compatible with the speaker system. For a more technical discussion about how sound cards produce sound, read the High-Tech Talk article on page 328.

satellite speakers

subwoofer

center speaker

satellite speakers

FIGURE 6-26 Most personal computer users add high-quality surround sound speaker systems to their computers.

When using speakers, anyone in listening distance can hear the output. In a computer laboratory or other crowded environment, speakers might not be practical. Instead, users can plug a headset in a port on the sound card, in a speaker, or on the front of the system unit. With the **headset**, only the individual wearing the headset hears the sound from the computer (Figure 6-27). Read At Issue 6-3 for a related discussion.

Electronically produced voice output is growing in popularity. **Voice output** occurs when you hear a person's voice or when the computer talks to you through the speakers on the computer. In some software applications, the computer can speak the contents of a document through voice output. On the Web, you can listen to (or download and then listen to) interviews, talk shows, sporting events, news, recorded music, and live concerts from many radio and television stations. Some Web sites dedicate themselves to providing voice output, where you can hear songs, quotes, historical lectures, speeches, and books (Figure 6-28).

WEB LINK 6-7

Speakers and Headsets

For more information, visit scsite.com/ dc2006/ch6/weblink and then click Speakers and Headsets.

FIGURE 6-27 In a crowded environment where speakers are not practical, users wear headsets to hear audio output.

FIGURE 6-28 Users can listen to book contents from the Web. Shown here is a sample audio broadcast of the book titled *Around the World In Eighty Days*. For users desiring to hear the entire book, they can purchase and download the entire audio file.

AT ISSUE 6-3

Wearable Web Devices: Help or Hindrance?

In addition to the time, a new watch from Microsoft can deliver news headlines, sports notes, local weather, and stock prices. The service uses portions of the FM radio band and can import several types of information, including calendar items and personal messages sent through MSN Messenger. Microsoft's watch may be only the tip of the iceberg. A Hewlett-Packard executive predicts that someday the boundary between people and the Internet may disappear. The reason for its dissolution is a concept called *Internet wearables*, which consist of portable, wireless output devices that people can wear to access the Internet. On the surface, these devices may appear as innocuous as eyeglasses or a hearing aid. But, when a wearer speaks into a tiny microphone attached to the device, information from a remote computer or a Web site is seen on a lens of the eyeglasses or heard through a speaker in the hearing aid. Advocates say products like Microsoft's new watch and Internet wearables will make people more efficient by providing immediate material to those who need it. Critics argue, however, that people could become over-dependent on, or easily distracted by, the devices. Will Internet wearables help people be more productive? Why or why not? When would Internet wearables be a good idea? When would they not be a good idea? Why?

Very often, voice output works with voice input. For example, when you call an airline to check the status of gates, terminals, and arrival times, your voice interacts with a computer-generated voice output. Another example is *Internet telephony*, which allows users to speak to other users over the Internet using their desktop computer, mobile computer, or mobile device.

Sophisticated programs enable the computer to converse with you. Talk into the microphone and say, "I'd like today's weather report." The computer replies, "For which city?" You reply, "Chicago." The computer says, "Sunny and 80 degrees."

OTHER OUTPUT DEVICES

In addition to display devices, printers, and speakers, many other output devices are available for specific uses and applications. These devices include fax machines and fax modems, multifunction peripherals, data projectors, and force-feedback joysticks and wheels.

Fax Machines and Fax Modems

A **fax machine** is a device that codes and encodes documents so they can be transmitted over telephone lines. The documents can contain text, drawings, or photographs, or can be handwritten. The term *fax* refers to a document that you send or receive via a fax machine.

A stand-alone fax machine scans an original document, converts the image into digitized data, and transmits the digitized image (Figure 6-29). A fax machine at the receiving end reads the incoming data, converts the digitized data back into an image, and prints or stores a copy of the original image.

Many computers include fax capability by using a fax modem. A *fax modem* is a modem that also allows you to send (and sometimes receive) electronic documents as faxes (Figure 6-30). A fax modem transmits computer-prepared documents, such as a word processing letter, or documents that have been digitized with a scanner or digital camera. A fax modem transmits these faxes to a fax machine or to another fax modem.

FIGURE 6-29 A stand-alone fax machine.

PC Card fax modem

internal fax modem card in system unit

fax machine

FIGURE 6-30 A fax modem allows users to send (and sometimes receive) electronic documents as faxes to a fax machine or another computer.

When a computer (instead of a fax machine) receives a fax, users can view the fax on the screen, saving the time and expense of printing it. If necessary, you also can print the fax. The quality of a viewed or printed fax is less than that of a word processing document because the fax actually is an image. Optical character recognition (OCR) software, which was discussed in Chapter 5, enables you to convert the image to text and then edit it.

A fax modem can be an external device that plugs in a port on the system unit, an internal adapter card inserted in an expansion slot on the motherboard, a chip integrated on the motherboard, or a PC Card that inserts in a PC Card slot.

Multifunction Peripherals

A **multifunction peripheral** is a single device that looks like a copy machine but provides the functionality of a printer, scanner, copy machine, and perhaps a fax machine (Figure 6-31). The features of these devices, which sometimes are called *all-in-one devices*, vary. For example, some use color ink-jet printer technology, while others include a black-and-white laser printer.

Small offices and home office (SOHO) users have multifunction peripherals because these devices require less space than having a separate printer, scanner, copy machine, and fax machine. Another advantage of these devices is they are significantly less expensive than if you purchase each device separately. If the device breaks down, however, you lose all four functions, which is the primary disadvantage.

Data Projectors

A **data projector** is a device that takes the text and images displaying on a computer screen and projects them on a larger screen so an audience can see the image clearly (Figure 6-32). For example, many classrooms use data projectors so all students easily can see an instructor's presentation on the screen.

Some data projectors are large devices that attach to a ceiling or wall in an auditorium. Others are small portable devices. Two types of smaller, lower-cost units are LCD projectors and DLP projectors.

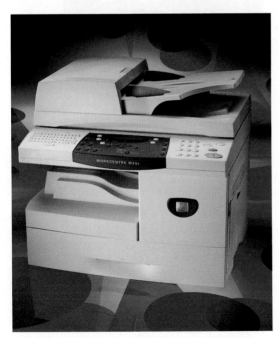

FIGURE 6-31 This multifunction peripheral is a color printer, scanner, copy machine, and fax machine all-in-one device.

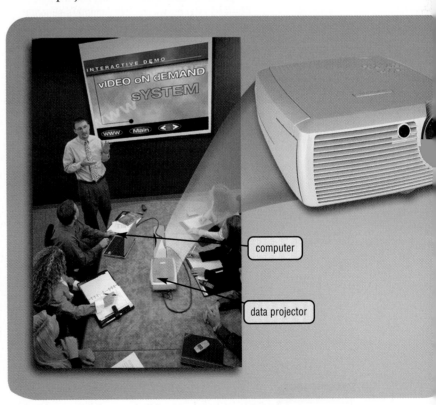

FIGURE 6-32 A data projector projects an image from a computer screen on a larger screen so an audience easily can see the image.

An *LCD projector*, which uses liquid crystal display technology, attaches directly to a computer, and uses its own light source to display the information shown on the computer screen. Because LCD projectors tend to produce lower-quality images, users often prefer DLP projectors for their sharper, brighter images.

A *digital light processing (DLP) projector* uses tiny mirrors to reflect light, which produces crisp, bright, colorful images that remain in focus and can be seen clearly even in a well-lit room. Read Looking Ahead 6-2 for a look at the next generation of digital cinema projectors.

Force-Feedback Joysticks and Wheels

As discussed in Chapter 5, joysticks and wheels are input devices for computer simulations and games used to control actions of a player or movements of a vehicle. Today's joysticks and wheels also include *force feedback*, which is a technology that sends resistance to the device in response to actions of the user (Figure 6-33). For example, as you use the simulation software to drive from a smooth road onto a gravel alley, the steering wheel trembles or vibrates, making the driving experience as realistic as possible. In addition to games, these devices are used in practical training applications such as in the military and aviation.

LOOKING AHEAD 6-2

Digital Cinema Just the Right Picture

Computers have influenced the motion picture business by modifying how movies are produced, distributed, and exhibited. Digital technology is expected to replace film by 2007, and the new technology's superior sound and visual clarity have been heralded as the greatest innovations since talkies replaced silent movies 80 years ago.

The seven larger Hollywood movie studios have cleared the final hurdle in the digital cinema process: agreeing on a compression scheme to deliver the movies to theaters. Called *JPG 2000*, this image coding system will allow the studios to distribute the movies without having to make thousands of prints, thus saving millions of dollars annually.

With the compression standard in place, manufacturers now can intensify their efforts to develop digital cinema projectors. For more information, visit scsite.com/dc2006/ch6/looking and then click Digital Cinema.

FIGURE 6-33 Joysticks, wheels, and other gaming devices often provide force feedback, giving the user a realistic experience.

PUTTING IT ALL TOGETHER

Many factors influence the type of output devices you should use: the type of output desired, the hardware and software in use, and the anticipated cost. Figure 6-34 outlines several suggested monitors, printers, and other output devices for various types of computer users.

SUGGESTED OUTPUT DEVICES BY USER

User	Monitor	Printer	Other
HOME	• 17- or 19-inch LCD monitor	• Ink-jet color printer; or • Photo printer	• Speakers • Headset • Force-feedback joystick and wheel
SMALL OFFICE/ HOME OFFICE	• 19- or 21-inch LCD monitor • Color LCD screen on Tablet PC, PDA, or smart phone	• Multifunction peripheral; or • Ink-jet color printer; or • Laser printer • Label printer • Postage printer	• Fax machine • Speakers
MOBILE	• 15.7-inch LCD screen on notebook computer • Color LCD screen on Tablet PC, PDA, or smart phone	• Mobile color printer • Ink-jet color printer; or • Laser printer for in-office use • Photo printer	• Fax modem • Headset • DLP data projector
POWER	• 23-inch LCD monitor	• Laser printer • Plotter or large-format printer; or • Photo printer; or • Dye-sublimation printer	• Fax machine or fax modem • Speakers • Headset
LARGE BUSINESS	• 19- or 21-inch LCD monitor • Color LCD screen on Tablet PC, PDA, or smart phone	• High-speed laser printer • Laser printer, color • Line printer (for large reports from a mainframe) • Label printer	• Fax machine or fax modem • Speakers • Headset • DLP data projector

FIGURE 6-34 This table recommends suggested output devices for various types of users.

OUTPUT DEVICES FOR PHYSICALLY CHALLENGED USERS

As Chapter 5 discussed, the growing presence of computers has generated an awareness of the need to address computing requirements for those with physical limitations. Read At Issue 6-4 for a related discussion.

For users with mobility, hearing, or vision disabilities, many different types of output devices are available. Hearing-impaired users, for example, can instruct programs to display words instead of sounds. With the Windows XP operating system, users also can set options to make programs easier to use. The Magnifier command, for example, enlarges text and other items in a window on the screen (Figure 6-35).

Visually impaired users can change Windows XP settings, such as increasing the size or changing the color of the text to make the words easier to read. Instead of using a monitor, blind users can work with voice output. That is, the computer reads the information that is displayed on the screen. Another alternative is a *Braille printer*, which prints information on paper in Braille (Figure 6-36).

FIGURE 6-36
A Braille printer.

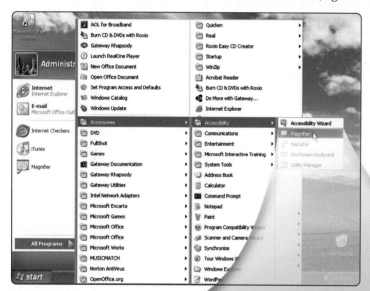

location of line that contains mouse pointer is magnified at top of screen

FIGURE 6-35 The Magnifier command in Windows XP enlarges text and other on-screen items for visually impaired users.

AT ISSUE 6-4

Should Web Sites Geared for Physically Challenged People Be Held Accountable for Accessibility Levels?

The World Wide Web Consortium (W3C) has published accessibility guidelines for Web sites. The guidelines specify measures that Web site designers can take to increase accessibility for physically challenged users. Among its guidelines, the W3C urges Web site designers to provide equivalent text for audio or visual content, include features that allow elements to be activated and understood using a variety of input and output devices, and make the user interface follow principles of accessible design. A recent report found that most Web sites do not meet all of the W3C guidelines. This failure is disappointing, because many physically challenged users could benefit from the Web's capability to bring products and services into the home. Ironically, a survey discovered that more than 50 percent of the Web sites run by disability organizations also fail to meet the W3C guidelines. Critics contend that these Web sites neglect the needs of their users and fail to lead by example. Web site apologists contend, however, that many sponsoring organizations lack the funding necessary to comply with the guidelines. Should all Web sites meet the W3C accessibility guidelines? Why or why not? Do Web sites run by disability organizations have a moral obligation to meet the guidelines? Why? What can be done to encourage sponsors to make their Web sites more accessible?

Test your knowledge of pages 320 through 327 in Quiz Yourself 6-3.

QUIZ YOURSELF 6-3

Instructions: Find the true statement below. Then, rewrite the remaining false statements so they are true.

1. A digital light processing (DLP) projector uses tiny lightbulbs to reflect light.
2. A stand-alone fax machine scans an original document, converts the image into digitized data, and transmits the digitized image.
3. Many personal computer users add surround sound printer systems to their computers to generate a higher-quality sound.
4. Multifunction peripherals require more space than having a separate printer, scanner, copy machine, and fax machine.
5. Some joysticks and wheels include real-time action, which is a technology that sends resistance to the device in response to actions of the user.

Quiz Yourself Online: To further check your knowledge of speakers and headsets, other output devices, and output for physically challenged users, visit scsite.com/dc2006/ch6/quiz and then click Objectives 8 – 10.

CHAPTER SUMMARY

Computers process and organize data (input) into information (output). This chapter described the various methods of output and several commonly used output devices. Output devices presented were flat-panel displays, CRT monitors, printers, speakers and headsets, fax machines and fax modems, multifunction peripherals, data projectors, and force-feedback joysticks and wheels.

Graphic Designer/Illustrator

Graphic designers and *graphic illustrators* are artists, but many do not create original works. Instead, they portray visually the ideas of their clients. Illustrators create pictures for books and other publications and sometimes for commercial products, such as greeting cards. They work in fields such as fashion, technology, medicine, animation, or even cartoons. Illustrators often prepare their images on a computer. Designers combine practical skills with artistic talent to convert abstract concepts into designs for products and advertisements. Many use computer-aided design (CAD) tools to create, visualize, and modify designs. Designer careers usually are specialized in particular areas, such as:

- Graphic designers — book covers, stationery, and CD covers
- Commercial and industrial designers — products and equipment
- Costume and theater designers — costumes and settings for theater and television
- Interior designers — layout, decor, and furnishings of homes and buildings
- Merchandise displayers — commercial displays
- Fashion designers — clothing, shoes, and other fashion accessories

Certificate, two-year, four-year, and masters-level educational programs are available within design areas. About 30 percent of graphic illustrators/designers choose to freelance, while others work with advertising agencies, publishing companies, design studios, or specialized departments within large companies. Salaries range from $25,000 to $80,000-plus, based on experience and educational background. For more information, visit scsite.com/dc2006/ch6/careers and then click Graphic Designer/Illustrator.

High-Tech Talk

SOUND CARDS: BRINGING YOUR COMPUTER TO LIFE

Speakers, headsets, and other audio output devices rely on sound cards or integrated sound card functionality to produce sounds such as music, voice, beeps, and chimes. Sound cards contain the chips and circuitry to record and play back a wide range of sounds using analog-to-digital conversion and digital-to-analog conversion, as described in the Chapter 1 High-Tech Talk on page 38.

To record a sound, the sound card must be connected to an input device, such as a microphone or audio CD player. The input device sends the sound to the sound card as an analog signal. The analog signal flows to the sound card's analog-to-digital-converter (ADC). The ADC converts the signal into digital (binary) data of 1s and 0s by sampling the signal at set intervals.

The analog sound is a continuous waveform, with a range of frequencies and volumes. To represent the waveform in a recording, the computer would have to store the waveform's value at every instant in time. Because this is not possible, the sound is recorded using a sampling process. *Sampling* involves breaking up the waveform into set intervals and representing all values during that interval with a single value.

Several factors in the sampling process — sampling rate, audio resolution, and mono or stereo recording — affect the quality of the recorded sound during playback.

- *Sampling rate*, also called sampling frequency, refers to the number of times per second the sound is recorded. The more frequently a sound is recorded, the smaller the intervals and the better the quality. The sampling frequency used for audio CDs, for example, is 44,100 times per second, which is expressed in hertz (Hz) as 44,100 Hz. Cassette-tape-quality multimedia files use a sampling rate of 22,050 Hz; and basic Windows sounds use a sampling rate of 11,025 Hz.

- *Audio resolution* — defined as a bit rate such as 8-bit, 16-bit, or 24-bit — refers to the number of bytes used to represent the sound at any one interval. A sound card using 8-bit resolution, for example, represents a sound with any 1 of 256 values (2^8). A 16-bit sound card uses any 1 of 65,536 values (2^{16}) for each interval. Using a higher resolution provides a finer measurement scale, which results in a more accurate representation of the value of each sample and better sound quality. With 8-bit resolution, the sound quality is like that of an AM radio; 16-bit resolution gives CD-quality sound, and a 24-bit resolution is used for high-quality digital audio editing.

- Mono or stereo recording refers to the number of channels used during recording. *Mono* means that the same sound emits from both the left and right speaker during playback; *stereo* means that two separate channels exist in the recording: one each for the left and right speakers. Most sound cards support stereo recording for better playback.

After the ADC converts the analog sound through sampling, the digital data flows to the digital signal processor (DSP) on the sound card. The DSP then requests instructions from the sound card's memory chip on how to process the digital data. Typically, the DSP then compresses the digital data to save space. Finally, the DSP sends the compressed data to the computer's main processor, which stores the data in .WAV, .MP3, or other audio file format.

To play a recorded sound, such as a WAV, an MP3, or a CD track, the main processor retrieves the sound file from a hard disk, CD, or other storage device (Figure 6-37). The processor then sends the digital data to the DSP, which decompresses the data and looks to the memory chip to determine how to recreate the sound.

The DSP then sends the digital signals to the sound card's digital-to-analog converter (DAC), which converts the sound in digital format back to an analog electrical voltage. An output device, such as a speaker, uses an amplifier to strengthen the electrical voltage. This causes the speaker's cone to vibrate, recreating the sound.

All of this happens in an instant. The next time your computer beeps or chirps, consider the complex process required to make that simple sound. Then, insert your favorite CD and hear your computer come to life with the sweet music provided courtesy of the sound card. For more information, visit scsite.com/dc2006/ch6/tech and then click Sound Cards.

FIGURE 6-37
The path of sound from media to speakers.

Companies on the Cutting Edge

HEWLETT-PACKARD
TECHNOLOGY FOR BUSINESS AND LIFE

If you have printed a document recently, chances are the printer manufacturer was *Hewlett-Packard (HP)*. Market analysts estimate that 60 percent of printers sold today bear the HP logo, and HP says it ships one million printers each week.

HP is noted for a range of high-quality printers, disk storage systems, UNIX and Windows servers, and notebook, desktop, and handheld computers. In 2002, HP enlarged its presence in the computer market with a $25 billion buyout of Compaq Computer Corporation.

William Hewlett and David Packard started the company in a one-car garage in 1939 with the goal of manufacturing test and measurement equipment. HP has been developing personal information devices, including calculators and computers, for the past 30 years. For more information, visit scsite.com/dc2006/ch6/companies and then click Hewlett-Packard.

VIEWSONIC
VISUAL TECHNOLOGY LEADER

We live in a "display-centric world" according to industry leaders at *ViewSonic*. Our computer displays, whether viewed on a PDA, a desktop monitor, or a flat-panel screen, influence how we access and control the informative and entertaining output.

ViewSonic's products focus on visual technology, including CRT and LCD monitors, data projectors, plasma screens, and high-definition television. The company also designs mobile products, such as Tablet PCs and wireless monitors.

President and CEO James Chu founded ViewSonic in 1987 with the goal of increasing workers' productivity while creating an ergonomically comfortable workspace. He developed the company's logo consisting of three colorful Gouldian finches to represent outstanding quality and value, radiant color, and crisp resolution. For more information, visit scsite.com/dc2006/ch6/companies and then click ViewSonic.

Technology Trailblazers

STEVE JOBS
APPLE COMPUTER AND PIXAR COFOUNDER

Steve Jobs has an uncompromising drive for perfection. He helped build the first desktop personal computer, cofounded Apple Computer Corporation, marketed a revolutionary operating system, and became a millionaire all before his 35th birthday.

He also is known as being a brilliant motivator and having the ability to bring out the best performance from his employees. They explain that Jobs's "reality-distortion field" allows him to make seemingly unreasonable ideas appear reasonable. The Macintosh computer incorporated one of these ideas: a graphical interface controlled by a mouse.

Under Jobs's supervision, Pixar's award-winning animation studios have created some of the most beloved animated films, such as *Toy Story*, *Toy Story 2*, *A Bug's Life*, *Monsters, Inc.*, and *Finding Nemo*. For more information, visit scsite.com/dc2006/ch6/people and then click Steve Jobs.

DONNA DUBINSKY
palmOne DIRECTOR

PDAs are ubiquitous, partly due to the efforts of *Donna Dubinsky*. In the mid-1990s, she sensed that people wanted to own an electronic version of their paper appointment books. She and Jeff Hawkins introduced the original Palm Pilot prototype made of mahogany and cardboard at Palm Computing in 1996. Sales of more than two million units made the Palm Pilot the most rapidly adopted new computing product ever manufactured.

Dubinsky and Hawkins left Palm in 1998 to cofound Handspring, where they introduced several successful products, including the Treo smart phone. In 2003, Handspring merged with the Palm hardware group to create palmOne.

Dubinsky currently serves as a director of palmOne and of Intuit Corporation. For more information, visit scsite.com/dc2006/ch6/people and then click Donna Dubinsky.

Chapter Review

The Chapter Review section summarizes the concepts presented in this chapter. To listen to the audio version of this Chapter Review, visit scsite.com/dc2006/ch6/review. To obtain help from other students regarding any subject in this chapter, visit scsite.com/dc2006/ch6/forum and post your thoughts or questions.

(1) What Are the Four Categories of Output? **Output** is data that has been processed into a useful form. Four categories of output are text, graphics, audio, and video. An **output device** is any hardware component that conveys information to one or more people.

(2) What Are LCD Monitors, LCD Screens, Plasma Monitors, and HDTVs? LCD monitors, LCD screens, plasma monitors, and many HDTVs are types of flat-panel displays. A *flat-panel display* is a display with a shallow depth that typically uses LCD or gas plasma technology. An **LCD** monitor is a desktop monitor that uses a liquid crystal display to produce images. A **liquid crystal display (LCD)** uses a liquid compound to present information on a display. A **plasma monitor** is a display device that uses gas plasma technology, which substitutes a layer of gas for the liquid crystal material in an LCD monitor. **HDTV** *(high-definition television)* is the most advanced form of digital television, working with digital broadcasting signals, transmitting digital sound, supporting wide screens, and providing resolutions up to 1920 × 1080 pixels.

(3) What Is a CRT Monitor, and What Factors Affect Its Quality? A **CRT monitor** is a desktop monitor that contains a *cathode-ray tube (CRT)*. The screen on the front of the CRT is coated with tiny dots of red, green, and blue phosphor that combine to make up each *pixel*, which is a single element in an electronic image. As an electron beam inside the CRT moves back and forth across the back of the screen, the dots glow, which produces an image. The quality of a CRT monitor depends largely on its resolution, dot pitch, and refresh rate. **Resolution** is the number of horizontal and vertical pixels in a display device. *Dot pitch*, sometimes called *pixel pitch*, is the distance in millimeters between pixels on a display device. *Refresh rate* is the speed that a monitor redraws the images on the screen.

(4) How Are Graphics Chips and CRT Monitors Related? Many CRT monitors use an analog signal to produce an image. A cable on the CRT monitor plugs in a port on the system unit, which enables communications from a graphics chip. If the graphics chip is on a video card, the card converts digital output from the computer into an analog video signal and sends the signal through a cable to the CRT monitor, which displays output on the screen.

connect
Visit scsite.com/dc2006/ch6/quiz or click the Quiz Yourself button. Click Objectives 1 – 4.

(5) What Are the Various Ways to Print? Users can print by connecting a computer to a printer with a cable that plugs in a port on the computer. *Bluetooth printing* uses radio waves to transmit output to a printer. With *infrared* printing, a device communicates with the printer via infrared light waves. Some digital cameras connect directly to a printer via a cable; others store images on media cards that can be removed and inserted in the printer. Networked computers can communicate with the network printer via cables or wirelessly.

(6) How Is a Nonimpact Printer Different from an Impact Printer? A **printer** is an output device that produces text and graphics on a physical medium, such as paper or transparency film. A **nonimpact printer** forms characters and graphics on a piece of paper without actually striking the paper. Commonly used nonimpact printers are ink-jet printers, photo printers, laser printers, thermal printers, mobile printers, label and postage printers, plotters, and large-format printers. An **impact printer** forms characters and graphics on a piece of paper by striking a mechanism against an inked ribbon that physically contacts the paper. Two commonly used types of impact printers are a **dot-matrix printer** and a **line printer**.

Chapter Review

(7) **What Are Ink-Jet Printers, Photo Printers, Laser Printers, Thermal Printers, Mobile Printers, Label and Postage Printers, and Plotters and Large-Format Printers?** An ink-jet **printer** is a type of nonimpact printer that forms characters and graphics by spraying tiny drops of liquid ink onto a piece of paper. A **photo printer** is a color printer that produces photo-lab-quality pictures. A **laser printer** is a high-speed, high-quality nonimpact printer that operates in a manner similar to a copy machine, creating images using a laser beam and powdered ink, called *toner*. A **thermal printer** generates images by pushing electronically heated pins against heat-sensitive paper. A **mobile printer** is a small, lightweight, battery-powered printer that allows a mobile user to print from a notebook computer. A **label printer** is a small printer that prints on an adhesive-type material that can be placed on a variety of items. A *postage printer* is a special type of label printer that has a built-in scale and prints postage stamps. **Plotters** are sophisticated printers used to produce high-quality drawings. A **large-format printer** uses ink-jet technology on a large scale to create photo-realistic-quality color prints.

> connect
> Visit scsite.com/dc2006/ch6/quiz or click the Quiz Yourself button. Click Objectives 5 – 7.

(8) **How Are Speakers and Headsets Used?** Speakers and headsets are two commonly used audio output devices. An **audio output device** is a component of a computer that produces sound. Many personal computer users add stereo **speakers** to their computers to generate a higher-quality sound. With a **headset**, only the individual wearing the headset hears the sound from the computer.

(9) **What Are Fax Machines and Fax Modems, Multifunction Peripherals, Data Projectors, Joysticks, and Wheels?** A **fax machine** is a device that codes and encodes documents so they can be transmitted over telephone lines. A document sent or received via a fax machine is a *fax*. Many computers include fax capability using a *fax modem,* which is a modem that allows you to send (and sometimes receive) electronic documents as faxes. A **multifunction peripheral** is a single device that looks like a copy machine but provides the functionality of a printer, scanner, copy machine, and perhaps a fax machine. A **data projector** is a device that takes the text and images displaying on a computer screen and projects them onto a larger screen so an audience of people can see the image clearly. Joysticks and wheels are input devices used to control actions of a player or vehicle. Today's joysticks and wheels also include *force feedback*, which is a technology that sends resistance to the device in response to actions of the user.

(10) **What Output Options Are Available for Physically Challenged Users?** Hearing-impaired users can instruct programs to display words instead of sound. With Windows XP, visually impaired users can enlarge items on the screen and change other settings, such as increasing the size or changing the color of text to make words easier to read. Blind users can work with voice output instead of a monitor. Another alternative is a *Braille printer*, which prints information in Braille on paper.

> connect
> Visit scsite.com/dc2006/ch6/quiz or click the Quiz Yourself button. Click Objectives 8 – 10.

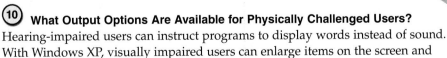

Key Terms

You should know the Primary Terms and be familiar with the Secondary Terms. Use the list below to help focus your study. To further enhance your understanding of the Key Terms in this chapter, visit scsite.com/dc2006/ch6/terms. See an example of and a definition for each term, and access current and additional information about the term from the Web.

Primary Terms

(shown in bold-black characters in the chapter)

audio output device (320)
CRT monitor (307)
data projector (323)
display device (302)
dot-matrix printer (319)
ENERGY STAR program (307)
fax machine (322)
HDTV (306)
headset (321)
impact printer (318)
ink-jet printer (312)
label printer (318)
large-format printer (318)
laser printer (315)
LCD monitor (302)
line printer (319)
liquid crystal display (LCD) (304)
mobile printer (317)
monitor (302)
multifunction peripheral (323)
nonimpact printer (312)
output (300)
output device (301)
photo printer (314)
plasma monitor (306)
plotters (318)
printer (310)
resolution (304)
speakers (320)
thermal printer (317)
voice output (321)

Secondary Terms

(shown in italic characters in the chapter)

active-matrix display (304)
all-in-one devices (323)
band printer (319)
bit depth (306)
Bluetooth printing (311)
Braille printer (326)
candela (304)
cathode-ray tube (CRT) (307)
color depth (306)
continuous-form paper (319)
digital light processing (DLP) projector (324)
digital photo printer (317)
digital television (DTV) (306)
display (302)
dot pitch (304)
dots per inch (dpi) (313)
DVI (Digital Video Interface) port (305)
dye-sublimation printer (317)
electromagnetic radiation (EMR) (308)
fax (322)
fax modem (322)
flat-panel monitor (302)
flat-panel display (302)
footprint (302)
force feedback (324)
graphics processing unit (305)
hard copy (310)
high-definition television (306)
infrared printing (311)
interactive TV (307)
Internet postage (318)
Internet telephony (322)
landscape orientation (310)
LCD projector (324)
monochrome (302)
MPR II (308)
native resolution (304)
near letter quality (NLQ) (318)
nit (304)
organic LED (OLED) (304)
page description language (PDL) (316)
passive-matrix display (304)
PCL (Printer Control Language) (316)
pixel (304)
pixel pitch (304)
portrait orientation (310)
postage printer (318)
PostScript (316)
printout (310)
refresh rate (308)
response time (304)
satellite speakers (320)
scan rate (308)
shuttle-matrix printer (319)
soft copy (302)
subwoofer (320)
S-video port (305)
SVGA (305)
SXGA (305)
TFT (thin-film transistor) display (304)
thermal wax-transfer printer (317)
toner (316)
UGA (305)
viewable size (307)
XGA (305)

Checkpoint

Use the Checkpoint exercises to check your knowledge level of the chapter. The Beyond the Book exercises will help broaden your understanding of the concepts presented in this chapter. To complete the Checkpoint exercises interactively, visit scsite.com/dc2006/ch6/check.

 Label the Figure
Identify the ports on this video card.

a. DVI port
b. standard monitor port
c. S-video port

1.____

2.____

3.____

 True/False
Mark T for True and F for False. (See page numbers in parentheses.)

_____ 1. A computer generates several types of output, depending on the hardware and software being used and the requirements of the user. (300)

_____ 2. Information on a display device sometimes is called hard copy. (302)

_____ 3. Most mobile computers and devices integrate the display and other components into the same physical case. (302)

_____ 4. A flat-panel display is a display device with a shallow depth that uses CRT technology. (302)

_____ 5. A pixel is a unit of visible light intensity equal to one candela per square meter. (304)

_____ 6. LCD monitors use an analog signal to produce a picture. (305)

_____ 7. Plasma monitors offer larger screen sizes and higher display quality than LCD monitors. (306)

_____ 8. A printout in portrait orientation is wider than it is tall. (310)

_____ 9. With Bluetooth printing, a device transmits output to a printer via radio waves. (311)

_____ 10. A photo printer is a color printer that produces photo-lab-quality pictures. (314)

_____ 11. Operating in a manner similar to a copy machine, a thermal printer creates images using a laser beam and powdered ink, called toner. (316)

_____ 12. A multifunction peripheral is a single device that looks like a copy machine but provides the functionality of a printer, scanner, copy machine, and perhaps a fax machine. (323)

Checkpoint

 Multiple Choice   Select the best answer. (See page numbers in parentheses.)

1. Examples of text-based documents are _____. (300)
   a. drawings, clip art, and photographs
   b. letters, reports, and mailing labels
   c. music, narrations, and speeches
   d. home movies and live performances

2. A passive-matrix display _____ an active matrix display. (304)
   a. uses more transistors than
   b. requires more power than
   c. often is not as bright as
   d. is more expensive than

3. An LCD monitor's _____ is the time in milliseconds that it takes to turn a pixel on or off. (304)
   a. candela
   b. pixel pitch
   c. response time
   d. dot pitch

4. The number of colors a graphics processing unit displays is determined by _____. (306)
   a. candela
   b. pixel pitch
   c. dot pitch
   d. bit depth

5. For a display device to show images as defined by a video standard, both the display device and the graphics processing unit must _____. (305)
   a. be the same size
   b. contain a heat sink or fan
   c. use an analog signal
   d. support the same video standard

6. Plasma monitors offer larger screens _____. (306)
   a. but lower display quality than LCD monitors and are less expensive
   b. but lower display quality than LCD monitors and are more expensive
   c. and higher display quality than LCD monitors but are less expensive
   d. and higher display quality than LCD monitors but are more expensive

7. The viewable size of a monitor is the _____ measurement of the actual viewing area provided by the screen in the monitor. (307)
   a. horizontal
   b. vertical
   c. diagonal
   d. three-dimensional

8. Printer resolution is measured by the number of _____ a printer can print. (313)
   a. pages per minute (ppm)
   b. dots per inch (dpi)
   c. lines per minute (lpm)
   d. pixels per inch (ppi)

9. Laser printers usually cost _____. (315)
   a. more than ink-jet printers and are faster
   b. less than ink-jet printers and are faster
   c. more than ink-jet printers and are slower
   d. less than ink-jet printers and are slower

10. The speed of a(n) _____ is measured by the number of characters per second (cps) it can print. (319)
    a. dot-matrix printer
    b. laser printer
    c. ink-jet printer
    d. thermal printer

11. _____ allows users to speak to other users over the Web using their desktop computer, mobile computer, or mobile device. (322)
    a. A plotter
    b. A fax modem
    c. Force feedback
    d. Internet telephony

12. When a computer receives a fax, _____ software enables the user to convert the image to text and then edit it. (323)
    a. optical character recognition (OCR)
    b. magnetic-ink character recognition (MICR)
    c. optical mark recognition (OMR)
    d. bar code recognition (BCR)

13. The disadvantage of multifunction peripherals is that _____. (323)
    a. they require more space than having separate devices
    b. they are significantly more expensive than purchasing each device separately
    c. if the multifunction peripheral breaks down, all functions are lost
    d. all of the above

14. The _____ command in Windows XP enlarges text and other on-screen items for visually impaired users. (326)
    a. Magnifier
    b. On-Screen Keyboard
    c. Narrator
    d. Utility Manager

Checkpoint

Matching　　　　　　　　Match the terms with their definitions. (See page numbers in parentheses.)

_____ 1. soft copy (302)

_____ 2. monochrome (302)

_____ 3. pixel pitch (304)

_____ 4. nit (304)

_____ 5. graphics processing unit (305)

_____ 6. electromagnetic radiation (EMR) (308)

_____ 7. hard copy (310)

_____ 8. near letter quality (NLQ) (318)

_____ 9. LCD projector (324)

_____ 10. DLP projector (324)

a. uses many shades of gray from white to black to enhance the quality of graphics

b. printed information that exists physically and is a more permanent form of output

c. distance in millimeters between pixels on a display device

d. changes the brightness and contrast of pixels surrounding each letter

e. graphics chip that controls the manipulation and display of graphics on a display device

f. unit of visible light intensity equal to one candela

g. uses tiny mirrors to reflect light, which produces crisp, bright, colorful images

h. information on a display device that exists electronically and appears for a temporary period

i. magnetic field that travels at the speed of light

j. print quality slightly less clear than what is acceptable for business letters

k. information appears in one color on a different background color

l. attaches directly to a computer and uses its own light source to display information

Short Answer　　　　　　　　Write a brief answer to each of the following questions.

1. What factors determine a CRT monitor's quality? _____ What is the ENERGY STAR program? _____

2. What determines the quality of an LCD monitor or LCD screen? _____ What are the differences between active-matrix and passive-matrix displays? _____

3. What advantages do digital television signals provide over analog signals? _____ What is interactive TV? _____

4. How is portrait orientation different from landscape orientation? _____ What is continuous-form paper? _____

5. What is a page description language? _____ How is PCL different from PostScript? _____

Beyond the Book　　　Read the following book elements, learn more about each using the Web, and then write a brief report.

1. At Issue — Ink-Jet Ink Wars? (314), Who Is Responsible for Stopping Counterfeiting? (315), Wearable Web Devices: Help or Hindrance? (321), or Should Web Sites Geared for Physically Challenged People Be Held Accountable for Accessibility Levels? (327)

2. Career Corner — Graphic Designer/Illustrator (327)

3. Companies on the Cutting Edge — Hewlett-Packard (329) or ViewSonic (329)

4. FAQs (302, 303, 306, 306, 307, 308, 308, 312, 315, 316)

5. High-Tech Talk — Sound Cards: Bringing Your Computer to Life (328)

6. Looking Ahead — Flexible Screens Lock and Roll (304), or Digital Cinema Just the Right Picture (324)

7. Making Use of the Web — Government (122)

8. Picture Yourself Saving Money Using a Computer (298)

9. Technology Trailblazers — Steve Jobs (329) or Donna Dubinsky (329)

10. Web Links (304, 306, 308, 314, 315, 316, 321, 322, 323, 324)

Learn It Online

Use the Learn It Online exercises to reinforce your understanding of the chapter concepts. To access the Learn It Online exercises, visit scsite.com/dc2006/ch6/learn.

 At the Movies — Plasma vs. LCD

To view the Plasma vs. LCD movie, click the number 1 button. Locate your video and click the corresponding High-Speed or Dial-Up link, depending on your Internet connection. Watch the movie and then complete the exercise by answering the questions that follow. Basic differences exist between plasma and LCD-display TVs, and those differences may affect your choice as a consumer. By understanding those differences, you will be able to choose the display options that best suit your needs. Compare and contrast the two technologies using simple criteria such as cost and size. What are the pros and cons of each display technology? How does a plasma TV display its picture? What are the disadvantages of plasma?

 At the Movies — Essential Dorm Room Gadgets

To view the Essential Dorm Room Gadgets movie, click the number 2 button. Locate your video and click the corresponding High-Speed or Dial-Up link, depending on your Internet connection. Watch the movie and then complete the exercise by answering the questions that follow. As a rule, most college students have little, if any, disposable income. Some great and affordable gadgets are available, however, that can make a dorm room more functional for study and more fun for play. How would a network interface improve a dorm room?

 Student Edition Labs — Peripheral Devices

Click the number 3 button. When the Student Edition Labs menu appears, click *Peripheral Devices* to begin. A new browser window will open. Follow the on-screen instructions to complete the Lab. When finished, click the Exit button. If required, submit your results to your instructor.

4 Student Edition Labs — Working with Graphics

Click the number 4 button. When the Student Edition Labs menu appears, click *Working with Graphics* to begin. A new browser window will open. Follow the on-screen instructions to complete the Lab. When finished, click the Exit button. If required, submit your results to your instructor.

 Practice Test

Click the number 5 button. Answer each question. When completed, enter your name and click the Grade Test button to submit the quiz for grading. Make a note of any missed questions. If required, submit your results to your instructor.

6 Who Wants To Be a Computer Genius²?

Click the number 6 button to find out if you are a computer genius. Directions about how to play the game will be displayed. When you are ready to play, click the Play button. Submit your score to your instructor.

 Wheel of Terms

Click the number 7 button to reinforce important terms you learned in this chapter by playing the Shelly Cashman Series version of this popular game. Directions about how to play the game will be displayed. When you are ready to play, click the Play button. Submit your score to your instructor.

Learn It Online

(8) DC Track and Field

Click the number 8 button to use what you have learned in this chapter to compete against other students in three track and field events. Directions about how to play the game will be displayed. When you are ready to play, click the start first event button. If required, submit your score to your instructor.

(9) You're Hired!

Click the number 9 button to use what you have learned in this chapter to embark on the path to a career in computers. Directions about how to play the game will be displayed. When you are ready to play, click the begin game button. If required, submit your score to your instructor.

(10) Crossword Puzzle Challenge

Click the number 10 button. Complete the puzzle to reinforce skills you learned in this chapter. Directions about how to play the game will be displayed. When you are ready to play, click the Submit button. Submit the completed puzzle to your instructor.

(11) Lab Exercises

Click the number 11 button. When the Lab Exercises menu appears, click the exercise assigned by your instructor. A new browser window will open. Follow the on-screen instructions to complete the exercise. When finished, click the Exit button. If required, submit your results to your instructor.

(12) Choosing a Printer

The printer is a key component of any new personal computer that you purchase. Whether you are printing black-and-white reports or producing photo-lab-quality pictures, determining which printer is best for your individual needs requires some research. Printers are available in a range of speeds and capabilities. Click the number 12 button for a tutorial about how to select the printer that is best for your particular requirements.

(13) In the News

Display device technology continues to advance. Not long ago, computer users would have considered connecting their $1,000 computers to a color television instead of paying outrageous prices for a color monitor. Today, you can purchase a 20-inch monitor that is faster and sharper than that color television for less than $300. Yet, as prices fall, consumers surely will purchase the display devices for HDTV and crystal-clear Internet access. Click the number 13 button and then read a news article about a new or improved output device. What is the device? Who manufactures it? How is the output device better than, or different from, earlier devices? Who do you think is most likely to use the device? Why?

(14) Chapter Discussion Forum

Select an objective from this chapter on page 299 about which you would like more information. Click the number 14 button and post a short message listing a meaningful message title accompanied by one or more questions concerning the selected objective. In two days, return to the threaded discussion by clicking the number 14 button. Submit to your instructor your original message and at least one response to your message.

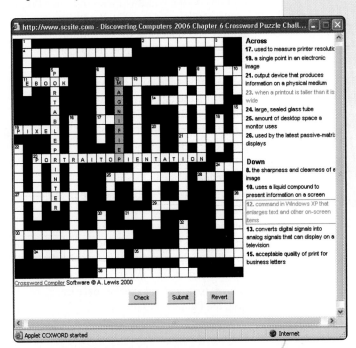

Learn How To

Use the Learn How To activities to learn fundamental skills when using a computer and accompanying technology. Complete the exercises and submit them to your instructor. Visit scsite.com/dc2006/ch6/howto to obtain more information pertaining to each activity.

LEARN HOW TO 1: Adjust the Sound on a Computer

Every computer today contains a **sound card** and associated hardware and software that allow you to play and record sound. You can adjust the sound by completing the following steps:

1. Click the Start button on the Windows taskbar and then click Control Panel on the Start menu.
2. When the Control Panel window opens, click Sounds, Speech, and Audio Devices and then click Adjust the system volume; or double-click Sounds and Audio Devices. *The Sounds and Audio Devices Properties dialog box is displayed (Figure 6-38).*
3. To adjust the volume for all devices connected to the sound card, drag the Device volume slider left or right to decrease or increase the volume.
4. If you want to mute the sound on the computer, click the Mute check box so it contains a check mark, and then click the OK button or the Apply button.
5. If you want to place the volume icon on the Windows taskbar, click the Place volume icon in the taskbar check box so it contains a check mark, and then click the OK button or the Apply button. You can click the icon on the taskbar to set the volume level or mute the sound.
6. To make sound and other adjustments for each device on the computer, click the Advanced button in the Device volume area. *The Play Control or Recording Control window opens, depending on prior choices for this window (Figure 6-39).*
7. If the Recording Control window is opened, click Options on the window menu bar, click Properties on the Options menu, click the Playback option button, and then click the OK button.
8. In the Play Control window, Play Control volume is the same as the volume adjusted in the Sounds and Audio Devices Properties dialog box. The other columns in the Play Control window refer to devices found on the computer. To select the columns that are displayed, click Options on the menu bar and then click Properties. With Playback selected, place checks in the check boxes for those devices you want to be displayed in the Control window.
9. To adjust volumes, drag the Volume sliders up or down for each device. To adjust the speaker balance, drag the Balance sliders.

FIGURE 6-38

FIGURE 6-39

Learn How To

10. If the Advanced button is not displayed in the Play Control window, click Options on the menu bar and then click Advanced Controls on the Options menu. Click the Advanced button. You can control the Bass and Treble settings by using the sliders in the Tone Controls area of the Advanced Controls for Play Control dialog box.

Exercise

1. Open the Control Panel window and then display the Sounds and Audio Devices Properties dialog box. What kind of sound card is on the computer? Click the Place volume icon in the taskbar check box and then click the Apply button. What change did you notice on the Windows taskbar? Do the same thing again. What change occurred on the Windows taskbar? Click the Advanced button in the Device volume area. Ensure the Play Control window is open. What devices are chosen for control in the Play Control window? How would you change what devices are chosen? Submit your answers to your instructor.

LEARN HOW TO 2: Control Printing on Your Computer

When you print using a computer, you control printing at two different points: first, before the printing actually begins, and second, after the document has been sent to the printer and either is physically printing or is waiting to be printed. To set the parameters for printing and then print the document, complete the following steps:

1. Click File on the menu bar of the program that will be used for printing and then click Print on the File menu. *The Print dialog box is displayed (Figure 6-40). The Print dialog box will vary somewhat depending on the program used.*

2. In the Print dialog box, make the selections for what printer will be used, what pages will be printed, the number of copies to be printed, and any other choices available. For further options, click the Properties button (or, sometimes, the Preferences button) or click the Options button.

3. Click the OK button or the Print button. The document being printed is sent to a **print queue**, which is an area on disk storage from which documents actually are printed.

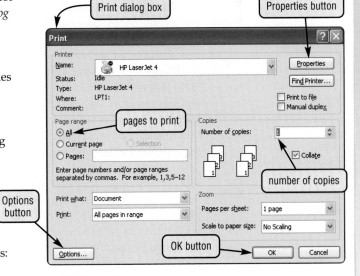

FIGURE 6-40

When you click the Print button to send the document to the print queue, a printer icon [🖨] may appear on the Windows taskbar. To see the print queue and control the actual printing of documents on the printer, complete the following steps:

1. If the printer icon appears on the Windows taskbar, double-click it; otherwise, click the Start button on the Windows taskbar, click Printers and Faxes on the Start menu, and then double-click the printer icon with the check mark. The check mark indicates the default printer. *A window opens with the name of the printer on the title bar. All the documents either printing or waiting to be printed are listed in the window. The Status column indicates whether the document is printing or waiting. In addition, the owner of the file, number of pages, size, date and time submitted, and printer port are listed.*

2. If you click Printer on the menu bar in the printer window, you can set printing preferences from the Printer menu. In addition, you can pause all printing and cancel all printing jobs from the Printer menu.

3. If you select a document in the document list and then click Document on the menu bar, you can cancel the selected document for printing, or you can pause the printing for the selected document. To continue printing for the selected document, click Document on the menu bar and then click Resume on the Document menu.

Exercise

1. Start WordPad from the Accessories submenu. Type The Print dialog box is displayed by clicking Print on the File menu.
2. Display the Print dialog box and then click the Preferences button. What choices do you have in the Layout sheet? Close the Printing Preferences dialog box. How do you select the number of copies you want to print? How would you print pages 25–35 of a document? Submit your answers to your instructor.

Web Research

Use the Internet-based Web Research exercises to broaden your understanding of the concepts presented in this chapter. Visit scsite.com/dc2006/ch6/research to obtain more information pertaining to each exercise. To discuss any of the Web Research exercises in this chapter with other students, post your thoughts or questions at scsite.com/dc2006/ch6/forum.

① Scavenger Hunt Use one of the <u>search engines</u> listed in Figure 2-10 in Chapter 2 on page 78 or your own favorite search engine to find the answers to the questions below. Copy and paste the Web address from the Web page where you found the answer. Some questions may have more than one answer. If required, submit your answers to your instructor. (1) What company introduced the first laser printer? When? (2) What is the most common type of ink-jet technology? (3) Who developed the liquid crystal display? (4) What is the purpose of backlight on an LCD screen? (5) What is an ambient light sensor on a monitor?

② Search Sleuth Some search engines use computers to index the World Wide Web automatically, so they generally find more Web sites that human indexers can catalog. One of the most aggressive automatic, or robot, search engines is <u>AltaVista</u> (altavista.com), which attempts to catalog the entire World Wide Web. AltaVista and many other search engines have a wildcard matching feature. Assume that you want to search for all information pertaining to printers, including ink-jet, photo, laser, and wireless. In this instance, you could use the wildcard symbol (*) to indicate missing letters. Your search query would be *printer, where the * substitutes for any variation of the word, printer. Visit this Web site and then use your word processing program to answer the following questions. Then, if required, submit your answers to your instructor. (1) Click the Help link and then click the Search link. Scroll down and then read about the features AltaVista emphasizes in its Web search results page. What are these features? (2) Click your browser's Back button or press the BACKSPACE key twice to return to the AltaVista home page. (3) Use the wildcard option and type *printer. (4) Scroll through the results until you reach the AltaVista News section. Read at least two of the news stories and then write a 50-word summary.

③ Journaling Respond to your readings in this chapter by writing at least one page about your reactions, evaluations, and reflections about using <u>output devices</u>. For example, have you printed photos taken with a digital camera? Do you purchase recyclable printer supplies, such as toner or ink-jet cartridges? Where would you dispose of old monitors and printers and used toner? Have you listened to audio books? Should all employers accommodate the needs of physically challenged employees by making computers accessible? You also can write about the new terms you learned by reading this chapter. If required, submit your journal to your instructor.

④ Expanding Your Understanding If you are using a Tablet PC and your coworker is using a PDA, it is cumbersome to transfer files from one device to the other. Engineers are developing <u>digital pens</u> that might ease the file exchange process. Using this special pen, one user can select a file on his computer and then place the pen on the other user's computer to transfer the file. Other digital pens allow users to write or draw and then retrieve all the handwritten information on a computer. Visit a local electronics store or Web site to learn more about digital pens. Compare their features, cost, file transfer process, and warranty. Write a report summarizing your findings, focusing on comparing and contrasting the digital pens. If required, submit your report to your instructor.

⑤ Ethics in Action <u>Internet addiction disorder</u> (IAD) may be affecting some Internet users. People claim to be addicted when they spend up to 10 hours a day online, they occasionally binge for extended Internet sessions, and they suffer withdrawal symptoms when they have not been online for some time. "Netomania" is not a recognized disorder, however, and some researchers believe the Internet problem is just a symptom of other psychiatric disorders, such as manic-depression. View online sites that provide information about IAD, including the Center for Online and Internet Addiction (netaddiction.com). Write a report summarizing your findings and include a table of links to Web sites that provide additional details. If required, submit your report to your instructor.

Case Studies

Use the Case Studies to apply the concepts presented in the chapter to real-world situations. Visit scsite.com/dc2006/ch6/cases to obtain more information pertaining to each exercise. To discuss the Case Studies in this chapter with other students, visit scsite.com/dc2006/ch6/forum and post your thoughts or questions.

Case Study 1 – Class Discussion   You are a manager of a 25-member telemarketing group. Your company provides desktop computers for each of the telemarketers. The current computers have 15-inch CRT monitors. The telemarketers have been complaining that the monitors are too small. Use the Web and/or print media to investigate the costs associated with upgrading the current monitors to 17-inch or 19-inch <u>flat-panel display devices</u>. What are the advantages and disadvantages of flat-panel display devices? What is the best screen size? Why? When you have finished reviewing flat-panel display device characteristics, write a brief report to your supervisor summarizing your recommendations. Include a list of the five factors you think are the most important to consider when purchasing a flat-panel display device. Be prepared to discuss your recommendations in class.

Case Study 2 — Class Discussion   The price of <u>laser printers</u> has dropped considerably over the past few years to a point where the price between a laser printer and ink-jet printer is not as significant as it once was. The company, at which you are employed as a buyer, has decided to upgrade the dot-matrix printers used by its administrative staff throughout the company to either ink-jet printers or laser printers. Your manager has asked you to send him a brief report that lists the advantages and disadvantages of purchasing an ink-jet printer and a laser printer. Include both initial and recurring cost estimates for both black-and-white and color printers. Be prepared to discuss your recommendations in class.

Case Study 3 — Research   Printing requirements vary greatly among users. The local insurance agency where you are employed part time is shopping for a <u>printer</u>. The owner is aware that you are taking a computer class and has asked you to assist her in making a decision on what printer to buy. Figure 6-12 on page 310 lists several questions that should be considered when choosing a printer. Use what you learned in class to answer the questions posed in Figure 6-12. Answer each question according to what you believe to be your employer's needs. Then, use the Web and/or print media to find at least two printers that fit the requirements. List the name of each printer and note their advantages and disadvantages. Which of the two printers would you buy? Why? Prepare a report and/or PowerPoint presentation and share your findings with your class.

Case Study 4 — Research   While printers produce an image on a page from top to bottom, <u>plotters</u> can draw on any part of a page at random, and then move on to any other part. This capability, coupled with their capacity to use large sheets of paper, makes plotters particularly valuable to people who produce maps or blueprints. A local engineering firm that has used hand drawings for the past 50 years has hired you to assist them in purchasing three 42-inch plotters with a maximum print length of 300 feet and at least 1200 × 600 dpi. What is the advantage or disadvantage of using a plotter compared to simply creating a drawing by hand? Use the Web and/or print media to research both the initial and recurring costs of plotters that meet the stated requirements from three different manufacturers. Include in your research how long each plotter takes to produce an image and other noteworthy information. Prepare a report and/or PowerPoint presentation summarizing your findings.

Case Study 5 — Team Challenge   Three accountants at the company you work for want to go off on their own and set up a small accounting office with approximately 20 to 25 employees. They have hired your group as consultants to help with the setup. The goal is to determine the type of output devices you think they will need within the office. Consider the types and number of printers, types and number of display devices, <u>audio devices</u>, microphones, LCD projectors, considerations for the physically challenged, and whether fax machines, fax modems, and/or multifunction peripherals are needed. Form a three-member team and assign each team member one or more categories of output devices. Have the team members use the Web and/or print media to research their assignments. Combine your findings in a table listing the advantages and disadvantages of the various devices, your team's recommendations, and a short explanation of why the team selected each device. Share your findings with your class.

Digital Imaging and Video Technology

Everywhere you look, people are capturing moments they want to remember. They take pictures or make movies of their vacations, birthday parties, activities, accomplishments, sporting events, weddings, and more. Because of the popularity of digital cameras and digital video cameras, increasingly more people desire to capture their memories digitally, instead of on film. With digital technology, photographers have the ability to modify and share the digital images and videos they create. When you use special hardware and/or software, you can copy, manipulate, print, and distribute digital images and videos using your personal computer and the Internet. Amateurs can create professional quality results by using more sophisticated hardware and software.

digital camera (input)

digital video camera (input)

FireWire or USB 2.0

television (output)

FIGURE 1 The top portion of the figure shows a typical home digital imaging setup, and the lower portion of the figure shows a typical home setup for editing personal video.

Digital photography and recordings deliver significant benefits over film-based photography and movie making. With digital cameras, no developing is needed. Instead, the images reside on storage media such as a hard disk, DVD, or flash memory card. Unlike film, storage media can be reused, which reduces costs, saves time, and provides immediate results. Digital technology allows greater control over the creative process, both while taking pictures and video and in the editing process. You can check results immediately after capturing a picture or video to determine whether it meets your expectations. If you are dissatisfied with a picture or video, you can erase it and recapture it, again and again.

As shown in the top portion of Figure 1, a digital camera functions as an input device when it transmits pictures through a cable to a personal computer via a USB port or FireWire port. Using a digital camera in this way allows you to edit the pictures, save them on storage media, and print them on a photographic-quality printer via a parallel port or USB port.

The lower portion of Figure 1 illustrates how you might use a digital video camera with a personal computer. The process typically is the same for most digital video cameras. You capture the images or video with the video camera. Next, you connect the video camera to your personal computer using a FireWire or USB 2.0 port, or you place the storage media used on the camera in the computer. The video then is copied or downloaded to the computer's hard disk. Then, you can edit the video using video editing software. If desired, you can preview the video during the editing process on a television. Finally, you save the finished result to the desired media, such as a VHS tape or DVD+RW or, perhaps, e-mail the edited video. In this example, a VCR and a DVD player also can be used to input video from a VHS tape or a DVD.

USB

USB

photographic-quality printer
(output)

personal computer

S-video-in

DVD recorder
(input, output, storage)

S-video

S-video-out

VCR (input, output, storage)

DIGITAL IMAGING TECHNOLOGY

Digital imaging technology involves capturing and manipulating still photographic images in an electronic format. The following sections outline the steps involved in the process of using digital imaging technology.

① Select a Digital Camera

A **digital camera** is a type of camera that stores photographed images electronically instead of on traditional film. Digital cameras are divided into three categories (Figure 2) based mainly on image resolution, features, and of course, price. The image resolution is measured in pixels (short for picture element). The image quality increases with the number of pixels. The image resolution usually is measured in **megapixels** (million of pixels), often abbreviated as **MP**. Features of digital cameras include red-eye reduction, zoom, autofocus, flash, self-timer, and manual mode for fine-tuning settings. Figure 3 summarizes the three categories of digital cameras.

TYPES OF DIGITAL CAMERAS

Type	Resolution Range	Features	Price
Point and shoot	Less than 6 MP	Fully automatic; fits in your pocket; easy to use; ideal for average consumer usage.	Less than $600
Field cameras	Greater than 5 MP	Used by photojournalists; portable but flexible; provides ability to change lenses and use other attachments; great deal of control over exposure and other photo settings.	$800 to $2,000
Studio cameras	Greater than 5 MP	Stationary camera used for professional studio work; flexible; widest range of lenses and settings.	$1,500 and up

FIGURE 3 Digital cameras often are categorized by image resolution, features, and price.

(a) point-and-shoot

(b) field

(c) studio

FIGURE 2 The point-and-shoot digital camera (a) requires no adjustments before shooting. The field digital camera (b) offers improved quality and features that allow you to make manual adjustments before shooting and use a variety of lenses. The studio digital camera (c) offers better color and resolution and greater control over exposure and lenses.

② Take Pictures

Digital cameras provide you with several options that are set before a picture is taken. Three of the more important options are the resolution, compression, and image file format in which the camera should save the picture. While a camera may allow for a very high resolution for a large print, you may choose to take a picture at a lower resolution if the image does not require great detail or must be a small size. For example, you may want to use the image on a Web page where smaller image file sizes are beneficial.

Compression results in smaller image file sizes. Figure 4 illustrates the image file sizes for varying resolutions and compressions under standard photographic conditions using a 4 megapixel digital camera. Figure 4 also shows the average picture size for a given resolution. The camera may take more time to save an image at lower compression, resulting in a longer delay before the camera is ready to take another picture. A higher compression, however, may result in some loss of image quality. If a camera has a 16 MB flash memory card, you can determine the number of pictures the card can hold by dividing 16 MB by the file size. Flash memory cards are available in sizes from 16 MB to 8 GB.

Most digital cameras also allow you to choose an image file format. Two popular file formats are TIFF and JPEG. The **TIFF** file format saves the image uncompressed. All of the image detail is captured and stored, but the file sizes can be large. The **JPEG** file format is compressed. The resolution of the image may be the same as a TIFF file, but some detail may be lost in the image.

Finally, before you take the photograph, you should choose the type of media on which to store the resulting image file. Some cameras allow for a choice of media to which you can store the image, such as a CompactFlash card or Memory Stick, while others allow for only one type of storage media. One major advantage of a digital camera is that you easily can erase pictures from its media, freeing up space for new pictures.

IMAGE FILE SIZE WITH A FOUR MEGAPIXEL DIGITAL CAMERA

Resolution in Pixels	COMPRESSION			Picture Size in Inches
	Low	Medium	High	
	Resulting Image File Size			
2272 × 1704	2 MB	1.1 MB	556 KB	11 by 17
1600 × 1200	1 MB	558 KB	278 KB	8 by 10
1024 × 768	570 KB	320 KB	170 KB	4 by 6
640 × 480	249 KB	150 KB	84 KB	3 by 5

FIGURE 4 Image file sizes for varying resolutions and compressions under standard photographic conditions using a 4 megapixel digital camera.

③ Transfer and Manage Image Files

The method of transferring images from the camera to the personal computer differs greatly depending on the capabilities of both. Digital cameras use a variety of storage media (Figure 5). If your camera uses a flash memory card such as a CompactFlash, Memory Stick, SmartMedia, or Secure Digital (SD), you can remove the media from the camera and place it in a slot on the personal computer or in a device, such as a card reader, connected to the personal computer. The Microdrive media shown in Figure 5 is a type of CompactFlash media. Your camera or card reader also may connect to the personal computer using a USB, USB 2.0, or FireWire (Figure 6) port. When you insert the memory card or connect the camera, software on the personal computer guides you through the process of transferring the images to the hard disk. Some operating systems and software recognize a memory card or camera as though it is another hard disk on the computer. This feature allows you to access the files, navigate them, and then copy, delete, or rename the files while the media still is in the camera.

After you transfer the files to the hard disk on your personal computer, you should organize the files by sorting them or renaming them so that information, such as the subject, date, time, and purpose, is saved along with the image. Finally, before altering the images digitally or using the images for other purposes, you should back up the images to another location, such as a CD or DVD, so the original image is recoverable.

FIGURE 5 Microdrives, CompactFlash, and Memory Sticks are popular storage devices for digital cameras.

FIGURE 6 Using a USB or FireWire connection, you can add a card reader to your personal computer.

④ Edit Images

Image editing software allows you to edit digital images. The following list summarizes the more common image enhancements or alterations:

- Adjust the contrast and brightness; correct lighting problems; or help give the photograph a particular feeling, such as warm or stark.
- Remove red-eye.
- Crop an image to remove unnecessary elements and resize it.
- Rotate the image to change its orientation.
- Add elements to the image, such as descriptive text, a date, a logo, or decorative items; create collages or add missing elements.
- Replace individual colors with a new color.
- Add special effects, such as texture or motion blurring to enhance the image.

Figure 7 shows some of the effects available in Jasc's Paint Shop Pro on the Artistic Effects submenu.

FIGURE 7 The capability of applying effects separates digital photography from film photography.

⑤ Print Images

Once an image is digitally altered, it is ready to be printed. You can print images on a personal color printer or send them to a professional service that specializes in digital photo printing.

When printing the images yourself, make sure that the resolution used to create the image was high enough for the size of the print you want to create. For example, if the camera used a resolution of 640 × 480 pixels, then the ideal print size is a wallet size. If you print such an image at a size of 8-by-10 inches, then the image will appear **pixilated**, or blurry. Use high-quality photo paper for the best results. A photo printer gives the best results when printing digital photography.

Many services print digital images, either over the Internet or through traditional photo developing locations and kiosks (Figure 8), such as those found in drug stores or shopping marts. Some services allow you to e-mail or upload the files to the service, specify the size, quality, and quantity of print; and then receive the finished prints via the postal service. Other services allow you to drop off flash memory cards, CD-ROMs, or floppy disks at a photo shop and later pick up the prints, just as you do with traditional photo developing shops.

FIGURE 8
A Pixel Magic Imaging Photo Ditto kiosk allows you to print digital images in high resolution on photo paper.

6 Distribute Images Electronically

Rather than printing images, you often need to use the images electronically. Depending on the electronic use of the image, the image may require additional processing. If you use the images on a Web site or want to e-mail a photo, you probably want to send a lower-resolution image. Image editing software allows you to lower the resolution of the image, resulting in a smaller file size. You also should use standard file formats when distributing an electronic photo. The JPEG format is viewable using most personal computers or Web browsers.

You can store very high resolution photos on a DVD or a CD. **DVD and CD mastering software** (Figure 9) allows you to create slide show presentations on a recordable DVD or CD that can play in many home DVD players or personal computer DVD drives.

Finally, you should back up and store images that you distribute electronically with the same care as you store your traditional film negatives.

FIGURE 9 Nero PhotoShow Elite and similar software applications allow you to create your own photo slide show on DVD or CD.

DIGITAL VIDEO TECHNOLOGY

Digital video technology allows you to input, edit, manage, publish, and share your videos using a personal computer. With digital video technology, you can transform home videos into Hollywood-style movies by enhancing the videos with scrolling titles and transitions, cutting out or adding scenes, and adding background music and voice-over narration. The following sections outline the steps involved in the process of using digital video technology.

1 Select a Video Camera

Video cameras record in either analog or digital format. **Analog formats** include 8mm, Hi8, VHS, VHS-C, and Super VHS-C. The last three formats use the types of tapes similar to those used in a standard VCR. **Digital formats** include Mini-DV, MICROMV, Digital8, and DVD. Consumer digital video cameras are by far the most popular type among consumers. They fall into three general categories: high-end consumer, consumer, and webcasting and monitoring (Figure 10). Digital video cameras provide more features than analog video cameras, such as a higher level of zoom, better sound, or greater control over color and lighting.

(a) high-end consumer

(b) consumer

(c) webcasting and monitoring

FIGURE 10 The high-end consumer digital video camera (a) can produce professional-grade results. The consumer digital video camera (b) produces amateur-grade results. The webcasting and monitoring digital video camera (c) is appropriate for webcasting and security monitoring.

2 Record a Video

Most video cameras provide you with a choice of recording programs, which sometimes are called automatic settings. Each recording program includes a different combination of camera settings, so you can adjust the exposure and other functions to match the recording environment. Usually, several different programs are available, such as point and shoot, point and shoot with manual adjustment, sports, portrait, spotlit scenes, and low light. You also have the ability to select special digital effects, such as fade, wipe, and black and white. If you are shooting outside on a windy day, then you can enable the wind screen to prevent wind noise. If you are shooting home videos, then the point-and-shoot recording program is sufficient.

3 Transfer and Manage Videos

After recording the video, the next step is to transfer the video to your personal computer. Most video cameras connect directly to a USB 2.0 or FireWire port on your personal computer (Figure 11). Transferring video with a digital camera is easy, because the video already is in a digital format that the computer can understand.

An analog camcorder or VCR requires additional hardware to convert the analog signals to a digital format before the video can be manipulated on a personal computer. The additional hardware includes a special video capture card using a standard RCA video cable or an S-video cable (Figure 12). *S-video* cables provide sharper

images and greater overall quality. When you use video capture hardware with an analog video, be sure to close all open programs on your computer because capturing video requires a great deal of processing power.

FIGURE 11 A digital video camera is connected to the personal computer via a FireWire or USB 2.0 port. No additional hardware is needed.

FIGURE 12 An analog camcorder or VCR is connected to the personal computer via an S-video port on a video capture card.

When transferring video, plan to use approximately 15 to 30 gigabytes of hard disk storage space per hour of digital video. A typical video project requires about four times the amount of raw footage as the final product. Therefore, at the high end, a video that lasts an hour may require up to 120 gigabytes of storage for the raw footage, editing process, and final video. This storage requirement can vary depending on the software you use to copy the video from the video camera to the hard disk and the format you select to save the video. For example, Microsoft claims that the latest version of its Windows Movie Maker can save 15 hours of video in 10 gigabytes when creating video for playback on a computer, but saves only 1 hour of video in 10 gigabytes when creating video for playback on a DVD or VCR.

The video transfer requires application software on the personal computer (Figure 13). Windows XP includes the Windows Movie Maker software that allows you to transfer the video from your video camera. Depending on the length of video and the type of connection used, the video may take a long time to download. Make certain that no other programs are running on your personal computer while transferring the video.

When transferring video, the software may allow you to choose a file format and a codec to store the video. A video **file format** holds the video information in a manner specified by a vendor, such as Apple or Microsoft. Three of the more popular file formats are listed in Figure 14.

File formats support codecs to encode the audio and video into the file formats. A particular file format may be able to store audio and video in a number of different codecs. A **codec** specifies how the audio and video is compressed and stored within the file. Figure 15 shows some options available for specifying a file format and codec in a video capture application. The dialog box in Figure 15 allows the user to determine whether the video is smoother in playback or if the video is more crisp, meaning that it includes more detail. The file format and codec you choose often is based on what you plan to do with the movie. For example, if you plan to stream video over the Web using RealNetworks software, the best choice for the file format is the RealMedia format, which uses the RealVideo codec.

After transferring the video to a personal computer, and before manipulating the video, you should store the video files in appropriate folders, named correctly, and backed up. Most video transfer application software helps manage these tasks.

POPULAR VIDEO FILE FORMATS

File Format	File Extensions
Apple QuickTime	.MOV or .QT
Microsoft Windows Media Video	.WMV or .ASF
RealNetworks RealMedia	.RM or .RAM

FIGURE 14 Apple, Microsoft, and RealNetworks offer the more popular video file formats.

FIGURE 13 Some video editing software allows you to transfer your video from any video source to a hard disk. This dialog box allows the user to set various video parameters for capturing video from a camera or other device.

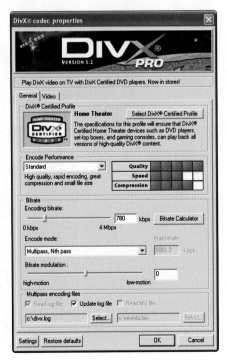

FIGURE 15 Video editing software applications allow you to specify a combination of file format and codec when saving a video.

4 Edit a Video

Once the video is stored on your hard disk, the next step is to edit, or manipulate, the video. If you used a video capture card to transfer analog video to your computer (Figure 12 on page 348), the files may require extra initial processing. When you use a video capture card, some of the video frames may be lost in the transfer process. Some video editing programs allow you to fix this problem with **frame rate correction** tools.

The first step in the editing process is to split the video into smaller pieces, or *scenes*, that you can manipulate more easily. This process is called *splitting*. Most video software automatically splits the video into scenes, thus sparing you the task. After splitting, you should cut out unwanted scenes or portions of scenes. This process is called *pruning*.

After you create the scenes you want to use in your final production, you edit each individual scene. You can *crop*, or change the size of, scenes. That is, you may want to cut out the top or a side of a scene that is irrelevant. You also can resize the scene. For example, you may be creating a video that will be displayed in a Web browser.

Making a smaller video, such as 320 × 200 pixels instead of 640 × 480 pixels, results in a smaller file that transmits faster over the Internet.

If video has been recorded over a long period, using different cameras or under different lighting conditions, the video may need color correction. *Color correction tools* (Figure 16) analyze your video and match brightness, colors, and other attributes of video clips to ensure a smooth look to the video.

You can add logos, special effects, or titles to scenes. You can place a company logo or personal logo in a video to identify yourself or the company producing the video. Logos often are added on the lower-right corner of a video and remain for the duration of the video. Special effects include warping, changing from color to black and white, morphing, or zoom motion. *Morphing* is a special effect in which one video image is transformed into another image over the course of several frames of video, creating the illusion of metamorphosis. You usually add titles at the beginning and end of a video to give the video context. A training video may have titles throughout the video to label a particular scene, or each scene may begin with a title.

FIGURE 16 Color correction tools in video editing software allow a great deal of control over the mood of your video creation.

The next step in editing a video is to add audio effects, including voice-over narration and background music. Many video editing programs allow you to add additional tracks, or *layers*, of sound to a video in addition to the sound that was recorded on the video camera. You also can add special audio effects.

The final step in editing a video is to combine the scenes into a complete video (Figure 17). This process involves ordering scenes and adding transition effects between scenes (Figure 18). Video editing software allows you to combine scenes and separate each scene with a transition. *Transitions* include fading, wiping, blurry, bursts, ruptures, erosions, and more.

FIGURE 17 In Windows Movie Maker 2, scenes, shown on the top, are combined into a sequence on the bottom of the screen.

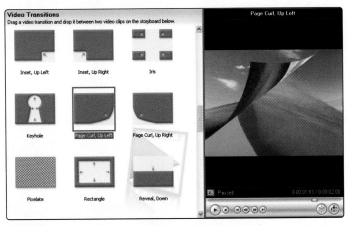

FIGURE 18 Smooth and dynamic transitions eliminate the hard cuts between scenes typically found in raw footage.

⑤ Distribute the Video

After editing the video, the final step is to distribute it or save it on an appropriate medium. You can save video in a variety of formats. Using special hardware, you can save the video on standard video tape. *A digital-to-analog converter* is necessary to allow your personal computer to transmit video to a VCR. A digital-to-analog converter may be an external device that connects to both the computer and input device, or may be a video capture card inside the computer.

Video also can be stored in digital formats in any of several DVD formats, on CD-R, or on video CD (VCD). *DVD* or *CD creation software*, which often is packaged with video editing software, allows you to create, or *master*, DVDs and CDs. You can add interactivity to your DVDs. For example, you can allow viewers to jump to certain scenes using a menu (Figure 19). A *video CD* (*VCD*) is a CD format that stores video on a CD-R that can be played in many DVD players.

You also can save your video creation in electronic format for distribution over the Web or via e-mail. Your video editing software must support the file format and codec you want to use. For example, RealNetworks's Helix media delivery system allows you to save media files in the RealVideo file formats.

Professionals use hardware and software that allow them to create a film version of digital video that can be played in movie theaters. This technology is becoming increasingly popular and has been used in such movies as the recent *Lord of the Rings* movies. Some Hollywood directors believe that eventually, all movies will be recorded and edited digitally.

After creating your final video for distribution or your personal video collection, you should backup the final video file. You can save your scenes for inclusion in other video creations or create new masters using different effects, transitions, and ordering of scenes.

FIGURE 19 DVD mastering software allows you to create interactive menus on your DVD.

CHAPTER SEVEN

Storage

Picture Yourself Working with Mobile Storage Media

At the end of the job interview, the supervisor asks, "When can you start?" You are thrilled to get this job with the local newspaper. The flexible hours are a perfect arrangement with your school schedule. As an added bonus, the job will give you experience toward your major — computer technology.

You will be working with the photojournalists in the office — more precisely, with their mobile media. The photojournalists take many pictures while on various assignments. All of them use digital cameras. Your job is to print pictures taken by the photojournalists. Because the photojournalists each use different makes and models of cameras, the digital pictures are stored on a variety of mobile media. Some of the cameras use flash memory cards such as CompactFlash cards, xD Picture cards, and Memory Sticks. One photojournalist transfers his pictures to a USB flash drive, from which you print the images. Some copy their pictures on a CD, and another gives you a Zip disk containing all her pictures.

After you receive the media, you insert it in the appropriate card reader, card slot, drive, or port. You then begin the process of storing the images on a hard disk and finally printing the images. The office has a very liberal personal use policy that allows you to print your own digital pictures during off-the-clock time — as long as you supply the paper. When you are away from the office, however, you print personal pictures using an in-store kiosk.

To learn about these various types of mobile media, read Chapter 7 and discover many other types of storage devices.

OBJECTIVES

After completing this chapter, you will be able to:

1. Differentiate between storage devices and storage media
2. Describe the characteristics of magnetic disks
3. Differentiate between floppy disks and Zip disks
4. Describe the characteristics of a hard disk
5. Describe the characteristics of optical discs
6. Differentiate among CD-ROMs, recordable CDs, rewritable CDs, DVD-ROMs, recordable DVDs, and rewritable DVDs
7. Identify the uses of tape
8. Discuss PC Cards and the various types of miniature mobile storage media
9. Identify uses of microfilm and microfiche

CONTENTS

STORAGE

Storage holds data, instructions, and information for future use. Every computer uses storage to hold system software and application software. To start up, a computer locates an operating system (system software) in storage and loads it into memory. When a user issues a command to start application software, such as a word processing program or a Web browser, the operating system locates the program in storage and loads it into memory.

In addition to programs, users store a variety of data and information on mainframe computers, servers, desktop computers, notebook computers, Tablet PCs, handheld computers, PDAs, and smart phones. For example, all types of users store digital photographs; appointments, schedules, and contact/address information; and correspondence, such as letters and e-mail messages. Other items stored by specific types of users include the following:

- The home user might also store budgets, bank statements, a household inventory, records of stock purchases, tax data, homework assignments, recipes, music, and videos.
- The small office/home office user also often stores faxes, business reports, financial records, tax data, travel records, customer orders, payroll records, inventory records, and Web pages.

floppy disk

Zip disk

microfiche

Storage

USB flash drive

flash memory card

PC Card

FIGURE 7-1 A variety of storage media.

- The mobile user usually also stores faxes, presentations, travel records, homework assignments, and quotations.
- The power user also stores diagrams, drawings, blueprints, designs, marketing literature, corporate newsletters, product catalogs, videos, audio recordings, multimedia presentations, and Web pages.
- The large business user also accesses many stored items such as tax data, inventory records, presentations, contracts, marketing literature, and Web pages. The large business user accesses hundreds or thousands of employee, customer, and vendor records, including data and information about orders, invoices, payments, and payroll.

Storage requirements among these users vary greatly. Home users, small office/home office users, and mobile users typically have much smaller storage requirements than the large business user or power user. For example, a home user may need 80 billion bytes of storage, while large businesses may require 50 trillion bytes of storage.

A **storage medium** (media is the plural), also called *secondary storage*, is the physical material on which a computer keeps data, instructions, and information. Examples of storage media are floppy disks, Zip disks, hard disks, CDs and DVDs, tape, PC Cards, flash memory cards, USB flash drives, and microfiche (Figure 7-1). Memory, by contrast, typically consists of one or more chips on the motherboard or some other circuit board in the computer.

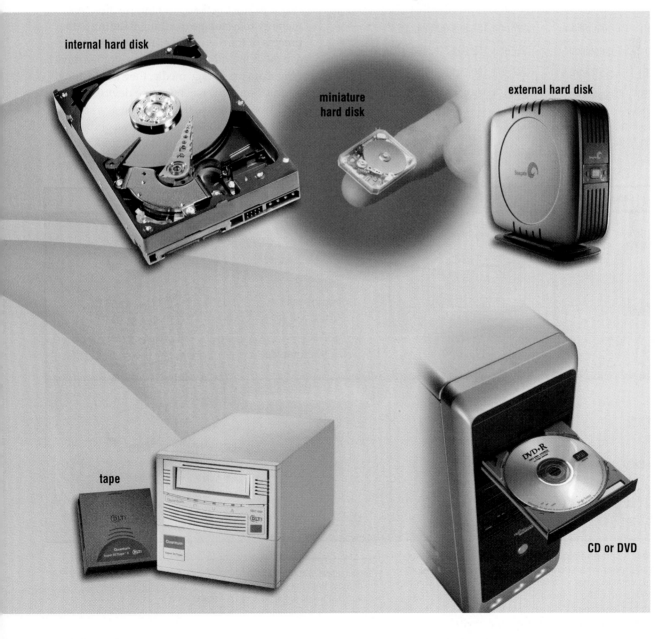

internal hard disk

miniature hard disk

external hard disk

tape

CD or DVD

Capacity is the number of bytes (characters) a storage medium can hold. Figure 7-2 identifies the terms manufacturers use to define the capacity of storage media. For example, a typical floppy disk can store up to 1.44 MB of data (approximately 1.4 million bytes) and a typical hard disk has 80 GB (approximately 80 billion bytes) of storage capacity.

Items on a storage medium remain intact even when power is removed from the computer. Thus, a storage medium is nonvolatile. Most memory, by contrast, holds data and instructions temporarily and thus is volatile. Figure 7-3 illustrates the concept of volatility. For an analogy, think of a filing cabinet that holds file folders as a storage medium, and the top of your desk as memory. When you want to work with a file, you remove it from the filing cabinet (storage medium) and place it on your desk (memory). When you are finished with the file, you remove it from your desk (memory) and return it to the filing cabinet (storage medium).

A **storage device** is the computer hardware that records and/or retrieves items to and from storage media. **Writing** is the process of transferring data, instructions, and information from memory to a storage medium. **Reading** is the process of transferring these items from a storage medium into memory. When storage devices write data on storage media, they are creating output. Similarly, when storage devices read from storage media, they function as a source of input. Nevertheless, they are categorized as storage devices, not as input or output devices.

STORAGE TERMS

Storage Term	Approximate Number of Bytes	Exact Number of Bytes
Kilobyte (KB)	1 thousand	2^{10} or 1,024
Megabyte (MB)	1 million	2^{20} or 1,048,576
Gigabyte (GB)	1 billion	2^{30} or 1,073,741,824
Terabyte (TB)	1 trillion	2^{40} or 1,099,511,627,776
Petabyte (PB)	1 quadrillion	2^{50} or 1,125,899,906,842,624
Exabyte (EB)	1 quintillion	2^{60} or 1,152,921,504,606,846,976
Zettabyte (ZB)	1 sextillion	2^{70} or 1,180,591,620,717,411,303,424
Yottabyte (YB)	1 septillion	2^{80} or 1,208,925,819,614,629,174,706,176

FIGURE 7-2 The capacity of a storage medium is measured by the amount of bytes it can hold.

AN ILLUSTRATION OF VOLATILITY

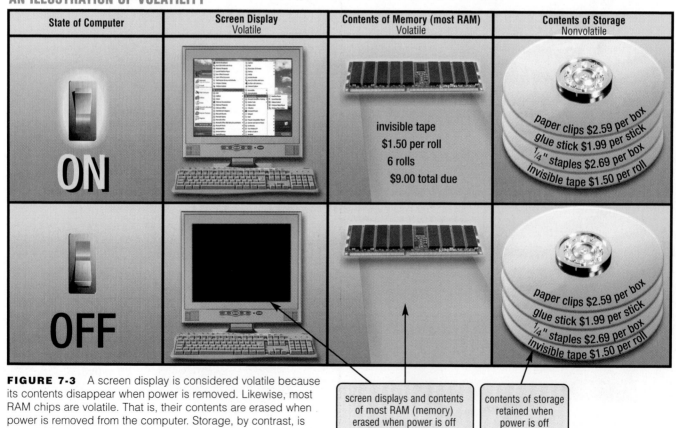

FIGURE 7-3 A screen display is considered volatile because its contents disappear when power is removed. Likewise, most RAM chips are volatile. That is, their contents are erased when power is removed from the computer. Storage, by contrast, is nonvolatile. Its contents remain when power is off.

screen displays and contents of most RAM (memory) erased when power is off

contents of storage retained when power is off

The speed of storage devices and memory is defined by access time. **Access time** measures (1) the amount of time it takes a storage device to locate an item on a storage medium or (2) the time required to deliver an item from memory to the processor. The access time of storage devices is slow, compared with the access time of memory. Memory (chips) accesses items in billionths of a second (nanoseconds). Storage devices, by contrast, access items in thousandths of a second (milliseconds).

Instead of, or in addition to access time, some manufacturers state a storage device's transfer rate because it affects access time. *Transfer rate* is the speed with which data, instructions, and information transfer to and from a device. Transfer rates for disks are stated in *KBps* (kilobytes per second) and *MBps* (megabytes per second).

Numerous types of storage media and storage devices exist to meet a variety of users' needs. Figure 7-4 shows how different types of storage media and memory compare in terms of transfer rates and uses. This chapter discusses these and other storage media.

FIGURE 7-4 A comparison of different types of storage media and memory in terms of relative speed and uses. Memory is faster than storage but is expensive and not practical for all storage requirements. Storage is less expensive but is slower than memory.

MAGNETIC DISKS

Magnetic disks use magnetic particles to store items such as data, instructions, and information on a disk's surface. Depending on how the magnetic particles are aligned, they represent either a 0 bit or a 1 bit. Recall from Chapter 4 that a bit (binary digit) is the smallest unit of data a computer can process. Thus, the alignment of the magnetic particles represents the data.

Before any data can be read from or written on a magnetic disk, the disk must be formatted. **Formatting** is the process of dividing the disk into tracks and sectors (Figure 7-5), so the operating system can store and locate data and information on the disk. A *track* is a narrow recording band that forms a full circle on the surface of the disk. The disk's storage locations consist of pie-shaped sections, which break the tracks into small arcs called *sectors*. On a magnetic disk, a sector typically stores up to 512 bytes of data.

For reading and writing purposes, sectors are grouped into clusters. A *cluster* is the smallest unit of disk space that stores data and information. Each cluster, also called an *allocation unit*, consists of two to eight sectors (the number varies depending on the operating system). Even if a file consists of only a few bytes, it uses an entire cluster. Each cluster holds data from only one file. One file, however, can span many clusters.

FIGURE 7-5 Tracks form circles on the surface of a magnetic disk. The disk's storage locations are divided into pie-shaped sections, which break the tracks into small arcs called sectors.

Sometimes, a sector has a flaw and cannot store data. When you format a disk, the operating system marks these bad sectors as unusable. For a technical discussion about formatting, read the High-Tech Talk article on page 382.

Three types of magnetic disks are floppy disks, Zip disks, and hard disks. Some of these disks are portable; others are not. With respect to a storage medium, the term *portable* means you can remove the medium from one computer and carry it to another computer. The following sections discuss specific types of magnetic disks.

Floppy Disks

A **floppy disk**, also called a *diskette*, is a portable, inexpensive storage medium that consists of a thin, circular, flexible plastic Mylar film with a magnetic coating enclosed in a square-shaped plastic shell. Although the exterior of current floppy disks is not bendable, users refer to this storage medium as a floppy disk because of the flexible film inside the rigid plastic 3.5-inch outer cover.

A standard floppy disk can store up to 500 double-spaced pages of text, several digital photographs, or a small audio file. Floppy disks are not as widely used as they were 15 years ago because of their low storage capacity. They are used, however, for specific applications. For example, some users work with floppy disks to transport small files to and from nonnetworked personal computers, such as from school or work to home.

A **floppy disk drive** is a device that reads from and writes on a floppy disk. A user inserts a floppy disk in and removes it from a floppy disk drive. Desktop personal computers and notebook computers may have a floppy disk drive installed inside the system unit (Figure 7-6a). Some computers use an *external floppy disk drive*, in which the drive is a separate device with a cable that plugs in a port on the system unit (Figure 7-6b). These external drives are attached to the computer only when the user needs to access items on a floppy disk.

If a personal computer has one floppy disk drive, it is named drive A. To read from or write on a floppy disk, a floppy disk drive must support that floppy disk's density. *Density* is the number of bits in an area on a storage medium. A disk with a higher density has more bits in an area and thus has a larger storage capacity. Most standard floppy disks today are high density (*HD*).

The average time it takes a current floppy disk drive to locate an item on a disk (access time) is 84 milliseconds, or approximately 1/12 of a second. The transfer rates range from 250 to 500 KBps.

You can read from and write on a floppy disk any number of times. To protect a floppy

FIGURE 7-6a (floppy disk drive installed inside a desktop computer)

FIGURE 7-6b (external floppy disk drive attached to computer with a cable)

FIGURE 7-6 Two types of floppy disk drives.

disk from accidentally being erased, the plastic outer shell on the disk contains a write-protect notch in its corner. A **write-protect notch** is a small opening that has a tab you slide to cover or expose the notch (Figure 7-7). If the write-protect notch is open, the drive cannot write on the floppy disk. If the write-protect notch is covered, or closed, the drive can write on the floppy disk. A floppy disk drive can read from a floppy disk whether the write-protect notch is open or closed. On the opposite corner, some floppy disks have a second opening without a small tab. This opening identifies the disk as a high-density floppy disk.

As mentioned earlier, a floppy disk is a type of magnetic media that stores data in tracks and sectors. A typical floppy disk stores data on both sides of the disk, has 80 tracks on each side of the recording surface, and has 18 sectors per track. To compute a disk's storage capacity, you multiply the number of sides on the disk, the number of tracks on the disk, the number of sectors per track, and the number of bytes in a sector. For example, the following is the formula for a high-density 3.5-inch floppy disk: 2 (sides) × 80 (tracks) × 18 (sectors per track) × 512 (bytes per sector) = 1,474,560 bytes (Figure 7-8). Disks often store system files in some tracks, which means the available capacity on a disk may be less than the total possible capacity.

CHARACTERISTICS OF A 3.5-INCH HIGH-DENSITY FLOPPY DISK

Capacity	1.44 MB
Sides	2
Tracks	80
Sectors per track	18
Bytes per sector	512
Sectors per disk	2,880

FIGURE 7-8   Most of today's personal computers use high-density disks.

Zip Disks

A **Zip disk** is a type of portable magnetic media that can store from 100 MB to 750 MB of data. The larger capacity Zip disks hold about 500 times more than a standard floppy disk. These large capacities make it easy to transport many files or large items such as graphics, audio, or video files. Another popular use of Zip disks is to back up important data and information. A **backup** is a duplicate of a file, program, or disk that you can use in case the original is lost, damaged, or destroyed. Chapter 8 discusses backup utilities.

Zip disks are slightly larger than and about twice as thick as a 3.5-inch floppy disk. A **Zip drive** is a high-capacity disk drive developed by Iomega Corporation that reads from and writes on a Zip disk (Figure 7-9). These drives cannot read standard 3.5-inch floppy disks.

Many users prefer to purchase an external Zip drive, which connects to a USB port or FireWire port on the system unit. The external Zip drive is convenient for users with multiple computers, because it allows them to move the drive from computer to computer as needed. As an alternative, some users prefer to order a computer with a built-in Zip drive.

WEB LINK 7-1

Floppy Disks
For more information, visit scsite.com/dc2006/ch7/weblink and then click Floppy Disks.

WEB LINK 7-2

Zip Disks
For more information, visit scsite.com/dc2006/ch7/weblink and then click Zip Disks.

Zip disk

FIGURE 7-9   An external Zip drive and Zip disk.

write-protected

not write-protected

hole on this side means disk is high density

notch open means you cannot write on the disk

notch closed means you can write on the disk

FIGURE 7-7   To protect data from being erased accidentally, floppy disks have a write-protect notch. By sliding a small tab, you either can cover or expose the notch.

Hard Disks

A **hard disk**, also called a *hard disk drive*, is a storage device that contains one or more inflexible, circular platters that magnetically store data, instructions, and information. Home users store documents, spreadsheets, presentations, databases, e-mail messages, Web pages, digital photographs, music, videos, and software on hard disks. Businesses use hard disks to store correspondence, reports, financial records, e-mail messages, customer orders and invoices, payroll records, inventory records, presentations, contracts, marketing literature, schedules, and Web sites.

The system unit on most desktop and notebook computers contains at least one hard disk. The entire device is enclosed in an airtight, sealed case to protect it from contamination. A hard disk that is mounted inside the system unit sometimes is called a *fixed disk* because it is not portable (Figure 7-10). Portable hard disks are discussed later in this chapter.

Current personal computer hard disks have storage capacities from 40 to 300 GB and more (read Looking Ahead 7-1 for a look at the next generation of hard disk storage capacities).

Hard disks are read/write storage media. That is, you can read from and write on a hard disk any number of times. If the computer contains only one hard disk, the operating system designates it as drive C. Additional hard disks are assigned the next available drive letter.

FAQ 7-1

Have personal computer hard disk capacities grown much since their inception?

Yes, hard disk capacities have grown phenomenally over the past several years, as shown in the chart below. This trend is expected to continue at a rate of 60 percent annually. For more information, visit scsite.com/dc2006/ch7/faq and then click Hard Disk Capacities.

Personal Computer Hard Disk Growth
(Historical and Projected)

LOOKING AHEAD 7-1

Heat Increases Disk Capacity

Things are heating up in the data storage industry. Engineers at IBM Research are testing the use of heat to record data inexpensively on magnetic media, such as hard disks.

Within the next ten years, the researchers predict that this new technique will allow storage of more than one terabit per square inch; today's magnetic media can store approximately 60 gigabits per square inch. With this capacity, a hard disk drive that can store seven terabits will be commonplace.

IBM calls this new storage system *Millipede*. It uses heated tips mounted on the ends of cantilevers, in a fashion similar to the way the stylus on an old phonograph sat on the grooves of vinyl records. For more information, visit scsite.com/dc2006/ch7/looking and then click Heated Storage.

front of system unit

FIGURE 7-10 The hard disk in a desktop personal computer is enclosed inside an airtight, sealed case inside the system unit.

CHARACTERISTICS OF A HARD DISK

Characteristics of a hard disk include its capacity, platters, read/write heads, cylinders, sectors and tracks, revolutions per minute, transfer rate, and access time. Figure 7-11 shows characteristics of a sample 120 GB hard disk. The following paragraphs discuss each of these characteristics.

The capacity of a hard disk is determined from the number of platters it contains, together with composition of the magnetic coating on the platters. A *platter* is made of aluminum, glass, or ceramic and is coated with an alloy material that allows items to be recorded magnetically

on its surface. The coating usually is three millionths of an inch thick.

On desktop computers, platters most often have a *form factor*, or size, of approximately 3.5 inches in diameter; on notebook computers and mobile devices, the form factor is 2.5 inches or less. A typical hard disk has multiple platters stacked on top of one another. Each platter has two read/write heads, one for each side. The hard disk has arms that move the read/write heads to the proper location on the platter (Figure 7-12). A *read/write head* is the mechanism that reads items and writes items in the drive as it barely touches the disk's recording surface.

SAMPLE HARD DISK CHARACTERISTICS

Advertised capacity	120 GB
Platters	3
Read/write heads	6
Cylinders	16,383
Bytes per sector	512
Sectors per track	63
Sectors per drive	234,441,648
Revolutions per minute	7,200
Transfer rate	133 MB per second
Access time	8.9 ms

FIGURE 7-11 Characteristics of a sample 120 GB hard disk. The actual disk's capacity sometimes is different from the advertised capacity because of bad sectors on the disk.

FIGURE 7-12 HOW A HARD DISK WORKS

Step 1:
The circuit board controls the movement of the head actuator and a small motor.

Step 2:
A small motor spins the platters while the computer is running.

Step 3:
When software requests a disk access, the read/write heads determine the current or new location of the data.

Step 4:
The head actuator positions the read/write head arms over the correct location on the platters to read or write data.

The location of the read/write heads often is referred to by its cylinder. A *cylinder* is the vertical section of a track that passes through all platters (Figure 7-13). A single movement of the read/write head arms accesses all the platters in a cylinder. If a hard disk has two platters (four sides), each with 1,000 tracks, then it will have 1,000 cylinders with each cylinder consisting of 4 tracks (2 tracks for each platter).

While the computer is running, the platters in the hard disk rotate at a high rate of speed. This spinning, which usually is 5,400 to 15,000 *revolutions per minute* (*rpm*), allows nearly instant access to all tracks and sectors on the platters. The platters typically continue to spin until power is removed from the computer. (On many computers, the hard disk stops spinning after a specified time to save power.) The spinning motion creates a cushion of air between the platter and its read/write head. This cushion ensures that the read/write head floats above the platter instead of making direct contact with the platter surface. The distance between the read/write head and the platter is about two millionths of one inch.

As shown in Figure 7-14, this close clearance leaves no room for any type of contamination. Dirt, hair, dust, smoke, and other particles could cause the hard disk to have a head crash. A *head crash* occurs when a read/write head touches the surface of a platter, usually resulting in a loss of data or sometimes loss of the entire drive. Although current internal hard disks are built to withstand shocks and are sealed tightly to keep out contaminants, head crashes do occasionally still occur. Thus, it is crucial that you back up your hard disk regularly. Chapter 8 discusses backup techniques.

Depending on the type of hard disk, transfer rates range from 15 MBps to 320 MBps. Access time for today's hard disks ranges from approximately 3 to 12 ms (milliseconds). The average hard disk access time is at least seven times faster than the average floppy disk drive.

FIGURE 7-13 A cylinder is the vertical section of track through all platters on a hard disk.

FIGURE 7-14 The clearance between a disk read/write head and the platter is about two millionths of an inch. A smoke particle, dust particle, human hair, or other contaminant could render the drive unusable.

Hard disks improve their access time by using disk caching. *Disk cache* (pronounced cash), sometimes called a buffer, consists of a memory chip(s) on a hard disk that stores frequently accessed items such as data, instructions, and information (Figure 7-15). Disk cache and memory cache work in a similar fashion. When a processor requests data, instructions, or information from the hard disk, the hard disk first checks its disk cache — before moving any mechanical parts to access the platters. If the requested item is in disk cache, the hard disk sends it to the processor. If the hard disk does not find the requested item in the disk cache, then the processor must wait for the hard disk to locate and transfer the item from the disk to the processor. Hard disks today contain between 2 MB and 16 MB of disk cache. The greater the disk cache, the faster the hard disk.

FIGURE 7-15   HOW DISK CACHE WORKS

processor

Step 3:
The controller transfers the requested item to the processor.

Step 2b:
If the controller does not find the requested item in disk cache, it locates the requested item on the hard disk's platters.

Step 1:
A special-purpose chip on the hard disk, called a controller, receives a request for data, instructions, or information from the processor.

disk cache

controller

Step 2a:
The controller first checks disk cache for the requested item.

MINIATURE HARD DISKS   Many mobile devices and consumer electronics include miniature hard disks, which provide users with greater storage capacities than flash memory. These tiny hard disks, some of which have form factors of less than 1 inch (Figure 7-16), are found in devices such as music players, digital cameras, smart phones, and PDAs. Miniature hard disks have storage capacities that range from 2 GB to 100 GB.

FIGURE 7-16   This hard disk has a form factor of 0.85 inch and storage capacities up to 4 GB.

PORTABLE HARD DISKS Portable hard disks either are external or removable and have storage capacities up to 250 GB or higher.

An **external hard disk**, shown in the top picture in Figure 7-17, is a separate free-standing hard disk that connects with a cable to a USB port or FireWire port on the system unit. As with the internal hard disk, the entire hard disk is enclosed in an airtight, sealed case.

A **removable hard disk** is a hard disk that you insert and remove from either a dock or a drive. Sometimes the dock or drive is built in the system unit. Others are external devices that connect with a cable to a USB port or FireWire port on the system unit. Removable hard disks that insert in a dock are self-contained units, similar to external hard disks. Removable hard disks that insert in a

drive, shown in the bottom picture in Figure 7-17, operate in a manner similar to a floppy disk drive, reading from and writing on the removable hard disk.

External hard disks and removable hard disks offer the following advantages over internal hard disks (fixed disks):
- Transport a large number of files
- Back up important files or an entire internal hard disk
- Easily store large audio and video files
- Secure your data; for example, at the end of a work session, remove the hard disk and lock it up, leaving no data in the computer
- Add storage space to a notebook computer or Tablet PC
- Add storage space to a desktop computer without having to open the system unit
- Share a drive with multiple computers

As the prices of portable hard disks drop, increasingly more users will purchase one to supplement a home or office internal hard disk. Keep in mind, though, that external or removable hard disks transfer data at slower rates than internal hard disks.

HARD DISK CONTROLLERS A *disk controller* consists of a special-purpose chip and electronic circuits that control the transfer of data, instructions, and information from a disk to and from the system bus and other components in the computer. That is, it controls the interface between the hard disk and the system bus. A disk controller for a hard disk, called the hard disk controller, may be part of a hard disk or the motherboard, or it may be a separate adapter card inside in the system unit.

In their personal computer advertisements, vendors usually state the type of hard disk interface supported by the hard disk controller. Thus, you should understand the types of available hard disk interfaces. In addition to USB and FireWire (external hard disk interfaces), three other types of hard disk interfaces for internal use in personal computers are SATA, EIDE, and SCSI.
- *SATA (Serial Advanced Technology Attachment)*, the newest type of hard disk interface, uses serial signals to transfer data, instructions, and information. The primary advantage of SATA interfaces is their cables are thinner, longer, more flexible, and less susceptible to interference than cables used by hard disks

external hard disk

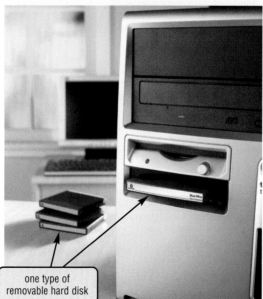

one type of removable hard disk

FIGURE 7-17 Examples of portable hard disks.

that use parallel signals. SATA interfaces have data transfer rates of up to 300 MBps. In addition to hard disks, SATA interfaces support connections to CD and DVD drives.

- *EIDE* (*Enhanced Integrated Drive Electronics*) is a hard disk interface that uses parallel signals to transfer data, instructions, and information. EIDE interfaces can support up to four hard disks at 137 GB per disk. These interfaces have data transfer rates up to 100 MBps. EIDE interfaces also provide connections for CD and DVD drives and tape drives. Some manufacturers market their EIDE interfaces as Fast ATA or Ultra ATA.

- *SCSI* interfaces, which also use parallel signals, can support up to eight or fifteen peripheral devices. Supported devices include hard disks, CD and DVD drives, tape drives, printers, scanners, network cards, and much more. Recall from Chapter 4 that SCSI is an acronym for Small Computer System Interface. Some computers have a built-in SCSI interface, while others use an adapter card to add a SCSI interface. SCSI interfaces provide up to 320 MBps data transfer rates.

FAQ 7-3

What are the transfer rates of USB and FireWire?

USB 2.0, also called *Hi-Speed USB*, has transfer rates up to 480 *Mbps* (megabits per second). FireWire has transfer rates up to 800 Mbps. For more information, visit scsite.com/dc2006/ch7/faq and then click USB and FireWire.

MAINTAINING DATA STORED ON A HARD DISK
Most manufacturers guarantee their hard disks to last approximately three to five years. Many last much longer with proper care. To prevent the loss of items stored on a hard disk, you regularly should perform preventive maintenance such as defragmenting or scanning the disk for errors. Chapter 8 discusses these and other utilities in depth.

ONLINE STORAGE Some users choose online storage instead of storing data locally on a hard disk. **Online storage** is a service on the Web that provides hard disk storage to computer users,

usually for a minimal monthly fee (Figure 7-18). Fee arrangements for use of these Internet hard disks vary. For example, one online storage service charges $10 per month for 5 GB of storage. Many offer free trial periods.

Users subscribe to an online storage service for a variety of reasons:

- To access files on the Internet hard disk from any computer or device that has Internet access
- To store large audio, video, and graphics files on an Internet hard disk instantaneously, instead of spending time downloading to a local hard disk
- To allow others to access files on their Internet hard disk so others can listen to an audio file, watch a video clip, or view a picture — instead of e-mailing the file to them
- To view time-critical data and images immediately while away from the main office or location; for example, doctors can view x-ray images from another hospital, home, or office, or while on vacation
- To store offsite backups of data (Chapter 8 presents this and other backup strategies)

Once users subscribe to the online storage service, they can save on the Internet hard disk in the same manner they save on their local hard disk or any other drive.

FIGURE 7-18 An example of one Web site advertising its online storage service.

Test your knowledge of pages 354 through 365 in Quiz Yourself 7-1.

QUIZ YOURSELF 7-1

Instructions: Find the true statement below. Then, rewrite the remaining false statements so they are true.

1. Floppy disks are a type of optical disc.

2. Hard disks contain one or more inflexible, circular platters that magnetically store data, instructions, and information.

3. SATA is a hard disk interface that uses parallel signals to transfer data, instructions, and information.

4. Storage media is the computer hardware that records and/or retrieves items to and from a storage device.

5. Three types of manual disks are floppy disks, Zip disks, and hard disks.

6. Users can move an internal Zip drive from computer to computer as needed by connecting the drive to a USB port or FireWire port on the system unit.

Quiz Yourself Online: To further check your knowledge of storage devices and storage media, magnetic disks, floppy disks, Zip disks, and hard disks, visit scsite.com/dc2006/ch7/quiz and then click Objectives 1 – 4.

OPTICAL DISCS

An *optical disc* is a type of storage media that consists of a flat, round, portable disc made of metal, plastic, and lacquer that is written and read by a laser. (Recall from Chapter 1 that the term disk is used for magnetic media, and disc is used for optical media.) Optical discs used in personal computers are 4.75 inches in diameter and less than one-twentieth of an inch thick. Smaller computers and devices, however, use *mini discs* that have a diameter of 3 inches or less.

Optical discs primarily store software, data, digital photographs, movies, and music. Some optical disc formats are read only, meaning users cannot write (save) on the media. Others are read/write, which allows users to save on the disc just as they save on a hard disk.

Nearly every personal computer today has some type of optical disc drive installed in a drive bay. On these drives, you push a button to slide out a tray, insert the disc, and then push the same button to close the tray (Figure 7-19). Other convenient features on most of these drives include a volume control button and a headphone port (or jack) so you can use head-phones to listen to audio without disturbing others nearby.

With some discs, you can read and/or write on one side only. Manufacturers usually place a silk-screened label on the top layer of these single-sided discs. You insert a single-sided disc in the drive with the label side up. Other discs are double-sided. Simply remove the disc from the drive, flip it over, and reinsert it in the drive

Push the button to slide out the tray.

Insert the disc, label side up.

Push the same button to close the tray.

FIGURE 7-19   On optical disc drives, you push a button to slide out a tray, insert the disc, and then push the same button to close the tray.

to use the other side of the disc. Double-sided discs often have no label; instead each side of the disc is identified with small writing around the center of the disc.

The drive designation of an optical disc drive usually follows alphabetically after that of all the hard disks and portable disks. For example, if the computer has one hard disk (drive C), a Zip disk drive (drive D), and an external hard disk (drive E), then the first optical disc drive is drive F. A second optical disc drive would be drive G.

Optical discs store items by using microscopic pits (indentations) and lands (flat areas) that are in the middle layer of the disc (Figure 7-20). A high-powered laser light creates the pits. A lower-powered laser light reads items from the disc by reflecting light through the bottom of the disc, which usually is either solid gold or silver in color. The reflected light is converted into a series of bits the computer can process. A land causes light to reflect, which is read as binary digit 1. Pits absorb the light; this absence of light is read as binary digit 0.

Optical discs commonly store items in a single track that spirals from the center of the disc to the edge of the disc. As with a hard disk, this single track is divided into evenly sized sectors on which items are stored (Figure 7-21).

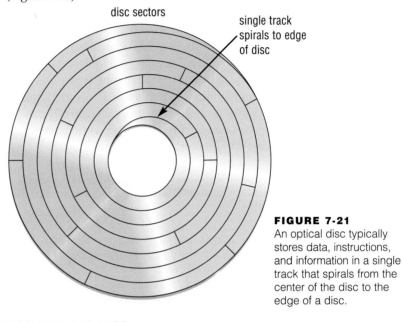

disc sectors

single track spirals to edge of disc

FIGURE 7-21
An optical disc typically stores data, instructions, and information in a single track that spirals from the center of the disc to the edge of a disc.

FIGURE 7-20   HOW A LASER READS DATA ON AN OPTICAL DISC

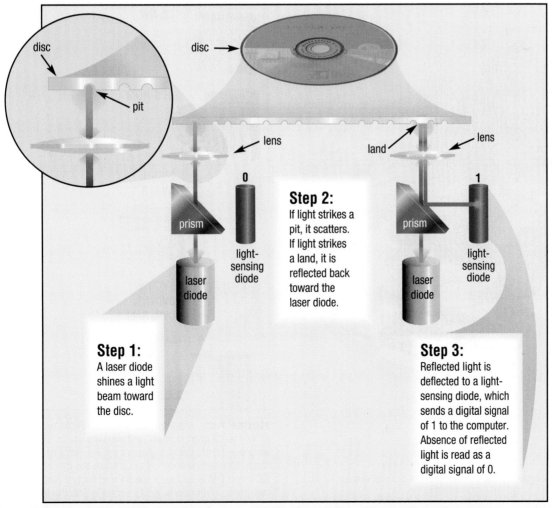

disc

disc

pit

lens

land

lens

0

1

prism

prism

light-sensing diode

light-sensing diode

laser diode

laser diode

Step 2:
If light strikes a pit, it scatters. If light strikes a land, it is reflected back toward the laser diode.

Step 1:
A laser diode shines a light beam toward the disc.

Step 3:
Reflected light is deflected to a light-sensing diode, which sends a digital signal of 1 to the computer. Absence of reflected light is read as a digital signal of 0.

Care of Optical Discs

Manufacturers claim that a properly cared for high-quality optical disc will last 5 years but could last up to 100 years. Figure 7-22 offers some guidelines for the proper care of optical discs. Never bend a disc; it may break. Do not expose discs to extreme temperatures or humidity. The ideal temperature range for disc storage is 50 to 70 degrees Fahrenheit. Stacking discs, touching the underside of discs, or exposing them to any type of contaminant may scratch a disc. Place an optical disc in its protective case, called a *jewel box*, when you are finished using it and store in an upright (vertical) position.

FAQ 7-4

Can I clean a disc?

Yes, you can remove dust, dirt, smudges, and fingerprints from the surface of an optical disc. Moisten a soft cloth with warm water or rubbing alcohol and then wipe the disc in straight lines from the center outward. You also can repair scratches on the surface with a specialized disc repair kit. For more information, visit scsite.com/dc2006/ch7/faq and then click Cleaning and Repairing Discs.

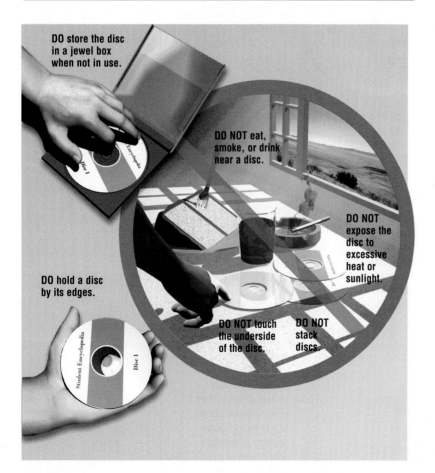

DO store the disc in a jewel box when not in use.

DO NOT eat, smoke, or drink near a disc.

DO NOT expose the disc to excessive heat or sunlight.

DO hold a disc by its edges.

DO NOT touch the underside of the disc.

DO NOT stack discs.

FIGURE 7-22   Some guidelines for the proper care of optical discs.

Types of Optical Discs

Many different formats of optical discs exist today. Two general categories are CDs and DVDs, with DVDs having a much greater storage capacity than CDs. Specific formats include CD-ROM, CD-R, CD-RW, DVD-ROM, DVD-R, DVD+R, DVD-RW, DVD+RW, and DVD+RAM. Figure 7-23 identifies each of these optical disc formats and specifies whether a user can read from the disc, write to the disc, and/or erase the disc. The following sections describe characteristics unique to each of these disc formats.

OPTICAL DISC FORMATS

Optical Disc		Read	Write	Erase
	CD-ROM	Y	N	N
	CD-R	Y	Y	N
	CD-RW	Y	Y	Y
	DVD-ROM	Y	N	N
	DVD-R DVD+R	Y	Y	N
	DVD-RW DVD+RW DVD+RAM	Y	Y	Y

FIGURE 7-23   Manufacturers sell CD-ROM and DVD-ROM media prerecorded (written) with audio, video, and software. Users cannot change the contents of these discs. Users, however, can purchase the other formats of CDs and DVDs as blank media and record (write) their own data, instructions, and information on these discs.

CD-ROMs

A **CD-ROM** (pronounced SEE-DEE-rom), or *compact disc read-only memory*, is a type of optical disc that users can read but not write (record) or erase — hence, the name read-only. Manufacturers write the contents of standard CD-ROMs. A standard CD-ROM is called a *single-session disc* because manufacturers write all items on the disc at one time. Software manufacturers often distribute their programs using CD-ROMs (Figure 7-24).

A typical CD-ROM holds from 650 MB to 1 GB of data, instructions, and information. This is equivalent to about 450 high-density 3.5-inch floppy disks.

To read a CD-ROM, insert the disc in a **CD-ROM drive** or a CD-ROM player. Because audio CDs and CD-ROMs use the same laser technology, you may be able to use a CD-ROM drive to listen to an audio CD while working on the computer. Some music companies, however, configure their CDs so the music will not play on a computer. They do this to protect themselves from customers illegally copying and sharing the music. Read At Issue 7-1 for a related discussion.

The speed of a CD-ROM drive determines how fast it installs programs and accesses the disc. Original CD-ROM drives were single-speed drives with transfer rates of 150 KBps (kilobytes per second). Manufacturers measure all optical disc drives relative to this original CD-ROM drive. They use an X to denote the original transfer rate of 150 KBps. For example, a 48X CD-ROM drive has a data transfer rate of 7,200 (48 × 150) KBps, or 7.2 MBps.

Current CD-ROM drives have transfer rates, or speeds, ranging from 48X to 75X or faster. The higher the number, the faster the CD-ROM drive. Faster CD-ROM drives are more expensive than slower drives.

WEB LINK 7-5

CD-ROMs

For more information, visit scsite.com/dc2006/ch7/weblink and then click CD-ROMs.

AT ISSUE 7-1

Does Music Sharing Harm CD Sales?

With over a billion songs illegally available on file sharing networks, such as Kazaa, the music industry claims that sharing music is harming CD sales, which results in less money in the artists' pockets. A recent study by researchers at Harvard University and the University of North Carolina showed that the availability and sharing of recent CD releases did not have an effect on the sales of the CDs. The researchers found that those who obtained the music from the Internet were often the least likely to purchase the CDs in the first place. While record companies have seen a modest decline in sales since the advent of music sharing, they have released significantly fewer titles, and some claim that the quality of music has declined. Also, CD sales may have been exceptionally high in the 1990s as people replaced older media, such as cassette tapes and vinyl albums, with the newer CD format. While clearly in violation of the music publishers' copyright, does music sharing harm CD sales? Why? Is it possible that music sharing actually results in higher sales for record companies in some cases? Why or why not? What are some possible strategies the music industry can adopt in response to the music sharing phenomenon?

FIGURE 7-24 Encyclopedias, games, simulations, and many other programs are distributed on CD-ROM.

PICTURE CDs   A Kodak **Picture CD** is a single-session CD-ROM that stores digital versions of a single roll of film using a jpg file format. Many film developers offer Picture CD service for consumers when they drop off film to be developed. That is, in addition to printed photographs and negatives, you also receive a Picture CD containing the film's pictures. The resolution of images stored on a Picture CD usually is 1024 × 1536 pixels. The additional cost for a Picture CD is about $10 per roll of film.

Most optical disc drives can read a Picture CD. Using photo editing software and photographs on the Picture CD, you can remove red eye, crop the photograph, enhance colors, trim away edges, adjust the lighting, and edit just about any aspect of a photograph. In addition, a Picture CD allows you to print copies of the photographs on glossy paper with an ink-jet printer. If you do not have a printer to print the images, many stores have kiosks at which you can print pictures from a Picture CD (Figure 7-25).

WEB LINK 7-6

Picture CDs

For more information, visit scsite.com/ dc2006/ch7/weblink and then click Picture CDs.

FAQ 7-5

How do I share my digital pictures with others?

You can send them as e-mail attachments, copy them to online storage, or post them to a personal Web page or a photo community. At a *photo community*, users can create online photo albums and share their digital photographs on the Web. Some photo communities provide free, unlimited storage space; others charge a nominal fee. For more information, visit scsite.com/dc2006/ch7/faq and then click Photo Communities.

FIGURE 7-25   HOW A PICTURE CD WORKS

Step 1:
Drop off the film to be developed. Mark the Picture CD box on the film-processing envelope.

Step 2:
When you pick up prints and negatives, a Picture CD contains digital images of each photograph.

Step 3:
At home, print images from the Picture CD on your ink-jet or photo printer. At a store, print images from the Picture CD at a kiosk.

CD-Rs and CD-RWs

A **CD-R** (*compact disc-recordable*) is a multisession optical disc on which users can write, but not erase, their own items such as text, graphics, and audio. *Multisession* means you can write on part of the disc at one time and another part at a later time. Each part of a CD-R, however, can be written on only one time, and the disc's contents cannot be erased.

Writing on the CD-R requires a *CD recorder* or a **CD-R drive**. A CD-R drive usually can read both audio CDs and standard CD-ROMs. These drives read at speeds of 48X or more and write at speeds of 40X or more. Manufacturers often list the write speed first, for example, as 40/48.

A **CD-RW** (*compact disc-rewritable*) is an erasable multisession disc you can write on multiple times. CD-RW overcomes the major disadvantage of CD-R because it allows users to write and rewrite data, instructions, and information on the CD-RW disc multiple times — instead of just once. Reliability of the disc tends to drop, however, with each successive rewrite.

To write on a CD-RW disc, you must have CD-RW software and a **CD-RW drive**. These drives have write speeds of 52X or more, rewrite speeds of 24X or more, and read speeds of 52X or more. Manufacturers state the speeds in this order; that is, write speed, rewrite speed, and read speed is stated as 52/24/52. Most CD-RW drives can read audio CDs, CD-ROMs, CD-Rs, and CD-RWs.

Many personal computers today include a CD-RW drive as a standard feature so users can burn their own discs. The process of writing on an optical disc is called *burning*. Some operating systems, such as Windows XP, include the capability of burning discs.

Using a CD-RW disc, users easily back up large files from a hard disk. Another popular use of CD-RW and CD-R discs is to create audio CDs. For example, users can record their own music and save it on a CD, purchase and download MP3 songs from the Web, or rearrange tracks on a purchased music CD. The process of copying an individual song from a purchased audio CD and converting it to a digital format is called *ripping*. Read At Issue 7-2 for a related discussion.

WEB LINK 7-7

CD-Rs and CD-RWs
For more information, visit scsite.com/ dc2006/ch7/weblink and then click CD-Rs and CD-RWs.

FAQ 7-6

Is it legal to copy songs to a CD?

It is legal to copy songs from an audio CD that you obtained legally, if you use the copied music for your own personal use. If you share the copy with a friend, however, you are violating copyright law. It is legal to download copyrighted music if the song's copyright holder has granted permission for users to download and play the song. In most cases, you pay a fee for the song. For more information, visit scsite.com/dc2006/ch7/faq and then click Copying Music.

AT ISSUE 7-2

Is It Ethical to Copy CDs or DVDs?

A musician's recent release quickly became the second most-played CD in computer CD drives — before the CD even appeared on store shelves. CD-R and DVD-R technology makes copying music and movies easy and affordable. People use CD-R and DVD-R technology to copy CDs and DVDs they have purchased, borrowed, or pirated on the Internet. At some campuses, students use college servers to create music Web sites, download copyrighted music, and then record and distribute unauthorized copies. The recording industry claims this practice is unfair to the industry and, in essence, steals from the recording artists. Others, however, insist that bootlegged music actually is a marketing vehicle, influencing listeners who pay to attend concerts eventually to purchase the CD. The music industry has gone as far as placing technology on CDs that makes them impossible or very difficult to copy. Opponents to this practice say that these measures infringe on the CD owner's right to fair use, such as making personal backup copies, which courts have upheld as exceptions to copyright laws. Is it ethical to download and copy portions of a music CD, or an entire music CD, from the Internet? Why? If you purchase a CD, is it ethical to make copies for yourself? For a friend? Why? Should recording or movie companies be able to use formatting techniques to keep people from copying CDs or DVDs? What practices should be allowed within the doctrine of fair use?

DVD-ROMs

A **DVD-ROM** (*digital versatile disc-read-only memory* or *digital video disc-read-only memory*) is an extremely high-capacity optical disc on which users can read but not write or erase. Manufacturers write the contents of DVD-ROMs and distribute them to consumers. DVD-ROMs store movies, music, music videos, huge databases, and complex software (Figure 7-26).

The storage capacity of a DVD-ROM is more than enough to hold a telephone book containing every resident in the United States. Not only is the storage capacity of a DVD-ROM greater than that of a CD, a DVD-ROM's quality also far surpasses that of CDs because images are stored at higher resolution.

To read a DVD-ROM, you must have a **DVD-ROM drive** or DVD player. Most DVD-ROM drives also can read audio CDs, CD-ROMs, CD-Rs, and CD-RWs. DVD-ROM drives can read DVDs at speeds of 16X or more and CDs at speeds of 52X or more.

Although the size and shape of a CD-ROM and DVD-ROM are similar, a DVD-ROM stores data, instructions, and information in a slightly different manner and thus achieves a higher storage capacity. Widely used DVD-ROMs are capable of storing 4.7 GB to 17 GB, depending on the storage techniques used (Figure 7-27). The first storage technique involves making the disc denser by packing the pits closer together. The second involves using two layers of pits. For this technique to work, the lower layer of pits is semitransparent so the laser can read through it to the upper layer. This technique doubles the capacity of the disc. Finally, some DVD-ROMs are double-sided. A newer, quite expensive type of DVD, called a *Blu-Ray disc*, currently has storage capacities of 27 GB, with expectations of exceeding 50 GB in the future. Read Looking Ahead 7-2 for a look at a future application of Blu-Ray technology.

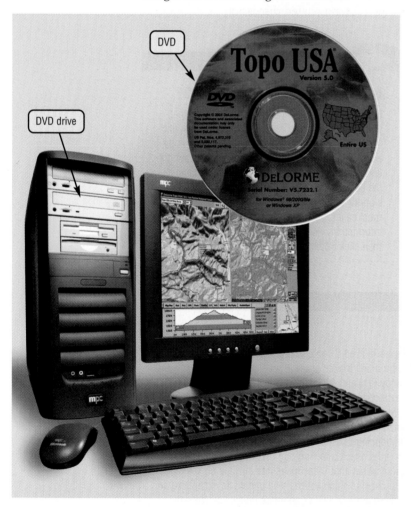

FIGURE 7-26 A DVD-ROM is an extremely high-capacity optical disc.

FAQ 7-7

What is a DVD/CD-RW drive?

It is a combination drive that reads DVD and CD media; it also writes to CD-RW media. This drive allows you to watch a DVD or burn a CD. For more information, visit scsite.com/dc2006/ch7/faq and then click DVD/CD-RW Drives.

DVD-ROM STORAGE CAPACITIES

Sides	Layers	Storage Capacity
1	1	4.7 GB
1	2	8.5 GB
2	1	9.4 GB
2	2	17 GB

FIGURE 7-27 Storage capacities of DVD-ROMs.

Paper Discs Offer Increased Capacity

The next generation high-capacity optical storage media will be composed of 51 percent paper and will hold as much as 50 GB of data. These discs will store more than 13 hours of video, which is more than five times the 8.5 GB capacity of current DVD discs. This recording capacity will become increasingly important as consumers purchase more high-definition television products and desire to record and view movies, photos, and other digital content on these devices.

The products are expected to cost no more than a currently priced DVD disc when produced in mass quantities and will be based on Blu-Ray disc technology. Destroying unwanted or sensitive data will be easy: just cut the disc with scissors. For more information, visit scsite.com/dc2006/ch7/looking and then click Paper Discs.

Recordable and Rewritable DVDs

Many types of recordable and rewritable DVD formats are available. *DVD-R* and *DVD+R* are competing DVD-recordable formats, each with up to 4.7 GB storage capacity. Both allow users to write on the disc once and read (play) it many times. In concept, DVD-R and DVD+R are similar to CD-R.

Instead of recordable DVDs, however, most users work with rewritable DVDs because these discs can be written on multiple times and also erased. Three competing rewritable DVD formats exist, each with storage capacities up to 4.7 GB per side: **DVD-RW**, **DVD+RW**, and **DVD+RAM**. These rewritable DVDs are similar in concept to CD-RW. With DVD-RW and DVD+RW discs, a user can erase and write (record) more than 1,000 times. To write on these discs, you must have a DVD-RW drive, a DVD+RW drive, or a DVD recorder. DVD-RW and DVD+RW drives have rewrite speeds of 12X or more, and read speeds of 40X or more. The drives usually can read DVD-ROM, DVD-R, DVD+R, and all CD media, and they can write on DVD-RW or DVD+RW, DVD-R, CD-R, and CD-RW media.

DVD+RAM (DVD+random access memory) allows users to erase and record on a DVD+RAM disc more than 100,000 times. These discs can be read by DVD+RAM drives and some DVD-ROM drives and players.

As the cost of DVD technologies becomes more reasonable, many industry professionals expect that DVD eventually will replace all CD media.

Do any digital video cameras record movies on DVD?

Yes. Video cameras that store at least 120 minutes of recording on mini-DVD media are available. Once recorded, users can view the DVD media in a standard computer DVD drive or a DVD player. Many video cameras include the capability of editing the video right in the camera. For more information, visit scsite.com/dc2006/ch7/faq and then click DVD Video Recorders.

 WEB LINK 7-8

DVDs
For more information, visit scsite.com/dc2006/ch7/weblink and then click DVDs.

Test your knowledge of pages 366 through 373 in Quiz Yourself 7-2.

Instructions: Find the true statement below. Then, rewrite the remaining false statements so they are true.

1. A CD-RW is a type of optical disc on which users can read but not write (record) or erase.

2. A DVD-RAM is a single-session disc that stores digital versions of a single roll of film using a jpg file format.

3. DVDs have the same storage capacities as CDs.

4. Optical discs are written and read by mirrors.

5. Single session means you can write on part of the disc at one time and another part at a later time.

6. Three competing rewritable DVD formats are DVD-RW, DVD+RW, and DVD+RAM.

Quiz Yourself Online: To further check your knowledge of optical discs and various optical disc formats, visit scsite.com/dc2006/ch7/quiz and then click Objectives 5 – 6.

TAPE

One of the first storage media used with mainframe computers was tape. **Tape** is a magnetically coated ribbon of plastic capable of storing large amounts of data and information at a low cost. Tape no longer is used as a primary method of storage. Instead, business and home users utilize tape most often for long-term storage and backup.

Comparable to a tape recorder, a **tape drive** reads and writes data and information on a tape. Although older computers used reel-to-reel tape drives, today's tape drives use tape cartridges. A *tape cartridge* is a small, rectangular, plastic housing for tape (Figure 7-28). Tape cartridges that contain quarter-inch-wide tape are slightly larger than audiocassette tapes. Business and home users sometimes back up personal computer hard disks to tape. Transfer rates of tape drives range from 1.25 MBps to 6 MBps.

Some personal computers have external tape units. Others have the tape drive built into the system unit. On larger computers, tape cartridges are mounted in a separate cabinet called a *tape library*.

Tape storage requires *sequential access*, which refers to reading or writing data consecutively. As with a music tape, you must forward or rewind the tape to a specific point to access a specific piece of data. For example, to access item W requires passing through points A through V sequentially.

Floppy disks, Zip disks, hard disks, CDs, and DVDs all use direct access. *Direct access*, also called *random access*, means that the device can locate a particular data item or file immediately, without having to move consecutively through items stored in front of the desired data item or file. When writing or reading specific data, direct access is much faster than sequential access.

FIGURE 7-28 A tape drive and a tape cartridge.

PC CARDs

As discussed in Chapter 4, a **PC Card** is a thin, credit-card-sized device that fits into a PC Card slot. Different types and sizes of PC Cards add storage, additional memory, fax/modem, networking, sound, and other capabilities to a desktop or notebook computer. PC Cards commonly are used in notebook computers (Figure 7-29).

Originally, PC Cards were called PCMCIA cards. Three kinds of PC Cards are available: Type I, Type II, and Type III (Figure 7-30). The only difference in size among the three types is their thickness. Some digital cameras use a Type II or Type III PC Card to store photographs. PC Cards that house a hard disk have storage capacities up to 5 GB. The advantage of a PC Card for storage is portability. You easily can transport large amounts of data, instructions, and information from one computer to another using a Type II or Type III PC Card.

FIGURE 7-29 A PC Card in a notebook computer.

PC CARDS

Category	Thickness	Use
Type I	3.3 mm	RAM, SRAM, flash memory
Type II	5.0 mm	Modem, LAN, SCSI, sound, TV tuner, hard disk, or other storage
Type III	10.5 mm	Rotating storage such as a hard disk

FIGURE 7-30 Various uses of PC Cards.

MINIATURE MOBILE STORAGE MEDIA

Miniature mobile storage media allow mobile users easily to transport digital images, music, or documents to and from computers and other devices (Figure 7-31). Many desktop computers, notebook computers, Tablet PCs, PDAs, smart phones, digital cameras, and music players have built-in slots or ports to read from and write on miniature mobile storage media. For computers or devices without built-in slots, users insert the media in separate peripherals such as a card reader/writer, which typically plugs in a USB port, or a device such as a *digital photo viewer*, which connects to a television port for on-screen picture viewing. The following sections discuss the widely used miniature storage media: flash memory cards, USB flash drives, and smart cards.

FIGURE 7-31   Many types of computers and devices use miniature mobile storage media.

Flash Memory Cards

Previously, this chapter discussed miniature hard disks (magnetic media) and mini discs (optical media). Flash memory cards, by contrast, are a type of *solid-state media*, which means they consist entirely of electronic components and contain no moving parts. Common types of flash memory cards include *CompactFlash* (CF), *SmartMedia*, *Secure Digital* (SD), *xD Picture Card*, and *Memory Stick*. The table in Figure 7-32 compares storage capacities and uses of these media.

Depending on the device, manufacturers claim miniature mobile storage media can last from 10 to 100 years. Transfer rates range from about 1 MBps to 10 MBps or more, depending on the device. Flash memory cards are quite expensive compared to other storage media.

For example, the cost of a 2 GB CompactFlash card is three times that of a 120 GB hard disk.

To view, edit, or print images and information stored on miniature mobile storage media, you transfer the contents to your desktop computer or other device such as a digital photo viewer. Some printers have slots to read PC Cards and flash memory cards. If your computer or printer does not have a built-in slot, you can purchase a *card reader/writer*, which is a device that reads and writes data, instructions, and information stored on PC Cards or flash memory cards. Card reader/writers usually connect to the USB port, FireWire port, or parallel port on the system unit. The type of card you have will determine the type of card reader/writer needed. Figure 7-33 shows how one type of flash memory card works with a card reader/writer.

WEB LINK 7-10

Flash Memory Cards

For more information, visit scsite.com/ dc2006/ch7/weblink and then click Flash Memory Cards.

VARIOUS FLASH MEMORY CARDS

Media Name	Storage Capacity	Use
CompactFlash	32 MB to 4 GB	Digital cameras, PDAs, smart phones, photo printers, music players, notebook computers, desktop computers
SmartMedia	32 MB to 128 MB	Digital cameras, PDAs, smart phones, photo printers, music players
Secure Digital	64 MB to 1 GB	Digital cameras, digital video cameras, PDAs, smart phones, photo printers, music players
xD Picture Card	64 MB to 512 MB	Digital cameras, photo printers
Memory Stick	256 MB to 2 GB	Digital cameras, digital video cameras, PDAs, photo printers, smart phones, notebook computers

FIGURE 7-32 A variety of flash memory cards.

FIGURE 7-33 HOW ONE TYPE OF FLASH MEMORY CARD WORKS

Step 1:
When you insert a memory card in a card reader/writer or card slot, the memory card's metallic conductors make contact with connectors in the card reader/writer or card slot, allowing the transfer of pictures and other items between the card and the reading/writing device.

metallic conductors

write-protect switch

card reader/writer

memory card

Step 4:
Some memory cards contain write-protect switches, which prevent users from accidentally erasing pictures and other items stored on the flash memory chips.

controller chip

notch

registers

flash memory chips

Step 2:
A notch on the side of the memory card prevents the card from accidentally slipping out of the card reader/writer or card slot.

Step 3:
Flash memory chips store pictures and other types of data and information. When requested, the controller transfers items stored on the flash memory chips to the metallic conductors, using registers for temporary storage, as needed.

USB Flash Drives

A **USB flash drive**, sometimes called a *pen drive*, is a flash memory storage device that plugs in a USB port on a computer or mobile device (Figure 7-34). USB flash drives are convenient for mobile users because they are small and lightweight enough to be transported on a keychain or in a pocket. Current USB flash drives have data transfer rates of about 12 MBps and storage capacities up to 4 GB.

Experts predict that USB flash drives will become the mobile user's primary portable storage device, eventually making the floppy disk obsolete because they have much greater storage capacities and are much more convenient to carry.

FIGURE 7-34 A USB flash drive.

Smart Cards

A **smart card**, which is similar in size to a credit card or ATM card, stores data on a thin microprocessor embedded in the card. Smart cards contain a processor and have input, process, output, and storage capabilities. When you insert the smart card in a specialized card reader, the information on the smart card is read and, if necessary, updated (Figure 7-35).

Uses of smart cards include storing medical records, vaccination data, and other health-care and identification information; tracking information such as customer purchases or employee attendance; storing a prepaid amount of money; and authenticating users such as for Internet purchases. Read At Issue 7-3 for a related discussion.

FAQ 7-9

Are some credit cards smart cards?

Yes. More than 60 million people around the world have a smart Visa card, which contains a microchip filled with their personal information. Credit card smart cards offer the consumer the convenience of using the card to make purchases in stores and online. For more information, visit scsite.com/dc2006/ch7/faq and then click Credit Card Smart Cards.

AT ISSUE 7-3

Should the World Become a Cashless Society?

Do you toss your loose change in a jar with the hopes of making a special purchase with the savings someday? Futurists predict that this practice may one day go the way of making purchases with silver and gold. Some forecasters say that the world is moving toward a cashless society. One form of payment that could end the need for cash is the smart card, which can store a dollar amount on a thin microprocessor and update the amount whenever a transaction is made. Advocates claim that smart cards would eliminate muggings and robberies, make it difficult to purchase illegal goods, and reduce taxes by identifying tax cheats. Smart cards already are common in Europe, but many Americans cite privacy concerns as reasons to avoid them. In a recent survey, most Americans said that they would not use a smart card even if privacy was guaranteed. A cash purchase usually is anonymous. Yet, a smart card purchase preserves a record of the transaction that could become available to other merchants, advertisers, government agencies, or hackers. Considering the advantages and disadvantages, should the world become a cashless society? Why or why not? Would you be comfortable using a smart card instead of cash? Why?

computer chip

smart card

card reader

FIGURE 7-35 A smart card and smart card reader.

MICROFILM AND MICROFICHE

Microfilm and microfiche store microscopic images of documents on roll or sheet film. **Microfilm** is a 100- to 215-foot roll of film. **Microfiche** is a small sheet of film, usually about 4 inches by 6 inches. A *computer output microfilm recorder* is the device that records the images on the film. The stored images are so small that you can read them only with a microfilm or microfiche reader (Figure 7-36).

Applications of microfilm and microfiche are widespread. Libraries use these media to store back issues of newspapers, magazines, and genealogy records. Large organizations use microfilm and microfiche to archive inactive files. Banks use them to store transactions and canceled checks. The U.S. Army uses them to store personnel records.

The use of microfilm and microfiche provides a number of advantages. They greatly reduce the amount of paper firms must handle. They are inexpensive and have the longest life of any storage media (Figure 7-37).

ENTERPRISE STORAGE

A large business, commonly referred to as an enterprise, has hundreds or thousands of employees in offices across the country or around the world. Enterprises use computers and computer networks to manage and store huge volumes of data and information about customers, suppliers, and employees.

To meet their large-scale needs, enterprises use special hardware geared for heavy use, maximum availability, and maximum efficiency. One or more servers on the network have the sole purpose of providing storage to connected users. For high-speed storage access, entire networks are dedicated exclusively to connecting devices that provide storage to other servers. In an enterprise, some storage systems can provide more than 185 terabytes (trillion bytes) of storage capacity. CD-ROM servers and DVD-ROM servers hold hundreds of CD-ROMs or DVD-ROMs.

An enterprise's storage needs usually grow daily. Thus, the storage solutions an enterprise chooses must be able to store its data and information requirements today and tomorrow. Read At Issue 7-4 for a related discussion.

FIGURE 7-36 Images on microfilm can be read only with a microfilm reader.

MEDIA LIFE EXPECTANCIES (when using high-quality media)

Media Type	Guaranteed Life Expectancy	Potential Life Expectancy
Magnetic disks	3 to 5 years	20 to 30 years
Optical discs	5 to 10 years	50 to 100 years
Microfilm	100 years	500 years

FIGURE 7-37 Microfilm is the medium with the longest life.

AT ISSUE 7-4

Who Is Looking at Your Medical Records?

A medical transcriber based in Pakistan and hired by a U.S. medical center threatened to post private medical records to the Internet if she was not paid more. With the widespread use of computers and an explosion in data storage capacity around the world, private information, such as medical records, requires increased diligence by companies, governments, and individuals to maintain this privacy. Updates to the Health Insurance Portability and Accountability Act (HIPAA) effective in 2003 set rigorous standards for medical record privacy. The law, however, still leaves much of your medical information at risk. The law does not cover financial records, education records, or employment records — each of which may contain medical information about you. Your medical information also may be examined by insurance companies, government agencies, the Medical Information Bureau (MIB), employers, and the courts. You also inadvertently may pass on medical information to direct marketers when you participate in informal health screenings or surveys. Some people have found that discussing medical conditions via Internet chat rooms or newsgroups has resulted in unwanted attention, and they later regret the disclosures. You can limit the amount of information available about you by discussing confidentiality with your medical providers and by requesting additional restrictions when you sign waivers to release your medical records, such as when applying for a job or applying for insurance. Should more limits be placed on what other people can do with your medical information? Why or why not? What are the advantages of increased access to medical records? What are the disadvantages?

PUTTING IT ALL TOGETHER

Many factors influence the type of storage devices you should use: the amount of data, instructions, and information to be stored; the hardware and software in use; and the desired cost. The table in Figure 7-38 outlines several suggested storage devices for various types of computer users.

CATEGORIES OF USERS

User	Typical Storage Devices
HOME	• 80 GB hard disk • Online storage • CD or DVD drive • Card reader/writer • USB flash drive and/or 3.5-inch floppy disk drive
SMALL OFFICE/ HOME OFFICE	• 750 MB Zip drive • 120 GB hard disk • Online storage • CD or DVD drive • External hard disk for backup • USB flash drive and/or 3.5-inch floppy disk drive
MOBILE 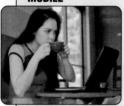	• 80 GB hard disk • Online storage • CD or DVD drive • Card reader/writer • Portable hard disk for backup • USB flash drive, and/or 2 GB PC Card hard disk, and/or 3.5-inch floppy disk drive
POWER	• CD or DVD drive • 300 GB hard disk • Online storage • Portable hard disk for backup • USB flash drive and/or 3.5-inch floppy disk drive
LARGE BUSINESS	• Desktop Computer - 160 GB hard disk - CD or DVD drive - Smart card reader - Tape drive - USB flash drive and/or 3.5-inch floppy disk drive • Server or Mainframe - Network storage server - 40 TB hard disk system - CD-ROM or DVD-ROM server - Microfilm or microfiche

FIGURE 7-38 Recommended storage devices for various users.

Test your knowledge of pages 374 through 380 in Quiz Yourself 7-3.

QUIZ YOURSELF 7-3

Instructions: Find the true statement below. Then, rewrite the remaining false statements so they are true.

1. A smart card stores data on a thin magnetic stripe embedded in the card.

2. A USB flash drive is a flash memory storage device that plugs in a parallel port on a computer or mobile device.

3. Flash memory cards are a type of magnetic media, which means they consist entirely of electronic components and contain no moving parts.

4. Microfilm and microfiche have the shortest life of any storage media.

5. Tape storage requires direct access, which refers to reading or writing data consecutively.

6. The only difference in size among Type I, Type II, and Type III PC Cards is their thickness.

Quiz Yourself Online: To further check your knowledge of tape, PC Cards, miniature mobile storage media, and microfilm and microfiche, visit scsite.com/dc2006/ch7/quiz and then click Objectives 7 – 9.

CHAPTER SUMMARY

Storage holds data, instructions, and information, which includes pictures, music, and videos, for future use. Users depend on storage devices to provide access to their storage media for years and decades to come. Read At Issue 7-5 for a discussion about the future of storage.

This chapter identified and discussed various storage media and storage devices. Storage media covered included floppy disks, Zip disks, internal hard disks, portable hard disks, CD-ROMs, recordable CDs, rewritable CDs, DVD-ROMs, recordable DVDs, rewritable DVDs, tape, PC Cards, flash memory cards, USB flash drives, smart cards, and microfilm and microfiche.

AT ISSUE 7-5

Will Digital Data Last Forever?

Up to 75 percent of today's data was born digital and never existed on paper. Historical data from hundreds or thousands of years ago still exists because it was written down. Although written documents can be read hundreds of years after they are created, rapid changes in computer technology can make digital records almost inaccessible in just one decade. For most computer users, hardware changes have made data stored on once-popular 5.25-inch floppy disks, or on the 8-inch floppy disks used in the early '70s, unavailable today. Loss of data on aging CDs and DVDs threatens the stored photo and video memories of countless families. Software changes also take a toll. One computer expert claims that trying to read material written with an obsolete word processing program is like trying to interpret Egyptian hieroglyphics without the Rosetta stone. Pennsylvania State University recently admitted that almost 3,000 student and school files could not be accessed due to lost or outdated software. Is the potential unavailability of digital data a problem? Why or why not? What can be done to keep today's digital information available in the future?

CAREER CORNER

Computer Technician

The demand for computer technicians is growing in every organization and industry. For many, this is the entry point for a career in the computer/information technology field. The responsibilities of a *computer technician*, also called a computer service technician, include a variety of duties. Most companies that employ someone with this title expect the technician to have basic across-the-board knowledge of concepts in the computer electronics field. Some of the tasks are hardware repair and installation; software installation, upgrade, and configuration; and troubleshooting client and/or server problems. Because the computer field is changing rapidly, technicians must work to remain abreast of current technology and become aware of future developments. Computer technicians generally work with a variety of users, which requires expert people skills, especially the ability to work with groups of non-technical users.

Most entry-level computer technicians possess the *A+ certification*. This certification attests that a computer technician has demonstrated knowledge of core hardware and operating system technology including installation, configuration, diagnosing, preventive maintenance and basic networking that meets industry standards and has at least six months of experience in the field. The Electronics Technicians Association also provides a Computer Service Technician (CST) certification program.

Because this is an entry-level position, the pay scale is not as high as other more demanding and skilled positions. Individuals can expect an average annual starting salary of around $28,000 to $42,000. Companies pay more for computer technicians with experience and certification. For more information, visit scsite.com/dc2006/ch7/careers and then click Computer Technician.

High-Tech Talk

DISK FORMATTING AND FILE SYSTEMS

Formatting a disk can be compared to starting a library. Before any books can be put in place, you must install the bookshelves and a catalog system. Similarly, a disk must have a file system set up to make it ready to receive data. This is true of many different storage media — including floppy disks, hard disks, removable hard disks, and CDs and DVDs — all of which must be formatted, to allow a way to organize and find files saved on the disk.

This discussion focuses on the formatting process required to take a hard disk from its newly manufactured state to a fully functional storage medium. Three main steps are involved in the process of formatting a hard disk: (1) low-level (physical) formatting, (2) partitioning, and (3) high-level (logical) formatting.

A hard disk must be formatted physically before it can be formatted logically. The hard disk manufacturer usually performs a hard disk's physical formatting, or *low-level formatting*. A hard drive physically formats a hard disk by writing a pattern of 1s and 0s on the surface of the disk. The 1s and 0s act as small electronic markers, which divide the hard disk platter into its basic physical elements: tracks, sectors, and cylinders.

These elements define the way data is written on and read from the disk physically. As the read/write head moves over the spinning disks, it reads the electronic markers that define the tracks, sectors, and cylinders to determine where it is in relation to the data on the disk's surface.

Once a hard disk has been formatted physically, it can be partitioned. *Partitioning* is the process of dividing the hard disk into regions called partitions. Each partition occupies a group of adjacent cylinders. Partitioning allows you to organize a hard disk into segments and lets you run multiple operating systems on a single computer. You also can keep the entire hard disk as one partition. After a disk partition has been formatted, it is referred to as a *volume*.

After a hard disk has been formatted physically and partitioned, it must be formatted logically. Logical formatting, known as *high-level formatting*, places a file system on the disk. A *file system* allows an operating system, such as Windows XP or Linux, to use the space available on a hard disk to store and retrieve files. The operating system uses the file system to store information about the disk's directory, or folder, structure.

The file system also defines the size of the clusters used to store data on the hard disk. A cluster, or *block*, is made up of two or more sectors on a single track on a hard disk. A cluster is the minimum unit the operating system uses to store information. Even if a file has a size of 1 byte, a cluster as large as 64 KB might be used to store the file on large drives. The number of sectors and tracks and, therefore, the number of clusters that a drive can create on a disk's surface determine the capacity of the disk.

While creating the file system during logical formatting, the drive creates a special table in the disk's first sector, sector 0. This table stores entries that the operating system uses to locate files on a disk. Each entry in the table takes up a certain number of bits, which is why file systems often are referred to as 12-bit, 16-bit, or 32-bit. The content of each entry consists of a whole number, which identifies one or more clusters where the file is stored.

Depending on the operating system used to format the disk, the file system can be one of several types, as shown in the table in Figure 7-39. Whatever file system is used, the file system is the interface between the operating system and drives. For more information, visit scsite.com/dc2006/ch7/tech and then click Disk Formatting.

File System	Description	Key Features
FAT (also called FAT12 and FAT16)	The standard file system for DOS and Windows. Because of its widespread use, FAT also is accessible by most other operating systems.	• FAT12 is used for floppy disk drives and very small hard disks (up to 16 MB) • FAT16 is used for small to moderate-sized hard disk volumes (up to 2 GB)
VFAT (Virtual FAT)	A newer protected-mode version of the FAT file system, introduced with Windows 95.	• Supports long file names up to 255 characters • Faster than FAT because the computer can read files at least 32 bits at a time
FAT32	A 32-bit version of FAT, introduced with Windows 95.	• Same key features as VFAT • Used for medium-sized to very large hard disk volumes (up to 2 terabytes)
NTFS (NT File System)	The 32-bit file system currently used for Windows NT, Windows 2000, and Windows XP.	• 32- or 64-bit entries in file system table • Fully recoverable file system, designed to restore consistency after a system crash • Used for medium-sized to very large hard disk volumes (up to 16 billion GB)

FIGURE 7-39 Comparison of various file systems.

Companies on the Cutting Edge

MAXTOR
INFORMATION STORAGE SUPPLIER

Computer-industry experts predict that 68 million hard disks will be needed for consumer electronic applications by 2007. *Maxtor* is poised to meet the demands of this rapidly growing market with its hard disks manufactured for the digital video recorder/personal video recorder (DVR/PVR) market.

Maxtor is a leading manufacturer of hard disks and storage solutions for desktop computers, high-performance servers, and consumer electronics, including digital video recorders and game consoles. Its wholly owned subsidiary, MMC Technology, manufactures nearly 50 million disks each year.

Maxtor's 250 GB OneTouch external hard disk was honored as the "Product of the Year" by *CRN* magazine and received a World Class Award from *PC World* in 2004. For more information, visit scsite.com/dc2006/ch7/companies and then click Maxtor.

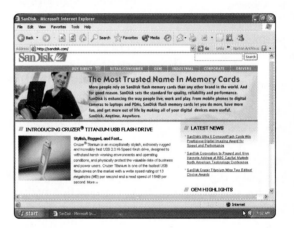

SANDISK CORPORATION
WORLD'S LARGEST FLASH MEMORY CARD SUPPLIER

The next time you buy milk at the grocery store or shampoo at the drug store, you might want to purchase a flash memory card for your digital camera, too. *SanDisk Corporation* products can be found in more than 10,000 retail stores across the United States, including Rite Aid and Kmart.

With retail sales of flash memory cards soaring, SanDisk executives believe consumers buy multiple flash memory cards to store their digital photographs in much the same manner as they formerly stored film negatives in shoe boxes. They also prefer to take a separate flash memory card to digital photo processing centers, which produce high-quality prints.

SanDisk also designs, develops, and manufactures USB flash drives and readers, Memory Sticks, and Wi-Fi cards. For more information, visit scsite.com/dc2006/ch7/companies and then click SanDisk.

Technology Trailblazers

AL SHUGART
STORAGE EXPERT

Al Shugart enjoys fixing broken items and developing new technology. The day after receiving his bachelor's degree in 1951, he went to work at IBM to repair broken machines. IBM then promoted him to supervisor of the product development team that developed the first removable rigid read/write disk drive.

He left IBM in 1969 and went to work as vice president of product development for Memorex. In 1973, he started Shugart Associates, a pioneer in the manufacture of floppy disks. Six years later, he and some associates founded Seagate Technology, Inc., which is a leader in designing and manufacturing storage products.

Today he serves as president, chairman, and CEO of Al Shugart International, a venture capital firm in California. For more information, visit scsite.com/dc2006/ch7/people and then click Al Shugart.

MARK DEAN
IBM INVENTOR

The next generation of IBM's hardware and software might be the work of *Mark Dean*. As vice president of IBM's Almaden Research Center lab in California, Dean is responsible for developing innovative products.

His designs are used in more than 40 million personal computers manufactured each year. He has more than 40 patents or patents pending, including four of the original seven for the architecture of the original personal computer.

Dean joined IBM in 1979 after graduating at the top of his class at the University of Tennessee. Dean earned his Ph.D. degree at Stanford, and he headed a team at IBM that invented the first CMOS microprocessor to operate at 1 gigahertz (1,000 MHz). For more information, visit scsite.com/dc2006/ch7/people and then click Mark Dean.

Chapter Review

The Chapter Review section summarizes the concepts presented in this chapter. To listen to the audio version of this Chapter Review, visit scsite.com/dc2006/ch7/review. To obtain help from other students regarding any subject in this chapter, visit scsite.com/dc2006/ch7/forum and post your thoughts or questions.

(1) **How Are Storage Devices Different from Storage Media?** A **storage medium** (media is the plural) is the physical material on which a computer keeps data, instructions, and information, which includes pictures, music, and videos. The number of bytes (characters) a storage medium can hold is its **capacity**. A **storage device** is the computer hardware that records and/or retrieves items to and from storage media. **Writing** is the process of transferring items from memory to a storage medium, and **reading** is the process of transferring these items from a storage medium into memory.

(2) **What Are the Characteristics of Magnetic Disks?** *Magnetic disks* use magnetic particles to store data, instructions, and information on a disk's surface. Before any data can be read from or written on a magnetic disk, the disk must be formatted. **Formatting** is the process of dividing the disk into *tracks* and *sectors*. Three types of magnetic disks are floppy disks, Zip disks, and hard disks.

(3) **What Are the Differences between Floppy Disks and Zip Disks?** A **floppy disk** is a portable, inexpensive storage medium that consists of a thin, circular, flexible plastic Mylar film with a magnetic coating enclosed in a square-shaped plastic shell. A standard floppy disk can store up to 500 double-spaced pages of text, several digital photographs, or a small audio file. A **floppy disk drive** is a device that reads from and writes on a floppy disk. A **Zip disk** is a type of portable magnetic media that can store up to 500 times more than a standard floppy disk. These large capacities make it easy to transport many files or large items. Another popular use of Zip disks is to make a **backup**, or duplicate, of a file, program, or disk that you can use in case the original is lost, damaged, or destroyed.

(4) **What Are the Characteristics of a Hard Disk?** A **hard disk**, also called a *hard disk drive*, is a storage device that contains one or more inflexible, circular platters that store data, instructions, and information. A *platter* is made of aluminum, glass, or ceramic and is coated with a material that allows items to be recorded magnetically on its surface. Each platter has two read/write heads, one for each side. The location of a *read/write head* often is referred to by its *cylinder*, which is the vertical section of a track that passes through all platters. While the computer is running, the platters rotate at 5,400 to 15,000 *revolutions per minute* (*rpm*), which allows nearly instant access to all tracks and sectors on the platters. The spinning creates a cushion of air between the platters and the read/write heads. A *head crash* occurs when a read/write head touches the surface of a platter, usually resulting in a loss of data.

Visit scsite.com/dc2006/ch7/quiz or click the Quiz Yourself button. Click Objectives 1 – 4.

(5) **What Are the Characteristics of Optical Discs?** An *optical disc* is a type of storage media that consists of a flat, round, portable disc made of metal, plastic, and lacquer that is written and read by a laser. Optical discs, which primarily store software, data, digital photographs, movies, and music, contain microscopic pits (indentations) and lands (flat areas) in their middle layer. Optical discs commonly store items in a single track that spirals from the center

Chapter Review

of the disc to its edge. Like a hard disk, the single track is divided into evenly sized sectors. Common optical discs used today are CD-ROM, CD-R, CD-RW, DVD-ROM, DVD-R, DVD+R, DVD-RW, DVD+RW, and DVD+RAM.

⑥ How Are CD-ROMs, Recordable CDs, Rewritable CDs, DVD-ROMs, Recordable DVDs, and Rewritable DVDs Different? A **CD-ROM**, or *compact disc read-only memory*, is a type of optical disc that uses laser technology to store items. A typical CD-ROM holds from 650 MB to 1 GB of data, instructions, and information. Users can read the contents of standard CD-ROMs but cannot erase or modify their contents. A **CD-R** (*compact disc-recordable*) is a *multisession* disc on which users can record their own items. Each part of a CD-R can be written on only one time, and the disc's contents cannot be erased. A **CD-RW** (*compact disc-rewritable*) is an erasable disc that can be written on multiple times. A **DVD-ROM** (*digital versatile disc-ROM* or *digital video disc-ROM*) is an extremely high capacity optical disk capable of storing from 4.7 GB to 17 GB. Not only is the storage capacity of a DVD-ROM greater than that of a CD-ROM, a DVD-ROM's quality also far surpasses that of a CD-ROM. **DVD-RW** and **DVD+RW** discs are a recordable version of DVD that allows users to erase and record more than 1,000 times. **DVD+RAM** allows users to erase and record on a DVD+RAM more than 100,000 times.

> connect
> Visit scsite.com/dc2006/ch7/quiz or click the Quiz Yourself button. Click Objectives 5 – 6.

⑦ How Is Tape Used? **Tape** is a magnetically coated ribbon of plastic capable of storing large amounts of data and information at a low cost. A **tape drive** reads and writes data and information on tape. Businesses and home users sometimes back up personal computer hard disks on tape.

⑧ What Are PC Cards and Other Types of Miniature Mobile Storage Media? A **PC Card** is a thin, credit-card-sized device that fits into a PC Card slot to add storage or other capabilities to a desktop or notebook computer. Many desktop and notebook computers, Tablet PCs, PDAs, smart phones, digital cameras, and music players have built-in slots or ports for miniature mobile storage media. Common types of miniature mobile storage media include flash memory cards, USB flash drives, and smart cards. A **USB flash drive** is a flash memory storage device that plugs in a port on a computer or mobile device. Common flash memory cards include *CompactFlash* (*CF*), *SmartMedia*, *Secure Digital* (*SD*), *xD Picture Card*, and *Memory Stick*. A **smart card**, which is similar in size to a credit or ATM card, stores data on a thin microprocessor embedded in the card.

⑨ How Are Microfilm and Microfiche Used? **Microfilm** is a 100- to 215-foot roll of film. **Microfiche** is a small sheet of film, usually about 4 inches by 6 inches. Libraries use microfilm and microfiche to store back issues of newspapers, magazines, and records; large organizations use them to archive inactive files; banks use them to store transactions and canceled checks; and the U.S. Army uses them to store personnel records.

> connect
> Visit scsite.com/dc2006/ch7/quiz or click the Quiz Yourself button. Click Objectives 7 – 9.

Key Terms

You should know the Primary Terms and be familiar with the Secondary Terms. Use the list below to help focus your study. To further enhance your understanding of the Key Terms in this chapter, visit scsite.com/dc2006/ch7/terms. See an example of and a definition for each term, and access current and additional information about the term from the Web.

Primary Terms

(shown in bold-black characters in the chapter)

access time (357)
backup (359)
capacity (356)
CD-R (371)
CD-R drive (371)
CD-ROM (369)
CD-ROM drive (369)
CD-RW (371)
CD-RW drive (371)
DVD+RAM (373)
DVD+RW (373)
DVD-ROM (372)
DVD-ROM drive (372)
DVD-RW (373)
external hard disk (364)
floppy disk (358)
floppy disk drive (358)
formatting (357)
hard disk (360)
microfiche (379)
microfilm (379)
online storage (365)
PC Card (374)
Picture CD (370)
reading (356)

removable hard disk (364)
smart card (378)
storage device (356)
storage medium (355)
tape (374)
tape drive (374)
USB flash drive (377)
write-protect notch (359)
writing (356)
Zip disk (359)
Zip drive (359)

Secondary Terms

(shown in italic characters in the chapter)

allocation unit (357)
Blu-Ray disc (372)
burning (371)
card reader/writer (376)
CD recorder (371)
cluster (357)
compact disc read-only memory (369)
compact disc-recordable (371)
compact disc-rewritable (371)
CompactFlash (CF) (376)
computer output microfilm recorder (379)
cylinder (362)
density (358)
digital photo viewer (375)
digital versatile disc-read-only memory (372)
digital video disc-read-only memory (372)
direct access (374)
disk cache (363)
disk controller (364)
diskette (358)
DVD+R (373)
DVD-R (373)
EIDE (Enhanced Integrated Drive Electronics) (365)
external floppy disk drive (358)

fixed disk (360)
form factor (361)
hard disk drive (360)
head crash (362)
HD (358)
jewel box (368)
KBps (357)
magnetic disks (357)
MBps (357)
Memory Stick (376)
mini discs (366)
multisession (371)
optical disc (366)
pen drive (377)
platter (361)
portable (358)
random access (374)
read/write head (361)
revolutions per minute (rpm) (362)
ripping (371)
SATA (Serial Advanced Technology Attachment) (364)
SCSI (365)
secondary storage (355)
sectors (357)
Secure Digital (SD) (376)
sequential access (374)
single-session disc (369)
SmartMedia (376)
solid-state media (376)
storage (354)
tape cartridge (374)
tape library (374)
track (357)
transfer rate (357)
xD Picture Card (376)

Checkpoint

Use the Checkpoint exercises to check your knowledge level of the chapter. The Beyond the Book exercises will help broaden your understanding of the concepts presented in this chapter. To complete the Checkpoint exercises interactively, visit scsite.com/dc2006/ch7/check.

Label the Figure

Identify the storage media.

a. CD or DVD
b. external hard disk
c. tape
d. miniature hard disk
e. Zip disk
f. flash memory card
g. USB flash drive

True/False

Mark T for True and F for False. (See page numbers in parentheses.)

_____ 1. Every computer uses storage to hold software, specifically, system software and application software. (354)

_____ 2. A storage medium is the physical material on which a computer keeps data, instructions, and information. (355)

_____ 3. Reading is the process of transferring data, instructions, and information from memory to a storage medium. (356)

_____ 4. A sector is a narrow recording band that forms a full circle on the surface of the disk. (357)

_____ 5. A cluster can hold data from only one file. (357)

_____ 6. A typical hard disk contains only one platter. (361)

_____ 7. An external hard disk is a separate, free-standing hard disk that connects with a cable to a port on the system unit. (364)

_____ 8. SCSI, the newest type of hard disk interface, uses serial signals to transfer data, instructions, and information. (364)

_____ 9. All optical discs are double-sided. (366)

_____ 10. Optical discs commonly store items in a single track. (367)

_____ 11. When writing or reading specific data, direct access is much slower than sequential access. (374)

_____ 12. A smart card sometimes is called a pen drive. (377)

Checkpoint

 Multiple Choice   Select the best answer. (See page numbers in parentheses.)

1. Examples of storage media include all of the following, except _____. (355)
   a. monitors and printers
   b. floppy disks and hard disks
   c. CDs and DVDs
   d. tape and PC Cards

2. A _____ is a narrow recording band that forms a full circle on the surface of a floppy disk. (357)
   a. track
   b. cluster
   c. shutter
   d. sector

3. On a floppy disk, if the write-protect notch is closed, the floppy disk drive _____. (359)
   a. can write on but cannot read from the floppy disk
   b. can write on and read from the floppy disk
   c. can read from but cannot write on the floppy disk
   d. cannot read from or write on the floppy disk

4. A Zip disk can store from _____ of data. (359)
   a. 10 MB to 75 MB
   b. 100 MB to 750 MB
   c. 10 GB to 75 GB
   d. 100 GB to 750 GB

5. If a computer contains only one hard disk drive, the operating system designates it as drive _____. (360)
   a. A   b. B
   c. C   d. D

6. Portable hard disks offer all of the following advantages over internal hard disks, except _____. (364)
   a. they can transport a large number of files
   b. they can add storage space to a notebook computer
   c. they can be shared with multiple computers
   d. they can transfer data at much faster rates

7. Users store data and information on online storage to _____. (365)
   a. save time by storing large files instantaneously
   b. allow others to access files
   c. store offsite backups of data
   d. all of the above

8. When a laser light reads CDs or DVDs, a land _____. (367)
   a. causes light to reflect, which is read as binary digit 0
   b. causes light to reflect, which is read as binary digit 1
   c. absorbs the light, which is read as binary digit 0
   d. absorbs the light, which is read as binary digit 1

9. All of the following are guidelines for the proper care of optical discs except _____. (368)
   a. do not expose the disc to extreme temperatures
   b. do not stack discs
   c. do not hold a disc by its edges
   d. do not eat, smoke, or drink near a disc

10. The process of writing on an optical disc is called _____. (371)
    a. formatting   b. ripping
    c. burning   d. reading

11. A storage technique that a DVD-ROM uses to achieve a higher storage capacity than a CD-ROM is _____. (372)
    a. making the disc denser by packing the pits closer together
    b. using two layers of pits
    c. using both sides of the disc
    d. all of the above

12. _____ storage requires sequential access. (374)
    a. Hard disk
    b. Tape
    c. Floppy disk
    d. CD

13. Which of the following is not true of flash memory cards? (376)
    a. they are a type of solid-state media
    b. they contain moving parts
    c. they can last 10 to 100 years
    d. they are quite expensive compared to other storage media

14. Microfilm and microfiche _____. (379)
    a. greatly increase the amount of paper firms must handle
    b. are expensive
    c. have the longest life of any storage media
    d. all of the above

Checkpoint

Matching

Match the terms with their definitions. (See page numbers in parentheses.)

_____ 1. transfer rate (357)

_____ 2. cluster (357)

_____ 3. form factor (361)

_____ 4. cylinder (362)

_____ 5. disk cache (363)

_____ 6. disk controller (364)

_____ 7. Picture CD (370)

_____ 8. Blu-Ray disc (372)

_____ 9. tape library (374)

_____ 10. pen drive (377)

a. memory chips that the processor uses to store frequently accessed items

b. speed with which data, instructions, and information move to and from a device

c. flash memory storage device that plugs in a USB port

d. piece of metal on a floppy disk that slides to expose the surface of the disk

e. smallest unit of disk space that stores data and information

f. size of hard disk platters on desktop computers

g. compact disc that stores digital versions of a single roll of film

h. newer, expensive type of DVD with storage capacities of 27 GB

i. vertical section of a track that passes through all platters

j. separate cabinet on which tape cartridges are mounted on larger computers

k. special-purpose chip and electronic circuits that control the transfer of items to and from the system bus

Short Answer

Write a brief answer to each of the following questions.

1. What is access time? _____ Why is the average hard disk access time faster than the average floppy disk access time? _____

2. What is density? _____ What is the purpose of a write-protect notch, and how does it work? _____

3. Why is a hard disk inside the system unit sometimes called a fixed disk? _____ What are the different types of portable hard disks? _____

4. How is a single-session disc different from a multisession disc? _____ How is a CD-R different from a CD-RW? _____

5. What are PC Cards, and why are they used? _____ What is the advantage of a PC Card? _____

Beyond the Book

Read the following book elements, learn more about each using the Web, and then write a brief report.

1. At Issue — Does Music Sharing Harm CD Sales? (369), Is It Ethical to Copy CDs or DVDs? (371), Should the World Become a Cashless Society? (378), Who Is Looking at Your Medical Records? (379), or Will Digital Data Last Forever? (381)

2. Career Corner — Computer Technician (381)

3. Companies on the Cutting Edge — Maxtor or SanDisk Corporation (383)

4. FAQs (360, 363, 365, 368, 370, 371, 372, 373, 378)

5. High-Tech Talk — Disk Formatting and File Systems (382)

6. Looking Ahead — Heat Increases Disk Capacity (360) or Paper Discs Offer Increased Capacity (373)

7. Making Use of the Web — Shopping (123)

8. Picture Yourself Working with Mobile Storage Media (352)

9. Technology Trailblazers — Al Shugart or Mark Dean (383)

10. Web Links (359, 364, 365, 369, 370, 371, 373, 374, 376, 378)

Quizzes and Learning Games

Computer Genius
Crossword Puzzle
DC Track and Field
Practice Test
Quiz Yourself
Wheel of Terms
You're Hired!

Exercises

Case Studies
Chapter Review
Checkpoint
Key Terms
Learn How To
▶ Learn It Online
Web Research

Beyond the Book

Career Corner
Companies
FAQs
High-Tech Talk
Looking Ahead
Making Use of the Web
Trailblazers
Web Links

Features

Chapter Forum
Install Computer
Lab Exercises
Maintain Computer
Tech News
Timeline 2006

Learn It Online

Use the Learn It Online exercises to reinforce your understanding of the chapter concepts. To access the Learn It Online exercises, visit scsite.com/dc2006/ch7/learn.

① At the Movies — Repair Your CD Scratches

To view the Repair Your CD Scratches movie, click the number 1 button. Locate your video and click the corresponding High-Speed or Dial-Up link, depending on your Internet connection. Watch the movie and then complete the exercise by answering the questions that follow. Just because your favorite CD has a few scratches is no reason to discard it. A few options are available to help you keep those scratched CDs playing smoothly longer. How does resurfacing work to restore your scratched CDs? What common household product can be used to repair a CD?

② At the Movies — Online Data Storage Options

To view the Online Data Storage Options movie, click the number 2 button. Locate your video and click the corresponding High-Speed or Dial-Up link, depending on your Internet connection. Watch the movie and then complete the exercise by answering the question that follows. Online data storage broadens your options for file sharing and frees up space on your personal computer. If you store files online, anyone who knows the password can access them from anywhere in the world. Several free storage systems offer a moderate amount of space; however, if you need more you can sign up and pay for additional storage for as little as $15 a month. What are some of the most important reasons for backing up your files online?

③ Student Edition Labs — Maintaining a Hard Drive

Click the number 3 button. When the Student Edition Labs menu appears, click *Maintaining a Hard Drive* to begin. A new browser window will open. Follow the on-screen instructions to complete the Lab. When finished, click the Exit button. If required, submit your results to your instructor.

④ Student Edition Labs — Managing Files and Folders

Click the number 4 button. When the Student Edition Labs menu appears, click *Managing Files and Folders* to begin. A new browser window will open. Follow the on-screen instructions to complete the Lab. When finished, click the Exit button. If required, submit your results to your instructor.

⑤ Practice Test

Click the number 5 button. Answer each question. When completed, enter your name and click the Grade Test button to submit the quiz for grading. Make a note of any missed questions. If required, submit your results to your instructor.

⑥ Who Wants To Be a Computer Genius²?

Click the number 6 button to find out if you are a computer genius. Directions about how to play the game will be displayed. When you are ready to play, click the Play button. Submit your score to your instructor.

⑦ Wheel of Terms

Click the number 7 button to reinforce important terms you learned in this chapter by playing the Shelly Cashman Series version of this popular game. Directions about how to play the game will be displayed. When you are ready to play, click the Play button. Submit your score to your instructor.

Learn It Online

8 DC Track and Field

Click the number 8 button to use what you have learned in this chapter to compete against other students in three track and field events. Directions about how to play the game will be displayed. When you are ready to play, click the start first event button. If required, submit your score to your instructor.

9 You're Hired!

Click the number 9 button to use what you have learned in this chapter to embark on the path to a career in computers. Directions about how to play the game will be displayed. When you are ready to play, click the begin game button. If required, submit your score to your instructor.

10 Crossword Puzzle Challenge

Click the number 10 button. Complete the puzzle to reinforce skills you learned in this chapter. Directions about how to play the game will be displayed. When you are ready to play, click the Submit button. Submit the completed puzzle to your instructor.

11 Lab Exercises

Click the number 11 button. When the Lab Exercises menu appears, click the exercise assigned by your instructor. A new browser window will open. Follow the on-screen instructions to complete the exercise. When finished, click the Exit button. If required, submit your results to your instructor.

12 In the News

Hitachi sells a small disk drive, about the size of a quarter, which is capable of storing up to 4 GB of information, as much as 50 CDs. The drive is used in devices such as PDAs or digital cameras. What other storage devices are on the horizon? Click the number 12 button and read a news article about a new or improved storage device. What is the device? Who manufactures it? How is the storage device better than, or different from, earlier devices? How will the device be used? Why?

13 Chapter Discussion Forum

Select an objective from this chapter on page 353 about which you would like more information. Click the number 13 button and post a short message listing a meaningful message title accompanied by one or more questions concerning the selected objective. In two days, return to the threaded discussion by clicking the number 13 button. Submit to your instructor your original message and at least one response to your message.

Learn How To

Use the Learn How To activities to learn fundamental skills when using a computer and accompanying technology. Complete the exercises and submit them to your instructor. Visit scsite.com/dc2006/ch7/howto to obtain more information pertaining to each activity.

LEARN HOW TO 1: Maintain a Hard Disk

A computer's hard disk is used for the majority of storage requirements. It is important, therefore, to ensure that each hard disk on a computer is operating at peak efficiency.

Three tasks that maximize disk operations are detecting and repairing disk errors by using the Check Disk utility program; removing unused or unnecessary files and folders by using the Disk Cleanup utility program; and, consolidating files and folders into contiguous storage areas using the Disk Defragmenter utility program.

A. Check Disk
To detect and repair disk errors using the Check Disk utility program, complete the following steps:
1. Click the Start button on the Windows taskbar and then click My Computer on the Start menu.
2. When the My Computer window opens, right-click the hard disk icon for drive C (or any other hard disk you want to select), and then click Properties on the shortcut menu.
3. In the Properties dialog box, if necessary click the Tools tab. *The Tools sheet contains buttons to start the Check Disk program, the Defragment program, and the Backup program (Figure 7-40).*
4. Click the Check Now button. *The Check Disk dialog box is displayed.*
5. To do a complete scan of the disk and correct any errors that are found, place a check mark in the Scan for and attempt recovery for bad sectors check box, and then click the Start button. Four phases of checking the disk will occur. While the checking is in progress, the disk being checked cannot be used for any purpose whatsoever; furthermore, once it has started, the process cannot be stopped.
6. When the four phases are complete (this may take more than one-half hour, depending on the size of the hard disk and how many corrections must occur), a dialog box is displayed with the message, Disk Check Complete. Click the OK button in the dialog box.

FIGURE 7-40

B. Cleanup Disk
After checking the disk, your next step can be to clean up the disk by removing any programs and data that are not required for the computer. To do so, complete the following steps:
1. Click the General tab (Figure 7-40) in the disk drive Properties dialog box to display the General sheet.
2. Click the Disk Cleanup button in the General sheet.
3. The Disk Cleanup dialog box is displayed and contains a message that indicates the amount of space that can be freed up is being calculated.
4. After the calculation is complete, the Disk Cleanup dialog box specifies the amount of space that can be freed up and the files to delete, some of which are checked automatically (Figure 7-41 on the next page). Select those items from which you wish to delete files.
5. Click the OK button in the Disk Cleanup dialog box.
6. A dialog box asks if you are sure you want to perform these actions. Click the Yes button. The Disk Cleanup dialog box illustrates the progress of the cleanup. When the cleanup is complete, the dialog box closes.

Learn How To

C. Defragment Disk

The next step in disk maintenance is to **defragment** all the files on the disk. When a file is stored on disk, the data in the file sometimes is stored contiguously, and other times is stored in a noncontiguous manner. When a file is stored in a noncontiguous manner, it can take significantly longer to find and retrieve data from the file. Therefore, one of the more useful utilities to speed up disk operations is the defragmentation program, which combines all files so that no files are stored in a noncontiguous manner. To use the defragmentation program, complete the following steps:

1. If necessary, click the Tools tab in the Properties dialog box for the hard disk to be defragmented.
2. Click the Defragment Now button in the Tools sheet. *The Disk Defragmenter window opens (Figure 7-42). This window displays the hard disks on the computer and shows the size and amount of free space for each disk. During defragmentation, the Estimated disk usage before defragmentation area and the Estimated disk usage after defragmentation area display the layout of the data on the disk. If you click the Analyze button, the disk will be analyzed for its data layout but defragmentation will not occur.*
3. Click the Defragment button. The defragmentation process begins. The amount of processing completed is shown on the status bar at the bottom of the window. The defragmentation process can consume more than one hour in some cases. You can pause or stop the operation at any time by clicking the Pause or Stop button in the Disk Defragmenter window.
4. When the process is complete, the Disk Defragmenter dialog box displays the message, Defragmentation is complete for (C:). Click the View Report button to see a complete report about the hard disk.
5. Click the Close button to close the Disk Defragmenter dialog box.

FIGURE 7-41

FIGURE 7-42

Exercise

Caution: The exercises for this chapter that require the actual disk maintenance are optional. If you are performing these exercises on a computer that is not your own, obtain explicit permission to complete these exercises. Keep in mind that these exercises can require significant computer time and the computer may be unusable during this time.

1. Display the Properties dialog box for a hard disk found on the computer. Display the Tools sheet. Click the Check Now button and then place a check mark in the Scan for and attempt recovery for bad sectors check box. Click the Start button. How long did it take to complete the check of the hard disk? Were any errors discovered and corrected? Submit your answers to your instructor.
2. Display the Properties dialog box for a hard disk found on the computer. Display the General sheet. What is the capacity of the hard disk? How much space is used? How much free space is available? Click the Disk Cleanup button. How much space can be freed up if you use the Disk Cleanup program? Click the OK button to clean up the disk. How long did it take to perform the disk cleanup? Submit your answers to your instructor.
3. Display the Properties dialog box for a hard disk found on the computer. Display the Tools sheet. Click the Defragment Now button. In the Disk Defragmenter window, click the Analyze button. Does the hard disk need to be defragmented? Click the View Report button. How many files are stored on the disk? What is the average size of the files stored on the disk? If necessary, click the Defragment button in the Analysis Report window. How long did defragmentation require? Submit your answers to your instructor.

Web Research

Use the Internet-based Web Research exercises to broaden your understanding of the concepts presented in this chapter. Visit scsite.com/dc2006/ch7/research to obtain more information pertaining to each exercise. To discuss any of the Web Research exercises in this chapter with other students, post your thoughts or questions at scsite.com/dc2006/ch7/forum.

(1) **Scavenger Hunt**   Use one of the <u>search engines</u> listed in Figure 2-10 in Chapter 2 on page 78 or your own favorite search engine to find the answers to the questions that follow. Copy and paste the Web address from the Web page where you found the answer. Some questions may have more than one answer. If required, submit your answers to your instructor. (1) What are the three different laser powers used in a CD-rewritable recorder? How do two of the powers affect the recording layer? During writing, to what temperature does the laser beam selectively heat areas of the recording material? (2) Daniel Bernoulli's principle has many practical applications. Describe two of them, and then explain how Iomega used the principle in its Bernoulli drive. (3) What is the Red Book standard? (4) What is the function of a hard disk's actuator? (5) What is areal density? What unit of measurement is used to describe this density?

(2) **Search Sleuth**   Many computer users search the World Wide Web by typing words in the search text box, and often they are overwhelmed when the search engine returns thousands of possible Web sites. You can narrow your search by typing quotation marks around phrases and by adding words that give details about the phrase. <u>Go.com</u> is a Web portal developed by the Walt Disney Internet Group. It features a search engine, the latest ABC news and ESPN sports stories, stock market quotes, weather forecasts, maps, and games. Visit this Web site and then use your word processing program to answer the following questions. Then, if required, submit your answers to your instructor. (1) Click the Search for text box at the top of the page. Type `hard disk` in the box. How many search results are returned that are not sponsored links? (2) Type `"hard disk"` in the Search for box. How many search results are returned that are not sponsored links? (3) Scroll down to the bottom of the page and then type `"access time"` in the text box to search within the "hard disk" results and narrow your results. How many search results are returned that are not sponsored links? (4) Review the Hard Disks section of your textbook for additional words that give details about this device. Perform two more searches with these words. Review your search results and then write a 50-word summary of your findings.

(3) **Journaling**   Respond to your readings in this chapter by writing at least one page about your reactions, evaluations, and reflections about using <u>storage devices</u>. For example, have you used USB flash drives, smart cards, or Zip disks? How do you care for your floppy disks? Have you ever encountered a corrupt floppy disk? What is the storage capacity of your school, office, or home computer's hard disk? Do you clean your CDs and DVDs? You also can write about the new terms you learned by reading this chapter. If required, submit your journal to your instructor.

(4) **Expanding Your Understanding**   Bill Gates, Microsoft's chief software architect, considers <u>holographic storage</u> an impressive new storage system. The holographic process can store more than 100 movie, photo, and music files on one disc holding one terabyte of data. View Web sites to learn more about holographic storage. What factors are driving the rush to develop this system? How are images stored? What companies are researching and developing this technology? Write a report summarizing your findings, focusing on the possible uses of this storage medium and current engineering efforts to commercialize the technology. If required, submit your report to your instructor.

(5) **Ethics in Action**   The United States Federal Bureau of Investigation uses a controversial program to monitor and store the e-mail and Internet activity of suspected criminals. Originally called Carnivore, the surveillance program has been renamed <u>DCS1000</u>. The program is designed to track the activities of potential terrorists, spies, drug traffickers, and organized crime ring members. FBI agents must obtain a court order to monitor an individual, but privacy advocates claim the software tracks people not covered under the court order. View online sites that provide information about DCS1000 or Carnivore, including HowStuffWorks (computer.howstuffworks.com/carnivore.htm). Write a report summarizing your findings, and include a table of links to Web sites that provide additional details. If required, submit your report to your instructor.

Case Studies

Use the Case Studies to apply the concepts presented in the chapter to real-world situations. Visit scsite.com/dc2006/ch7/cases to obtain more information pertaining to each exercise. To discuss the Case Studies in this chapter with other students, visit scsite.com/dc2006/ch7/forum and post your thoughts or questions.

CASE STUDY 1 — Class Discussion   The owner of the tractor repair shop where you are employed as a part-time office manager is tired of continually upgrading the company's computer system. After attending a seminar on how small businesses can make use of the Internet, she asked you to look into the feasibility of using <u>online storage</u> (also called an Internet hard disk, rather than purchasing additional storage for the company's computer. Write a brief report outlining the advantages and disadvantages of using online storage. Compare Yahoo! and Google's online storage offerings. Which company offers the best arrangement? Why? Be prepared to discuss your recommendations in class.

CASE STUDY 2 — Class Discussion   PJ Cement Company has hired you as an IT consultant. The company plans to purchase 15 computers for use in the accounting department. The first task assigned to you by the president of the company is to recommend the number and types of <u>CD and DVD drives</u> to include with the computers they plan to purchase. They want to use CDs and/or DVDs to share data and information between employees and to back up critical files. Create a brief memo that includes a table summarizing the advantages and disadvantages of using CD-ROM, recordable CD, rewritable CD, DVD-ROM, recordable DVD, and rewritable DVD. Include in the table both the approximate cost of the drive and the media. Be prepared to discuss your findings in class.

CASE STUDY 3 — Research   An old aphorism claims, "You never can have too much money." Many computer users support a similar maxim, "You never can have too much storage." Your manager at MJ National Bank where you are employed as an analyst, however, is tired of buying more hardware to meet the bank's storage needs. She wants you to investigate alternative ways to improve <u>storage capacity</u>. Use the Web and/or print media to find out more about hard disk partitions and data compression as a means of increasing storage capacity. How do partitions increase the capacity of hard disks? What kind of data compression is most suitable for communications devices? What are the most well known data compression algorithms? How can compression ratios of different algorithms be compared? What are some formats for data compression archives? Prepare a report and/or PowerPoint presentation and share your findings with your class.

CASE STUDY 4 — Research   A major national retail chain, where you are employed as a technology buyer, has grown enormously over the past few years. The growth has required the company to triple its storage capacity each year to keep pace with its expanding business. Your manager, who is up for promotion, wants to impress his boss by expanding the storage capacity by tenfold this year while staying under the budget earmarked for storage improvements. He has asked you to look into the latest cutting-edge <u>storage technologies</u>, such as holographic and heat-assisted storage. Use the Web and/or print media to develop a features/benefits breakdown that compares the latest storage technologies to the more traditional hard disk technology. What do the different technologies entail? Are they available today? If not, when? What are their costs? Prepare a report and/or PowerPoint presentation summarizing your findings.

CASE STUDY 5 — Team Challenge   Your team has been assigned to do IT research for a new local magazine-subscription telemarketing company that is about to open for business. The company's business plan calls for 150 telemarketers to make a minimum of 100 calls a day. If a telemarketer does not meet the minimum number of calls, then he or she is required to finish the calls from home. The company plans to buy used computers for each telemarketer to use at home. The company also has to decide on the type of <u>storage device</u> to provide the telemarketers so that when they have to make calls from home, they have a way to take the necessary data home with them. Senior management has narrowed down their choice to three storage devices — floppy disks, USB flash drives, or Zip drives. Form a three-member team and have each team member choose a different storage device. Using the Web and/or print media, have each team member determine the advantages and disadvantages of their chosen device. Include such features as capacity, access time, durability of media, and cost. As a team, merge your findings into a team report and/or PowerPoint presentation and share your recommendations with your class.

CHAPTER EIGHT

Operating Systems and Utility Programs

Picture Yourself Getting a Virus through E-Mail

With a break between classes, you and some classmates sit outside and enjoy the nice weather. Everyone decides to exchange e-mail addresses and phone numbers, so you can communicate while away from school.

Later that night at home, you notice a classmate has sent you a picture via e-mail. As soon as you open the picture, your computer freezes. You click the mouse button. Nothing happens. You press a key on the keyboard. The computer beeps. You click the mouse again. Still no response. You restart the computer. The Windows XP desktop never appears.

At that moment, your smart phone rings. A panicked friend says his computer stopped working as soon as he opened that picture. Realizing the picture file probably had a virus, you call a technical support hotline. After explaining the situation, the support technician asks you several questions, and you answer: Did you have antivirus software installed on the computer? "No." Were the operating system's firewall settings enabled? "I don't know." Do you have a backup of the computer's hard disk? "No, I haven't learned how to burn CDs to make backups." Can you find the computer's recovery disc? "Yes, it's right here." The bad news is you lost *everything* on your computer and had to reinstall Windows XP — the good news is your computer is functional again. Now, you need to protect your computer from future infections.

Read Chapter 8 to learn about antivirus software, firewall settings, backups, and recovery discs, and discover features of most operating systems and utility programs.

SYSTEM SOFTWARE

When you purchase a personal computer, it usually has system software installed on its hard disk. **System software** consists of the programs that control or maintain the operations of the computer and its devices. System software serves as the interface between the user, the application software, and the computer's hardware.

Two types of system software are operating systems and utility programs. Several types of utility programs are provided with an operating system. Other utility programs are available stand-alone, that is, as programs separate from the operating system. This chapter discusses the operating system and its functions, as well as several types of utility programs for personal computers.

OPERATING SYSTEMS

An **operating system (OS)** is a set of programs containing instructions that coordinate all the activities among computer hardware resources. Most operating systems perform similar functions that include starting a computer, providing a user interface, managing programs, managing memory, scheduling jobs, configuring devices, establishing an Internet connection,

start the computer

administer security

control a network

provide file management and other utilities

operating system

FIGURE 8-1   Most operating systems perform the functions illustrated in this figure.

monitoring performance, and providing file management utilities. Some operating systems also allow users to control a network and administer security (Figure 8-1).

In most cases, the operating system is installed and resides on the computer's hard disk. On handheld computers and many mobile devices such as PDAs and smart phones, however, the operating system may reside on a ROM chip.

Different sizes of computers typically use different operating systems. For example, a mainframe computer does not use the same operating system as a personal computer. Even the same types of computers, such as desktop computers, may not use the same operating system. Furthermore, the application software designed for a specific operating system may not run when using another operating system. For example, PCs often use Windows XP, and iMacs use Mac OS X. When purchasing application software, you must ensure that it works with the operating system installed on your computer.

The operating system that a computer uses sometimes is called the *platform*. On purchased application software, the package identifies the required platform (operating system). A *cross-platform* program is one that runs the same on multiple operating systems.

provide a user interface

manage programs

manage memory

establish an Internet connection

schedule jobs and configure devices

monitor performance

OPERATING SYSTEM FUNCTIONS

Many different operating systems exist, designed for all types of computers. Regardless of the size of the computer, however, most operating systems provide similar functions. The following sections discuss functions common to most operating systems. The operating system handles many of these functions automatically, without requiring any instructions from a user.

Starting a Computer

The process of starting or restarting a computer is called **booting**. When turning on a computer that has been powered off completely, you are performing a **cold boot**. A **warm boot**, by contrast, is the process of using the operating system to restart a computer. A warm boot properly closes any open processes and programs. With Windows XP, you can perform a warm boot by clicking the Start button on the taskbar, clicking Turn Off Computer on the Start menu, and then clicking Restart in the Turn off computer dialog box (Figure 8-2). Some computers have a reset button that when pressed restarts a computer as if it had been powered off. A reset button does not properly close open processes.

When you install new software, often an on-screen prompt instructs you to restart the computer. In this case, a warm boot is appropriate. If your computer stops responding, try to restart it with a warm boot first. If it does not respond to the warm boot, then try pushing the reset button on the computer, if the computer has a reset button. As a last resort, restart the computer with a cold boot; that is, push the power button.

Each time you boot a computer, the kernel and other frequently used operating system instructions are loaded, or copied, from the hard disk (storage) into the computer's memory (RAM). The *kernel* is the core of an operating

FIGURE 8-2 To reboot a running computer, click the Restart button in the Turn off computer dialog box.

system that manages memory and devices, maintains the computer's clock, starts applications, and assigns the computer's resources, such as devices, programs, data, and information. The kernel is *memory resident*, which means it remains in memory while the computer is running. Other parts of the operating system are *nonresident*, that is, these instructions remain on the hard disk until they are needed.

When you boot a computer, a series of messages may be displayed on the screen. The actual information displayed varies depending on the make and type of the computer and the equipment installed. The boot process, however, is similar for large and small computers.

The steps in the following paragraphs explain what occurs during a cold boot on a personal computer using the Windows XP operating system. The steps in Figure 8-3 illustrate and correspond to the steps discussed in the following paragraphs.

Step 1: When you turn on the computer, the power supply sends an electrical signal to the components in the system unit.

Step 2: The charge of electricity causes the processor chip to reset itself and find the ROM chip(s) that contains the BIOS. The **BIOS** (pronounced BYE-ose), which stands for *basic input/output system*, is firmware that contains the computer's startup instructions.

Step 3: The BIOS executes a series of tests to make sure the computer hardware is connected properly and operating correctly. The tests, collectively called the *power-on self test* (POST), check the various system components including the buses, system clock, adapter cards, RAM chips, mouse, keyboard, and drives. As the POST executes, LEDs (tiny lights) flicker on devices such as the disk drives and keyboard. Several beeps also sound, and messages are displayed on the screen.

Step 4: The POST results are compared with data in a CMOS chip. As discussed in Chapter 4, CMOS is a technology that uses battery power to retain information when the computer is off. The CMOS chip stores configuration information about the computer, such as the amount of memory; type of disk drives, keyboard, and monitor; the current date and time; and other startup information. It also detects any new devices connected to the computer. If any problems are identified, the computer may beep, display error messages, or cease operating — depending on the severity of the problem.

Step 5: If the POST completes successfully, the BIOS searches for specific operating system files called *system files*. The BIOS may look first to see if a disk in the floppy disk drive or a disc in a CD or DVD drive contain the system files. If these drives do not contain media or if the system files are not on media

in the drive, the BIOS looks in drive C (the designation usually given to the first hard disk) for the system files.

Step 6: Once located, the system files load into memory (RAM) from storage (usually the hard disk) and execute. Next, the kernel of the operating system loads into memory. Then, the operating system in memory takes control of the computer.

Step 7: The operating system loads system configuration information. In Windows XP,

WEB LINK 8-1

BIOS
For more information, visit scsite.com/ dc2006/ch8/weblink and then click BIOS.

FIGURE 8-3   HOW A PC BOOTS UP

Step 1:
The power supply sends a signal to the components in the system unit.

Step 2:
The processor finds the ROM chip(s) that contains the BIOS (basic input/output system).

Step 3:
The BIOS performs the POST (power-on self test), which checks components, such as the mouse, keyboard, and adapter cards.

Step 4:
The results of the POST are compared with data in a CMOS chip.

Step 5:
The BIOS sometimes looks for the system files in drive A (floppy disk drive) or a CD or DVD drive, and then drive C (hard disk).

Step 6:
The system files and the kernel of the operating system load into memory (RAM) from storage (hard disk).

Step 7:
The operating system loads configuration information, may request user information, and displays the desktop on the screen.

the *registry* consists of several files that contain the system configuration information. Windows XP constantly accesses the registry during the computer's operation for information such as installed hardware and software devices and individual user preferences for mouse speed, passwords, and other information.

Necessary operating system files are loaded into memory. On some computers, the operating system verifies that the person attempting to use the computer is a legitimate user. Finally, the Windows XP desktop and icons are displayed on the screen. The operating system executes programs in the *Startup folder*, which contains a list of programs that open automatically when you boot the computer.

RECOVERY DISK A **boot drive** is the drive from which your personal computer boots (starts). In most cases, drive C (the hard disk) is the boot drive. Sometimes a hard disk becomes damaged and the computer cannot boot from the hard disk. In this case, you can boot from a special disk, called a **recovery disk** or a **boot disk**, that contains a few system files that will start the computer. When you purchase a computer, it usually includes a recovery disk in the form of a CD. If you do not have a recovery disk, the operating system usually provides a means to create one.

FAQ 8-1

When I am finished using the computer, can I simply turn it off?

No! You must use the operating system's shut-down procedure so various processes are closed in sequence and items in memory released properly. Depending on the computer, several shut-down options exist. The Turn Off command removes power from the computer. Restart does a warm boot. *Hibernate* saves all documents in memory and then turns off the computer. *Stand By* places the entire computer in a low-power state but does not turn it off. With Hibernate and Stand By, the next time you resume work on the computer, the desktop is restored to exactly how you left it. For more information, visit scsite.com/dc2006/ch8/faq and then click Shut-Down Options.

Providing a User Interface

You interact with software through its user interface. That is, a **user interface** controls how you enter data and instructions and how information is displayed on the screen. Three types of user interfaces are command-line, menu-driven, and graphical. Operating systems often use a combination of these interfaces to define how a user interacts with a computer.

COMMAND-LINE INTERFACE To configure devices, manage system resources, and trouble-shoot network connections, network administrators and other advanced users work with a command-line interface. In a *command-line interface*, a user types commands or presses special keys on the keyboard (such as function keys or key combinations) to enter data and instructions (Figure 8-4a). Command-line interfaces often are difficult to use because they require exact spelling, grammar, and punctuation. Minor errors, such as a missing period, generate an error message. Command-line interfaces, however, give a user more control to manage detailed settings. For a technical discussion about a command-line interface, read the High-Tech Talk article on page 430.

When working with a command-line interface, the set of commands entered into the computer is called the *command language*. Programs that contain command language instructions are called *scripts*. Network administrators and Web page programmers often use scripts.

MENU-DRIVEN INTERFACE A *menu-driven interface* provides menus as a means of entering commands (Figure 8-4b). Menu-driven interfaces are easier to learn than command-line interfaces because users do not have to learn the rules of entering commands.

GRAPHICAL USER INTERFACE Most users today work with a graphical user interface. With a *graphical user interface* (*GUI*), you interact with menus and visual images such as buttons and other graphical objects to issue commands. Many current GUI operating systems incorporate features similar to those of a Web browser. The Windows XP screen shown in Figure 8-4c, for example, contains links and navigation buttons such as the Back button and the Forward button.

FIGURE 8-4a (command-line)

FIGURE 8-4b (menu-driven)

FIGURE 8-4c (graphical)

FIGURE 8-4 Examples of command-line, menu-driven, and graphical user interfaces.

Managing Programs

Some operating systems support a single user and only one running program at a time. Others support thousands of users running multiple programs. How an operating system handles programs directly affects your productivity.

A *single user/single tasking* operating system allows only one user to run one program at a time. For example, if you are working in a graphics program and want to check e-mail messages, you must quit the graphics program before you can run the e-mail program. Early systems were single user/single tasking. Most of today's operating systems are multitasking. PDAs, smart phones, and other small computing devices, however, often use a single user/single tasking operating system.

A *single user/multitasking* operating system allows a single user to work on two or more programs that reside in memory at the same time. Using the example just cited, if you are working with a single user/multitasking operating system, you do not have to quit the graphics program to run the e-mail program. Both programs can run concurrently. Users today typically run multiple programs concurrently. It is common to have an e-mail program and Web browser open at all times, while working with application programs such as word processing or graphics.

When a computer is running multiple programs concurrently, one program is in the foreground and the others are in the background. The one in the *foreground* is the active program, that is, the one you currently are using. The other programs running but not in use are in the *background*. In Figure 8-5, the PowerPoint program, which is showing a slide show, is in the foreground, and three other programs are running in the background (Paint Shop Pro, Encarta Encyclopedia, and iTunes). For example, iTunes can be playing music while you are modifying the slide show.

The foreground program typically displays on the desktop, and the background programs are partially or completely hidden behind the foreground program. You easily can switch between foreground and background programs. To make a program active (in the foreground) in Windows XP, click its program button on the taskbar. This causes the operating system to place all other programs in the background.

In addition to application programs, an operating system manages other processes. These processes include utilities or routines that provide support to other programs or hardware.

FIGURE 8-5 The foreground program, PowerPoint, is displayed on the desktop. The other programs (Paint Shop Pro, Encarta Encyclopedia, and iTunes) are in the background.

Some are memory resident. Others run as they are required. Figure 8-6 shows a list of all processes running on a Windows XP computer. The list contains the applications programs running, as well as other programs and processes.

Some operating systems use preemptive multitasking to prevent any one process from monopolizing the computer's resources. With *preemptive multitasking*, the operating system interrupts a program that is executing and passes control to another program waiting to be executed. An advantage of preemptive multitasking is the operating system regains control if one program stops operating properly.

A *multiuser* operating system enables two or more users to run programs simultaneously. Networks, midrange servers, mainframes, and supercomputers allow hundreds to thousands of users to connect at the same time, and thus are multiuser.

A *multiprocessing* operating system supports two or more processors running programs at the same time. Multiprocessing involves the coordinated processing of programs by more than one processor. Multiprocessing increases a computer's processing speed.

A computer with separate processors also can serve as a fault-tolerant computer. A *fault-tolerant computer* continues to operate when one of its components fails, ensuring that no data is lost. Fault-tolerant computers have duplicate components such as processors, memory, and disk drives. If any one of these components fails, the computer switches to the duplicate component and continues to operate. Airline reservation systems, communications networks, automated teller machines, and other systems that must be operational at all times use fault-tolerant computers.

Managing Memory

The purpose of **memory management** is to optimize the use of random access memory (RAM). As discussed in Chapter 4, RAM consists of one or more chips on the motherboard that hold items such as data and instructions while the processor interprets and executes them. The operating system allocates, or assigns, data and instructions to an area of memory while they are being processed. Then, it carefully monitors the contents of memory. Finally, the operating system releases these items from being monitored in memory when the processor no longer requires them.

If you have multiple programs running simultaneously, it is possible to run out of RAM. For example, assume an operating system requires 128 MB of RAM, an antivirus program — 128 MB of RAM, a Web browser — 32 MB of RAM, a business software suite — 64 MB of RAM, and a photo editing program — 128 MB of RAM. With all these programs running simultaneously, the total RAM required would be 480 MB of RAM (128 + 128 + 32 + 64 + 128). If the computer has only 256 MB of RAM, the operating system may have to use virtual memory to solve the problem.

FIGURE 8-6 An operating system manages multiple programs and processes while you use the computer.

With **virtual memory**, the operating system allocates a portion of a storage medium, usually the hard disk, to function as additional RAM (Figure 8-7). As you interact with a program, part of it may be in physical RAM, while the rest of the program is on the hard disk as virtual memory. Because virtual memory is slower than RAM, users may notice the computer slowing down while it uses virtual memory.

The area of the hard disk used for virtual memory is called a *swap file* because it swaps (exchanges) data, information, and instructions between memory and storage. A *page* is the amount of data and program instructions that can swap at a given time. The technique of swapping items between memory and storage, called *paging*, is a time-consuming process for the computer.

When an operating system spends much of its time paging, instead of executing application software, it is said to be *thrashing*. If application software, such as a Web browser, has stopped responding and the hard disk's LED blinks repeatedly, the operating system probably is thrashing.

FAQ 8-2

How can I stop a computer from thrashing?

Try to quit the program that stopped responding. If the computer does not respond and continues to thrash, do a warm boot. When the computer reboots, check whether the available hard disk space is less than 200 MB. If it is, remove unnecessary files from the hard disk and if possible uninstall seldom used programs. Defragment the hard disk (discussed later in this chapter). If thrashing continues to occur, you may need to install more RAM in the computer. For more information, visit scsite.com/dc2006/ch8/faq and then click Optimizing Memory.

Scheduling Jobs

The operating system determines the order in which jobs are processed. A **job** is an operation the processor manages. Jobs include receiving data from an input device, processing instructions, sending information to an output device, and transferring items from storage to memory and from memory to storage.

FIGURE 8-7 HOW A COMPUTER MIGHT USE VIRTUAL MEMORY

RAM (physical memory)

page swapped out

disk (virtual memory)

swap file

Step 1:
The operating system transfers the least recently used data and program instructions from RAM to the hard disk because RAM is needed for other functions.

Step 2:
The operating system transfers data and program instructions from the hard disk to RAM when they are needed.

page swapped in

A mulituser operating system does not always process jobs on a first-come, first-served basis. Sometimes, one user may have a higher priority than other users. In this case, the operating system adjusts the schedule of jobs.

Sometimes, a device already may be busy processing one job when it receives a second job. This occurs because the processor operates at a much faster rate of speed than peripheral devices. For example, if the processor sends five print jobs to a printer, the printer can print only one document at a time.

While waiting for devices to become idle, the operating system places items in buffers. A **buffer** is a segment of memory or storage in which items are placed while waiting to be transferred from an input device or to an output device.

The operating system commonly uses buffers with print jobs. This process, called **spooling**, sends print jobs to a buffer instead of sending them immediately to the printer. The buffer holds the information waiting to print while the printer prints from the buffer at its own rate of speed. By spooling print jobs to a buffer, the processor can continue interpreting and executing instructions while the printer prints. This allows users to work on the computer for other tasks while a printer is printing. Multiple print jobs line up in a **queue** (pronounced Q)

in the buffer. A program, called a *print spooler*, intercepts print jobs from the operating system and places them in the queue (Figure 8-8).

Configuring Devices

A **driver**, short for *device driver*, is a small program that tells the operating system how to communicate with a specific device. Each device on a computer, such as the mouse, keyboard, monitor, printer, card reader/writer, and scanner, has its own specialized set of commands and thus requires its own specific driver. When you boot a computer, the operating system loads each device's driver. These devices will not function without their correct drivers.

If you attach a new device to a computer, such as a printer or scanner, its driver must be installed before you can use the device. Today, many devices and operating systems support Plug and Play. As discussed in Chapter 4, **Plug and Play** means the operating system automatically configures new devices as you install them. Specifically, it assists you in the device's installation by loading the necessary drivers automatically and checking for conflicts with other devices. With Plug and Play, a user plugs in a device, turns on the computer, and then uses the device without having to configure the system manually.

FIGURE 8-8 Spooling increases both processor and printer efficiency by placing print jobs in a buffer on disk before they are printed. This figure illustrates three jobs in the queue with one job printing.

For devices that are not Plug and Play, Windows XP provides a wizard to guide users through the installation steps. Figure 8-9 shows how to install a driver for a printer. You follow the same general steps to install drivers for any type of hardware. For many devices, the computer's operating system may include the necessary drivers. If it does not, you can install the drivers from the CD or disk provided with the purchased device.

When you attach a Plug and Play device to a computer, the operating system determines an

FIGURE 8-9 HOW TO INSTALL DRIVERS FOR NEW HARDWARE IN WINDOWS XP

Step 1:
Open the Control Panel window. Point to the Printers and Other Hardware link.

Step 2:
Click the Printers and Other Hardware link. Point to the Add a printer link.

Step 4:
The Add Printer Wizard searches for Plug and Play printers on your computer. If it finds any such printers, it installs them.

Step 3:
Click the Add a printer link. Follow the on-screen instructions.

Step 5:
If the Add Printer Wizard cannot find any Plug and Play printers, you can select the type of printer you want to install. An on-screen prompt may ask you to insert the floppy disk, CD-ROM, or DVD-ROM that contains the necessary driver files to complete the installation of the printer.

appropriate IRQ to use. An *IRQ* (*interrupt request line*) is a communications line between a device and the processor. If the operating system uses an IRQ that already is assigned to another device, an IRQ conflict may occur and the computer may not work properly. If an IRQ conflict occurs, you will have to obtain the correct IRQ for the device. This information typically is located in the installation directions that accompany the device. Most personal computers have 16 IRQs.

FAQ 8-3

What if I do not have the driver for a device?

When reinstalling an operating system, you may have to supply a device's driver. If you do not have the original driver disk, visit the manufacturer's Web site. Most post drivers for download at no cost, or they may suggest a similar driver that will work. If you do not have Internet access, call the manufacturer and request a new disk via the postal service. For more information, visit scsite.com/dc2006/ch8/faq and then click Drivers.

Establishing an Internet Connection

Operating systems typically provide a means to establish Internet connections. For example, Windows XP includes a New Connection Wizard that guides users through the process of setting up a connection between a computer and an Internet service provider (Figure 8-10).

Some operating systems also include a Web browser and an e-mail program, enabling you to begin using the Web and communicate with others as soon as you set up the Internet connection. Some also include a built-in firewall to protect computers from unauthorized intrusions.

Monitoring Performance

Operating systems typically contain a performance monitor. A **performance monitor** is a program that assesses and reports information about various computer resources and devices (Figure 8-11). For example, users can monitor the processor, disks, memory, and network usage. A performance monitor also can check the number of reads and writes to a disk.

The information in performance reports helps users and administrators identify a problem with resources so they can try to resolve any problems. If a computer is running extremely slow, for example, the performance monitor may determine that the computer's memory is being used to its maximum. Thus, you might consider installing additional memory in the computer.

FIGURE 8-11 The System Monitor above is tracking the kernel usage and the amount of unused physical memory.

FIGURE 8-10 To display the New Connection Wizard in Windows XP, click the Start button, point to All Programs, point to Accessories, point to Communications, and then click New Connection Wizard on the Communications submenu.

Providing File Management and Other Utilities

Operating systems often provide users with the capability of managing files, viewing images, securing a computer from unauthorized access, uninstalling programs, scanning disks, defragmenting disks, diagnosing problems, backing up files and disks, and setting up screen savers. A later section in the chapter discusses these utilities in depth. Read At Issue 8-1 for a related discussion.

AT ISSUE 8-1

Who Is Responsible for Operating System Security?

A few years ago, the Sasser worm infected almost one million computers in the stretch of a weekend. Surprisingly, most computer users already had the necessary means to stop this worm before it even got started. The Windows XP operating system comes equipped with built-in firewall protection, but, by default, the feature was turned off. Microsoft later released a service pack, or update, for the operating system in which the feature was turned on by default. Most operating system manufacturers allow users automatically to download and install up-to-date security patches. It is up to the users to make use of this service properly and make certain that their operating system software is up-to-date. Sometimes, as was the case with the Sasser worm, the updates come too late. Often, users are not technically savvy enough to keep up with the security updates or to configure a network connection with a firewall properly. Who should be responsible for operating system security? Why? Should operating system manufacturers be required to send security updates to computer users? Why or why not? Should users be required to take responsibility for worms and viruses that they spread to others due to lax security? Why or why not?

Controlling a Network

Some operating systems are network operating systems. A **network operating system**, or *network OS*, is an operating system that organizes and coordinates how multiple users access and share resources on a network. Resources include hardware, software, data, and information. For example, a network OS allows multiple users to share a printer, Internet access, files, and programs.

Some operating systems have network features built into them. In other cases, the network OS is a set of programs separate from the operating system on the client computers that access the network. When not connected to the network, the client computers use their own operating system. When connected to the network, the network OS may assume some of the operating system functions.

The *network administrator*, the person overseeing network operations, uses the network OS to add and remove users, computers, and other devices to and from the network. The network administrator also uses the network operating system to install software and administer network security.

Administering Security

The network administrator uses the network OS to establish permissions to resources. These permissions define who can access certain resources and when they can access those resources.

For each user, the network administrator establishes a user account, which enables a user to access, or **log on** to, a computer or a network. Each user account typically consists of a user name and password (Figure 8-12). A **user name**, or **user ID**, is a unique combination of characters, such as letters of the alphabet or numbers, that identifies one specific user. Many users select a combination of their first and last names as their user name. A user named Henry West might choose H West as his user name.

A **password** is a private combination of characters associated with the user name that allows access to certain computer resources. Some operating systems allow the network

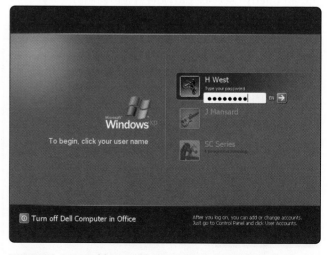

FIGURE 8-12 Most multiuser operating systems allow each user to log on, which is the process of entering a user name and a password into the computer.

administrator to assign passwords to files and commands, restricting access to only authorized users.

To prevent unauthorized users from accessing computer resources, keep your password confidential. While entering your password, most computers hide the actual password characters by displaying some other characters, such as asterisks (*) or dots. After entering a user name and password, the operating system compares the user's entry with a list of authorized user names and passwords. If the entry matches the user name and password kept on file, the operating system grants the user access. If the entry does not match, the operating system denies access to the user.

The operating system records successful and unsuccessful logon attempts in a file. This allows the network administrator to review who is using or attempting to use the computer. Network administrators also use these files to monitor computer usage.

To protect sensitive data and information further as it travels over the network, a network operating system may encrypt it. *Encryption* is the process of encoding data and information into an unreadable form. Network administrators can set up a network to encrypt data as it travels over the network to prevent unauthorized users from reading the data. When an authorized user attempts to read the data, it automatically is decrypted, or converted back into a readable form.

Test your knowledge of pages 398 through 411 in Quiz Yourself 8-1.

QUIZ YOURSELF 8-1

Instructions: Find the true statement below. Then, rewrite the remaining false statements so they are true.

1. A buffer is a small program that tells the operating system how to communicate with a specific device.
2. A cold boot is the process of using the operating system to restart a computer.
3. A password is a public combination of characters associated with the user name that allows access to certain computer resources.
4. Firmware that contains the computer's startup instructions is called the kernel.
5. The program you currently are using is in the background, and the other programs running but not in use are in the foreground.
6. Two types of system software are operating systems and application programs.
7. With virtual memory, the operating system allocates a portion of a storage medium, usually the hard disk, to function as additional RAM.

Quiz Yourself Online: To further check your knowledge of system software and features common to most operating systems, visit scsite.com/dc2006/ch8/quiz and then click Objectives 1 – 4.

OPERATING SYSTEM UTILITY PROGRAMS

A **utility program**, also called a **utility**, is a type of system software that allows a user to perform maintenance-type tasks, usually related to managing a computer, its devices, or its programs. Most operating systems include several built-in utility programs (Figure 8-13). Users often buy stand-alone utilities, however, because they offer improvements over those included with the operating system.

FAQ 8-4

What are the guidelines for selecting a good password?

Choose a password that no one could guess. Do not use any part of your first or last name, your spouse's or child's name, telephone number, street address, license plate number, Social Security number, and so on. Be sure your password is at least six characters long, mixed with letters and numbers. For more information, visit scsite.com/dc2006/ch8/faq and then click Passwords.

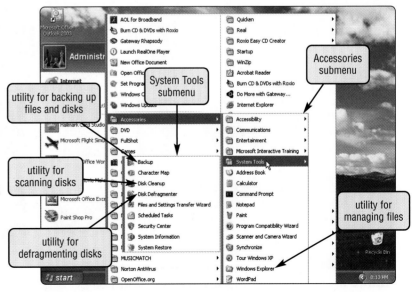

FIGURE 8-13 Many utilities available in Windows XP are accessible through the Accessories and System Tools submenus.

Utility programs included with most operating systems provide the following functions: managing files, viewing images, securing a computer from unauthorized access, uninstalling programs, scanning disks, defragmenting disks, diagnosing problems, backing up files and disks, and setting up screen savers. The following sections briefly discuss each of these utilities.

File Manager

A **file manager** is a utility that performs functions related to file and disk management. Windows XP includes a file manager called *Windows Explorer*. Some of the file and disk management functions that a file manager performs are formatting and copying disks; displaying a list of files on a storage medium (Figure 8-14); checking the amount of used or free space on a storage medium; organizing, copying, renaming, deleting, moving, and sorting files; and creating shortcuts. A **shortcut** is an icon on the desktop that provides a user with immediate access to a program or file.

Formatting is the process of preparing a disk for reading and writing. Most floppy and hard disk manufacturers preformat their disks. If you must format a floppy disk or other media, you can do so using the file manager. For a technical discussion about formatting, read the High-Tech Talk article on page 382 in Chapter 7.

Image Viewer

An **image viewer** is a utility that allows users to display, copy, and print the contents of a graphics file. With an image viewer, users can see images without having to open them in a paint or image editing program. Windows XP includes an image viewer called *Windows Picture and Fax Viewer* (Figure 8-15). To display a file in this image viewer, simply double-click the thumbnail of the image in the file manager. For example, double-clicking a thumbnail in Windows Explorer (Figure 8-14) displays the image in a Windows Picture and Fax Viewer window.

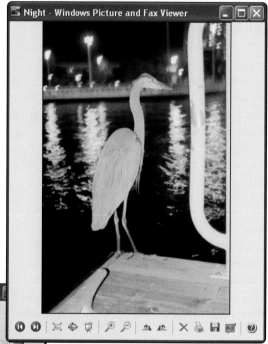

FIGURE 8-15 Windows Picture and Fax Viewer allows users to see the contents of a graphics file.

FIGURE 8-14 With Windows Explorer, which is the file manager included with Windows XP, users can display a list of graphics files on a disk. In this case, thumbnails of the files are displayed.

Personal Firewall

A **personal firewall** is a utility that detects and protects a personal computer from unauthorized intrusions. Personal firewalls constantly monitor all transmissions to and from a computer.

When connected to the Internet, your computer is vulnerable to attacks from a hacker. A *hacker* is someone who tries to access a computer or network illegally. Users with broadband Internet connections, such as through DSL and Internet cable television service, are even more susceptible than those with dial-up access because the Internet connection is always on.

The latest update to Windows XP automatically enables the built-in personal firewall upon installation. This firewall, called Windows Firewall, is easy to access and configure (Figure 8-16). If your operating system does not include a personal firewall or you want additional protection, you can purchase a standalone personal firewall utility or a hardware firewall, which is a device such as a router that has a built-in firewall.

Uninstaller

An **uninstaller** is a utility that removes a program, as well as any associated entries in the system files. In Windows XP, the uninstaller is available through the Add/Remove Programs command in the Control Panel.

When you install a program, the operating system records the information it uses to run the software in the system files. The uninstaller deletes files and folders from the hard disk, as well as removes program entries from the system files.

FAQ 8-5

Should I use the file manager to delete a program?

No! If you remove software from a computer by deleting the files and folders associated with the program without running the uninstaller, the system file entries are not updated. This may cause the operating system to display error messages when you start the computer. If the program has an uninstaller, always use it to remove software. For more information, visit scsite.com/dc2006/ch8/faq and then click Uninstalling Programs.

FIGURE 8-16 Through the Security Center in the Control Panel of Windows XP, users can configure Windows Firewall, which is a personal firewall utility built into the latest upgrade of Windows XP.

WEB LINK 8-3

Personal Firewalls

For more information, visit scsite.com/dc2006/ch8/weblink and then click Personal Firewalls.

Disk Scanner

A **disk scanner** is a utility that (1) detects and corrects both physical and logical problems on a hard disk and (2) searches for and removes unnecessary files. A physical disk problem is a problem with the media such as a scratch on the surface of the disk. A logical disk problem is a problem with the data, such as a corrupt file. Windows XP includes two disk scanner utilities. One detects problems and the other searches for and removes unnecessary files such as temporary files (Figure 8-17).

FIGURE 8-17 Disk Cleanup searches for and removes unnecessary files.

Disk Defragmenter

A **disk defragmenter** is a utility that reorganizes the files and unused space on a computer's hard disk so the operating system accesses data more quickly and programs run faster. When an operating system stores data on a disk, it places the data in the first available sector on the disk. It attempts to place data in sectors that are contiguous (next to each other), but this is not always possible. When the contents of a file are scattered across two or more noncontiguous sectors, the file is *fragmented*.

Fragmentation slows down disk access and thus the performance of the entire computer. **Defragmenting** the disk, or reorganizing it so the files are stored in contiguous sectors, solves this problem (Figure 8-18). Windows XP includes a disk defragmenter available on the System Tools submenu.

FIGURE 8-18 A fragmented disk has many files stored in noncontiguous sectors. Defragmenting reorganizes the files so they are located in contiguous sectors, which speeds access time.

Diagnostic Utility

A **diagnostic utility** compiles technical information about your computer's hardware and certain system software programs and then prepares a report outlining any identified problems. For example, Windows XP includes the diagnostic utility, *Dr. Watson*, which diagnoses problems as well as suggests courses of action (Figure 8-19). Information in the report assists technical support staff in remedying any problems.

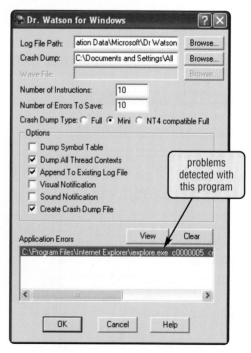

FIGURE 8-19 Dr. Watson is a diagnostic utility included with Windows.

Backup Utility

A **backup utility** allows users to copy, or *back up*, selected files or an entire hard disk to another storage medium. During the backup process, the backup utility monitors progress and alerts you if it needs additional discs or tapes. Many backup programs *compress*, or shrink the size of, files during the backup process. By compressing the files, the backup program requires less storage space for the backup files than for the original files.

Because they are compressed, you usually cannot use backup files in their backed up form. In the event you need to use a backup file, a **restore program** reverses the process and returns backed up files to their original form. Backup utilities include restore programs.

You should back up files and disks regularly in the event your originals are lost, damaged, or destroyed. Windows XP includes a backup utility (Figure 8-20). Instead of backing up to a local disk storage device, some users opt to use online storage to back up their files. As described in Chapter 7, online storage is a service on the Web that provides hard disk storage to computer users, usually for a minimal monthly fee.

FIGURE 8-20 A backup utility allows users to copy files or an entire hard disk to another storage medium.

Screen Saver

A **screen saver** is a utility that causes a display device's screen to show a moving image or blank screen if no keyboard or mouse activity occurs for a specified time (Figure 8-21). When you press a key on the keyboard or move the mouse, the screen saver disappears and the screen returns to the previous state.

FIGURE 8-21 A Windows XP screen saver.

Screen savers originally were developed to prevent a problem called *ghosting*, in which images could be permanently etched on a monitor's screen. Although ghosting is not as severe of a problem with today's displays, manufacturers continue to recommend that users install screen savers for this reason. Screen savers also are popular for security, business, and entertainment purposes. To secure a computer, users configure their screen saver to require a password to deactivate. In addition to those included with the operating system, many screen savers are available in stores and on the Web for free or a minimal fee.

TYPES OF OPERATING SYSTEMS

Many of the first operating systems were device dependent and proprietary. A *device-dependent* program is one that runs only on a specific type or make of computer. *Proprietary software* is privately owned and limited to a specific vendor or computer model. Some operating systems still are device dependent. The trend today, however, is toward *device-independent* operating systems that run on computers provided by a variety of manufacturers. The advantage of device-independent operating systems is you can retain existing application software and data files even if you change computer models or vendors.

WEB LINK 8-4

Screen Savers
For more information, visit scsite.com/dc2006/ch8/weblink and then click Screen Savers.

When you purchase a new computer, it typically has an operating system preinstalled. As new versions of the operating system are released, users upgrade their existing computers to incorporate features of the new version. An upgrade usually costs less than purchasing the entire operating system.

Some software manufacturers, such as Microsoft and IBM, release free downloadable updates to their software, often called a *service pack*. Users also can order service packs on CD for a minimal shipping fee. Service packs provide enhancements to the original software and fix bugs (errors) in the software. Read At Issue 8-2 for a related discussion.

New versions of an operating system usually are downward compatible. That is, they recognize and work with application software written for an earlier version of the operating system (or platform). The application software, by contrast, is said to be upward compatible, meaning it will run on new versions of the operating system.

The three basic categories of operating systems that exist today are stand-alone, network, and embedded. The table in Figure 8-22 lists specific names of operating systems in each category. The following pages discuss the operating systems listed in the table.

AT ISSUE 8-2

Should Software Manufacturers Be Liable for Defective Software?

Several years ago in Panama, 28 patients receiving radiation treatment were given massive overdoses of radiation due to a software bug. Over the next several years, five of these patients died due to radiation poisoning and others were considered to be at risk of developing further complications. In another mishap, bugs in retail tax return preparation software caused erroneous tax calculations on individuals' tax returns. It is estimated that defective software costs U.S. businesses approximately $60 billion annually. In a software license, software manufacturers usually include a disclaimer that limits the manufacturer's liability in the event that software malfunctions. Due to the increase in viruses, worms, and well-publicized software failures, such as the one that caused the power blackout in much of the northeastern U.S. a few years ago, many people are calling for the government to force software manufacturers to assume more liability. Software manufacturers claim that more liability — and consequently more cost — will result in less software and fewer features. Should the government enact more rules regarding software quality and liability? Why or why not? Who should be held accountable, if anyone, when faulty software causes injury or financial loss? Why? Will the free market eventually force makers of bug-ridden software to go out of business?

CATEGORIES OF OPERATING SYSTEMS

Category	Operating System Name
Stand-alone	• DOS • Early Windows versions (Windows 3.x, Windows 95, Windows NT Workstation, Windows 98, Windows 2000 Professional, Windows Millennium Edition) • Windows XP • Mac OS X • UNIX • Linux
Network	• NetWare • Early Windows Server versions (Windows NT Server, Windows 2000 Server) • Windows Server 2003 • UNIX • Linux • Solaris
Embedded	• Windows CE • Windows Mobile • Palm OS • Embedded Linux • Symbian OS

FIGURE 8-22 Examples of stand-alone, network, and embedded operating systems. Some stand-alone operating systems include the capability of configuring small home or office networks.

STAND-ALONE OPERATING SYSTEMS

A **stand-alone operating system** is a complete operating system that works on a desktop computer, notebook computer, or mobile computing device. Some stand-alone operating systems are called *client operating systems* because they also work in conjunction with a network operating system. Client operating systems can operate with or without a network. Other stand-alone operating systems include networking capabilities, allowing the home and small business user to set up a small network.

Examples of stand-alone operating systems are DOS, Windows XP, Mac OS X, UNIX, and Linux. The following paragraphs briefly discuss these operating systems.

DOS

The term **DOS** (*Disk Operating System*) refers to several single user operating systems developed in the early 1980s by Microsoft for personal computers. The two more widely used versions of DOS were PC-DOS and MS-DOS. The functionality of these two operating systems was essentially the same.

DOS used a command-line interface when Microsoft first developed it. Later versions included both command-line and menu-driven user interfaces. At its peak, DOS was a widely used operating system, with an estimated 70 million computers running it. DOS hardly is used today because it does not offer a graphical user interface and it cannot take full advantage of modern 32-bit personal computer processors.

Windows XP

In the mid-1980s, Microsoft developed its first version of Windows, which provided a graphical user interface (GUI). Since then, Microsoft continually has updated its Windows operating system, incorporating innovative features and functions with each subsequent version (Figure 8-23). **Windows XP** is Microsoft's fastest, most reliable Windows operating system yet, providing quicker startup, better performance, and a simplified visual look.

FAQ 8-6

How many people use Windows?

According to Microsoft, the number of Windows PCs will grow to more than one billion by 2010. Studies by industry analysts estimate that 96 percent of desktop computers worldwide currently use Windows. For more information, visit scsite.com/dc2006/ch8/faq and then click Windows Users.

HIGHLIGHTS OF STAND-ALONE WINDOWS VERSIONS

Windows Version	Year Released	Highlights
Windows 3.x	1990	• Provided a GUI • An operating environment only — worked in combination with DOS
Windows NT 3.1	1993	• Client OS that connected to a Windows NT Advanced Server • Interface similar to Windows 3.x
Windows 95	1995	• True multitasking operating system • Improved GUI • Included support for networking, Plug and Play technology, longer file names, and e-mail
Windows NT Workstation 4.0	1996	• Client OS that connected to a Windows NT Server • Interface similar to Windows 95 • Network integration
Windows 98	1998	• Upgrade to Windows 95 • More integrated with the Internet; included *Internet Explorer* (a Web browser) • Faster system startup and shutdown, better file management, support for multimedia technologies (e.g., DVDs), and USB connectivity
Windows Millennium Edition	2000	• Upgrade to Windows 98 • Designed for the home user who wanted music playing, video editing, and networking capabilities
Windows 2000 Professional	2000	• Upgrade to Windows NT Workstation 4.0 • Complete multitasking client OS designed for business personal computers • Certified device drivers, faster performance, adaptive Start menu, image viewer, enhanced for mobile users
Windows XP	2001	• Upgrade to Windows Millennium Edition called Windows XP Home Edition • Upgrade to Windows 2000 Professional called Windows XP Professional • Windows XP Tablet PC Edition designed for Tablet PC users • Windows XP Media Center Edition designed for PCs used for home entertainment • Windows XP 64-bit Edition designed for workstations with an Itanium 2 processor • Improved interface and increased performance in all editions
Windows XP SP2 (Service Pack 2)	2004	• Enhancement to Windows XP that offers more built-in security technologies • Improved firewall utility • Automatic blocking of Internet pop-up advertisements

FIGURE 8-23 Microsoft released many versions of Windows before Windows XP.

Windows XP is available in five editions: Home Edition, Professional (Figure 8-24), Media Center Edition, Tablet PC Edition, and 64-bit Edition. The table in Figure 8-25 highlights features in all editions of Windows XP; the following page identifies the differences. Read Looking Ahead 8-1 for a look at the next generation of the Windows operating system.

FIGURE 8-24 Windows XP, with its simplified look, is the fastest and most reliable Windows operating system to date.

 LOOKING AHEAD 8-1

The Future of Windows

Searching for computer files can be a frustrating experience. Microsoft, however, plans to simplify the process with an eventual add-on to its next version of the Windows operating system, currently code-named *Longhorn*.

 With this search feature, called *WinFS* (Windows Future Storage), users will be able to locate e-mail messages, documents, and multimedia images, no matter what their format, on a stand-alone computer and on a network.

Longhorn is being developed as a consumer-friendly product with a completely object-oriented interface. When this major update to Windows XP is released in 2006 or later, it will recognize users and tailor the systems for their specific needs. It also will feature new security technology called Palladium, an antivirus program, and recordable DVD capabilities. For more information, visit scsite.com/dc2006/ch8/looking and then click Longhorn.

WINDOWS XP FEATURES

Appearance and Performance
- New look and feel to the user interface
- Increased reliability and security
- Increased performance to run programs faster
- Redesigned Start menu and Control Panel
- Minimized clutter on the taskbar with multiple open windows organized into groups
- Crisper display of images on LCD screens with ClearType

Administration
- Improved interface for creating multiple user accounts and switching among accounts
- Enhanced system recovery from failure with System Restore, without causing loss of data
- Easy-to-install home or small office network
- Windows Firewall to protect a home or small office network from hackers
- Improved wireless network support
- Improved battery-life management for notebook computers

Help and Support
- Comprehensive Help and Support system
- Remote Assistance that allows another person (with your permission) to control your computer remotely to demonstrate a process or solve a problem

Communications and the Web
- New version of Windows Messenger to send instant messages; communicate in real time using text, graphics, video, and voice to other online users; and a whiteboard available for use in video conferences
- New version of Internet Explorer with improved look
- Remote Desktop to access data and applications on your desktop computer while away from the computer using another Windows-based computer with a network or Internet connection
- Publish, store, and share text, graphics, photographs, and other items on the Web

Digital Media
- New version of Windows Media Player to listen to more than 3,000 Internet radio stations, play MP3 and Microsoft's WMA music format, copy music and data onto blank CDs, and watch DVD movies
- New version of Movie Maker
- Transfer images from a digital camera or scanner to your computer

FIGURE 8-25 Some features of Windows XP.

WINDOWS XP HOME EDITION *Windows XP Home Edition* is an upgrade to Windows Millennium Edition. In addition to providing the capabilities of Windows Millennium Edition, Windows XP Home Edition offers features and functionality that allow users to perform the following tasks:

- Acquire, organize, and share digital pictures
- Download, store, and playback high-quality music through Windows Media Player
- Create, edit, and share videos with Windows Movie Maker
- Easily network and share multiple home computers
- Use built-in instant messaging and video conferencing with Windows Messenger
- Recover from problems with easy-to-use tools

WINDOWS XP PROFESSIONAL *Windows XP Professional* is an upgrade to Windows 2000 Professional. In addition to providing the capabilities of Windows 2000 Professional, Windows XP Professional includes all the capabilities of Windows XP Home Edition and offers the following features and functionality:

- Greater data security through encryption of files and folders
- Remote access to a computer, its data, and its files from any other computer anywhere
- Simpler administration of groups of users or computers
- Multiple language user interface
- Support for secured wireless network access

WINDOWS XP MEDIA CENTER EDITION *Windows XP Media Center Edition* includes all the features of Windows XP Professional and is designed for Media Center PCs. A *Media Center PC* is a home entertainment personal computer that includes a mid- to high-end processor, large-capacity hard disk, CD and DVD drives, a remote control, and advanced graphics and audio capabilities. These computers often use a television as their display device. Windows XP Media Center Edition offers the following media features:

- Access to digital entertainment including live and recorded television programs, movies, music, radio, and photographs via a remote control device (Figure 8-26)
- Up-to-date online television program guide
- Parental control for television programs
- Capability to record television programs while away from the computer
- On-screen telephone call notification alert
- Download, play, copy, and listen to music
- Listen to Internet and FM radio stations

FIGURE 8-26 With Windows XP Media Center Edition, users access recorded videos, pictures, music, television programs, radio stations, or movies via a remote control device.

FAQ 8-7

How do I connect a television to a Media Center PC?
Plug one end of a cable in the TV out port on the Media Center PC and the other end of the cable in the input port on the television. Many users have two display devices for a Media Center PC: a monitor for computing purposes and a television for entertainment. For more information, visit scsite.com/dc2006/ch8/faq and then click Media Center PC.

WINDOWS XP TABLET PC EDITION *Windows XP Tablet PC Edition* includes all the features of Windows XP Professional and provides the following additional features that are designed to make users more productive while working on their Tablet PCs:

- Write on screen or issue instructions to the Tablet PC using a digital pen
- Save documents in handwritten form or convert them to typewritten text for use in other application software
- Add handwritten notes to documents created in other application software
- Enter text and instructions by speaking into the Tablet PC

WINDOWS XP 64-BIT EDITION *Windows XP 64-bit Edition* is designed for workstations that use an Itanium 2 processor and offers the following features and functionality:

- Supports up to 16 GB of RAM and 16 TB of virtual memory
- Supports multiprocessing
- Integrates 64-bit and 32-bit applications

WEB LINK 8-5

Windows XP

For more information, visit scsite.com/dc2006/ch8/weblink and then click Windows XP.

Mac OS X

Since it was released in 1984 with Macintosh computers, Apple's **Macintosh operating system** has set the standard for operating system ease of use and has been the model for most of the new GUIs developed for non-Macintosh systems. The latest version, **Mac OS X**, is a multitasking operating system available only for computers manufactured by Apple (Figure 8-27).

Mac OS X includes features from previous versions of the Macintosh operating system such as large photo-quality icons, built-in networking support, e-mail, online shopping, enhanced speech recognition, CD burning, and enhanced multimedia capabilities. In addition, Mac OS X includes these features:

- Built-in AOL-compatible instant messenger
- 3-D video conferencing
- Voice chats
- Filter to eliminate junk e-mail messages
- Contact lists synchronized with PDA or Bluetooth-enabled smart phone
- Web search without a browser
- Latest version of QuickTime to listen to music and view videos on the Internet
- Easy networking of computers and devices
- Conversion of handwritten text to typewritten text
- Windows network connection and shared Windows documents

WEB LINK 8-6

Mac OS X

For more information, visit scsite.com/dc2006/ch8/weblink and then click Mac OS X.

UNIX

UNIX (pronounced YOU-nix) is a multitasking operating system developed in the early 1970s by scientists at Bell Laboratories. Bell Labs (a subsidiary of AT&T) was prohibited from actively promoting UNIX in the commercial marketplace because of federal regulations. Bell Labs instead licensed UNIX for a low fee to numerous colleges and universities, where UNIX obtained a wide following. UNIX was implemented on many different types of computers. After deregulation of the telephone companies in the 1980s, UNIX was licensed to many hardware and software companies.

Several versions of this operating system exist, each slightly different. When programmers move application software from one UNIX version to another, they sometimes have to rewrite some of the programs. Although some versions of UNIX have a command-line interface, most versions of UNIX offer a graphical user interface (Figure 8-28).

Today, a version of UNIX is available for most computers of all sizes. Power users often work with UNIX because of its flexibility and power. Manufacturers such as Sun and IBM sell personal computers and workstations with a UNIX operating system.

WEB LINK 8-7

UNIX

For more information, visit scsite.com/dc2006/ch8/weblink and then click UNIX.

FIGURE 8-27 Mac OS X is the operating system used with Apple Macintosh computers.

FIGURE 8-28 Some versions of UNIX have a graphical user interface.

Linux

Linux is one of the faster growing operating systems. **Linux** (pronounced LINN-uks) is a popular, multitasking UNIX-type operating system. In addition to the basic operating system, Linux also includes many free programming languages and utility programs.

Linux is not proprietary software like the operating systems discussed thus far. Instead, Linux is *open source software*, which means its code is provided for use, modification, and redistribution. It has no restrictions from the copyright holder regarding modification of the software's internal instructions and redistribution of the software. Many programmers have donated time to modify and redistribute Linux to make it the best possible version of UNIX. Promoters of open source software state two main advantages: users who modify the software share their improvements with others, and customers can personalize the software to meet their needs. Read At Issue 8-3 for a related discussion.

Some versions of Linux are command-line. Others are GUI. The two most popular GUIs available for Linux are GNOME and KDE. Some companies such as Red Hat market software applications that run on their own version of Linux (Figure 8-29). Many application programs, utilities, and plug-ins have Linux versions, including OpenOffice.org, StarOffice, Mozilla, Netscape, Yahoo! Messenger, RealPlayer, QuickTime, and Acrobat Reader.

Users obtain Linux in a variety of ways. Some download it free from the Web. Others purchase it from vendors such as Red Hat or IBM, who bundle their own software with the operating system. Linux CD-ROMs are included in many Linux books and also are available for purchase from vendors. Some retailers such as Dell will preinstall Linux on a new computer's hard disk on request. Read Looking Ahead 8-2 for a look at the next generation of Linux.

AT ISSUE 8-3

Closed Source vs. Open Source Software

Linux is a fast-growing, innovative operating system. One of the features that make it different from other operating systems is that Linux is open source and its source code, along with any changes, remains public. Since its introduction in 1991, Linux has been altered, adapted, and improved by hundreds of programmers. Unlike Linux, most operating systems are proprietary, and their program code often is a zealously guarded secret. At one large software developer, an employee reported that application programmers had little opportunity to contribute to operating system programs because they had no access to the operating system program source code. Supporters of open source maintain that source code should be open to the public so that it can be scrutinized, corrected, and enhanced. In light of concerns about security and fears of possible virus problems, however, some people are not sure open source software is a good idea. Besides, they argue, programmers should be able to control, and profit from, the operating systems they create. On the other hand, open source software can be scrutinized for errors by a much larger group of people and changes can be made immediately. Is open source software a good idea? Why or why not? Can the concerns about open source software be addressed? How? What are the advantages and disadvantages of open versus closed source software? Does open source software lead to better software?

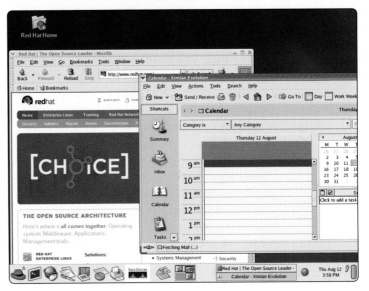

FIGURE 8-29   Red Hat provides a version of Linux called Red Hat Linux.

LOOKING AHEAD 8-2

The Future of Linux

The Linux operating system has been altered and enhanced since Linus Torvalds wrote the initial source code in 1991. With hundreds of programmers donating their time to make Linux the best possible version of UNIX, the software literally has changed on a daily basis.

As these developers work to improve Linux, their efforts are helping to shape the software's future. Experts predict the operating system may change by establishing a consistent desktop environment that is easy for all computer users to use. They also believe that hardware manufacturers will promote Linux-approved systems that maximize the software's features. Others forecast that a few major distributors will issue the software, in contrast to the hundreds of independent distributors that now exist. For more information, visit scsite.com/dc2006/ch8/looking and then click Linux Future.

Test your knowledge of pages 411 through 421 in Quiz Yourself 8-2.

QUIZ YOURSELF 8-2

Instructions: Find the true statement below. Then, rewrite the remaining false statements so they are true.

1. A file manager is a utility that detects and protects a personal computer from unauthorized intrusions.

2. Fragmenting a disk is the process of reorganizing it so the files are stored in contiguous sectors.

3. Linux is available in five editions: Home Edition, Professional, Media Center Edition, Tablet PC Edition, and 64-bit Edition.

4. Mac OS X is a multitasking operating system available only for computers manufactured by Apple.

5. Windows XP is a UNIX-type operating system that is open source software.

6. You should uninstall files and disks regularly in the event your originals are lost, damaged, or destroyed.

Quiz Yourself Online: To further check your knowledge of utilities included with most operating systems and stand-alone operating systems, visit scsite.com/dc2006/ch8/quiz and then click Objectives 5 – 6.

NETWORK OPERATING SYSTEMS

As discussed earlier in this chapter, a network operating system is an operating system that is designed specifically to support a network. A network operating system typically resides on a server. The client computers on the network rely on the server(s) for resources. Many of the client operating systems discussed in the previous section work in conjunction with a network operating system.

Some of the stand-alone operating systems discussed in the previous section include networking capability; however, network operating systems are designed specifically to support all sizes of networks, including medium to large-sized businesses and Web servers. Examples of network operating systems include NetWare, Windows Server 2003, UNIX, Linux, and Solaris.

NetWare

Novell's *NetWare* is a network operating system designed for client/server networks. NetWare has a server portion that resides on the network server and a client portion that resides on each client computer connected to the network. NetWare supports open source software and runs on all types of computers from mainframes to personal computers.

The server portion of NetWare allows users to share hardware devices attached to the server (such as a printer), as well as e-mail, databases, or any other files and software

stored on the server. The client portion of NetWare communicates with the server. Client computers also can have their own stand-alone operating system such as Windows XP, Mac OS X, or a Linux-based client.

Windows Server 2003

Windows Server 2003 is an upgrade to Windows 2000 Server, which was an upgrade to Windows NT Server. Windows Server 2003, which includes features of previous server versions, offers the following capabilities:

- Web site management and hosting
- Delivery and management of multimedia across intranets and the Internet
- Document storage in Web folders
- Central information repository about network users and resources with *Active Directory*
- Client support using Windows XP and earlier versions of Windows, Mac OS X, UNIX, and Linux

To meet the needs of all sizes of businesses, the **Windows Server 2003 family** includes five products:

- *Windows Small Business Server 2003* designed for businesses with fewer than 75 users and limited networking expertise
- *Windows Server 2003, Standard Edition* for the typical small- to medium-sized business network
- *Windows Server 2003, Enterprise Edition* for medium- to large-sized businesses, including those with e-commerce operations; available in 64-bit version

- *Windows Server 2003, Datacenter Edition* for businesses with huge volumes of transactions and large-scale databases; available in 64-bit version
- *Windows Server 2003, Web Edition* for Web server and Web hosting businesses

Windows Server 2003 is part of Windows Server System. In addition to Windows Server 2003, *Windows Server System* provides developers with dynamic development tools that allow businesses and customers to connect and communicate easily via the Internet. Through Windows Server System, programmers have the ability to use *Web services*, which are Web applications created with any programming language or any operating system to communicate and share data seamlessly.

UNIX

In addition to being a stand-alone operating system, UNIX also is a network operating system. That is, UNIX is capable of handling a high volume of transactions in a multiuser environment and working with multiple processors using multiprocessing. For this reason, some computer professionals call UNIX a *multipurpose operating system* because it is both a stand-alone and network operating system. Many Web servers use UNIX as their operating system.

Linux

Some network servers use Linux as their operating system. Thus, Linux also is a multipurpose operating system. With Linux, a network administrator can configure the network, administer security, run a Web server, and process e-mail. Clients on the network can run Linux, UNIX, or Windows. Versions of Linux include both the Netscape and Mozilla Web browsers.

FAQ 8-8

How widespread is Linux usage?

Forecasters predict that Linux will command one-third of the server market by 2008. Desktop personal computers, however, have a much lower Linux usage — only one percent worldwide. For more information, visit scsite.com/dc2006/ch8/faq and then click Linux Users.

Solaris

Solaris, a version of UNIX developed by Sun Microsystems, is a network operating system designed specifically for e-commerce applications. Solaris manages high-traffic accounts and incorporates security necessary for Web transactions. Client computers often use a desktop program, such as GNOME desktop, that communicates with the Solaris operating system.

EMBEDDED OPERATING SYSTEMS

The operating system on most PDAs and small devices, called an **embedded operating system**, resides on a ROM chip. Popular embedded operating systems today include Windows CE, Windows Mobile, Palm OS, Embedded Linux, and Symbian OS. The following sections discuss these operating systems.

Windows CE

Windows CE is a scaled-down Windows operating system designed for use on communications, entertainment, and computing devices with limited functionality. For example, set-top boxes, which enable you to access the Internet on a television, often use Windows CE. A widely used communications application of Windows CE is Internet telephony (Figure 8-30).

FIGURE 8-30 Windows CE often is used in an Internet telephony environment. As shown here, users can dial a call, forward a call, adjust phone volume, and set ring tones using a Windows CE interface that converts their desktop computer into an Internet telephone.

Windows CE is a GUI that supports color, sound, multitasking, multimedia, e-mail, Internet access, and Web browsing. A built-in file viewer allows users to view files created in popular applications such as Word, Excel, and PowerPoint.

Devices equipped with Windows CE can communicate wirelessly with computers and other devices using Bluetooth or other wireless technologies, as long as the device is equipped with the necessary communications hardware.

Windows Mobile

Windows Mobile enhances Windows CE to include functionality, applications, and a user interface designed for a specific type of PDA, called a **Pocket PC**, and smart phones (Figure 8-31). With this operating system and a Pocket PC or smart phone, users have access to all the basic PIM (personal information manager) functions such as contact lists, schedules, tasks, calendars, and notes. Information on the PDA or smart phone easily synchronizes with a personal computer or prints on a printer using a cable or a wireless technology.

Windows Mobile, which has a Windows XP look, also provides numerous additional features that allow users to check e-mail, browse the Web, listen to music, watch a video, send and receive instant messages, record a voice message, manage finances, or read an e-book. Many applications, such as Word, Excel, Outlook, and Internet Explorer, have scaled-down versions that run with Windows Mobile.

Some devices with Windows Mobile also support handwriting and voice input. With the Pocket PC Phone Edition devices, users can make telephone calls and send text messages using the PDA.

Palm OS

A competing operating system to Windows Mobile is *Palm OS*, which runs on PDAs and smart phones (Figure 8-32). With Palm OS devices, users manage schedules and contacts, telephone messages, project notes, reminders, task and address lists, and important dates and appointments. Information on the PDA or smart phone easily synchronizes with a personal computer or prints on a printer using a cable or a wireless technology. Palm users also can exchange information with other Palm users wirelessly through IrDA technology.

Palm OS includes handwriting recognition software, called Graffiti. Many Palm OS devices allow users to connect wirelessly to the Internet; browse the Web; and send and receive e-mail messages and instant messages. The latest version of Palm OS includes improved security for data transmission, allows for biometric identification, and supports the use of smart cards.

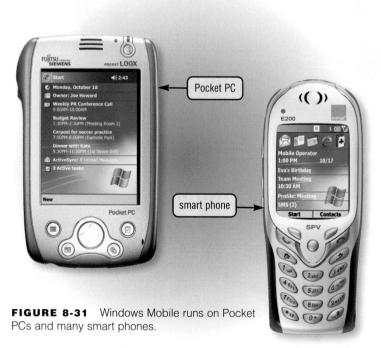

FIGURE 8-31 Windows Mobile runs on Pocket PCs and many smart phones.

FIGURE 8-32 Palm OS runs on PDAs and smart phones.

Embedded Linux

Embedded Linux is a scaled-down Linux operating system designed for PDAs, smart phones, smart watches, set-top boxes, Internet telephones, and many other types of devices and computers requiring an embedded operating system (Figure 8-33). PDAs and smart phones with embedded Linux offer calendar and address book and other PIM functions, touch screens, and handwriting recognition. Many also allow you to connect to the Internet, take pictures, play videos, listen to music, and send e-mail and instant messages. Devices that use embedded Linux synchronize with desktop computers using a variety of technologies including Bluetooth.

FIGURE 8-33
A PDA that uses embedded Linux.

Symbian OS

Symbian OS is an open source multitasking operating system designed for smart phones (Figure 8-34). In addition to making telephone calls, users of Symbian OS can maintain contact lists; save appointments; browse the Web; and send and receive text and picture messages, e-mail messages, and faxes using a smart phone. Users enter data by pressing keys on the keypad or keyboard, touching the screen, writing on the screen with a stylus, or speaking into the smart phone. Symbian OS allows users to communicate wirelessly using a variety of technologies including Bluetooth and IrDA.

FIGURE 8-34 This smart phone uses the Symbian OS.

STAND-ALONE UTILITY PROGRAMS

Although operating systems typically include some built-in utilities, many stand-alone utility programs are available for purchase. For example, you can purchase personal firewall, backup utilities, and screen savers. These stand-alone utilities typically offer improvements over those features built into the operating system or provide features not included in an operating system.

Other functions provided by stand-alone utilities include protecting against viruses, removing spyware, filtering Internet content, compressing files, converting files, burning CDs and DVDs, and maintaining a personal computer. The following sections discuss each of these utilities.

Antivirus Programs

The term, computer **virus**, describes a potentially damaging computer program that affects, or infects, a computer negatively by altering the way the computer works without the user's knowledge or permission. More specifically, a computer virus is a segment of program code from some outside source that implants itself in a computer. Once the virus is in a computer, it can spread throughout and may damage your files and operating system.

Currently, more than 81,000 known virus programs exist with an estimated 6 new virus programs discovered each day. Computer viruses do not generate by chance. The programmer of a virus, known as a *virus author*, intentionally writes a virus program. Some virus authors find writing viruses a challenge. Others write virus programs to cause destruction. Writing a virus program usually requires significant programming skills.

Some viruses are harmless pranks that simply freeze a computer temporarily or display sounds or messages. The Music Bug virus, for example, instructs the computer to play a few chords of music. Other viruses destroy or corrupt data stored on the hard disk of the infected computer. If you notice any unusual changes in your computer's performance, it may be infected with a virus. Figure 8-35 outlines some common symptoms of virus infection.

SIGNS OF VIRUS INFECTION

- An unusual message or image is displayed on the computer screen
- An unusual sound or music plays randomly
- The available memory is less than what should be available
- A program or file suddenly is missing
- An unknown program or file mysteriously appears
- The size of a file changes without explanation
- A file becomes corrupted
- A program or file does not work properly
- System properties change

FIGURE 8-35 Viruses attack computers in a variety of ways. This list indicates some of the more common signs of virus infection.

Viruses are just one type of malicious-logic program. A *malicious-logic program* is a program that acts without a user's knowledge and deliberately alters the computer's operations. In addition to viruses, other malicious-logic programs are worms and Trojan horses.

A **worm**, such as Sasser or CodeRed, copies itself repeatedly, for example, in memory or over a network, using up system resources and possibly shutting the system down. A **Trojan horse** (named after the Greek myth) hides within or looks like a legitimate program such as a screen saver. A certain condition or action usually triggers the Trojan horse. Unlike a virus or worm, a Trojan horse does not replicate itself to other computers. For a more technical discussion about computer viruses, read the High-Tech Talk article in Chapter 3 on page 168.

To protect a computer from virus attacks, users should install an antivirus program and update it frequently. An **antivirus program** protects a computer against viruses by identifying and removing any computer viruses found in memory, on storage media, or on incoming files (Figure 8-36). Most antivirus programs also protect against worms and Trojan horses. When you purchase a new computer, it often includes antivirus software.

The two more popular antivirus programs are McAfee VirusScan and Norton AntiVirus. As an alternative to purchasing these products on CD, both McAfee and Norton offer Web-based antivirus programs. That is, during your paid subscription period, the program continuously protects the computer against viruses.

FAQ 8-9

What steps should I take to prevent virus infections on my computer?

Set up the antivirus software to scan on a regular basis. Update your virus definitions regularly. Never open an e-mail attachment unless you are expecting the attachment and it is from a trusted source. If you use Windows, install the latest updates. Set macro security in programs such as word processing and spreadsheet so you can enable or disable macros. Back up files regularly. For more information, visit scsite.com/dc2006/ ch8/faq and then click Preventing Virus Infections.

Spyware Removers

Spyware is a program placed on a computer without the user's knowledge that secretly collects information about the user, often related to Web browsing habits. Spyware often enters a computer as a result of a user installing a new program. The spyware program communicates information it collects to some outside source while you are online.

A **spyware remover** is a program that detects and deletes spyware. Most spyware removers cost less than $50; some are available on the Web at no cost.

Internet Filters

Filters are programs that remove or block certain items from being displayed. Three widely used Internet filters are anti-spam programs, Web filters, and pop-up blockers.

ANTI-SPAM PROGRAMS *Spam* is an unsolicited e-mail message or newsgroup posting sent to many recipients or newsgroups at once. Spam is Internet junk mail. The content of spam ranges from selling a product or service, to promoting a business opportunity, to advertising offensive material. An **anti-spam program** is a filtering program that attempts to remove spam before it reaches your inbox. If your e-mail program does not include an anti-spam program, many anti-spam programs are available at no cost on the Web.

FIGURE 8-36 An antivirus program scans memory, disks, and incoming e-mail messages and attachments for viruses and attempts to remove any viruses it finds.

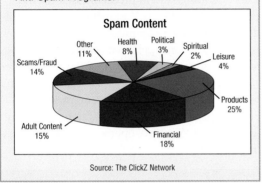

Should anti-spam programs be installed on home computers?

Yes. With more than 65 percent of all e-mail categorized as spam, home and business users could lose valuable time sifting through messages related to the variety of subjects shown in the chart below. For more information, visit scsite.com/dc2006/ch8/faq and then click Anti-Spam Programs.

Spam Content

Other 11%, Health 8%, Political 3%, Spiritual 2%, Leisure 4%, Products 25%, Scams/Fraud 14%, Adult Content 15%, Financial 18%

Source: The ClickZ Network

WEB FILTERS Web filtering software is a program that restricts access to certain material on the Web. Some restrict access to specific Web sites; others filter sites that use certain words or phrases. Many businesses use Web filtering software to limit employee's Web access. Some schools, libraries, and parents use this software to restrict access to minors.

POP-UP BLOCKERS A *pop-up ad* is an Internet advertisement that appears in a new window in the foreground of a Web page displayed in your browser. A **pop-up blocker** is a filtering program that stops pop-up ads from displaying on Web pages. If your operating system does not block pop-up ads, many pop-up blockers can be downloaded from the Web at no cost.

File Compression

A **file compression utility** shrinks the size of a file(s). A compressed file takes up less storage space than the original file (Figure 8-37). Compressing files frees up room on the storage media and improves system performance. Attaching a compressed file to an e-mail message, for example, reduces the time needed for file transmission. Uploading and downloading compressed files to and from the Internet reduces the file transmission time.

Compressed files, sometimes called **zipped files**, usually have a .zip extension. When you receive or download a compressed file, you must uncompress it. To **uncompress**, or *unzip*, a file, you restore it to its original form. Some operating systems such as Windows XP include uncompress capabilities. To compress a file, however, you need a stand-alone file compression utility. Two popular stand-alone file compression utilities are PKZIP and WinZip.

FIGURE 8-37 This file (Vacation) contains four compressed files. Without being compressed, these files consume 4,574 KB. Compressing them reduced the amount of storage by about 50 percent.

File Conversion

A *file conversion utility* transforms the contents of a file or data from one format to another. When a business develops a new information system, often the data in the current system is not in the correct format for the new system. Thus, part of the system development process is to convert data — instead of having users reenter all the existing data in the new system. On a smaller scale, when home users purchase new software, they may need to convert files so the files will be displayed properly in the new software.

CD/DVD Burning

CD/DVD burning software writes text, graphics, audio, and video files on a recordable or rewritable CD or DVD. This software enables the home user easily to back up contents of their hard disk on a CD/DVD and make duplicates of uncopyrighted music or movies. CD/DVD burning software usually also includes photo editing, audio editing, and video editing capabilities (Figure 8-38).

When you buy a recordable or rewritable CD or DVD, it typically includes CD/DVD burning software. You also can buy CD/DVD burning software for a cost of less than $100.

Personal Computer Maintenance

Operating systems typically include a diagnostic utility that diagnoses computer problems but does not repair them. A **personal computer maintenance utility** identifies and fixes operating system problems, detects and repairs disk problems, and includes the capability of improving a computer's performance. Additionally, some personal computer maintenance utilities continuously monitor a computer while you use it to identify and repair problems before they occur. Norton SystemWorks is a popular personal computer maintenance utility designed for Windows operating systems (Figure 8-39).

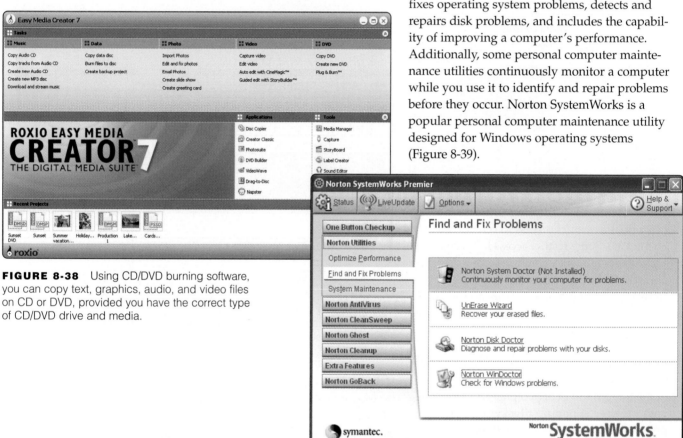

FIGURE 8-38 Using CD/DVD burning software, you can copy text, graphics, audio, and video files on CD or DVD, provided you have the correct type of CD/DVD drive and media.

FIGURE 8-39 A popular maintenance program for Windows users.

Test your knowledge of pages 422 through 428 in Quiz Yourself 8-3.

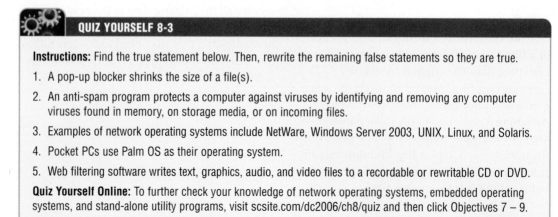

QUIZ YOURSELF 8-3

Instructions: Find the true statement below. Then, rewrite the remaining false statements so they are true.

1. A pop-up blocker shrinks the size of a file(s).

2. An anti-spam program protects a computer against viruses by identifying and removing any computer viruses found in memory, on storage media, or on incoming files.

3. Examples of network operating systems include NetWare, Windows Server 2003, UNIX, Linux, and Solaris.

4. Pocket PCs use Palm OS as their operating system.

5. Web filtering software writes text, graphics, audio, and video files to a recordable or rewritable CD or DVD.

Quiz Yourself Online: To further check your knowledge of network operating systems, embedded operating systems, and stand-alone utility programs, visit scsite.com/dc2006/ch8/quiz and then click Objectives 7 – 9.

CHAPTER SUMMARY

This chapter defined an operating system and then discussed the functions common to most operating systems. Next, it introduced several utility programs commonly found in operating systems (read At Issue 8-4 for a related discussion). The chapter discussed a variety of stand-alone operating systems, network operating systems, and embedded operating systems. Finally, the chapter described several stand-alone utility programs.

AT ISSUE 8-4

What Should Be in an Operating System?

Microsoft includes a Web browser, movie making software, a word processing program, plug-ins, a personal firewall, and other programs, utilities, and features with its Windows operating system. Apple bundles QuickTime, CD burning software, and other programs, utilities, and features into Mac OS X. Manufacturers say that combining additional features and programs with their operating systems is a convenience for consumers and sometimes integral to the operating systems' performance. Microsoft's built-in personal firewall, for example, helps protect computers from malicious attacks. Yet, because other developers create programs and features similar to those included with operating systems, some consumer advocates argue that bundling applications is unfair and leads to monopolies. Microsoft's bundling of its Web browser with its Windows operating system was the proximate cause of an antitrust action against the software giant. Critics also insist that bundling applications with an operating system forces consumers to pay for programs they may never use. Is bundling applications with an operating system fair, or is it a monopolistic practice? Why? Who should decide what an operating system should include? Why? Should computer manufacturers be allowed to choose which bundled applications are installed on computers that they ship to customers? Why or why not?

CAREER CORNER

Systems Programmer

System software is a key component in any computer. A *systems programmer* evaluates, installs, and maintains system software and provides technical support to the programming staff.

Systems programmers work with the programs that control computers, such as operating systems, network operating systems, and database systems. They identify current and future processing needs and then recommend the software and hardware necessary to meet those needs. In addition to selecting and installing system software, systems programmers must be able to adapt system software to the requirements of an organization, provide regular maintenance, measure system performance, determine the impact of new or updated software on the system, design and implement special software, and provide documentation. Because they are familiar with the entire system, systems programmers often help application programmers to diagnose technical problems.

Systems programmers must be acquainted thoroughly with a variety of operating systems. They must be able to think logically, pay attention to detail, work with abstract concepts, and devise solutions to complex problems. Systems programmers often work in teams and interact with programmers and nontechnical users, so communications skills are important.

Most systems programmers have a four-year B.S. degree in Computer Science or Information Technology. Depending on responsibilities and experience, salaries range from $53,000 to more than $100,000. For more information, visit scsite.com/dc2006/ch8/careers and then click Systems Programmer.

High-Tech Talk

WINDOWS XP: A USEFUL WAY TO COMPLETE A WIDE RANGE OF TASKS

When Microsoft developed the Windows XP operating system, it gave it a fresh, new graphical user interface. You still, however, can complete many important tasks using the command-line interface. Microsoft's first operating system, MS-DOS, was based entirely on a command-line interface. Today, Windows XP supports many of the original MS-DOS commands — and many new commands that help you complete tasks.

With Windows XP, you enter commands via a command shell. A *command shell* is a program with a nongraphical, command-line interface that provides an environment to run text-based application software and utility programs. The Windows XP command shell is called *Command Prompt*; the file name for the Command Prompt application is cmd.exe.

To open the Command Prompt window, click the Start button and point to All Programs, point to Accessories on the All Programs submenu, and then click Command Prompt on the Accessories submenu. Clicking Run on the Start menu and then typing **cmd** in the Run dialog box also opens the Command Prompt window. To execute a command, type one command per line and then press the ENTER key. Many commands allow you to enter one or more *options*, or *arguments*, which are additions to a command that change or refine the command in a specified manner. To close the Command Prompt window, type **exit** and then press the ENTER key or click the Close button in the Command Prompt window.

The Command Prompt window allows you to complete a wide range of tasks, including troubleshooting network connections. The *ping command*, for example, allows you to test TCP/IP connectivity for network and Internet connections (Figure 8-4a on page 403). When you enter the ping command with an IP address, your computer sends a special packet called ICMP Echo to that address. If everything is working, a reply comes back; if not, the ping times out. You also can use *TRACERT* (*traceroute*), a command-line utility that traces a data packet's path to its destination. When you enter **tracert scsite.com**, for example, the tracert utility traces the path from your computer to the Shelly Cashman Web server (Figure 8-40). The tracert command sends information to each device (called a hop) three times. The traceroute program sends the information three times to give you some idea of the variance in transit times. The time it takes for the device to respond each time is displayed. When you access a Web site, your request usually will pass through several routers before you connect to the destination server. For example, the tracert command for scsite.com passed through 15 other routers before connecting to the destination server (www.scsite.com).

You also can use the Windows XP Command Prompt to help manage your computer. When you enter the *systeminfo command*, Command Prompt queries your computer for basic system information, including operating system configuration and hardware properties, such as RAM and disk space. If you enter the *tasklist command*, the Command Prompt window returns a list of processes running on a computer, with each process identified by a process ID (PID). You can terminate any process by entering the *taskkill command* and the PID as the argument. Network administrators can use this command to fix problems on networked computers by closing applications.

The Windows XP Command Prompt also supports commands used to manage the files and file system on your hard disk. The *chkdsk command* checks for and corrects errors on the disk. You also can defragment your hard disk by entering the *defrag command*, with an argument specifying the drive to defragment (for example, defrag c:). When you are done working, you can use the *shutdown command* to shut down or restart your local or a remote computer.

Windows XP Command Prompt window

tracert scsite.com command

time required for device to respond to request

names of routers along path

hops required to reach destination

destination address

FIGURE 8-40
An example of the tracert command.

In most cases, the command-line tools perform functions similar to the GUI application. The Disk Defragmenter utility and the defrag command, for example, provide similar functionality. In others, the command-line tools provide additional functionality. For instance, the *diskpart command* starts the command-line version of the DiskPart utility and gives you access to advanced features not available in the GUI version.

The commands discussed here are just some of the wide range of commands supported by Windows XP. For more information, visit scsite.com/dc2006/ch8/tech and then click Windows XP Command Prompt.

Companies on the Cutting Edge

RED HAT
SHARING OPEN SOURCE SOFTWARE

When you were young, you were taught to share. University professors share their research with colleagues throughout the world; and *Red Hat* shares software code, or instructions, with computer users.

Red Hat is the largest supplier of open source software, which allows buyers to view, modify, and perhaps improve, the software. The company delivers the software improvements to customers through the Red Hat Network, the company's Internet service.

Bob Young and Marc Ewing founded Red Hat in 1994 and started distributing a version of the Red Hat Linux operating system complete with documentation and support. Today, Linux is Red Hat's most well-known product. In addition, its open source Apache Web server commands 67 percent of the market, according to E-Soft, a consulting firm that tracks online services. For more information, visit scsite.com/dc2006/ch8/companies and then click Red Hat.

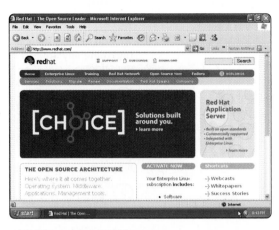

SYMBIAN
HANDHELD COMPUTING DEVICES MANUFACTURER

The next time you send a text message using your smart phone, you may be using an operating system developed by *Symbian*. This British company's operating system is the global industry standard and is licensed to leading cellular telephone manufacturers, including Ericsson, Matsushita (Panasonic), Motorola, Nokia, and Psion, which account for more than 80 percent of annual worldwide mobile phone sales.

In 1994, former CEO Colly Myers began experimenting with his programming expertise with the goal of developing a full operating system for a handset rivaling that found on a mainframe computer. Four years later, he convinced Ericsson, Motorola, and Nokia to invest in his product.

The Symbian open standards allow manufacturers to customize services and user interfaces, including graphics, e-mail, and touch screens. For more information, visit scsite.com/dc2006/ch8/companies and then click Symbian.

Technology Trailblazers

ALAN KAY
COMPUTER PIONEER

Chances are that every time you use your computer you use one of *Alan Kay*'s ideas. More than 35 years ago — long before the personal computer became ubiquitous — he was developing a notebook computer complete with a flat screen, wireless network, and storage. More than 20 years ago, he engineered a graphical user interface, object-oriented languages, and personal computer networks.

Kay did much of his early work at the U.S. Defense Department's Advance Research Project Agency (DARPA) and Xerox's Palo Alto Research Center (PARC). Today he is a senior fellow at HP Labs and a computer science professor at UCLA. In 2004, he won three major awards for his breakthrough inventions that have enhanced society scientifically, culturally, and spiritually. For more information, visit scsite.com/dc2006/ch8/people and then click Alan Kay.

LINUS TORVALDS
LINUX CREATOR

When *Linus Torvalds* developed a new operating system in 1991, he announced his project in an Internet newsgroup, made the source code available, and asked for suggestions. Computer users responded by reviewing the system and offering enhancements. Three years later, Torvalds released a much-enhanced version of open source operating system he called Linux.

Torvalds decided to create the innovative operating system when he was a 21-year-old computer science student in Finland. Today, Linux is estimated to be running on at least 10 percent of computers and is Microsoft's main competitor. Torvalds leads the development of Linux as a fellow at OSDL (Open Source Development Labs), a not-for-profit consortium of companies dedicated to developing and promoting the operating system. For more information, visit scsite.com/dc2006/ch8/people and then click Linus Torvalds.

Chapter Review

The Chapter Review section summarizes the concepts presented in this chapter. To listen to the audio version of this Chapter Review, visit scsite.com/dc2006/ch8/review. To obtain help from other students regarding any subject in this chapter, visit scsite.com/dc2006/ch8/forum and post your thoughts or questions.

① What Are the Types of System Software?   **System software** consists of the programs that control or maintain the operations of a computer and its devices. Two types of system software are operating systems and utility programs. An **operating system (OS)** contains instructions that coordinate all the activities among computer hardware resources. A **utility program** performs maintenance-type tasks, usually related to managing a computer, its devices, or its programs.

② What Is the Startup Process on a Personal Computer?   **Booting** is the process of starting or restarting a computer. When a user turns on a computer, the power supply sends a signal to the system unit. The processor chip finds the ROM chip(s) that contains the **BIOS**, which is firmware with the computer's startup instructions. The BIOS performs the *power-on self test (POST)* to check system components and compares the results with data in a CMOS chip. If the POST completes successfully, the BIOS searches for the *system files* and the *kernel* of the operating system, which manages memory and devices, and loads them into memory from storage. Finally, the operating system loads configuration information, requests any necessary user information, and displays the desktop on the screen.

③ What Are the Functions of an Operating System?   The operating system provides a user interface, manages programs, manages memory, schedules jobs, configures devices, establishes an Internet connection, and monitors performance. The **user interface** controls how data and instructions are entered and how information is displayed. Three types of user interfaces are a *command-line interface*, a *menu-driven interface*, and a *graphical user interface (GUI)*. Managing programs refers to how many users, and how many programs, an operating system can support at one time. An operating system can be *single user/single tasking*, *single user/multitasking*, *multiuser*, or *multiprocessing*. **Memory management** optimizes the use of random access memory (RAM). If memory is insufficient, the operating system may use **virtual memory**, which allocates a portion of a storage medium to function as additional RAM. Scheduling jobs determines the order in which jobs are processed. A **job** is an operation the processor manages. Configuring devices involves loading each device's driver when a user boots the computer. A **driver** is a program that tells the operating system how to communicate with a specific device. Establishing an Internet connection sets up a connection between a computer and an Internet service provider. A **performance monitor** is an operating system program that assesses and reports information about computer resources and devices.

④ How Can Operating Systems Help Administrators Control a Network and Manage Security?   A **network operating system**, or *network OS*, is an operating system that organizes and coordinates how multiple users access and share network resources. A *network administrator* uses the network OS to add and remove users, computers, and other devices to and from the network. A network administrator also uses the network OS to administer network security. For each user, the network administrator establishes a user account that enables the user to **log on**, or access, the network by supplying the correct **user name** and **password**.

> *connect*
> Visit scsite.com/dc2006/ch8/quiz or click the Quiz Yourself button. Click Objectives 1 – 4.

⑤ What Is the Purpose of the Utilities Included with Most Operating Systems?   Most operating systems include several built-in utility programs. A **file manager** performs functions related to file and disk management. An **image viewer** displays, copies, and prints the contents of a graphics file. A **personal firewall** detects and protects a computer from unauthorized intrusions. An **uninstaller** removes a program and any associated entries in the system files. A **disk scanner** detects and corrects problems on a disk and searches for and removes unnecessary files. A **disk defragmenter** reorganizes the files and unused space on a computer's hard disk. A

Chapter Review

diagnostic utility compiles and reports technical information about a computer's hardware and certain system software programs. A **backup utility** is used to copy, or *back up*, selected files or an entire hard disk. A **screen saver** displays a moving image or blank screen if no keyboard or mouse activity occurs for a specified time.

(6) **What Are Features of Several Stand-Alone Operating Systems?**   A **stand-alone operating system** is a complete operating system that works on a desktop computer, notebook computer, or mobile computing device. Stand-alone operating systems include DOS, Windows XP, Mac OS X, UNIX, and Linux. **DOS** (*Disk Operating System*) refers to several single user, command-line operating systems developed for personal computers. **Windows XP** is Microsoft's fastest, most reliable Windows operating system, providing better performance and a simplified look. **Mac OS X** is a multitasking operating system available only for Apple computers. **UNIX** is a multitasking operating system developed at Bell Laboratories. **Linux** is a popular, multitasking UNIX-type operating system that is *open source software*, which means its code is available to the public.

connect
Visit scsite.com/dc2006/ch8/quiz or click the Quiz Yourself button. Click Objectives 5 – 6.

(7) **What Are Various Network Operating Systems?**   Network operating systems include NetWare, Windows Server 2003, UNIX, Linux, and Solaris. Novell's *NetWare* is a network OS designed for client/server networks. **Windows Server 2003** is an upgrade to Windows 2000 Server and includes features of previous server versions. Linux, like UNIX, is a *multipurpose operating system* because it is both a stand-alone and network operating system. *Solaris*, a version of UNIX developed by Sun Microsystems, is a network OS designed for e-commerce applications.

(8) **What Devices Use Embedded Operating Systems?**   Most PDAs and small devices have an **embedded operating system** that resides on a ROM chip. Popular embedded operating systems include Windows CE, Windows Mobile, Palm OS, embedded Linux, and Symbian OS. **Windows CE** is a scaled-down Windows operating system designed for use on communications, entertainment, and computing devices with limited functionality. **Windows Mobile** enhances Windows CE and provides a user interface designed for a specific type of PDA, called the **Pocket PC**. *Palm OS* is an operating system used on PDAs and smart phones. *Embedded Linux* is a scaled-down operating system for PDAs, smart phones and watches, and other devices with embedded operating systems. *Symbian OS* is an open source multitasking operating system designed for smart phones.

(9) **What Is the Purpose of Several Stand-Alone Utility Programs?**   Stand-alone utility programs offer improvements over features built into the operating system or provide features not included in the operating system. An **antivirus program** protects computers against a **virus**, or potentially damaging computer program, by identifying and removing any computer viruses. A

spyware remover detects and deletes *spyware*. Internet filter programs can include an **anti-spam** program, **Web filtering software**, and a **pop-up blocker**. A **file compression utility** shrinks the size of a file so that it takes up less storage space. A *file conversion utility* transforms the contents of a file from one format to another. **CD/DVD burning software** writes to a recordable or rewritable CD or DVD. A **personal computer maintenance utility** identifies and repairs operating system problems or disk problems, and improves a computer's performance.

connect
Visit scsite.com/dc2006/ch8/quiz or click the Quiz Yourself button. Click Objectives 7 – 9.

Key Terms

You should know the Primary Terms and be familiar with the Secondary Terms. Use the list below to help focus your study. To further enhance your understanding of the Key Terms in this chapter, visit scsite.com/dc2006/ch8/terms. See an example of and a definition for each term, and access current and additional information about the term from the Web.

Primary Terms

(shown in bold-black characters in the chapter)

anti-spam program (426)
antivirus program (426)
backup utility (415)
BIOS (400)
boot disk (402)
boot drive (402)
booting (400)
buffer (407)
CD/DVD burning software (428)
cold boot (400)
defragmenting (414)
diagnostic utility (414)
disk defragmenter (414)
disk scanner (414)
DOS (417)
driver (407)
embedded operating system (423)
file compression utility (427)
file manager (412)
formatting (412)
image viewer (412)
job (406)
Linux (421)
log on (410)
Mac OS X (420)
Macintosh operating system (420)
memory management (405)
network operating system (410)
operating system (OS) (398)
password (410)
performance monitor (409)

personal computer maintenance utility (428)
personal firewall (413)
Plug and Play (407)
Pocket PC (424)
pop-up blocker (427)
queue (407)
recovery disk (402)
restore program (415)
screen saver (415)
shortcut (412)
spooling (407)
spyware remover (426)
stand-alone operating system (416)
system software (398)
Trojan horse (426)
uncompress (427)
uninstaller (413)
UNIX (420)
user ID (410)
user interface (402)
user name (410)
utility (411)
utility program (411)
virtual memory (406)
virus (425)
warm boot (400)
Web filtering software (427)
Windows Mobile (424)
Windows Server 2003 (422)
Windows Server 2003 family (422)
Windows CE (423)
Windows XP (417)
worm (426)
zipped files (427)

Secondary Terms

(shown in italic characters in the chapter)

Active Directory (422)
back up (415)
background (404)
basic input/output system (400)
client operating systems (416)
command language (402)
command-line interface (402)
compress (415)
cross-platform (399)
device driver (407)
device-dependent (415)
device-independent (415)
Disk Operating System (417)
Dr. Watson (414)
embedded Linux (425)
encryption (411)
fault-tolerant computer (405)
file conversion utility (427)
foreground (404)
fragmented (414)
ghosting (415)
graphical user interface (GUI) (402)
hacker (413)
IRQ (interrupt request line) (409)
kernel (400)
malicious-logic program (426)
Media Center PC (419)
memory resident (400)
menu-driven interface (402)
multiprocessing (405)
multipurpose operating system (423)
multiuser (405)
NetWare (422)
network administrator (410)
network OS (410)
nonresident (400)
open source software (421)
page (406)
paging (406)
Palm OS (424)
platform (399)
pop-up ad (427)
power-on self test (POST) (400)

preemptive multitasking (405)
print spooler (407)
proprietary software (415)
registry (402)
scripts (402)
service pack (416)
single user/multitasking (403)
single user/single tasking (403)
Solaris (423)
spam (426)
spyware (426)
Startup folder (402)
swap file (406)
Symbian OS (425)
system files (401)
thrashing (406)
unzip (427)
virus author (425)
Web services (423)
Windows Explorer (412)
Windows Picture and Fax Viewer (412)
Windows Server 2003, Datacenter Edition (423)
Windows Server 2003, Enterprise Edition (422)
Windows Server 2003, Standard Edition (422)
Windows Server 2003, Web Edition (423)
Windows Server System (423)
Windows Small Business Server 2003 (422)
Windows XP 64-bit Edition (419)
Windows XP Home Edition (419)
Windows XP Media Center Edition (419)
Windows XP Professional (419)
Windows XP Tablet PC Edition (419)

Checkpoint

Use the Checkpoint exercises to check your knowledge level of the chapter. The Beyond the Book exercises will help broaden your understanding of the concepts presented in this chapter. To complete the Checkpoint exercises interactively, visit scsite.com/dc2006/ch8/check.

Label the Figure

Identify the various elements of virtual memory.

a. disk (virtual memory)
b. page swapped in
c. swap file
d. page swapped out
e. RAM (physical memory)

True/False

Mark T for True and F for False. (See page numbers in parentheses.)

_____ 1. All sizes of computers typically use the same operating system. (399)

_____ 2. Booting is the process of starting or restarting a computer. (400)

_____ 3. A user interface controls how you enter data and instructions and how information is displayed on the screen. (402)

_____ 4. By spooling print jobs to a buffer, a processor can continue interpreting and executing instructions while the printer prints, which allows users to work on the computer for other tasks. (407)

_____ 5. A utility program is a program that assesses and reports information about various computer resources and devices. (409)

_____ 6. A disk scanner is a utility that reorganizes the files and unused space on a computer's hard disk so the operating system accesses data more quickly and programs run faster. (414)

_____ 7. Some stand-alone operating systems are called client operating systems because they also work in conjunction with a network operating system. (416)

_____ 8. Some versions of Linux are command-line, and others are GUI. (421)

_____ 9. Most antivirus programs do not protect against worms or Trojan horses. (426)

_____ 10. A spyware remover is a utility program that detects and protects a personal computer from unauthorized intrusions. (426)

Quizzes and Learning Games

Checkpoint

 Multiple Choice Select the best answer. (See page numbers in parentheses.)

1. The _____ chip, which uses battery power, stores configuration information about the computer. (400)
   a. BIOS
   b. POST
   c. CMOS
   d. RAM

2. In Windows XP, the _____ consists of several files that contain the system configuration information. (401)
   a. shortcut
   b. page
   c. registry
   d. swap file

3. Many current _____ operating systems incorporate features similar to those of a Web browser, such as links and navigation buttons. (402)
   a. command-line interface
   b. menu-driven interface
   c. graphical user interface
   d. all of the above

4. When an operating system spends much of its time paging, instead of executing application software, it is said to be _____. (406)
   a. booting
   b. thrashing
   c. spooling
   d. formatting

5. Encryption is the process of _____. (411)
   a. encoding data and information into an unreadable form
   b. recording successful and unsuccessful logon attempts in a file
   c. establishing a user account that allows a user to log on to a network
   d. entering a user name and password

6. Defragmenting reorganizes the files on a disk so they are located in _____ access time. (414)
   a. noncontiguous sectors, which slows
   b. noncontiguous sectors, which speeds
   c. contiguous sectors, which slows
   d. contiguous sectors, which speeds

7. Windows XP includes the _____, Dr. Watson, which detects problems as well as suggests courses of action. (414)
   a. file manager
   b. backup utility
   c. image viewer
   d. diagnostic utility

8. _____ used a command-line interface when Microsoft first developed it, although later versions included menu-driven user interfaces. (417)
   a. Windows XP
   b. DOS
   c. Mac OS X
   d. UNIX

9. Apple's _____ has set the standard for operating system ease of use and has been the model for most of the new GUIs. (420)
   a. UNIX operating system
   b. Macintosh operating system
   c. Windows XP operating system
   d. Linux operating system

10. In addition to being a stand-alone operating system, _____ also is a network operating system. (423)
    a. DOS
    b. UNIX
    c. NetWare
    d. Windows XP

11. _____, developed by Sun Microsystems, manages high-traffic accounts and incorporates security necessary for Web transactions. (423)
    a. Solaris
    b. Linux
    c. Windows Server 2003
    d. Netware

12. _____ is an open source multitasking operating system designed for smart phones. (425)
    a. Solaris
    b. Linux
    c. Symbian OS
    d. Palm OS

13. A _____ is a malicious-logic program that does not replicate itself to other computers. (426)
    a. virus
    b. Trojan horse
    c. worm
    d. all of the above

14. Web filtering software _____. (427)
    a. shrinks the size of a file
    b. enters a computer without a user's knowledge and secretly collects information about the user
    c. restricts access to certain material on the Web
    d. all of the above

Checkpoint

Matching

Match the terms with their definitions. (See page numbers in parentheses.)

_____ 1. kernel (400)

_____ 2. fault-tolerant computer (405)

_____ 3. page (406)

_____ 4. buffer (407)

_____ 5. IRQ (409)

_____ 6. user name (410)

_____ 7. shortcut (412)

_____ 8. restore program (415)

_____ 9. proprietary software (415)

_____ 10. uncompress (427)

a. communications line between a device and the processor

b. program that tells the operating system how to communicate with a device

c. continues to operate when one of its components fails

d. unique combination of characters that identifies one specific user

e. reverses the backup process and restores backed up files

f. core of an operating system that manages memory and devices, maintains system clock, starts applications, and other tasks

g. restore a zipped file to its original form

h. with virtual memory, the amount of data and program instructions that can be swapped at a given time

i. icon on the desktop that provides immediate access to a program or file

j. privately owned and limited to a specific vendor or computer model

k. segment of memory or storage in which items are placed while waiting to be transferred

l. contains a list of programs that open when a computer boots up

Short Answer

Write a brief answer to each of the following questions.

1. How is a cold boot different from a warm boot? _____ How is a memory-resident part of an operating system different from a nonresident part of an operating system? _____

2. What is a user interface? _____ How are a command-line interface, a menu-driven interface, and a graphical user interface different? _____

3. How is a single user/single tasking operating system different from a single user/multitasking operating system? _____ What is preemptive multitasking? _____

4. What is the difference between device-dependent and device-independent software? _____ What is proprietary software? _____

5. What is a malicious-logic program? _____ How is a worm different from a Trojan horse? _____

Beyond the Book

Read the following book elements, learn more about each using the Web, and then write a brief report.

1. At Issue — Who Is Responsible for Operating System Security? (410), Should Software Manufacturers Be Liable for Defective Software? (416), Closed Source vs. Open Source Software (421), or What Should Be in an Operating System? (429)

2. Career Corner — Systems Programmer (429)

3. Companies on the Cutting Edge – Red Hat or Symbian (431)

4. FAQs (402, 406, 409, 411, 413, 417, 419, 423, 426, 427)

5. High-Tech Talk — Windows XP: A Useful Way to Complete a Wide Range of Tasks (430)

6. Looking Ahead — The Future of Windows (418) or The Future of Linux (421)

7. Making Use of the Web — Weather, Sports, and News (124)

8. Picture Yourself Getting a Virus through E-Mail (396)

9. Technology Trailblazers — Alan Kay or Linus Torvalds (431)

10. Web Links (401, 407, 413, 415, 419, 420, 422, 424, 426)

Learn It Online

Use the Learn It Online exercises to reinforce your understanding of the chapter concepts. To access the Learn It Online exercises, visit scsite.com/dc2006/ch8/learn.

(1) At the Movies — Windows XP Media Center Edition

To view the Windows XP Media Center Edition movie, click the number 1 button. Locate your video and click the corresponding High-Speed or Dial-Up link, depending on your Internet connection. Watch the movie and then complete the exercise by answering the questions that follow. Windows XP Media Center Edition 2004 is software that easily can enable advanced multimedia interactivity on your computer. With one touch of the remote control, you can activate your music, photographs, videos, radio shows, or television programs. Why is the Windows XP Media Center prone to viruses? How can you make sure your computer is protected from viruses?

(2) At the Movies — Beam DVDs From Room to Room

To view the Beam DVDs From Room to Room movie, click the number 2 button. Locate your video and click the corresponding High-Speed or Dial-Up link, depending on your Internet connection. Watch the movie and then complete the exercise by answering the question that follows. With a moderately priced audio/video sender and receiver system you easily could hook up a small camera and monitor in any room in the house. What are the pros and cons of using video monitoring in your home?

(3) Student Edition Labs — Installing and Uninstalling Software

Click the number 3 button. When the Student Edition Labs menu appears, click *Installing and Uninstalling Software* to begin. A new browser window will open. Follow the on-screen instructions to complete the Lab. When finished, click the Exit button. If required, submit your results to your instructor.

(4) Practice Test

Click the number 4 button. Answer each question. When completed, enter your name and click the Grade Test button to submit the quiz for grading. Make a note of any missed questions. If required, submit your results to your instructor.

(5) Who Wants To Be a Computer Genius^2?

Click the number 5 button to find out if you are a computer genius. Directions about how to play the game will be displayed. When you are ready to play, click the Play button. Submit your score to your instructor.

(6) Wheel of Terms

Click the number 6 button to reinforce important terms you learned in this chapter by playing the Shelly Cashman Series version of this popular game. Directions about how to play the game will be displayed. When you are ready to play, click the Play button. Submit your score to your instructor.

(7) DC Track and Field

Click the number 7 button to use what you have learned in this chapter to compete against other students in three track and field events. Directions about how to play the game will be displayed. When you are ready to play, click the start first event button. If required, submit your score to your instructor.

Learn It Online

 You're Hired!

Click the number 8 button to use what you have learned in this chapter to embark on the path to a career in computers. Directions about how to play the game will be displayed. When you are ready to play, click the begin game button. If required, submit your score to your instructor.

 Crossword Puzzle Challenge

Click the number 9 button. Complete the puzzle to reinforce skills you learned in this chapter. Directions about how to play the game will be displayed. When you are ready to play, click the Submit button. Submit the completed puzzle to your instructor.

 Lab Exercises

Click the number 10 button. When the Lab Exercises menu appears, click the exercise assigned by your instructor. A new browser window will open. Follow the on-screen instructions to complete the exercise. When finished, click the Exit button. If required, submit your results to your instructor.

 In the News

When Windows XP was introduced in October 2001, hundreds queued up at computer outlets. It is unclear, however, whether the anticipation was caused by the new operating system or by the promotions many dealers offered. Click the number 11 button and read a news article about the impact, quality, or promotion of an operating system. What operating system was it? What was done to sell the operating system? Is the operating system recommended? Why or why not?

 Chapter Discussion Forum

Select an objective from this chapter on page 397 about which you would like more information. Click the number 12 button and post a short message listing a meaningful message title accompanied by one or more questions concerning the selected objective. In two days, return to the threaded discussion by clicking the number 12 button. Submit to your instructor your original message and at least one response to your message.

Learn How To

Use the Learn How To activities to learn fundamental skills when using a computer and accompanying technology. Complete the exercises and submit them to your instructor. Visit scsite.com/dc2006/ch8/howto to obtain more information pertaining to each activity.

LEARN HOW TO 1: Install a Computer

Once you have purchased a computer, you must install it for use. Based on years of experience, a set of guidelines for installing and using your computer has been developed. To examine these guidelines, complete the following steps:

1. Start the browser on your computer.
2. Type the Web address `scsite.com/dc2006` in the Address box and then press the ENTER key.
3. Click the Chapter 8 link in the top navigation bar.
4. Click Install Computer in the left sidebar below the heading, Features.
5. Read the material presented about how to install a computer.

Exercise

1. Using your Web search skills, research the latest recommendations with respect to proper ergonomics for using a computer. What information did you find that you did not know before? What changes would you make to your current computer setup that might make you more productive? Submit your answers to your instructor.
2. Many people report illnesses or injuries from using computers. Perform research in a library or on the Web to discover the five most common ailments associated with using a computer. Determine the actions people can take to minimize or eliminate these ailments. Submit a report to your instructor describing your findings.
3. Your computer lab at school contains multiple computers for student use. Using the knowledge you have obtained from this Learn How To activity, evaluate the computer installation in your school lab. In a report to your instructor, specify those items you think can be improved in the lab.

LEARN HOW TO 2: Maintain a Computer

While computers are amazingly resilient and reliable, you still should perform certain activities to ensure they maintain peak performance. To learn about these activities, complete the following steps:

1. Start the browser on your computer.
2. Type the Web address `scsite.com/dc2006` in the Address box and then press the ENTER key.
3. Click the Chapter 8 link in the top navigation bar.
4. Click Maintain Computer in the left sidebar below the heading, Features.
5. Read the material presented about how to maintain a computer.

Exercise

1. On either your computer or the computer on which you are working, perform a hardware and software inventory of at least five hardware devices and five application programs on the computer. List the vendor, product, vendor Web address, vendor e-mail address, and vendor support telephone number. Submit your inventory to your instructor.
2. Record the serial number of the computer on which you are working. Then, record the serial number for seven different application programs on the computer. Submit this information to your instructor.

Learn How To

LEARN HOW TO 3: Keep Windows XP Up-to-Date

Keeping Windows XP up-to-date is a critical part of keeping your computer in good working order. The updates made available by Microsoft for no charge over the Internet will keep errors from occurring on your computer and will ensure that all security safeguards are in place. To **update Windows**, complete the following steps:

1. Click the Start button on the Windows taskbar, point to All Programs, and then click Windows Update on the All Programs submenu (Figure 8-41). *A browser window will open and display the Windows Update page.*
2. Click the Express Install (Recommended) link. Your computer will be examined and then a list of recommended updates for your computer will be shown.
3. If necessary, select those updates you wish to install and then click the Install button. Be aware that some updates might take 20 minutes or more to download and install, based primarily on your Internet access speed.
4. Often, after installation of updates, you must restart your computer to allow those updates to take effect. Be sure to save any open files before restarting your computer.

FIGURE 8-41

    You also can schedule automatic updates for your computer. To do so, complete the following steps:

1. Click the Start button on the Windows taskbar and then click Control Panel on the Start menu.
2. In the Control Panel window, ensure that Category view is displayed, and then click Performance and Maintenance.
3. In the Performance and Maintenance window, click System.
4. In the System Properties dialog box, click the Automatic Updates tab. *The Automatic Updates sheet is displayed in the System Properties dialog box (Figure 8-42).*
5. Select the option you want to use for Windows updates. Microsoft, together with all security and operating system experts, strongly recommends you select Automatic so updates will be installed on your computer automatically. Notice that if you select Automatic, you also should select a time when your computer will be on and be connected to the Internet. A secondary choice is to download the suggested updates and then choose when you want to install them.
6. When you have made your selection, click the OK button in the System Properties dialog box.

FIGURE 8-42

    Updating Windows on your computer is vital to maintain security and operational integrity.

Exercise

1. Open the Windows Update window in your browser. Make a list of the recommended updates to Windows XP on the computer you are using. Add to the list the Custom Install updates that are available. If you are using your own computer, install the updates of your choice on your computer. Submit the list of updates to your instructor.
2. Optional: If you are not using your own computer, do not complete this exercise. Display the Automatic Updates sheet in the System Properties dialog box. Select the level of automatic updates you want to use. Write a report justifying your choice of automatic updates and then submit the report to your instructor.

Web Research

Use the Internet-based Web Research exercises to broaden your understanding of the concepts presented in this chapter. Visit scsite.com/dc2006/ch8/research to obtain more information pertaining to each exercise. To discuss any of the Web Research exercises in this chapter with other students, post your thoughts or questions at scsite.com/dc2006/ch8/forum.

(1) Scavenger Hunt   Use one of the <u>search engines</u> listed in Figure 2-10 in Chapter 2 on page 78 or your own favorite search engine to find the answers to the questions that follow. Copy and paste the Web address from the Web page where you found the answer. Some questions may have more than one answer. If required, submit your answers to your instructor. (1) What are the three file systems for disk partitions on a computer running the Windows XP operating system? Which of the three does Microsoft recommend using? Why? (2) If you use Microsoft Office on a computer running Windows XP, can you use the same software on a computer running the UNIX or Linux operating system? Why or why not? (3) What did Gary Kildall develop in 1974 while working for Intel? What is the basis of the lawsuit Caldera Inc. filed against Microsoft in 1996?

(2) Search Sleuth   A search engine using a <u>concept-based search system</u> seeks Web sites containing a search term along with related concepts. For example, if you search for "operating systems," this type of search engine also returns links to books, professional organizations, and other operating system-related topics. Many researchers consider Excite (excite.com) the best concept-based search engine. Visit this Web site and then use your word processing program to answer the following questions. Then, if required, submit your answers to your instructor. (1) Click the Member Info link at the bottom of the page. What are the benefits of free membership? (2) Click the Web search text box and type "`utility programs`" in the box. How many search results are returned that are not sponsored links? (3) Click the View By Search Engine option button near the top of the page. What are three search engines Excite used to return results? Which search engine returned the most links? (4) Click two of the unsponsored links that discuss backing up and recovering files. Review these articles and then write a 50-word summary of your findings.

(3) Journaling   Respond to your readings in this chapter by writing at least one page about your reactions, evaluations, and reflections about using <u>stand-alone utility programs</u>. For example, does your computer have an antivirus program? If so, how often do you check for new virus definition updates? Has a virus ever infected one of your files or your computer? Do you have a backup of your hard disk? Do you have a recovery disk? Do you have a personal firewall? You also can write about the new terms you learned by reading this chapter. If required, submit your journal to your instructor.

(4) Expanding Your Understanding   Instant messaging (IM) is moving into the workplace. According to America Online, 59 percent of Internet users use IM, and 27 percent of these people use IM at work. Computer industry analysts predict this method of electronic communication will overtake e-mail during the next few years. With IM's popularity comes <u>spim</u>, a junk message. Yahoo! reports that 2 percent of the instant messages sent over its network are spim. View Web sites to learn more about IM's popularity and spim. What programs allow you to filter instant messages? Write a report summarizing your findings, focusing on the possible uses of this method of communication in the workplace. If required, submit your report to your instructor.

(5) Ethics in Action   Several automobile insurers, including Progressive Casualty Insurance Company, are promising drivers insurance premium discounts if they install a data recorder in their cars to track their driving and then exercise good driving behavior. Progressive customers voluntarily taking part in this <u>TripSense</u> program upload the data from their monitors monthly and hope to decrease their insurance bills by a maximum of 25 percent. Privacy experts predict more insurance companies will offer this monitoring system and that it eventually will become mandatory. These critics fear that negative data will be used against poor drivers and possibly be subpoenaed in litigation. View online sites that provide information about vehicle monitoring devices. Write a report summarizing your findings and include a table of links to Web sites that provide additional details. If required, submit your report to your instructor.

Case Studies

Use the Case Studies to apply the concepts presented in the chapter to real-world situations. Visit scsite.com/dc2006/ch8/cases to obtain more information pertaining to each exercise. To discuss the Case Studies in this chapter with other students, visit scsite.com/dc2006/ch8/forum and post your thoughts or questions.

CASE STUDY 1 — Class Discussion   Many students at the local college have been using the college's computers to download music from the Internet. You have been asked to serve on a student committee to draft a policy addressing this questionable use of the college's computers. Is it the college's responsibility to block music downloads? Why or why not? How would the college prevent students from **downloading music**? What is the difference between taping a song heard on the radio and downloading music from the Internet? Should violators be expelled, fined, required to attend a seminar on the ethical use of computers, or given a verbal warning? What recommendations would you give to the committee regarding the downloading of music? Draft a memo addressed to all students regarding this matter. Be prepared to discuss your recommendations in class.

CASE STUDY 2 — Class Discussion   It is legal to **copy songs from a CD**, provided it was purchased legally. A principal at a local high school, however, has learned that students have been copying popular tracks from purchased music CDs to other CDs using the school's computer and then selling the CDs for $1.00 each. As the dean of students, what action would you take against the students copying the CDs? What action would you take against students buying the illegal copies? Write a brief report, and be prepared to discuss your recommendations in class.

CASE STUDY 3 — Research   Your neighbor is buying a new computer both for personal use and to run her floral business, which she operates out of her home. She is undecided on the Windows operating system to purchase with her new computer. **Windows XP** Professional Edition is intended for business and power users. Windows XP Home Edition is designed for home computing. She has asked you to help her decide if she should buy one or the other. Use the Web and/or print media to develop a report that lists the differences. Which Windows XP Professional Edition features are not available in Windows XP Home Edition? Submit your report or use PowerPoint to create a presentation and share your findings with your class.

CASE STUDY 4 — Research   Many programs are available for users of personal computers. The owner of the pet store, Friendly Pets, where you work part time is interested in purchasing an **antivirus program**. Because you are taking a computer class, she has asked you to help her choose the best program. Choose at least two competing manufacturers of antivirus programs. Use the Web and/or print media and compare the programs. For each program, answer the following questions: What is the program's function? What are the system requirements? How easy is the program to use? Does it include a firewall? Does it protect against spam and spyware? How do you obtain updates to the program? How much does the program cost? In your opinion, is the program worth the price? Why or why not? Which one would you buy? Why? Write a brief report or use PowerPoint to create a presentation and share your findings with your class.

CASE STUDY 5 — Team Challenge   Your team members are employed as analysts at Soap-n-Suds, an international manufacturer of laundry soaps. The company currently uses an early version of the Windows operating system on its 5,000 desktop computers. Next year, the company plans to upgrade the operating system and, if necessary, its desktop computers. The vice-president of information technology has asked your team to compare the latest desktop versions of the Windows operating system, the **Mac operating system**, and the Linux operating system. Assign each member of your team an operating system. Have each member use the Web and/or print media to develop a feature/benefit report. What is the initial cost of the operating system per computer? What are the memory and storage requirements? Will the operating system require the company to purchase new computers? Are training costs involved? Which one is best at avoiding viruses, spam, and spyware? Which operating system is easier to use? Why? Can Microsoft Office run under the operating system? As a team, merge your findings into a team report and/or PowerPoint presentation and share your findings with your class.

Buyer's Guide 2006:
How to Purchase a Personal Computer

(a) desktop computer

At some point, perhaps while you are taking this course, you may decide to buy a personal computer. The decision is an important one and will require an investment of both time and money. Like many buyers, you may have little computer experience and find yourself unsure of how to proceed. You can get started by talking to your friends, coworkers, and instructors about their computers. What type of computers did they buy? Why? For what purposes do they use their computers? You also should answer the following four questions to help narrow your choices to a specific computer type, before reading this Buyer's Guide.

(b) mobile computer (notebook computer or Tablet PC)

(c) personal mobile device (smart phone or PDA)

Should I buy a desktop or mobile computer or personal mobile device?

For what purposes will I use the computer?

Should I buy a Mac or PC?

Should the computer I buy be compatible with the computers at school or work?

1 **Do you want a desktop computer, mobile computer, or personal mobile device?** A desktop computer (Figure 1a) is designed as a stationary device that sits on or below a desk or table in a location such as a home, office, or dormitory room. A desktop computer must be plugged into an electrical outlet to operate. A mobile computer, such as a notebook computer or Tablet PC (Figure 1b), is smaller than a desktop computer, more portable, and has a battery that allows you to operate it for a period without an electrical outlet. A personal mobile device (Figure 1c) runs on a battery for a longer period of time than a notebook computer or Tablet PC and can fit in your pocket.

Desktop computers are a good option if you work mostly in one place and have plenty of space in your work area. Desktop computers generally give you more performance for your money.

Increasingly, more desktop computer users are buying mobile computers to take advantage of their portability to work in the library, at school, while traveling, and at home. The past disadvantages of mobile computers, such as lower processor speeds, poor-quality monitors, weight, short battery life, and significantly higher prices, have all but disappeared when compared with desktop computers.

FIGURE 1

If you are thinking of using a mobile computer to take notes in class or in business meetings, then consider a Tablet PC with handwriting and drawing capabilities. Typically, note-taking involves writing text notes and drawing charts, schematics, and other illustrations. By allowing you to write and draw directly on the screen with a digital pen, a Tablet PC eliminates the distracting sound of the notebook keyboard tapping and allows you to capture drawings. Some notebook computers can convert to Tablet PCs.

A personal mobile device, such as a smart phone or a PDA, is ideal if you require a pocket-sized computing device as you move from place to place. Personal mobile devices provide personal organizer functions, such as a calendar, appointment book, address book, and many other applications. The small size of the processor, screen, and keyboard, however, limit a personal mobile device's capabilities when compared with a desktop or notebook computer or a Tablet PC. For this reason, most people who purchase personal mobile devices also have a desktop or notebook computer to handle heavy-duty applications.

Drawbacks of mobile computers and personal mobile devices are that they tend to have a shorter useful lifetime than desktop computers and lack the high-end capabilities. Their portability makes them susceptible to vibrations, heat or cold, and accidental drops, which can cause components such as hard disks or display devices to fail. Also, because of their size and portability, they are easy to lose and are the prime targets of thieves.

2 **For what purposes will you use the computer?** Having a general idea of the purposes for which you want to use your computer will help you decide on the type of computer to buy. At this point in your research, it is not necessary to know the exact application software titles or version numbers you might want to use. Knowing that you plan to use the computer primarily to create word processing, spreadsheet, database, and presentation documents, however, will point you in the direction of a desktop or notebook computer. If you want the portability of a smart phone or PDA, but you need more computing power, then a Tablet PC may be the best alternative. You also must consider that some application software runs only on a Mac, while others run only on a PC with the Windows operating system. Still other software may run only on a PC running the UNIX or Linux operating system.

3 **Should the computer be compatible with the computers at school or work?** If you plan to bring work home, telecommute, or take distance education courses, then you should purchase a computer that is compatible with those at school or work.

Compatibility is primarily a software issue. If your computer runs the same operating system version, such as Microsoft Windows XP, and the same application software, such as Microsoft Office, then your computer will be able to read documents created at school or work and vice versa. Incompatible hardware can become an issue if you plan to connect directly to a school or office network using a cable or wireless technology. You usually can obtain the minimum system requirements from the Information Technology department at your school or workplace.

4 **Should the computer be a Mac or PC?** If you ask a friend, coworker, or instructor, which is better — a Mac or a PC — you may be surprised by the strong opinion expressed in the response. No other topic in the computer industry causes more heated debate. The Mac has strengths, especially in the areas of graphics, movies, photos, and music. The PC, however, has become the industry standard with 95 percent of the market share. Figure 2 compares features of the Mac and PC in several different areas. Overall, the Mac and PC have more similarities than differences, and you should consider cost, compatibility, and other factors when choosing whether to purchase a Mac or PC.

Area	Comparison
Cost and availability	A Mac is priced slightly higher than a PC. Mac peripherals also are more expensive. The PC offers more available models from a wide range of vendors. You can custom build, upgrade, and expand a PC for less money than a Mac.
Exterior design	The Mac has a more distinct and stylish appearance than most PCs.
Free software	Although free software for the Mac is available on the Internet, significantly more free software applications are available for the PC.
Market share	The PC dominates the personal computer market. While the Mac sells well in education, publishing, Web design, graphics, and music, the PC is the overwhelming favorite of businesses.
Operating system	Users claim that Mac OS X provides a better all-around user experience than Microsoft Windows XP. Both the Mac and PC supports other operating systems, such as Linux and UNIX.
Program control	Both have simple and intuitive graphical user interfaces. The Mac relies more on the mouse and less on keyboard shortcuts than the PC. The mouse on the Mac has one button, whereas the mouse on a PC has a minimum of two buttons.
Software availability	The basic application software most users require, such as Microsoft Office, is available for both the Mac and PC. More specialized software, however, often is available only for PCs. Many programs are released for PCs long before they are released for Macs.
Speed	The PC provides faster processors than the Mac.
Viruses	Dramatically fewer viruses attack Macs. Mac viruses also generally are less infectious than PC viruses.

FIGURE 2 Comparison of Mac and PC features.

After evaluating the answers to these four questions, you should have a general idea of how you plan to use your computer and the type of computer you want to buy. Once you have decided on the type of computer you want, you can follow the guidelines presented in this Buyer's Guide to help you purchase a specific computer, along with software, peripherals, and other accessories.

Many of the desktop computer guidelines presented also apply to the purchase of a notebook computer, Tablet PC, and personal mobile device. Later in this Buyer's Guide, sections on purchasing a notebook computer or Tablet PC address additional considerations specific to those computer types.

This Buyer's Guide concentrates on recommendations for purchasing a desktop computer or mobile computer. For recommendations on purchasing a personal mobile device, see page 296 in the Personal Mobile Devices feature that follows Chapter 5.

Type of Computer	Web Site	Web Address
PC	CNET Shopper	shopper.cnet.com
	PC World Magazine	pcworld.com
	BYTE Magazine	byte.com
	PC Magazine	zdnet.com/reviews
	Yahoo! Computers	computers.yahoo.com
	MSN Shopping	eshop.msn.com
	Dave's Guide to Buying a Home Computer	css.msu.edu/PC-Guide
Mac	Macworld Magazine	macworld.com
	Apple	apple.com
	Switch to Mac Campaign	apple.com/switch

For an updated list of hardware and software reviews and their Web site addresses, visit scsite.com/dc2006/ch8/buyers.

FIGURE 3 Hardware and software reviews.

HOW TO PURCHASE A DESKTOP COMPUTER

Once you have decided that a desktop computer is most suited to your computing needs, the next step is to determine specific software, hardware, peripheral devices, and services to purchase, as well as where to buy the computer.

1 Determine the specific software you want to use on your computer. Before deciding to purchase software, be sure it contains the features necessary for the tasks you want to perform. Rely on the computer users in whom you have confidence to help you decide on the software to use. The minimum requirements of the software you select may determine the operating system (Microsoft Windows XP, Linux, UNIX, Mac OS X) you need. If you have decided to use a particular operating system that does not support software you want to use, you may be able to purchase similar software from other manufacturers.

Many Web sites and trade magazines, such as those listed in Figure 3, provide reviews of software products. These Web sites frequently have articles that rate computers and software on cost, performance, and support.

Your hardware requirements depend on the minimum requirements of the software you will run on your computer. Some software requires more memory and disk space than others, as well as additional input, output, and storage devices. For example, suppose you want to run software that can copy one CD's or DVD's contents directly to another CD or DVD, without first copying the data to your hard disk. To support that, you should consider a desktop computer or a high-end notebook computer, because the computer will need two CD or DVD drives: one that reads from a CD or DVD, and one that reads from and writes on a CD or DVD. If you plan to run software that allows your computer to work as an entertainment system, then you will need a CD or DVD drive, quality speakers, and an upgraded sound card.

2 Look for bundled software. When you purchase a computer, it may come bundled with software. Some sellers even let you choose which software you want. Remember, however, that bundled software has value only if you would have purchased the software even if it had not come with the computer. At the very least, you probably will want word processing software and a browser to access the Internet. If you need additional applications, such as a spreadsheet, a database, or presentation graphics, consider purchasing Microsoft Works, Microsoft Office, OpenOffice.org, or Sun StarOffice, which include several programs at a reduced price.

3 Avoid buying the least powerful computer available. Once you know the application software you want to use, you then can consider the following important criteria about the computer's components: (1) processor speed, (2) size and types of memory (RAM) and storage, (3) types of input/output devices, (4) types of ports and adapter cards, and (5) types of communications devices. The information in Figures 4 and 5 can help you determine what system components are best for you. Figure 4 outlines considerations for specific hardware components. Figure 5 (on page 449) provides a Base Components worksheet that lists PC recommendations for each category of user discussed in this book: Home User,

Small Office/Home Office User, Mobile User, Power User, and Large Business User. In the worksheet, the Home User category is divided into two groups: Application Home User and Game Home User. The Mobile User recommendations list criteria for a notebook computer, but do not include the PDA or Tablet PC options.

Computer technology changes rapidly, meaning a computer that seems powerful enough today may not serve your computing needs in a few years. In fact, studies show that many users regret not buying a more powerful computer. To avoid this, plan to buy a computer that will last you for two to three years. You can help delay obsolescence by purchasing the fastest processor, the most memory, and the largest hard disk you can afford. If you must buy a less powerful computer, be sure you can upgrade it with additional memory, components, and peripheral devices as your computer requirements grow.

CD/DVD Drives: Most computers come with a 32X to 48X speed CD-ROM drive that can read CDs. If you plan to write music, audio files, and documents on a CD, then you should consider upgrading to a CD-RW. An even better alternative is to upgrade to a DVD+RW combination drive. It allows you to read DVDs and CDs and to write data on (burn) a DVD or CD. A DVD has a capacity of at least 4.7 GB versus the 650 MB capacity of a CD.

Card Reader/Writer: A card reader/writer is useful for transferring data directly to and from a removable flash memory card, such as the ones used in your camera or music player. Make sure the card reader/writer can read from and write on the flash memory cards that you use.

Digital Camera: Consider an inexpensive point-and-shoot digital camera. They are small enough to carry around, usually operate automatically in terms of lighting and focus, and contain storage cards for storing photographs. A 2- to 4-megapixel camera with an 8 MB or 16 MB storage card is fine for creating images for use on the Web or to send via e-mail.

Digital Video Capture Device: A digital video capture device allows you to connect your computer to a camcorder or VCR and record, edit, manage, and then write video back on a VCR tape, a CD, or a DVD. The digital video capture device can be an external device or an adapter card. To create quality video (true 30 frames per second, full-sized TV), the digital video capture device should have a USB 2.0 or FireWire port. You will find that a standard USB port is too slow to maintain video quality. You also will need sufficient storage: an hour of data on a VCR tape takes up about 5 GB of disk storage.

Floppy Disk Drive: If you plan to use a floppy disk drive, then make sure the computer you purchase has a standard 3.5", 1.44 MB floppy disk drive. A floppy disk drive is useful for backing up and transferring files.

Hard Disk: It is recommended that you buy a computer with 40 to 60 GB if your primary interests are browsing the Web and using e-mail and Office suite-type applications; 60 to 80 GB if you also want to edit digital photographs; 80 to 100 GB if you plan to edit digital video or manipulate large audio files even occasionally; and 100 to 160 GB if you will edit digital video, movies, or photography often; store audio files and music; or consider yourself to be a power user.

Joystick/Wheel: If you use your computer to play games, then you will want to purchase a joystick or a wheel. These devices, especially the more expensive ones, provide for realistic game play with force feedback, programmable buttons, and specialized levers and wheels.

Keyboard: The keyboard is one of the more important devices used to communicate with the computer. For this reason, make sure the keyboard you purchase has 101 to 105 keys, is comfortable and easy to use, and has a USB connection. A wireless keyboard should be considered, especially if you have a small desk area.

Microphone: If you plan to record audio or use speech recognition to enter text and commands, then purchase a close-talk headset with gain adjustment support.

Modem: Most computers come with a modem so that you can use your telephone line to dial out and access the Internet. Some modems also have fax capabilities. Your modem should be rated at 56 Kbps.

Monitor: The monitor is where you will view documents, read e-mail messages, and view pictures. A minimum of a 17" screen is recommended, but if you are planning to use your computer for graphic design or game playing, then you may want to purchase a 19" or 21" monitor. The LCD flat panel monitor should be considered, especially if space is an issue.

FIGURE 4 Hardware guidelines.

(continued on next page)

(continued from previous page)

Mouse: As you work with your computer, you use the mouse constantly. For this reason, spend a few extra dollars, if necessary, and purchase a mouse with an optical sensor and USB connection. The optical sensor replaces the need for a mouse ball, which means you do not need a mouse pad. For a PC, make sure your mouse has a wheel, which acts as a third button in addition to the top two buttons on the left and right. An ergonomic design is also important because your hand is on the mouse most of the time when you are using your computer. A wireless mouse should be considered to eliminate the cord and allow you to work at short distances from your computer.

Network Card: If you plan to connect to a network or use broadband (cable or DSL) to connect to the Internet, then you will need to purchase a network card. Broadband connections require a 10/100 PCI Ethernet network card.

Printer: Your two basic printer choices are ink-jet and laser. Color ink-jet printers cost on average between $50 and $300. Laser printers cost from $200 to $2,000. In general, the cheaper the printer, the lower the resolution and speed, and the more often you are required to change the ink cartridge or toner. Laser printers print faster and with a higher quality than an ink-jet, and their toner on average costs less. If you want color, then go with a high-end ink-jet printer to ensure quality of print. Duty cycle (the number of pages you expect to print each month) also should be a determining factor. If your duty cycle is on the low end — hundreds of pages per month — then stay with a high-end ink-jet printer, rather than purchasing a laser printer. If you plan to print photographs taken with a digital camera, then you should purchase a photo printer. A photo printer is a dye-sublimation printer or an ink-jet printer with higher resolution and features that allow you to print quality photographs.

Processor: For a PC, a 2.8 GHz Intel or AMD processor is more than enough processor power for application home and small office/home office users. Game home, large business, and power users should upgrade to faster processors.

RAM: RAM plays a vital role in the speed of your computer. Make sure the computer you purchase has at least 512 MB of RAM. If you have extra money to invest in your computer, then consider increasing the RAM to 1 GB or more. The extra money for RAM will be well spent.

Scanner: The most popular scanner purchased with a computer today is the flatbed scanner. When evaluating a flatbed scanner, check the color depth and resolution. Do not buy anything less than a color depth of 48 bits and a resolution of 1200 x 2400 dpi. The higher the color depth, the more accurate the color. A higher resolution picks up the more subtle gradations of color.

Sound Card: Most sound cards today support the Sound Blaster and General MIDI standards and should be capable of recording and playing digital audio. If you plan to turn your computer into an entertainment system or are a game home user, then you will want to spend the extra money and upgrade from the standard sound card.

Speakers: Once you have a good sound card, quality speakers and a separate subwoofer that amplifies the bass frequencies of the speakers can turn your computer into a premium stereo system.

PC Video Camera: A PC video camera is a small camera used to capture and display live video (in some cases with sound), primarily on a Web page. You also can capture, edit, and share video and still photos. The camera sits on your monitor or desk. Recommended minimum specifications include 640 x 480 resolution, a video with a rate of 30 frames per second, and a USB 2.0 or FireWire connection.

USB Flash Drive: If you work on different computers and need access to the same data and information, then this portable miniature mobile storage device is ideal. USB flash drive capacity varies from 16 MB to 4 GB.

Video Graphics Card: Most standard video cards satisfy the monitor display needs of application home and small office users. If you are a game home user or a graphic designer, you will want to upgrade to a higher quality video card. The higher refresh rates will further enhance the display of games, graphics, and movies.

Wireless LAN Access Point: A Wireless LAN Access Point allows you to network several computers, so they can share files and access the Internet through a single cable modem or DSL connection. Each device that you connect requires a wireless card. A Wireless LAN Access Point can offer a range of operations up to several hundred feet, so be sure the device has a high-powered antenna.

Zip Drive: Consider purchasing a Zip drive to back up important files. The Zip drive, which has a capacity of up to 750 MB, is sufficient for most users. An alternative to purchasing a backup drive is to purchase a CD-RW or DVD+RW and burn backups of key files on a CD or DVD.

BASE COMPONENTS

	Application Home User	Game Home User	Small Office/Home Office User	Mobile User	Large Business User	Power User
HARDWARE						
Processor	Pentium 4 at 2.8 GHz	Pentium 4 at 3.0 GHz	Pentium 4 at 3.0 GHz	Pentium 4M at 2.4 GHz	Pentium 4 at 3.4 GHz	Multiple Itanium at 1.6 GHz
RAM	512 MB	1 GB	512 MB	512 MB	1 GB	2 GB
Cache	256 KB L2	512 KB L2	512 KB L2	512 KB L2	512 KB L2	2 MB L3
Hard Disk	80 GB	120 GB	120 GB	60 GB	160 GB	300 GB
Monitor/LCD Flat Panel	17" or 19"	21"	19" or 21"	15.7" Wide Display	19" or 21"	23"
Video Graphics Card	256 MB	512 MB	256 MB	32 MB	128 MB	256 MB
CD/DVD Bay 1	48x CD-ROM	48x CD-RW Drive	48x CD-ROM	24X CD-RW/DVD	48x CD-RW Drive	16x DVD-ROM
CD/DVD Bay 2	8x DVD+RW	12x DVD+RW	8x DVD+RW	4x DVD+RW	12x DVD+RW	8x DVD+RW
Floppy Disk Drive	3.5"	3.5"	3.5"	3.5"	3.5"	3.5"
Printer	Color Ink-Jet	Color Ink-Jet	18 ppm Laser	Portable Ink-Jet	50 ppm Laser	10 ppm Laser
PC Video Camera	Yes	Yes	Yes	Yes	Yes	Yes
Fax/Modem	Yes	Yes	Yes	Yes	Yes	Yes
Microphone	Close-Talk Headset with Gain Adjustment	Close-Talk Headset with Gain Adjustment	Close-Talk Headset with Gain Adjustment	Close-Talk Headset with Gain Adjustment	Close-Talk Headset with Gain Adjustment	Close-Talk Headset with Gain Adjustment
Speakers	Stereo	Full-Dolby Surround	Stereo	Stereo	Stereo	Full-Dolby Surround
Pointing Device	IntelliMouse or Optical Mouse	Laser Mouse and Joystick	IntelliMouse or Optical Mouse	Touchpad or Pointing Stick and Laser Mouse	IntelliMouse or Optical Mouse	IntelliMouse or Laser Mouse and Joystick
Keyboard	Yes	Yes	Yes	Built-In	Yes	Yes
Backup Disk/Tape Drive	250 MB Zip®	External or Removable Hard Disk	External or Removable Hard Disk	External or Removable Hard Disk	Tape Drive	External or Removable Hard Disk
USB Flash Drive	128 MB	256 MB	256 MB	256 MB	4 GB	2 GB
Sound Card	Sound Blaster Compatible	Sound Blaster Audigy 2	Sound Blaster Compatible	Built-In	Sound Blaster Compatible	Sound Blaster Audigy 2
Network Card	Yes	Yes	Yes	Yes	Yes	Yes
TV-Out Connector	Yes	Yes	Yes	Yes	Yes	Yes
USB Port	6	8	6	2	8	8
FireWire Port	2	2	2	1	2	2
SOFTWARE						
Operating System	Windows XP Home Edition with Service Pack 2	Windows XP Home Edition with Service Pack 2	Windows XP Professional with Service Pack 2	Windows XP Professional with Service Pack 2	Windows XP Professional with Service Pack 2	Windows XP Professional with Service Pack 2
Application Suite	Office 2003 Standard Edition	Office 2003 Standard Edition	Office 2003 Small Business Edition	Office2003 Small Business Edition	Office 2003 Professional	Office 2003 Professional
Antivirus	Yes, 12-Mo. Subscription	Yes, 12-Mo. Subscription	Yes, 12-Mo. Subscription	Yes, 12-Mo. Subscription	Yes, 12-Mo. Subscription	Yes, 12-Mo. Subscription
Internet Access	Cable, DSL, or Dial-up	Cable or DSL	Cable, DSL, or Dial-up	Wireless or Dial-up	LAN/WAN (T1/T3)	Cable or DSL
OTHER						
Surge Protector	Yes	Yes	Yes	Portable	Yes	Yes
Warranty	3-Year Limited, 1-Year Next Business Day On-Site Service	3-Year Limited, 1-Year Next Business Day On-Site Service	3-year On-Site Service	3-Year Limited, 1-Year Next Business Day On-Site Service	3-year On-Site Service	3-year On-Site Service
Other		Wheel	Postage Printer	Docking Station Carrying Case Fingerprint Scanner Portable Data Projector		Graphics Tablet Plotter or Large-Format Printer

Optional Components for All Categories	
802.11g Wireless Card	Graphics Tablet
Bluetooth Enabled	iPod Music Player
Biometric Input Device	IrDa Port
Card Reader/Writer	Mouse Pad/Wrist Rest
Digital Camera	Multifunction Peripheral
Digital Video Capture	Photo Printer
Digital Video Camera	Portable Data Projector
Dual-Monitor Support with Second Monitor	Scanner
Ergonomic Keyboard	TV/FM Tuner
External Hard Disk	Uninterruptible Power Supply

FIGURE 5 Base desktop and mobile computer components and optional components. A copy of the Base Components worksheet is on the Data Disk. To obtain a copy of the Data Disk, see the inside cover of this book for instructions.

4 Consider upgrades to the mouse, keyboard, monitor, printer, microphone, and speakers.
You use these peripheral devices to interact with your computer, so you should make sure they are up to your standards. Review the peripheral devices listed in Figure 4 on pages 447 and 448 and then visit both local computer dealers and large retail stores to test the computers on display. Ask the salesperson what input and output devices would be best for you and whether you should upgrade beyond what comes standard. Consider purchasing a wireless keyboard and wireless mouse to eliminate bothersome wires on your desktop. A few extra dollars spent on these components when you initially purchase a computer can extend its usefulness by years.

5 Determine whether you want to use telephone lines or broadband (cable or DSL) to access the Internet. If your computer has a modem, then you can access the Internet using a standard telephone line. Ordinarily, you call a local or toll-free 800 number to connect to an ISP (see Guideline 6 on the next page). Using a dial-up Internet connection is relatively inexpensive but slow.

DSL and cable connections provide much faster Internet connections, which are ideal if you want faster file download speeds for software, digital photos, and music. As you would expect, they also are more expensive. DSL, which is available through local telephone companies, also may require that you subscribe to an ISP. Cable is available through your local cable television provider and some online service providers (OSPs). If you get cable, then you would not use a separate Internet service provider or online service provider.

6 **If you are using a dial-up or wireless connection to connect to the Internet, then select an ISP or OSP.** You can access the Internet via telephone lines in one of two ways: an ISP or an OSP. Both provide Internet access for a monthly fee that ranges from $6 to $25. Local ISPs offer Internet access to users in a limited geographic region, through local telephone numbers. National ISPs provide access for users nationwide (including mobile users), through local and toll-free telephone numbers and cable. Because of their size, national ISPs generally offer more services and have a larger technical support staff than local ISPs. OSPs furnish Internet access as well as members-only features for users nationwide. Figure 6 lists several national ISPs and OSPs. Before you choose an ISP or OSP, compare such features as the number of access hours, monthly fees, available services (e-mail, Web page hosting, chat), and reliability.

Company	Service	Web Address
America Online	OSP	aol.com
AT&T Worldnet	ISP	www.att.net
Comcast	OSP	comcast.net
CompuServe	OSP	compuserve.com
EarthLink	ISP	earthlink.net
Juno	OSP	juno.com
NetZero	OSP	netzero.com
MSN	OSP	msn.com
SBC Prodigy	ISP/OSP	prodigy.net

For an updated list of national ISPs and OSPs and their Web site addresses, visit scsite.com/dc2006/ch8/buyers.

FIGURE 6 National ISPs and OSPs.

7 **Use a worksheet to compare computers, services, and other considerations.** You can use a separate sheet of paper to take notes on each vendor's computer and then summarize the information on a worksheet, such as the one shown in Figure 7. You can use Figure 7 to compare prices for either a PC or a Mac. Most companies advertise a price for a base computer that includes components housed in the system unit (processor, RAM, sound card, video card), disk drives (floppy disk, hard disk, CD-ROM, CD-RW, DVD-ROM, and DVD+RW), a keyboard, mouse, monitor, printer, speakers, and modem. Be aware, however, that some advertisements list prices for computers with only some of these components. Monitors and printers, for example, often are not included in a base computer's price. Depending on how you plan to use the computer, you may want to invest in additional or more powerful components. When you are comparing the prices of computers, make sure you are comparing identical or similar configurations.

FIGURE 7 A worksheet is an effective tool for summarizing and comparing components and prices of different computer vendors. A copy of the PC or Mac Cost Comparison Worksheet is on the Data Disk. To obtain a copy of the Data Disk, see the inside cover of this book for instructions.

8 **If you are buying a new computer, you have several purchasing options: buying from your school bookstore, a local computer dealer, a local large retail store, or ordering by mail via telephone or the Web.** Each purchasing option has certain advantages. Many college bookstores, for example, sign exclusive pricing agreements with computer manufacturers and, thus, can offer student discounts. Local dealers and local large retail stores, however, more easily can provide hands-on support. Mail-order companies that sell computers by telephone or online via the Web (Figure 8) often provide the lowest prices, but extend less personal service. Some major mail-order companies, however, have started to provide next-business-day, on-site services. A credit card usually is required to buy from a mail-order company. Figure 9 lists some of the more popular mail-order companies and their Web site addresses.

9 **If you are buying a used computer, stay with name brands such as Dell, Gateway, Hewlett-Packard, and Apple.** Although brand-name equipment can cost more, most brand-name computers have longer, more comprehensive warranties, are better supported, and have more authorized centers for repair services. As with new computers, you can purchase a used computer from local computer dealers, local large retail stores, or mail

order via the telephone or the Web. Classified ads and used computer sellers offer additional outlets for purchasing used computers. Figure 10 lists several major used computer brokers and their Web site addresses.

10 **If you have a computer and are upgrading to a new one, then consider selling or trading in the old one.** If you are a replacement buyer, your older computer still may have value. If you cannot sell the computer through the classified ads, via a Web site, or to a friend, then ask if the computer dealer will buy your old computer. An increasing number of companies are taking trade-ins, but do not expect too much money for your old computer. Other companies offer free disposal of your old PC.

11 **Be aware of hidden costs.** Before purchasing, be sure to consider any additional costs associated with buying a computer, such as an additional telephone line, a cable or DSL modem, an uninterruptible power supply (UPS), computer furniture, a USB flash drive, paper, and computer training classes you may want to take. Depending on where you buy your computer, the seller may be willing to include some or all of these in the computer purchase price.

Type of Computer	Company	Web Address
PC	CNET Shopper	shopper.cnet.com
	Hewlett-Packard	hp.com
	CompUSA	compusa.com
	Dartek	dartek.com
	Dell	dell.com
	Gateway	gateway.com
Macintosh	Apple Computer	store.apple.com
	ClubMac	clubmac.com
	MacConnection	macconnection.com
	PC & MacExchange	macx.com

For an updated list of new mail-order computer companies and their Web site addresses, visit scsite.com/dc2006/ch8/buyers.

FIGURE 9 Computer mail-order companies.

FIGURE 8 Mail-order companies, such as Dell, sell computers online.

Company	Web Address
Amazon.com	amazon.com
Off-Lease Computers	off-leasecomputers.com
American Computer Exchange	www.amcoex.com
U.S. Computer Exchange	usce.org
eBay	ebay.com

For an updated list of used computer mail-order companies and their Web site addresses, visit scsite.com/dc2006/ch8/buyers.

FIGURE 10 Used computer mail-order companies.

12 **Consider more than just price.** The lowest-cost computer may not be the best long-term buy. Consider such intangibles as the vendor's time in business, the vendor's regard for quality, and the vendor's reputation for support. If you need to upgrade your computer often, you may want to consider a leasing arrangement, in which you pay monthly lease fees, but can upgrade or add on to your computer as your equipment needs change. No matter what type of buyer you are, insist on a 30-day, no-questions-asked return policy on your computer.

13 **Avoid restocking fees.** Some companies charge a restocking fee of 10 to 20 percent as part of their money-back return policy. In some cases, no restocking fee for hardware is applied, but it is applied for software. Ask about the existence and terms of any restocking policies before you buy.

14 **Use a credit card to purchase your new computer.** Many credit cards offer purchase protection and extended warranty benefits that cover you in case of loss of or damage to purchased goods. Paying by credit card also gives you time to install and use the computer before you have to pay for it. Finally, if you are dissatisfied with the computer and are unable to reach an agreement with the seller, paying by credit card gives you certain rights regarding withholding payment until the dispute is resolved. Check your credit card terms for specific details.

15 **Consider purchasing an extended warranty or service plan.** If you use your computer for business or require fast resolution to major computer problems, consider purchasing an extended warranty or a service plan through a local dealer or third-party company. Most extended warranties cover the repair and replacement of computer components beyond the standard warranty. Most service plans ensure that your technical support calls receive priority response from technicians. You also can purchase an on-site service plan that states that a technician will come to your home, work, or school within 24 hours. If your computer includes a warranty and service agreement for a year or less, think about extending the service for two or three years when you buy the computer.

HOW TO PURCHASE A NOTEBOOK COMPUTER

If you need computing capability when you travel or to use in lecture or meetings, you may find a notebook computer to be an appropriate choice. The guidelines mentioned in the previous section also apply to the purchase of a notebook computer. The following are additional considerations unique to notebook computers.

1 **Purchase a notebook computer with a sufficiently large active-matrix screen.** Active-matrix screens display high-quality color that is viewable from all angles. Less expensive, passive-matrix screens sometimes are difficult to see in low-light conditions and cannot be viewed from an angle. Notebook computers typically come with a 12.1-inch, 13.3-inch, 14.1-inch, or 15.7-inch display. For most users, a 14.1-inch display is satisfactory. If you intend to use your notebook computer as a desktop computer replacement, however, you may opt for a 15.7-inch display. Notebook computers with these larger displays weigh seven to ten pounds, however, so if you travel a lot and portability is essential, you might want a lighter computer with a smaller display. The lightest notebook computers, which weigh less than 3 pounds, are equipped with a 12.1-inch display. Regardless of size, the resolution of the display should be at least 1024 x 768 pixels. To compare the monitor size on various notebook computers, visit the company Web sites in Figure 11.

Type of Notebook	Company	Web Address
PC	Acer	global.acer.com
	Dell	dell.com
	Fujitsu	fujitsu.com
	Gateway	gateway.com
	Hewlett-Packard	hp.com
	IBM	ibm.com
	NEC	nec.com
	Sony	sony.com
	Toshiba	toshiba.com
Mac	Apple	apple.com

For an updated list of companies and their Web site addresses, visit scsite.com/dc2006/ch8/buyers.

FIGURE 11 Companies that sell notebook computers.

CENTURY COMPUTERS
Performance Guarantee
(See reverse for terms & conditions of this contract)

Invoice #: 1984409   Effective Date: 10/12/07
Invoice Date: 10/12/07   Expiration Date: 10/12/10

Customer Name: Leon, Richard   System & Serial Numbers
Date: 10/12/07   IMB computer
Address: 1123 Roxbury   S/N: US759290C
         Sycamore, IL 60178
Day phone: (815) 555-0303
Evening Phone: (728) 555-0203

John Smith   *10/12/07*
Print Name of Century's Authorized Signature   Date

2 **Experiment with different keyboards and pointing devices.** Notebook computer keyboards are far less standardized than those for desktop computers. Some notebook computers, for example, have wide wrist rests, while others have none. Notebook computers also use a range of pointing devices, including pointing sticks, touchpads, and trackballs. Before you purchase a notebook computer, try various types of keyboard and pointing devices to determine which is easiest for you to use. Regardless of the pointing device you select, you also may want to purchase a regular mouse to use when you are working at a desk or other large surface.

3 **Make sure the notebook computer you purchase has a CD and/or DVD drive.** Loading and installing software, especially large Office suites, is much faster if done from a CD-ROM, CD-RW, DVD-ROM, or DVD+RW. Today, most notebook computers come with an internal or external CD-ROM drive. Some notebook computers even come with a CD-ROM drive and a CD-RW drive or a DVD-ROM drive and a CD-RW or DVD+RW drive. Although DVD drives are slightly more expensive, they allow you to play CDs and DVD movies using your notebook computer and a headset.

4 **If necessary, upgrade the processor, memory, and disk storage at the time of purchase.** As with a desktop computer, upgrading your notebook computer's memory and disk storage usually is less expensive at the time of initial purchase. Some disk storage is custom designed for notebook computer manufacturers, meaning an upgrade might not be available in the future. If you are purchasing a lightweight notebook computer, then it should include at least a 2.4 GHz processor, 512 MB RAM, and 80 GB of storage.

5 **The availability of built-in ports on a notebook computer is important.** A notebook computer does not have a lot of room to add adapter cards. If you know the purpose for which you plan to use your notebook computer, then you can determine the ports you will need. Most notebooks come with common ports, such as a mouse port, IrDA port, serial port, parallel port, video port, and USB port. If you plan to connect your notebook computer to a TV, however, then you will need a PCtoTV port. If you want to connect to networks at school or in various offices, make sure the notebook computer you purchase has a built-in network card. If your notebook computer does not come with a built-in network wireless card, then you will have to purchase an external network card that slides into an expansion slot in your notebook computer, as well as a network cable. If you expect to connect an iPod portable digital music player to your notebook computer, then you will need a FireWire port.

6 **If you plan to use your notebook computer for note-taking at school or in meetings, consider a notebook computer that converts to a Tablet PC.** Some computer manufacturers have developed convertible notebook computers that allow the screen to rotate 180 degrees on a central hinge and then fold down to cover the keyboard and become a Tablet PC (Figure 12). You then can use a stylus to enter text or drawings into the computer by writing on the screen.

FIGURE 12 The Toshiba Protégé M200 notebook computer converts to a Tablet PC.

7 **Consider purchasing a notebook computer with a built-in wireless card to connect to your home network.** Many users today are setting up wireless home networks. With a wireless home network, the desktop computer functions as the server, and your notebook computer can access the desktop computer from any location in the house to share files and hardware, such as a printer, and browse the Web. If your notebook computer does not come with a built-in wireless card, you can purchase an external one that slides into your notebook computer. Most home wireless networks allow connections from distances of 150 to 800 feet.

8 **If you are going to use your notebook computer for long periods without access to an electrical outlet, purchase a second battery.** The trend among notebook computer users today is power and size over battery life, and notebook computer manufacturers have picked up on this. Many notebook computer users today are willing to give up longer battery life for a larger screen, faster processor, and more storage. In addition, some manufacturers typically sell the notebook with the lowest capacity battery. For this reason, you need to be careful in choosing a notebook computer if you plan to use it without access to electrical outlets for long periods, such as an airplane flight. You also might want to purchase a second battery as a backup. If you anticipate running your notebook computer on batteries frequently, choose a computer that uses lithium-ion batteries, which last longer than nickel cadmium or nickel hydride batteries.

9 **Purchase a well-padded and well-designed carrying case.** An amply padded carrying case will protect your notebook computer from the bumps it will receive while traveling. A well-designed carrying case will have room for accessories such as spare floppy disks, CDs and DVDs, a user manual, pens, and paperwork (Figure 13).

FIGURE 13
A well-designed notebook computer carrying case.

10 **If you travel overseas, obtain a set of electrical and telephone adapters.** Different countries use different outlets for electrical and telephone connections. Several manufacturers sell sets of adapters that will work in most countries.

11 **If you plan to connect your notebook computer to a video projector, make sure the notebook computer is compatible with the video projector.** You should check, for example, to be sure that your notebook computer will allow you to display an image on the computer screen and projection device at the same time (Figure 14). Also, ensure that your notebook computer has the ports required to connect to the video projector.

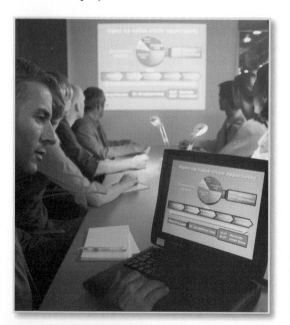

FIGURE 14
A notebook computer connected to a video projector projects the image displayed on the screen.

12 **For improved security, consider a fingerprint scanner.** More than a quarter of a million notebook computers are stolen or lost each year. If you have critical information stored on your notebook computer, then consider purchasing one with a fingerprint scanner (Figure 15) to protect the data if your computer is stolen or lost. Fingerprint security offers a level of protection that extends well beyond the standard password protection.

FIGURE 15 Fingerprint scanner technology offers greater security than passwords.

HOW TO PURCHASE A TABLET PC

The Tablet PC (Figure 16) combines the mobility features of a traditional notebook computer with the simplicity of pencil and paper, because you can create and save Office-type documents by writing and drawing directly on the screen with a digital pen. Tablet PCs use the Windows XP Tablet PC Edition operating system, which expands on Windows XP Professional by including digital pen and speech capabilities. A notebook computer and a Tablet PC have many similarities. For this reason, if you are considering purchasing a Tablet PC, review the guidelines for purchasing a notebook computer, as well as the guidelines below.

FIGURE 16
The lightweight Tablet PC, with its handwriting capabilities, is the latest addition to the family of mobile computers.

① Make sure the Tablet PC fits your mobile computing needs.   The Tablet PC is not for every mobile user. If you find yourself in need of a computer in class or you are spending more time in meetings than in your office, then the Tablet PC may be the answer. Before you invest money in a Tablet PC, however, determine the programs you plan to use on it. You should not buy a Tablet PC simply because it is a new and interesting type of computer. For additional information on the Tablet PC, visit the Web sites listed in Figure 17. You may have to use the search capabilities on the home page of the companies listed to locate information about the Tablet PC.

Company	Web Address
Fujitsu	fujitsu.com
Hewlett-Packard	hp.com
Microsoft	microsoft.com/windowsxp/tabletpc
ViewSonic	viewsonic.com

For an updated list of companies and their Web site addresses, visit scsite.com/dc2006/ch8/buyers.

FIGURE 17   Companies involved with Tablet PCs and their Web sites.

② Decide whether you want a convertible or pure Tablet PC.   Convertible Tablet PCs have an attached keyboard and look like a notebook computer. You rotate the screen and lay it flat against the computer for note-taking. The pure Tablet PCs are slim and lightweight, weighing less than four pounds. They have the capability of easily docking at a desktop to gain access to a large monitor, keyboard, and mouse. If you spend a lot of time attending lectures or meetings, then the pure Tablet PC is ideal. Acceptable specifications for a Tablet PC are shown in Figure 18.

TABLET PC SPECIFICATIONS

Dimensions	12" × 9" × 1.2"
Weight	Less than 4 Pounds
Processor	Pentium III processor-M at 1.33 GHz
RAM	512 MB
Hard Disk	40 GB
Display	12.1" XGA TFT
Digitizer	Electromagnetic Digitizer
Battery	4-Cell (3-Hour)
USB	2
FireWire	1
Docking Station	Grab and Go with CD-ROM, Keyboard, and Mouse
Bluetooth Port	Yes
Wireless	802.11b/g Card
Network Card	10/100 Ethernet
Modem	56 Kbps
Speakers	Internal
Microphone	Internal
Operating System	Windows XP Tablet PC Edition
Application Software	Office Small Business Edition
Antivirus Software	Yes – 12 Month Subscription
Warranty	1-Year Limited Warranty Parts and Labor

FIGURE 18   Tablet PC specifications.

③ Be sure the weight and dimensions are conducive to portability.   The weight and dimensions of the Tablet PC are important because you carry it around like a notepad. The Tablet PC you buy should weigh four pounds or less. Its dimensions should be approximately 12 inches by 9 inches by 1.2 inches.

4 **Port availability, battery life, and durability are even more important with a Tablet PC than they are with a notebook computer.**
Make sure the Tablet PC you purchase has the ports required for the applications you plan to run. As with any mobile computer, battery life is important especially if you plan to use your Tablet PC for long periods without access to an electrical outlet. A Tablet PC must be durable because if you use it the way it was designed to be used, then you will be handling it much like you handle a pad of paper.

5 **Experiment with different models of the Tablet PC to find the digital pen that works best for you.** The key to making use of the Tablet PC is to be comfortable with its handwriting capabilities and on-screen keyboard. Not only is the digital pen used to write on the screen (Figure 19), you also use it to make gestures to complete tasks, in a manner similar to the way you use a mouse. Figure 20 compares the standard point-and-click of a mouse with the gestures made with a digital pen. Other gestures with the digital pen replicate some of the commonly used keys on a keyboard.

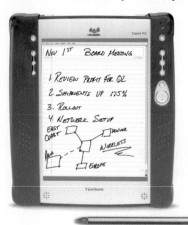

FIGURE 19 A Tablet PC lets you handwrite notes and draw on the screen using a digital pen.

Mouse	Digital Pen
Point	Point
Click	Tap
Double-click	Double-tap
Right-click	Tap and hold
Click and drag	Drag

FIGURE 20 Standard point-and-click of a mouse compared with the gestures made with a digital pen.

6 **Check out the comfort level of handwriting in different positions.** You should be able to handwrite on a Tablet PC with your hand resting on the screen. You also should be able to handwrite holding the Tablet PC in one hand, as well as with it sitting in your lap.

7 **Make sure the LCD display device has a resolution high enough to take advantage of Microsoft's ClearType technologies.**
Tablet PCs use a digitizer under a standard 10.4-inch motion-sensitive LCD display to make the digital ink on the screen look like real ink on paper. To ensure you get the maximum benefits from the new ClearType technology, make sure the LCD display has a resolution of 800 × 600 in landscape mode and a 600 × 800 in portrait mode.

8 **Test the built-in Tablet PC microphone and speakers.** With many application software packages recognizing human speech, such as Microsoft Office, it is important that the Tablet PC's built-in microphone operates at an acceptable level. If the microphone is not to your liking, you may want to purchase a close-talk headset with your Tablet PC. Increasingly more users are sending information as audio files, rather than relying solely on text. For this reason, you also should check the speakers on the Tablet PC to make sure they meet your standards.

9 **Consider a Tablet PC with a built-in PC video camera.** A PC video camera adds streaming video and still photography capabilities to your Tablet PC, while still allowing you to take notes in lectures or meetings.

10 **Review the docking capabilities of the Tablet PC.**
The Microsoft Windows XP Tablet PC Edition operating system supports a grab-and-go form of docking, so you can pick up and take a docked Tablet PC with you, just as you would pick up a notepad on your way to a meeting (Figure 21).

FIGURE 21 A Tablet PC docked to create a desktop computer with the Tablet PC as the monitor.

11 **Wireless access to the Internet and your e-mail is essential with a Tablet PC.** Make sure the Tablet PC has wireless networking, so you can access the Internet and your e-mail anytime and anywhere. Your Tablet PC also should include standard network connections, such as dial-up and Ethernet connections.

12 **Review available accessories to purchase with your Tablet PC.** Tablet PC accessories include docking stations, mouse units, keyboards, security cables, additional memory and storage, protective handgrips, screen protectors, and various types of digital pens.

Communications
and Networks

Picture Yourself Communicating Wirelessly

While driving to a small, quaint village for a weekend getaway, you realize you forgot to pay bills before leaving on the trip. All you need is an Internet connection because you pay your bills online. Along the roadside, you see a Starbucks Coffee billboard that says, "Stay connected with T-Mobile Hot Spot." After four hours of driving, a white chocolate mocha latte sounds real good. Not sure how to get to the Starbucks Coffee advertised on the billboard, you pull off the road and use the GPS feature of your PDA to access a city map.

At the coffee shop, you order your coffee, sit down at a table, open up your notebook computer that has Intel's built-in Centrino wireless technology, connect to the Internet, access your bank's Web site, and pay your bills.

Later that night at the bed and breakfast, you decide to check e-mail messages. Although the inn provides a central telephone line for dial-up Internet connections, you use your wireless PC modem card to connect to your wireless Internet service provider and download e-mail messages wirelessly. This way you can stay in your room and relax.

While shopping for antiques the next day, you see a clock your mom would love. Before buying it, you take a picture of it with your smart phone and use picture messaging to send the picture to your dad's e-mail address — you want to be sure she does not have it already. He sends back a text message that says, "Buy It!"

Read Chapter 9 to learn about wireless communications with a notebook computer, PDA, and smart phone and to discover other uses of communications.

After completing this chapter, you will be able to:

1. Discuss the components required for successful communications

2. Identify various sending and receiving devices

3. Describe uses of computer communications

4. List advantages of using a network

5. Differentiate among client/server, peer-to-peer, and P2P networks

6. Describe the various network communications standards

7. Explain the purpose of communications software

8. Describe various types of lines for communications over the telephone network

9. Describe commonly used communications devices

10. Discuss different ways to set up a home network

11. Identify various physical and wireless transmission media

CONTENTS

COMMUNICATIONS

Computer **communications** describes a process in which two or more computers or devices transfer data, instructions, and information. Today, even the smallest computers and devices communicate directly with one another, with hundreds of computers on a company network, or with millions of other computers around the globe — often via the Internet.

Figure 9-1 shows a sample communications system. Some communications involve cables and wires; others are sent wirelessly through the air. For successful communications, you need the following:

- A **sending device** that initiates an instruction to transmit data, instructions, or information.
- A communications device that connects the sending device to a communications channel.
- A **communications channel**, or transmission media on which the data, instructions, or information travel.

FIGURE 9-1　An example of a communications system. Some devices that serve as sending devices and receiving devices are (a) mainframe computers, (b) servers, (c) desktop computers, (d) notebook computers, (e) Tablet PCs, (f) smart phones, (g) Internet-enabled PDAs, and (h) GPS receivers. The communications channel consists of telephone lines, cable television and other underground lines, microwave stations, and satellites.

- A communications device that connects the communications channel to a receiving device.
- A **receiving device** that accepts the transmission of data, instructions, or information.

As shown in Figure 9-1, all types of computers and mobile devices serve as sending and receiving devices in a communications system. This includes mainframe computers, servers, desktop computers, notebook computers, Tablet PCs, smart phones, PDAs, and GPS receivers. One type of communications device that connects a communications channel to a sending or receiving device such as a computer is a modem. Two examples of communications channels are cable television lines and telephone lines.

This chapter presents various uses of communications, discusses different types of networks, and then examines several types of communications devices and communications channels.

USES OF COMPUTER COMMUNICATIONS

Computer communications are everywhere. Many require that users subscribe to an Internet access provider. With other computer communications, an organization such as a business or school provides communications services to employees, students, or customers. The following pages discuss a variety of computer communications.

Internet, Web, E-Mail, Instant Messaging, Chat Rooms, Newsgroups, Internet Telephony, FTP, Web Folders, Video Conferencing, and Fax

Previous chapters discussed many uses of computer communications as they related to a particular topic. In the course of a day, it is likely you use, or use information generated by, one or more of these previously discussed communications technologies. The table in Figure 9-2 reviews the features of these modes of communications.

PREVIOUSLY DISCUSSED USES OF COMMUNICATIONS

Internet — Worldwide collection of networks that links millions of businesses, government agencies, educational institutions, and individuals

Web — Worldwide collection of electronic documents on the Internet that users access through a Web browser (read At Issue 9-1 for a related discussion)

E-Mail — Transmission of messages and files via a computer network

Instant Messaging — Real-time Internet communications service that notifies you when one or more people are online and then allows you to exchange messages, pictures, files, audio, and video

Chat Rooms — Real-time typed conversation that takes place on a computer connected to a network that also may allow the exchange of messages, pictures, files, audio, and video

Newsgroups — Online areas in which users have written discussions about a particular subject

Internet Telephony — Conversation that takes place over the Internet using a telephone connected to a desktop computer, mobile computer, or mobile device

FTP — Internet standard that permits users to upload and download files to and from FTP servers on the Internet

Web Folders — Location on a Web server to which users publish documents and other files

Video Conferencing — Real-time meeting between two or more geographically separated people who use a network to transmit audio and video data

Fax Machine or Computer Fax/Modem — Transmits and receives documents over telephone lines

FIGURE 9-2 Uses of communications discussed in earlier chapters.

The following pages discuss a variety of other uses of communications that have not been discussed previously. These include wireless messaging services, public Internet access points, global positioning systems, groupware, collaboration, voice mail, and Web services.

 AT ISSUE 9-1

Should Companies Be Able to Track Your Online Habits?

When you visit a Web site that includes an advertisement, someone probably is recording the fact that you visited that Web site and viewed the advertisement with your browser. Over time, companies that specialize in tracking who views which online advertisements can amass an enormous amount of information about your online Web surfing habits. This collection of information is considered to be part of your online profile. One company claims that through the use of advertisements on Web pages, it can track well over one billion Web page views per day.

Through tracking the Web sites a user visits, the products they buy, and the articles they read, a company may attempt to profile the visitor's beliefs, associations, and habits. Although a user may think he or she is anonymous while navigating the Web, the company can attempt through various means to link the user's true identity with the user's online profile. The company can sell online profiles, with or without the user's true identity, to other advertisers or organizations. Should organizations be allowed to track your Web surfing habits? Why or why not? Should organizations be allowed to associate your real identity with your online identity and profit from the information? Who should have access to information about your online habits?

Wireless Messaging Services

Users can send and receive wireless messages to and from smart phones, cellular telephones, or PDAs using three techniques: text messaging, wireless instant messaging, and picture messaging (Figure 9-3). The type of messaging you use depends primarily on the services offered by the wireless Internet service provider (WISP) that works with the cellular phone or PDA you select. In most cases, you can receive these messages at no cost but pay a per use or monthly fee to send messages to others.

FIGURE 9-3 Users can send and receive text messages, wireless instant messages, and picture messages to and from their smart phones and other computers and devices.

TEXT MESSAGING A mobile device with **text messaging**, also called **SMS** (*short message service*), capability allows users to send and receive short text messages on a smart phone or PDA. Most text messaging services limit messages to a specific number of characters, usually fewer than 300 characters. Text messaging services typically provide users with several options for sending and receiving messages:

- Mobile to Mobile: send the message from your mobile device to another mobile device
- Mobile to E-Mail: send the message from your mobile device to an e-mail address anywhere in the world
- Web to Mobile: send the message from a text messaging Web site to a mobile device

Most services store incoming text messages for about 72 hours. After that time, the WISP deletes any unread messages from its server.

WIRELESS INSTANT MESSAGING Wireless instant messaging (IM) is a real-time Internet communications service that allows wireless mobile devices to exchange messages with one or more mobile devices or online users. Some WISPs partner with IM services so you can use your smart phone or PDA to send and receive wireless instant messages. AT&T Wireless service, for example, allows communications through various instant messengers such as AOL Instant Messenger, Yahoo! Messenger, and MSN Messenger. With a compatible IM service, users have these IM options:

- Mobile to Mobile: use a wireless instant messenger to communicate between two mobile devices
- Mobile to Personal Computer: use a wireless instant messenger to communicate between a mobile device and a personal computer

Many services also allow users to forward wireless instant messages from a personal computer to their smart phone.

PICTURE MESSAGING   Users can send graphics, pictures, video clips, and sound files, as well as short text messages with **picture messaging**, also called *MMS* (*multimedia message service*) to another smart phone, PDA, or computer. Smart phones and PDAs with picture messaging capability typically have a digital camera built into the device. Read At Issue 9-2 for a related discussion.

Picture messaging services typically provide users these options for sending and receiving messages:

- Mobile to Mobile: send the picture from your mobile device to another mobile device
- Mobile to E-Mail: send the picture from your mobile device to an e-mail address anywhere in the world

If you send a picture message to a cellular phone that does not have picture messaging capability, the cellular phone usually displays a text message directing the user to a Web page that contains the picture message.

Public Internet Access Points

In many public locations, people connect wirelessly to the Internet through a **public Internet access point** using mobile computers or other devices. Two types of public Internet access points are hot spots and cybercafés.

A *hot spot* is a wireless network that provides Internet connections to mobile computers and other devices. Through the hot spot, mobile users check e-mail, browse the Web, and access any service on the Internet — as long as their computers or devices have built-in wireless capability or the appropriate wireless network card or PC Card (Figure 9-4). Hot spots are appearing in airports, hotels, schools, shopping malls, bookstores, restaurants, and coffee shops. Most hot spots span from 100 to 300 feet; some can extend to 15 miles and cover entire cities.

Some hot spots provide free Internet access, some charge a per-use fee, and others require users to subscribe to a WISP, to which they pay per access fees, daily fees, or a monthly fee. Per access fees average $3, daily fees range from $5 to $20, and monthly fees range from $30 to $50 for unlimited access.

When mobile users travel without their notebook computer or Internet-enabled mobile device, they can visit a cybercafé to access e-mail, the Web, and other Internet services. A **cybercafé** is a coffee house or restaurant that provides personal computers with Internet access to its customers (Figure 9-5). More than 6,300 cybercafés exist in cities around the world. Although some provide free Internet access, most charge a per-hour or per-minute fee. Some cybercafés also are hot spots, providing wireless Internet connections to users with mobile computers and devices.

AT ISSUE 9-2

High-Tech Cheating via Wireless Messaging Services

Several schools have banned student cellular telephones claiming that they disrupt classes and sometimes are used for illegal activities, such as drug sales. Now, schools may have another reason to prohibit cellular telephones and other wireless devices among students.

Once, teachers only had to watch test-takers to make sure that no one was copying from a neighbor's paper or secretly referring to notes concealed under a desk. Recently, however, students were caught using their cellular phones' messaging service to send each other answers to test questions. Others have been caught using camera-enabled cellular phones to take pictures of tests and forwarding the images to other students who were scheduled to take the test at a later time. Some teachers fear that more students soon may be using wireless devices to communicate covertly with classmates during a test, or even to receive messages from sources outside the classroom. To eliminate this high-tech method of cheating, should cellular telephones, digital cameras, notebook computers, Tablet PCs, PDAs, and other wireless devices be banned during lectures and exams? Why or why not? Short of banning these devices, what, if anything, can schools do to prevent students from using them to cheat? Should schools seek a point of compromise so that they can both embrace the new technology and control it?

FAQ 9-1

What are the typical fee structures in a cybercafé?

Internet connection fees at a cybercafé usually range from $1.50 to $10.00 per hour. To print, the fees range from $0.25 per page to $3.00 per page. Some cybercafés offer lower or waived rates to customers who purchase food or become a member of the café. For more information, visit scsite.com/dc2006/ch9/faq and then click Cybercafés.

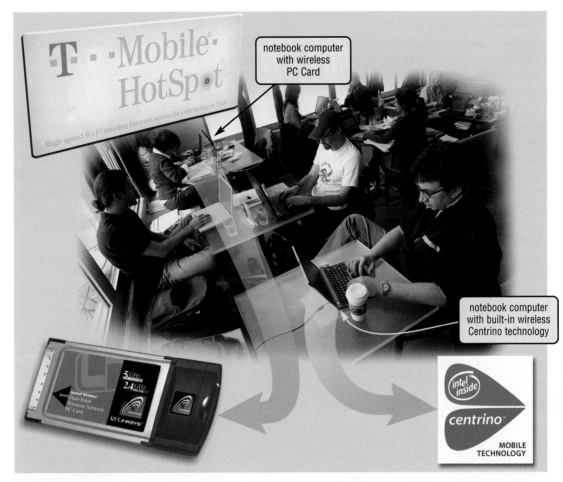

notebook computer
with wireless
PC Card

notebook computer
with built-in wireless
Centrino technology

WEB LINK 9-1

Hot Spots
For more information,
visit scsite.com/
dc2006/ch9/weblink
and then click Hot
Spots.

FIGURE 9-4   Mobile users in this hot spot access the Internet through their notebook computers. One computer uses a wireless network PC Card. The other has Intel's built-in wireless Centrino technology.

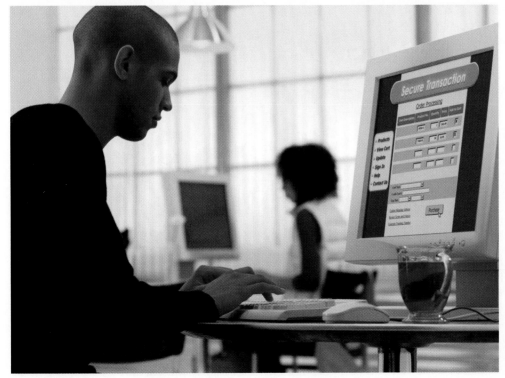

FIGURE 9-5   People using Internet-connected computers and drinking beverages in a cybercafé.

Global Positioning System

A **global positioning system (GPS)** is a navigation system that consists of one or more earth-based receivers that accept and analyze signals sent by satellites in order to determine the receiver's geographic location (Figure 9-6). A *GPS receiver* is a handheld, mountable, or embedded device that contains an antenna, a radio receiver, and a processor. Many include a screen display that shows an individual's location on a map.

Many mobile devices such as PDAs and smart phones have GPS capability built into the device or as an add-on feature. Some users carry a handheld GPS receiver; others mount a receiver to an object such as an automobile, boat, airplane, farm and construction equipment, or computer.

The first and most used application of GPS technology is to assist people with determining where they are located. The data obtained from a GPS, however, can be applied to a variety of other uses: creating a map, ascertaining the best route between two points, locating a lost person or stolen object, or monitoring the movement of a person or object. Many vehicles use GPSs to provide drivers with directions or other information, automatically call for help if the airbag is deployed, dispatch roadside assistance, unlock the driver's side door if keys are locked in the car, and track the vehicle if it is stolen. Hikers and remote campers may carry GPS receivers in case they need emergency help or directions.

For applications that locate or track people, the GPS receiver typically works in conjunction

WEB LINK 9-2

GPS

For more information, visit scsite.com/ dc2006/ch9/weblink and then click GPS.

FIGURE 9-6   HOW A GPS WORKS

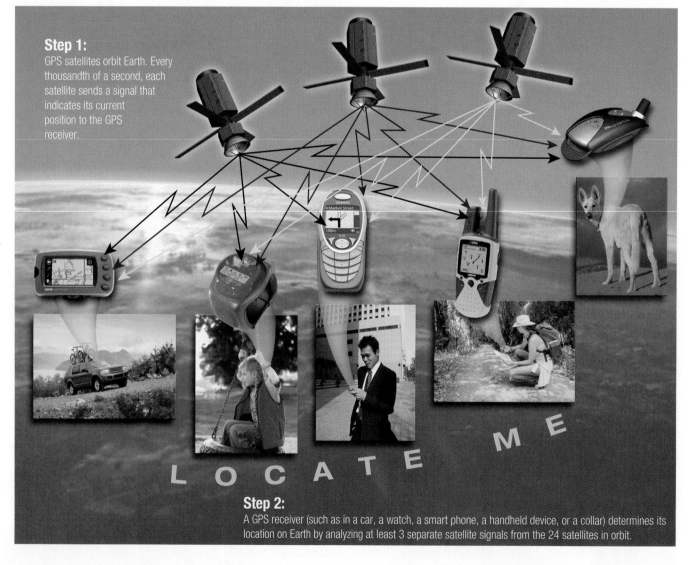

Step 1:
GPS satellites orbit Earth. Every thousandth of a second, each satellite sends a signal that indicates its current position to the GPS receiver.

L O C A T E   M E

Step 2:
A GPS receiver (such as in a car, a watch, a smart phone, a handheld device, or a collar) determines its location on Earth by analyzing at least 3 separate satellite signals from the 24 satellites in orbit.

with a cellular wireless network. When a user presses a button on the GPS receiver or at regularly scheduled times, the GPS receiver captures data from the satellite and sends location information to a cellular wireless network. Once the cellular wireless network receives the data, its computer calculates the exact location of a person or object.

A new use of GPS places the GPS receiver on a computer chip that is worn as a wristwatch or chain or woven into fabric. The chip measures and sends a person's biological information to a cellular wireless network. If the information relayed indicates a person needs medical attention, dispatchers use data from the GPS receiver to calculate the person's location and immediately send emergency medical help. Other possible uses include locating a missing person or pet, tracking parolees, and protecting valuables.

Collaboration

Many programs provide a means to **collaborate**, or work online, with other users connected to a server. With Microsoft Office, for example, users can conduct online meetings (Figure 9-7). An *online meeting* allows users to share documents with others in real time. That is, all participants see the document at the same time. As someone changes the document, everyone in the meeting sees the changes being made. During the online meeting, participants have the ability to open a separate window and type messages to one another. Some programs refer to this window as a chat room.

Instead of interacting in a live meeting, users often collaborate via e-mail. For example, if users want others to review a document, they can attach a routing slip to the document and send it via e-mail to everyone on the routing slip. When the first person on the routing slip receives the document, he or she may add comments to the document. As changes are made to the document, both the original text and the changes are displayed. When subsequent persons on the routing slip receive the document via e-mail, they see all the previous users' changes and can make additional changes. Once everyone on the routing slip has reviewed the document, it automatically returns to the sender.

FIGURE 9-7 When you start an online meeting from a Microsoft Office product, the participants use NetMeeting to collaborate on the document.

Groupware

Groupware is software that helps groups of people work together on projects and share information over a network. Groupware is a component of a broad concept called *workgroup computing*, which includes network hardware and software that enables group members to communicate, manage projects, schedule meetings, and make group decisions. To assist with these activities, most groupware provides personal information manager (PIM) functions, such as an electronic appointment calendar, an address book, and a notepad. A major feature of groupware is group scheduling, in which a group calendar tracks the schedules of multiple users and helps coordinate appointments and meeting times.

Voice Mail

Voice mail, which functions much like an answering machine, allows someone to leave a voice message for one or more people. Unlike answering machines, however, a computer in the voice mail system converts an analog voice message into digital form. Once digitized, the message is stored in a voice mailbox. A *voice mailbox* is a storage location on a hard disk in the voice mail system.

A voice mail system usually provides individual voice mailboxes for many users (for example, employees in a company or students and faculty at a college). By accessing their voice mailboxes, recipients of a call listen to messages, may add comments to a message, and reply or forward a message to another voice mailbox in the voice mail system. Some voice mail systems allow users to broadcast a message, which sends the same message to a group of people or to everyone listed in the system's database. Colleges, for example, might use voice mail to notify every student of registration deadlines and weather-related school closings.

Web Services

Web services describe standardized software that enables programmers to create applications that communicate with other remote computers over the Internet or on an internal business network (Figure 9-8). Businesses are the primary users of Web services because this technology provides a means for departments to communicate with each other, suppliers, vendors, and with clients. For example, third-party vendors can use Web services to communicate with their online retailer's Web site to manage their inventory levels.

Web services do not require a specific programming language, operating system, or Web browser. Different applications from different platforms can communicate with each other by sending properly formatted *XML* (eXtensible Markup Language) files to the Web services. A Windows application, for example, can communicate with a UNIX application. Web services do not have a user interface because the application's user interface interacts with the Web service.

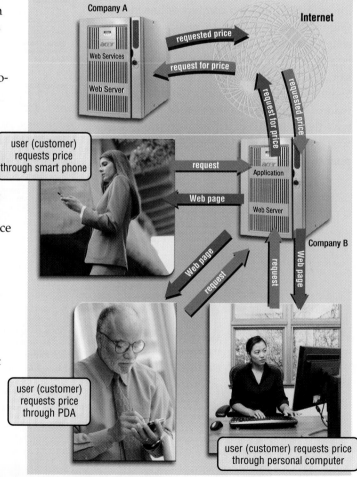

FIGURE 9-8 An example of Web services.

Test your knowledge of pages 460 through 468 in Quiz Yourself 9-1.

QUIZ YOURSELF 9-1

Instructions: Find the true statement below. Then, rewrite the remaining false statements so they are true.

1. A cybercafé is a wireless network that provides Internet connections to mobile computers and other devices.

2. A Web folder is a navigation system that consists of one or more earth-based receivers that accept and analyze signals sent by satellites in order to determine the receiver's geographic location.

3. Web services describe standardized software that enables programmers to create applications that communicate with other remote computers over the Internet or on an internal business network.

4. Receiving devices initiate an instruction to transmit data, instructions, or information.

5. Users can send graphics, pictures, video clips, and sound files, as well as short text messages with text messaging.

Quiz Yourself Online: To further check your knowledge of required components for communications, sending and receiving devices, and uses of computer communications, visit scsite.com/dc2006/ch9/quiz and then click Objectives 1 – 3.

NETWORKS

As discussed in Chapter 1, a **network** is a collection of computers and devices connected together via communications devices and transmission media. Many businesses network their computers together to facilitate communications, share hardware, share data and information, share software, and transfer funds (Figure 9-9). The next page elaborates on how businesses use networks.

FIGURE 9-9 Businesses use networks to facilitate communications, share hardware, share data and information, share software, and transfer funds.

A network can be internal to an organization or span the world by connecting itself to the Internet. Networks facilitate communications among users and allow users to share resources, such as data, information, hardware, and software, with other users. The following paragraphs explain the advantages of using a network.

- Facilitating communications — Using a network, people communicate efficiently and easily via e-mail, instant messaging, chat rooms, video telephone calls, video conferencing, Internet telephony, wireless messaging services, and groupware. Some of these communications, such as e-mail, occur within a business's internal network. Other times, they occur globally over the Internet.

- Sharing hardware — In a networked environment, each computer on the network has access to hardware on the network. Business and home users network their hardware to save money. That is, it may be too costly to provide each user with the same piece of hardware such as a printer. If the computers and a laser printer are connected to a network, the computer users each access the laser printer on the network, as they need it.

- Sharing data and information — In a networked environment, any authorized computer user can access data and information stored on other computers on the network. A large company, for example, might have a database of customer information. Any authorized person, including a mobile user with a PDA or smart phone connected to the network, has access to the database.

  Most businesses use a standard, such as *EDI* (*electronic data interchange*), that defines how data transmits across telephone lines or other means. For example, companies use EDI to handle product catalog distribution, bids, requests for quotations, proposals, order placement, shipping notifications, invoicing, and payment processing. EDI enables businesses to operate with a minimum amount of paperwork.

- Sharing software — Users connected to a network have access to software on the network. To support multiple users' access of software, most vendors sell network versions or site licenses of their software, which usually cost less than buying individual copies of the software for each computer. A *network license* is a legal agreement that allows multiple users to access the software on a server simultaneously. The network license fee usually is based on the number of users or the number of computers attached to the network. A *site license* is a legal agreement that permits users to install the software on multiple computers — usually at a volume discount.

- Transferring funds — Called *electronic funds transfer* (*EFT*), it allows users connected to a network to transfer money from one bank account to another via transmission media. Both businesses and consumers use EFT. Consumers use an ATM to access their bank account. Businesses deposit payroll checks directly in employees' bank accounts. Consumers use credit cards to make purchases from a retail Web site. Businesses use EFT to purchase and pay for goods purchased from vendors. Both businesses and consumers pay bills online, with which they instruct a bank to use EFT to pay creditors.

Instead of using the Internet or investing in and administering an internal network, some companies hire a value-added network provider for network functions. A *value-added network* (*VAN*) is a third-party business that provides networking services such as secure data and information transfer, storage, e-mail, and management reports. Some VANs charge an annual or monthly fee; others charge by service used.

For a technical discussion about networks, read the High-Tech Talk article on page 498.

LANs, MANs, and WANs

Networks usually are classified as a local area network, metropolitan area network, or wide area network. The main differentiation among these classifications is their area of coverage, as described in the following paragraphs.

LAN A **local area network (LAN)** is a network that connects computers and devices in a limited geographical area such as a home, school computer laboratory, office building (Figure 9-10), or closely positioned group of buildings. Each computer or device on the network, called a *node*, often shares resources such as printers, large hard disks, and programs. Often, the nodes are connected via cables.

A **wireless LAN (WLAN)** is a LAN that uses no physical wires. Computers and devices that access a wireless LAN must have built-in wireless capability or the appropriate wireless network card, PC Card, or flash card. Very often, a WLAN communicates with a wired LAN for access to its resources, such as software, hardware, and the Internet (Figure 9-11).

customer service offices

marketing department offices

computer center

FIGURE 9-10 An example of a local area network (LAN) in an office building.

Internet

high-speed Internet connection

wired network

wireless access point

wireless network

FIGURE 9-11
Computers on a wireless LAN often communicate via an access point with a wired LAN to access its software, printer, the Internet, and other resources.

MAN A *metropolitan area network* (*MAN*) is a high-speed network that connects local area networks in a metropolitan area such as a city or town and handles the bulk of communications activity across that region. A MAN typically includes one or more LANs, but covers a smaller geographic area than a WAN. The state of Pennsylvania, for example, has a MAN that connects state agencies and individual users in the region around the state capital.

A MAN usually is managed by a consortium of users or by a single network provider that sells the service to the users. Local and state governments, for example, regulate some MANs. Telephone companies, cable television operators, and other organizations provide users with connections to the MAN.

WAN A **wide area network** (**WAN**) is a network that covers a large geographic area (such as a city, country, or the world) using a communications channel that combines many types of media such as telephone lines, cables, and radio waves (Figure 9-12). A WAN can be one large network or can consist of two or more LANs connected together. The Internet is the world's largest WAN.

Network Architectures

The design of computers, devices, and media in a network, sometimes called the *network architecture*, is categorized as either client/server or peer-to-peer. The following paragraphs discuss these network architectures.

CLIENT/SERVER On a **client/server network**, one or more computers act as a server, and the other computers on the network request services from the server (Figure 9-13). A **server**, sometimes called a *host computer*, controls access to the hardware, software, and other resources on the network and provides a centralized storage area for programs, data, and information. The **clients** are other computers and mobile devices on the network that rely on the server for its resources. For example, a server might store a database of customers. Clients on the network (company employees) access the customer database on the server.

FIGURE 9-13 On a client/server network, one or more computers act as a server, and the clients access the server(s).

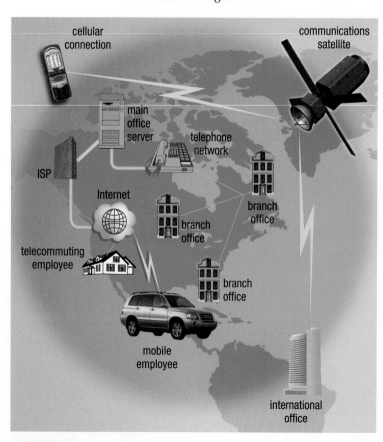

FIGURE 9-12 An example of a WAN.

Some servers, called *dedicated servers*, perform a specific task and can be placed with other dedicated servers to perform multiple tasks. For example, a *file server* stores and manages files. A *print server* manages printers and print jobs. A *database server* stores and provides access to a database. A *network server* manages network traffic (activity).

Although it can connect a smaller number of computers, a client/server network typically provides an efficient means to connect 10 or more computers. Most client/server networks require a person to serve as a network administrator because of the large size of the network.

PEER-TO-PEER One type of *peer-to-peer network* is a simple, inexpensive network that typically connects fewer than 10 computers. Each computer, called a *peer*, has equal responsibilities and capabilities, sharing hardware (such as a printer), data, or information with other computers on the peer-to-peer network (Figure 9-14). Each computer stores files on its own storage devices. Thus, each computer on the network contains both the network operating system and application software. All computers on the network share any peripheral device(s) attached

to any computer. For example, one computer may have a laser printer and a scanner, while another has an ink-jet printer and an external hard disk.

Peer-to-peer networks are ideal for very small businesses and home users. Some operating systems, such as Windows, include a peer-to-peer networking utility that allows users to set up a peer-to-peer network.

INTERNET PEER-TO-PEER Another type of peer-to-peer, called *P2P*, describes an Internet network on which users access each other's hard disks and exchange files directly over the Internet (Figure 9-15). This type of peer-to-peer network sometimes is called a *file sharing network* because users with compatible software and an Internet connection copy files from someone else's hard disk to their hard disks. As more users connect to the network, each user has access to shared files on other users' hard disks. When users log off the network, others no longer have access to their hard disks. To maintain an acceptable speed for communications, some implementations of P2P limit the number of users.

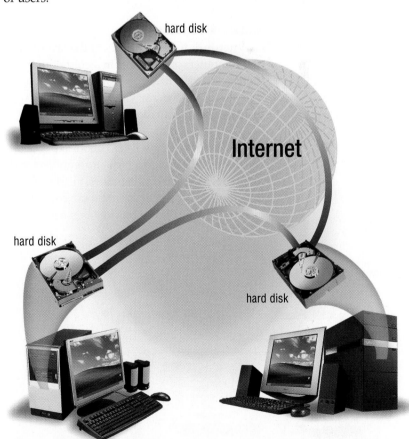

FIGURE 9-14 Each computer on a peer-to-peer network shares its hardware and software with other computers on the network.

printer may be used by all computers on network

network operating system and application software installed on each computer

hard disk

Internet

hard disk

hard disk

FIGURE 9-15 P2P describes an Internet network on which users connect to each other's hard disks and exchange files directly.

Examples of networking software that support P2P are BitTorrent, Grokster, Gnutella, and Kazaa, which allow users to swap MP3 music files via the Web. For example, when one user requests a song, the program searches through lists of shared files – which are stored on one or more connected computers, called supernodes. If a match is found, the MP3 file is copied from the computer on which it resides to the requesting computer. These programs initially stirred much controversy with respect to copyright infringement of music because they allowed users easily to copy MP3 music files free from one computer to another. To help reduce copyright infringement, today's music-sharing services typically are fee based, and music files often are encrypted as they travel across the Internet.

Many businesses also see an advantage to using P2P. That is, companies and employees can exchange files using P2P, freeing the company from maintaining a network server for this purpose. Business-to-business e-commerce Web sites find that P2P easily allows buyers and sellers to share company information such as product databases.

WEB LINK 9-4

P2P

For more information, visit scsite.com/dc2006/ch9/weblink and then click P2P.

Network Topologies

A **network topology** refers to the layout of the computers and devices in a communications network. Three commonly used network topologies are bus, ring, and star. Networks usually use combinations of these topologies.

BUS NETWORK A *bus network* consists of a single central cable, to which all computers and other devices connect (Figure 9-16). The *bus* is the physical cable that connects the computers and other devices. The bus in a bus network

transmits data, instructions, and information in both directions. When a sending device transmits data, the address of the receiving device is included with the transmission so the data is routed to the appropriate receiving device.

Bus networks are popular on LANs because they are inexpensive and easy to install. One advantage of the bus network is that computers and other devices can be attached and detached at any point on the bus without disturbing the rest of the network. Another advantage is that failure of one device usually does not affect the rest of the bus network. The greatest risk to a bus network is that the bus itself might become inoperable. If that happens, the network remains inoperative until the bus is back in working order.

RING NETWORK On a *ring network*, a cable forms a closed loop (ring) with all computers and devices arranged along the ring (Figure 9-17). Data transmitted on a ring network travels from device to device around the entire ring, in one direction. When a computer or device sends data, the data travels to each computer on the ring until it reaches its destination.

FIGURE 9-17 On a ring network, all connected devices form a continuous loop.

personal computer

personal computer

personal computer personal computer personal computer

FIGURE 9-16 Devices in a bus network share a single data path.

If a computer or device on a ring network fails, all devices before the failed device are unaffected, but those after the failed device cannot function. A ring network can span a larger distance than a bus network, but it is more difficult to install. The ring topology primarily is used for LANs, but also is used in WANs.

STAR NETWORK On a *star network*, all of the computers and devices (nodes) on the network connect to a central device, thus forming a star (Figure 9-18). The central device that provides a common connection point for nodes on the network often is called the *hub*. All data that transfers from one node to another passes through the hub.

Star networks are fairly easy to install and maintain. Nodes can be added to and removed from the network with little or no disruption to the network.

On a star network, if one node fails, only that node is affected. The other nodes continue to operate normally. If the hub fails, however, the entire network is inoperable until the hub is repaired. Most large star networks, therefore, keep backup hubs available in case the primary hub fails.

Intranets

Recognizing the efficiency and power of the Internet, many organizations apply Internet and Web technologies to their own internal networks. An *intranet* (intra means within) is an internal network that uses Internet technologies. Intranets generally make company information accessible to employees and facilitate working in groups.

Simple intranet applications include electronic publishing of organizational materials such as telephone directories, event calendars, procedure manuals, employee benefits information, and job postings. Additionally, an intranet typically includes a connection to the Internet. More sophisticated uses of intranets include groupware applications such as project management, chat rooms, newsgroups, group scheduling, and video conferencing.

An intranet essentially is a small version of the Internet that exists within an organization. It has a Web server, supports multimedia Web pages coded in HTML, and is accessible via a Web browser such as Microsoft Internet Explorer or Netscape Navigator. Users update information on the intranet by creating and posting a Web page, using a method similar to that used on the Internet.

Sometimes a company uses an *extranet*, which allows customers or suppliers to access part of its intranet. Package shipping companies, for example, allow customers to access their intranet to print air bills, schedule pickups, and even track shipped packages as the packages travel to their destinations.

FIGURE 9-18 A star network contains a single, centralized hub through which all the devices in the network communicate.

NETWORK COMMUNICATIONS STANDARDS

Today's networks connect terminals, devices, and computers from many different manufacturers across many types of networks, such as wide area, local area, and wireless. For the different devices on various types of networks to be able to communicate, the network must use similar techniques of moving data through the network from one application to another. For example, an IBM mainframe computer cannot communicate directly with an Apple Macintosh network — some form of translation must occur for devices on these two types of networks to communicate.

To alleviate the problems of incompatibility and ensure that hardware and software components can be integrated into any network, various organizations such as ANSI and IEEE (pronounced I triple E) propose, develop, and approve network standards. A *network standard* defines guidelines that specify the way computers access the medium to which they are attached, the type(s) of medium used, the speeds used on different types of networks, and the type(s) of physical cable and/or the wireless technology used. A standard that outlines characteristics of how two network devices communicate is called a *protocol*. Specifically, a protocol may define data format, coding schemes, error handling, and sequencing techniques. Hardware and software manufacturers design their products to meet the guidelines specified in a particular standard, so their devices can communicate with the network.

The following sections discuss some of the more widely used network communications standards and protocols for both wired and wireless networks including Ethernet, token ring, TCP/IP, 802.11, Bluetooth, IrDA, RFID, and WAP. Oftentimes, these network standards and protocols work together to move data through a network. Some of these standards define how a network is arranged physically; others specify how messages travel along the network, and so on. Thus, as data moves through the network from one application to another, it may use one or more of these standards.

Ethernet

Ethernet is a network standard that specifies no central computer or device on the network (nodes) should control when data can be transmitted; that is, each node attempts to transmit data when it determines the network is available to receive communications. If two computers on an Ethernet network attempt to send data at the same time, a collision will occur, and the computers must attempt to send their messages again.

Ethernet is based on a bus topology, but Ethernet networks can be wired in a star pattern. The Ethernet standard defines guidelines for the physical configuration of a network, e.g., cabling, network cards, and nodes. Today, Ethernet is the most popular network standard for LANs because it is relatively inexpensive and easy to install and maintain.

Ethernet networks often use cables to transmit data. At a 10 Mbps (million bits per second) data transfer rate, the original Ethernet standard is not very fast by today's standards. A more recent Ethernet standard, called *Fast Ethernet*, has a data transfer rate of 100 Mbps, ten times faster than the original standard. *Gigabit Ethernet* provides an even higher speed of transmission, with transfer rates of 1 Gbps (1 billion bits per second). The *10-Gigabit Ethernet* standard supports transfer rates up to 10 Gbps.

Token Ring

The second most popular network standard for LANs is token ring. The **token ring** standard specifies that computers and devices on the network share or pass a special signal, called a token, in a unidirectional manner and in a preset order. A *token* is a special series of bits that function like a ticket. The device with the token can transmit data over the network. Only one token exists per network. This ensures that only one computer transmits data at a time.

Token ring is based on a ring topology (although it can use a star topology). The token ring standard defines guidelines for the physical configuration of a network, e.g., cabling, network cards, and devices. Some token ring networks connect up to 72 devices. Others use a special type of wiring that allows up to 260 connections. The data transfer rate on a token ring network can be 4 Mbps, 16 Mbps, or up to 100 Mbps.

TCP/IP

Short for *Transmission Control Protocol/Internet Protocol*, **TCP/IP** is a network standard, specifically a protocol, that defines how messages (data) are routed from one end of a network to the other, ensuring the data arrives correctly. TCP/IP describes rules for dividing messages into small pieces, called *packets*; providing addresses for each packet; checking for and detecting errors; sequencing packets; and regulating the flow of messages along the network.

TCP/IP has been adopted as a network standard for Internet communications. Thus, all hosts on the Internet follow the rules defined in this standard. As shown in Figure 9-19, Internet communications also use other standards, such as the Ethernet standard, as data is routed to its destination.

When a computer sends data over the Internet, the data is divided into packets. Each packet contains the data, as well as the recipient (destination), the origin (sender), and the sequence information used to reassemble the data at the destination. Each packet travels along the fastest individual available path to the recipient's computer via communications devices called routers.

This technique of breaking a message into individual packets, sending the packets along the best route available, and then reassembling the data is called *packet switching*.

FAQ 9-2

Do HTTP, SMTP, and POP work with TCP/IP?

Yes. HTTP (Hypertext Transfer Protocol), SMTP (Simple Mail Transfer Protocol), and POP (Post Office Protocol) are standards that define the format of data as it transmits over networks that use the TCP/IP standard. HTTP works with Web browsers, and SMTP and POP work with e-mail programs. For more information, visit scsite.com/dc2006/ch9/faq and then click HTTP, SMTP, and POP.

EXAMPLE OF HOW COMMUNICATIONS STANDARDS WORK TOGETHER

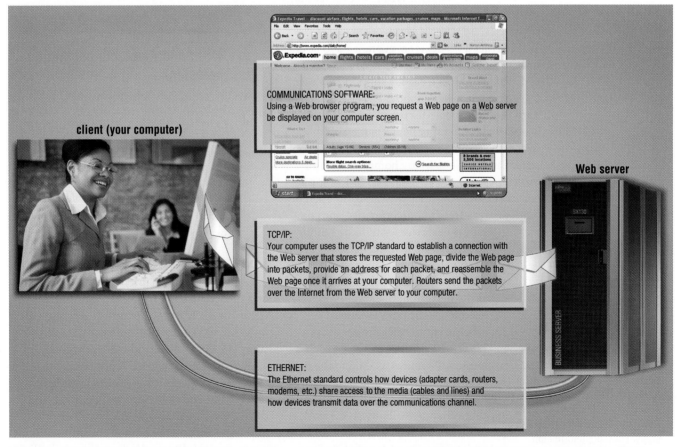

client (your computer)

COMMUNICATIONS SOFTWARE:
Using a Web browser program, you request a Web page on a Web server be displayed on your computer screen.

Web server

TCP/IP:
Your computer uses the TCP/IP standard to establish a connection with the Web server that stores the requested Web page, divide the Web page into packets, provide an address for each packet, and reassemble the Web page once it arrives at your computer. Routers send the packets over the Internet from the Web server to your computer.

ETHERNET:
The Ethernet standard controls how devices (adapter cards, routers, modems, etc.) share access to the media (cables and lines) and how devices transmit data over the communications channel.

FIGURE 9-19   Network communications use a variety of standards to ensure that data travels correctly to its destination. Some standards used in Internet communications include the TCP/IP and Ethernet standards, as shown in this figure.

802.11

Developed by IEEE, **802.11** is a series of network standards that specifies how two wireless devices communicate over the air with each other. Using the 802.11 standard, wireless computers or devices communicate via radio waves with other computers or devices. The table in Figure 9-20 outlines various 802.11 standards and their data transfer rates. As shown in the table, *802.11g* currently has the fastest data transfer rate of 54 Mbps and higher. An *802.11i* network standard specifies enhanced security for wireless communications.

The 802.11 standard often is called the *wireless Ethernet standard* because it uses techniques similar to the Ethernet standard to specify how physically to configure a wireless network. Thus, 802.11 networks easily can be integrated with wired Ethernet networks. When an 802.11 network accesses the Internet, it works in conjunction with the TCP/IP network standard.

The term **Wi-Fi** (*wireless fidelity*) identifies any network based on the 802.11 series of standards. Wi-Fi Certified products are guaranteed to be able to communicate with each other. Windows XP and Windows Mobile include support for Wi-Fi.

One popular use of the Wi-Fi network standard is in hot spots (discussed earlier in this chapter) that offer mobile users the ability to connect to the Internet with their wireless computers and devices. Many homes and small businesses also use Wi-Fi to network computers and devices together wirelessly. In open or outdoor areas free from interference, the computers or devices should be within 800 feet of each other. In closed areas, the wireless network range is about 150 feet. To obtain communications at the maximum distances, you may need to install extra antennas.

Some entire cities are set up as a *Wi-Fi mesh network*, in which each mesh node routes its data to the next available node until the data reaches its destination — usually an Internet connection. A Wi-Fi mesh network is more flexible than a hot spot because each node in a mesh network does not have to be directly connected to the Internet.

802.11 SERIES OF STANDARDS

Standard	Transfer Rates
802.11	1 or 2 Mbps
802.11a	Up to 54 Mbps
802.11b	Up to 11 Mbps
802.11g	54 Mbps and higher

FIGURE 9-20 A comparison of standards in the 802.11 series.

FAQ 9-3

How prevalent are hot spots?

Very. By 2007, experts predict that more than 120,000 hot spots will exist worldwide. The United States has the most hot spots, followed by the United Kingdom, France, Germany, and Japan. In the United States, New York City has the most hot spots. For more information, visit scsite.com/dc2006/ch9/faq and then click Hot Spots.

Bluetooth

Bluetooth is a network standard, specifically a protocol, that defines how two Bluetooth devices use short-range radio waves to transmit data. The data transfers between devices at a rate of up to 2 Mbps. To communicate with each other, Bluetooth devices often must be within about 10 meters (about 33 feet) but can be extended to 100 meters with additional equipment.

A Bluetooth device contains a small chip that allows it to communicate with other Bluetooth devices. Examples of Bluetooth-enabled devices can include desktop computers, notebook computers, handheld computers, PDAs, smart phones, headsets, microphones, digital cameras, fax machines, and printers. For computers and devices not Bluetooth-enabled, you can purchase a Bluetooth wireless port adapter that will convert an existing USB port or serial port into a Bluetooth port. Windows XP has built-in Bluetooth support that allows users easily to configure Bluetooth communications.

FAQ 9-4

Are Wi-Fi and Bluetooth competing technologies?

Not really. Bluetooth is designed for limited data transfer between two devices, one of which usually is a mobile device (e.g., a notebook computer and a printer, a digital camera and a desktop computer, two PDAs). Wi-Fi, which supports much faster data transfer rates, allows users to network many computers and devices together wirelessly. For more information, visit scsite.com/dc2006/ch9/faq and then click Wi-Fi and Bluetooth.

IrDA

As discussed in Chapter 4, some computers and devices use the **IrDA** standard to transmit data wirelessly to each other via infrared (IR) light waves. The devices transfer data at rates from 115 Kbps (thousand bits per second) to 4 Mbps between their IrDA ports.

Infrared requires a *line-of-sight transmission*; that is, the sending device and the receiving device must be in line with each other so that nothing obstructs the path of the infrared light wave. Because Bluetooth does not require line-of-sight transmission, some industry experts predict that Bluetooth will replace infrared.

RFID

RFID (*radio frequency identification*) is a standard, specifically a protocol, that defines how a network uses radio signals to communicate with a tag placed in or attached to an object, an animal, or a person. The tag, called a transponder, consists of an antenna and a memory chip that contains the information to be transmitted via radio waves. Through an antenna, an RFID reader, also called a transceiver, reads the radio signals and transfers the information to a computer or computing device.

RFID tags are passive or active. An active RFID tag contains a battery that runs the chip's circuitry and broadcasts a signal to the RFID reader. A passive RFID tag does not contain a battery and thus cannot send a signal until the reader activates the tag's antenna by sending out electromagnetic waves. Because passive RFID tags contain no battery, these can be small enough to be embedded in skin.

Depending on the type of RFID reader, the distance between the tag and the reader ranges from 5 inches to 15 feet. Readers can be handheld or embedded in an object such as the tollbooth shown in Figure 9-21. Read At Issue 9-3 for a related discussion.

FAQ 9-5

Are RFID tags implanted in people?

To date, more than 1,000 people have been implanted with RFID tags. The most common application of human-implanted RFID tags is to control access to buildings and other secure areas. For more information, visit scsite.com/dc2006/ch9/faq and then click Implanting RFID tags.

AT ISSUE 9-3

Will We Be Safer in the Upcoming Surveillance Society?

Cameras that photograph real-time situations are everywhere — in parking garages, at day-care centers, in public buildings, at tollbooths, and even at street corners. In hundreds of cities, video cameras and radar devices are installed at intersections to catch speeding motorists and those who run red lights. When a violator is spotted, the devices transmit an image and other information to the local police network, and computers automatically send a citation to the vehicle's owner. Supporters of the video cameras say the systems promote safety and free police officers for other duties. Yet, critics express concerns about privacy issues. As more devices and agencies are networked together, the law enforcement community has an unprecedented look at a person's movement through society. A U.S. congressman who opposes the video cameras questions how long tapes and other information are kept, what safeguards are in place to prevent the tapes and information from being misused, and whether the systems violate a defendant's right to face his or her accuser. Are video cameras at intersections a good idea? Why or why not? How can the concerns of opponents of the systems be answered?

FIGURE 9-21 HOW ELECTRONIC RFID TOLL COLLECTION WORKS

Step 1:
Motorist purchases an RFID transponder or RFID tag and attaches it to the vehicle's windshield.

Step 2:
As vehicle approaches the tollbooth, the RFID reader in the tollbooth sends a radio wave that activates the windshield-mounted RFID tag. The activated tag sends vehicle information to the RFID reader.

video camera

RFID tag

RFID reader

Step 3:
The RFID reader sends the vehicle information to the lane controller. The lane controller, which is part of a local area network, transmits the vehicle information to a central computer that subtracts the toll from the motorist's account. If the vehicle does not have an RFID tag, the video camera takes a picture of the license plate and the computer prints a violation notice, which is mailed to the motorist.

WAP

The **Wireless Application Protocol (WAP)** is a standard, specifically a protocol, that specifies how some wireless mobile devices such as smart phones and PDAs can display the content of Internet services such as the Web, e-mail, chat rooms, and newsgroups. For example, to display a Web page on a smart phone, the phone would be WAP enabled and contain a microbrowser. WAP works in conjunction with the TCP/IP network standard.

WAP uses a client/server network. The wireless device contains the client software, which connects to the Internet service provider's server. On WAP-enabled devices, data transfer rates range from 9.6 to 153 Kbps depending on the type of service.

WEB LINK 9-6

WAP

For more information, visit scsite.com/ dc2006/ch9/weblink and then click WAP.

COMMUNICATIONS SOFTWARE

Communications software consists of programs that (1) help users establish a connection to another computer or network; (2) manage the transmission of data, instructions, and information; and (3) provide an interface for users to communicate with one another. The first two are system software and the third is application software. Chapter 3 presented a variety of examples of application software for communications: e-mail, FTP, Web browser, newsgroup/message boards, chat rooms, instant messaging, video conferencing, and Internet telephony. Read At Issue 9-4 for a discussion related to Web browser communications.

Sometimes, communications devices are preprogrammed to accomplish communications tasks. Other communications devices require separate communications software to ensure proper transmission of data. Communications software works with the network standards and protocols just discussed to ensure data moves through the network or the Internet correctly. Communications software usually is bundled with the operating system or purchased network devices.

Often, a computer has various types of communications software, each serving a different purpose. One type of communications software, for example, helps users establish an Internet connection using wizards, dialog boxes, and other on-screen messages. Another allows home and small office users to configure wired and wireless networks and connect devices to an existing network (Figure 9-22).

FIGURE 9-22   Windows XP includes communications software that guides a user through setting up a wireless network.

COMMUNICATIONS OVER THE TELEPHONE NETWORK

The *public switched telephone network* (*PSTN*) is the worldwide telephone system that handles voice-oriented telephone calls (Figure 9-23). Nearly the entire telephone network today uses digital technology, with the exception of the final link from the local telephone company to a home, which often is analog.

The telephone network is an integral part of computer communications. Data, instructions, and information are transmitted over the telephone network using dial-up lines or dedicated lines. The following sections discuss dial-up lines and the various types of dedicated lines that use the telephone network for data communications.

Dial-Up Lines

A **dial-up line** is a temporary connection that uses one or more analog telephone lines for communications. A dial-up connection is not permanent. Using a dial-up line to transmit data is similar to using the telephone to make a call. A modem at the sending end dials the telephone number of a modem at the receiving end. When the modem at the receiving end answers the call, a connection is established and data can be transmitted. When either modem hangs up, the communications end.

Using a dial-up line to connect computers costs no more than making a regular telephone call. Computers at any two locations establish an Internet or network connection using modems and the telephone network. Mobile users, for example, can use dial-up lines in hotels to connect to their main office network to read e-mail messages, access the Internet, and upload files.

FIGURE 9-23   A sample telephone network configuration.

Dedicated Lines

A **dedicated line** is a type of always-on connection that is established between two communications devices (unlike a dial-up line where the connection is reestablished each time it is used). The quality and consistency of the connection on a dedicated line are better than a dial-up line because dedicated lines provide a constant connection.

Businesses often use dedicated lines to connect geographically distant offices. Dedicated lines can be either analog or digital. Digital lines increasingly are connecting home and business users to networks around the globe because they transmit data and information at faster rates than analog lines.

Four popular types of digital dedicated lines are ISDN lines, DSL, T-carrier lines, and ATM. Although cable television (CATV) lines and fixed wireless are not a type of standard telephone line, they are very popular ways for the home user to connect to the Internet. Fixed wireless Internet connections use an antenna on your house or business to communicate with a tower location via radio signals. Later sections in this chapter discusses the use of CATV lines and radio signals to connect to the Internet.

The table in Figure 9-24 lists the approximate monthly costs of various types of Internet connections and transfer rates (speeds), as compared with dial-up lines. The following sections discuss ISDN lines, DSL, T-carrier lines, and ATM.

SPEEDS OF VARIOUS INTERNET CONNECTIONS

Type of Line	Approximate Monthly Cost	Transfer Rates
Dial-up	Local or long-distance rates	Up to 56 Kbps
ISDN	$10 to $40	Up to 128 Kbps
DSL	$30 to $80	128 Kbps to 8.45 Mbps
Cable TV (CATV)	$30 to $50	128 Kbps to 36 Mbps
Fixed Wireless	$35 to $70	256 Kbps to 10 Mbps
Fractional T1	$200 to $700	128 Kbps to 768 Kbps
T1	$500 to $1,000	1.544 Mbps
T3	$5,000 to $15,000	44.736 Mbps
ATM	$3,000 or more	155 Mbps to 622 Mbps, can reach 10 Gbps

FIGURE 9-24 The speeds of various lines that can be used to connect to the Internet.

ISDN Lines

For the small business and home user, an ISDN line provides faster transfer rates than dial-up telephone lines. *ISDN* (*Integrated Services Digital Network*) is a set of standards for digital transmission of data over standard copper telephone lines. With ISDN, the same telephone line that could carry only one computer signal now can carry three or more signals at once through the same line, using a technique called *multiplexing*.

ISDN requires that both ends of the connection have an ISDN modem. This type of modem is different from the type used in dial-up connections. The ISDN modem at your location must be within about 3.5 miles of the telephone company's ISDN modem. Thus, ISDN may not be an option for rural residents. ISDN lines also may require a special ISDN telephone for voice communications.

DSL

DSL is another digital line alternative for the small business or home user. **DSL** (*Digital Subscriber Line*) transmits at fast speeds on existing standard copper telephone wiring. Some DSL installations include a dial tone, providing users with both voice and data communications. Others share services with an existing telephone line.

To connect to DSL, a customer must have a special network card and a DSL modem. Similar to an ISDN modem, a DSL modem is different from the modem used for dial-up connections.

Not all areas offer DSL service because the local telephone company or the lines in the area may not be capable of supporting DSL technology. As with ISDN, DSL may not be an option for rural residents because the user's location (and DSL modem) and the telephone company's DSL modem must be located within about 3.5 miles of each other.

ADSL is one of the more popular types of DSLs. As shown in Figure 9-25, *ADSL* (*asymmetric digital subscriber line*) is a type of DSL that supports faster transfer rates when receiving data (the *downstream rate*) than when sending data (the *upstream rate*). ADSL is ideal for Internet access because most users download more information from the Internet than they upload. Some experts predict that DSL eventually will replace ISDN because it is much easier to install and provides much faster data transfer rates.

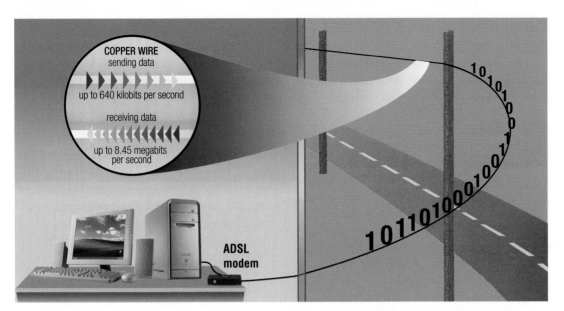

COPPER WIRE
sending data

up to 640 kilobits per second

receiving data

up to 8.45 megabits
per second

ADSL
modem

1 0 1 1 0 1 0 0 0 1 0 0 1 1
1 0 1 0 1 0 0

WEB LINK 9-7

DSL

For more information, visit scsite.com/dc2006/ch9/weblink and then click DSL.

FIGURE 9-25 ADSL connections transmit data downstream (receiving) at a much faster rate than upstream (sending).

T-Carrier Lines

A **T-carrier line** is any of several types of long-distance digital telephone lines that carry multiple signals over a single communications line. Whereas a standard dial-up telephone line carries only one signal, digital T-carrier lines use multiplexing so that multiple signals share the line. T-carrier lines provide very fast data transfer rates. Only medium to large companies usually can afford the investment in T-carrier lines because these lines are so expensive.

The most popular T-carrier line is the *T1 line*. Businesses often use T1 lines to connect to the Internet. Many Internet access providers use T1 lines to connect to the Internet backbone. Home and small business users purchase *fractional T1*, in which they share a connection to the T1 line with other users. Fractional T1 is slower than a dedicated T1 line, but it also is less expensive. Users who do not have other high-speed Internet access in their areas can opt for fractional T1.

A *T3 line* is equal in speed to 28 T1 lines. T3 lines are quite expensive. Main users of T3 lines include large companies, telephone companies, and Internet access providers connecting to the Internet backbone. The Internet backbone itself also uses T3 lines.

ATM

ATM (*Asynchronous Transfer Mode*) is a service that carries voice, data, video, and multimedia at very high speeds. Telephone networks, the

Internet, and other networks with large amounts of traffic use ATM. Some experts predict that ATM eventually will become the Internet standard for data transmission, replacing T3 lines.

Test your knowledge of pages 469 through 483 in Quiz Yourself 9-2.

QUIZ YOURSELF 9-2

Instructions: Find the true statement below. Then, rewrite the remaining false statements so they are true.

1. A wireless LAN is a LAN that uses physical wires.

2. An intranet is an internal network that uses video conferencing technologies.

3. Four popular types of digital dial-up lines are ISDN lines, DSL, T-carrier lines, and ATM.

4. In a client/server network, servers on the network access resources on the client.

5. In a networked environment, any unauthorized computer user can access data and information stored on other computers on the network.

6. P2P describes an Internet network on which users access each other's hard disks and exchange files directly over the Internet.

Quiz Yourself Online: To further check your knowledge of networks, network communications standards, communications software, and communications over the telephone network, visit scsite.com/dc2006/ch9/quiz and then click Objectives 4 – 8.

COMMUNICATIONS DEVICES

A **communications device** is any type of hardware capable of transmitting data, instructions, and information between a sending device and a receiving device. At the sending end, a communications device sends the data, instructions, or information from the sending device to a communications channel. At the receiving end, a communications device receives the signals from the communications channel.

One type of communications device that connects a communications channel to a sending or receiving device such as a computer is a modem. Computers process data as digital signals. Data, instructions, and information travel along a communications channel in either analog or digital form, depending on the communications channel. An *analog signal* consists of a continuous electrical wave. A *digital signal* consists of individual electrical pulses that represent bits grouped together into bytes.

For communications channels that use digital signals (such as cable television lines), the modem transfers the digital signals between the computer and the communications channel (Figure 9-26a). If a communications channel uses analog signals (such as some telephone lines), however, the modem first converts between analog and digital signals (Figure 9-26b).

The following pages describe these types of communications devices: dial-up modems, ISDN and DSL modems, cable modems, network cards, wireless access points, routers, and hubs.

FIGURE 9-26a   (all digital communications channel)

FIGURE 9-26b   (digital to analog to digital communications channel)

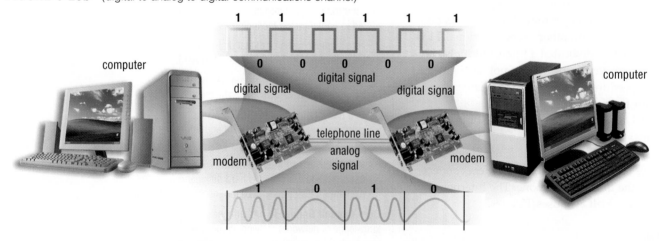

FIGURE 9-26   A modem connects a communications channel, such as a cable television line or a telephone line, to a sending or receiving device such as a computer. Depending on the type of communications channel, a modem may need to convert digital signals to analog signals (and vice versa) before transferring data, instructions, and information to or from a sending or receiving device.

Dial-Up Modems

As previously discussed, a computer's digital signals must be converted to analog signals before they are transmitted over standard telephone lines. The communications device that performs this conversion is a **modem**, sometimes called a *dial-up modem*. The word, modem, is derived from the combination of the words, *modulate*, to change into an analog signal, and *demodulate*, to convert an analog signal into a digital signal.

Both the sending and receiving ends of a standard telephone line (communications channel) must have a dial-up modem for data transmission to occur. For example, a dial-up modem connected to a sending computer converts the computer's digital signals into analog signals. The analog signals then can travel over a standard telephone line. At the receiving end, if necessary, another dial-up modem converts the analog signals back into digital signals that a receiving computer can process.

A dial-up modem usually is in the form of an adapter card that you insert in an expansion slot on a computer's motherboard (Figure 9-27). One end of a standard telephone cord attaches to a port on the modem card and the other end plugs into a telephone outlet. Devices other than computers also use modems. A standalone fax machine, for example, has a modem that converts a scanned digitized image into an analog signal that is sent to a recipient's fax machine.

If a notebook or other mobile computer does not have built-in modem capabilities, mobile users can insert a PC Card modem in a PC Card slot on the computer. The PC Card modem attaches to a telephone outlet with a standard telephone cord. Mobile users without access to a telephone outlet also can use a special cable to attach the PC Card modem to a cellular telephone, thus enabling them to transmit data over a cellular telephone.

ISDN and DSL Modems

If you access the Internet using ISDN or DSL, you need a communications device to send and receive the digital ISDN or DSL signals. A *digital modem* is a modem that sends and receives data and information to and from a digital telephone line such as ISDN or DSL. An *ISDN modem* sends digital data and information from a computer to an ISDN line and receives digital data and information from an ISDN line. A **DSL modem** sends digital data and information from a computer to a DSL line and receives digital data and information from a DSL line. ISDN and DSL modems usually are external devices, in which one end connects to the telephone line and the other end connects to a port on the system unit.

WEB LINK 9-8
Dial-Up Modems
For more information, visit scsite.com/dc2006/ch9/weblink and then click Dial-Up Modems.

FAQ 9-6

Are digital modems really modems?

According to the definition of a modem (to convert from analog to digital signals and vice versa), the use of the term modem in this context is not correct. Although the original term for these devices was terminal adapter, the industry refers to ISDN, DSL, and cable modems as digital modems. For more information, visit scsite.com/dc2006/ch9/faq and then click Digital Modems.

Cable Modems

A **cable modem**, sometimes called a *broadband modem*, is a digital modem that sends and receives digital data over the cable television (CATV) network. With more than 100 million homes wired for cable television, cable modems provide a faster Internet access alternative to dial-up for the home user and have speeds similar to DSL. Cable modems currently can transmit data at speeds that are much faster than either a dial-up modem or ISDN (Figure 9-24 on page 482).

FIGURE 9-27 A dial-up modem for a desktop computer usually is in the form of an adapter card you install in the system unit.

As shown in Figure 9-28, CATV service enters your home through a single line. To access the Internet using the CATV service, the CATV company installs a splitter inside your house. From the splitter, one part of the cable runs to your televisions and the other part connects to the cable modem. Many CATV operators provide a cable modem as part of the installation; some offer a rental plan; and others require that you purchase one separately. A cable modem usually is an external (separate) device, in which one end of a cable connects to a CATV wall outlet and the other end plugs in a port, such as on an Ethernet card, in the system unit. An Ethernet card is a type of network card. A later section discusses network cards.

FAQ 9-7

Which is better, DSL or cable Internet service?
Each has its own advantages. DSL uses a line that is not shared with other users in the neighborhood. With cable Internet service, by contrast, users share the node with up to 500 other cable Internet users. Simultaneous access by many users can cause the cable Internet service to slow down. Cable Internet service, however, has widespread availability. For more information, visit scsite.com/dc2006/ch9/faq and then click DSL and Cable Internet Service.

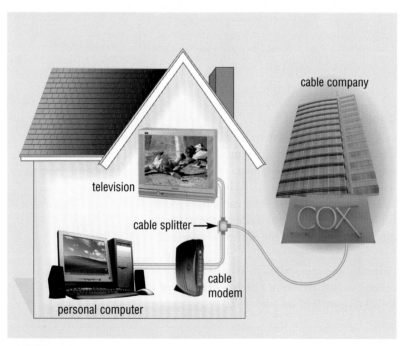

FIGURE 9-28 A typical cable modem installation.

Wireless Modems

Some mobile users have a **wireless modem** that allows access to the Web wirelessly from a notebook computer, a PDA, a smart phone, or other mobile device (Figure 9-29). Wireless modems, which have an antenna, typically use the same waves used by cellular telephones. These modems are available as PC Cards and flash cards.

FIGURE 9-29 Wireless modems, in the form of a PC Card or flash card, allow users to access the Internet wirelessly using their mobile computers and devices.

Network Cards

A **network card**, sometimes called a *network interface card* (*NIC* pronounced nick), is an adapter card, PC Card, or flash card that enables the computer or device to access a network. Although some computers and devices have networking capabilities integrated in their circuitry, most personal computers on a LAN contain a network card. The network card coordinates the transmission and receipt of data, instructions, and information to and from the computer or device containing the network card.

Network cards are available in a variety of styles (Figure 9-30). A network card for a desktop computer is an adapter card that has a port to which a cable connects. A network card for mobile computers and devices is in the form of a Type II PC Card or a flash card. Many of these network cards have more than one type of port, which enable different types of cables to attach to the card. For example, some cable modems and DSL modems require that one end of a cable plug in the modem and the other end in a network card. (If your computer does not have a network card, these modems often allow connections to a USB port also.)

Network cards that provide wireless data transmission also are available. This type of card, called a *wireless network card*, often has an antenna. Sometimes the antenna is detachable, allowing the user to position it in a location with the best signal strength. Some network cards include support for both wired and wireless networks.

A network card follows the guidelines of a particular network communications standard, such as Ethernet or token ring. An Ethernet card is the most common type of network card. Depending on the type of wiring used, the transfer rate on an Ethernet network is 10 Mbps, 100 Mbps, or 1,000 Mbps (1 Gbps). Ethernet cards typically support one or more of these speeds. For example, some are called 10/100 because they support both 10 Mbps and 100 Mbps. Some network cards also are a combination Ethernet and dial-up modem card.

FAQ 9-8

Do I need a wireless network card to access a wireless network?

No. Some computers and devices have built-in 802.11 (Wi-Fi) hardware, such as those with Intel's *Centrino technology.* For computers and devices requiring a wireless network card, some users purchase a wireless USB network adapter that connects to a USB port on the computer instead of a network card. Wireless USB network adapters are ideal for users who have no empty expansion slots in their computers or for users not comfortable working inside the system unit. For more information, visit scsite.com/dc2006/ch9/faq and then click Wireless Network Cards and Adapters.

Wireless Access Points

A *wireless access point* is a central communications device that allows computers and devices to transfer data wirelessly among themselves or to transfer data wirelessly to a wired network (Figure 9-31). Wireless access points have high-quality antennas for optimal signals. For the best signal, some manufacturers suggest positioning the wireless access point at the highest possible location.

FIGURE 9-30 Network cards are available for both desktop and notebook computers.

FIGURE 9-31 Wireless access points around campus allow students to access the school network wirelessly from their classrooms, the library, dorms, and other campus locations. To access the network, the notebook computer or mobile device must have built-in wireless capability or a wireless network card.

Routers

A *router* is a communications device that connects multiple computers or other routers together and transmits data to its correct destination on the network. A router can be used on any size of network. On the largest scale, routers along the Internet backbone forward data packets to their destination using the fastest available path. For smaller business and home networks, a router allows multiple computers to share a single high-speed Internet connection such as through a cable modem or DSL modem (Figure 9-32). These routers connect from 2 to 250 computers.

To prevent unauthorized users from accessing files and computers, many routers are protected by a built-in firewall, called a *hardware firewall*. Some also have built-in antivirus protection. Routers also support wireless communications, eliminating the need for a separate wireless access point in a wireless network. If the network has a separate wireless access point, it connects to the router via a cable. Some routers also include additional functionality such as including a built-in print server.

Connecting Networks

Today, thousands of computer networks exist, ranging from small networks operated by home users to global networks operated by numerous telecommunications firms. Interconnecting these many types of networks requires various types of communications devices. For example, as shown in Figure 9-33, a *hub* is a device that provides a central point for cables in a network. Some hubs include routers. That is, the hub receives data from many directions and then forwards it to one or more destinations.

FAQ 9-9

How fast do routers transfer data across the Internet?

Cisco Systems manufacturers the fastest router, which transfers 92 trillion bits per second across the Internet backbone. At this speed, you could download everything contained in the United States Library of Congress in 4.6 seconds. On your dial-up modem, this same task would take about 82 years. For more information, visit scsite.com/dc2006/ch9/faq and then click World's Fastest Router.

WEB LINK 9-9

Hardware Firewalls

For more information, visit scsite.com/ dc2006/ch9/weblink and then click Hardware Firewalls.

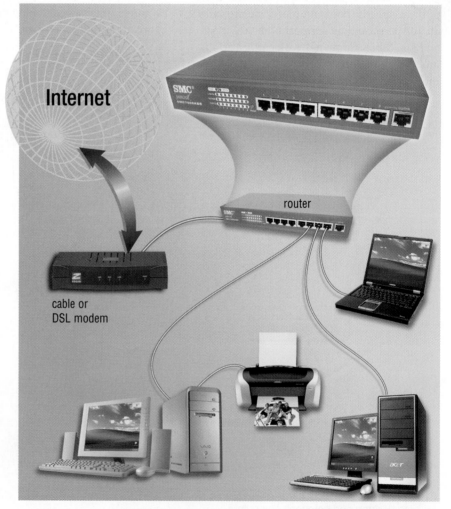

FIGURE 9-32 Through a router, home and small business networks can share access to a high-speed Internet connection such as through a cable or DSL modem.

- Share peripherals such as a printer, scanner, external hard disk, or DVD drive
- Play multiplayer games with players on other computers in the house

Many vendors offer home networking packages that include all the necessary hardware and software to network your home using wired or wireless techniques. Some of these packages also offer intelligent networking capabilities. An *intelligent home network* extends the basic home network to include features such as lighting control, thermostat adjustment, and a security system.

Wired Home Networks

As with other networks, a home network can use wires, be wireless, or use a combination of wired and wireless. Three types of wired home networks are Ethernet, powerline cable, and phoneline.

ETHERNET Some home users have an Ethernet network. As discussed earlier in this chapter, traditional Ethernet networks require that each computer have built-in network capabilities or contain a network card, which connects to a central network hub or similar device with a physical cable. This may involve running cable through walls, ceilings, and floors in the house. For the average home user, the hardware and software of an Ethernet network can be difficult to configure.

POWERLINE CABLE NETWORK A home *powerline cable network* is a network that uses the same lines that bring electricity into the house. This network requires no additional wiring. One end of a cable plugs in the computer's parallel or USB port and the other end of the cable plugs in a wall outlet. The data transmits through the existing power lines in the house.

PHONELINE NETWORK A *phoneline network* is an easy-to-install and inexpensive network that uses existing telephone lines in the home. With this network, one end of a cable connects to an adapter card or PC Card in the computer and the other end plugs in a wall telephone jack. The phoneline network does not interfere with voice and data transmissions on the telephone lines. That is, you can talk on the telephone and use the same line to connect to the Internet. One slight disadvantage is that the room with the computer must have a wall telephone jack.

FIGURE 9-33 A hub is a central point that connects several devices in a network together.

HOME NETWORKS

An estimated 39 million homes have more than one computer. Thus, many home users are connecting multiple computers and devices together in a **home network**. Home networking saves the home user money and provides many conveniences. Each networked computer in the house has the following capabilities:
- Connect to the Internet at the same time
- Share a single high-speed Internet connection
- Access files and programs on the other computers in the house

Wireless Home Networks

To network computers and devices that span multiple rooms or floors in a home, it may be more convenient to use a wireless strategy. One advantage of wireless networks is that you can take a mobile computer outside, for example in the backyard, and connect to the Internet through the home network, as long as you are in the network's range. Two types of wireless home networks are HomeRF and Wi-Fi.

A *HomeRF* (*radio frequency*) *network* uses radio waves, instead of cables, to transmit data. A HomeRF network sends signals through the air over distances up to 150 feet. One end of a cable connects to a special card in the computer and the other end connects to a transmitter/receiver that has an antenna to pick up signals.

A HomeRF network usually can connect up to 10 computers.

Another home network that uses radio waves is a Wi-Fi network, which sends signals over a wider distance than the HomeRF network — up to 1,500 feet in some configurations. A Wi-Fi home network is more expensive than a HomeRF network. Despite the higher costs, increasingly more home users set up Wi-Fi networks in their homes because they are fairly easy to configure. Each computer that accesses the network needs built-in wireless networking capabilities (such as Intel's Centrino technology) or a wireless network card, which communicates either with a wireless access point or a combination router/wireless access point (Figure 9-34). Even in a wireless home network,

FIGURE 9-34   HOW TO SET UP HARDWARE FOR A WI-FI HOME NETWORK

Step 1:
Sign up for high-speed Internet service, such as through a cable or DSL modem.

Step 2:
Using a cable, connect the network card in a desktop computer to the combination router/wireless access point.

Step 3:
Using a cable, connect the combination router/wireless access point to the cable modem.

Step 4:
Install a wireless network card or network adapter in other desktop computers in the home network.

Step 5:
Insert a wireless PC Card in each notebook computer that will access the home network or purchase a notebook computer with built-in wireless networking capabilities.

Step 6:
Insert a wireless compact flash card in each PDA that will access the home network.

wireless PDA

cable/DSL modem

desktop computer

router/wireless access point

wireless desktop computer

wireless notebook computer

one desktop computer usually connects to the router/wireless access point using a cable.

Wireless networks do have the disadvantage of interference. Walls, ceilings, and electrical devices such as cordless telephones and microwave ovens can disrupt wireless communications.

COMMUNICATIONS CHANNEL

As described at the beginning of the chapter, a communications channel is the transmission media on which data, instructions, or information travel in a communications system. The amount of data, instructions, and information that can travel over a communications channel sometimes is called the **bandwidth**. The higher the bandwidth, the more the channel transmits. For example, a cable modem has more bandwidth than a dial-up modem.

For transmission of text only, a lower bandwidth is acceptable. For transmission of music, graphics, photographs, virtual reality images, or 3-D games, however, you need a higher bandwidth. When the bandwidth is too low for the application, you will notice a considerable slow-down in system performance.

Latency is the time it takes a signal to travel from one location to another on a network. Several factors that negatively can affect latency include the distance between the two points, the type of transmission media, and the number of nodes through which the data must travel over the communications channel. For best performance, bandwidth should be high and latency low.

A communications channel consists of one or more transmission media. **Transmission media** consists of materials or substances capable of carrying one or more signals. When you send data from a computer, the signal that carries the data may travel over various transmission media. This is especially true when the transmission spans a long distance.

Figure 9-35 illustrates a typical communications channel and shows the variety of transmission media used to complete the connection. Although many media and devices are involved, the entire communications process could take less than one second.

FIGURE 9-35 AN EXAMPLE OF SENDING A REQUEST OVER THE INTERNET USING A COMMUNICATIONS CHANNEL

Step 1:
The sending device requests information using either physical transmission media or wireless transmission media.

sending device

modem

microwave station

Step 2:
When the request leaves the ISP, it travels over T1 lines, and possibly microwave stations, earth-based stations, and communications satellites, until it reaches the Internet backbone.

mainframe

T1 lines

ISP

Step 3:
The request travels over T3 lines along the Internet backbone.

T3 lines

Internet backbone

Step 4:
The request travels over T1 lines until it reaches the destination network server.

destination network server

T1 lines

mainframe

Baseband media transmit only one signal at a time. By contrast, **broadband** media transmit multiple signals simultaneously. Broadband media transmit signals at a much faster speed than baseband media. Home and business users today opt for broadband Internet access because of the much faster transfer rates. Two previously discussed services that offer broadband transmission are DSL and the cable television Internet service. Satellites also offer broadband transmission. Read Looking Ahead 9-1 for a look at the future of broadband.

Transmission media are one of two types: physical or wireless. *Physical transmission media* use wire, cable, and other tangible materials to send communications signals. *Wireless transmission media* send communications signals through the air or space using radio, microwave, and infrared signals. The following sections discuss these types of media.

PHYSICAL TRANSMISSION MEDIA

Physical transmission media used in communications include twisted-pair cable, coaxial cable, and fiber-optic cable. These cables typically are used within or underground between buildings. Ethernet and token ring LANs often use physical transmission media. The table in Figure 9-36 lists the transfer rates of LANs using various physical transmission media. The following sections discuss each of these types of cables.

TRANSFER RATES FOR VARIOUS TYPES OF LANS USING PHYSICAL TRANSMISSION MEDIA

Type of Cable and LAN	Maximum Transfer Rate
Twisted-Pair Cable	
• 10Base-T (Ethernet)	10 Mbps
• 100Base-T (Fast Ethernet)	100 Mbps
• 1000Base-T (Gigabit Ethernet)	1 Gbps
• Token ring	4 Mbps to 16 Mbps
Coaxial Cable	
• 10Base2 (ThinWire Ethernet)	10 Mbps
• 10Base5 (ThickWire Ethernet)	10 Mbps
Fiber-Optic Cable	
• 10Base-F (Ethernet)	10 Mbps
• 100Base-FX (Fast Ethernet)	100 Mbps
• FDDI (Fiber Distributed Data Interface) token ring	100 Mbps
• Gigabit Ethernet	1 Gbps
• 10-Gigabit Ethernet	10 Gbps

FIGURE 9-36 The speeds of various physical communications media when they are used in LANs.

FAQ 9-10

Do many home users have a broadband Internet connection?

As shown in the chart below, the number of home users with a broadband Internet connection has grown to more than 75 percent. For more information, visit scsite.com/dc2006/ch9/faq and then click Broadband Usage.

Broadband Growth Trend - US Home Users

(Extrapolated by Web Site Optimization, LLC from Nielson//NetRatings Data)

Market Penetration %

90.0%, 80.0%, 70.0%, 60.0%, 50.0%, 40.0%, 30.0%, 20.0%, 10.0%, 0.0%

Oct-99, Feb-00, Jun-00, Oct-00, Feb-01, Jun-01, Oct-01, Feb-02, Jun-02, Oct-02, Feb-03, Jun-03, Oct-03, Feb-04, Jun-04, Oct-04, Feb-05, Jun-05, Oct-05, Feb-06

LOOKING AHEAD 9-1

Broadband Sparks Portal Services

When the Internet was in its infancy, many computer users were satisfied with a stable telephone connection and a variety of Web sites. With broadband becoming more commonplace, however, users are demanding superfast connection speeds and Web sites that offer easily accessible information.

Super Web portals are being developed in response to these demands. Portals offer many services in one convenient location, so a user can find a variety of related content at a single Web site. For example, yahoo.rogers.com and Sympatico.MSN.ca are media-intensive portals for people desiring to upload photos, download music, and play games.

As broadband becomes more ubiquitous, look for the convergence of the television and online communities, where viewers watch programs and simultaneously or soon afterwards find related premium content online. For more information, visit scsite.com/dc2006/ch9/looking and then click Broadband Future.

Twisted-Pair Cable

One of the more widely used transmission media for network cabling and telephone systems is twisted-pair cable. **Twisted-pair cable** consists of one or more twisted-pair wires bundled together (Figure 9-37). Each *twisted-pair wire* consists of two separate insulated copper wires that are twisted together. The wires are twisted together to reduce noise. **Noise** is an electrical disturbance that can degrade communications.

Coaxial Cable

Coaxial cable, often referred to as *coax* (pronounced KO-ax), consists of a single copper wire surrounded by at least three layers: (1) an insulating material, (2) a woven or braided metal, and (3) a plastic outer coating (Figure 9-38).

Cable television (CATV) network wiring often uses coaxial cable because it can be cabled over longer distances than twisted-pair cable. Most of today's computer networks, however, do not use coaxial cable because other transmission media such as fiber-optic cable transmit signals at faster rates.

Fiber-Optic Cable

The core of a **fiber-optic cable** consists of dozens or hundreds of thin strands of glass or plastic that use light to transmit signals. Each strand, called an *optical fiber*, is as thin as a human hair. Inside the fiber-optic cable, an insulating glass cladding and a protective coating surround each optical fiber (Figure 9-39).

Fiber-optic cables have the following advantages over cables that use wire, such as twisted-pair and coaxial cables:

- Capability of carrying significantly more signals than wire cables
- Faster data transmission
- Less susceptible to noise (interference) from other devices such as a copy machine
- Better security for signals during transmission because they are less susceptible to noise
- Smaller size (much thinner and lighter weight)

Disadvantages of fiber-optic cable are it costs more than twisted-pair or coaxial cable and can be difficult to install and modify. Despite these limitations, many local and long-distance telephone companies are replacing existing telephone lines with fiber-optic cables. Businesses also are using fiber-optic cables in high-traffic networks or as the backbone in a network.

FIGURE 9-37 A twisted-pair cable consists of one or more twisted-pair wires. Each twisted-pair wire usually is color coded for identification. Telephone networks and LANs often use twisted-pair cable.

FIGURE 9-38 On a coaxial cable, data travels through a copper wire. This illustration shows computers networked together with coaxial cable.

FIGURE 9-39 A fiber-optic cable consists of hair-thin strands of glass or plastic that carry data as pulses of light.

WIRELESS TRANSMISSION MEDIA

Many users opt for wireless transmission media because it is more convenient than installing cables. In addition to convenience, businesses use wireless transmission media in locations where it is impossible to install cables.

Types of wireless transmission media used in communications include infrared, broadcast radio, cellular radio, microwaves, and communications satellites. The table in Figure 9-40 lists transfer rates of various wireless transmission media. The following sections discuss these types of wireless transmission media.

TRANSFER RATES FOR VARIOUS TYPES OF WIRELESS TRANSMISSION MEDIA

Transmission Medium	Maximum Transfer Rate
Infrared	115 Kbps to 4 Mbps
Broadcast radio	
• Bluetooth	1 to 2 Mbps
• HomeRF	1.6 Mbps to 10 Mbps
• 802.11b	11 Mbps
• 802.11g	54 Mbps
• 802.11a	54 Mbps
Cellular radio	
• 2G	9.6 Kbps to 19.2 Kbps
• 3G	144 Kbps to 2.4 Mbps
Microwave radio	150 Mbps
Communications satellite	1 Gbps

FIGURE 9-40 The transfer rates of various wireless transmission media.

Infrared

As discussed earlier in the chapter, *infrared* (*IR*) is a wireless transmission medium that sends signals using infrared light waves. Mobile computers and devices, such as a mouse, printer, and smart phone, often have an IrDA port that enables the transfer of data from one device to another using infrared light waves. If your notebook computer has an IrDA port, simply position the port in front of the IrDA port on a printer to print a document wirelessly. Many PDAs also have IrDA ports that allow users to transfer data to another PDA or a network wirelessly.

Broadcast Radio

Broadcast radio is a wireless transmission medium that distributes radio signals through the air over long distances such as between cities, regions, and countries and short distances such as within an office or home.

For radio transmissions, you need a transmitter to send the broadcast radio signal and a receiver to accept it. To receive the broadcast radio signal, the receiver has an antenna that is located in the range of the signal. Some networks use a transceiver, which both sends and receives signals from wireless devices. Broadcast radio is slower and more susceptible to noise than physical transmission media but it provides flexibility and portability.

Bluetooth, HomeRF, and Wi-Fi communications technologies discussed earlier in this chapter use broadcast radio signals. Bluetooth is an alternative to infrared communications, and HomeRF and Wi-Fi are competing technologies for home and small business networks. Hot spots also use Wi-Fi networks. In a Wi-Fi business network, employees have access to the network from their notebook computers while roaming from one meeting room to another.

Cellular Radio

Cellular radio is a form of broadcast radio that is used widely for mobile communications, specifically wireless modems and cellular telephones (Figure 9-41). A cellular telephone is a telephone device that uses high-frequency radio waves to transmit voice and digital data messages. Because only a limited number of radio frequencies exist, cellular network providers reuse frequencies so they can accommodate the large number of users.

Some mobile users connect their notebook computer or other mobile computer to a cellular telephone to access the Web, send and receive e-mail, enter a chat room, or connect to an office or school network while away from a standard telephone line. Read At Issue 9-5 for a related discussion.

Several categories of cellular transmissions exist, defining the development of cellular networks:
- *1G* (first generation) transmitted analog data
- *2G* (second generation) transmit digital data at speeds from 9.6 Kbps to 19.2 Kbps
- *3G* (third generation) transmit digital data at speeds from 144 Kbps to 2.4 Mbps

Examples of 3G standards include *GSM* (Global System for Mobile Communications), *UMTS* (Universal Mobile Telecommunications System), *GPRS* (General Packet Radio Service), and *CDMA* (Code Division Multiple Access). These 3G standards allow users quickly to

FIGURE 9-41 As a person with a cellular telephone drives from one cell to another, the radio signals transfer from the base station (microwave station) in one cell to a base station in another cell.

AT ISSUE 9-5

Should Cell Phones Be Banned in Public Places?

Most people would never consider cutting in line at the bank or checking out with too many items in the 10-items-or-fewer lane at the grocery store. This courtesy, however, seems to elude many people when it comes to cellular phone etiquette. In movie theatres, libraries, schools, restaurants, and on the sidewalk, more and more people are engaging in loud cell phone conversations with coworkers, friends, and family. Psychologists have found that it may not be the cell phone users' speech volume that annoys us, but rather that the person is having a seemingly one-way conversation with no one, which is a much more difficult background noise for the brain to filter out. New York City recently banned the use of cell phones in places of public performance, including theatres, lectures, museums, and libraries. Some states have banned the use of cell phones while driving, or required the use of hands-free devices while driving and using a cell phone. Should governments do more to discourage the use of cell phones in public places? Why or why not? Should simple rules of etiquette for cell phone use be more publicized or enforced? Why or why not? If so, by whom?

---

display multimedia and graphics, browse the Web, watch television or a video, have a video conference, and transfer data on a cellular device. Providers that offer 3G service include Sprint, Verizon, AT&T, Cingular, Motorola, Ericsson, and Nokia.

Personal Communications Services (*PCS*) is the term used by the U. S. Federal Communications Commission (FCC) to identify all wireless digital communications. Devices that use PCS include cellular telephones, PDAs, pagers, and fax machines. These devices have voice mail, call forwarding, fax capability, caller ID, and wireless modems for Internet and e-mail access.

Microwaves

Microwaves are radio waves that provide a high-speed signal transmission. Microwave transmission, often called *fixed wireless*, involves sending signals from one microwave station to another (Figure 9-42). Microwaves can transmit data at rates up to 4,500 times faster than a dial-up modem.

A *microwave station* is an earth-based reflective dish that contains the antenna, transceivers, and other equipment necessary for microwave communications. As with infrared, microwaves use line-of-sight transmission. To avoid possible obstructions, such as buildings or mountains, microwave stations often sit on the tops of buildings, towers, or mountains.

microwave stations

FIGURE 9-42 A microwave station is a ground-based reflective dish that contains the antenna and other equipment necessary for microwave communications.

Microwave transmission typically is used in environments where installing physical transmission media is difficult or impossible and where line-of-sight transmission is available. For example, microwave transmission is used in wide-open areas such as deserts or lakes; between buildings in a close geographic area; or to communicate with a satellite. Current users of microwave transmission include universities, hospitals, city governments, cable television providers, and telephone companies. Homes and small businesses who do not have other high-speed Internet connections available in their area also opt for lower-cost fixed wireless plans. A newer communications standard, called *WiMAX* (Worldwide Interoperability for Microwave Access), enables broadband wireless to extend up to 30 miles.

Communications Satellite

A **communications satellite** is a space station that receives microwave signals from an earth-based station, amplifies (strengthens) the signals, and broadcasts the signals back over a wide area to any number of earth-based stations (Figure 9-43).

These earth-based stations often are microwave stations. Other devices, such as PDAs and GPS receivers, also can function as earth-based stations. Transmission from an earth-based station to a satellite is an *uplink*. Transmission from a satellite to an earth-based station is a *downlink*.

Applications such as air navigation, television and radio broadcasts, weather forecasting, video conferencing, paging, global positioning systems, and Internet connections use communications satellites. With the proper satellite dish and a satellite modem card, consumers can access the Internet using satellite technology. With satellite Internet connections, however, uplink transmissions usually are slower than downlink transmissions. This difference in speeds usually is acceptable to most Internet satellite users because they download much more data than they upload. Although a satellite Internet connection is more expensive than cable Internet or DSL connections, sometimes it is the only high-speed Internet option in remote areas. Read Looking Ahead 9-2 for a look at the next generation of satellite communications.

communications satellite

earth-based station　**earth-based station**

FIGURE 9-43 Communications satellites are placed about 22,300 miles above the Earth's equator.

LOOKING AHEAD 9-2

Hear the Music on a Smart Phone

Listening to music, watching television, and using a cellular telephone probably are part of your daily life, and you soon may be able to perform all three activities on one device: your smart phone.

The next generation of smart phones and other pocket devices might add the capability of receiving digital terrestrial and satellite broadcasts. A satellite co-owned by Japan's Mobile Broadcasting and South Korea's TU Media beams 30 channels of audio and 7 channels of video to subscribers. The nonstop music channels feature a variety of genres and radio stations, and the video channels include news, financial information, and MTV.

The subscription service is expected to cost approximately $15 per month for audio and $23 for both audio and video. For more information, visit scsite.com/dc2006/ch9/looking and then click Satellite Broadcasts.

Test your knowledge of pages 484 through 496 in Quiz Yourself 9-3.

QUIZ YOURSELF 9-3

Instructions: Find the true statement below. Then, rewrite the remaining false statements so they are true.

1. A cable modem converts a computer's digital signals to analog signals before they are transmitted over standard telephone lines.

2. A hardware firewall is a communications device that allows computers and devices to transfer data wirelessly among themselves or to transfer data wirelessly to a wired network.

3. A network card is an adapter card, PC Card, or flash card that enables the computer or device to access a network.

4. Analog signals consist of individual electrical pulses that represent bits grouped together into bytes.

5. Physical transmission media send communications signals through the air or space using radio, microwave, and infrared signals.

6. The lower the bandwidth, the more data, instructions, and information the channel transmits.

7. Two types of wireless home networks are HomeRF and powerline cable.

Quiz Yourself Online: To further check your knowledge of communications devices, home networks, and transmission media, visit scsite.com/dc2006/ch9/quiz and then click Objectives 9 – 11.

CHAPTER SUMMARY

This chapter provided an overview of communications terminology and applications. It also discussed how to join computers into a network, allowing them to communicate and share resources such as hardware, software, data, and information. It also explained various communications devices, media, and procedures as they relate to computers.

CAREER CORNER

Network Specialist

As more companies rely on networks, the demand for network specialists will continue to grow. A *network specialist* must have a working knowledge of local area networks and their application within wide area networks. A network specialist also must be familiar with the Internet, its connectivity to LANs and WANs, and Web server management. Responsibilities of a network specialist include installing, configuring, and troubleshooting network systems. Other responsibilities may include managing system and client software, Web page integration and creation, network security measures, user accounting, and monitoring network event logs for problem resolution. A network specialist must possess good problem-solving skills and the ability to work independently. They also must have the ability to concentrate on detailed projects for long periods of time. Good oral, written, and team-oriented interpersonal skills also are beneficial.

Many institutions offer two-year network specialist programs. In addition to a college degree, industry certifications are available for further career enhancement. Two of the more notable certifications are the Novell CNA (Certified Novell Administrator) and the Cisco CCNA (Certified Cisco Networking Associate). Network specialist salaries will vary depending on education, certifications, and experience. Individuals with certifications can expect an approximate starting salary between $43,000 and $55,000. For more information, visit scsite.com/dc2006/ch9/careers and then click Network Specialist.

High-Tech Talk

OSI REFERENCE MODEL: THE DRIVING FORCE BEHIND NETWORK COMMUNICATIONS

Every message sent over a network — even the simplest e-mail message — must be divided into discrete packages of data and routed via transmission media such as telephone lines. While traveling from the sending computer to the receiving computer, each data package can take a different path over the network. How do these messages get to their destination, intact and accurate?

The *Open Systems Interconnection (OSI) reference model*, a communications standard developed by the International Organization for Standardization (ISO), offers an answer. The OSI reference model describes the flow of data in a network through seven layers, from the user's application to the physical transmission media.

A simple way to understand the OSI reference model is to think of it as an elevator (Figure 9-44). On the sending end, data enters at the top floor (the application layer) and travels to the bottom floor (the physical layer). Each layer communicates with the layers immediately above and below it. When a layer receives data, it performs specific functions, adds control information to the data, and passes it to the next layer. The control information contains error-checking, routing, and other information needed to ensure proper transmission along the network.

The top layer, the *application layer*, serves as the interface between the user and the network. Using application software, such as an e-mail program, a user can type a message and specify a recipient. The application then prepares the message for delivery by converting the message data into bits and attaching a header identifying the sending and receiving computers.

The *presentation layer* translates the converted message data into a language the receiving computer can process (from ASCII to EBCDIC, for example) and also may compress or encrypt the data. Finally, the layer attaches another header specifying the language, compression, and encryption schemes.

The next layer, called the *session layer*, establishes and maintains communications sessions. A *session* is the period between establishment of a connection, transmission of the data, and termination of the connection.

The *transport layer*, also called the end-to-end layer, ensures that data arrives correctly and in proper sequence. The transport layer divides the data into segments and creates a *checksum*, a mathematical sum based on the data, and puts this information in the transport header. The checksum later is used to determine if the data was scrambled during transmission.

The *network layer* routes the message from sender to receiver. This layer splits the data segments from the transport layer into smaller groups of bits called *packets*. Next, it adds a header containing the packet sequence, the receiving computer address, and routing information. The network layer also manages network problems by rerouting packets to avoid network congestion.

The *data link layer* supervises the transmission of the message to the next network node by specifying the network technology (such as Ethernet or token ring) and grouping data accordingly. The data link layer also calculates the checksum and keeps a copy of each packet until it receives confirmation that the packet arrived undamaged at the next node.

Finally, the *physical layer* encodes the packets into a signal recognized by the medium that will carry them — such as an analog signal to be sent over a telephone line — and sends the packets along that medium to the receiving computer.

At the receiving computer, the process is reversed and the data moves back through the seven layers from the physical layer to the application layer, which identifies the recipient, converts the bits into readable data, removes some of the error-checking and control information from the data, and directs it to the appropriate application. The next time you send an e-mail message to a friend, consider the network communications processes described by the OSI reference model, which ensure that your message travels safely over many networks to your friend's computer. For more information, visit scsite.com/dc2006/ch9/tech and then click OSI Reference Model.

FIGURE 9-44   The seven layers of the OSI model.

Companies on the Cutting Edge

CISCO SYSTEMS
NETWORKING THE INTERNET

As the world leader in networking equipment, *Cisco Systems* strives to empower the Internet generation by connecting people and networks regardless of differences in locations, time, or types of computers. The company offers a broad line of networking equipment for transporting data within a building, across a campus, or across the globe.

A group of computer scientists from Stanford University founded Cisco in 1984. From the start, the company focused on communicating over networks. Today, Cisco's Internet Protocol-based (IP) networking equipment is the basis of the Internet and most networks.

Its key products focus on the areas of home and wireless networking, network security, and communications. The company set a Guinness world record for having the highest capacity Internet router of 92 terabits (92 trillion bits per second). For more information, visit scsite.com/dc2006/ch9/companies and then click Cisco.

QUALCOMM
WIRELESS COMMUNICATIONS LEADER

When you speak into your cellular telephone, your voice is converted into digital information that is transmitted as a radio signal with a unique code. This wireless communications process is based on Code Division Multiple Access (CDMA), which *QUALCOMM* engineers first conceptualized in 1988.

Commercial CDMA networks were unveiled in 1995, and they provided about 10 times the capacity of analog networks. Today, QUALCOMM is the world's largest provider of 3G technology and has shipped more than 1 million chips to the 125 telecommunications equipment manufacturers using the CDMA standard.

QUALCOMM has been selected as a FORTUNE 500 company and has been named to *FORTUNE* magazine's lists of the 100 Fastest-Growing Companies in America, 100 Best Companies to Work for in America, and America's Most Admired Companies. For more information, visit scsite.com/dc2006/ch9/companies and then click QUALCOMM.

Technology Trailblazers

ROBERT METCALFE
ETHERNET INVENTOR

The Internet will be filled with video within 20 years, according to *Robert Metcalfe*. His prediction is likely to be correct based on his visionary track record. While studying for his doctorate degree at Harvard and working at Xerox's Palo Alto Research Center (PARC), he combined hardware with a high-speed network interface and envisioned that his invention would be used widely. This network technology developed into Ethernet, today's most popular LAN technology that links millions of computers worldwide.

In 1979, Metcalfe left Xerox to found 3Com Corporation and make Ethernet the standard for computer communications. After he retired from that company, he became a columnist for *InfoWorld* magazine. He also has written three books and been a venture capitalist with Polaris Ventures. For more information, visit scsite.com/dc2006/ch9/people and then click Robert Metcalfe.

PATRICIA RUSSO
LUCENT TECHNOLOGIES CHAIRMAN AND CEO

As captain of her high school cheerleading squad, *Patricia Russo* had to project a spirit of optimism, build teamwork, and solve problems. She uses these same skills in her current job as chairman and chief executive officer of Lucent Technologies, which designs and delivers communications hardware, software, and services to communications service providers worldwide.

Russo helped found Lucent in 1996 and oversaw various critical corporate functions, including global sales, strategy and business development, human resources, and public relations. She left Lucent to serve as CEO for Eastman Kodak, but nine months later Lucent asked her to return and appointed her CEO in 2002 and chairman the following year. Prior to her Lucent tenure, she headed AT&T's Business Communications System unit (now Avaya Inc.) and worked in sales and marketing at IBM. For more information, visit scsite.com/dc2006/ch9/people and then click Patricia Russo.

Chapter Review

The Chapter Review section summarizes the concepts presented in this chapter. To listen to the audio version of this Chapter Review, visit scsite.com/dc2006/ch9/review. To obtain help from other students regarding any subject in this chapter, visit scsite.com/dc2006/ch9/forum and post your thoughts or questions.

(1) What Components Are Required for Successful Communications? Computer **communications** describes a process in which two or more computers or devices transfer data, instructions, and information. Successful communications requires a **sending device** that initiates a transmission instruction, a communications device that connects the sending device to a communications channel, a **communications channel** on which the data travels, a communications device that connects the communications channel to a receiving device, and a **receiving device** that accepts the transmission.

(2) What Are Various Sending and Receiving Devices? All types of computers and mobile devices serve as sending and receiving devices. This includes mainframe computers, servers, desktop computers, notebook computers, Tablet PCs, smart phones, PDAs, and GPS receivers.

(3) How Are Computer Communications Used? Communications technologies include the Internet, Web, e-mail, instant messaging, chat rooms, newsgroups, Internet telephony, FTP, Web folders, video conferencing, and fax machine or computer fax/modem. Users can send and receive wireless messages to and from smart phones, cellular telephones, or PDAs using **text messaging**, wireless instant messaging, and **picture messaging**. A **public Internet access point** lets people connect wirelessly to the Internet. A *hot spot* is a wireless network that provides Internet connections to mobile computers and devices. A **cybercafé** is a coffee house or restaurant that provides computers with Internet access. A **global positioning system** (**GPS**) analyzes signals sent by satellites to determine an earth-based receiver's geographic location. Many software products provide a means to **collaborate**, or work online with other users. **Groupware** is software that helps people share information over a network. **Voice mail** allows someone to leave a voice message for one or more people. *Web services* describe standardized software that enables programmers to create applications that communicate over the Internet or an internal network.

Visit scsite.com/dc2006/ch9/quiz or click the Quiz Yourself button. Click Objectives 1 – 3.

(4) What Are Advantages of Using a Network? A **network** is a collection of computers and devices connected together via communications devices and transmission media. Advantages of using a network include facilitating communications, sharing hardware, sharing data and information, sharing software, and transferring funds.

(5) How Are Client/Server, Peer-to-Peer, and P2P Networks Different? On a **client/server network**, one or more computers acts as a **server**, which controls access to network resources and provides a centralized storage area, while the other computers on the network are **clients** that rely on the server for resources. A *peer-to-peer network* is a simple network that typically connects fewer than 10 computers, each called a *peer*, that have equal responsibilities and capabilities. *P2P* is an Internet peer-to-peer network on which users connect directly to each other's hard disks and exchange files over the Internet.

(6) What Are Various Network Communications Standards? A *network standard* defines guidelines that specify the way computers access a medium, the type(s) of medium, the speeds on different types of networks, and the type of physical cable or wireless technology used. Network communications standards include Ethernet, token ring, TCP/IP, 802.11, Bluetooth, IrDA, RFID, and WAP. **Ethernet** allows nodes to contend for access to the network. **Token ring** requires devices to share or pass a special signal, called a *token*. **TCP/IP** divides data up into *packets*. **802.11** is a

Chapter Review

series of standards for wireless devices. **Bluetooth** uses short-range radio waves to transmit data. **IrDA** transmits data wirelessly via infrared light waves. **RFID** uses radio signals for communications. The **Wireless Application Protocol** (**WAP**) allows wireless mobile devices to access the Internet.

(7) What Is the Purpose of Communications Software?   **Communications software** helps users establish a connection to another computer or network, manages the transmission of data, and provides an interface for users to communicate with one another.

(8) What Are Various Types of Lines for Communications Over the Telephone Network? The telephone network uses dial-up lines or dedicated lines. A **dial-up line** is a temporary connection that uses one or more analog telephone lines for communications. A **dedicated line** is an always-on connection established between two communications devices. Dedicated lines include ISDN lines, DSL, T-carrier lines, and ATM. *ISDN* is a set of standards for digital transmission over standard copper telephone lines. **DSL** transmits at fast speeds on existing standard copper telephone wiring. A **T-carrier line** is a long-distance digital telephone line that carries multiple signals over a single communications line. **ATM** (*Asynchronous Transfer Mode*) is a service that carries voice, data, video, and multimedia at extremely high speeds.

> *connect*
> Visit scsite.com/dc2006/ch9/quiz or click the Quiz Yourself button. Click Objectives 5 – 8.

(9) What Are Commonly Used Communications Devices?   A **communications device** is hardware capable of transmitting data between a sending device and a receiving device. A **modem** converts a computer's digital signals to analog signals for transmission over standard telephone lines. An *ISDN modem* transmits digital data to and from an ISDN line, while a **DSL modem** transmits digital data to and from a DSL line. A **cable modem** is a digital modem that sends and receives digital data over the cable television network. A **wireless modem** allows wireless access to the Web. A **network card** is an adapter card, PC Card, or flash card that enables a computer or device to access a network. A *wireless access point* allows computers and devices to transfer data wirelessly. A *router* connects multiple computers together and transmits data to its destination on the network. A *hub* provides a central point for cables in a network.

(10) How Can a Home Network Be Set Up?   A **home network** connects multiple computers and devices in a home. An Ethernet network connects each computer to a hub with a physical cable. A home *powerline cable network* uses the same lines that bring electricity into the house. A *phoneline network* uses existing telephone lines in a home. A *HomeRF* (*radio frequency*) *network* and **Wi-Fi** network use radio waves, instead of cable, to transmit data.

(11) What Are Various Physical and Wireless Transmission Media?   **Transmission media** consists of materials or substances capable of carrying one or more signals. *Physical transmission media* use tangible materials to send communications signals. **Twisted-pair cable** consists of one or more twisted-pair wires bundled together. **Coaxial cable** consists of a single copper wire surrounded by at least three layers: an insulating material, a woven or braided metal, and a plastic outer coating. **Fiber-optic cable** consists of thin strands of glass or plastic that use light to transmit signals. *Wireless transmission media* send communications signals through the air or space. *Infrared* (*IR*) sends signals using infrared light waves. **Broadcast radio** distributes radio signals through the air over long and short distances. **Cellular radio** is a form of broadcast radio that is used widely for mobile communications. **Microwaves** are radio waves that provide a high-speed signal transmission. A **communications satellite** is a space station that receives microwave signals from an earth-based station, amplifies the signals, and broadcasts the signals back over a wide area.

> *connect*
> Visit scsite.com/dc2006/ch9/quiz or click the Quiz Yourself button. Click Objectives 9 – 11.

Key Terms

You should know the Primary Terms and be familiar with the Secondary Terms. Use the list below to help focus your study. To further enhance your understanding of the Key Terms in this chapter, visit scsite.com/dc2006/ch9/terms. See an example of and a definition for each term, and access current and additional information about the term from the Web.

Primary Terms

(shown in bold-black characters in the chapter)

802.11 (478)
ATM (483)
bandwidth (491)
Bluetooth (478)
broadband (492)
broadcast radio (494)
cable modem (485)
cellular radio (494)
client/server network (472)
clients (472)
coaxial cable (493)
collaborate (467)
communications (460)
communications channel (460)
communications device (484)
communications satellite (496)
communications software (480)
cybercafé (464)
dedicated line (482)
dial-up line (481)
DSL (482)
DSL modem (485)
Ethernet (476)
fiber-optic cable (493)
global positioning system (GPS) (466)
groupware (468)
home network (489)
IrDA (478)

latency (491)
local area network (LAN) (471)
microwaves (495)
modem (485)
network (469)
network card (486)
network topology (474)
noise (493)
picture messaging (464)
public Internet access point (464)
receiving device (461)
RFID (479)
sending device (460)
server (472)
SMS (463)
text messaging (463)
T-carrier line (483)
TCP/IP (477)
token ring (476)
transmission media (491)
twisted-pair cable (493)
voice mail (468)
wide area network (WAN) (472)
Wi-Fi (478)
Wireless Application Protocol (WAP) (480)
wireless LAN (WLAN) (471)
wireless modem (486)

Secondary Terms

(shown in italic characters in the chapter)

802.11g (478)
802.11i (478)
10-Gigabit Ethernet (476)
1G (494)
2G (494)
3G (494)
ADSL (asymmetric digital subscriber line) (482)
analog signal (484)
Asynchronous Transfer Mode (483)
baseband (492)
broadband modem (485)
bus (474)
bus network (474)
CDMA (494)
coax (493)
database server (473)
dedicated servers (473)
demodulate (485)
dial-up modem (485)
digital modem (485)
digital signal (484)
Digital Subscriber Line (482)
downlink (496)
downstream rate (482)
EDI (electronic data interchange) (470)
electronic funds transfer (EFT) (470)
extranet (475)
Fast Ethernet (476)
file server (473)
file sharing network (473)
fixed wireless (495)
fractional T1 (483)
Gigabit Ethernet (476)
GPRS (494)
GPS receiver (466)
GSM (494)
hardware firewall (488)
HomeRF (radio frequency) network (490)
host computer (472)
hot spot (464)
hub (connecting networks) (488)
hub (star network) (475)
infrared (IR) (494)
intelligent home network (489)
intranet (475)
ISDN (Integrated Services Digital Network) (482)
ISDN modem (485)
line-of-sight transmission (478)
metropolitan area network (MAN) (472)

microwave station (495)
MMS (multimedia message service) (464)
modulate (485)
multiplexing (482)
network architecture (472)
network interface card (NIC) (486)
network license (470)
network server (473)
network standard (476)
node (471)
online meeting (467)
optical fiber (493)
P2P (473)
packet switching (477)
packets (477)
peer (473)
peer-to-peer network (473)
Personal Communications Services (PCS) (495)
phoneline network (489)
physical transmission media (492)
powerline cable network (489)
print server (473)
protocol (476)
public switched telephone network (PSTN) (481)
radio frequency identification (479)
ring network (474)
router (488)
short message service (463)
site license (470)
star network (475)
T1 line (483)
T3 line (483)
token (476)
Transmission Control Protocol/Internet Protocol (477)
twisted-pair wire (493)
UMTS (494)
uplink (496)
upstream rate (482)
value-added network (VAN) (470)
voice mailbox (468)
Web services (468)
Wi-Fi mesh network (478)
WiMAX (496)
wireless fidelity (478)
wireless access point (487)
wireless Ethernet standard (478)
wireless network card (487)
wireless transmission media (492)
workgroup computing (468)
XML (468)

Checkpoint

Use the Checkpoint exercises to check your knowledge level of the chapter. The Beyond the Book exercises will help broaden your understanding of the concepts presented in this chapter. To complete the Checkpoint exercises interactively, visit scsite.com/dc2006/ch9/check.

Label the Figure

Identify the elements in this sample communications system.

a. Tablet PCs

b. GPS receivers

c. desktop computers

d. smart phones

e. mainframe computers

f. notebook computers

g. Internet-enabled PDAs

h. servers

True/False

Mark T for True and F for False. (See page numbers in parentheses.)

_____ 1. A communications channel is the media on which data, instructions, or information travel. (460)

_____ 2. Groupware is software that helps groups of people work together on projects and share information over a network. (468)

_____ 3. Businesses are the primary users of Web services. (468)

_____ 4. A network is a collection of computers and devices connected together via communications devices and transmission media. (469)

_____ 5. A local area network (LAN) is a network that covers a large geographic area using a communications channel that combines many types of media such as telephone lines, cables, and radio waves. (472)

_____ 6. On a ring network, all of the computers and devices on the network connect to a central device. (475)

_____ 7. A packet is a special series of bits that function like a ticket. (476)

_____ 8. Bluetooth requires line-of-sight transmission. (478)

_____ 9. A cable modem is a digital modem that sends and receives digital data over the cable television network. (485)

_____ 10. Bandwidth is the time it takes a signal to travel from one location to another on a network. (491)

_____ 11. Because microwaves use line-of-sight transmission, microwave stations often sit on the tops of buildings, towers, or mountains. (495)

Checkpoint

 Multiple Choice   Select the best answer. (See page numbers in parentheses.)

1. Sending and receiving devices include _____. (461)
   a. mainframe computers and servers
   b. desktop computers and notebook computers
   c. Tablet PCs, smart phones, and PDAs
   d. all of the above

2. An online meeting allows users to _____. (467)
   a. share documents with other users in real time
   b. leave voice messages for one or two people
   c. determine the receiver's geographic location
   d. print to a Web address associated with a particular printer

3. Different applications can communicate with each other by sending XML files to the _____. (468)
   a. Internet telephony
   b. instant messenger
   c. Web services
   d. global positioning system

4. Many businesses network their computers together to _____. (469)
   a. facilitate communications
   b. share hardware, software, data, and information
   c. transfer funds
   d. all of the above

5. A(n) _____ is a legal agreement that allows multiple users to access the software on a server simultaneously. (470)
   a. site license
   b. EDI
   c. value-added network
   d. network license

6. Because of its larger size, most _____ networks require a person to serve as a network administrator. (473)
   a. client/server   b. peer-to-peer
   c. P2P   d. all of the above

7. Today, _____ is the most popular network standard for LANs because it is relatively inexpensive and easy to install and maintain. (476)
   a. token ring   b. Ethernet
   c. TCP/IP   d. Bluetooth

8. When a computer uses TCP/IP to send data over the Internet, the data is divided into small pieces, or _____. (477)
   a. tokens   b. packets
   c. hubs   d. nodes

9. Communications software consists of programs that do all of the following except _____. (480)
   a. help users establish a connection to another computer or network
   b. manage the transmission of data, instructions, and information
   c. provide an interface for users to communicate with one another
   d. convert a computer's analog signals into digital signals for transmission

10. With ISDN, a telephone line can carry three or more signals at once using a technique called _____. (482)
    a. packet switching
    b. multiplexing
    c. file sharing
    d. collaborating

11. The most popular T-carrier line is the _____. (483)
    a. T1 line
    b. ATM
    c. T3 line
    d. DSL

12. Many CATV operators provide a(n) _____ as part of the installation. (486)
    a. dial-up modem
    b. ISDN modem
    c. cable modem
    d. DSL modem

13. Two types of wireless home networks are _____. (490)
    a. Ethernet and powerline
    b. phoneline and HomeRF
    c. Ethernet and Wi-Fi
    d. HomeRF and Wi-Fi

14. When compared to cables that use wire, fiber-optic cables _____. (493)
    a. are capable of carrying significantly more signals
    b. provide slower data transmission
    c. are more susceptible to noise
    d. have larger size (much thicker and greater weight)

Checkpoint

 Matching　　　　Match the terms with their definitions. (See page numbers in parentheses.)

_____ 1. text messaging (463)

_____ 2. cybercafé (464)

_____ 3. groupware (468)

_____ 4. Web services (468)

_____ 5. intranet (475)

_____ 6. extranet (475)

_____ 7. network standard (476)

_____ 8. T-carrier line (483)

_____ 9. bandwidth (491)

_____ 10. latency (491)

a. guidelines that specify the way computers access a medium, type of medium, speed, and physical technology used

b. allows customers or suppliers to access part of a company's intranet

c. coffee house or restaurant that provides computers with Internet access

d. standardized software that enables programmers to create applications that communicate over the Internet or an internal network

e. any of several types of long-distance digital telephone lines that carry multiple signals over a single communications line

f. amount of data, instructions, and information that can travel over a communications channel

g. internal network that uses Internet technologies

h. time it takes a signal to travel from one network location to another

i. online area in which users have written discussions about a subject

j. type of media that transmits only one signal at a time

k. allows smart phone or PDA users to send and receive brief text messages

l. software that helps groups of people share information over a network

 Short Answer　　　　Write a brief answer to each of the following questions.

1. What is a public Internet access point? _____ What is a hot spot? _____

2. How are a local area network (LAN), a metropolitan area network (MAN), and a wide area network (WAN) different? _____ What is a wireless LAN? _____

3. What is a dedicated server? _____ How are a file server, a print server, a database server, and a network server different? _____

4. What is a network topology? _____ How are a bus network, a ring network, and a star network different? _____

5. What is a network standard? _____ What is a protocol? _____

Beyond the Book　　　　Read the following book elements, learn more about each using the Web, and then write a brief report.

1. At Issue — Should Companies Be Able to Track Your Online Habits? (462), High-Tech Cheating via Wireless Messaging Services (464), Will We Be Safer in the Upcoming Surveillance Society? (479), Librarians Caught in Middle of Internet Censorship Battle (480), and Should Cell Phones Be Banned in Public Places? (495)

2. Career Corner — Network Specialist (497)

3. Companies on the Cutting Edge — Cisco Systems or QUALCOMM (499)

4. FAQs (464, 477, 478, 478, 479, 485, 486, 487, 488, 492)

5. High-Tech Talk — OSI Reference Model: The Driving Force Behind Network Communications (498)

6. Looking Ahead — Broadband Sparks Portal Services (492) and Hear the Music on a Smart Phone (496)

7. Making Use of the Web — Learning (125)

8. Picture Yourself Communicating Wirelessly (458)

9. Technology Trailblazers — Robert Metcalfe or Patricia Russo (499)

10. Web Links (465, 466, 471, 474, 476, 480, 483, 485, 488, 489, 494)

Learn It Online

Use the Learn It Online exercises to reinforce your understanding of the chapter concepts. To access the Learn It Online exercises, visit scsite.com/dc2006/ch9/learn.

① At the Movies — Bluetooth in Action

To view the Bluetooth in Action movie, click the number 1 button. Locate your video and click the corresponding High-Speed or Dial-Up link, depending on your Internet connection. Watch the movie and then complete the exercise by answering the questions that follow. When Bluetooth works, it can be a great way to optimize your personal area network (PAN). How can Bluetooth change your personal area network (PAN) into a wireless network? What are the dangers of using Bluetooth without proper security?

② At the Movies — Tracking Kids With GPS

To view the Tracking Kids With GPS movie, click the number 2 button. Locate your video and click the corresponding High-Speed or Dial-Up link, depending on your Internet connection. Watch the movie and then complete the exercise by answering the questions that follow. Inventors using a new miniaturization process have merged cellular and GPS tracking technology into a valuable instrument for parents who want an extra measure of security in protecting their children. Disguised as a simple wristwatch, this device is able to provide parents with a way to track children who may become lost in a crowd or become a victim of kidnapping. By placing the

watch on their child and signing up for a tracking service, parents can locate lost or stolen children in a short period of time. What are the pros and cons of using technologies such as Digital Angel to track children? Under what situations might the watch become a danger to the child?

③ Student Edition Labs — Networking Basics

Click the number 3 button. When the Student Edition Labs menu appears, click *Networking Basics* to begin. A new browser window will open. Follow the on-screen instructions to complete the Lab. When finished, click the Exit button. If required, submit your results to your instructor.

④ Student Edition Labs — Wireless Networking

Click the number 4 button. When the Student Edition Labs menu appears, click *Wireless Networking* to begin. A new browser window will open. Follow the on-screen instructions to complete the Lab. When finished, click the Exit button. If required, submit your results to your instructor.

⑤ Practice Test

Click the number 5 button. Answer each question. When completed, enter your name and click the Grade Test button to submit the quiz for grading. Make a note of any missed questions. If required, submit your results to your instructor.

⑥ Who Wants To Be a Computer Genius²?

Click the number 6 button to find out if you are a computer genius. Directions about how to play the game will be displayed. When you are ready to play, click the Play button. Submit your score to your instructor.

Learn It Online

 7 Wheel of Terms

Click the number 7 button to reinforce important terms you learned in this chapter by playing the Shelly Cashman Series version of this popular game. Directions about how to play the game will be displayed. When you are ready to play, click the Play button. Submit your score to your instructor.

 8 DC Track and Field

Click the number 8 button to use what you have learned in this chapter to compete against other students in three track and field events. Directions about how to play the game will be displayed. When you are ready to play, click the start first event button. If required, submit your score to your instructor.

9 You're Hired!

Click the number 9 button to use what you have learned in this chapter to embark on the path to a career in computers. Directions about how to play the game will be displayed. When you are ready to play, click the begin game button. If required, submit your score to your instructor.

 10 Crossword Puzzle Challenge

Click the number 10 button. Complete the puzzle to reinforce skills you learned in this chapter. Directions about how to play the game will be displayed. When you are ready to play, click the Submit button. Submit the completed puzzle to your instructor.

 11 Lab Exercises

Click the number 11 button. When the Lab Exercises menu appears, click the exercise assigned by your instructor. A new browser window will open. Follow the on-screen instructions to complete the exercise. When finished, click the Exit button. If required, submit your results to your instructor.

12 In the News

Theoretically, business travelers can access e-mail, fax documents, and transmit data from anywhere in the world. In practice, however, incompatible telephone standards and mismatched telephone jacks can frustrate even experienced globetrotters. The 3Com Megahertz LAN PC Card addresses this problem. The modem and accompanying software allow travelers to use computer communications with more than 250 telephone systems worldwide simply by selecting the appropriate country from a menu and attaching a suitable adapter plug. Click the number 12 button and read a news article about a product that is changing computer communications. What is the product? What does it do? Who is likely to use this product?

13 Chapter Discussion Forum

Select an objective from this chapter on page 459 about which you would like more information. Click the number 13 button and post a short message listing a meaningful message title accompanied by one or more questions concerning the selected objective. In two days, return to the threaded discussion by clicking the number 13 button. Submit to your instructor your original message and at least one response to your message.

Learn How To

Use the Learn How To activities to learn fundamental skills when using a computer and accompanying technology. Complete the exercises and submit them to your instructor. Visit scsite.com/dc2006/ch9/howto to obtain more information pertaining to each activity.

LEARN HOW TO 1: Set Up and Install a Wi-Fi Home Network

In this chapter you learned about home networks and their advantages (see page 489, Home Networks). Creating a <u>Wi-Fi home network</u> consists of four phases: 1) subscribe to a high-speed Internet connection; 2) purchase the Wi-Fi equipment; 3) connect the physical devices; and 4) create the network through the use of software.

SUBSCRIBE TO A HIGH-SPEED INTERNET CONNECTION   A high-speed Internet connection is advisable to connect all computers on the home network to the Internet. The three primary ways for home users to obtain a fast connection to the Internet are DSL, cable, and satellite. DSL is provided by telephone companies, cable is provided by cable TV companies, and satellite connections are provided by satellite TV providers. Each has its advantages and disadvantages, including the minimum and maximum speed of Internet access, cost, and availability.

Determining the optimal high-speed Internet connection depends largely on where the network will be located, local costs, and service availability. The way to obtain the best high-speed Internet connection is to research the options available in your area.

Exercise

1. Assume you live near Coeur d'Alene, Idaho. You have decided that high-speed Internet access and a Wi-Fi network would be advantageous for your at-home business. Find answers to the following questions for this Idaho town or a town specified by your instructor: What methods of high-speed Internet access are available? Which provides the best service? Which is the cheapest? Based on the information you gather, write a plan for subscribing to a high-speed Internet connection service. Submit the answers to the questions and your plan to your instructor.

PURCHASE THE WI-FI EQUIPMENT   As part of the service when you subscribe to fast access on the Internet, you receive a modem that is capable of connecting to the Internet. In most cases, the modem is not a wireless transmitter. So, in order to establish a wireless connection between the Internet and the home network, you will need a wireless router that establishes the wireless access point.

You can visit any retail electronics store and find a wide variety of wireless routers. A key to purchasing the correct router is to ensure it will work with your modem and Internet access service. Some Internet service providers support only certain brands of routers and, while it is true that other routers may work, you might be taking a risk if you purchase an unsupported router. With the popularity of wireless home networks, though, some Internet service providers now provide a wireless router as part of the subscription service, often for an additional fee. You should investigate closely the needs for the Wi-Fi router to ensure compatibility with your Internet access service.

In addition to the router, each computer that is to be part of the Wi-Fi network needs a wireless network adapter. This device allows the computers to communicate with one another. Most external wireless network adapters plug in either a PC Card slot or a USB connection. Many notebook computers have a built-in wireless network adapter.

Finally, in the better designed home networks, one computer is designated the Internet Connection Sharing (ICS) host. This is the computer that is connected directly to the wireless router, then to the modem and the Internet. Most of the time, this computer, which normally is a desktop and the most powerful computer in the network, is connected using an Ethernet network adapter and cable.

Once the Wi-Fi equipment is assembled, you are ready to connect your home network.

Learn How To

Exercise

1. Using your Web research skills, determine the type of IEEE 802.11 standard used by modems available from Internet service providers. What percentage use 802.11b? What percentage use 802.11g? If your modem uses 802.11b but your wireless network router is 802.11g, what happens? Based on your research, which router do you recommend? Submit your answers to your instructor.

CONNECT THE PHYSICAL DEVICES Once you have assembled your equipment, you can connect the devices in the network. Usually, the modem will be connected to the source of the Internet transmission (DSL, cable, or satellite). Then the modem is connected to the wireless router, which in turn is connected to the Internet Connection Sharing computer.

After these connections are completed, each of the computers that will be used in the network that do not have a built-in wireless network adapter must have the adapter attached, often by using a USB connection. Once these connections are made, the network can be created.

CREATE THE NETWORK To establish a network, operating system software must be configured based on the design of your network. To begin the process on a Windows XP computer with Service Pack 2, you should run the Wireless Network Setup Wizard by completing the following steps:

1. Click the Start button on the Windows taskbar and then click Control Panel on the Start menu.
2. In Category view, click Network and Internet Connections.
3. In the Network and Internet Connections window, click Set up a wireless network for home or small office. *The first Wireless Network Setup Wizard dialog box is displayed.*
4. Click the Next button. If the next Wireless Network Setup Wizard dialog box asks "What do you want to do?," click Set up a new wireless network and then click the Next button.
5. In the Network name (SSID) text box, type a name for the wireless network you are creating. Use a name that you will recognize as the name for the network. Make sure the Automatically assign a network key option button is selected. If your devices are so equipped, click the Use WPA encryption instead of WEP check box. This will give your network stronger security. Then, click the Next button.
6. In the next Wireless Network Setup Wizard dialog box (Figure 9-45), click Use a USB flash drive if you have a USB drive to use; otherwise, click Set up a network manually (these steps assume you have a USB drive). Click the Next button.
7. Insert your flash drive in a USB port and wait for the drive letter to appear. Click the Next button.
8. Follow the steps specified in the wizard to configure each computer in the network and then click the Next button.
9. The network has been created. Click the Finish button to close the wizard.

FIGURE 9-45

Next, you must run the Network Setup Wizard to configure the network by completing the following steps:

1. Open the Network and Internet Connections window in Control Panel. Click Set up or change your home or small office network. *The Network Setup Wizard is displayed (Figure 9-46).*
2. Follow the instructions in the wizard.

FIGURE 9-46

Exercise

1. Form a three-person team whose responsibility is to create a Wi-Fi network for a small business in your local area. Assign tasks to each member of the team. Write a detailed plan for creating the Wi-Fi network, including the brand and type of equipment to be purchased, costs, and a schedule for completing the work. Submit the plan to your instructor.

Web Research

Use the Internet-based Web Research exercises to broaden your understanding of the concepts presented in this chapter. Visit scsite.com/dc2006/ch9/research to obtain more information pertaining to each exercise. To discuss any of the Web Research exercises in this chapter with other students, post your thoughts or questions at scsite.com/dc2006/ch9/forum.

① Scavenger Hunt   Use one of the search engines listed in Figure 2-10 in Chapter 2 on page 78 or your own favorite search engine to find the answers to the questions that follow. Copy and paste the Web address from the Web page where you found the answer. Some questions may have more than one answer. If required, submit your answers to your instructor. (1) How is the IEEE 802.3 standard applied in home entertainment systems? (2) Which operating system has TCP/IP built into it? (3) What is the most common bridge used to connect two dissimilar networks? (4) What company developed the token ring protocol? What is the data transfer rate for token ring technology? (5) What is the purpose of the Bluetooth Special Interest Group? Where is the headquarters of this organization? (6) How many cybercafés are located in Paris, France? In China?

② Search Sleuth   Subject directories are used to find specialized topics, such as information about automobiles, travel, and real estate. Most subject directories are arranged by topic and then displayed in a series of menus. Yahoo! is one of the more popular directories. Visit this Web site and then use your word processing program to answer the following questions. Then, if required, submit your answers to your instructor. (1) Click the Shopping link in the Shop area and then click the Software link in the Computers category. What are the top three software products displayed and their prices? (2) Click your browser's Back button or press the BACKSPACE key to return to the Yahoo! home page. Click the Search text box and type "digital camera" and "5.0 megapixels" in the box. Sort the cameras by lowest price by clicking the Lowest Price link near the top of the page. Which camera is the least expensive? (3) Click your browser's Back button or press the BACKSPACE key several times to return to the Yahoo! home page. Click the College and University link in the Education area of the Web Site Directory. Click two of the links in the Site Listings area and review the articles. Write a 50-word summary of your findings.

③ Journaling   Respond to your readings in this chapter by writing at least one page about your reactions, evaluations, and reflections on computer communications. For example, have you visited a cybercafé? Have you used a device equipped with a global positioning system? How would you react if a classmate used a cell phone with text and picture messaging to cheat on an exam? You also can write about the new terms you learned by reading this chapter. If required, submit your journal to your instructor.

④ Expanding Your Understanding   More than a million drivers are finding their commutes more enjoyable with the advent of satellite radio. The two major providers, XM Radio and Sirius, offer hundreds of channels of specific music, talk shows, news, and sports programming. Traditional broadcasters have complained to the Federal Communication Commission, stating that the satellite companies have violated their original licenses because they have expanded their channels to include local weather and traffic advisories and plan to introduce video channels to air on back seat video screens. View Web sites to learn more about satellite radio's popularity. What is the monthly subscription fee for both services? What programming is available in your area? Write a report summarizing your findings, focusing on the broadcasters' objections. If required, submit your report to your instructor.

⑤ Ethics in Action   Products such as cell phones with global positioning system tracking capabilities certainly can be beneficial. The tracking information, however, could be used in detrimental ways if your electronic device always is turned on, according to privacy experts. If, for example, you regularly eat at fast-food establishments, your health insurance company could obtain the data regarding your whereabouts and then increase your premiums. Your automobile insurance company could drop your coverage if it learns you drive farther to work than you stated on your application. View online sites that provide arguments about trading privacy for information. Write a report summarizing your findings, and include a table of links to Web sites that provide additional details. If required, submit your report to your instructor.

Case Studies

Use the Case Studies to apply the concepts presented in the chapter to real-world situations. Visit scsite.com/dc2006/ch9/cases to obtain more information pertaining to each exercise. To discuss the Case Studies in this chapter with other students, visit scsite.com/dc2006/ch9/forum and post your thoughts or questions.

CASE STUDY 1 — Class Discussion   Your cousin owns a major architectural firm on the west coast. The company specializes in designing condominium complexes for retirees throughout the United States. One of her biggest expenses is the cost of her sales force and architects traveling to meetings with customers. She recently learned about the collaboration features of Microsoft Office. She is aware that you are studying about computers and has asked you to examine <u>online collaboration</u> as an alternative to some or all of the face-to-face meetings with customers. What are the advantages and disadvantages of collaborating online? What is a whiteboard? How are online meetings set up? What is NetMeeting? Does collaboration require additional hardware? Write a brief report and be prepared to discuss your findings in class.

CASE STUDY 2 — Class Discussion   You work as an intern in the Information Technology department for the *Star Journal*, a local newspaper. The newspaper's board of directors recently approved a budget for redesigning the interior of its century-old building as part of an inner-city rehabilitation project. Your manager has been asked to recommend the type of <u>transmission media</u> (hardwire or wireless) to use for the newspaper's local area network. He has asked you to submit a feature/benefit report that summarizes the advantages of hardwiring the building versus using wireless transmission media. Which transmission media would have a greater startup cost? Which transmission media do you think is the most secure? Do the walls in the building present a problem for a wireless network? Does a wireless network present any health hazards? Be prepared to discuss your findings in class.

CASE STUDY 3 — Research   You are employed as a communications advisor at Telemark, a telemarketing firm with over 1,500 telemarketers. The president of the company recently attended the annual Internet Telephony Conference & Expo and came away with the idea that the company can save hundreds of thousands of dollars annually on local, long distance, and international calls by using <u>Internet telephony</u>, rather than the conventional public switched telephone network (PSTN). She has asked you to look into the feasibility of making the switch. Use the Web and/or print media to research the advantages and disadvantages of Internet telephony. How does Internet telephony work? What type of hardware and software must the company purchase to make calls over the Internet? Submit your report or use PowerPoint to create a presentation and share your findings with your class.

CASE STUDY 4 — Research   You recently were hired as a network consultant by P. J. Hoff Enterprises, the only local supplier of business equipment and office supplies in Macomb County. Because of the lack of competition, the owners have not reinvested in the business. A nationally recognized competitor recently opened for business with plans to put P. J. Hoff out of business. In response, the owners have decided to reinvest substantial sums of money in the company. One of their first projects is to develop a <u>local area network</u> that will link employee computers. Before they invest money in the network, they want to know more about networks. Use the Web and/or print media material to answer the following questions put forward by the owners. What are the advantages of having a network? What are the disadvantages? What type of network is best suited for our company — a peer-to-peer network or a client/server network? What transmission media should the company use? Why? What types of problems can we expect with a network? Write a brief report or use PowerPoint to create a presentation and share your findings with your class.

CASE STUDY 5 — Team Challenge   Your school offers free student-intern assistance to the county government. The county in turn assigns a manager to each team of students, who is responsible for defining the project assigned to the student team and ensuring that dates are met. Your team has been assigned to the manager of communications in the information technology department. Next year, he plans to select an <u>ISP — DSL, cable, or wireless</u> — to handle all Internet communications in the county buildings. Form a three-member team and have each team member choose a different type of ISP. Using the Web and/or print media, have each team member determine the advantages and disadvantages of their chosen ISP. Include such features as start-up costs, e-mail disk storage, speed, online protection, and recurring costs. As a team, merge your findings into a team report and/or PowerPoint presentation and share your recommendations with your class.

CHAPTER TEN

Database Management

Picture Yourself Using Web Databases

During a break, you think about everything you have to do after work today. Grocery shop . . . stop by the bank . . . pick up your niece — you promised her a movie and pizza tonight. Before leaving the office at the end of the day, you check show times using the Internet Movie Database (IMDb) Web site. You notice the movie has a rating of 8.2 out of 10 — it must be pretty good. The movie starts at 7:30 p.m., which gives you plenty of time.

At home, you log on to the grocery store's Web site and begin filling your shopping cart. Each time you search for an item, the screen says "accessing our database of thousands of products." When finished shopping, you select a time for the groceries to be delivered to your house, enter credit card information, and then click the Submit Order button.

Next, you drop off the application for a personal loan at the bank. The loan officer explains that the credit check, which is done online through Equifax's credit database, will take just a few minutes. Approved! You can pick up your check in the morning. While leaving the bank, you run into a friend you have not seen since high school. He asks if you are going to the class reunion next month. You ask him for more information because you had not heard about it. He explains if you log on to classmates.com and enter the year you graduated from high school, you will have access to the reunion information — and your high school classmates in the database of more than 38 million people.

To learn about Web databases, read Chapter 10 and discover the many features and functions of databases and database software.

DATABASES, DATA, AND INFORMATION

As presented in Chapter 3, a **database** is a collection of data organized in a manner that allows access, retrieval, and use of that data. *Data* can include text, numbers, images, audio, and video. For example, you can type text on a keyboard, talk into a computer's microphone, transfer photographs taken with a digital camera to a computer, and capture motion and sounds with a video camera and store the recordings on a computer.

Information is processed data; that is, it is organized, meaningful, and useful. In addition to documents, information can be in the form of audio, images, and video. For example, voice communications can be sent in an e-mail message for a family member, friend, or coworker to hear. You can post photographs taken with a digital camera on a Web page for others to view. With a PC video camera, others can see you in real time during a conference call.

Computers process data in a database into information. A database at a members-only discount warehouse, for example, contains data about its club members, e.g., member data, purchases data, etc. When someone wishes to become a warehouse club member, a membership services associate enters several

FIGURE 10-1 HOW A MEMBERS-ONLY DISCOUNT WAREHOUSE MIGHT PROCESS DATA INTO INFORMATION

Step 1:
A membership services associate uses a digital camera to take a photograph of the new member and uses a keyboard to enter other member data into the computer.

data items into a computer. The associate also uses a digital camera to photograph the new member. This picture, along with the other entered data, is stored in a database on a server's hard disk. A computer at the discount warehouse then processes the new member data and then sends receipt information to a laser printer and member ID card information to an ID card printer (Figure 10-1).

With **database software**, often called a **database management system** (**DBMS**), users create a computerized database; add, change, and delete data in the database; sort and retrieve data from the database; and create forms and reports from the data in the database. A discount warehouse might use Microsoft Access as its database software.

Database software includes many powerful features, as you will discover later in this chapter.

Most companies realize that data is one of their more valuable assets — because data is used to generate information. Many business transactions take less time when employees have instant access to information. For example, if membership services associates at a discount warehouse have instant access to member records, they can determine when a membership is due for renewal upon member request. When employees are more productive, customers (members, in this case) usually are more satisfied. When customers are happy, typically they become loyal to that business. Loyal customers can lead to referrals and an increase in profits.

Step 2:
The member data, including the photograph, is stored in a database on a hard disk.

DATABASE

Benjamin Tu

2204 Elm Court

Indianapolis, IN 46259

tu@indi.net

9/4/2007 BP <picture object>

data stored on disk

processing

Step 3:
A computer extracts the member data from the disk and obtains the amount due based on the type of membership plan.

information

Step 4:
When the amount due is paid, the receipt prints.

receipt

Step 5:
The membership services associate hands the ID card to the new member.

National Discount Warehouse

Benjamin Tu
2204 Elm Court
Indianapolis, IN 46259

EXP. 09-04-08

To ensure that data is accessible on demand, a company must manage and protect its data just as it would any other resource. Thus, it is vital that the data has integrity and is kept secure. Read At Issue 10-1 for a related discussion. Chapter 11 discusses data security.

AT ISSUE 10-1

Are Portable Storage Devices a Threat to Businesses?

For years, and to the dismay of many companies, workers carted home floppy disks loaded with valuable company information. The capacity of floppy disks, however, is miniscule compared with today's powerhouse devices, such as USB flash drives and MP3 players that contain small hard disks. Not only are the capacities of these devices far superior to floppy disks — sometimes topping out at 60 GB — but the devices often are smaller than floppy disks. Companies now must be concerned with disgruntled employees walking off with complete customer lists, employee databases, or secret product designs and strategies in their shirt pockets. Some companies have gone as far as banning some MP3 players and other portable storage devices from the company premises. Other companies have begun disabling USB and FireWire ports on employee computers, thereby preventing the devices from being used at all.

How can companies control employee use of portable storage devices to copy company information? Should companies be allowed to dictate the types of personal devices that employees bring to work? Why or why not? Is the problem solvable, just manageable, or should the company find other ways to secure its information? Why?

Data Integrity

For a computer to produce correct information, the data that is entered into a database must have integrity. *Data integrity* identifies the quality of the data. An erroneous member address in a member database is an example of incorrect data. When a database contains this type of error, it loses integrity. The more errors the data contains, the lower its integrity.

Garbage in, garbage out (*GIGO*) is a computing phrase that points out the accuracy of a computer's output depends on the accuracy of the input. If you enter incorrect data into a computer (garbage in), the computer will produce incorrect information (garbage out).

Data integrity is important because computers and people use information to make decisions and take actions. When you sign up for a warehouse club membership and pay with a credit card, a process begins that charges an amount to your credit card. If the membership price is not correct in the discount warehouse's database, an incorrect amount will be billed to your credit card. This type of error causes both you and the membership services associate extra time and effort to remedy.

Qualities of Valuable Information

The information that data generates also is an important asset. People make decisions daily using all types of information such as receipts, bank statements, pension plan summaries, stock analyses, and credit reports. At school, students use grade reports and degree audits to make decisions. In a business, managers make decisions based on sales trends, competitors' products and services, production processes, and even employee skills.

To assist with sound decision making, the information must have value. For it to be valuable, information should be accurate, verifiable, timely, organized, accessible, useful, and cost-effective.

- *Accurate information* is error free. Inaccurate information can lead to incorrect decisions. For example, consumers assume their credit report is accurate. If your credit report incorrectly shows past due payments, a bank may not lend you money for a car or house.

- *Verifiable information* can be proven as correct or incorrect. For example, a ticket agent at an airport usually requests some type of photo identification to verify that you are the person named on the ticket.

- *Timely information* has an age suited to its use. A decision to build additional schools in a particular district should be based on the most recent census report — not on one that is 20 years old. Most information loses value with time. Some information, such as information about trends, gains value as time passes and more information is obtained. For example, your transcript gains value as you take more classes.

- *Organized information* is arranged to suit the needs and requirements of the decision maker. Two different people may need the same information presented in a different manner. For example, an inventory manager may want an inventory report to list out-of-stock items first. The purchasing agent, instead, wants the report alphabetized by vendor.

- *Accessible information* is available when the decision maker needs it. Having to wait for information may delay an important decision. For example, a sales manager cannot decide which sales representative deserves the award for highest annual sales if the final sales have not yet been placed in the database.

- *Useful information* has meaning to the person who receives it. Most information is important only to certain people or groups of people. Always consider the audience when collecting and reporting information. Avoid distributing useless information. For example, an announcement of an alumni association meeting is not useful to students not yet graduated.

- *Cost-effective information* should give more value than it costs to produce. A company occasionally should review the information it produces to determine if it still is cost-effective to produce. Sometimes, it is not easy to place a value on information. For this reason, some companies create information only on demand, that is, as people request it, instead of on a regular basis. Many companies make information available online. Users then can access and print online information as they need it. For example, sending a printed benefits manual to each employee in a company could be quite costly. Instead, employees can access an online benefits manual, when they need to review it.

FAQ 10-1

How can I tell if information is useful?

If you stop distributing information and find that those who had received it do not notify you, then it might be that the information was not very useful. In many cases, what was useful information at one time now may end up in the wastebasket or recycle bin — possibly without even being reviewed. For more information, visit scsite.com/dc2006/ch10/faq and then click Useful Information.

THE HIERARCHY OF DATA

Data is organized in layers. In the computer profession, data is classified in a hierarchy. Each higher level of data consists of one or more items from the lower level. For example, a member has an address, and an address consists of letters and numbers. Depending on the application and the user, different terms describe the various levels of the hierarchy.

As shown in Figure 10-2, a database contains files, a file contains records, a record contains fields, and a field is made up of one or more characters. The Discount Warehouse database contains four files: Member, Membership Plans, Member Purchases, and Products. The Member file contains records about current members. The Membership Plans file contains records identifying a type of membership and its annual fee. The Member Purchases file contains records about members' purchases at the discount warehouse, and the Products file contains records about items for sale.

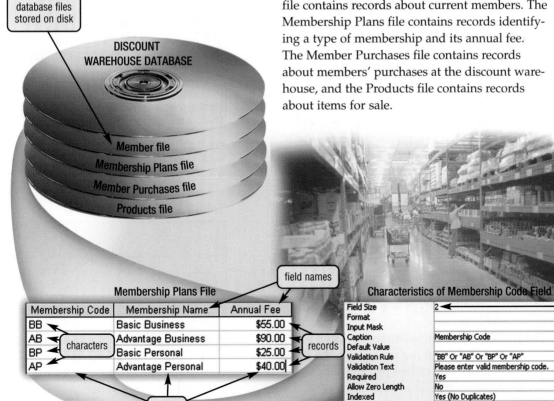

FIGURE 10-2 A sample discount warehouse database with four files: Member, Membership Plans, Member Purchases, and Products. The sample Membership Plans file contains four records. Each record contains three fields. The Membership Code field can contain a maximum of two characters (bytes).

Characters

As discussed in Chapter 4, a bit is the smallest unit of data the computer can process. Eight bits grouped together in a unit comprise a byte. In the ASCII and EBCDIC coding schemes, each byte represents a single **character**, which can be a number (4), letter (R), punctuation mark (?), or other symbol (&). The Unicode coding scheme, by contrast, uses one or two bytes to represent a character. (Read Appendix A for more information about coding schemes.)

Fields

A **field** is a combination of one or more related characters or bytes and is the smallest unit of data a user accesses. A **field name** uniquely identifies each field. When searching for data in a database, you often specify the field name. Field names for the data in the Membership Plans file are Membership Code, Membership Name, and Annual Fee.

A database uses a variety of characteristics, such as field size and data type, to define each field. The **field size** defines the maximum number of characters a field can contain. For example, the Membership Code field contains two characters. Valid entries include BB (Basic Business), AB (Advantage Business), BP (Basic Personal), and AP (Advantage Personal). Thus, as shown in Figure 10-2 on the previous page, the Membership Code field has a field size of 2.

The type of data in a field is an important consideration. Figure 10-3 identifies the data types for fields in the Membership Plans and Member files. The **data type** specifies the kind of data a field can contain and how the field is used. Common data types include:

• Text (also called *alphanumeric*) — letters, numbers, or special characters
• Numeric — numbers only
• AutoNumber — unique number automatically assigned by the DBMS to each added record
• Currency — dollar and cent amounts or numbers containing decimal values
• Date — month, day, year, and sometimes time information
• Memo — lengthy text entries
• Yes/No (also called *Boolean*) — only the values Yes or No (or True or False)
• Hyperlink — Web address that links to a document or a Web page

• Object (also called *BLOB* for binary large object) — photograph, audio, video, or a document created in other programs such as word processing or spreadsheet

In the Membership Plans file, two fields (Membership Code and Membership Name) have a text data type; the third field (Annual Fee) has a currency data type (Figure 10-3). In the Member file, the Member ID field has an AutoNumber data type. The First Name, Last Name, Address, City, State, Postal Code, and Membership Code fields have a text data type. E-mail Address field has a hyperlink data type, Date Joined a date/time data type, and Photograph an object data type.

Membership Plans file

Membership Code	Text
Membership Name	Text
Annual Fee	Currency

data types

Member file

Member ID	AutoNumber
First Name	Text
Last Name	Text
Address	Text
City	Text
State	Text
Postal Code	Text
E-mail Address	Hyperlink
Date Joined	Date/Time
Membership Code	Text
Photograph	Object

FIGURE 10-3 Data types of fields in the Membership Plans and Member files.

SAMPLE MEMBER FILE

Member ID	First Name	Last Name
2295	Milton	Brewer
3876	Louella	Drake
3928	Adelbert	Ruiz
4872	Elena	Gupta

records

key field

fields

Records

A **record** is a group of related fields. For example, a member record includes a set of fields about one member. A **key field**, or **primary key**, is a field that uniquely identifies each record in a file. The data in a key field is unique to a specific record. For example, the Member ID field uniquely identifies each member because no two members can have the same Member ID.

Files

A **data file** is a collection of related records stored on a storage medium such as a hard disk, CD, or DVD. A Member file at a discount warehouse might consist of hundreds of individual member records. Each member record in the file contains the same fields. Each field, however, contains different data. Figure 10-4 shows a small sample Member file that contains four member records, each with eleven fields. Typical fields about people often include First Name, Last Name, Address, City, State, Postal Code, and E-mail Address.

A database includes a group of related data files. With a DBMS, users access data and set relationships among the data in data files. Read At Issue 10-2 for a discussion related to a use of databases.

FAQ 10-2

Do users enter a primary key value?

Users enter a primary key value only if the program requests one, such as a driver's license number or student identification number. Often, the database program automatically assigns a unique primary key number to each newly added record. For more information, visit scsite.com/dc2006/ch10/faq and then click Primary Key Fields.

AT ISSUE 10-2

Is a National Identification Card Necessary for the Security of the Nation?

Calls for a national identification card in the United States have sparked heated debate, although such cards are the norm in many parts of the world. A *national ID card* could do more than simply assert the cardholder's identity. Some card proponents have called for embedding a biometric identifier, such as a fingerprint or facial scan, in the cards as an added security measure. Larry Ellison, Oracle CEO, proposes tying the cards to a combination of national databases related to personal information. Law enforcement officials contend that national ID cards would provide tamper-resistant proof of identification and improve national security. Civil liberties groups fear that the cards would facilitate information sharing among government agencies, increase police power, and lead to unjustified suspicion when someone fails to produce a card. Should the United States require a national identification card? Why or why not? If a national ID card is used, should it have biometric identifiers or be tied to a national database? Why?

Address	City	State	Postal Code	E-mail Address	Date Joined	Membership Code	Photograph
54 Lucy Court	Shelbyville	IN	46176		6/10/2006	AB	
33 Timmons Place	Cincinnati	OH	45208	lou@world.com	8/9/2006	AP	
99 Tenth Street	Carmel	IN	46033		10/8/2006	BP	
2 East Penn Drive	Pittsboro	IN	46167	eg@earth.net	11/6/2006	BB	

fields

FIGURE 10-4   A sample data file, stored on a hard disk, that contains four records, each with eleven fields.

MAINTAINING DATA

File maintenance refers to the procedures that keep data current. File maintenance procedures include adding records to, changing records in, and deleting records from a file.

Adding Records

Users add new records to a file when they obtain new data. If a new member wants to join the discount warehouse club, a membership services associate adds a new record to the Member file at the discount warehouse. The process required to add this record to the file might include the following steps:

1. A membership services associate displays a Member Maintenance form that gives him or her access to the Member file. The associate then clicks the New Record button, which begins the process of adding a record to the Member file.

2. The associate fills in the fields of the member record with data (except for the Member ID, which automatically is assigned by the program). In this example, the data entered is kept to a minimum.

3. The associate takes a picture of the member using a digital camera. The program stores this picture in the Member file and prints it on a member ID card.

4. The membership services associate verifies the data on the screen and then presses a key on the keyboard or clicks a button on the screen to add the new member record to the Member file. The system software determines where to write the record on the disk, depending on the location of enough free space on the disk. In some cases, it writes the new record at the end of the file. In other cases, such as illustrated in Figure 10-5, it writes the new record for Benjamin Tu between existing records in the file.

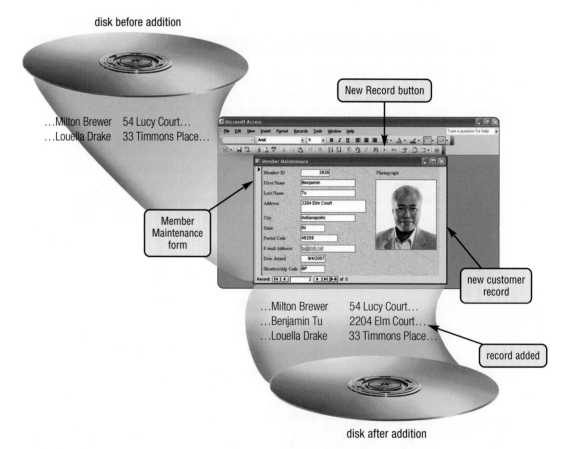

FIGURE 10-5 Using the Member Maintenance form, a membership services associate adds a new member record for Benjamin Tu. After the associate takes the photograph with the digital camera and confirms the data is correct, he or she adds the record to the database file.

Changing Records

Generally, users change a record in a file for two reasons: (1) to correct inaccurate data or (2) to update old data with new data.

As an example of the first type of change, assume that a membership services associate enters a member's e-mail address as ge@earth.net, instead of eg@earth.net. The member notices the error when she reviews her membership agreement at home. The next time she visits the discount warehouse, she requests that a membership services associate correct her e-mail address.

A more common reason to change a record is to update old data with new data. Suppose, for example, that Benjamin Tu moves from 2204 Elm Court to 76 Ash Street. The process to change the address and update Benjamin Tu's record might include the following steps:

1. The membership services associate displays the Member Maintenance form.

2. Assuming Benjamin Tu is present, the associate inserts Benjamin's member ID card in a card reader to display his member record on the screen. If Benjamin did not have his ID card or was not present, the associate could enter Benjamin's member ID — if Benjamin knew it. Otherwise, the associate could enter Tu in the Last Name field, which would retrieve all members with that same last name. The associate then would scroll through all of the retrieved records to determine which one is Benjamin's.

3. The program displays data about Benjamin Tu so that the associate can confirm the correct member record is displayed.

4. The associate enters the new street address, 76 Ash Street.

5. The membership services associate verifies the data on the screen and then clicks the Save button to change the record in the Member file. The program changes the record on the disk (Figure 10-6).

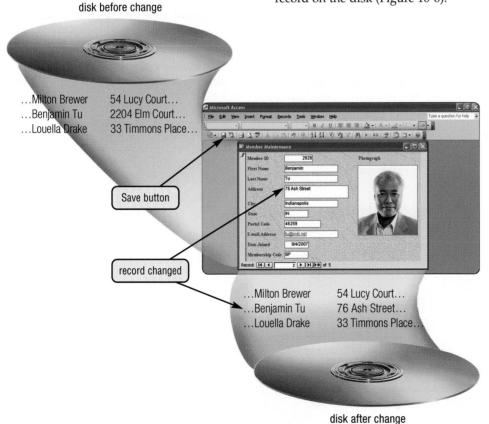

disk before change

Save button

record changed

disk after change

FIGURE 10-6   The membership services associate scans the membership ID card to display the member's record. After looking at the photograph on the screen to confirm that the correct member record is displayed, the associate changes the member's address.

Deleting Records

When a record no longer is needed, a user deletes it from a file. Assume a member named Elena Gupta is moving out of the country. The process required to delete a record from a file includes the following steps:

1. The membership services associate displays the Member Maintenance form.
2. The associate displays Elena Gupta's member record on the screen.
3. The associate confirms the correct member record is displayed. Then, the associate clicks the Delete Record button to delete the record from the Member file and then clicks the Save button to save the modified file.

Programs use a variety of techniques to manage deleted records. Sometimes, the program removes the record from the file immediately. Other times, the record is flagged, or marked, so the program will not process it again. In this case, the program places an asterisk (*) or some other character at the beginning of the record (Figure 10-7).

Programs that maintain inactive data for an extended period commonly flag records. For example, a discount warehouse might flag canceled memberships. When a program flags a deleted record, the record remains physically on the disk. The record, however, is deleted logically because the program will not process it. Programs will ignore flagged records unless an instruction is issued to process them.

From time to time, users should run a utility program that removes flagged records and reorganizes current records. For example, the discount warehouse may remove from disk any accounts that have been canceled for more than one year. Deleting unneeded records reduces the size of files and frees up storage space.

Validating Data

Validation is the process of comparing data with a set of rules or values to find out if the data is correct. Many programs perform a *validity check* that analyzes entered data to help ensure that it is correct. For instance, when a membership services associate adds or changes data in a member record, the DBMS tests the entered data.

With an annual membership fee, you would expect to see numbers before and after a decimal point. For example, a valid annual membership fee is 30.00. An entry of XR.WP clearly is not correct. If the entered data fails a validity check, the computer should display an error message that instructs the user to enter the data again. Validity checks, sometimes called *validation rules*, reduce data entry errors and thus enhance the data's integrity.

Various types of validity checks include alphabetic checks, numeric checks, range checks, consistency checks, and completeness checks. Check digits also validate data accuracy. The following paragraphs describe the purpose of these validity checks. The table in Figure 10-8 illustrates several of these validity checks and shows valid data that passes the check and invalid data that fails the check.

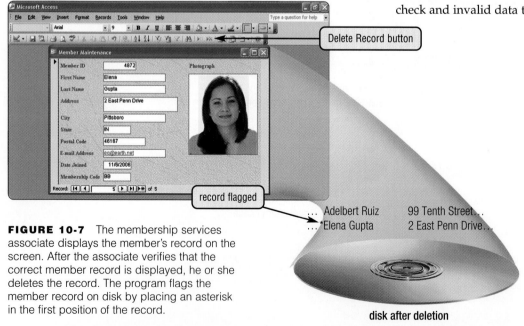

FIGURE 10-7 The membership services associate displays the member's record on the screen. After the associate verifies that the correct member record is displayed, he or she deletes the record. The program flags the member record on disk by placing an asterisk in the first position of the record.

disk after deletion

SAMPLE VALID AND INVALID DATA

Validity Check	Field Being Checked	Valid Data	Invalid Data
Alphabetic Check	First Name	Karen	Ka24n
Numeric Check	Postal Code	46322	4tr22
Range Check	Annual Fee	$30.00	$120.00
Consistency Check	Date Joined Birth Date	9/20/2006 8/27/1983	9/20/2006 8/27/2007
Completeness Check	Last Name	Tu	

FIGURE 10-8 In this table of sample valid and invalid data, the first column lists commonly used validity checks. The second column lists the name of the field that contains data being checked. The third column shows valid data that passes the validity checks. The fourth column shows invalid data that fails the validity checks.

ALPHABETIC/NUMERIC CHECK An *alphabetic check* ensures that users enter only alphabetic data into a field. A *numeric check* ensures that users enter only numeric data into a field. For example, data in a First Name field should contain only characters from the alphabet. Data in a postal code field should contain numbers (with the exception of the special characters such as a hyphen).

RANGE CHECK A *range check* determines whether a number is within a specified range. Assume the lowest annual membership fee at the discount warehouse is $25.00 and the highest is $90.00. A range check on the Annual Fee field ensures it is a value between $25.00 and $90.00.

CONSISTENCY CHECK A *consistency check* tests the data in two or more associated fields to ensure that the relationship is logical. For example, the value in a Date Joined field cannot occur earlier in time than a value in a Birth Date field.

COMPLETENESS CHECK A *completeness check* verifies that a required field contains data. For example, in many programs, you cannot leave the Last Name field blank. The completeness check ensures that data exists in the Last Name field.

CHECK DIGIT A *check digit* is a number(s) or character(s) that is appended to or inserted in a primary key value. A check digit often confirms the accuracy of a primary key value. Bank account, credit card, and other identification numbers often include one or more check digits.

A program determines the check digit by applying a formula to the numbers in the primary key value. An oversimplified illustration of a check digit formula is to add the numbers in the primary key. For example, if the primary key is 1367, this formula would add these numbers (1 + 3 + 6 + 7) for a sum of 17. Next, the

formula would add the numbers in the result (1 + 7) to generate a check digit of 8. The primary key then is 13678. This example began with the original primary key value, 1367, then the check digit, 8, was appended.

When a data entry clerk enters the primary key of 13678, for example, to look up an existing record, the program determines whether the check digit is valid. The program applies the check digit formula to the first four digits of the primary key. If the calculated check digit matches the entered check digit (8, in this example), the program assumes the entered primary key is valid. If the clerk enters an incorrect primary key, such as 13778, the check digit entered (8) will not match the computed check digit (9). In this case, the program displays an error message that instructs the user to enter the primary key value again.

WEB LINK 10-1

Check Digits
For more information, visit scsite.com/dc2006/ch10/weblink and then click Check Digits.

Test your knowledge of pages 514 through 523 in Quiz Yourself 10-1.

QUIZ YOURSELF 10-1

Instructions: Find the true statement below. Then, rewrite the remaining false statements so they are true.

1. A coding scheme is a number(s) or character(s) that is appended to or inserted in a primary key value.
2. A database is a combination of one or more related characters or bytes and is the smallest unit of data a user accesses.
3. A record is a collection of data organized in a manner that allows access, retrieval, and use of that data.
4. Data is processed information.
5. Hierarchy of data procedures include adding records to, changing records in, and deleting records from a file.
6. To be valuable, information should be accurate, verifiable, timely, organized, accessible, useful, and cost-effective.

Quiz Yourself Online: To further check your knowledge of databases, qualities of valuable information, the hierarchy of data, and file maintenance techniques, visit scsite.com/dc2006/ch10/quiz and then click Objectives 1 – 5.

FILE PROCESSING VERSUS DATABASES

Almost all application programs use either the file processing approach or the database approach to store and manage data. The next sections discuss these two approaches.

File Processing Systems

In the past, many organizations used file processing systems to store and manage data. In a typical **file processing system**, each department or area within an organization has its own set of files. The records in one file may not relate to the records in any other file.

Companies have used file processing systems for many years. A lot of these systems, however, have two major weaknesses: they have redundant data and they isolate data.

- Data Redundancy — Each department or area in a company has its own files in a file processing system. Thus, the same fields are stored in multiple files. If a file processing system is used at the discount warehouse, for example, the Member file and the Member Purchases file store the same members' names and addresses.

  Duplicating data in this manner wastes resources such as storage space and people's time. When new members are added or member data is changed, file maintenance tasks consume additional time because people must update multiple files that contain the same data.

  Data redundancy also can increase the chance of errors. If a member changes his or her address, for example, the discount warehouse must update the address wherever it appears. In this example, the Address field is in the Member file and also in the Member Purchases file. If the Address field is not changed in all the files where it is stored, then discrepancies among the files exist.

- Isolated Data — Often it is difficult to access data stored in separate files in different departments. Assume that the member e-mail addresses exist in the Member files, and items on sale are in the Products files. To send an e-mail message informing members about items on sale, data is needed from both the Member file and the Products file. Sharing data from multiple, separate files to generate such a list in a file processing system often is a complicated procedure and usually requires the experience of a computer programmer.

The Database Approach

When a company uses the **database approach**, many programs and users share the data in the database. A discount warehouse's database most likely contains data about members, membership plans, member purchases, and products. As shown in Figure 10-9, various areas within the discount warehouse share and

Programs on Computer for Checkout Lanes

Programs on Membership Services Associate's Computer

Database Management System

Member File
Membership Plans File
Member Purchases File
Products File

Discount Warehouse Database

FIGURE 10-9 In a discount warehouse that uses a database, the computer used by the membership services associate and the computer used in the checkout lane access data in a single database through the DBMS.

interact with the data in this database. The database does secure its data, however, so only authorized users can access certain data items.

Users can access the data in the database via application software called a DBMS. While a user is working with the database, the DBMS resides in the memory of the computer. Instead of working directly with the DBMS, some users interact with a front end. A *front end* is a program that generally has a more user-friendly interface than the DBMS. For example, a membership services associate interacts with the Membership program. This front-end program interacts with the DBMS, which in turn, interacts with the database. Many programs today have a Web page as their front end. An application that supports a front-end program sometimes is called the *back end*. In this case, the DBMS is the back end.

The database approach addresses many of the weaknesses associated with file processing systems. The following paragraphs present some strengths of the database approach.

- Reduced Data Redundancy — Most data items are stored in only one file, which greatly reduces duplicate data. For example, a discount warehouse's database would record a member's name and address only once. When member data is entered or changed, one employee makes the change once. Figure 10-10 demonstrates the differences between how a database application and a file processing application might store data.

- Improved Data Integrity — When users modify data in the database, they make changes to one file instead of multiple files. Thus, the database approach increases the data's integrity by reducing the possibility of introducing inconsistencies.

- Shared Data — The data in a database environment belongs to and is shared, usually over a network, by the entire organization. This data is independent of, or separate from, the programs that access the data. Companies that use databases typically have security settings to define who can access, add, change, and delete the data in a database. Read At Issue 10-3 for a related discussion.

- Easier Access — The database approach allows nontechnical users to access and maintain data, providing they have the necessary privileges. Many computer users also can develop smaller databases themselves, without professional assistance.

- Reduced Development Time — It often is easier and faster to develop programs that use the database approach. Many DBMSs include several tools to assist in developing programs, which further reduces the development time. The next section discusses these tools and other DBMS features.

File Processing Example

Database Example

FIGURE 10-10 In the file processing environment, both files contain all three membership plans data fields. In a database environment, only the Membership Plans file contains the Membership Name and Annual Fee fields. Other files, however, such as the Member file, contain the Membership Code, which links to the Membership Plans file when membership plans data is needed.

AT ISSUE 10-3

Should States Share Criminal Databases?

California was the first state to employ a controversial database. Based on Megan's Law — the statute named for a seven year old girl who was violated and killed by a paroled felon — the database listed the names and addresses of people convicted of crimes against children. Today, all states employ similar databases and are required to share the information with a national database. In some communities, when a paroled offender moves in, the police inform the local school system, which in turn sends parents a notification that includes a history, address, and picture of the wrongdoer. Touted as a valuable tool in crime prevention, some feel that publishing this information makes it impossible for an offender to lead a normal life and can result in vigilantism — one paroled lawbreaker's car was firebombed only days after his name was released. Should a database of people paroled or released for crimes against children be made public? Why or why not? Who should have access to the database? Why? Should such a database also include accused, but not convicted, offenders? Why or why not?

Databases have many advantages as well as some disadvantages. A database can be more complex than a file processing system. People with special training usually develop larger databases and their associated applications. Databases also require more memory, storage, and processing power than file processing systems.

Data in a database is more vulnerable than data in file processing systems. A database stores most data in a single file. Many users and programs share and depend on this data. If the database is not operating properly or is damaged or destroyed, users may not be able to perform their jobs. In some cases, certain programs may stop working. To protect their valuable database resource, individuals and companies should establish and follow security procedures. Chapter 11 discusses a variety of security methods.

Despite these limitations, many business and home users work with databases because of their tremendous advantages. Although the hardware and software costs to set up a database may seem expensive, long-term benefits exceed the initial costs.

FAQ 10-3

Can a database eliminate redundant data completely?

No, a database reduces redundant data — it does not eliminate it. Files in a database link together based on values in key fields. For example, the Member ID field will exist in any file that requires access to member data. Thus, the Member ID is duplicated (exists in many files) in the database. For more information, visit scsite.com/dc2006/ch10/faq and then click Database Relationships.

DATABASE MANAGEMENT SYSTEMS

As previously discussed, a database management system (DBMS), or database program, is software that allows you to create, access, and manage a database. DBMSs are available for many sizes and types of computers (Figure 10-11). Whether designed for a small or large computer, most DBMSs perform common functions. The following pages discuss functions common to most DBMSs.

POPULAR DATABASE MANAGEMENT SYSTEMS

Database	Manufacturer	Computer Type
Access	Microsoft Corporation	Personal computer, server, PDA
Adabas	Software AG	Midrange server, mainframe
D³	Raining Data	Personal computer, midrange server
DB2	IBM Corporation	Personal computer, midrange server, mainframe
Essbase	Hyperion Solutions Corporation	Personal computer, server
FastObjects	FastObjects Inc.	Personal computer, midrange server
GemFire	GemStone Systems, Inc.	Midrange server
Informix	IBM Corporation	Personal computer, midrange server, mainframe
Ingres	Computer Associates International, Inc.	Personal computer, midrange server, mainframe
InterBase	Borland Software Corporation	Personal computer, server
JDataStore	Borland Software Corporation	Personal computer, server
KE Texpress	KE Software, Inc.	Personal computer, server
MySQL	MySQL AB	Personal computer, midrange server
ObjectStore	Progress Software Corporation	Personal computer, midrange server
Oracle	Oracle Corporation	Personal computer, midrange server, mainframe, PDA
SQL Server	Microsoft Corporation	Server, personal computer, PDA
Sybase	Sybase Inc.	Personal computer, midrange server, PDA
Versant	Versant Corporation	Personal computer, midrange server
Visual FoxPro	Microsoft Corporation	Personal computer, server

FIGURE 10-11 Many database management systems run on multiple types of computers.

FAQ 10-4

Which companies have the largest database presence?

As shown in the chart below, Oracle has the largest market share, followed by IBM and Microsoft. For more information, visit scsite.com/dc2006/ch10/faq and then click Database Market Share.

Database Vendor Market Share

☐ Oracle ■ IBM ☐ Microsoft ■ Others

IBM 31%
Microsoft 12%
Others 17%
Oracle 40%

Source: IDC

Data Dictionary

A **data dictionary**, sometimes called a *repository*, contains data about each file in the database and each field in those files. For each file, it stores details such as the file name, description, the file's relationship to other files, and the number of records in the file. For each field, it stores details such as the field name, description, field type, field size, default value, validation rules, and the field's relationship to other fields. Figure 10-12 shows how a data dictionary might list data for a Member file.

Because the data dictionary contains details about data, some call it *metadata* (meta means more comprehensive). Sometimes, a data dictionary also contains data about programs and users. It might keep track of who accessed data and when they accessed it. The data dictionary is a crucial backbone to a DBMS. Thus, only skilled professionals should update the contents of a data dictionary.

A DBMS uses the data dictionary to perform validation checks. When users enter data, the data dictionary verifies that the entered data matches the field's data type. For example, the data dictionary allows only numbers to be entered in a Postal Code field. The data dictionary also can limit the type of data that can be entered, often allowing a user to select from a list. For example, the data dictionary ensures that the State field contains a valid two-letter state code, such as IN, by presenting a list of valid state codes to the user. By validating data, the data dictionary helps to maintain the integrity of the data.

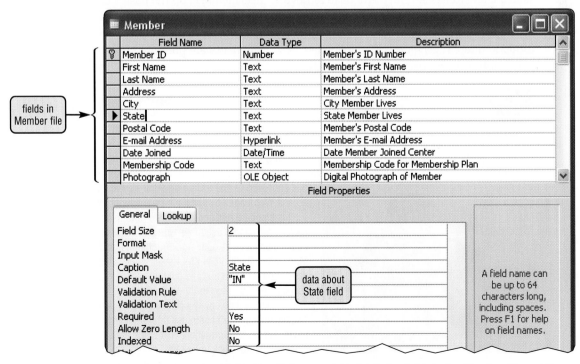

FIGURE 10-12 A sample data dictionary entry shows the fields in the Member file and the properties of the State field.

A data dictionary allows users to specify a default value for a field. A *default value* is a value that the DBMS initially displays in a field. If most members who join the warehouse club live in Indiana, then the DBMS initially could display IN in the State field. The user does not have to type in a default value. Displaying a default value reduces the possibility of errors. A user typically can override a default value if it does not apply for a certain record. For example, you can change the value from IN to OH if the member lives in Ohio.

File Retrieval and Maintenance

A DBMS provides several tools that allow users and programs to retrieve and maintain data in the database. As discussed earlier in this chapter, file maintenance involves adding new records, changing data in existing records, and removing unwanted records from the database.

To retrieve or select data in a database, you query it. A **query** is a request for specific data from the database. Users can instruct the DBMS to display, print, or store the results of a query. The capability of querying a database is one of the more powerful database features.

To meet the needs of a wide variety of database users, from trained experts to nontechnical staff, a DBMS offers several methods to retrieve and maintain its data. The four more commonly used are query languages, query by example, forms, and report generators. The following paragraphs describe each of these methods.

QUERY LANGUAGE A **query language** consists of simple, English-like statements that allow users to specify the data to display, print, or store. Each query language has its own grammar and vocabulary. A person without a programming background usually can learn a query language in a short time.

Although a query language can be used to maintain (add, change, and delete) data, most users only retrieve (query) data with a query language. To simplify the query process, many DBMSs provide wizards to guide users through the steps of creating a query. Figure 10-13 shows how to use the Simple Query Wizard in Microsoft Access to display the First Name, Last Name, and E-mail Address fields from the Member file.

Instead of using the Simple Query Wizard, you could enter the query language statement shown in Figure 10-13 directly in the DBMS to display the results shown in Step 3. Read Looking Ahead 10-1 for a look at the next generation of query languages.

QUERY BY EXAMPLE Most DBMSs include **query by example** (**QBE**), a feature that has a graphical user interface to assist users with retrieving data. Figure 10-14 shows a sample QBE screen for a query that searches for and lists members on the Basic Personal plan; that is, their Membership Code field value is equal to BP. Later in the chapter, specific query languages are presented in more depth.

WEB LINK 10-3

Data Dictionary

For more information, visit scsite.com/dc2006/ch10/weblink and then click Data Dictionary.

LOOKING AHEAD 10-1

Having a Voice with Web Databases

Travel agents, financial advisors, and other workers who routinely query databases may one day have a new tool to increase efficiency: their voices. The World Wide Web Consortium (W3C), which sets Web standards, has approved verbal technology that allows individuals to access Web pages by speaking on a telephone.

This standard, termed *VoiceXML (eXtensible Markup Language)*, can be used to create and access Internet databases, such as catalogs, stock quotations, and sports scores. More than 10,000 VoiceXML-based applications have been developed for such uses as customer care and directory assistance, according to the VoiceXML Forum.

The voice technology will be practical for people who are visually impaired or cannot use or are not located near a keyboard. For more information, visit scsite.com/dc2006/ch10/looking and then click VoiceXML.

FIGURE 10-13 HOW TO USE THE SIMPLE QUERY WIZARD

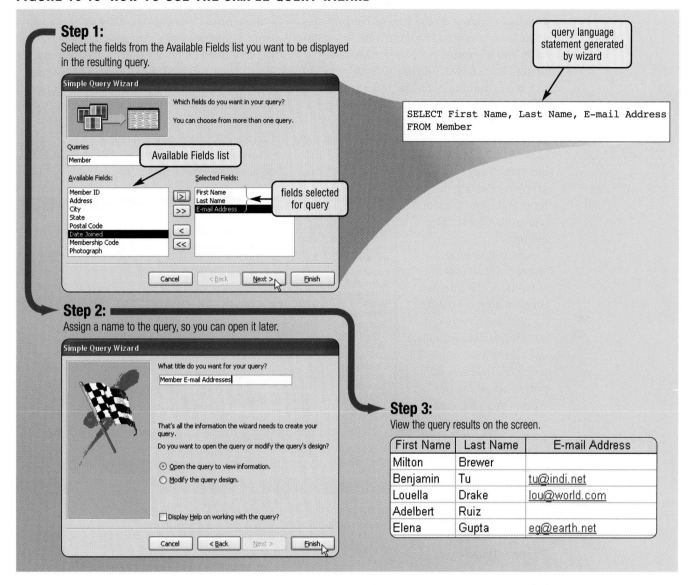

Step 1:
Select the fields from the Available Fields list you want to be displayed in the resulting query.

Available Fields list

fields selected for query

query language statement generated by wizard

```
SELECT First Name, Last Name, E-mail Address
FROM Member
```

Step 2:
Assign a name to the query, so you can open it later.

Step 3:
View the query results on the screen.

First Name	Last Name	E-mail Address
Milton	Brewer	
Benjamin	Tu	tu@indi.net
Louella	Drake	lou@world.com
Adelbert	Ruiz	
Elena	Gupta	eg@earth.net

FIGURE 10-14a (query by example screen)

	Last Name	Address	City	State	Postal Code	E-mail Address	Date Joined	Membership Code
								BP

criteria

FIGURE 10-14b (query results)

		Last Name	Address	City	State	Postal Code	E-mail Address	Date Joined	Membership Code
▶	+	Tu	76 Ash Street	Indianapolis	IN	46259	tu@indi.net	9/4/2007	BP
	+	Ruiz	99 Tenth Street	Carmel	IN	46033		10/8/2006	BP

Record: 1 of 2 (Filtered)

FIGURE 10-14 Access has many QBE capabilities. One QBE technique is Filter by Form, which uses a form to show available fields. The database program retrieves records that match criteria you enter in the form fields. This example searches for members whose Membership Code is equal to BP.

FORM A **form**, sometimes called a *data entry form*, is a window on the screen that provides areas for entering or changing data in a database. You use forms (such as the Member Maintenance form in Figure 10-5 on page 520) to retrieve and maintain the data in a database.

To reduce data entry errors, well-designed forms should validate data as it is entered. When designing a form using a DBMS, you can make the form attractive and easy to use by incorporating color, shading, lines, boxes, and graphics; varying the fonts and font styles; and using other formatting features.

A form that sends entered data across a network or the Internet is called an *e-form*, short for *electronic form* (Figure 10-15). E-forms generally use a means to secure the data while it is transported across the network. Often, the data in the e-form automatically enters in, or updates existing data in, a database on the network or the Internet. Thus, many DBMSs include the capability of creating e-forms.

Data Security

Sometimes, users accidentally delete the data from a database; others misuse the data intentionally (read At Issue 10-4 for a related discussion). Thus, a DBMS provides means to ensure that only authorized users access data at permitted times. In addition, most DBMSs allow different levels of access privileges to be identified for each field in the database. These access privileges define the actions that a specific user or group of users can perform.

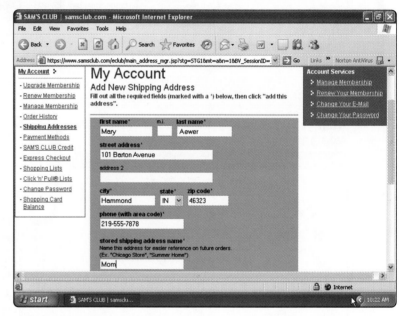

FIGURE 10-15 This e-form adds a shipping address to an online membership database.

REPORT GENERATOR A **report generator**, also called a *report writer*, allows users to design a report on the screen, retrieve data into the report design, and then display or print the report (Figure 10-16). Unlike a form, you use a report generator only to retrieve data. Report generators usually allow you to format page numbers and dates; titles and column headings; subtotals and totals; and fonts, font sizes, color, and shading.

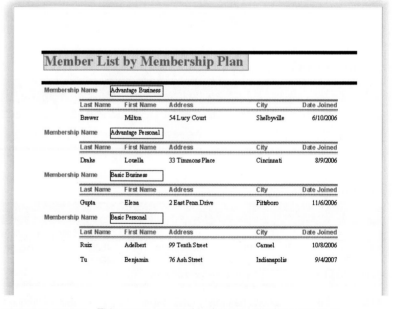

FIGURE 10-16 This report, created in Access, displays member information by the type of membership in which members are enrolled.

Who Should Be Granted Access to Student Records?

Most database management systems specify various access privileges. When a database is created, access policies are determined. Individuals may be granted no access privileges, read only privileges (data can be read but not changed), limited access privileges (only certain data can be read and/or changed), or full update privileges (all data can be read and changed). A student file, for example, contains each student's name, address, and grades, and also may contain data about ethnicity, gender, finances, family, health, activities, discipline, and so on. In a recent case, due to lax security and a simple desire to "see if it could be done," a student at a community college accessed and read all of the grades of students at the school. Being satisfied that he had done nothing wrong, the student did not alter any of the information. Using this situation as an example, what access privileges should be granted to the student, other students, faculty, administrators, financial aid officers, potential employers, and other outside groups? Explain your answers. Is it a crime to access confidential information without authorization? Why? Does it depend on the information? Does it depend on whether the information is altered? Does it depend on how the information is used? Would it be a crime for a student to access a school database of instructors' salaries? Why or why not?

Access privileges for data involve establishing who can enter new data, change existing data, delete unwanted data, and view data. In the Products file, a checkout clerk might have read-only privileges for product prices. That is, the clerk could view the prices, but cannot change them. An inventory manager, by contrast, would have full-update privileges to product data, meaning he or she can view and change the data. Finally, some users have no access privileges to the data; that is, they cannot view or change any data in the database. Chapter 11 discusses access privileges and other security techniques in more depth.

Backup and Recovery

Occasionally a database is damaged or destroyed because of hardware failure, a problem with the software, human error, or a catastrophe such as fire or flood. A DBMS provides a variety of techniques to restore the database to a usable form in case it is damaged or destroyed.

- A **backup**, or copy, of the entire database should be made on a regular basis. Some DBMSs have their own built-in backup utilities. Others require users to purchase a separate backup utility, or use one included with the operating system.
- More complex DBMSs maintain a **log**, which is a listing of activities that change the contents of the database. If a membership services associate modifies a member's address, for example, the change appears in the log. The DBMS places the following in the log: (1) a copy of the member record prior to the change, called the *before image* (Figure 10-17a); (2) the actual change of address data (Figure 10-17b); and (3) a copy of the member record after the change, called the *after image* (Figure 10-17c). The log also might store who made the change, when it was made, and from which computer it was made.

FIGURE 10-17a (before image)

FIGURE 10-17b (change)

FIGURE 10-17c (after image)

FIGURE 10-17 When the contents of a record are changed, the DBMS places three items in the log: the before image of the record, the actual change, and the after image of the record.

- A DBMS that creates a log usually provides a recovery utility. A **recovery utility** uses the logs and/or backups to restore a database when it becomes damaged or destroyed. The recovery utility restores the database using rollforward and rollback techniques. In a *rollforward*, also called *forward recovery*, the DBMS uses the log to reenter changes made to the database since the last save or backup. In a *rollback*, also called *backward recovery*, the DBMS uses the log to undo any changes made to the database during a certain period, such as an hour. The rollback restores the database to its condition prior to the failure. Then, users reenter any transactions entered after the failure.

Depending on the type of failure, the DBMS determines which type of recovery technique to use. For example, if the database is destroyed by a lightning strike, the DBMS would rollforward from the last backup. Assume, however, that a power failure happens at 3:15 p.m. and shuts down all computers, but does not destroy any data. Because some users may have been in the middle of entering transactions, the DBMS needs to undo any partial transactions. Thus, it would rollback the database to 3:00 p.m. and send a message to all users that they need to reenter any transactions made after that time.

WEB LINK 10-4

Backup and Recovery

For more information, visit scsite.com/ dc2006/ch10/weblink and then click Backup and Recovery.

Test your knowledge of pages 524 through 532 in Quiz Yourself 10-2.

QUIZ YOURSELF 10-2

Instructions: Find the true statement below. Then, rewrite the remaining false statements so they are true.

1. A DBMS is hardware that allows you to create, access, and manage an operating system.
2. A query contains data about files and fields in the database.
3. Backup and recovery procedures for data involve establishing who can enter new data, change existing data, delete unwanted data, and view data.
4. Strengths of the database approach include increased data redundancy, reduced data integrity, shared data, easier access, and increased development time.
5. To reduce data entry errors, well-designed forms should rollback data as it is entered.
6. Two major weaknesses of file processing systems are data redundancy and isolated data.

Quiz Yourself Online: To further check your knowledge of file processing systems versus databases and functions of a DBMS, visit scsite.com/ dc2006/ch10/quiz and then click Objectives 6 – 7.

RELATIONAL, OBJECT-ORIENTED, AND MULTIDIMENSIONAL DATABASES

Every database and DBMS is based on a specific data model. A **data model** consists of rules and standards that define how the database organizes data. A data model defines how users view the organization of the data. It does not define how the operating system actually arranges the data on the disk.

Three popular data models in use today are relational, object-oriented, and multidimensional. A database typically is based on one data model. For example, when using a relational database, users work with the relational data model. Some databases are called *object-relational databases* because they combine features of the relational and object-oriented data models.

The table in Figure 10-18 lists some popular DBMSs and the data model on which they are based. The following sections discuss the features of relational, object-oriented, and multidimensional databases.

DATA MODELS FOR POPULAR DBMSs

Data Model	Popular DBMSs
Relational	Access Adabas Informix Ingres InterBase MySQL SQL Server Sybase
Object-oriented	FastObjects GemFire KE Texpress ObjectStore Versant
Object-relational	DB2 JDataStore Oracle Polyhedra PostgreSQL Visual FoxPro
Multidimensional	D^3 Essbase Oracle Express

FIGURE 10-18 Four popular data models are relational, object-oriented, object-relational, and multidimensional. Most DBMSs are based on one of these models.

How big is the largest database?

The world's largest database stores more than 895 TB (trillion bytes) of physics data in about 850,000 files. It requires 2,000 processors and 100 servers. More than 600 physicists and engineers contribute to the database. For more information, visit scsite.com/dc2006/ch10/faq and then click World's Largest Database.

Relational Databases

Today, a relational database is a widely used type of database. A **relational database** is a database that stores data in tables that consist of rows and columns. Each row has a primary key and each column has a unique name.

As discussed earlier in this chapter, a file processing environment uses the terms file, record, and field to represent data. A relational database uses terms different from a file processing system. A developer of a relational database refers to a file as a *relation*, a record as a *tuple*, and a field as an *attribute*. A user of a relational database, by contrast, refers to a file as a **table**, a record as a **row**, and a field as a **column**. Figure 10-19 summarizes this varied terminology.

In addition to storing data, a relational database also stores data relationships. A **relationship** is a connection within the data. In a relational database, you can set up a relationship between tables at any time. The tables must have a common column (field). For example, you would relate the Member table and the Membership Plans table using the Membership Code column. Figure 10-20 illustrates these relational database concepts. In a relational database, the only data redundancy (duplication) exists in the common columns (fields). The database uses these common columns for relationships.

Applications best suited for relational databases are those whose data can be organized into a two-dimensional table. Many businesses use relational databases for payroll, accounts receivable, accounts payable, general ledger, inventory, order entry, invoicing, and other business-related functions.

DATA TERMINOLOGY

File Processing Environment	Relational Database Developer	Relational Database User
File	Relation	Table
Record	Tuple	Row
Field	Attribute	Column

FIGURE 10-19   In this data terminology table, the first column identifies the terms used in a file processing environment. The second column presents the terms used by developers of a relational database. The third column indicates terms to which the users of a relational database refer.

FIGURE 10-20   The Member table is linked to the Membership Plans table through the Membership Code column. The Member table is linked to the Member Purchases table through the Member ID column. The Products table is linked to the Member Purchases table through the Product ID column.

WEB LINK 10-5

Relational Databases

For more information, visit scsite.com/ dc2006/ch10/weblink and then click Relational Databases.

A developer of relational databases uses normalization to organize the data. *Normalization* is a process designed to ensure the data within the relations (tables) contains the least amount of duplication. For a technical discussion about normalization, read the High-Tech Talk article on page 540.

SQL Structured Query Language (**SQL**) is a query language that allows users to manage, update, and retrieve data. SQL has special keywords and rules that users include in SQL statements. For example, the SQL statement in Figure 10-21a shows how to write the join operation that creates the results shown in Figure 10-21b. The statement displays the First Name, Last Name, and Annual Fee fields in alphabetical order by last name for all records in the Member table.

Most relational database products for midrange servers and mainframes include SQL. Many personal computer databases also include SQL.

WEB LINK 10-6

SQL

For more information, visit scsite.com/ dc2006/ch10/weblink and then click SQL.

FIGURE 10-21a (SQL statement)

```
SELECT FIRST NAME, LAST NAME, ANNUAL FEE
FROM MEMBER, MEMBERSHIP PLANS
WHERE MEMBER.MEMBERSHIP CODE =
  MEMBERSHIP PLANS.MEMBERSHIP CODE
ORDER BY LAST NAME
```

FIGURE 10-21b (SQL statement results)

First Name	Last Name	Annual Fee
Milton	Brewer	$90.00
Louella	Drake	$40.00
Elena	Gupta	$55.00
Adelbert	Ruiz	$25.00
Benjamin	Tu	$25.00

FIGURE 10-21 A sample SQL statement and its results.

Object-Oriented Databases

An **object-oriented database** (**OODB**) stores data in objects. An **object** is an item that contains data, as well as the actions that read or process the data. A Member object, for example, might contain data about a member such as Member ID, First Name, Last Name, Address, and so on. It also could contain instructions about how to print the member record or the formula required to calculate a member's balance due. A record in a relational database, by contrast, would contain only data about a member.

WEB LINK 10-7

Object-Oriented Databases

For more information, visit scsite.com/ dc2006/ch10/weblink and then click Object-Oriented Databases.

Object-oriented databases have several advantages compared with relational databases: they can store more types of data, access this data faster, and allow programmers to reuse objects. An object-oriented database stores unstructured data more efficiently than a relational database. Unstructured data includes photographs, video clips, audio clips, and documents. When users query an object-oriented database, the results often are displayed more quickly than the same query of a relational database. If an object already exists, programmers can reuse it instead of recreating a new object — saving on program development time.

Examples of applications appropriate for an object-oriented database include the following:

- A *multimedia database* stores images, audio clips, and/or video clips. For example, a geographic information system (GIS) database stores maps. A voice mail system database stores audio messages. A television news station database stores audio and video clips.

- A *groupware database* stores documents such as schedules, calendars, manuals, memos, and reports. Users perform queries to search the document contents. For example, you can search people's schedules for available meeting times.

- A *computer-aided design* (CAD) *database* stores data about engineering, architectural, and scientific designs. Data in the database includes a list of components of the item being designed, the relationship among the components, and previous versions of the design drafts.

- A *hypertext database* contains text links to other types of documents. A *hypermedia database* contains text, graphics, video, and sound. The Web contains a variety of hypertext and hypermedia databases. You can search these databases for items such as documents, graphics, audio and video clips (Figure 10-22), and links to Web pages.

- A *Web database* links to an e-form on a Web page. The Web browser sends and receives data between the form and the database. A later section in this chapter discusses Web databases in more depth.

FIGURE 10-22 This hypermedia database stores pictures of cars for sale and show.

OBJECT QUERY LANGUAGE Object-oriented and object-relational databases often use a query language called *object query language* (*OQL*) to manipulate and retrieve data. OQL is similar to SQL. OQL and SQL use many of the same rules, grammar, and keywords. Because OQL is a relatively new query language, not all object databases support it.

Multidimensional Databases

A **multidimensional database** stores data in dimensions. Whereas a relational database is a two-dimensional table, a multidimensional database can store more than two dimensions of data. These multiple dimensions, sometimes known as a *hypercube*, allow users to access and analyze any view of the database data.

A Webmaster at a retailing business may want information about product sales and customer sales for each region spanning a given time. A manager at the same business may want information about product sales by department for each sales representative spanning a given time. A multidimensional database can consolidate this type of data from multiple dimensions at very high rates of speed.

The number of dimensions in a multidimensional database varies. A retailing business might have four dimensions: products, customers, regions, and time. A multidimensional database for a hospital procedure could have six dimensions: time, procedure type, patient, hospital, physician, and diagnosis. A multidimensional database for an insurance policy may include five dimensions: time, policy type, agent, customer, and coverage. Nearly every multidimensional database has a dimension of time. The content of other dimensions varies depending on the subject.

The key advantage of the multidimensional database is that it can consolidate data much faster than a relational database. A relational database typically does not process and summarize large numbers of records efficiently. With a multidimensional database, users obtain summarized results very quickly. For example, a query that takes minutes or hours to execute in a relational database will take only seconds to execute in a multidimensional database.

No standard query language exists for multidimensional databases. Each database uses its own language. Most are similar to SQL.

WEB LINK 10-8

Multidimensional Databases

For more information, visit scsite.com/dc2006/ch10/weblink and then click Multidimensional Databases.

DATA WAREHOUSES   One application that uses multidimensional databases is a data warehouse. A **data warehouse** is a huge database that stores and manages the data required to analyze historical and current transactions. Through a data warehouse, managers and other users access transactions and summaries of transactions quickly and efficiently. Some major credit card companies monitor and manage customers' credit card transactions using a data warehouse. Additionally, consumers can access their own transactions in the data warehouse via the Web. A data warehouse typically has a user-friendly interface, so users easily can interact with its data.

The databases in a data warehouse usually are quite large. Often, the database is distributed. The data in a *distributed database* exists in many separate locations throughout a network or the Internet. The data is accessible through a single server. The data's location is transparent to the user, who usually is unaware that the data is stored in multiple servers.

Data warehouses often use a process called *data mining* to find patterns and relationships among data. A state government could mine through data to check if the number of births

has a relationship to income level. Many e-commerce sites use data mining to determine customer preferences.

A smaller version of a data warehouse is the *data mart*. A data mart contains a database that helps a specific group or department make decisions. Marketing and sales departments may have their own separate data marts. Individual groups or departments often extract data from the data warehouse to create their data marts.

WEB DATABASES

One of the more profound features of the Web is the vast amount of information it provides. The Web offers information about jobs, travel destinations, television programming, movies and videos (Figure 10-23), local and national weather, sporting events, legislative information, and movies. You can shop for just about any product or service, buy or sell stocks, search for a job, and make airline reservations. Much of this and other information on the Web exists in databases. Read At Issue 10-5 for a related discussion.

FIGURE 10-23   Through the Internet Movie Database (IMDb) Web site, users can access a huge database loaded with content about current and classic movies.

Can the Government Be Trusted with Personal Data?

Despite laws, policies, and procedures to the contrary, a New York state government subcontractor posted a confidential database containing information about children involved in various government programs. The database remained on the Web until a news organization notified the state of the security breach. In another case of government mishandling data, a judge ordered all of the Web sites of the Interior Department to be shut down for 10 weeks because a database system handling billions of dollars of payments to Native Americans was found to be vulnerable to hackers. In a recent survey, concern over many well-publicized security lapses and computer crime incidents resulted in 63 percent of adults being less likely to provide personal information to the government. In addition, 81 percent worried about the government misusing the information. Because of the volumes of information kept by the government in massive databases, the lack of resources, and an increase in outsourcing work to subcontractors, information is increasingly insecure in many government agencies. Who should be held accountable for lapses in security? Why? Should governments be limited in any way in the amount of information they store, types of information they store, or the duration for which they store the information? Why or why not?

To access data in a Web database, you fill in a form on a Web page. The Web page is the front end to the database. Many search engines such as Yahoo! use databases to store Web site descriptions. Thus, the search engine's home page is the front end to the database. To access the database, you enter search text into the search engine.

A Web database usually resides on a database server. A *database server* is a computer that stores and provides access to a database. One type of program that manages the sending and receiving of data between the front end and the database server is a *CGI* (*Common Gateway Interface*) script. CGI scripts run automatically — as soon as you click the button to send or receive information. Writing a CGI script requires computer programming skills.

In addition to accessing information, users provide information to Web databases. Many Web sites request users to enter personal information, such as name, address, telephone number, and preferences, into an e-form. The database then stores this personal information for future use. A company, for example, may send e-mail messages to certain groups of customers. If you are a frequent flyer, you may receive travel information.

For smaller databases, many personal computer database programs provide a variety of Web publishing tools. Microsoft FrontPage, for example, has a Database Results Wizard that requires no computer programming. The wizard publishes a Web page that links to your existing database such as a Microsoft Access or Oracle database.

DATABASE ADMINISTRATION

Managing a company's database requires a great deal of coordination. The role of coordinating the use of the database belongs to the database analysts and administrators. To carry out their responsibilities, these IT (information technology) professionals follow database design guidelines and need cooperation from all database users.

Database Design Guidelines

A carefully designed database makes it easier for a user to query the database, modify the data, and create reports. The guidelines shown in Figure 10-24 apply to databases of all sizes.

DATABASE DESIGN GUIDELINES

1. Determine the purpose of the database.
2. Design the tables.
   - Design tables on paper first.
   - Each table should contain data about one subject. The Member table, for example, contains data about members.
3. Design the records and fields for each table.
   - Be sure every record has a unique primary key.
   - Use separate fields for logically distinct items. For example, a name could be stored in six fields: Title (Mr., Mrs., Dr., etc.), First Name, Middle Name, Last Name, Suffix (Jr., Sr., etc.), and Nickname.
   - Do not create fields for information that can be derived from entries in other fields. For example, do not include a field for Age. Instead, store the birthdate and compute the age.
   - Allow enough space for each field.
   - Set default values for frequently entered data.
4. Determine the relationships among the tables.

FIGURE 10-24 Guidelines for developing a database.

Role of the Database Analysts and Administrators

The database analysts and administrators are responsible for managing and coordinating all database activities. The **database analyst (DA)**, or *data modeler*, focuses on the meaning and usage of data. The DA decides on the proper placement of fields, defines the relationships among data, and identifies users' access privileges. The **database administrator (DBA)** requires a more technical inside view of the data. The DBA creates and maintains the data dictionary, manages security of the database, monitors the performance of the database, and checks backup and recovery procedures.

In small companies, one person often is both the DA and DBA. In larger companies, the responsibilities of the DA and DBA are split among two or more people.

FAQ 10-6

Does DBA have two meanings?

Yes; DBA stands for either database administration or database administrator. The first, database administration, is the act of managing a database. The second, database administrator, is the person who manages the database. For more information, visit scsite.com/dc2006/ch10/faq and then click DBA.

Role of the Employee as a User

Employees should learn how to use the data in the database effectively. The amount of information available often amazes first-time database users. Instant access to this information helps employees perform their jobs more effectively. For example, assume a car backed into your parked car. You call your insurance agent to find out where to repair your car. The agent instantly reads to you a list of authorized car repair shops in your area. Today, employees access databases from their office desktop computers, notebook computers, or even smart phones and PDAs (Figure 10-25).

Employees also must take an active role in identifying new data for the database. For example, maybe the insurance agent does not have access to the list of car repair shops on the computer. Instead, the agent looks them up in the telephone book. The agent's job would be much easier if this information was available on the computer.

The maintenance of a database is an ongoing task that companies measure constantly against their overall goals. Users can take part in designing the database that will help them achieve those goals.

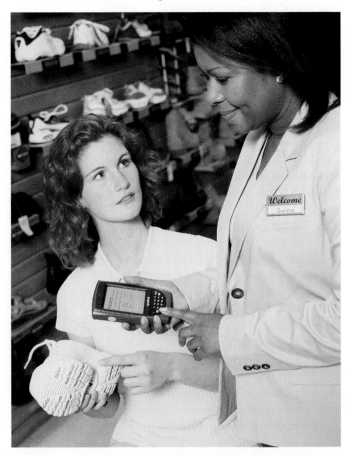

FIGURE 10-25 This sales clerk checks inventory to see if the requested shoe size is in inventory.

Test your knowledge of pages 532 through 538 in Quiz Yourself 10-3.

QUIZ YOURSELF 10-3

Instructions: Find the true statement below. Then, rewrite the remaining false statements so they are true.

1. Data warehouses often use a process called OQL to find patterns and relationships among data.

2. Object-oriented databases store data in tables.

3. One type of program that manages the sending and receiving of data between the front end and the database server is a CGI script.

4. Relational database users refer to a file as a table, a record as a column, and a field as a row.

5. SQL is a data modeling language that allows users to manage, update, and retrieve data.

6. The database analyst requires a more technical inside view of the data than does the database administrator.

Quiz Yourself Online: To further check your knowledge of relational, object-oriented, and multidimensional databases; Web databases; and database administration, visit scsite.com/dc2006/ch10/quiz and then click Objectives 8 – 10.

CHAPTER SUMMARY

This chapter discussed how data and information are valuable assets to an organization (read Looking Ahead 10-2 for a look at the next generation of preserving data and information). The chapter also presented methods for maintaining high-quality data and assessing the quality of valuable information. It then discussed the advantages of organizing data in a database and described various types of databases. It also presented the roles of the database analysts and administrators.

LOOKING AHEAD 10-2

Preserving Electronic Files for Future Generations

Historians and researchers are concerned that Web content and rare and unique electronic works may be lost forever because they exist only in digital form.

In an attempt to gather, organize, and preserve digital files, the United States Congress approved the *National Digital Information Infrastructure & Preservation Program* and commissioned The Library of Congress to supervise the project. Six digital formats have been identified: large Web sites, electronic journals, electronic books, digitally recorded sound, digital moving images, and digital television.

Library officials have partnered with industry and educational experts to discuss how to create and maintain the database. In addition, the National Science Foundation has awarded research grants to address these preservation issues. For more information, visit scsite.com/dc2006/ch10/looking and then click Preservation.

CAREER CORNER

Database Administrator

Most businesses and organizations are built around databases. Access to timely, accurate, and relevant information is a company's lifeline. A database administrator (DBA) creates, applies, supports, and administers the policies and procedures for maintaining a company's database. Database administrators construct logical and physical descriptions of the database, establish database parameters, develop data models characterizing data elements, ensure database integrity, and coordinate database security measures including developing and implementing disaster recovery and archiving procedures. They also use query languages to obtain reports of the information in the database. With the large amounts of sensitive data generated, data integrity, backup, and security have become increasingly important aspects of the administrator's responsibilities.

Administering a database requires a great deal of mental work and the ability to focus on finite details. Database administrators must be able to read and comprehend business related information, organize data in a logical manner, apply general rules to specific problems, identify business principles and practices, and communicate clearly with database users. Being proficient with a particular database such as Oracle, Informix, or SQL Server is an added advantage. The real key, however, is learning, understanding, and becoming an expert in database design.

Database administrators usually have a bachelor or associate degree and experience with computer programming, relational databases, query languages, and online analytical processing. Typical salaries for database administrators are between $69,000 and $95,000, depending on experience. For more information, visit scsite.com/dc2006/ch10/careers and then click Database Administrator.

High-Tech Talk

ENSURE CONSISTENCY OF YOUR DATA WITH NORMALIZATION

Normalization organizes a database into one of several normal forms to remove ambiguous relationships between data and minimize data redundancy. In *zero normal form* (*0NF*), the database is completely nonnormalized, and all of the data fields are included in one relation or table. Repeating groups are listed within parentheses (Figure 10-26a). The table has large rows due to the repeating groups and wastes disk space when an order has only one item.

To normalize the data from 0NF to *1NF* (*first normal form*), you remove the repeating groups (fields 3 through 7 and 8 through 12) and place them in a second table (Figure 10-26b). You then assign a primary key to the second table (Line Item), by combining the primary key of the nonrepeating group (Order #) with the primary key of the repeating group (Product #). Primary keys are underlined to distinguish them from other fields.

To further normalize the database from 1NF to *2NF* (*second normal form*), you remove partial dependencies. A *partial dependency* exists when fields in the table depend on only part of the primary key. In the Line Item table (Figure 10-26b), Product Name is dependent on Product #, which is only part of the primary key. Second normal form requires you to place the product information in a separate Product table to remove the partial dependency (Figure 10-26c).

To move from 2NF to *3NF* (*third normal form*), you move transitive dependencies. A *transitive dependency* exists when a nonprimary key field depends on another nonprimary key field. As shown in Figure 10-26c, Vendor Name is dependent on Vendor #, both of which are nonprimary key fields. If Vendor Name is left in the Order table, the database will store redundant data each time a product is ordered from the same vendor.

Third normal form requires Vendor Name to be placed in a separate Vendor table, with Vendor # as the primary key. The field that is the primary key in the new table — in this case, Vendor # — also remains in the original table as a *foreign key* and is identified by a dotted underline (Figure 10-26d). In 3NF, the database now is logically organized in four separate tables and is easier to maintain. For instance, to add, delete, or change a Vendor or Product Name, you make the change in just one table. For more information, visit scsite.com/dc2006/ch10/tech and then click Normalization.

FIGURE 10-26
The process of normalizing a database.

Order Table

				repeating group I				repeating group II			
Order #	Order Date	Product #	Product Name	Qty Ordered	Vendor #	Vendor Name	Product #	Product Name	Qty Ordered	Vendor #	Vendor Name
1001	6/8/2006	605	8.5" x 11" White Copy Paper	2	321	Hammermill	203	CD Jewel Cases	5	110	Fellowes
1002	6/10/2006	751	Ballpoint Pens	6	166	Pilot					
1003	6/10/2006	321	1" Ring Binder, Blue	12	450	Globe					
1004	6/11/2006	605	8.5" x 11" White Copy Paper	2	321	Hammermill	102	Interior File Folders	2	450	Globe

(a) Zero Normal Form (0NF)
(Order #, Order Date, (Product #, Product Name, Quantity Ordered, Vendor #, Vendor Name))

(b) First Normal Form (1NF)
Order (Order #, Order Date)
Line Item (Order # + Product #, Product Name, Quantity Ordered, Vendor #, Vendor Name)

(c) Second Normal Form (2NF)
Order (Order #, Order Date)
Line Item (Order # + Product #, Quantity Ordered, Vendor #, Vendor Name)
Product (Product #, Product Name)

(d) Third Normal Form (3NF)
Order (Order #, Order Date)
Line Item (Order # + Product #, Quantity Ordered, Vendor #)
Product (Product #, Product Name)
Vendor (Vendor #, Vendor Name)

Order

Order #	Order Date
1001	6/8/2006
1002	6/10/2006
1003	6/10/2006
1004	6/11/2006

Line Item

Order # + Product #	Qty Ordered	Vendor #
1001605	2	321
1001203	5	110
1002751	6	166
1003321	12	450
1004605	2	321
1004102	2	450

Product

Product #	Product Name
102	Interior File Folders
203	CD Jewel Cases
321	1" Ring Binder, Blue
605	8.5" x 11" White Copy Paper
751	Ballpoint Pens

Vendor

Vendor #	Vendor Name
110	Fellowes
166	Pilot
321	Hammermill
450	Globe

Companies on the Cutting Edge

ORACLE
DATABASE SOFTWARE DEVELOPER

More than half of the FORTUNE 100 companies use an *Oracle* product as their primary database, but Oracle's quest, according to CEO Larry Ellison, is to have its customers convert all their database applications to Oracle's software.

Ellison and two partners founded the company in 1977 with the intent of developing a commercially viable relational database. When their Oracle database was released, it was an immediate success and changed the way companies stored and managed information. For the first time, separate data tables could be connected by a common field.

The company is the world's second largest independent software company behind Microsoft. With the recent $10.3 billion acquisition of PeopleSoft, Oracle also will control 25 percent of the corporate application-software market. For more information, visit scsite.com/dc2006/ch10/companies and then click Oracle.

SYBASE
MANAGING DATA FOR THE UNWIRED ENTERPRISE

Researchers at the University of California, Berkeley, estimate that 95 percent of the data produced by major corporations never is used after it is stored in a database because it is disorganized and inaccessible.

Sybase helps companies unlock and use this data whenever and wherever needed through its unwired enterprise. This data access solution helps mobile database users tap into corporate networks, often wirelessly. The company focuses especially on Enterprise Portal (EP) solutions, which convert stored data into information that can be used by customers, partners, and suppliers.

For more than 20 years, Sybase has produced software that links platforms, servers, databases, applications, and mobile devices. Many of its customers are part of the financial services, telecommunications, and health care professions. For more information, visit scsite.com/dc2006/ch10/companies and then click Sybase.

Technology Trailblazers

E. F. CODD
RELATIONAL DATABASE MODEL INVENTOR

The majority of large and small databases are structured on the relational model, which is considered one of the greatest technological inventions of the 20th Century. *E. F. Codd* single-handedly is credited with developing and promoting that model in a series of research papers beginning with his 1969 IBM Research Report, "Derivability, Redundancy, and Consistency of Relations Stored in Large Data Banks."

Edgar F. Codd began his career in 1949 when he joined IBM as a programming mathematician after graduating from Oxford University. Throughout the 1950s he helped develop several IBM computers and then turned his attention to database management. Among his achievements is earning the prestigious A. M. Turing Award, which is the Association for Computing Machinery's highest technical achievement honor given to an individual, for his relational database theory. For more information, visit scsite.com/dc2006/ch10/people and then click E. F. Codd.

LARRY ELLISON
ORACLE CEO

On a visit to Kyoto, Japan, *Larry Ellison* became intrigued with the country's culture and the citizens' combination of confidence and humility. He says he applies these philosophical principles to his work at Oracle, where he serves as CEO.

As a young man, Ellison was interested in science and mathematics. He was inspired by E. F. Codd's relational database model and founded Oracle in 1977 under the name Software Development Laboratories with a $1,200 investment.

Under Ellison's leadership, the company doubled its sales in 11 of its first 12 years. He is known for his uncanny ability to motivate his employees and business partners toward a common goal, including a demand for a 100 percent growth in his company's software sales. For more information, visit scsite.com/dc2006/ch10/people and then click Larry Ellison.

s the concepts presented in this chapter. To listen to the audio
ite.com/dc2006/ch10/review. To obtain help from other students
sit scsite.com/dc2006/ch10/forum and post your thoughts or

se is a collection of data organized in a manner that allows
Database software, often called a **database management**
e a computerized database; add, change, and delete the data;
orms and reports from the data.

able Information? *Data* can include text, numbers, images,
data into information. *Information* is processed data; that is, it
For information to be valuable, it should be accurate,
le, useful, and cost-effective.

Organization? Because data is used to generate information,
many companies realize that data is one of their more valuable assets. *Data integrity* identifies the
quality of data. Data integrity is important because computers and people use information to make
decisions and take actions. For a computer to produce correct information, the data that is entered
in a database must have integrity.

(4) **What Is Meant by Character, Field, Record, and File?** Data is classified in a hierarchy,
with each level of data consisting of one or more items from the lower level. A bit is the smallest
unit of data a computer can process. Eight bits grouped together in a unit form a byte, and each
byte represents a single **character**. A **field** is a combination of one or more related characters and
is the smallest unit of data a user accesses. A **record** is a group of related fields. A **data file** is a
collection of related records stored on a storage medium such as a hard disk, CD, or DVD.

(5) **How Are Files Maintained?** **File maintenance** refers to the procedures that keep data
current. File maintenance procedures include adding records when new data is obtained, changing
records to correct inaccurate data or to update old data with new data, and deleting records when
they no longer are needed. **Validation** is the process of comparing data with a set of rules or values
to find out if the data is correct. Many programs perform a *validity
check* that analyzes entered data to help ensure that it is correct.
Types of validity checks include an *alphabetic check*, a *numeric
check*, a *range check*, a *consistency check*, a *completeness check*, and a
check digit.

connect

Visit scsite.com/dc2006/ch10/quiz
or click the Quiz Yourself button. Click
Objectives 1 – 5.

(6) **How Is a File Processing System Approach Different from the Database Approach?**
In a **file processing system**, each department or area within an organization has its own set of data
files. Two major weaknesses of file processing systems are redundant data (duplicated data) and
isolated data. With a **database approach**, many programs and users share the data in a database.
The database approach reduces data redundancy, improves data integrity, shares data, permits easier access, and reduces development time. A database, however, can be more complex than a file
processing system, requiring special training and more computer memory, storage, and processing
power. Data in a database also is more vulnerable than data in file processing systems.

(7) **What Functions Are Common to Most DBMSs?** Most DBMSs perform common
functions. A **data dictionary** contains data about each file in the database and each field within
those files. A DBMS offers several methods to maintain and retrieve data, such as query languages,
query by example, forms, and report generators. A **query language** consists of simple, English-like

Companies on the Cutting Edge

ORACLE
DATABASE SOFTWARE DEVELOPER

More than half of the FORTUNE 100 companies use an *Oracle* product as their primary database, but Oracle's quest, according to CEO Larry Ellison, is to have its customers convert all their database applications to Oracle's software.

Ellison and two partners founded the company in 1977 with the intent of developing a commercially viable relational database. When their Oracle database was released, it was an immediate success and changed the way companies stored and managed information. For the first time, separate data tables could be connected by a common field.

The company is the world's second largest independent software company behind Microsoft. With the recent $10.3 billion acquisition of PeopleSoft, Oracle also will control 25 percent of the corporate application-software market. For more information, visit scsite.com/dc2006/ch10/companies and then click Oracle.

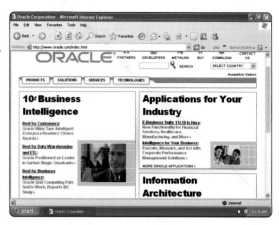

SYBASE
MANAGING DATA FOR THE UNWIRED ENTERPRISE

Researchers at the University of California, Berkeley, estimate that 95 percent of the data produced by major corporations never is used after it is stored in a database because it is disorganized and inaccessible.

Sybase helps companies unlock and use this data whenever and wherever needed through its unwired enterprise. This data access solution helps mobile database users tap into corporate networks, often wirelessly. The company focuses especially on Enterprise Portal (EP) solutions, which convert stored data into information that can be used by customers, partners, and suppliers.

For more than 20 years, Sybase has produced software that links platforms, servers, databases, applications, and mobile devices. Many of its customers are part of the financial services, telecommunications, and health care professions. For more information, visit scsite.com/dc2006/ch10/companies and then click Sybase.

Technology Trailblazers

E. F. CODD
RELATIONAL DATABASE MODEL INVENTOR

The majority of large and small databases are structured on the relational model, which is considered one of the greatest technological inventions of the 20th Century. *E. F. Codd* single-handedly is credited with developing and promoting that model in a series of research papers beginning with his 1969 IBM Research Report, "Derivability, Redundancy, and Consistency of Relations Stored in Large Data Banks."

Edgar F. Codd began his career in 1949 when he joined IBM as a programming mathematician after graduating from Oxford University. Throughout the 1950s he helped develop several IBM computers and then turned his attention to database management. Among his achievements is earning the prestigious A. M. Turing Award, which is the Association for Computing Machinery's highest technical achievement honor given to an individual, for his relational database theory. For more information, visit scsite.com/dc2006/ch10/people and then click E. F. Codd.

LARRY ELLISON
ORACLE CEO

On a visit to Kyoto, Japan, *Larry Ellison* became intrigued with the country's culture and the citizens' combination of confidence and humility. He says he applies these philosophical principles to his work at Oracle, where he serves as CEO.

As a young man, Ellison was interested in science and mathematics. He was inspired by E. F. Codd's relational database model and founded Oracle in 1977 under the name Software Development Laboratories with a $1,200 investment.

Under Ellison's leadership, the company doubled its sales in 11 of its first 12 years. He is known for his uncanny ability to motivate his employees and business partners toward a common goal, including a demand for a 100 percent growth in his company's software sales. For more information, visit scsite.com/dc2006/ch10/people and then click Larry Ellison.

Chapter Review

The Chapter Review section summarizes the concepts presented in this chapter. To listen to the audio version of this Chapter Review, visit scsite.com/dc2006/ch10/review. To obtain help from other students regarding any subject in this chapter, visit scsite.com/dc2006/ch10/forum and post your thoughts or questions.

① What Is a Database?   A **database** is a collection of data organized in a manner that allows access, retrieval, and use of that data. **Database software**, often called a **database management system** (**DBMS**), allows users to create a computerized database; add, change, and delete the data; sort and retrieve the data; and create forms and reports from the data.

② What Are the Qualities of Valuable Information?   *Data* can include text, numbers, images, audio, and video. Computers process data into information. *Information* is processed data; that is, it is organized, meaningful, and useful. For information to be valuable, it should be accurate, verifiable, timely, organized, accessible, useful, and cost-effective.

③ Why Is Data Important to an Organization?   Because data is used to generate information, many companies realize that data is one of their more valuable assets. *Data integrity* identifies the quality of data. Data integrity is important because computers and people use information to make decisions and take actions. For a computer to produce correct information, the data that is entered in a database must have integrity.

④ What Is Meant by Character, Field, Record, and File?   Data is classified in a hierarchy, with each level of data consisting of one or more items from the lower level. A bit is the smallest unit of data a computer can process. Eight bits grouped together in a unit form a byte, and each byte represents a single **character**. A **field** is a combination of one or more related characters and is the smallest unit of data a user accesses. A **record** is a group of related fields. A **data file** is a collection of related records stored on a storage medium such as a hard disk, CD, or DVD.

⑤ How Are Files Maintained?   **File maintenance** refers to the procedures that keep data current. File maintenance procedures include adding records when new data is obtained, changing records to correct inaccurate data or to update old data with new data, and deleting records when they no longer are needed. **Validation** is the process of comparing data with a set of rules or values to find out if the data is correct. Many programs perform a *validity check* that analyzes entered data to help ensure that it is correct. Types of validity checks include an *alphabetic check*, a *numeric check*, a *range check*, a *consistency check*, a *completeness check*, and a *check digit*.

Visit scsite.com/dc2006/ch10/quiz or click the Quiz Yourself button. Click Objectives 1 – 5.

⑥ How Is a File Processing System Approach Different from the Database Approach? In a **file processing system**, each department or area within an organization has its own set of data files. Two major weaknesses of file processing systems are redundant data (duplicated data) and isolated data. With a **database approach**, many programs and users share the data in a database. The database approach reduces data redundancy, improves data integrity, shares data, permits easier access, and reduces development time. A database, however, can be more complex than a file processing system, requiring special training and more computer memory, storage, and processing power. Data in a database also is more vulnerable than data in file processing systems.

⑦ What Functions Are Common to Most DBMSs?   Most DBMSs perform common functions. A **data dictionary** contains data about each file in the database and each field within those files. A DBMS offers several methods to maintain and retrieve data, such as query languages, query by example, forms, and report generators. A **query language** consists of simple, English-like

Chapter Review

statements that allow users to specify the data to display, print, or store. **Query by example (QBE)** has a graphical user interface that assists users with retrieving data. A **form** is a window on the screen that provides areas for entering or changing data. A **report generator** allows users to design a report on the screen, retrieve data into the report design, and then display or print the report. To supply security, most DBMSs can identify different levels of *access privileges* that define the actions a specific user or group of users can perform for each field in a database. If a database is damaged or destroyed, a DBMS provides techniques to return the database to a usable form. A **backup** is a copy of the database. A **log** is a listing of activities that change the contents of the database. A **recovery utility** uses the logs and/or backups to restore the database.

connect
Visit scsite.com/dc2006/ch10/quiz or click the Quiz Yourself button. Click Objectives 6 – 7.

(8) **What Are Characteristics of Relational, Object-Oriented, and Multidimensional Databases?** A **data model** consists of rules and standards that define how the database organizes data. Three popular data models are relational, object-oriented, and multidimensional. A **relational database** stores data in tables that consist of rows and columns. A relational database developer refers to a file as a *relation*, a record as a *tuple*, and a field as an *attribute*. A relational database user refers to a file as a **table**, a record as a **row**, and a field as a **column**. A **relationship** is a connection within the data in a relational database. **Structured Query Language (SQL)** allows users to manage, update, and retrieve data. An **object-oriented database (OODB)** stores data in objects. An **object** is an item that contains data, as well as the actions that read or process the data. Applications appropriate for an object-oriented database include a *multimedia database*, a *groupware database*, a *computer-aided design* (*CAD*) *database*, a *hypertext database*, a *hypermedia database*, and a *Web database*. Object-oriented databases often use an *object query language* (*OQL*) to manipulate and retrieve data. A **multidimensional database** stores data in dimensions. These multiple dimensions, sometimes known as a *hypercube*, allow users to access and analyze any view of the database data. One application that uses multidimensional databases is a **data warehouse**, which is a huge database that stores and manages the data required to analyze historical and current transactions. No standard query language exists for multidimensional databases.

(9) **How Do Web Databases Work?** To access data in a *Web database*, you fill in a form on a Web page, which is the *front end* to the database. A Web database usually resides on a *database server*, which is a computer that stores and provides access to a database. One type of program that manages the sending and receiving of data between the front end and the database is a *CGI* (*Common Gateway Interface*) *script*.

(10) **What Are the Responsibilities of Database Analysts and Administrators?** A **database analyst (DA)**, or *data modeler*, focuses on the meaning and usage of data. The DA decides on the placement of fields, defines data relationships, and identifies access privileges. A **database administrator (DBA)** requires a more technical view of the data. The DBA creates and maintains the data dictionary, manages database security, monitors database performance, and checks backup and recovery procedures.

connect
Visit scsite.com/dc2006/ch10/quiz or click the Quiz Yourself button. Click Objectives 8 – 10.

Quizzes and Learning Games

Computer Genius
Crossword Puzzle
DC Track and Field
Practice Test
Quiz Yourself
Wheel of Terms
You're Hired!

Exercises

Case Studies
Chapter Review
Checkpoint
▶ Key Terms
Learn How To
Learn It Online
Web Research

Beyond the Book

Career Corner
Companies
FAQs
High-Tech Talk
Looking Ahead
Making Use of the Web
Trailblazers
Web Links

Features

Chapter Forum
Install Computer
Lab Exercises
Maintain Computer
Tech News
Timeline 2006

Key Terms

You should know the Primary Terms and be familiar with the Secondary Terms. Use the list below to help focus your study. To further enhance your understanding of the Key Terms in this chapter, visit scsite.com/dc2006/ch10/terms. See an example of and a definition for each term, and access current and additional information about the term from the Web.

Primary Terms

(shown in bold-black characters in the chapter)

backup (531)
character (518)
column (533)
data dictionary (527)
data file (519)
data model (532)
data type (518)
data warehouse (536)
database (514)
database administrator (DBA) (538)
database analyst (DA) (538)
database approach (524)
database management system (DBMS) (515)
database software (515)
field (518)
field name (518)
field size (518)
file maintenance (520)
file processing system (524)
form (530)

key field (519)
log (531)
multidimensional database (535)
object (534)
object-oriented database (OODB) (534)
primary key (519)
query (528)
query by example (QBE) (528)
query language (528)
record (519)
recovery utility (532)
relational database (533)
relationship (533)
report generator (530)
row (533)
Structured Query Language (SQL) (534)
table (533)
validation (522)

Secondary Terms

(shown in italic characters in the chapter)

access privileges (531)
accessible information (516)
accurate information (516)
after image (531)
alphabetic check (523)
alphanumeric (518)
attribute (533)
back end (525)
backward recovery (532)
before image (531)
BLOB (518)
Boolean (518)
CGI (Common Gateway Interface) script (537)
check digit (523)
completeness check (523)
computer-aided design (CAD) database (534)
consistency check (523)
cost-effective information (517)
data (514)
data entry form (530)
data integrity (516)
data mart (536)
data mining (536)
data modeler (538)
database server (537)
default value (528)
distributed database (536)
e-form (530)
electronic form (530)

forward recovery (532)
front end (525)
garbage in, garbage out (GIGO) (516)
groupware database (534)
hypercube (535)
hypermedia database (534)
hypertext database (534)
information (514)
metadata (527)
multimedia database (534)
normalization (534)
numeric check (523)
object query language (OQL) (535)
object-relational databases (532)
organized information (516)
range check (523)
relation (533)
report writer (530)
repository (527)
rollback (532)
rollforward (532)
timely information (516)
tuple (533)
useful information (517)
validation rules (522)
validity check (522)
verifiable information (516)
Web database (534)

Checkpoint

Use the Checkpoint exercises to check your knowledge level of the chapter. The Beyond the Book exercises will help broaden your understanding of the concepts presented in this chapter. To complete the Checkpoint exercises interactively, visit scsite.com/dc2006/ch10/check.

Label the Figure

Identify the database elements.

a. column

b. relationships

c. table

d. row

True/False

Mark T for True and F for False. (See page numbers in parentheses.)

_____ 1. Data can include text, numbers, sounds, images, audio, and video. (514)

_____ 2. Garbage in, garbage out is a computing phrase that points out the accuracy of a computer's output depends on the accuracy of the input. (516)

_____ 3. A character is the smallest unit of data a computer can process. (518)

_____ 4. The data in a key field is the same for every record in a file. (519)

_____ 5. Validation is the process of comparing data with a set of rules or values to find out if the data is correct. (522)

_____ 6. A range check tests the data in two or more associated fields to ensure that the relationship is logical. (523)

_____ 7. Databases require less memory, storage, processing power, and training than a file processing system. (526)

_____ 8. To retrieve or select data in a database, you query it. (528)

_____ 9. Access privileges refer to the rules and standards that define how the database organizes data. (531)

_____ 10. A multidimensional database is a database that stores data in tables that consist of rows and columns. (533)

Checkpoint

 Multiple Choice   Select the best answer. (See page numbers in parentheses.)

1. Data _____ identifies the quality of data. (516)
   a. security
   b. modeling
   c. integrity
   d. mining

2. _____ information can be proven as correct or incorrect. (516)
   a. Timely
   b. Organized
   c. Cost-effective
   d. Verifiable

3. Accessible information _____. (516)
   a. is error free
   b. has an age suited to its use
   c. is available when the decision maker needs it
   d. has meaning to the person who receives it

4. The _____ data type is used for lengthy text entries. (518)
   a. memo
   b. numeric
   c. hyperlink
   d. data

5. A _____ is a collection of related records. (519)
   a. key field
   b. data file
   c. primary key
   d. data character

6. _____ analyzes entered data to help ensure that it is correct. (522)
   a. Data integrity
   b. A validity check
   c. An access privilege
   d. A data model

7. A completeness check _____. (523)
   a. ensures that users enter only alphabetic data into a field
   b. determines whether a number is within a specified range
   c. ensures that users enter only numeric data into a field
   d. verifies that a required field contains data

8. All of the following are strengths of the database approach, except _____. (525)
   a. less complexity
   b. improved data integrity
   c. easier access
   d. reduced development time

9. Because the _____ contains details about data, some call it metadata (meta means more comprehensive). (527)
   a. data mart
   b. data warehouse
   c. data modeler
   d. data dictionary

10. _____ has a graphical user interface that assists users with retrieving data. (528)
    a. A query language
    b. A form
    c. A report generator
    d. Query by example (QBE)

11. A(n) _____ sends entered data across a network or the Internet. (530)
    a. e-form
    b. groupware database
    c. report generator
    d. log

12. The data in a(n) _____ exists in many separate locations throughout a network or the Internet. (536)
    a. hypermedia database
    b. distributed database
    c. relational database
    d. object-oriented database

13. To access data in a Web database, users fill in a form on a Web page, which is the _____ to the database. (537)
    a. front end
    b. before image
    c. back end
    d. after image

14. The database analyst (DA) _____. (538)
    a. decides on the proper placement of fields
    b. creates and maintains the data dictionary
    c. monitors the performance of the database
    d. checks backup and recovery procedures

Checkpoint

Matching

Match the terms with their definitions. (See page numbers in parentheses.)

_____ 1. database (514)
_____ 2. field name (518)
_____ 3. field size (518)
_____ 4. data type (518)
_____ 5. key field (519)
_____ 6. default value (528)
_____ 7. query (528)
_____ 8. normalization (534)
_____ 9. object (534)
_____ 10. data mining (536)

a. collection of data organized in a manner that allows access, retrieval, and use of that data
b. request for specific data from a database
c. defines the maximum number of characters a field can contain
d. used by data warehouses to find patterns and relationships among data
e. value that a DBMS initially displays in a field
f. item that contains data and the actions that read or process the data
g. process that ensures data within relations (tables) contains the least amount of duplication
h. specifies the kind of data a field can contain and how the field is used
i. uniquely identifies each field
j. uniquely identifies each record in a file
k. smaller version of a data warehouse

Short Answer

Write a brief answer to each of the following questions.

1. How is a field different from a record? _____ What is a data file? _____
2. What is file maintenance? _____ When are records added, changed, or deleted in a file? _____
3. Why is data redundancy a weakness of file processing systems? _____ How does the database approach reduce data redundancy? _____
4. In a log, how is a before image different from an after image? _____ How is rollforward different from rollback? _____
5. What is an object-oriented database (OODB)? _____ What are some of OODB's advantages compared with relational databases? _____

Beyond the Book

Read the following book elements, learn more about each using the Web, and then write a brief report.

1. At Issue — Are Portable Storage Devices a Threat to Businesses? (516), Is a National Identification Card Necessary for the Security of the Nation? (519), Should States Share Criminal Databases? (525), Who Should Be Granted Access to Student Records? (531), or Can the Government Be Trusted with Personal Data? (537)
2. Career Corner — Database Administrator (539)
3. Companies on the Cutting Edge — Oracle or Sybase (541)
4. FAQs (517, 519, 526, 527, 533, 538)
5. High-Tech Talk — Ensure Consistency of Your Data with Normalization (540)
6. Looking Ahead — Having a Voice with Web Databases (528) or Preserving Electronic Files for Future Generations (538)
7. Making Use of the Web — Science (128)
8. Picture Yourself Using Web Databases (512)
9. Technology Trailblazers — E. F. Codd or Larry Ellison (541)
10. Web Links (523, 526, 528, 532, 534, 535, 536, 538)

Learn It Online

Use the Learn It Online exercises to reinforce your understanding of the chapter concepts. To access the Learn It Online exercises, visit scsite.com/dc2006/ch10/learn.

(1) At the Movies — Internet Movie Database

To view the Internet Movie Database movie, click the number 1 button. Locate your video and click the corresponding High-Speed or Dial-Up link, depending on your Internet connection. Watch the movie and then complete the exercise by answering the question that follows. Using Rottentomatoes.com could help you save time and money by allowing you to view movie trailers and view customer reviews. Explain how the "tomato picker" works and how using that feature of Rottentomatoes.com could save you time and money.

(2) At the Movies — National Identity Card

To view the National Identity Card movie, click the number 2 button. Locate your video and click the corresponding High-Speed or Dial-Up link, depending on your Internet connection. Watch the movie and then complete the exercise by answering the question that follows. Identity theft is a burgeoning problem. One solution is a national identity card, but other groups have proposed a national driver's license. Both of these ideas have spawned widespread controversy due to the ease with which the cards' opponents feel that the cards can be fraudulently reproduced. Explain the three security measures that AAMVA has proposed as safeguards against fraud should national driver's licenses be issued.

(3) Student Edition Labs — Advanced Databases

Click the number 3 button. When the Student Edition Labs menu appears, click *Advanced Databases* to begin. A new browser window will open. Follow the on-screen instructions to complete the Lab. When finished, click the Exit button. If required, submit your results to your instructor.

(4) Student Edition Labs — Advanced Spreadsheets

Click the number 4 button. When the Student Edition Labs menu appears, click *Advanced Spreadsheets* to begin. A new browser window will open. Follow the on-screen instructions to complete the Lab. When finished, click the Exit button. If required, submit your results to your instructor.

(5) Practice Test

Click the number 5 button. Answer each question. When completed, enter your name and click the Grade Test button to submit the quiz for grading. Make a note of any missed questions. If required, submit your results to your instructor.

(6) Who Wants To Be a Computer Genius²?

Click the number 6 button to find out if you are a computer genius. Directions about how to play the game will be displayed. When you are ready to play, click the Play button. Submit your score to your instructor.

Learn It Online

 Wheel of Terms

Click the number 7 button to reinforce important terms you learned in this chapter by playing the Shelly Cashman Series version of this popular game. Directions about how to play the game will be displayed. When you are ready to play, click the Play button. Submit your score to your instructor.

 DC Track and Field

Click the number 8 button to use what you have learned in this chapter to compete against other students in three track and field events. Directions about how to play the game will be displayed. When you are ready to play, click the start first event button. If required, submit your score to your instructor.

 You're Hired!

Click the number 9 button to use what you have learned in this chapter to embark on the path to a career in computers. Directions about how to play the game will be displayed. When you are ready to play, click the begin game button. If required, submit your score to your instructor.

10 Crossword Puzzle Challenge

Click the number 10 button. Complete the puzzle to reinforce skills you learned in this chapter. Directions about how to play the game will be displayed. When you are ready to play, click the Submit button. Submit the completed puzzle to your instructor.

 Lab Exercises

Click the number 11 button. When the Lab Exercises menu appears, click the exercise assigned by your instructor. A new browser window will open. Follow the on-screen instructions to complete the exercise. When finished, click the Exit button. If required, submit your results to your instructor.

12 In the News

To spare harried dispatchers, police officers used to request suspect information only when it was urgent. Now, IBM's eNetwork Law Enforcement Express lets officers directly access real-time databases of stolen cars, mug shots, and warrants. With a few taps on a notebook computer keyboard, police officers can search a database to see if a suspect in custody has a past criminal record. They also can find out if a suspect stopped for speeding is wanted for any more serious infractions. Click the number 12 button and read a news article about a database that is being used in a new way. Who is using the database? How is it being used? How will the database benefit the user?

13 Chapter Discussion Forum

Select an objective from this chapter on page 513 about which you would like more information. Click the number 13 button and post a short message listing a meaningful message title accompanied by one or more questions concerning the selected objective. In two days, return to the threaded discussion by clicking the number 13 button. Submit to your instructor your original message and at least one response to your message.

Learn How To

Use the Learn How To activities to learn fundamental skills when using a computer and accompanying technology. Complete the exercises and submit them to your instructor. Visit scsite.com/dc2006/ch10/howto to obtain more information pertaining to each activity.

LEARN HOW TO 1: Organize and Manage Files on a Computer

Introduction   In Learn How To 1 in Chapter 3 (page 178), you learned the procedure for saving a file. In this Learn How To activity, you will learn how to **manage files using folders** and how to find a file if you cannot remember where you saved it.

Folders   A folder is a virtual container where you can store a file on media. When you store any file, the file must be stored in a folder. The folder symbol, together with the folder name, identifies a folder.

You can create folders in a variety of ways. To create a folder on the desktop, complete the following steps:
1. Right-click the desktop in a location that does not contain an icon or toolbar.
2. Point to New on the shortcut menu that is displayed (Figure 10-27).
3. Click Folder on the New submenu.
4. When the folder icon is displayed on the desktop, type the name you want to assign to the folder and then press the ENTER key. You should choose a name that identifies the contents of the folder.

A folder can contain other folders. This allows you to organize your files in a hierarchical manner so that the highest level folder contains all the folders for a given subject, and lower-level folders contain more specific files and folders. For example, your highest level folder could be named Fall Semester 2006. For each class, such as Computer Information Systems 110, you could define a folder within the Fall Semester 2006 folder. Within each class folder, you could define folders for each week of the class, or for each project or assignment within the class. In this manner, you would have a set of folders, each designated for a specific use. You then would save your files in the appropriate folder.

To create a folder within a folder, complete the following steps:
1. Double-click the folder name either on the desktop or in the window or dialog box in which the folder name appears.
2. Right-click a blank space in the window that is displayed.
3. Point to New on the shortcut menu that is displayed and then click Folder on the New submenu.
4. When the folder icon is displayed, type the name you want to assign to the folder, and then press the ENTER key.

To delete a folder, complete the following steps:
1. Right-click the folder.
2. On the shortcut menu that is displayed (Figure 10-28), click Delete.
3. In the Confirm Folder Delete dialog box, click the Yes button.

FIGURE 10-27

FIGURE 10-28

Learn How To

When you delete a folder, all the files and folders contained in the folder you are deleting, together with all files and folders on the lower hierarchical levels, are deleted. If you accidentally delete a folder, complete the following steps:

1. Double-click the Recycle Bin icon on the desktop.
2. In the Recycle Bin window, select the folder you wish to restore.
3. Click File on the menu bar and then click Restore on the File menu.

Using folders effectively will aid you in keeping track of files you create for your classes.

Exercise

1. Assume you are taking the following courses: Computer Information Systems 120, History 210, English 145, Marketing 221, and Business Law 120. Define the hierarchy of folders you would create for these classes. In which folder would you store an assignment from English 145 that was assigned in the sixth week of class? Submit your answers to your instructor.

LEARN HOW TO 2: Search for Files and Folders

At times, you might store a file in a folder and then forget where you stored the file. The Search Companion feature of Windows XP enables you to search storage media on a computer to find the file. To use the Search Companion, complete the following steps:

1. Click the Start button on the Windows taskbar.
2. Click Search on the Start menu.
3. Click All files and folders in the What do you want to search for balloon.
4. In the All or part of the file name text box, type the name of the file for which you are searching. If you do not know the entire file name, enter as much of the file name as you can remember. If you do not know any portion of the file name, use the other options in the balloon to provide the search criteria (Figure 10-29).
5. Click the Search button in the balloon.
6. All items containing the file name or partial file name will be displayed in the Search Results window. If the file was not found, a message to that effect is displayed.
7. To open the file you found, double-click the file name in the list. The file will be opened by the appropriate program.

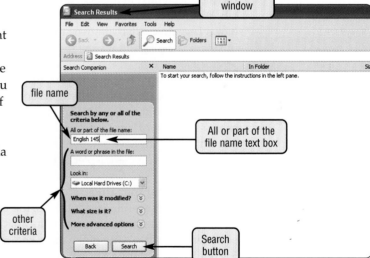

FIGURE 10-29

8. Before you close the Search Results window, make a note of the location of the file. If this is not the location where you want the file to be stored, store the file in the correct location.

Exercise

1. Using the **Windows XP Search Companion**, locate the file named Soap Bubbles. How many file names were returned? Which folder contains the Soap Bubbles file? Submit your answers to your instructor.
2. On the computer you are using, create a hierarchy of folders for your classes. Create a WordPad file that contains the following text: `This file will be found using Search Companion.` Save the file in one of the folders using a file name of your choice. Using Search Companion, search for the file you just created. How many files were returned from your search? Delete all folders and files you created in this exercise. Write a paragraph describing the steps you will take to organize your files for the coming semester. Submit your responses to your instructor.

Web Research

Use the Internet-based Web Research exercises to broaden your understanding of the concepts presented in this chapter. Visit scsite.com/dc2006/ch10/research to obtain more information pertaining to each exercise. To discuss any of the Web Research exercises in this chapter with other students, post your thoughts or questions at scsite.com/dc2006/ch10/forum.

(1) Scavenger Hunt   Use one of the <u>search engines</u> listed in Figure 2-10 in Chapter 2 on page 78 or your own favorite search engine to find the answers to the questions that follow. Copy and paste the Web address from the Web page where you found the answer. Some questions may have more than one answer. If required, submit your answers to your instructor. (1) How does click-stream analysis examine data from Web site usage patterns? (2) What geographic information system (GIS) functions does ArcExplorer perform? (3) What company developed SQL? What is the name of the original SQL prototype developed in 1974? (4) What is the definition of data modeling? (5) What is a knowledge engineer's primary job in developing expert systems?

(2) Search Sleuth   Major United States newspapers helped design <u>Clusty</u> the Clustering Engine (clusty.com). One of its unique features is returning search results for Web sites, news stories, images, and shopping sites in clusters, which are categories of folders, along with a list of links. Visit this Web site and then use your word processing program to answer the following questions. Then, if required, submit your answers to your instructor. (1) Click the Web+ tab, click the Request text box, and then type **"query by example"** or QBE in the box. Click the Cluster button. Browse the clusters on the left side of the page and then expand the SQL cluster by clicking the + icon next to the SQL link. What are the sub-cluster categories? (2) Click the Encyclopedia tab. What is one definition retrieved and its source? (3) Click the News tab and then click the News Page link. What are two stories listed in the Top News category? (4) Click two links in the Business category and review the articles. Write a 50-word summary of your findings.

(3) Journaling   Respond to your readings in this chapter by writing at least one page about your reactions, evaluations, and reflections on databases. For example, have you created a database to store details about your movie and music collections? Have you shopped online and accessed a merchant's database? Have you experienced problems with data integrity and tried to correct errors? Should Americans have a <u>national identification card</u>? You also can write about the new terms you learned by reading this chapter. If required, submit your journal to your instructor.

(4) Expanding Your Understanding   Public records contain details about professional licenses, civil court filings, adoptions, foreclosures, driving records, and much other personal data. The Internet makes searching for this data quite easy, and many of the databases can be browsed for free. One of the more comprehensive free public records databases is the <u>Search Systems Public Records Directories</u>. View Web sites to learn more about searching public records. Which databases are free, and which require a subscription fee? What state records are available where you live? Write a report summarizing your findings, focusing on searching the public records databases. If required, submit your report to your instructor.

(5) Ethics in Action   When you shop online, enter contests, and complete warranty registration cards, businesses automatically store data about you and your transactions in a marketing database. They often use this data to analyze sales and develop advertising campaigns. Unbeknownst to many consumers, some companies also sell this data to third parties for financial gain. Consumers can refuse to receive targeted e-mail messages and marketing materials, but they actively must search the Web sites or paper forms for check boxes to indicate these opt-out preferences. Some privacy experts, however, view this practice as unethical and urge businesses to default to not adding consumers' information to databases unless the consumer opts in to receive additional materials. View online sites that include <u>opt-in or opt-out provisions</u>. Write a report summarizing your findings, and include a table of links to Web sites that provide additional details about protecting consumers' data. If required, submit your report to your instructor.

Case Studies

Use the Case Studies to apply the concepts presented in the chapter to real-world situations. Visit scsite.com/dc2006/ch10/cases to obtain more information pertaining to each exercise. To discuss the Case Studies in this chapter with other students, visit scsite.com/dc2006/ch10/forum and post your thoughts or questions.

CASE STUDY 1 — Class Discussion   While attending college, you work 25 hours a week in the admissions office. You earn $7.00 an hour and are paid every two weeks. You recently received a payroll check that was $150.00 less than you expected for 50 hours of work. What error do you think the data entry clerk made that resulted in the wrong check being generated? Errors such as the one illustrated here show why <u>data integrity</u> is as important to a successful information management system as the hardware and software being used. The phrase garbage in, garbage out (GIGO) has been used to explain that you cannot create correct information from incorrect data. Write a brief report that includes your suggestion regarding the error made by the data entry clerk, and summarize the various data validation techniques described in this chapter. Be prepared to discuss your findings in class.

CASE STUDY 2 — Class Discussion   Reviews of movies on a video store's new release shelf are fairly easy to find, but critiques of other movies in stock may be less accessible. To help film buffs, information on more than 100,000 movie titles is available from a database on the World Wide Web. The Internet Movie Database Ltd. can be searched using a movie's title, cast members, year produced, characters, genre, awards, or other criteria. Each movie's page offers a brief description and rating and includes links to such items as stars, summary, trivia, reviews, quotes, goofs, and recommendations. Visit the movie database and write a brief report outlining how visitors can <u>query</u> the movie database. Search for several movies. How complete was the information provided? Who would benefit most from using the movie database? Why? Be prepared to discuss your findings in class.

CASE STUDY 3 — Research   While taking computer classes at the local community college, you also work as a data entry clerk for a car dealership. The dealership uses a network of personal computers and a twenty-year-old file processing system to handle its applications. Your manager has been told that it is time to convert the file processing system to a modern <u>database management system</u>. Because you are taking computer classes, he has asked you to submit an initial report that summarizes the features of three database management systems — Access, Visual FoxPro, and Oracle. Use the Web and/or print media to complete your evaluation. Which system is the least expensive to purchase? Which one offers the easiest conversion? Which one offers a query language, query by example, forms, a report generator, and backup and recovery procedures? Submit your report or use PowerPoint to create a presentation and share your findings with your class.

CASE STUDY 4 — Research   You recently were hired as a student intern to assist a local insurance agency in reorganizing their customer files. The agency employs a file processing system to maintain three distinct customer files — billing, claims, and promotion. The manager indicates that data entry has become unwieldy because of unclear relationships between data and data redundancy. Furthermore, customers are complaining about inconsistencies in the information they receive. The problem is beginning to affect business in a negative way. As a first step, she has asked you to prepare a report summarizing the benefits of <u>normalizing</u> the data in the three files. Use the Web and/or print media and High-Tech Talk on page 540 to gain an understanding of the normalization process. What is zero normal form? First normal form? Second normal form? Third normal form? Define and give an example of each of the following terms: data redundancy, primary key, and repeating group. Write a brief report or use PowerPoint to create a presentation and share your findings with your class.

CASE STUDY 5 – Team Challenge   When deciding on which database management system to use, companies have a choice of three <u>data models</u> — relational, object-oriented, and multidimensional. A major retail company has hired your team as database specialists to determine the data model best suited for their applications. Form a three-member team and have each team member choose a different data model. Have each member use the Web and/or print media to develop a feature/benefit report for each data model. Does the data model allow for query by example? How does the data model allow users to manage, update, and retrieve data? As a team, merge your findings into a team report and/or PowerPoint presentation and share your findings with your class.

CHAPTER ELEVEN

Computer Security, Ethics, and Privacy

Picture Yourself Aware of Computer-related Risks

According to the old adage, things happen in threes. If that is true, your streak of bad luck is over because you plan to prevent each of these three situations from ever occurring again.

While working at your computer last week, you received an e-mail message from your credit card company (or so you thought). The message explained that your account temporarily would be unavailable until you updated some information. You clicked a link to display what appeared to be the credit card company's Web page. You entered your credit card number, name, address, and telephone number. Unfortunately, you supplied enough information to the scammer who later used the information to make purchases in your name.

During a severe storm yesterday, a lightning strike caused a loss of power in your house. Once power was restored, you discovered that your printer no longer worked. After talking with a technician, you learned the printer will need to be replaced because it was damaged by a power surge.

At the doctor's office this morning, you were diagnosed with tendonitis in your arm. She said the tendonitis was caused from improperly using the mouse while working on the computer.

Each of these unfortunate incidents taught you valuable lessons about safeguarding against identity theft, protecting computer and devices, and preventing computer-related health injuries. Read Chapter 11 to learn about these and many other computer safeguards.

After completing this chapter, you will be able to:

1. Describe the types of computer security risks
2. Identify ways to safeguard against computer viruses, worms, Trojan horses, denial of service attacks, back doors, and spoofing
3. Discuss techniques to prevent unauthorized computer access and use
4. Identify safeguards against hardware theft and vandalism
5. Explain the ways software manufacturers protect against software piracy
6. Define encryption and explain why it is necessary
7. Discuss the types of devices available that protect computers from system failure
8. Explain the options available for backing up computer resources
9. Identify risks and safeguards associated with wireless communications
10. Recognize issues related to information accuracy, rights, and conduct
11. Discuss issues surrounding information privacy
12. Discuss ways to prevent health-related disorders and injuries due to computer use

CONTENTS

COMPUTER SECURITY RISKS

Today, people rely on computers to create, store, and manage critical information. Thus, it is important that the computers and the data they store are accessible and available when needed. It also is crucial that users take measures to protect their computers and data from loss, damage, and misuse. For example, businesses must ensure that information such as credit records, employee and customer data, and purchase information is secure and confidential. Home users must ensure that their credit card number is secure when they use it to purchase goods and services from Web-based businesses.

A **computer security risk** is any event or action that could cause a loss of or damage to computer hardware, software, data, information, or processing capability. Some breaches to computer security are accidental. Others are planned intrusions. Some intruders do no damage; they merely access data, information, or programs on the computer before logging off. Other intruders indicate some evidence of their presence either by leaving a message or by deliberately altering or damaging data.

An intentional breach of computer security often involves a deliberate act that is against the law. Any illegal act involving a computer generally is referred to as a **computer crime**. The term **cybercrime** refers to online or Internet-based illegal acts. Today, cybercrime is one of the FBI's top three priorities.

Perpetrators of cybercrime and other intrusions fall into seven basic categories: hacker, cracker, script kiddie, corporate spy, unethical employee, cyberextortionist, and cyberterrorist.

- The term **hacker**, although originally a complimentary word for a computer enthusiast, now has a derogatory meaning and refers to someone who accesses a computer or network illegally. Hackers often claim the intent of their security breaches is to improve security.
- A **cracker** also is someone who accesses a computer or network illegally but has the intent of destroying data, stealing information, or other malicious action. Both hackers and crackers have advanced computer and network skills.
- A **script kiddie** has the same intent as a cracker but does not have the technical skills and knowledge. Script kiddies often are teenagers that use prewritten hacking and cracking programs to break into computers.
- Some **corporate spies** have excellent computer and network skills and are hired to break into a specific computer and steal its proprietary data and information. Unscrupulous companies hire corporate spies, a practice known as corporate espionage, to gain a competitive advantage.
- **Unethical employees** break into their employers computers for a variety of reasons. Some simply want to exploit a security weakness. Others seek financial gains from selling confidential information. Disgruntled employees may want revenge.

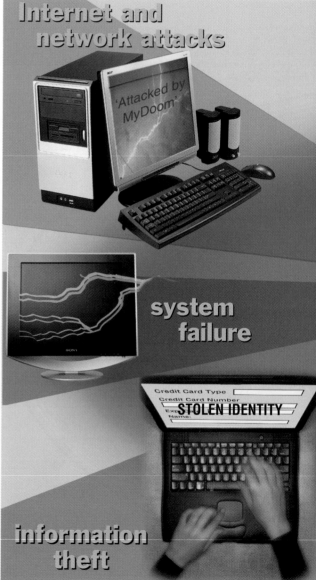

Internet and network attacks

'Attacked by MyDoom'

system failure

STOLEN IDENTITY

information theft

- A **cyberextortionist** is someone who uses e-mail as a vehicle for extortion. These perpetrators send a company a threatening e-mail message indicating they will expose confidential information, exploit a security flaw, or launch an attack that will compromise the company's network — if they are not paid a sum of money.

- A **cyberterrorist** is someone who uses the Internet or network to destroy or damage computers for political reasons. The extensive damage might destroy the nation's air traffic control system, electricity-generating companies, or a telecommunications infrastructure.

Cyberterrorism usually requires a team of highly skilled individuals, millions of dollars, and several years of planning.

Business and home users must protect, or safeguard, their computers from breaches of security and other computer security risks. The more common computer security risks include Internet and network attacks, unauthorized access and use, hardware theft, software theft, information theft, and system failure (Figure 11-1). The following pages describe these computer security risks and also discuss safeguards users might take to minimize or prevent their consequences.

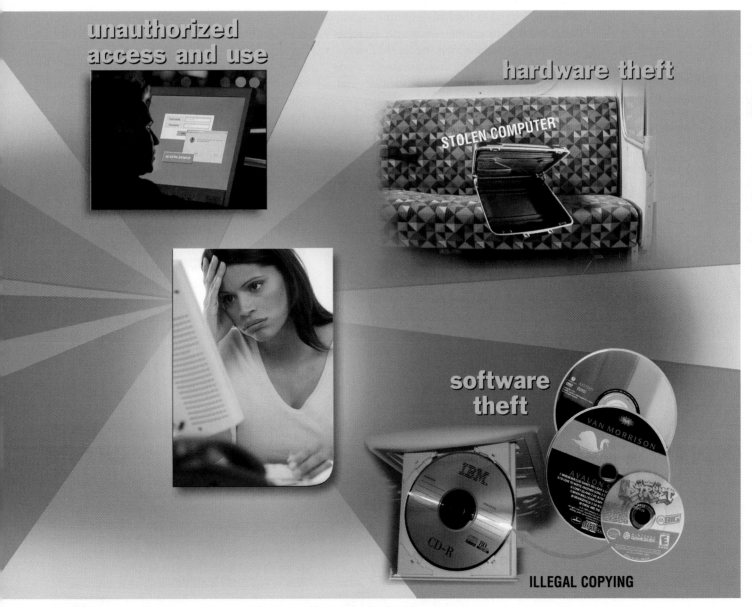

FIGURE 11-1 Computers are exposed to several types of security risks.

INTERNET AND NETWORK ATTACKS

Information transmitted over networks has a higher degree of security risk than information kept on a company's premises. In a business, network administrators usually take measures to protect a network from security risks. On the Internet, where no central administrator is present, the security risk is greater.

To determine if your computer is vulnerable to an Internet or network attack, you could use an online security service. An **online security service** is a Web site that evaluates your computer to check for Web and e-mail vulnerabilities. The service then provides recommendations of how to address the vulnerabilities.

Companies and individuals requiring assistance or information about Internet security breaches can contact or visit the Web site for the *Computer Emergency Response Team Coordination Center*, or *CERT/CC*, which is a federally funded Internet security research and development center.

Internet and network attacks that jeopardize security include computer viruses, worms, and Trojan horses; denial of service attacks; and spoofing. The following pages address these computer security risks and suggest measures businesses and individuals can take to protect their computers while on the Internet or connected to a network.

Computer Viruses, Worms, and Trojan Horses

Every unprotected computer is susceptible to the first type of computer security risk — a computer virus, worm, and/or Trojan horse.

- A computer **virus** is a potentially damaging computer program that affects, or infects, a computer negatively by altering the way the computer works without the user's knowledge or permission. Once the virus infects the computer, it can spread throughout and may damage files and system software, including the operating system.
- A **worm** is a program that copies itself repeatedly, for example in memory or on a network, using up resources and possibly shutting down the computer or network.
- A **Trojan horse** (named after the Greek myth) is a program that hides within or looks like a legitimate program. A certain condition or action usually triggers the Trojan horse. Unlike a virus or worm, a Trojan horse does not replicate itself to other computers.

Computer viruses, worms, and Trojan horses are classified as *malicious-logic programs*, which are programs that act without a user's knowledge and deliberately alter the computer's operations. Although these programs often are one of the three types (virus, worm, or Trojan horse), some have characteristics of two or all three types. For example, MyDoom and Blaster are worms; Melissa has elements of a virus, worm, and Trojan horse.

Unscrupulous programmers write malicious-logic programs and then test the programs to ensure they can deliver their payload (read At Issue 11-1 for a related discussion). The *payload* is the destructive event or prank the program is intended to deliver. A computer infected by a virus, worm, or Trojan horse often has one or more of the following symptoms:

- Screen displays unusual message or image
- Music or unusual sound plays randomly
- Available memory is less than expected
- Existing programs and files disappear
- Files become corrupted

WEB LINK 11-1

Computer Emergency Response Team Coordination Center

For more information, visit scsite.com/ dc2006/ch11/weblink and then click Computer Emergency Response Team Coordination Center.

AT ISSUE 11-1

How Should Virus Authors Be Punished?

Recently, the author of an Internet virus that caused millions or billions of dollars in alleged damages pleaded guilty to the crime and faced 18 to 37 months in prison — about the same as that for auto theft. Robert Morris, who created the first Internet worm in 1989, was sentenced to probation, community service, and a $10,000 fine. Many experts and computer administrators claim that the punishment for the crime is out of proportion with the damages caused by the crime. Some legal experts claim that lax security on the part of Internet users is to blame, and perhaps those who help to spread the viruses via lax security should be punished as well. Others claim that some companies provide exorbitant estimates of true damages that viruses cause and that these alleged damages provoke an emotional overreaction to the crimes. The types of crimes and international extent of possible damages is relatively new territory in criminal law. Should the government create new laws specifically aimed at punishing those who spread viruses and worms? Why or why not? Should virus authors be punished in proportion to the alleged damages that they cause? Why or why not? Because the Internet is an international medium, how should countries coordinate law enforcement and punishment for virus authors?

- Programs or files do not work properly
- Unknown programs or files mysteriously appear
- System properties change

Computer viruses, worms, and Trojan horses deliver their payload on a computer in four basic ways: when a user (1) opens an infected file, (2) runs an infected program, (3) boots the computer with an infected disk in a disk drive, or (4) connects an unprotected computer to a network. Today, a common way computers become infected with viruses, worms, and Trojan horses is through users opening infected e-mail attachments. Figure 11-2 shows how a virus can spread from one computer to another through an infected e-mail attachment.

Currently, more than 81,000 known viruses, worms, and Trojan horse programs exist with

an estimated 6 new programs discovered each day. Many Web sites maintain lists of all known malicious-logic programs. For a technical discussion about viruses, worms, and Trojan horses, read the High-Tech Talk article on page 168 in Chapter 3.

FAQ 11-1

How long is an unprotected computer safe from intruders?

One security expert maintains that an unprotected computer will be compromised by an intruder within 20 minutes. Slammer and Nimda, two devastating worms, wreaked worldwide havoc in 10 and 30 minutes, respectively. For more information, visit scsite.com/dc2006/ch11/faq and then click Viruses and Worms.

FIGURE 11-2 HOW A VIRUS CAN SPREAD THROUGH AN E-MAIL MESSAGE

Step 1:
Unscrupulous programmers create a virus program that deletes all files. They hide the virus in a Word document and attach the Word document to an e-mail message.

Step 2:
They use the Internet to send the e-mail message to thousands of users around the world.

Step 3a:
Some users open the attachment and their computers become infected with the virus.

Step 3b:
Other users do not recognize the name of the sender of the e-mail message. These users do not open the e-mail message — instead they immediately delete the e-mail message. These users' computers are not infected with the virus.

Safeguards against Computer Viruses, Worms, and Trojan Horses

Methods that guarantee a computer or network is safe from computer viruses, worms, and Trojan horses simply do not exist. Users can take several precautions, however, to protect their home and work computers from these malicious infections. The following paragraphs discuss these precautionary measures.

Do not start a computer with removable media in the drives. That is, CD and DVD drives should be empty, the floppy disk drive should not contain a floppy disk, etc. During the startup process, a computer may attempt to execute the boot sector on media in certain drives. Even if the attempt is unsuccessful, any virus on the boot sector of removable media can infect the computer's hard disk. If you must start the computer with media in a drive, for example, in the event the hard disk fails — be certain the media is uninfected.

Never open an e-mail attachment unless you are expecting the attachment *and* it is from a trusted source. A **trusted source** is a company or person you believe will not send a virus-infected file knowingly. If the e-mail message is from an unknown source or untrusted source, delete the e-mail message immediately — without opening or executing any attachments. If the e-mail message is from a trusted source, but you were not expecting an attachment, verify with the source that they intended to send you an attachment — before opening it.

Many e-mail programs allow users to preview an e-mail message before or without opening it. Some viruses and worms can deliver their payload when a user simply previews the message. Thus, you should turn off message preview in your e-mail program.

Some viruses are hidden in *macros*, which are instructions saved in an application such as a word processing or spreadsheet program. In applications that allow users to write macros, you should set the macro security level to medium (Figure 11-3a). With a medium security level, the application software warns users that a document they are attempting to open contains a macro (Figure 11-3b). From this warning, a user chooses to disable or enable the macro. If the document is from a trusted source, the user can enable the macro. Otherwise, it should be disabled.

Users should install an antivirus program and update it frequently. As discussed in Chapter 8, an **antivirus program** protects a computer against viruses by identifying and removing any computer viruses found in memory, on storage media, or on incoming files. Most antivirus programs also protect against worms and Trojan horses. When you purchase a new computer, it often includes antivirus software. The table in Figure 11-4 lists popular antivirus programs.

An antivirus program scans for programs that attempt to modify the boot program, the operating system, and other programs that normally are read from but not modified. In addition, many antivirus programs automatically scan files downloaded from the Web, e-mail attachments, opened files, and all types of removable media inserted into the computer.

FIGURE 11-3a   (dialog box to set macro security)

FIGURE 11-3b   (warning is displayed because security is set to medium)

FIGURE 11-3 Many application programs, such as Microsoft Word, allow users to set security levels for macros. To display the dialog box shown in Figure 11-3a in Word, click Tools on the menu bar, point to Macro, and then click Security.

POPULAR ANTIVIRUS PROGRAMS

- AVG Anti-Virus
- eTrust EZ Antivirus
- F-Secure Anti-Virus
- McAfee VirusScan
- Norton AntiVirus
- Trend Micro PC-cillin
- Vexira Antivirus

FIGURE 11-4 Popular antivirus programs.

One technique that antivirus programs use to identify a virus is to look for virus signatures. A **virus signature**, also called a **virus definition**, is a known specific pattern of virus code. Computer users should update their antivirus program's signature files regularly. Updating signature files downloads any new virus definitions that have been added since the last update (Figure 11-5). This extremely important activity allows the antivirus program to protect against viruses written since the antivirus program was released. Most antivirus programs contain an automatic update feature that regularly prompts users to download the virus signature. The vendor usually provides this service to registered users at no cost for a specified time.

Another technique that antivirus programs use to detect viruses is to inoculate existing program files. To **inoculate** a program file, the antivirus program records information such as the file size and file creation date in a separate inoculation file. The antivirus program then uses this information to detect if a virus tampers with the data describing the inoculated program file.

If an antivirus program identifies an infected file, it attempts to remove its virus, worm, or Trojan horse. If the antivirus program cannot remove the infection, it often quarantines the infected file. A **quarantine** is a separate area of a hard disk that holds the infected file until the infection can be removed. This step ensures other files will not become infected. Users also can quarantine suspicious files themselves.

In extreme cases, you may need to reformat the hard disk to remove a virus. Having uninfected, or clean, backups of all files is important. A later section in this chapter covers backup and restore techniques in detail.

In addition to an antivirus program, users often install a personal firewall program to protect a computer and its data from unauthorized intrusions. A later section discusses firewalls.

FIGURE 11-5 Many vendors of antivirus programs allow registered users to update virus signature files automatically from the Web at no cost for a specified time.

Finally, stay informed about new virus alerts and virus hoaxes. A **virus hoax** is an e-mail message that warns users of a nonexistent virus, worm, or Trojan horse. Often, these virus hoaxes are in the form of a chain letter that requests the user to send a copy of the e-mail message to as many people as possible. Instead of forwarding the message, visit a Web site that publishes a list of virus alerts and virus hoaxes.

The list in Figure 11-6 summarizes important tips for protecting your computer from virus, worm, and Trojan horse infection.

WEB LINK 11-2

Virus Hoaxes

For more information, visit scsite.com/dc2006/ch11/weblink and then click Virus Hoaxes.

FAQ 11-2

Should I inform others if my computer gets a virus, worm, or Trojan horse?

If you share data with other users, such as via e-mail attachments, instant message attachments, or removable media, then you should inform these users of your virus, worm, or Trojan horse infection. This courteous gesture allows fellow users to check their computers for the same type of infection. Be careful not to spread the virus inadvertently. For more information, visit scsite.com/dc2006/ch11/faq and then click Safeguards against Viruses, Worms, and Trojan Horses.

TIPS FOR PREVENTING VIRUS, WORM, AND TROJAN HORSE INFECTIONS

1. Never start a computer with removable media in the drives, unless the media is uninfected.
2. Never open an e-mail attachment unless you are expecting it *and* it is from a trusted source. Turn off message preview.
3. Set the macro security in programs so you can enable or disable macros. Enable macros only if the document is from a trusted source and you are expecting it.
4. Install an antivirus program on all of your computers. Obtain updates to the virus signature files on a regular basis.
5. Check all downloaded programs for viruses, worms, or Trojan horses. These malicious-logic programs often are placed in seemingly innocent programs, so they will affect a large number of users.
6. If the antivirus program flags an e-mail attachment as infected, delete the attachment immediately.
7. Before using any removable media, use the antivirus scan program to check the media for infection. Incorporate this procedure even for shrink-wrapped software from major developers. Some commercial software has been infected and distributed to unsuspecting users this way.
8. Install a personal firewall program.

FIGURE 11-6 With the growing number of new viruses, worms, and Trojan horses, it is crucial that users take steps to protect their computers.

Denial of Service Attacks

A **denial of service attack**, or **DoS attack**, is an assault whose purpose is to disrupt computer access to an Internet service such as the Web or e-mail. Perpetrators carry out a DoS attack in a variety of ways. For example, they may use an unsuspecting computer to send an influx of confusing data messages or useless traffic to a computer network. The victim computer network eventually jams, blocking legitimate visitors from accessing the network.

A more devastating type of DoS attack is the *DDoS* (*distributed DoS*) *attack*, in which multiple unsuspecting computers are used to attack multiple computer networks. DDoS attacks have been able to stop operations temporarily at numerous Web sites, including powerhouses such as Yahoo!, Amazon.com, eBay, and CNN.com.

The computer that a perpetrator uses to execute the DoS or DDoS attack, known as a *zombie*, is completely unaware it is being used to attack other systems.

Back Doors

A **back door** is a program or set of instructions in a program that allow users to bypass security controls when accessing a program, computer, or network. Once perpetrators gain access to unsecure computers, they often install a back door or modify an existing program to include a back door, which allows them to continue to access the computer remotely without the user's knowledge. Some worms leave back doors, which have been used to spread other worms or to distribute junk e-mail from the unsuspecting victim computers.

Programmers often build back doors into programs during system development. These back doors save development time because the programmer can bypass security controls while writing and testing programs. If the programmer fails to remove the back door before releasing the software, a perpetrator could use the back door to gain entry to a computer or network.

Spoofing

Spoofing is a technique intruders use to make their network or Internet transmission appear legitimate to a victim computer or network. Several types of spoofing schemes exist. One type, called IP spoofing, occurs when an intruder computer fools a network into believing its IP address is associated with a trusted source.

Perpetrators of IP spoofing trick their victims into interacting with the phony Web site. For example, the victim may provide confidential information or download files containing viruses, worms, or other malicious programs.

Safeguards against DoS Attacks, Back Doors, and IP Spoofing

Some of the latest antivirus programs include provisions to protect a computer from DoS and DDoS attacks. To further defend against these and other Internet and network attacks, users can implement firewall solutions, install intrusion detection software, and set up honeypots.

Firewalls

A **firewall** is hardware and/or software that protects a network's resources from intrusion by users on another network such as the Internet (Figure 11-7). All networked and online computer users should implement a firewall solution.

Companies use firewalls to protect network resources from outsiders and to restrict employees' access to sensitive data such as payroll or personnel records. Businesses can implement a firewall solution themselves or outsource their needs to a company specializing in providing firewall protection.

Large companies often route all their communications through a proxy server, which typically is a component of the firewall. A *proxy server* is a server outside the company's network that controls which communications pass into the company's network. That is, the proxy server carefully screens all incoming and outgoing messages. Proxy servers use a variety of screening techniques. Some check the domain name or IP address of the message for legitimacy. Others require that the messages have digital signatures. A section later in this chapter discusses digital signatures.

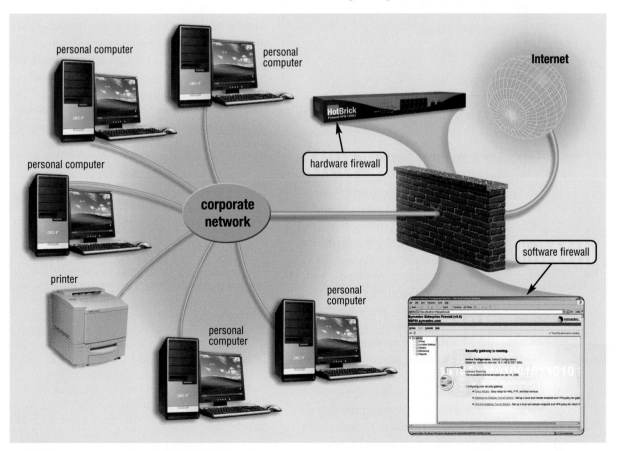

FIGURE 11-7 A firewall is hardware and/or software that protects a network's resources from intrusion by users on another network such as the Internet.

Home and small office/home office users often protect their computers with a personal firewall utility. As discussed in Chapter 8, a **personal firewall utility** is a program that detects and protects a personal computer and its data from unauthorized intrusions. Personal firewall utilities constantly monitor all transmissions to and from the computer and inform you of any attempted intrusion. Some operating systems, such as Windows XP, include personal firewalls. For enhanced firewall protection, many users purchase stand-alone personal firewall software (Figure 11-8), usually for less than $50.

Some small office/home office users purchase a hardware firewall, such as a router or other device that has a built-in firewall, in addition to or instead of personal firewall software. Hardware firewalls stop intrusions before they break in your computer.

PERSONAL FIREWALL SOFTWARE
BlackICE PC Protection
McAfee Personal Firewall Plus
Norton Personal Firewall
Sygate Personal Firewall
Tiny Personal Firewall
ZoneAlarm

FIGURE 11-8   Popular personal firewall software.

Intrusion Detection Software

To provide extra protection against hackers and other intruders, large companies sometimes use intrusion detection software to identify possible security breaches. *Intrusion detection software* automatically analyzes all network traffic, assesses system vulnerabilities, identifies any unauthorized intrusions, and notifies network administrators of suspicious behavior patterns or system breaches.

To utilize intrusion detection software requires the expertise of a network administrator because the programs are complex and difficult to use and interpret. These programs also are quite expensive. This software, however, when combined with a firewall, provides an added layer of protection to companies with highly sensitive data such as credit card databases.

Honeypots

Some companies use honeypots so they can analyze an attack being perpetrated. A *honeypot* is a vulnerable computer that is set up to entice an intruder to break into it. These computers, which appear real to the intruder, actually are separated safely from the company network. Honeypots allow the company to learn how intruders are exploiting its network. They also enable the company to attempt to catch perpetrators who have been doing damage elsewhere on the company's network. Large Web hosting companies, such as Yahoo! and AT&T, frequently use honeypots.

UNAUTHORIZED ACCESS AND USE

Another type of computer security risk is unauthorized access and use. **Unauthorized access** is the use of a computer or network without permission. **Unauthorized use** is the use of a computer or its data for unapproved or possibly illegal activities. Unauthorized use includes a variety of activities: an employee using an organization's computer to send personal e-mail messages, an employee using the organization's word processing software to track his or her child's soccer league scores, or someone gaining access to a bank computer and performing an unauthorized transfer. For the home user, most unauthorized use occurs on computers that have always-on Internet connections, such as through Internet cable or DSL.

FAQ 11-3

Why do hackers and other intruders want to access my home computer?

Some hackers and other intruders access home computers to use the computer's resources to spread malicious code, carry out a DoS attack, or get away with other nefarious acts. Once they break into your home computer, these intruders often install a back door so they can continue to use your computer as a launching pad for their activities. For more information, visit scsite.com/dc2006/ch11/faq and then click Protecting Home Computers.

Safeguards against Unauthorized Access and Use

Companies take several measures to help prevent unauthorized access and use. At a minimum, they should have a written acceptable use policy (AUP) that outlines the computer activities for which the computer and network may and may not be used. A company's AUP should specify the acceptable use of computers by employees for personal reasons. Some companies prohibit such use entirely. Others allow personal use on the employee's own time such as a lunch hour. Whatever the policy, a company should document and explain it to employees.

To protect your personal computer from unauthorized intrusions, you should disable file and printer sharing on your Internet connection (Figure 11-9). This security measure attempts to ensure that others cannot access your files or your printer. To display the dialog box shown in Figure 11-9 in Windows XP, click the Start button on the taskbar, point to All Programs, point to Accessories, point to Communications, and then click Network Connections. Right-click the appropriate network connection in the list and then click Properties on the shortcut menu.

Other measures that safeguard against unauthorized access and use include firewalls and intrusion detection software, which were discussed in the previous section, and identifying and authenticating users.

FAQ 11-4

Are Stand-Alone Browsers More Secure?

Some users believe that a browser independent of the operating system, such as Firefox or Opera, is more secure than a browser built in an operating system, such as Internet Explorer. For more information, visit scsite.com/dc2006/ch11/faq and then click Browser Security.

Identifying and Authenticating Users

Many companies use access controls to minimize the chance that a perpetrator intentionally may access or an employee accidentally may access confidential information on a computer. An *access control* is a security measure that defines who can access a computer, when they can access it, and what actions they can take while accessing the computer. In addition, the computer should maintain an **audit trail** that records in a file both successful and unsuccessful access attempts. An unsuccessful access attempt could result from a user mistyping his or her password, or it could result from a hacker trying thousands of passwords.

Companies should investigate unsuccessful access attempts immediately to ensure they are not intentional breaches of security. They also should review successful access for irregularities, such as use of the computer after normal working hours or from remote computers. In addition, a company regularly should review users' access privilege levels to determine whether they still are appropriate.

FIGURE 11-9   To protect files on your local hard disk from hackers and other intruders, turn off file and printer sharing on your Internet connection.

Many systems implement access controls using a two-phase process called identification and authentication. *Identification* verifies that an individual is a valid user. *Authentication* verifies that the individual is the person he or she claims to be. Three methods of identification and authentication include user names and passwords, possessed objects, and biometric devices. The technique(s) a company uses should correspond to the degree of risk associated with the unauthorized access. The following paragraphs discuss each of the identification and authentication methods.

USER NAMES AND PASSWORDS A **user name**, or *user ID* (identification), is a unique combination of characters, such as letters of the alphabet or numbers, that identifies one specific user. A **password** is a private combination of characters associated with the user name that allows access to certain computer resources.

Most multiuser (networked) operating systems require that users correctly enter a user name and a password before they can access the data, information, and programs stored on a computer or network. Many other systems that maintain financial, personal, and other confidential information also require a user name and password as part of their logon procedure (Figure 11-10).

Some systems assign a user name or user ID to each user. For example, a school may use the student identification number as a user ID. With other systems, users select their own user name or user ID. Many users select a combination of their first and last names.

Most systems require that users select their own passwords. Users typically choose an easy-to-remember word or series of characters for passwords. If your password is too obvious, however, such as your initials or birthday, others can guess it easily. Easy passwords make it simple for hackers and other intruders to break into a system. Hackers use computer automated tools to assist them with guessing passwords. Thus, you should select a password carefully. Longer passwords provide greater security than shorter ones. Each character added to a password significantly increases the number of possible combinations and the length of time it might take for someone or for a hacker's computer to guess the password (Figure 11-11).

In addition to a user name and password, some systems ask users to enter one of several pieces of personal information. Such items can include a spouse's first name, a birth date, a place of birth, or a mother's maiden name. As with a password, if the user's response does not match information on file, the system denies access.

FIGURE 11-10 Many Web sites that maintain personal and confidential data require a user to enter a user name (user ID) and password.

FAQ 11-5

How can I protect my password?

Once you select a password, change it frequently. Do not disclose it to anyone or write it on a slip of paper kept near the computer, especially taped to the monitor or under the keyboard. E-mail and telemarketing scams often ask unsuspecting users to disclose their password, so be wary if you did not initiate the inquiry or telephone call. For more information, visit scsite.com/dc2006/ch11/faq and then click Protecting Passwords.

PASSWORD PROTECTION		AVERAGE TIME TO DISCOVER	
Number of Characters	Possible Combinations	Human	Computer
1	36	3 minutes	.000018 second
2	1,300	2 hours	.00065 second
3	47,000	3 days	.02 second
4	1,700,000	3 months	1 second
5	60,000,000	10 years	30 seconds
10	3,700,000,000,000,000	580 million years	59 years

- Possible characters include the letters A–Z and numbers 0–9
- Human discovery assumes 1 try every 10 seconds
- Computer discovery assumes 1 million tries per second
- Average time assumes the password would be discovered in approximately half the time it would take to try all possible combinations

FIGURE 11-11 This table shows the effect of increasing the length of a password that consists of letters and numbers. The longer the password, the more effort required to discover it. Long passwords, however, are more difficult for users to remember.

POSSESSED OBJECTS A *possessed object* is any item that you must carry to gain access to a computer or computer facility. Examples of possessed objects are badges, cards, smart cards, and keys. The card you use in an automated teller machine (ATM) is a possessed object that allows access to your bank account (Figure 11-12).

FIGURE 11-12 The card you use in an automated teller machine (ATM) is a possessed object that allows access to your bank account.

Possessed objects often are used in combination with personal identification numbers. A **personal identification number (PIN)** is a numeric password, either assigned by a company or selected by a user. PINs provide an additional level of security. An ATM card typically requires a four-digit PIN. Most debit cards and some credit cards use PINs. If someone steals these cards, the thief must enter the user's PIN to access the account. PINs are passwords. Select them carefully and protect them as you do any other password.

BIOMETRIC DEVICES As discussed in Chapter 5, a **biometric device** authenticates a person's identity by translating a personal characteristic, such as a fingerprint, into a digital code that then is compared with a digital code stored in the computer verifying a physical or behavioral characteristic. If the digital code in the computer does not match the personal characteristic code, the computer denies access to the individual.

Biometric devices grant access to programs, computers, or rooms using computer analysis of some biometric identifier. Examples of biometric devices and systems include fingerprint scanners (Figure 11-13), hand geometry systems, face recognition systems, voice verification systems, signature verification systems, and iris recognition systems. Read Looking Ahead 11-1 for a look at the next generation of face recognition systems.

Biometric devices are gaining popularity as a security precaution because they are a virtually foolproof method of identification and authentication (read At Issue 11-2 for a related discussion). Users can forget their user names and passwords. Possessed objects can be lost, copied, duplicated, or stolen. Personal characteristics, by contrast, are unique and cannot be forgotten or misplaced.

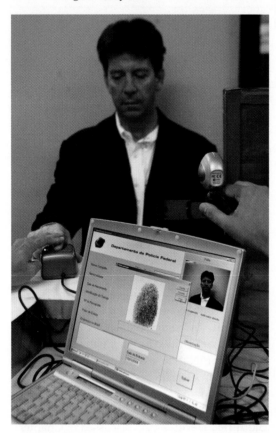

FIGURE 11-13 A fingerprint scanner verifies this traveler's identity.

AT ISSUE 11-2

Should Biometrics Be Required to Ride the School Bus or Eat Lunch?

An Ohio school system requires that students use a biometric thumbprint to pay for their school lunches. The school board cites the need to better track the number of free and subsidized lunches that the schools provide. A Florida school district requires that students provide a thumbprint both as they enter and as they leave their GPS-tracked school buses each day. The school system cites both safety and the fact that more accurate counting and tracking of bus usage will result in more state transportation funds. In both cases, the schools promise to provide digital ID cards for those opposed to the system and refusing to take part. Some experts feel that children are being trained very early to expect no privacy when they are adults. Others also are concerned that student eating habits can be tracked and then used against them in the future, or that the information could end up in the wrong hands. Should children be required to provide biometric information to engage in common public school-related activities? Why or why not? Do the school boards' reasons for the measures justify them? Why or why not? What are the privacy issues involved and should they be a concern?

LOOKING AHEAD 11-1

Three-Dimensional Facial Recognition Software — A Step Forward for Security

Your next passport may contain an added feature: a chip that communicates with a reader via radio frequency. The chip will contain at least one photograph of you and perhaps your fingerprints so you can be verified as the passport owner.

The facial recognition software market is expected to grow from $228 million in 2005 to $802 million in 2008 according to the International Biometric Group. Leading the way are three-dimensional systems that measure the width, height, and depth of an individual's face and then compare the dimensions to the original photographs. The software can identify an individual positively in a dark room or in a different pose than when the photographs were taken. For more information, visit scsite.com/dc2006/ch11/looking and then click Facial Recognition.

Biometric devices do have disadvantages. If you cut your finger, a fingerprint scanner might reject you as a legitimate user. Hand geometry readers can transmit germs. If you are nervous, a signature might not match the one on file. If you have a sore throat, a voice recognition system might reject you. Many people are uncomfortable with the thought of using an iris scanner.

Test your knowledge of pages 556 through 569 in Quiz Yourself 11-1.

QUIZ YOURSELF 11-1

Instructions: Find the true statement below. Then, rewrite the remaining false statements so they are true.

1. A back door attack is an assault whose purpose is to disrupt computer access to an Internet service such as the Web or e-mail.

2. All networked and online computer users should implement a firewall solution.

3. A biometric device translates a personal characteristic into an analog code that then is compared with a digital code stored in the computer.

4. Computer viruses, worms, and Trojan horses are malicious-logic programs that act with a user's knowledge.

5. Perpetrators of cybercrime and other intrusions fall into seven basic categories: hacker, cracker, CERT/CC, corporate spy, unethical employee, trusted source, and cyberterrorist.

6. Shorter passwords provide greater security than longer ones.

7. Updating an antivirus program's quarantine protects a computer against viruses written since the antivirus program was released.

Quiz Yourself Online: To further check your knowledge of security risks; safeguards against viruses, worms, Trojan horses, denial of service attacks, back doors, and spoofing; and preventing unauthorized computer access and use, visit scsite.com/dc2006/ch11/quiz and then click Objectives 1 – 3.

HARDWARE THEFT AND VANDALISM

Hardware theft and vandalism are other types of computer security risks. **Hardware theft** is the act of stealing computer equipment. **Hardware vandalism** is the act of defacing or destroying computer equipment. Hardware vandalism takes many forms, from someone cutting a computer cable to individuals breaking into a business or school computer lab and aimlessly smashing computers.

Hardware theft and vandalism do not really pose a threat to the home desktop computer user. Companies and schools and other organizations that house many computers, however, are at risk to hardware theft and vandalism.

Mobile users also are susceptible to hardware theft. It is estimated that more than 600,000 notebook computers are stolen each year. The size and weight of these computers make them easy to steal. Thieves often target notebook computers of company executives, so they can use the stolen computer to access confidential company information illegally.

Safeguards against Hardware Theft and Vandalism

To help reduce the chances of theft, companies and schools use a variety of security measures. Physical access controls, such as locked doors and windows, usually are adequate to protect the equipment. Many businesses, schools, and some homeowners install alarm systems for additional security. School computer labs and other areas with a large number of semifrequent users often attach additional physical security devices such as cables that lock the equipment to a desk (Figure 11-14), cabinet, or floor. Small locking devices also exist that require a key to access a hard disk or CD/DVD drive.

FIGURE 11-14
Using cables to lock computers can help prevent the theft of computer equipment.

Mobile computer users must take special care to protect their equipment. The best preventive measures are common sense and a constant awareness of the risk. Some users attach a physical device such as a cable to lock a mobile computer temporarily to a stationary object. For example, a hotel guest could lock a notebook computer to a desk or table in a hotel room when he or she leaves the room. Other mobile users install a mini-security system in the notebook computer. Some of these security systems shut down the computer and sound an alarm if the computer moves outside a specified distance. Others can track the location of the stolen notebook computer.

Some notebook computers use passwords, possessed objects, and biometrics as methods of security. When you boot up these computers, you must enter a password, slide a card in a card reader, or press your finger on a fingerprint scanner before the hard disk unlocks. This type of security does not prevent theft, but it renders the computer useless if it is stolen.

You also can password-protect many PDAs and smart phones. This allows only authorized users to access the device's data. You usually can instruct the password screen to display your name and telephone number, so a Good Samaritan can return it to you if lost. Several models also allow you to encrypt data in the device. A later section in this chapter discusses encryption.

SOFTWARE THEFT

Another type of computer security risk is software theft. **Software theft** occurs when someone (1) steals software media, (2) intentionally erases programs, or (3) illegally copies a program.

The first type of software theft involves a perpetrator physically stealing the media that contain the software. For example, an unscrupulous library patron might steal the Microsoft Encarta Encyclopedia CD-ROM.

The second type of software theft can occur when a programmer is terminated from, or stops working for, a company. Although the programs are company property, some dishonest programmers intentionally remove the programs they have written from company computers.

The third type of software theft occurs when software is stolen from software manufacturers. This type of theft, called piracy, is by far the most common form of software theft. Software **piracy** is the unauthorized and illegal duplication of copyrighted software.

Safeguards against Software Theft

To protect software media from being stolen, owners should keep original software boxes and media in a secure location, out of sight of prying eyes. When some companies terminate a programmer or if the programmer quits, they escort the employee off the premises immediately. These companies believe that allowing terminated employees to remain on the premises gives them time to sabotage files and other network procedures.

To protect themselves from software piracy, software manufacturers issue users license agreements. A **license agreement** is the right to use the software. That is, you do not own the software. The license agreement provides specific conditions for use of the software, which a user must accept before using the software (Figure 11-15). These terms usually are displayed when you install the software. Use of the software constitutes acceptance of the terms on the user's part.

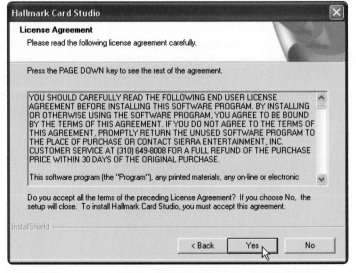

FIGURE 11-15   A user must accept the terms in the license agreement before using the software.

The most common type of license included with software purchased by individual users is a *single-user license agreement*, also called an *end-user license agreement* (*EULA*). A single-user license agreement typically includes many of the following conditions that specify a user's responsibility upon acceptance of the agreement.

Users are permitted to:

- Install the software on only one computer. (Some license agreements allow users to install the software on one desktop computer and one notebook computer.)
- Make one copy of the software as a backup.
- Give or sell the software to another individual, but only if the software is removed from the user's computer first.

Users are not permitted to:

- Install the software on a network, such as a school computer lab.
- Give copies to friends and colleagues, while continuing to use the software.
- Export the software.
- Rent or lease the software.

Unless otherwise specified by a license agreement, you do not have the right to copy, loan, borrow, rent, or in any way distribute software. Doing so is a violation of copyright law. It also is a federal crime. Despite this, some experts estimate for every authorized copy of software in use, at least one unauthorized copy exists.

Software piracy continues for several reasons. In some countries, legal protection for software does not exist. In other countries, laws rarely are enforced. In addition, many buyers believe they have the right to copy the software for which they pay hundreds, even thousands, of dollars. Finally, software piracy is a fairly simple crime to commit.

Software piracy, however, is a serious offense. For one, it introduces a number of risks into the software market. It increases the chance of spreading viruses, reduces your ability to receive technical support, and drives up the price of software for all users. Further, software companies take illegal copying seriously. In some cases, offenders have been prosecuted to the fullest extent of the law with penalties including fines up to $250,000 and five years in jail.

To promote a better understanding of software piracy problems and, if necessary, to take legal action, a number of major worldwide software companies formed the *Business Software Alliance* (*BSA*). The BSA operates a Web site and antipiracy hotlines in the United States and more than 60 other countries.

In an attempt to prevent software piracy, Microsoft and other manufacturers have incorporated an activation process into many of their consumer products. During the **product activation**, which is conducted either online or by telephone, users provide the software product's 25-character identification number to receive an installation identification number unique to the computer on which the software is installed. Usually, the software does not function or has limited functionality until you activate it via the Internet or telephone.

Many organizations and businesses also have strict written policies governing the installation and use of software and enforce their rules by checking networked or online computers periodically to ensure that all software is licensed properly. If you are not completely familiar with your school or employer's policies governing installation of software, check with the information technology department or your school's technology coordinator.

WEB LINK 11-5

Business Software Alliance

For more information, visit scsite.com/dc2006/ch11/weblink and then click Business Software Alliance.

FAQ 11-6

How prevalent is software piracy?

A recent study showed that more than half of 86 countries polled had a piracy rate greater than 60 percent. The chart below outlines some of the piracy rates around the world. For more information, visit scsite.com/dc2006/ch11/faq and then click Software Piracy.

Worldwide Piracy Rates

Source: United Press International

INFORMATION THEFT

Information theft is yet another type of computer security risk. **Information theft** occurs when someone steals personal or confidential information. If stolen, the loss of information can cause as much damage as (if not more than) hardware or software theft.

Both business and home users can fall victim to information theft. An unethical company executive may steal or buy stolen information to learn about a competitor. A corrupt individual may steal credit card numbers to make fraudulent purchases. Information theft often is linked to other types of computer crime. For example, an individual first might gain unauthorized access to a computer and then steal credit card numbers stored in a firm's accounting department.

Information transmitted over networks offers a higher degree of risk because unscrupulous users can intercept it during transmission. Every computer along the path of your data can see what you send and receive.

Safeguards against Information Theft

Most companies attempt to prevent information theft by implementing the user identification and authentication controls discussed earlier in this chapter. These controls are best suited for protecting information on computers located on a company's premises.

To protect information on the Internet and networks, companies and individuals use a variety of encryption techniques to keep data secure and private.

Encryption

Encryption is a process of converting readable data into unreadable characters to prevent unauthorized access. You treat encrypted data just like any other data. That is, you can store it or send it in an e-mail message. To read the data, the recipient must **decrypt**, or decipher, it into a readable form.

In the encryption process, the unencrypted, readable data is called *plaintext*. The encrypted (scrambled) data is called *ciphertext*. To encrypt the data, the originator of the data converts the plaintext into ciphertext using an encryption key. In its simplest form, an *encryption key* is a programmed formula that the recipient of the data uses to decrypt ciphertext. For a more technical discussion about encryption keys, read the High-Tech Talk article on page 592.

Many data encryption methods exist. Figure 11-16 shows examples of some simple encryption methods. Figure 11-17 shows the contents of a sample encrypted file. An encryption key (formula) often uses more than one of these methods, such as a combination of transposition and substitution. Most organizations use available software for encryption. Others develop their own encryption programs.

When users send an e-mail message over the Internet, they never know who might intercept it, who might read it, or to whom it might be forwarded. If a message contains personal or confidential information, users can protect the message by encrypting it or signing it digitally. One of the more popular e-mail encryption programs is called *Pretty Good Privacy* (PGP). PGP is freeware for personal, noncommercial users. Home users can download PGP from the Web at no cost.

A **digital signature** is an encrypted code that a person, Web site, or company attaches to an electronic message to verify the identity of the message sender. The code usually consists of the user's name and a hash of all or part of the message. A *hash* is a mathematical formula that generates a code from the contents of the message. Thus, the hash differs for each message. Receivers of the message decrypt the digital signature. The recipient then generates a new hash of the received message and compares it with one in the digital signature to ensure they match.

WEB LINK 11-6

Encryption

For more information, visit scsite.com/dc2006/ch11/weblink and then click Encryption.

SAMPLE ENCRYPTION METHODS

Name	Method	Plaintext	Ciphertext	Explanation
Transposition	Switch the order of characters	SOFTWARE	OSTFAWER	Adjacent characters swapped
Substitution	Replace characters with other characters	INFORMATION	WLDIMXQUWIL	Each letter replaced with another
Expansion	Insert characters between existing characters	USER	UYSYEYRY	Letter Y inserted after each character
Compaction	Remove characters and store elsewhere	ACTIVATION	ACIVTIN	Every third letter removed (T, A, O)

FIGURE 11-16   This table shows four simple methods of encryption. Most encryption programs use a combination of these four methods.

WEB LINK 11-7

PGP Encryption Program

For more information, visit scsite.com/ dc2006/ch11/weblink and then click PGP Encryption Program.

FIGURE 11-17 A sample encrypted file.

Digital signatures often are used to ensure that an impostor is not participating in an Internet transaction. That is, digital signatures help to prevent e-mail forgery. A digital signature also can verify that the content of a message has not changed.

Many Web browsers also use encryption. Some browsers offer a protection level known as *40-bit encryption*. Many also offer *128-bit encryption*, which is an even higher level of protection because it has a longer encryption key. Applications requiring more security, such as banks, brokerage firms, or online retailers that use credit card or other financial information, require 128-bit encryption.

A Web site that uses encryption techniques to secure its data is known as a **secure site**. Secure sites use digital certificates along with a security protocol. Two popular security protocols are Secure Sockets Layer and Secure HTTP. The following paragraphs briefly discuss digital certificates and these security protocols.

DIGITAL CERTIFICATES A **digital certificate** is a notice that guarantees a user or a Web site is legitimate. E-commerce applications commonly use digital certificates.

A *certificate authority* (*CA*) is an authorized person or a company that issues and verifies digital certificates. Users apply for a digital certificate from a CA (Figure 11-18). A digital certificate typically contains information such as the user's name, the issuing CA's name and signature, and the serial number of the certificate. The information in a digital certificate is encrypted.

FIGURE 11-18 A company called Thawte is a certificate authority that issues and verifies digital certificates.

SECURE SOCKETS LAYER *Secure Sockets Layer* (*SSL*) provides encryption of all data that passes between a client and an Internet server. SSL requires the client have a digital certificate. Once the server has a digital certificate, the Web browser communicates securely with the client. Web addresses of pages that use SSL typically begin with https, instead of http (Figure 11-19). SSL is available in both 40-bit and 128-bit encryption.

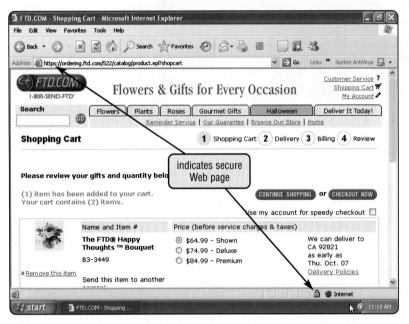

indicates secure
Web page

FIGURE 11-19 Web addresses of secure sites often begin with https instead of http. Secure sites also often display a lock symbol on the status bar.

SECURE HTTP *Secure HTTP (S-HTTP)* allows users to choose an encryption scheme for data that passes between a client and a server. With S-HTTP, the client and server both must have digital certificates. S-HTTP is more difficult to use than SSL, but it is more secure. Applications that must verify the authenticity of a client, such as for online banking, use S-HTTP.

Mobile users today often access their company networks through a virtual private network. When a mobile user connects to a main office using a standard Internet connection, a *virtual private network (VPN)* provides the mobile user with a secure connection to the company network server, as if the user has a private line. VPNs help ensure that data is safe from being intercepted by unauthorized people by encrypting data as it transmits from a notebook computer, Tablet PC, PDA, or other mobile device.

SYSTEM FAILURE

System failure is yet another type of computer security risk. A *system failure* is the prolonged malfunction of a computer. System failure also can cause loss of hardware, software, data, or information. A variety of causes can lead to system failure. These include aging hardware; natural disasters such as fires, floods, or hurricanes; random events such as electrical power problems; and even errors in computer programs.

One of the more common causes of system failure is an electrical power variation. Electrical power variations can cause loss of data and loss of equipment. If the computer equipment is networked, a single power disturbance can damage multiple systems. Electrical disturbances include noise, undervoltages, and overvoltages.

Noise is any unwanted signal, usually varying quickly, that is mixed with the normal voltage entering the computer. Noise is caused by external devices such as fluorescent lighting, radios, and televisions, as well as by components within the computer itself. Noise generally is not a risk to hardware, software, or data. Computer power supplies, however, do filter out noise.

An **undervoltage** occurs when the electrical supply drops. In North America, a wall plug usually supplies electricity at approximately 120 volts. Any significant drop below 120 volts is an undervoltage. A *brownout* is a prolonged undervoltage. A *blackout* is a complete power failure. Undervoltages can cause data loss but generally do not cause equipment damage.

An **overvoltage**, or **power surge**, occurs when the incoming electrical power increases significantly above the normal 120 volts. A momentary overvoltage, called a *spike*, occurs when the increase in power lasts for less than one millisecond (one thousandth of a second). Uncontrollable disturbances such as lightning bolts cause spikes. Overvoltages can cause immediate and permanent damage to hardware.

Safeguards against System Failure

To protect against overvoltages, use a surge protector. A **surge protector**, also called a *surge suppressor*, uses special electrical components to smooth out minor noise, provide a stable current flow, and keep an overvoltage from reaching the computer and other electronic equipment (Figure 11-20). Sometimes resembling a power strip, the computer and other devices plug in the surge protector, which plugs in the power source. The surge protector absorbs small overvoltages — generally without damage to the computer and equipment. To protect the computer and other equipment from large overvoltages, such as those caused by a lightning strike, some surge protectors completely stop working when an overvoltage reaches a certain level.

No surge protectors are 100 percent effective. Large power surges can bypass the protector. Repeated small overvoltages can weaken a surge protector permanently. Some experts recommend replacing a surge protector every two to three years. Typically, the amount of protection offered by a surge protector is proportional to its cost. That is, the more expensive, the more protection the protector offers.

The surge protector you purchase should meet the safety specification for surge suppression products. This specification, which is called the *Underwriters Laboratories* (*UL*) *1449 standard*, allows no more than 500 maximum volts to pass through the line. The response time of the surge protector should be less than one nanosecond. The surge protector also should have a Joule rating of at least 200. A *Joule* is the unit of energy a surge protection device can absorb before it can be damaged. The higher the Joule rating, the better the protection.

If your computer connects to a network or the Internet, also be sure to have protection for your modem, telephone lines, DSL lines, Internet cable lines, and network lines. Many surge protectors include plug-ins for telephone lines and other cables. If yours does not, you can purchase separate devices to protect these lines.

For additional electrical protection, some applications connect an uninterruptible power supply to the computer. An **uninterruptible power supply** (**UPS**) is a device that contains surge protection circuits and one or more batteries that can provide power during a temporary or permanent loss of power (Figure 11-21). A UPS connects between your computer and a power source.

Two types of UPS devices are standby and online. A *standby UPS*, sometimes called an *offline UPS*, switches to battery power when a problem occurs in the power line. The amount of time a standby UPS allows a user to continue working depends on the electrical requirements of the computer and the size of the batteries in the UPS. A UPS for a personal computer should provide from 10 to 30 minutes of use in the event of a total power loss. This should be enough time to save current work and shut down the computer properly. An *online UPS* always runs off the battery, which provides continuous protection. An online UPS is much more expensive than a standby UPS.

WEB LINK 11-8

Uninterruptible Power Supply

For more information, visit scsite.com/dc2006/ch11/weblink and then click Uninterruptible Power Supply.

FIGURE 11-20 Circuits inside a surge protector safeguard against overvoltages and undervoltages.

FIGURE 11-21 If power fails, an uninterruptible power supply (UPS), uses batteries to provide electricity for a limited amount of time.

Some companies use duplicate components or computers to protect against system failure. A *fault-tolerant computer* has duplicate components so it can continue to operate when one of its main components fail. Companies that must have their computers operational at all times may have two separate duplicate computers running simultaneously. Airline reservation systems, communications networks, and automated teller machines are examples of systems that duplicate components or computers to ensure that no data is lost in the event of a system failure.

FAQ 11-7

Should I use a surge protector on all my electronics?

It is a good idea to use a surge protector on high-end, expensive electronic equipment such as entertainment systems, DVD players, fax machines, and copy machines. A lightning strike or other substantial power surge could cause damage to any of this equipment. For more information, visit scsite.com/dc2006/ch11/faq and then click Surge Protectors.

BACKING UP — THE ULTIMATE SAFEGUARD

To prevent against data loss caused by system failure, computer users should back up files regularly. A **backup** is a duplicate of a file, program, or disk that can be used if the original is lost, damaged, or destroyed. Thus, to **back up** a file means to make a copy of it. In the case of system failure or the discovery of corrupted files, you **restore** the files by copying the backed up files to their original location on the computer.

You can use just about any media to store backups. Be sure to use high-quality media. A good choice for a home user might be CD-RWs or DVD+RWs.

Keep backup copies in a fireproof and heatproof safe or vault, or offsite. *Offsite* means in a location separate from the computer site. Home and business users keep backup copies offsite so that a single disaster, such as a fire, does not destroy both the original and the backup copy of the data. An offsite location can be a safe deposit box at a bank or a briefcase. A growing trend is to use online storage as an offsite location. As discussed in

Chapter 7, online storage is a service on the Web that provides storage to computer users.

Most backup programs for the home user provide for a full backup and a selective backup. A *full backup* copies all of the files in the computer. With a *selective backup*, users choose which folders and files to include in a backup.

Some users implement a *three-generation backup* policy to preserve three copies of important files. The *grandparent* is the oldest copy of the file. The *parent* is the second oldest copy of the file. The *child* is the most recent copy of the file.

Backup programs are available from many sources. Most operating systems include a backup program. Backup devices, such as tape and removable disk drives, also include backup programs. Numerous stand-alone backup utilities exist. Many of these can be downloaded from the Web at no cost.

Some companies choose to use an online backup service to handle their backup needs. An *online backup service* is a Web site that automatically backs up files to its online location. These sites usually charge a monthly or annual fee. If the system crashes, the online backup service typically sends the company one or more CDs that contains all of its backed up data. Users with high-speed Internet connections opt for online backup services. For slower connections, these services are not practical.

WIRELESS SECURITY

Wireless technology has made dramatic changes in the way computer users communicate worldwide. Billions of home and business users have notebook computers, PDAs, smart phones, and other devices to access the Internet, send e-mail and instant messages, chat online, or share network connections — all without wires. Home users set up wireless home networks. Mobile users access wireless networks in hot spots at airports, hotels, schools, shopping malls, bookstores, restaurants, and coffee shops. Schools have wireless networks so students can access the school network using their mobile computers and devices as they move from building to building.

Although wireless access provides many conveniences to users, it also poses additional security risks. One study showed that about 65 percent of wireless networks have no security protection. Some perpetrators connect to other's wireless networks to gain free Internet access; others may try to access a company's confidential data.

To access the network, the perpetrator must be in range of the wireless network. Some intruders intercept and monitor communications as they transmit through the air. Others connect to a network through an unsecured wireless access point (WAP). In one technique, called *war driving*, perpetrators attempt to connect to wireless networks via their notebook computer while driving a vehicle through areas they suspect have a wireless network. Some perpetrators instead use *war flying*, where they use airplanes instead of vehicles to detect unsecured wireless networks. Once located, some intruders use a GPS device to add the WAP to a war driving access point map on the Internet (Figure 11-22), making the wireless network vulnerable to future attacks.

In addition to using firewalls, some safeguards that improve the security of wireless networks include reconfiguring the wireless access point and ensuring equipment uses one or more wireless security standards such as Wired Equivalent Privacy, Wi-Fi Protected Access, and 802.11i.

- A wireless access point (WAP) should be configured so it does not broadcast a network name. The WAP also should be programmed so only certain devices can access it.
- *Wired Equivalent Privacy* (*WEP*) is a security standard that defines how to encrypt data as it travels across wireless networks. WEP supports both 40-bit and 128-bit encryption.
- *Wi-Fi Protected Access* (*WPA*) is a security standard that improves on WEP by authenticating network users and providing more advanced encryption techniques.
- An *802.11i* network, the most recent network security standard, conforms to the government's security standards and uses more sophisticated encryption techniques than both WPA and WEP.

By implementing these security measures, you can help to prevent unauthorized access to wireless networks.

FIGURE 11-22   This Web site marks all unsecured wireless networks located during a war drive.

Test your knowledge of pages 569 through 577 in Quiz Yourself 11-2.

QUIZ YOURSELF 11-2

Instructions: Find the true statement below. Then, rewrite the remaining false statements so they are true.

1. An end-user license agreement (EULA) permits users to give copies to friends and colleagues, while continuing to use the software.

2. Encryption is a process of converting ciphertext into plaintext to prevent authorized access.

3. Mobile users are not susceptible to hardware theft.

4. Overvoltages can cause immediate and permanent damage to hardware.

5. Three backup security standards are Wired Equivalent Privacy, Wi-Fi Protected Access, and 802.11i.

6. To prevent against data loss caused by a system failure, computer users should restore files regularly.

Quiz Yourself Online: To further check your knowledge of safeguards against hardware theft and vandalism, software piracy, encryption, protection against system failure, backing up resources, and wireless security, visit scsite.com/dc2006/ch11/quiz and then click Objectives 4 – 9.

ETHICS AND SOCIETY

As with any powerful technology, computers can be used for both good and bad intentions. The standards that determine whether an action is good or bad are known as ethics.

Computer ethics are the moral guidelines that govern the use of computers and information systems. Six frequently discussed areas of computer ethics are unauthorized use of computers and networks, software theft (piracy), information accuracy, intellectual property rights, codes of conduct, and information privacy. The questionnaire in Figure 11-23 raises issues in each of these areas.

Previous sections in this chapter discussed unauthorized use of computers and networks, and software theft (piracy). The following pages discuss issues related to information accuracy, intellectual property rights, codes of conduct, and information privacy.

	Ethical	Unethical
1. A company requires employees to wear badges that track their whereabouts while at work.	☐	☐
2. A supervisor reads an employee's e-mail.	☐	☐
3. An employee uses his computer at work to send e-mail messages to a friend.	☐	☐
4. An employee sends an e-mail message to several coworkers and blind copies his supervisor.	☐	☐
5. An employee forwards an e-mail message to a third party without permission from the sender.	☐	☐
6. An employee uses her computer at work to complete a homework assignment for school.	☐	☐
7. The vice president of your Student Government Association (SGA) downloads a photograph from the Web and uses it in a flier recruiting SGA members.	☐	☐
8. A student copies text from the Web and uses it in a research paper for his English Composition class.	☐	☐
9. An employee sends political campaign material to individuals on her employer's mailing list.	☐	☐
10. As an employee in the registration office, you have access to student grades. You look up grades for your friends, so they do not have to wait for delivery of grade reports from the postal service.	☐	☐
11. An employee makes a copy of software and installs it on her home computer. No one uses her home computer while she is at work, and she uses her home computer only to finish projects from work.	☐	☐
12. An employee who has been laid off installs a computer virus on his employer's computer.	☐	☐
13. A person designing a Web page finds one on the Web similar to his requirements, copies it, modifies it, and publishes it as his own Web page.	☐	☐
14. A student researches using only the Web to write a report.	☐	☐
15. In a society in which all transactions occur online (a cashless society), the government tracks every transaction you make and automatically deducts taxes from your bank account.	☐	☐
16. Someone copies a well-known novel to the Web and encourages others to read it.	☐	☐

FIGURE 11-23   Indicate whether you think the situation described is ethical or unethical. Discuss your answers with your instructor and other students.

Information Accuracy

Information accuracy today is a concern because many users access information maintained by other people or companies, such as on the Internet. Do not assume that because the information is on the Web that it is correct. As Chapter 2 discussed, users should evaluate the value of a Web page before relying on its content. Be aware that the company providing access to the information may not be the creator of the information.

In addition to concerns about the accuracy of computer input, some individuals and organizations raise questions about the ethics of using computers to alter output, primarily graphical output such as retouched photographs. Using graphics equipment and software, users easily can digitize photographs and then add, change, or remove images (Figure 11-24).

One group that completely opposes any manipulation of an image is the National Press Photographers Association. It believes that allowing even the slightest alteration eventually could lead to misrepresentative photographs. Others believe that digital photograph retouching is acceptable as long as the significant content or meaning of the photograph does not change. Digital retouching is an area in which legal precedents so far have not been established.

Intellectual Property Rights

Intellectual property (IP) refers to unique and original works such as ideas, inventions, art, writings, processes, company and product names, and logos. **Intellectual property rights** are the rights to which creators are entitled for their work. Certain issues arise surrounding IP today because many of these works are available digitally.

A **copyright** gives authors and artists exclusive rights to duplicate, publish, and sell their materials. A copyright protects any tangible form of expression.

A common infringement of copyright is piracy. People pirate (illegally copy) software, movies, and music. Many areas are not clear-cut with respect to the law, because copyright law gives the public fair use to copyrighted material. The issues surround the phrase, fair use, which allows use for educational and critical purposes.

FIGURE 11-24 A digitally altered photograph shows sports legend Michael Jordan (born in 1963) meeting the famous scientist Albert Einstein (who died in 1955).

This vague definition is subject to widespread interpretation and raises many questions:

- Should individuals be able to download contents of your Web site, modify it, and then put it on the Web again as their own?
- Should a faculty member have the right to print material from the Web and distribute it to all members of the class for teaching purposes only?
- Should someone be able to scan photographs or pages from a book, publish them to the Web, and allow others to download them?
- Should someone be able to put the lyrics of a song on the Web?
- Should students be able to post term papers they have written on the Web, making it tempting for other students to download and submit them as their own work?

These and many other issues are being debated strongly by members of society. Read At Issue 11-3 for a related discussion.

WEB LINK 11-9

Intellectual Property Rights

For more information, visit scsite.com/dc2006/ch11/weblink and then click Intellectual Property Rights.

AT ISSUE 11-3

Should Companies Be Able to Develop Software that Encourages Illegal Activity?

In 2001, the cutting-edge Napster file-sharing network was shut down effectively by courts because it contributed to the illegal sharing of copyrighted material. The main issue cited by the courts was that the service relied on a Napster-owned central database that contained the locations of files of copyrighted songs and movies. While the Napster software and service served a legitimate purpose by allowing millions of people to share legal information, the result was that most users of the service chose to engage in illegal sharing of copyrighted material.

Since then, other companies have developed similar services, but with one critical difference — the new services do not rely on a central database of the location of files. Instead, the information about the location of files is stored on many users' computers. To the dismay of the recording and motion picture industries, courts now have ruled that this technical difference in the software and services does not make the software companies liable for copyright infringement in which their users engage. Who is responsible for the enormous increase in copyright infringement: technology, software companies, or consumers? What can the recording and motion picture industries do to impede copyright infringement? Should software companies be allowed to distribute software that contributes to or encourages illegal activity?

Codes of Conduct

Recognizing that individuals need specific standards for the ethical use of computers, a number of computer-related organizations have established IT (information technology) codes of conduct (Figure 11-25). An IT **code of conduct** is a written guideline that helps determine whether a specific computer action is ethical or unethical.

IT CODE OF CONDUCT
1. Computers may not be used to harm other people.
2. Employees may not interfere with others' computer work.
3. Employees may not meddle in others' computer files.
4. Computers may not be used to steal.
5. Computers may not be used to bear false witness.
6. Employees may not copy or use software illegally.
7. Employees may not use others' computer resources without authorization.
8. Employees may not use others' intellectual property as their own.
9. Employees shall consider the social impact of programs and systems they design.
10. Employees always should use computers in a way that demonstrates consideration and respect for fellow humans.

FIGURE 11-25 Sample IT code of conduct employers may distribute to employees.

INFORMATION PRIVACY

Information privacy refers to the right of individuals and companies to deny or restrict the collection and use of information about them. In the past, information privacy was easier to maintain because information was kept in separate locations. Each retail store had its own credit files. Each government agency maintained separate records. Doctors had their own patient files.

Today, huge databases store this data online. Much of the data is personal and confidential and should be accessible only to authorized users. Many individuals and organizations, however, question whether this data really is private. That is, some companies and individuals collect and use this information without your authorization. Web sites often collect data about you, so they can customize advertisements and send you personalized e-mail messages. Some employers monitor your computer usage and e-mail messages.

Figure 11-26 lists measures you can take to make your personal data more private. The following sections address techniques companies and employers use to collect your personal data.

Electronic Profiles

When you fill out a form such as a magazine subscription, product warranty registration card, or contest entry form, the merchant that receives the form usually enters it into a database. Likewise, every time you click an advertisement on the Web or register software online, your information and preferences enter a database. Merchants then sell the contents of their databases to national marketing firms and Internet advertising firms. By combining this data with information from public sources such as driver's licenses and vehicle registrations,

HOW TO SAFEGUARD PERSONAL INFORMATION
1. Fill in only necessary information on rebate, warranty, and registration forms.
2. Do not preprint your telephone number or Social Security number on personal checks.
3. Have an unlisted or unpublished telephone number.
4. If Caller ID is available in your area, find out how to block your number from displaying on the receiver's system.
5. Do not write your telephone number on charge or credit receipts.
6. Ask merchants not to write credit card numbers, telephone numbers, Social Security numbers, and driver's license numbers on the back of your personal checks.
7. Purchase goods with cash, rather than credit or checks.
8. Avoid shopping club and buyer cards.
9. If merchants ask personal questions, find out why they want to know before releasing the information.
10. Inform merchants that you do not want them to distribute your personal information.
11. Request, in writing, to be removed from mailing lists.
12. Obtain your credit report once a year from each of the three major credit reporting agencies (Equifax, Experian, and TransUnion) and correct any errors.
13. Request a free copy of your medical records once a year from the Medical Information Bureau.
14. Limit the amount of information you provide to Web sites. Fill in only required information.
15. Install a cookie manager to filter cookies.
16. Clear your history file when you are finished browsing.
17. Set up a free e-mail account. Use this e-mail address for merchant forms.
18. Turn off file and printer sharing on your Internet connection.
19. Install a personal firewall.
20. Sign-up for e-mail filtering through your Internet service provider or use an anti-spam program such as Brightmail.
21. Do not reply to spam for any reason.
22. Surf the Web anonymously with a program such as Freedom WebSecure or through an anonymous Web site such as Anonymizer.com.

FIGURE 11-26 Techniques to keep personal data private.

these firms create an electronic profile of individuals. The information in these electronic profiles includes personal details such as your age, address, telephone number, spending habits, marital status, number of dependents, ages of dependents, and so on.

Direct marketing supporters say that using information in this way lowers overall selling costs, which lowers product prices. Critics contend that the information in an electronic profile reveals more about an individual than anyone has a right to know. They claim that companies should inform people if they plan to provide personal information to others, and people should have the right to deny such use. Many companies today allow people to specify whether they want their personal information distributed (Figure 11-27).

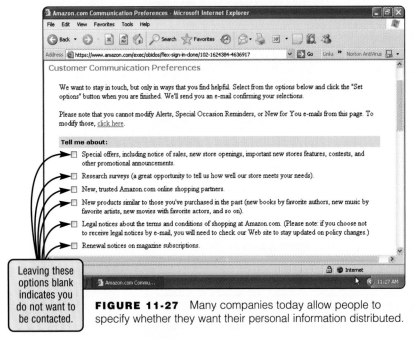

Leaving these options blank indicates you do not want to be contacted.

FIGURE 11-27   Many companies today allow people to specify whether they want their personal information distributed.

Cookies

E-commerce and other Web applications often rely on cookies to identify users and customize Web pages. A **cookie** is a small text file that a Web server stores on your computer. Cookie files typically contain data about you, such as your user name or viewing preferences.

Web sites use cookies for a variety of purposes.

- Most Web sites that allow for personalization use cookies to track user preferences. On such sites, users may be asked to fill in a form requesting personal information, such as their name, postal code, or site preferences. A news Web site, for example, might allow users to customize their viewing preferences to display certain stock quotes. The Web site stores their preferences in a cookie on the users' hard disks.
- Some Web sites use cookies to store users' passwords, so they do not need to enter it every time they log in to the Web site.
- Online shopping sites generally use a *session cookie* to keep track of items in a user's shopping cart. This way, users can start an order during one Web session and finish it on another day in another session. Session cookies usually expire after a certain time, such as a week or a month.
- Some Web sites use cookies to track how regularly users visit a site and the Web pages they visit while at the site.
- Web sites may use cookies to target advertisements. These sites store a user's interests and browsing habits in the cookie.

Many commercial Web sites send a cookie to your browser, and then your computer's hard disk stores the cookie. The next time you visit the Web site, your browser retrieves the cookie from your hard disk and sends the data in the cookie to the Web site. Figure 11-28 illustrates how Web sites work with cookies.

Some Web sites do sell or trade information stored in your cookie to advertisers — a practice many believe to be unethical. If you do not want your personal information distributed, you should limit the amount of information you provide to a Web site.

You can set your browser to accept cookies automatically, prompt you if you want to accept a cookie, or disable cookie use altogether. Keep in mind if you disable cookie use, you may not be able to use many of the e-commerce Web sites. As an alternative, you can purchase software that selectively blocks cookies.

FAQ 11-8

Can a Web site read data in all the cookie files on my computer's hard disk?

No, a Web site can read data only from its own cookie file stored on your hard disk. It cannot access or view any other data on your hard disk — including another cookie file. For more information, visit scsite.com/ dc2006/ch11/faq and then click Cookies.

FIGURE 11-28 HOW COOKIES WORK

Step 1:
When you type the Web address of a Web site in your browser window, the browser program searches your hard disk for a cookie associated with the Web site.

Step 2:
If the browser finds a cookie, it sends information in the cookie file to the Web site.

Web server for www.company.com

Step 3:
If the Web site does not receive cookie information, and is expecting it, the site creates an identification number for you in its database and sends that number to your browser. The browser in turn creates a cookie file based on that number and stores the cookie file on your hard disk. The Web site now can update information in the cookie file whenever you access the site.

Spyware and Adware

Spyware is a program placed on a computer without the user's knowledge that secretly collects information about the user. Spyware can enter a computer as a virus or as a result of a user installing a new program. The spyware program communicates information it collects to some outside source while you are online.

Some vendors or employers use spyware to collect information about program usage or employees. Internet advertising firms often collect information about users' Web browsing habits by hiding spyware in adware. *Adware* is a program that displays an online advertisement in a banner or pop-up window on Web pages, e-mail, or other Internet services.

Another type of spyware, called a *Web bug*, is hidden on Web pages or in e-mail messages in the form of graphical images. Web businesses use Web bugs to monitor online habits of Web site visitors. Often, Web bugs link to a cookie stored on the hard disk. (Cookies are not considered spyware because you know they exist.)

To remove spyware, you can purchase a special program that can detect and delete it. Read At Issue 11-4 for a related discussion.

AT ISSUE 11-4

Should Spyware Be Legal?

Legitimate businesses and illegitimate hackers use a variety of techniques to secretly install spyware on unsecured computers. Spyware can perform a number of tasks, such as monitoring the Web sites that you visit or controlling a computer remotely. Some Web pages also have cookies that count visitors and gather basic statistical information about a visitor's location and Web browser. Online advertising agencies or Internet service providers frequently place spyware cookies as part of a promotion, sometimes without the knowledge of the Web page's sponsor. When the collected information is stored in a Web database and shared among several sites, the technology can track a visitor's travels around the Web. If a visitor completes a registration, that information also can be distributed to other advertisers. Spyware and cookies help advertisers reach their markets and refine their messages, but opponents say the technology is little more than electronic stalking. Should spyware and/or cookies be banned, or is it the right of Web page owners and advertisers to collect information about visitors? Why? Should Web page authors and/or Web page visitors be made aware of spyware and cookies? Why or why not?

Spam

Spam is an unsolicited e-mail message or newsgroup posting sent to many recipients or newsgroups at once. Spam is Internet junk mail (Figure 11-29). The content of spam ranges from selling a product or service, to promoting a business opportunity, to advertising offensive material. One study indicates the average user receives more than 1,000 spam e-mail messages each year. Instead of via e-mail, some spam is sent through an instant massaging system and, thus, is called *spim*. Another type, called *spit*, is spam sent via Internet telephony.

Users can reduce the amount of spam they receive with a number of techniques. Some e-mail programs have built-in settings that allow users to delete spam automatically. Users also can sign up for e-mail filtering from their Internet service provider. **E-mail filtering** is a service that blocks e-mail messages from designated sources. These services typically collect the spam in a central location that users can view at anytime. An alternative to e-mail filtering is to purchase an **anti-spam program** that attempts to remove spam before it reaches your inbox. The disadvantage of e-mail filters and anti-spam programs is that sometimes they remove valid e-mail messages.

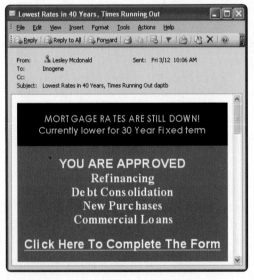

FIGURE 11-29   An example of spam.

Phishing

Phishing is a scam in which a perpetrator sends an official looking e-mail that attempts to obtain your personal and financial information. Some phishing e-mail messages ask you to reply with your information; others direct you to a phony Web site, or a pop-up window that looks like a Web site, that collects the information. Read At Issue 11-5 for a related discussion.

If you receive an e-mail message that looks legitimate and requests you update credit card numbers, Social Security numbers, bank account numbers, passwords, or other private information, the FTC recommends you visit the Web site directly to determine if the request is valid.

To help deter spam and phishing scams, Microsoft and others are developing standards that require e-mail messages contain sender identification so recipients can verify the legitimacy of messages.

FAQ 11-9

What do I do if I have been caught in a phishing scam?

If you have been trapped in a phishing scam, forward the phishing e-mail message to uce@ftc.gov or call the FTC help line at 1-877-FTC-HELP. For more information, visit scsite.com/dc2006/ch11/faq and then click Phishing Scams.

AT ISSUE 11-5

Are You Protecting Yourself from Identity Theft?

Using both spam and Web browser pop-up windows, scam artists are employing a technique known as phishing to try to steal your personal information, such as credit card numbers, banking information, and passwords. For example, an e-mail message may appear to be a request from your credit card company to verify your Social Security number and online banking password. Instead, the information you submit ends up in the hands of the scammer, who then either uses the information to access your accounts and take money, or sell and trade the information with other criminals. Sadly, the result often is identity theft. Law enforcement agencies believe that many of the phishing schemes are related to organized crime. Approximately 20 percent of those targeted by phishing provide the requested information. This high level of response emboldens the scammers. Social, technological, and legal solutions have been proposed to solve the phishing problem, but the phenomenon continues to grow. What can a person do to protect against phishing when e-mail messages are received from what appear to be legitimate organizations? What can be done to limit or stop the practice of phishing? Are companies and/or consumers to share in the blame for the success of phishing? Why or why not?

Privacy Laws

The concern about privacy has led to the enactment of federal and state laws regarding the storage and disclosure of personal data (Figure 11-30). Common points in some of these laws are outlined at the top of the next page.

Date	Law	Purpose
2003	CAN-SPAM Act	Gives law enforcement the right to impose penalties on people using the Internet to distribute spam.
2002	Sarbanes-Oxley Act	Requires corporate officers, auditors, and attorneys of publicly-traded companies follow strict financial reporting guidelines.
2001	Children's Internet Protection Act (CIPA)	Protects minors from inappropriate content when accessing the Internet in schools and libraries.
2001	Provide Appropriate Tools Required to Intercept and Obstruct Terrorism (PATRIOT) Act	Gives law enforcement the right to monitor people's activities, including Web and e-mail habits.
1999	Gramm-Leach-Bliley Act (GLBA) or Financial Modernization Act	Protects consumers from disclosure of their personal financial information and requires institutions to alert customers of information disclosure policies.
1998	Children's Online Privacy Protection Act (COPPA)	Requires Web sites protect personal information of children under 13 years of age.
1998	Digital Millennium Copyright Act (DMCA)	Makes it illegal to circumvent antipiracy schemes in commercial software; outlaws sale of devices that copy software illegally.
1997	No Electronic Theft (NET) Act	Closes a narrow loophole in the law that allowed people to give away copyrighted material (such as software) on the Internet without legal repercussions.
1996	Health Insurance Portability and Accountability Act (HIPAA)	Protects individuals against the wrongful disclosure of their health information.
1996	National Information Infrastructure Protection Act	Penalizes theft of information across state lines, threats against networks, and computer system trespassing.
1994	Computer Abuse Amendments Act	Amends 1984 act to outlaw transmission of harmful computer code such as viruses.
1992	Cable Act	Extends the privacy of the Cable Communications Policy Act of 1984 to include cellular and other wireless services.
1991	Telephone Consumer Protection Act	Restricts activities of telemarketers.
1988	Computer Matching and Privacy Protection Act	Regulates the use of government data to determine the eligibility of individuals for federal benefits.
1988	Video Privacy Protection Act	Forbids retailers from releasing or selling video-rental records without customer consent or a court order.
1986	Electronic Communications Privacy Act (ECPA)	Provides the same right of privacy protection for the postal delivery service and telephone companies to the new forms of electronic communications, such as voice mail, e-mail, and cellular telephones.
1984	Cable Communications Policy Act	Regulates disclosure of cable television subscriber records.
1984	Computer Fraud and Abuse Act	Outlaws unauthorized access of federal government computers.
1978	Right to Financial Privacy Act	Strictly outlines procedures federal agencies must follow when looking at customer records in banks.
1974	Privacy Act	Forbids federal agencies from allowing information to be used for a reason other than that for which it was collected.
1974	Family Educational Rights and Privacy Act	Gives students and parents access to school records and limits disclosure of records to unauthorized parties.
1970	Fair Credit Reporting Act	Prohibits credit reporting agencies from releasing credit information to unauthorized people and allows consumers to review their own credit records.

FIGURE 11-30 Summary of the major U.S. government laws concerning privacy.

1. Information collected and stored about individuals should be limited to what is necessary to carry out the function of the business or government agency collecting the data.

2. Once collected, provisions should be made to restrict access to the data to those employees within the organization who need access to it to perform their job duties.

3. Personal information should be released outside the organization collecting the data only when the person has agreed to its disclosure.

4. When information is collected about an individual, the individual should know that the data is being collected and have the opportunity to determine the accuracy of the data.

One law with an apparent legal loophole is the 1970 **Fair Credit Reporting Act**. The act limits the rights of others viewing a credit report to only those with a legitimate business need. The problem is that it does not define a legitimate business need. The result is that just about anyone can claim a legitimate business need and gain access to your credit report.

Computer Forensics

Computer forensics, also called *digital forensics*, *network forensics*, or *cyberforensics*, is the discovery, collection, and analysis of evidence found on computers and networks. Forensic analysis involves the examination of computer media, programs, data and log files on computers, servers, and networks. Many areas use computer forensics, including law enforcement, criminal prosecutors, military intelligence, insurance agencies, and information security departments in the private sector.

A computer forensics analyst must have knowledge of the law, technical experience with many types of hardware and software products, superior communication skills, familiarity with corporate structures and policies, a willingness to learn and update skills, and a knack for problem solving. For more information about computer forensics, read the Computer Forensics Special Feature that follows this chapter. For a look at the next generation of forensics, read Looking Ahead 11-2.

LOOKING AHEAD 11-2

Computer Knowledge Assessment Using Brain Fingerprinting

A powerful forensic tool may one day replace the traditional lie detector test. Brain fingerprinting examines a subset of brain waves generated involuntarily when an individual recognizes familiar information.

To conduct the test, researchers place a strap equipped with sensors on an individual's head and then present a variety of relevant and irrelevant words, pictures, and sounds. If the stimulus is familiar, the brain generates unique brain waves 300 to 800 milliseconds after receiving the stimulus.

Computers store and then analyze the series of unique brain waves to determine if the person's brain has stored critical details of a situation, such as a fraudulent or criminal act. Researchers also have determined that brain fingerprinting could help identify the onset of Alzheimer's disease. For more information, visit scsite.com/dc2006/ch11/looking and then click Brain Fingerprinting.

Employee Monitoring

Employee monitoring involves the use of computers to observe, record, and review an employee's use of a computer, including communications such as e-mail messages, keyboard activity (used to measure productivity), and Web sites visited. Many programs exist that easily allow employers to monitor employees. Further, it is legal for employers to use these programs.

A frequently debated issue is whether an employer has the right to read employee e-mail messages. Actual policies vary widely. Some companies declare that they will review e-mail messages regularly, and others state that e-mail is private. If a company does not have a formal e-mail policy, it can read e-mail messages without employee notification. One survey discovered that more than 73 percent of companies search and/or read employee files, voice mail, e-mail messages, Web connections, and other networking communications. Several lawsuits have been filed against employers because many believe that such internal communications should be private.

Another controversial issue relates to the use of cameras to monitor employees, customers, and the public. Many people feel that this use of video cameras is a violation of privacy.

Content Filtering

One of the more controversial issues that surround the Internet is its widespread availability of objectionable material, such as racist literature, violence, and obscene pictures. Some believe that such materials should be banned. Others believe that the materials should be filtered, that is, restricted. **Content filtering** is the process of restricting access to certain material on the Web. Content filtering opponents argue that banning any materials violates constitutional guarantees of free speech and personal rights.

Many businesses use content filtering to limit employees' Web access. These businesses argue that employees are unproductive when visiting inappropriate or objectionable Web sites. Some schools, libraries, and parents use content filtering to restrict access to minors.

One approach to content filtering is through a rating system of the *Internet Content Rating Association (ICRA)*, which is similar to those used for movies and videos. Major Web sites such as Yahoo!, AOL, and MSN use the rating system established by the ICRA. If content at the Web site goes beyond the rating limits set in the Web browser software, a user cannot access the Web site. Concerned parents can set the rating limits and prevent these limits from being changed by using a password.

Another approach to content filtering is to use filtering software. **Web filtering software** is a program that restricts access to specified Web sites. Some also filter sites that use specific words. Others allow you to filter e-mail messages, chat rooms, and programs. Many Internet security programs include a firewall, antivirus program, and filtering capabilities combined (Figure 11-31).

FIGURE 11-31   Many Internet security programs include content filtering capabilities, where users can block specified Web sites and applications.

WEB LINK 11-11

Internet Content Rating Association

For more information, visit scsite.com/ dc2006/ch11/weblink and then click Internet Content Rating Association.

HEALTH CONCERNS OF COMPUTER USE

Users are a key component in any information system. Thus, protecting users is just as important as protecting hardware, software, and data.

The widespread use of computers has led to some important health concerns. Users should be proactive and minimize their chance of risk. The following sections discuss health risks and preventions, along with measures users can take to keep the environment healthy.

Computers and Health Risks

A **repetitive strain injury (RSI)** is an injury or disorder of the muscles, nerves, tendons, ligaments, and joints. Computer-related RSIs include tendonitis and carpal tunnel syndrome. RSIs are the largest job-related injury and illness problem in the United States today. For this reason, OSHA (Occupational Safety and Health Administration) has developed industry-specific and task-specific guidelines designed to prevent workplace injuries with respect to computer usage.

Tendonitis is inflammation of a tendon due to repeated motion or stress on that tendon. *Carpal tunnel syndrome* (CTS) is inflammation of the nerve that connects the forearm to the palm of the wrist. Repeated or forceful bending of the wrist can cause CTS or tendonitis of the wrist. Symptoms of tendonitis of the wrist include extreme pain that extends from the forearm to the hand, along with tingling in the fingers. Symptoms of CTS include burning pain when the nerve is compressed, along with numbness and tingling in the thumb and first two fingers.

Long-term computer work can lead to tendonitis or CTS. Factors that cause these disorders include prolonged typing, prolonged mouse usage, or continual shifting between the mouse and the keyboard. If untreated, these disorders can lead to permanent damage to your body.

You can take many precautions to prevent these types of injuries. Take frequent breaks during the computer session to exercise your hands and arms (Figure 11-32). To prevent injury due to typing, place a wrist rest between the keyboard and the edge of your desk. To prevent injury while using a mouse, place the mouse at least six inches from the edge of the

desk. In this position, your wrist is flat on the desk. Finally, minimize the number of times you switch between the mouse and the keyboard, and avoid using the heel of your hand as a pivot point while typing or using the mouse.

Another type of health-related condition due to computer usage is **computer vision syndrome** (CVS). You may have CVS if you have sore, tired, burning, itching, or dry eyes; blurred or double vision; distance blurred vision after prolonged staring at a display device; headache or sore neck; difficulty shifting focus between a display device and documents; difficulty focusing on the screen image; color fringes or after-images when you look away from the display device; and increased sensitivity to light. Eyestrain associated with CVS is not thought to have serious or long-term consequences. Figure 11-33 outlines some techniques you can follow to ease eyestrain.

People who spend their workday using the computer sometimes complain of lower back pain, muscle fatigue, and emotional fatigue. Lower back pain sometimes is caused from poor posture. Always sit properly in the chair while you work. Take a break every 30 to 60

HAND EXERCISES

- Spread fingers apart for several seconds while keeping wrists straight.
- Gently push back fingers and then thumb.
- Dangle arms loosely at sides and then shake arms and hands.

TECHNIQUES TO EASE EYESTRAIN

- Every 10 to 15 minutes, take an eye break.
  - Look into the distance and focus on an object for 20 to 30 seconds.
  - Roll your eyes in a complete circle.
  - Close your eyes and rest them for at least one minute.
- Blink your eyes every five seconds.
- Place your display device about an arm's length away from your eyes with the top of the screen at eye level or below.
- Use large fonts.
- If you wear glasses, ask your doctor about computer glasses.
- Adjust the lighting.

FIGURE 11-32 To reduce the chance of developing tendonitis or carpal tunnel syndrome, take frequent breaks during computer sessions to exercise your hands and arms.

FIGURE 11-33 Following these tips may help reduce eyestrain while working on a computer.

minutes — stand up, walk around, or stretch. Another way to help prevent these injuries is to be sure your workplace is designed ergonomically, which is discussed in the next section.

Ergonomics and Workplace Design

Ergonomics is an applied science devoted to incorporating comfort, efficiency, and safety into the design of items in the workplace. Ergonomic studies have shown that using the correct type and configuration of chair, keyboard, display device, and work surface helps users work comfortably and efficiently and helps protect their health. For the computer work space, experts recommend an area of at least two feet by four feet. Figure 11-34 illustrates additional guidelines for setting up the work area.

Computer Addiction

Computers can provide entertainment and enjoyment. Some computer users, however, become obsessed with the computer and the Internet. **Computer addiction** occurs when the computer consumes someone's entire social life. Computer addiction is a growing health problem.

Symptoms of a user with computer addiction include the following:
• Craves computer time
• Overjoyed when at the computer
• Unable to stop computer activity
• Irritable when not at the computer
• Neglects family and friends
• Problems at work or school

Computer addiction is a treatable illness through therapy and support groups.

viewing angle: 20° to center of screen
viewing distance: 18 to 28 inches

arms: elbows at about 90° and arms and hands approximately parallel to floor

keyboard height: 23 to 28 inches depending on height of user

adjustable height chair with 4 or 5 legs for stability

feet flat on floor

FIGURE 11-34 A well-designed work area should be flexible to allow adjustments to the height and build of different individuals. Good lighting and air quality also are important considerations.

Green Computing

Green computing involves reducing the electricity and environmental waste while using a computer. People use, and often waste, resources such as electricity and paper while using a computer. Society has become aware of this waste and is taking measures to combat it.

As discussed in Chapter 6, personal computers, display devices, and printers should comply with guidelines of the ENERGY STAR program. For example, many devices switch to standby or power save mode after a specified number of inactive minutes or hours.

Users should not store obsolete computers and devices in their basement, storage room, attic, warehouse, or any other location. Computers, monitors, and other equipment contain toxic materials and potentially dangerous elements including lead, mercury, and flame retardants. In a landfill, these materials release into the environment. Recycling and refurbishing old equipment are much safer alternatives for the environment. Manufacturers can use the millions of pounds of recycled raw materials to make products such as outdoor furniture and automotive parts.

By the year 2007, experts estimate that more than 500 million personal computers will be obsolete. Because of the huge potential volumes of electronic waste, the U.S. federal government has proposed a bill that would require computer recycling across the country. Local governments are working on methods to make it easy for consumers to recycle this type of equipment. Many computer manufacturers, office supply stores, and other agencies offer free recycling to consumers and businesses.

To reduce the environmental impact of computing further, users simply can alter a few habits. Figure 11-35 lists the ways you can contribute to green computing.

FAQ 11-10

Should I turn off my computer every night?

Manufacturers claim if you use the hibernate feature of your operating system or the sleep feature on your computer, you save about the same amount of energy as when you turn off the computer. The ENERGY STAR program, however, recommends turning it off. For more information, visit scsite.com/dc2006/ch11/faq and then click ENERGY STAR.

GREEN COMPUTING SUGGESTIONS

1. Use computers and devices that comply with the ENERGY STAR program.
2. Do not leave the computer running overnight.
3. Turn off the monitor, printer, and other devices when not in use.
4. Use paperless methods to communicate.
5. Recycle paper.
6. Buy recycled paper.
7. Recycle toner cartridges.
8. Recycle old computers and printers.
9. Telecommute (saves gas).

FIGURE 11-35 A list of suggestions to make computing healthy for the environment.

WEB LINK 11-12

Green Computing

For more information, visit scsite.com/dc2006/ch11/weblink and then click Green Computing.

Test your knowledge of pages 578 through 590 in Quiz Yourself 11-3.

QUIZ YOURSELF 11-3

Instructions: Find the true statement below. Then, rewrite the remaining false statements so they are true.

1. A code of conduct gives authors and artists exclusive rights to duplicate, publish, and sell their materials.

2. Factors that cause CVS include prolonged typing, prolonged mouse usage, or continual shifting between the mouse and the keyboard.

3. Phishing is the discovery, collection, and analysis of evidence found on computers and networks.

4. Spam is Internet junk mail.

5. Users should store obsolete computers and devices in their basement or attic.

6. Web sites use electronic profiles to track user preferences, store users' passwords, keep track of items in a user's shopping cart, and track Web site browsing habits.

7. You can assume that information on the Web is correct.

Quiz Yourself Online: To further check your knowledge of information accuracy, intellectual property rights, codes of conduct, information privacy, and computer-related health disorders and preventions, visit scsite.com/dc2006/ch11/quiz and then click Objectives 10 – 12.

CHAPTER SUMMARY

This chapter identified some potential computer risks and the safeguards that schools, businesses, and individuals can implement to minimize these risks. Wireless security risks and safeguards also were discussed.

The chapter presented ethical issues surrounding information accuracy, intellectual property rights, codes of conduct, and information privacy. The chapter ended with a discussion of computer-related health issues, their preventions, and ways to keep the environment healthy.

CAREER CORNER

Computer Forensics Specialist

Computer forensics is a rapidly growing field that involves gathering and analyzing evidence from computers and networks. It is the responsibility of the *computer forensics specialist* to carefully take several steps to identify and retrieve possible evidence that may exist on a suspect's computer. These steps include protecting the suspect's computer, discovering all files, recovering deleted files, revealing hidden files, accessing protected or encrypted files, analyzing all the data, and providing expert consultation and/or testimony as required. A computer forensics specialist must have knowledge of all aspects of the computer, from the operating system to computer architecture and hardware design.

In the past, many computer forensics specialists were self-taught computer users who may have attended computer forensics seminars, or they may have been trained in the use of one or more computer forensics tools by software vendors. The computer forensics specialist of today needs extensive training, usually from several different sources. A degree in Computer Science should be supplemented with graduate courses and university level professional development certificates.

Entry level salaries for computer forensics specialists range from $45,000 to $75,000. With experience and certifications, salaries can exceed $125,000. For more information, read the Computer Forensics Special Feature that follows this chapter or visit scsite.com/dc2006/ch11/careers and then click Computer Forensics Specialist.

High-Tech Talk

THE KEY(S) TO MAKING ENCRYPTION WORK

Every day, hundreds of thousands of people carry notebook computers to and from work, even as other computer users interact electronically, via e-mail, Web sites, ATMs, and cellular telephones. The increase of electronically transmitted information has led to an increased reliance on encryption, which helps ensure that unauthorized individuals cannot obtain the contents of these electronic transmissions.

The two basic types of encryption are private key and public key. With *private key encryption*, also called *symmetric key encryption*, both the originator and the recipient use the same secret key to encrypt and decrypt the data. The most popular private key encryption system is *advanced encryption standard* (*AES*), which was adopted officially as the U.S. government standard in May 2002.

Public key encryption, also called *asymmetric key encryption*, uses two encryption keys: a public key and a private key. Public key encryption software generates both your private key and your public key. A message encrypted with your public key can be decrypted only with your private key, and vice versa.

The public key is made known to those with whom you communicate. For example, public keys are posted on a Web page or e-mailed. A central administrator can publish a list of public keys on a public key server. The private key, by contrast, should be kept confidential. To send an encrypted e-mail message with public key encryption, the sender uses the receiver's public key to encrypt the message. Then, the receiver uses his or her private key to decrypt the message (Figure 11-36). For example, if Mae wants to send Jonah an encrypted message, she would use Jonah's public key to encrypt the message. When Jonah receives the encrypted message, he would use his private key to decrypt it. Jonah's encryption software generated his public and private keys. Mae uses Jonah's public key to encrypt the message. Thus, only Jonah will be able to decrypt the message with his private key.

Windows XP includes a security feature called the *Encryption File System* (*EFS*). EFS uses a combination of public key and symmetric key encryption to ensure that files are protected from almost any method of unauthorized access. When a user encrypts a file, EFS generates a random number for the file that EFS calls the file's file encryption key (FEK) to encrypt the data. EFS then uses FEK to encrypt the file's contents with an encryption algorithm. The FEK then is encrypted with the user's public key using the RSA public-key-based encryption algorithm, and the encrypted FEK then is stored with the file. Of course, the entire encryption process happens behind the scenes for the user, who simply completes a few mouse clicks to encrypt a folder or file. That is part of the elegance of EFS: while it is simple for a user, it is very difficult for any unauthorized user without the correct keys to crack the encryption. In the end, that is the key to keeping your data safe and sound. For more information, visit scsite.com/dc2006/ch11/tech and then click Encryption.

FIGURE 11-36   AN EXAMPLE OF PUBLIC KEY ENCRYPTION

Step 1:
The sender creates a document to be e-mailed to the receiver.

Step 4:
The receiver can read or print the decrypted message.

CONFIDENTIAL

The new
plant will
be located...

message to be sent

Step 2:
The sender uses the receiver's public key to encrypt a message.

Step 3:
The receiver uses his or her private key to decrypt the message.

CONFIDENTIAL

The new
plant will
be located...

decrypted message

sender (Mae)

public key

AA311C253

43025OC
4CAD078
32EC8EF

encrypted message

private key

receiver (Jonah)

Companies on the Cutting Edge

MCAFEE
INTRUSION PREVENTION PRODUCTS DEVELOPER

Researchers in sixteen countries on five continents are hard at work at *McAfee* laboratories trying to prevent computer intrusions. The Anti-Virus Emergency Response Team (AVERT) protects desktop computers, servers, networks, and wireless devices by collecting and then disassembling malicious-logic programs. The researchers also monitor online bulletin board systems for suspicious messages and expect to find more than 18,000 new threats each year.

More than 70 million consumers, small- and medium-sized businesses, governmental agencies, and large corporations rely on McAfee's intrusion prevention products to shield them from viruses, worms, Trojan horses, spyware and adware, and phishing schemes. In 2004, the Santa Clara, California, company sold its network analysis division and changed its name from Network Associates to improve its brand recognition. For more information, visit scsite.com/dc2006/ch11/companies and then click McAfee.

SYMANTEC
COMPUTER SECURITY SOLUTIONS LEADER

Ninety percent of computer users have installed a virus protection program on their systems, but only twenty percent have a firewall to protect against malicious hackers, according to a survey conducted by Applied Marketing Research. *Symantec*'s line of Norton products, including AntiVirus, Personal Firewall, and AntiSpam, can provide these users with peace of mind knowing that their systems are as secure as possible.

Gordon Eubank founded Symantec in 1982. Since then, more than 120 million users worldwide have used that company's products, helping it grow to one of the world's premier Internet security technology companies with operations in more than 35 countries. *Black Enterprise* magazine named Symantec's chairman and chief executive officer, John Thompson, corporate executive of the year in 2004. For more information, visit scsite.com/dc2006/ch11/companies and then click Symantec.

Technology Trailblazers

DONN PARKER
CYBERCRIME AUTHORITY

Computer criminals are troubled people, according to *Donn Parker*, so they violate the law in an attempt to solve their problems. In an attempt to fight cybercrime, Parker founded the International Information Integrity Institute (I-4), then interviewed hundreds of computer criminals and analyzed thousands of security crime cases during the past 30 years.

Security systems within corporations are critical, he says, but they should evolve constantly to defend against attackers. Parker says that computer criminals are unpredictable and irrational, so companies need to stay motivated to enforce their technology risk management plans.

Parker has conducted security reviews for more than 250 companies and has written 6 computer security books. For more information, visit scsite.com/dc2006/ch11/people and then click Donn Parker.

CLIFFORD STOLL
COMPUTER PHILOSOPHER

Computers have become integrated in practically every phase of our lives, but *Clifford Stoll* wants us to think about their effect on our quality of life. He questions the benefits technology and the Internet presumably provide and the role computers play in schools.

In his books, *Silicon Snake Oil — Second Thoughts on the Information Highway* and *High Tech Heretic: Why Computers Don't Belong in the Classroom*, Stoll maintains that "life in the real world is far more interesting, far more important, far richer, than anything you'll ever find on a computer screen."

He first gained fame by tracking a hacker who was part of a spy ring selling computer secrets to the Soviet Union's KGB for money and drugs. For more information, visit scsite.com/dc2006/ch11/people and then click Clifford Stoll.

Chapter Review

The Chapter Review section summarizes the concepts presented in this chapter. To listen to the audio version of this Chapter Review, visit scsite.com/dc2006/ch11/review. To obtain help from other students regarding any subject in this chapter, visit scsite.com/dc2006/ch11/forum and post your thoughts or questions.

① What Are Types of Computer Security Risks? A **computer security risk** is any event or action that could cause a loss of or damage to computer hardware, software, data, information, or processing capability. Common computer security risks include computer viruses, worms, Trojan horses, denial of service attacks, and spoofing; unauthorized access and use; hardware theft and vandalism; software theft; information theft; and system failure.

② How Can Users Safeguard against Computer Viruses, Worms, Trojan Horses, Denial of Service Attacks, Back Doors, and Spoofing? A computer **virus** is a potentially damaging program that affects, or infects, a computer negatively by altering the way the computer works. A **worm** is a program that copies itself repeatedly, using up resources and possibly shutting down the computer or network. A **Trojan horse** is a program that hides within or looks like a legitimate program. Users can take precautions to guard against these *malicious-logic programs*. Do not start a computer with removable media in the drives. Never open an e-mail attachment unless it is from a trusted source. Disable *macros* in documents that are not from a trusted source. Install an **antivirus program** and a personal firewall. Stay informed about any new virus alert or **virus hoax**. To defend against a **denial of service attack**, improper use of a **back door**, and **spoofing**, users can install a **firewall**, install *intrusion detection software*, and set up a *honeypot*.

③ What Are Techniques to Prevent Unauthorized Computer Access and Use?
Unauthorized access is the use of a computer or network without permission. **Unauthorized use** is the use of a computer or its data for unapproved or illegal activities. A written acceptable use policy (AUP) outlines the activities for which the computer and network may and may not be used. A **firewall** consists of hardware and/or software that prevents unauthorized access to data, information, and storage media. *Intrusion detection software* analyzes network traffic, assesses vulnerability, identifies unauthorized intrusions, and notifies network administrators of suspicious behavior patterns or system breaches. An *access control* defines who can access a computer, when they can access it, and what actions they can take. Access controls include a **user name** and **password**, a *possessed object*, and a **biometric device**. An **audit trail** records in a file both successful and unsuccessful access attempts.

> *connect!* Visit scsite.com/dc2006/ch11/quiz or click the Quiz Yourself button. Click Objectives 1 – 3.

④ What Are Safeguards against Hardware Theft and Vandalism? **Hardware theft** is the act of stealing computer equipment. **Hardware vandalism** is the act of defacing or destroying computer equipment. The best preventive measures against hardware theft and vandalism are common sense and a constant awareness of the risk. Physical devices and practical security measures, passwords, possessed objects, and biometrics can reduce the risk of theft or render a computer useless if it is stolen.

⑤ How Do Software Manufacturers Protect against Software Piracy? Software **piracy** is the unauthorized and illegal duplication of copyrighted software. To protect themselves from software piracy, manufacturers issue a **license agreement** that provides specific conditions for use of the software. **Product activation** is a process during which users provide the product's identification number to receive an installation identification number unique to their computer.

⑥ What Is Encryption, and Why Is It Necessary? **Information theft** occurs when someone steals personal or confidential information. **Encryption** prevents information theft by converting readable data into unreadable characters. To read the data, a recipient must **decrypt**, or decipher, it into a readable form.

Chapter Review

(7) **What Types of Devices Are Available to Protect Computers from System Failure?**
A *system failure* is the prolonged malfunction of a computer. A common cause of system failure is
an electrical disturbance such as **noise**, an **undervoltage**, or an **overvoltage**. A **surge protector** uses
special electrical components to smooth out minor noise, provide a stable current flow, and keep
an overvoltage from reaching the computer. An **uninterruptible power supply** (**UPS**) contains surge
protection circuits and one or more batteries that can provide power during an undervoltage.

(8) **What Are Options for Backing Up Computer Resources?** A **backup** is a
duplicate of a file, program, or disk that can be used to **restore** the file if the original is
lost, damaged, or destroyed. Users can opt for a *full backup* or a *selective backup*. Most
operating systems and backup devices include a backup program, and numerous
stand-alone backup utilities exist. An *online backup service* is a Web site that
automatically backs up files to its online location.

(9) **What Are Risks and Safeguards Associated with Wireless Communications?** Wireless
access poses additional security risks. Intruders connect to other wireless networks to gain free Internet
access or a company's confidential data. Some intruders intercept and monitor communications as
they are transmitted. Others connect to a network through an
unsecured wireless access point (WAP). Some safeguards include
firewalls, reconfiguring the WAP, and ensuring equipment uses a
wireless security standard, such as *Wired Equivalent Privacy* (WEP),
Wi-Fi Protected Access (WPA), and *802.11i*.

> connect
> Visit scsite.com/dc2006/ch11/quiz
> or click the Quiz Yourself button. Click
> Objectives 4 – 9.

(10) **What Are Issues Related to Information Accuracy, Rights, and Conduct?** Computer
ethics govern the use of computers and information systems. Issues in computer ethics include the
responsibility for information accuracy and the **intellectual property rights** to which creators are
entitled for works that are available digitally. A **copyright** gives authors and artists exclusive rights
to duplicate, publish, and sell their materials. An IT (information technology) **code of conduct**
helps determine whether a specific computer action is ethical or unethical.

(11) **What Are Issues Surrounding Information Privacy?** **Information privacy** is the right of
individuals and companies to deny or restrict the collection and use of information about them. Issues
surrounding information privacy include electronic profiles, cookies, spyware and adware, spam,
phishing, computer forensics, and employee monitoring. An electronic profile combines data about an
individual's Web use with data from public sources, which then is sold. A **cookie** is a file that a Web
server stores on a computer to collect data about the user. *Spyware* is a program placed on a computer
that secretly collects information about the user. *Adware* is a program that displays an online advertisement in a banner or pop-up window. **Spam** is an unsolicited e-mail message or newsgroup posting
sent to many recipients. **Phishing** is a scam in which a perpetrator sends an official looking e-mail that
attempts to obtain personal or financial information. **Computer forensics** is the discovery, collection,
and analysis of evidence found on computers and networks. **Employee monitoring** uses computers to
observe, record, and review an employee's computer use.

(12) **How Can Health-Related Disorders and Injuries Due to Computer Use Be Prevented?**
A **repetitive strain injury** (**RSI**) is an injury or disorder of the muscles, nerves, tendons, ligaments,
and joints. Computer-related RSIs include *tendonitis* and *carpal tunnel syndrome* (*CTS*). Another
health-related condition is eyestrain associated with **computer vision syndrome** (*CVS*). To prevent
health-related disorders, take frequent breaks, use precautionary
exercises and techniques, and use *ergonomics* when planning the
workplace. **Computer addiction** occurs when the computer consumes someone's entire social life. Computer addiction is a
treatable illness through therapy and support groups.

> connect
> Visit scsite.com/dc2006/ch11/quiz
> or click the Quiz Yourself button. Click
> Objectives 10 – 12.

Key Terms

You should know the Primary Terms and be familiar with the Secondary Terms. Use the list below to help focus your study. To further enhance your understanding of the Key Terms in this chapter, visit scsite.com/dc2006/ch11/terms. See an example of and a definition for each term, and access current and additional information about the term from the Web.

Primary Terms

(shown in bold-black characters in the chapter)

anti-spam program (584)
antivirus program (560)
audit trail (565)
back door (562)
back up (576)
backup (576)
biometric device (567)
code of conduct (580)
computer addiction (589)
computer crime (556)
computer ethics (578)
computer forensics (586)
computer security risk (556)
computer vision syndrome (588)
content filtering (587)
cookie (582)
copyright (579)
cracker (556)
cybercrime (556)
cyberextortionist (557)
cyberterrorist (557)
decrypt (572)
denial of service attack (562)
digital certificate (573)
digital signature (572)
DoS attack (562)
e-mail filtering (584)
employee monitoring (586)
encryption (572)
Fair Credit Reporting Act (586)
firewall (563)
green computing (590)
hacker (556)
hardware theft (569)
hardware vandalism (569)
information privacy (580)

information theft (571)
inoculate (561)
intellectual property rights (579)
license agreement (570)
noise (574)
online security service (558)
overvoltage (574)
password (566)
personal firewall utility (564)
personal identification number (PIN) (567)
phishing (584)
piracy (570)
power surge (574)
product activation (571)
quarantine (561)
repetitive strain injury (RSI) (587)
restore (576)
script kiddie (556)
secure site (573)
software theft (570)
spam (584)
spoofing (563)
surge protector (574)
Trojan horse (558)
trusted source (560)
unauthorized access (564)
unauthorized use (564)
undervoltage (574)
uninterruptible power supply (UPS) (575)
user name (566)
virus (558)
virus definition (561)
virus hoax (562)
virus signature (561)
Web filtering software (587)
worm (558)

Secondary Terms

(shown in italic characters in the chapter)

128-bit encryption (573)
40-bit encryption (573)
802.11i (577)
access control (565)
adware (583)
authentication (566)
blackout (574)
brownout (574)
Business Software Alliance (BSA) (571)
carpal tunnel syndrome (CTS) (588)
CERT/CC (558)
certificate authority (CA) (573)
child (576)
ciphertext (572)
Computer Emergency Response Team Coordination Center (558)
CVS (588)
cyberforensics (586)
DDoS (distributed DoS) attack (562)
digital forensics (586)
encryption key (572)
end-user license agreement (EULA) (571)
ergonomics (589)
fault-tolerant computer (576)
full backup (576)
grandparent (576)
hash (572)
honeypot (564)
identification (566)
intellectual property (IP) (579)
Internet Content Rating Association (ICRA) (587)
intrusion detection software (564)
Joule (575)
macros (560)

malicious-logic programs (558)
network forensics (586)
offline UPS (575)
offsite (576)
online backup service 576)
online UPS (575)
parent (576)
payload (558)
plaintext (572)
possessed object (567)
Pretty Good Privacy (PGP) (572)
proxy server (563)
Secure HTTP (S-HTTP) (574)
Secure Sockets Layer (SSL) (574)
selective backup (576)
session cookie (582)
single-user license agreement (571)
spike (574)
spim (584)
spit (584)
spyware (583)
standby UPS (575)
surge suppressor (574)
system failure (574)
tendonitis (588)
three-generation backup (576)
Underwriters Laboratories (UL) 1449 standard (575)
user ID (566)
virtual private network (VPN) (574)
war driving (577)
war flying (577)
Web bug (583)
Wi-Fi Protected Access (WPA) (577)
Wired Equivalent Privacy (WEP) (577)
zombie (562)

Checkpoint

Use the Checkpoint exercises to check your knowledge level of the chapter. The Beyond the Book exercises will help broaden your understanding of the concepts presented in this chapter. To complete the Checkpoint exercises interactively, visit scsite.com/dc2006/ch11/check.

 Label the Figure   Identify these common computer security risks.

a. Internet and network attacks

b. hardware theft

c. information theft

d. software theft

e. system failure

f. unauthorized access and use

 True/False   Mark T for True and F for False. (See page numbers in parentheses.)

_____ 1. All breaches to computer security are planned. (556)

_____ 2. A worm is a program that hides within or looks like a legitimate program. (558)

_____ 3. Many methods exist to guarantee completely a computer or network is safe from computer viruses, worms, and Trojan horses. (560)

_____ 4. IP spoofing occurs when an intruder computer fools a network into believing its IP address is associated with a trusted source. (563)

_____ 5. A honeypot is a computer that is set up to entice an intruder to break into it. (564)

_____ 6. Software piracy reduces the chance of spreading viruses, increases your ability to receive technical support, and drives down the price of software. (571)

_____ 7. Noise generally is not a risk to hardware, software, or data. (574)

_____ 8. An online UPS switches to battery power when a problem occurs in a power line. (575)

_____ 9. To access a network, some perpetrators use a technique known as war driving, where they use airplanes to detect unsecured wireless networks. (577)

_____ 10. A cookie is a small text file that a Web server stores on your computer. (582)

_____ 11. A Web bug is a type of spyware hidden on Web pages or in e-mail messages in the form of graphical images. (583)

_____ 12. Web filtering software is a program that restricts access to specified Web sites. (587)

Checkpoint

 Multiple Choice   Select the best answer. (See page numbers in parentheses.)

1. The term cybercrime refers to _____. (556)
   a. events that damage computer hardware
   b. any illegal activities involving a computer
   c. online or Internet-based illegal acts
   d. destructive events or pranks

2. A computer infected by a virus, worm, or Trojan horse may have any of the following symptoms except _____. (558)
   a. available memory is more than expected
   b. system properties change
   c. existing programs and files disappear
   d. files become corrupted

3. _____ is a technique intruders use to make their network or Internet transmission appear legitimate to a victim computer or network. (563)
   a. A backdoor
   b. A DoS attack
   c. Spoofing
   d. A virus hoax

4. Physical access controls, such as locked doors and windows, usually are adequate to protect against _____. (569)
   a. software piracy
   b. unauthorized access
   c. hardware theft
   d. all of the above

5. Software piracy continues because _____. (571)
   a. in some countries, legal protection for software does not exist
   b. many buyers believe they have the right to copy software
   c. software piracy is a fairly simple crime to commit
   d. all of the above

6. Encrypted (scrambled) data is called _____. (572)
   a. hypertext
   b. ciphertext
   c. subtext
   d. plaintext

7. A(n) _____ is a notice that guarantees a user or a Web site is legitimate. (573)
   a. trusted source
   b. end-user license agreement
   c. surge protector
   d. digital certificate

8. A _____ is a complete power failure. (574)
   a. spike
   b. blackout
   c. joule
   d. brownout

9. To _____ a file means to make a copy of it. (576)
   a. inoculate
   b. back up
   c. quarantine
   d. encrypt

10. A _____ gives authors and artists exclusive rights to duplicate, publish, and sell their materials. (579)
   a. copyright
   b. license
   c. password
   d. firewall

11. _____ is a program placed on a computer without the user's knowledge that secretly collects information about the user. (583)
   a. A cookie
   b. Spam
   c. Adware
   d. Spyware

12. _____ is a program that displays an online advertisement in a banner or pop-up window on Web pages, e-mail, or other Internet services. (583)
   a. A cookie
   b. Spam
   c. Adware
   d. Spyware

13. Web filtering software is a program that _____. (587)
   a. restricts access to specified Web sites
   b. backs up files to an online location
   c. uses encryption to secure a transaction on the Web
   d. protects against computer viruses

14. _____ is inflammation of the nerve that connects the forearm to the palm of the wrist. (588)
   a. Tendonitis
   b. Computer vision syndrome (CVS)
   c. Computer addiction
   d. Carpal tunnel syndrome (CTS)

Checkpoint

Matching

Match the terms with their definitions. (See page numbers in parentheses.)

____ 1. cracker (556)

____ 2. cyberterrorist (557)

____ 3. quarantine (561)

____ 4. back door (562)

____ 5. personal firewall utility (564)

____ 6. password (566)

____ 7. biometric device (567)

____ 8. encryption (572)

____ 9. certificate authority (CA) (573)

____ 10. digital certificate (573)

a. program or set of instructions in a program that allows users to bypass security controls when accessing a program, computer, or network

b. area of the hard disk that holds an infected file until the infection can be removed

c. protects a personal computer from unauthorized intrusions

d. someone who uses the Internet or network to destroy or damage computers for political reasons

e. notice that guarantees a user or a Web site is legitimate

f. translates a personal characteristic into digital code

g. spyware hidden on Web pages or in e-mail messages in the form of a graphical image

h. contains an uninfected copy of key commands and startup information

i. someone who accesses a computer or network illegally with the intent of maliciously action

j. private combination of characters associated with a user name

k. converting readable data into unreadable characters

l. company that issues and verifies digital certificates

Short Answer

Write a brief answer to each of the following questions.

1. How do antivirus programs detect and identify a virus? _____ What is a virus hoax? _____

2. How is identification different from authentication? _____ What are three methods of identification and authentication? _____

3. What does a single-user license agreement typically permit users to do? _____ What does it not permit users to do? _____

4. What is an uninterruptible power supply (UPS)? _____ How is a standby UPS different from an online UPS? _____

5. How is a full backup different from a selective backup? _____ What is a three-generation backup policy? _____

Beyond the Book

Read the following book elements, learn more about each using the Web, and then write a brief report.

1. At Issue — How Should Virus Authors Be Punished? (558), Should Biometrics Be Required to Ride the School Bus or Eat Lunch? (568), Should Companies Be Able to Develop Software that Encourages Illegal Activity? (580), Should Spyware Be Legal? (583), or Are You Protecting Yourself from Identity Theft? (584)

2. Career Corner — Computer Forensics Specialist (591)

3. Companies on the Cutting Edge — McAfee or Symantec (593)

4. FAQs (559, 562, 564, 565, 566, 571, 576, 582, 584, 590)

5. High-Tech Talk — The Key(s) to Making Encryption Work (592)

6. Looking Ahead — Three-Dimensional Facial Recognition Software — A Step Forward for Security (568) or Computer Knowledge Assessment Using Brain Fingerprinting (586)

7. Making Use of the Web — Environment (127)

8. Picture Yourself Aware of Computer-related Risks (554)

9. Technology Trailblazers — Donn Parker and Clifford Stoll (593)

10. Web Links (558, 562, 564, 570, 571, 572, 573, 575, 580, 582, 587, 590)

Learn It Online

Use the Learn It Online exercises to reinforce your understanding of the chapter concepts. To access the Learn It Online exercises, visit scsite.com/dc2006/ch11/learn.

(1) At the Movies — Does Biometrics Violate Employee Privacy?

To view the Does Biometrics Violate Employee Privacy? movie, click the number 1 button. Locate your video and click the corresponding High-Speed or Dial-Up link, depending on your Internet connection. Watch the movie and then complete the exercise by answering the questions that follow. Many companies are turning to high-tech methods of identifying and tracking employees. Biometric identification methods, which include fingerprinting, iris, voice, hand, and facial scans, are gaining in popularity. These methods used to be associated with high-security facilities; but due to increased risks from terrorism, they are gaining popularity in other workplaces. Biometric identification will help employers with employee fraud and security issues. Can you think of any instances where biometric identification can be used as a safety measure for employees? Are there any circumstances under which biometric technology can be abused in the workplace?

(2) At the Movies — Stop Spam

To view the Stop Spam movie, click the number 2 button. Locate your video and click the corresponding High-Speed or Dial-Up link, depending on your Internet connection. Watch the movie and then complete the exercise by answering the question that follows. You have set every possible mail control and blocked every unknown e-mail address; yet each day when you open your

virtual mailbox, you find unwelcome advertisements. No matter how high your security features are set, you still are bound to find some spam in your e-mail. Besides setting your e-mail controls, what are some other steps you can take to stamp out spam?

(3) Student Edition Labs — Protecting Your Privacy Online

Click the number 3 button. When the Student Edition Labs menu appears, click *Protecting Your Privacy Online* to begin. A new browser window will open. Follow the on-screen instructions to complete the Lab. When finished, click the Exit button. If required, submit your results to your instructor.

(4) Student Edition Labs — Keeping Your Computer Virus Free

Click the number 4 button. When the Student Edition Labs menu appears, click *Keeping Your Computer Virus Free* to begin. A new browser window will open. Follow the on-screen instructions to complete the Lab. When finished, click the Exit button. If required, submit your results to your instructor.

(5) Practice Test

Click the number 5 button. Answer each question. When completed, enter your name and click the Grade Test button to submit the quiz for grading. Make a note of any missed questions. If required, submit your results to your instructor.

(6) Who Wants To Be a Computer Genius[2]?

Click the number 6 button to find out if you are a computer genius. Directions about how to play the game will be displayed. When you are ready to play, click the Play button. Submit your score to your instructor.

Learn It Online

⑦ Wheel of Terms

Click the number 7 button to reinforce important terms you learned in this chapter by playing the Shelly Cashman Series version of this popular game. Directions about how to play the game will be displayed. When you are ready to play, click the Play button. Submit your score to your instructor.

⑧ DC Track and Field

Click the number 8 button to use what you have learned in this chapter to compete against other students in three track and field events. Directions about how to play the game will be displayed. When you are ready to play, click the start first event button. If required, submit your score to your instructor.

⑨ You're Hired!

Click the number 9 button to use what you have learned in this chapter to embark on the path to a career in computers. Directions about how to play the game will be displayed. When you are ready to play, click the begin game button. If required, submit your score to your instructor.

⑩ Crossword Puzzle Challenge

Click the number 10 button. Complete the puzzle to reinforce skills you learned in this chapter. Directions about how to play the game will be displayed. When you are ready to play, click the Submit button. Submit the completed puzzle to your instructor.

⑪ Lab Exercises

Click the number 11 button. When the Lab Exercises menu appears, click the exercise assigned by your instructor. A new browser window will open. Follow the on-screen instructions to complete the exercise. When finished, click the Exit button. If required, submit your results to your instructor.

⑫ In the News

Why own the latest video game when you can rent it from the comfort of your personal computer? IGN Entertainment has agreements with leading video-game publishers — Ripcord Games, GameSpy.com, and FilePlanet.com — that will allow broadband users to download files from the IGN Entertainment Web site to play stand-alone or multiplayer games. The IGN Web site sends users all they need to get started playing the games, and as more bytes are needed, they are sent from the server to the users. Click the number 12 button and read a news article about online games and edutainment applications. What applications have been developed? Do you think the applications will be successful? Why or why not? Do you think online games will replace the traditional, local CD-ROM game?

⑬ Chapter Discussion Forum

Select an objective from this chapter on page 555 about which you would like more information. Click the number 13 button and post a short message listing a meaningful message title accompanied by one or more questions concerning the selected objective. In two days, return to the threaded discussion by clicking the number 13 button. Submit to your instructor your original message and at least one response to your message.

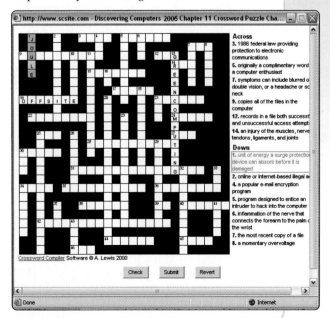

http://www.scsite.com - Discovering Computers 2006 Chapter 11 Crossword Puzzle Cha...

Across
3. 1986 federal law providing protection to electronic communications
5. originally a complimentary word; a computer enthusiast
7. symptoms can include blurred or double vision, or a headache or stiff neck
9. copies all of the files in the computer
12. records in a file both successful and unsuccessful access attempts
14. an injury of the muscles, nerves, tendons, ligaments, and joints

Down
1. unit of energy a surge protection device can absorb before it is damaged
2. online or Internet-based illegal act
4. a popular e-mail encryption program
5. program designed to entice an intruder to hack into the computer
6. inflammation of the nerve that connects the forearm to the palm of the wrist
7. the most recent copy of a file
8. a momentary overvoltage

Crossword Compiler Software © A. Lewis 2000

Check   Submit   Revert

Select a chapter: 1 2 3 4 5 6 7 8 9 10 **11** 12 13 14 15

Learn How To

Use the Learn How To activities to learn fundamental skills when using a computer and accompanying technology. Complete the exercises and submit them to your instructor. Visit scsite.com/dc2006/ch11/howto to obtain more information pertaining to each activity.

LEARN HOW TO 1: Backup Files on an Offsite Internet Server

Backing up files stored on your computer on another disk or computer located in a different geographical location is the ultimate safeguard for data on your computer. A good way to backup data is to use one of the services available on the Web. A leading service is found at www.IBackup.com. To subscribe to the IBackup service, complete the following steps:

1. Start a Web browser, type the Web address `www.IBackup.com` in the Address bar, and then press the ENTER key.
2. When the IBackup Web page is displayed, click Sign Up on the top horizontal toolbar.
3. Enter your e-mail address in the E-mail Address text box, and then click the Send Registration E-mail button.
4. In a short period, you will receive a subscription e-mail message. Because you want to subscribe to the backup service, click the backup link in the e-mail message. A form will be displayed in your browser (Figure 11-37).
5. Fill in the form. Select the plan you want in the Select a Storage Plan list. If you want to try the service for a short period of time before subscribing, select 50 MB Trial for 30 Days (Figure 11-37).
6. To continue, you must enter credit card information. If you select the 30 day trial, your credit card will not be charged, and an automatic billing at the end of 30 days will not occur. After entering the required information, click the Continue button at the bottom of the page.
7. A message is displayed that tells you the amount charged against your credit card. Also, you can click a link to go to the login page, or enter the Web address `https://www.IBackup.com`.

FIGURE 11-37

After establishing an account, you can use it for the time for which you subscribed. Complete the following steps to use the service:

1. Enter the Web address as noted in Step 7 above.
2. In the upper-left corner of the home page, enter your user name and password, and then click the Login button. *Your file/folder page is displayed (Figure 11-38). Initially, no files will be saved in your IBackup folder.*
3. To upload a file, click the Upload button on the IBackup toolbar, click a Browse button in the window that opened, browse your computer and locate the file you wish to upload, and then click the Upload file button. The file will be placed in the IBackup folder.

FIGURE 11-38

Learn How To

4. For further activities you can accomplish on this site for backing up your files, click the links in the File/Folder area and experiment.

Exercise

1. Visit the IBackup Web site. Click IBackup Tour and then follow the screen prompts to view all the services offered by IBackup. Which service is most appropriate for your home computer? Which service is most useful for the server that is used in the computer lab at your school? If you had critical data you needed to backup, would you use a service like this? Why or why not? Submit your answers to your instructor.

2. **Optional: Perform this exercise only for your own computer. Do not perform this exercise on a school computer.** Establish an account on IBackup.com. Upload two or more files from your computer. Right-click a file you uploaded on Ibackup.com and click Save Target As on the menu. What happened? Save the file on your computer. What message(s) were displayed? Download the files you uploaded back to your computer. Is this an efficient way to backup your files? Submit your answers to your instructor.

LEARN HOW TO 2: Use the Windows XP Firewall

When you use the Internet, data is sent both from your computer to the Internet and from computers on the Internet to your computer. A firewall is a barrier that checks information coming from the Internet and either turns it away or allows it to pass through to your computer, based on your firewall settings. It also checks data being sent from your computer to the Internet to ensure your computer is not sending unsolicited messages to other computers on the Internet. A firewall can be implemented using hardware or software.

Windows XP SP2 contains a software firewall that starts automatically when you boot your computer. To control the firewall usage on your computer, complete the following steps:

1. Click the Start button on the Windows taskbar, and then click Control Panel on the Start menu.

2. In the Category view of the Control Panel, click Security Center, and then click Windows Firewall in the Windows Security Center window. *The Windows Firewall dialog box is displayed (Figure 11-39).*

3. In the Windows Firewall dialog box, select On or Off to turn on or off the Windows firewall. The firewall automatically is on when you start your computer. You should NOT turn off the firewall unless you have a compelling reason to do so.

4. Click the Exceptions tab in the Windows Firewall dialog box. *The Exceptions sheet is displayed (Figure 11-40). The exceptions that are checked can communicate with the Internet without your clicking a link.*

5. You may want to allow programs that routinely communicate with the Internet, such as sports programs that display updated game scores, to have full access to your computer. To add a program to the Exceptions list, in the Exceptions sheet click the Add Program button. The Add a Program dialog box is displayed. Select a program and then click the OK button.

FIGURE 11-39

FIGURE 11-40

Exercise

1. Display the Windows Firewall dialog box. Click What else should I know about Windows Firewall in the General sheet. Read the information about Windows firewall. What did you learn that you did not know? What is a security log? How can you cause a security log to be created? Submit your answers to your instructor.

Web Research

Use the Internet-based Web Research exercises to broaden your understanding of the concepts presented in this chapter. Visit scsite.com/dc2006/ch11/research to obtain more information pertaining to each exercise. To discuss any of the Web Research exercises in this chapter with other students, post your thoughts or questions at scsite.com/dc2006/ch11/forum.

(1) **Scavenger Hunt**   Use one of the <u>search engines</u> listed in Figure 2-10 in Chapter 2 on page 78 or your own favorite search engine to find the answers to the questions that follow. Copy and paste the Web address from the Web page where you found the answer. Some questions may have more than one answer. If required, submit your answers to your instructor. (1) What is the $800 from Microsoft hoax? (2) What similarities do PGP (Pretty Good Privacy) and GPG (GNU Privacy Guard) share? (3) When did the first virus attack occur? What network was affected? (4) What company developed SSL? How does SSL differ from Secure HTTP (S-HTTP)? (5) At what university is the Computer Emergency Response Team Coordination Center (CERT/CC) located? What is one of the latest advisories or incident notes reported by this organization?

(2) **Search Sleuth**   Internet subject directories are used to find information on specialized topics. One of the oldest and more popular subject directories is the <u>WWW Virtual Library (VL)</u>. This Web site is administered by a group of volunteers who are experts in particular topics. Visit this Web site and then use your word processing program to answer the following questions. Then, if required, submit your answers to your instructor. (1) Click the Computing link and then click the Cryptology, PGP and Privacy link. Read two articles in the Online Documents section and then write a 50-word summary of your findings. (2) Click the Back button and then click The Virtual Museum of Computing link. When did the Museum open? What are three recent additions and events? (3) Click the Back button twice, click the Recreation link, and then click the American College Football link. Click the Official College Football Team Homepages (by State) link and then find the link for your college or a college in your state. What is a major story featured on this page?

(3) **Journaling**   Respond to your readings in this chapter by writing at least one page about your reactions, evaluations, and reflections on computer security, privacy, and ethics. For example, have you suffered from a <u>repetitive strain injury</u>? Does your employer monitor your computer use? Should an employer be able to read your e-mail messages? How have you tried to decrease spam and to safeguard your personal information? You also can write about the new terms you learned by reading this chapter. If required, submit your journal to your instructor.

(4) **Expanding Your Understanding**   Thousands of hackers are attempting to gain unauthorized access to computer systems across the world, according to computer security experts. Some of these hackers are experienced programmers, while others are <u>script kiddies</u> who are using tools developed by sophisticated programmers. All computers are vulnerable to script-kiddie assaults, especially home computers with always-on, high-speed connections. A personal firewall can help thwart these invasions. Visit a software vendor and locate a personal firewall program. What is the name of this software? Who is the manufacturer? What is the cost? What are the system requirements? How is the software installed? What tasks does the software perform? Write a report summarizing your findings. If required, submit your report to your instructor.

(5) **Ethics in Action**   <u>Radio frequency identification (RFID) tags</u> are expected to help merchants in many ways. By placing these tags on such items as prescription drugs, computer peripherals, and clothing, retailers hope to reduce theft, track inventory, reduce labor costs, and keep their shelves stocked. Privacy experts, however, claim the tags can store information about consumers' shopping habits and whereabouts. Law enforcement officials, lawyers, marketers, and even thieves could use this electronic detailed data to track people at all times of the day. View online sites that discuss using RFID tags in stores and the privacy issues that arise from their use. Write a report summarizing your findings, and include a table of links to Web sites that provide additional details about the developing field of RFID. If required, submit your report to your instructor.

Case Studies

Use the Case Studies to apply the concepts presented in the chapter to real-world situations. Visit scsite.com/dc2006/ch11/cases to obtain more information pertaining to each exercise. To discuss the Case Studies in this chapter with other students, visit scsite.com/dc2006/ch11/forum and post your thoughts or questions.

CASE STUDY 1 — Class Discussion   As manager of the information technology department, you are responsible for maintaining the company's **e-mail system**. Recently, you were sent a request by a member of the senior management team to make available for her review all e-mails sent and received by non-salaried employees over the past month. Your initial reaction was that such a request is not only unethical, but possibly illegal as well. Upon contacting the human resources department, you learn that an obscure statement in the employee handbook gives senior staff the right to read anything transmitted on media owned by the company without notifying the sender or recipient. Would you immediately honor the request, or would you first try to convince senior management that internal communications between employees should be private? Why or why not? Do you think such a policy is good for employee morale? Why or why not? Write a brief report and be prepared to discuss your recommendations in class.

CASE STUDY 2 — Class Discussion   Your best friend, Eric, spends all his free time writing computer programs that interact with the Windows operating system. He recently informed you that over the semester break he had written a **malicious-logic program** that randomly erases files and displays weird messages the day after July 4 at exactly 10:00 a.m. He plans to distribute the Trojan horse, called Happy Birthday America, via an e-mail attachment. Also included with the e-mail is a hidden program that sends the same e-mail to all the e-mail addresses in the user's address list. The e-mail with the attachment will be sent as spam the day after finals in May, so it will have plenty of time to be distributed to millions of computers worldwide before July 4. Upon learning of Eric's plan, what would you do? You know that a hefty reward of $250,000 is offered by a large software company for turning in unscrupulous programmers. Do you think it is right to inform on a friend when no profit is involved in the crime? Why or why not? Who would you notify (i.e., Eric's parents, the dean of students, the police, or the software company offering the reward)? Write a brief report and be prepared to discuss your recommendations in class.

CASE STUDY 3 — Research   Computer viruses have cost companies billions of dollars in lost revenue. In a recent six-month period, the number of **new viruses and worms** aimed at Microsoft's ubiquitous Windows operating system rose from 1,000 a year to nearly 5,000. You work as a network analyst for a large manufacturing company that uses Windows. After the most recent virus attack, your manager asked you to investigate the feasibility of switching to a different operating system, such as Linux or Unix. Use the Web and/or print media to research the advantages and disadvantages of switching operating systems. Are alternative operating systems as susceptible to viruses as Windows? Why or why not? What is Microsoft's approach to eliminating virus attacks? Why is Windows so prone to virus attacks? What types of costs are involved in changing operating systems? Submit your report or use PowerPoint to create a presentation and share your findings with your class.

CASE STUDY 4 — Research   Internet-based companies who take advantage of consumer trust are sneaking their spyware into computers for their own purposes. **Spyware** secretly collects information about a user's computer activities. The owner of a chain of fast-food restaurants, Burgers & Fries, where you are employed as an application analyst wants to purge spyware from the chain's computers. Use the Web and/or print media and compare the anti-spyware programs available. For each program, answer the following questions. What is the program's function? What are the system requirements? How easy is the program to use? How do you obtain updates to the program? How much does the program cost? In your opinion, is the program worth the price? Why or why not? Which one would you recommend? Why? Write a brief report or use PowerPoint to create a presentation and share your findings with your class.

CASE STUDY 5 — Team Challenge   A recent study conducted by the senior management at Consumer-Mart, a large retail company with worldwide sales, concluded that the company's computer system was at severe risk. Your team has been hired as consultants to deal with the following vulnerabilities: Internet and network attacks, unauthorized access and use, hardware theft and vandalism, software theft, information theft, system failure, and wireless security. Divide these areas of vulnerabilities between the team members. Using the Web and/or print media, have each team member summarize the issues associated with each of the areas of **computer security risk** assigned to them and make recommendations as to how the company can deal with them. As a team, merge your findings into a team report and/or PowerPoint presentation and share your recommendations with your class.

Special Feature

COMPUTER FORENSICS

Forensics is the use of science to investigate and establish facts in criminal or civil courts. Forensic scientists are able to examine a set of clues and rebuild a sequence of events. Computer forensics is the newest and fastest growing discipline in this field. As described earlier in Chapter 11, computer forensics, also called digital forensics, network forensics, or cyber-forensics, is the discovery, collection, and analysis of evidence found on computers and networks. Computer forensics techniques include analyzing log files, analyzing deleted files, analyzing chat logs, and reviewing trace nodes (Figure 1). This field of study integrates aspects of criminal justice, computer science, and computer forensics techniques.

(a) Analyze Log Files

```
1) Mar 13 03:11:55 watson ipop3d[16319]: pop3
   service init from 192.168.187.35

2) Mar 13 03:11:55 watson ipop3d[16319]: Login
   user=kumquat host=holmes.example.net
   [192.168.187.35] nmsgs=0/0

3) Mar 13 03:12:16 watson ipop3d[16319]: Logout
   user=kumquat host=holmes.example.net
   [192.168.187.35] nmsgs=0 ndele=0
```

(b) Analyze Deleted Files

Computer Forensics Examiner

(c) Analyze Chat Logs

```
Session Start: Tue Mar 23 15:50:33 2006
Session Ident: #Strong&40
* Now talking in #Strong&40
* Topic is 'Welcome to the BEST little channel on the net!    www.40plus.com.html '
* Set by Bunni on Tue Mar 23 10:31:01
<BettyF> I sure beats the 20's we've been having, Cary
<BettyF> Hi, billy
<billy89> Hi
<abc_m> hi Cary:)
<abc_m> hi billy89
<`Cary> hey cd  how  be?
<billy89> Hi
<abc_m> not bad a bit cold but doing okay
<BettyF> How ya doing, billy?
<billy89> So... I'm just lookin' around irc...
<BettyF> and lo and behold you found us
<billy89> Doin' ok... also cold where I am... Minnesota... Where're you?
<BettyF> Maine here
<billy89> Yep... here I am ... :-)
<abc_m> ottawa canada here
<billy89> Sunny Ontario! :-)
<BettyF> You had some really nasty spells in January, billy
<`Cary> I gotta go again.. laters  yawl.. play safe
* `Cary has left #Strong&40
<billy89> Bitter cold in Jan. dumped on by TWO bad snow storms in December
<BettyF> I talked with my old Ottawa friend a few days ago, cdn -- but only for
about a minute -- I think he had a date. lol
<abc_m> ohhhhhhhhhhhhh
<abc_m> they have those out here?
<BettyF> I have a friend in St. Paul, billy -- she was in her house with her jacket
on in January.
```

(d) Trace Nodes

FIGURE 1 Computer forensics is the discovery, collection, and analysis of evidence found on computers and networks.

THE SCOPE OF COMPUTER FORENSICS

Computer forensics focuses on computers and networks. The forensic analysis of computers specifically involves the examination of computer media, programs, and data and log files to reconstruct the activity in which a computer was engaged, such as instant messaging conversations, Internet chats, e-mail messages, Web sites visited, documents and spreadsheets created, and image and audio files viewed. The forensics analysis of networks focuses more on the activity of a network and includes the analysis of server contents, server and router log files, packet traffic, and information obtained from Internet access providers.

The science of computer forensics covers several overlapping areas (Figure 2). It is critical for law enforcement as an evidence gathering and criminal investigation tool. It is an increasingly important tool used for civilian and military intelligence gathering — including activities related to homeland defense. It is becoming widely employed by businesses and other private sector organizations for combating information security attacks. The core tools and skills are the same regardless of the application.

A computer forensics specialist also must have knowledge of the law regardless of whether the investigation is for law enforcement or civilian purposes. Additional complexity in this area exists because computer crime statutes and users' legitimate expectation of privacy vary widely from state to state and nation to nation. With the Internet and World Wide Web, jurisdictional boundaries are blurred, and an individual in one country can commit crimes almost anywhere in the world without ever leaving his or her keyboard.

Although most computer forensic specialists today are engaged in law enforcement investigations, the field is not by any means limited to finding evidence of criminal guilt. Computer forensics also is a rapidly growing subspecialty for information security professionals. The traditional information security manager is responsible for proactively protecting the information technology assets within an organization. Security intrusions and other events are inevitable, however, and the computer forensics specialist often leads the incident response function to learn how an event occurred, who was behind it, and how to prevent a recurrence.

Computer forensics is part of the toolkit of today's computer scientist. Many information security researchers purposely place a honeypot (vulnerable computer) on their networks for the specific purpose of analyzing the attacks that eventually will be perpetrated on those systems. Carefully examining the way in which a honeypot has been attacked can provide significant insight into new forms of attack which then can be translated into new defensive tools and strategies.

THE IMPORTANCE OF COMPUTER FORENSICS

Computer forensics is a rapidly growing field for the simple reason that computers and the Internet are the fastest growing technology used for criminal activity. As computers become smaller, lighter, cheaper, and easier to use, they appear at nearly every crime scene that police investigate. Some activities, such as illegal gambling and unauthorized access to computers, have been given new life because of the pervasiveness of computers and the Internet.

Cybercrimes are growing rapidly in both the number of incidents as well as the cost in dollars, largely because these crimes are safer and more lucrative than crimes in the "real" world. The average bank robber, for example, nets only a few thousand dollars, and most are caught and sent to jail. Conversely, white collar computer crimes such as auction fraud, credit card theft, identity theft, and other financial scams tend to net a much larger sum of money, and the perpetrators are more difficult to catch and convict. In addition, computer criminals tend to generate more sympathy with judges, juries, and the public than violent offenders. Compounding the problem is the fact that access to corporate network resources makes insider jobs by employees easier and easier. Figure 3 shows the dollar loss reported by 269 large companies in a recent year due to telecom and financial fraud, insider abuse, unauthorized network access, theft of proprietary information, and other computer-related crimes.

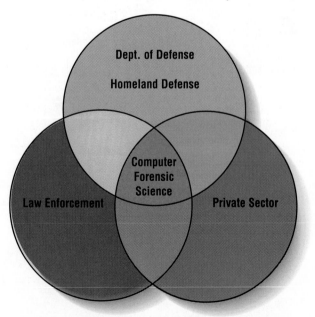

FIGURE 2 The domain of computer forensics is multidisciplinary, spanning the needs of the military and homeland defense, law enforcement, and the private sector.

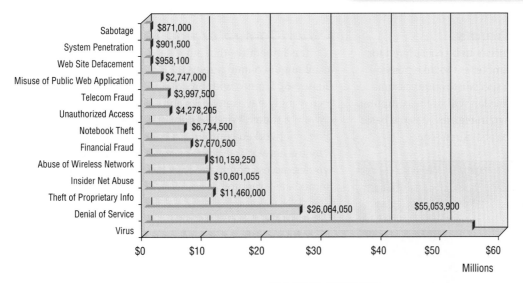

FIGURE 3
Total computer security losses of $141,496,560 reported by 269 respondents in a recent year.

Computer forensics is being used not just to combat cybercrime. Terrorists around the world are known to use computers and other digital devices, so computer forensics analysis is important as an antiterrorism tool for both criminal prosecution and intelligence gathering. All organizations that employ computers, ranging from nonprofit agencies and major corporations to government agencies and utility companies are at risk. As more information is stored digitally and more aspects of our society are under computer control, we all face increased exposure and vulnerability. Computer forensics is an important tool in understanding our digital information systems and keeping them safe, as well as tracking down the people who abuse those systems.

THE COMPUTER FORENSICS PROCESS

The computer forensics process can be simple or complex, depending upon the circumstances causing the investigation in the first place. The computer forensics specialist may be part of an investigative team, and the analysis of digital evidence may be just one part of the investigation as a whole. The specialist will look for information pertinent to the incident or event being investigated, which may be limited by a search warrant, time, and/or other circumstances.

The first step in the process is to gather the materials to analyze. This may not be quite as easy as it sounds. Law enforcement personnel will be guided by a search warrant in the seizure of materials while a corporate forensics specialist may be guided by what equipment is owned by the company. Even with clear guidelines, many items need to be considered for collection and examination as described in the following sections.

Computer Media

Computer media can be found in many places these days (Figure 4). This includes the obvious hard disk, Zip disk, floppy disk, and optical disc (CDs and DVDs). Also included are physically small, high-capacity memory devices such as USB flash drives (including the versions where the device is embedded in a watch, pen, or Swiss Army knife) and flash memory cards.

(a) hard disk

(b) Zip disk

(c) USB flash drives

(f) optical disk

(e) flash memory card

(d) floppy disk

FIGURE 4 Computer forensics experts analyze the data stored on various types of media.

Computers and Peripherals

Every part of the computer needs to be considered for examination, and it is generally important to take possession of all of the equipment. The specialist cannot assume that the spare keyboard back in the lab will fit the computer being seized. The computer shown in Figure 5 has the basic hardware one might expect to see at a crime scene.

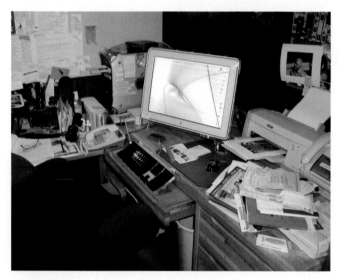

FIGURE 5 A typical scene a computer forensics specialist encounters.

Other Computer and Network Hardware

It is imperative that other hardware devices be examined, as all might contain important log or other information (Figure 6). Homes with broadband network connections increasingly have networks and, therefore, multiple computers and a router. Wireless networks make it relatively easy to hide a networked computer; a computer using a home's wireless network could be as far as 100 yards or so from the wireless access point, and thus be situated far outside of the immediate structure.

Computer Software

Although the computer forensics specialist generally will not run software directly from the suspect drive, it may be impossible to examine files without the proper application software. In some cases, the user of a suspect computer might have installed specialized, custom, or very old software to which the specialist generally will not have access; in that case, the specialist may have to install software found at the suspect site onto a forensics lab computer. This is one reason to look around the site where the computer is found and consider seizing distribution media and manuals of any software with which the specialist is not familiar. The papers and books found near the computer also will give the specialist a clue as to the sophistication of the user and the possible types of applications to be found on the system.

FIGURE 6 Common digital hardware devices examined by a computer investigator.

In the Computer Forensics Lab

Once the materials are in the computer forensics lab, the investigation can begin. The basic steps of a computer forensics analysis are:

1. **Preserve the media** — Computer forensics analysis never should be performed on the original media except under the most extraordinary circumstances because of the potential of accidentally making a change to the original evidence. The copy also needs to be made in such a way that the original information is not altered in any way and that it can be authenticated as containing the same information as the original. This process is known as **imaging a drive**.

2. **Extract evidence** — Based upon the guidelines of the investigation, the specialist needs to determine what kind of information on the computer is pertinent to the case. Clues as to what to search for will depend upon the type of case. Spreadsheets, for example, would be highly relevant to a business fraud case, while images are important for a case of suspected child pornography, and chat and e-mail logs are of use in a case of cyberstalking. Keywords, such as pertinent phrases, slang words, names, locations, etc., must be provided to the computer forensics specialist on the case.

3. **Analyze computer media** — The actual analysis of evidence and/or the root cause of the event is the most time-consuming aspect of the process. It is important to note that the information retrieved from the computer either can be incriminating (indicating guilt) or exculpatory (indicating innocence). In addition, the specialist has to look at the entire capacity of the medium because information can be hidden anywhere. Figure 7 summarizes the common items examined during a computer forensics investigation.

4. **Document results** — The results of a computer forensics exam must be documented thoroughly, particularly if the examination is being performed for legal purposes. Everything must be written down, from the configuration of the computer and BIOS settings to each and every step taken by the computer forensic specialist and any pertinent evidence that is found. All computer equipment, media, peripherals, or other items seized must be logged, and photographs should be taken of external and internal connections, if possible. The handling of the evidence also has to be logged carefully to demonstrate that no tampering occurred. Sample computer forensics evidence worksheets are shown in Figure 8. Figure 8a is an evidence worksheet used with a computer. Figure 8b is an evidence worksheet used with a hard disk.

1. Visited Web sites
2. Downloaded files
3. Dates when files were last accessed and modified
4. Attempts to conceal, destroy, or fabricate evidence
5. Deleted or overwritten files
6. Data from RAM
7. Use of cryptography or steganography
8. File directory structure
9. Image, movie, and sound files
10. Keyword search hits
11. Contents of system files, such as the print spool and swap files
12. Installed programs
13. E-mail, chat logs, instant messaging logs
14. Registry entries
15. Contents of the Recycle Bin and unallocated space
16. Antivirus, personal firewall, and spyware detection software, as well as the presence of viruses, Trojan horses, and spyware

FIGURE 7 Common items examined during a computer forensics investigation.

(a) Computer evidence worksheet

(b) Hard disk evidence worksheet

FIGURE 8 Computer and Hard Disk Evidence Worksheets (from *Forensic Examination of Digital Evidence: A Guide for Law Enforcement*, National Institute of Justice).

In general, specialized computer forensics tools are used to perform an analysis to ensure that no information is modified on the target media and that the examination is thorough. Booting a computer changes hundreds of registry, log, and/or data files; therefore, the original hard disk never should be used to boot a computer. In addition, many operating systems, such as Linux and Windows, maintain a number of time stamps associated with every file, including the creation, last access, and last modified dates; using ordinary operating system tools to examine the contents of files usually will cause at least the last-access date to be altered. Use of specialized analysis tools maintains the integrity of the original data so that the specialist can be sure that the results of the analysis are legally and technically valid. It is important that no harm be done to the original evidence.

In some cases, specialists prefer to image hard disks in the field rather than transporting entire computers to the lab; this often is the preferable approach when the device to be imaged is a company's critical server where seizing the computer might cause undue economic hardship to the owner. Devices such as Intelligent Computer Solutions' Road MASSter-II (Figure 10) is such a device; note that it fits into a small carrying case.

Notebook computers represent a particular challenge for forensic analysis because many notebook computer hard disks have proprietary or specialty interfaces; additional hardware is available specifically for imaging drives from various models of Dell, Gateway, HP, IBM, NEC, Toshiba, and other brands of notebook computers. Other specialized hardware allows for the imaging of PDAs, smart phones, and other digital devices.

COMPUTER FORENSICS TOOLS

A wide variety of computer forensics tools are available, each with its own applications, strengths, and weaknesses. Several companies make computer forensics hardware, primarily for purposes of disk imaging. Digital Intelligence, for example, makes several forensics hardware devices, including:

- The Forensic Recovery of Digital Evidence (FRED) hardware (Figure 9a) is a standalone forensics workstation that can acquire data from all types of hard disk media, including floppy and Zip disks. This system includes fixed hard disks for the workstation's operating system and analysis tools plus a number of bays for other drives to be inserted and removed. For imaging applications, the contents of the suspect disk are copied to a blank disk; the analysis then is performed on the newly copied disk.
- The FireChief hardware (Figure 9b) has two removable hard disk bays, one of which is write-protected (for the original disk). This device can be used to copy the contents of one disk to another. It is connected to a computer via a FireWire connection and is ideal for building a low-cost forensics workstation.
- The FireFly hardware (Figure 9c) can plug directly in an IDE hard drive and attach to the forensics computer via a FireWire connection.

(a) Forensic Recovery of Digital Evidence (FRED) forensics workstation

(b) FireChief hard disk replication and examination hardware

(c) FireFly hard disk examination hardware

FIGURE 9 Three computer forensics devices manufactured by Digital Intelligence, Inc.

(a) Details of the keyboard and working area of the Road MASSter

USB connectors for additional peripheral attachment

connector for evidence drive

auxiliary VGA video connector

platform for evidence drive

serial port for printing an evidence report on the thermal printer or seizing data from personal data assistants

A.C. power jack

power for CD-ROM and floppy drive

10/100 Base T connector for Ethernet connectivity

voltage selector switch

(b) The Road MASSter case

ECP parallel port for use with LapLink™

connector for floppy disk drive

connector for suspect's drive

under keyboard storage compartment

full QWERTY mini keyboard

connector for CD-ROM

FIGURE 10 The Intelligent Computer Solutions' Road MASSter-II is a portable computer forensics laboratory.

The primary computer forensics analysis tool is software. The most widely-used specialty forensics programs today are Guidance Software's EnCase and AccessData's Ultimate Toolkit (Figure 11). No single program can perform all aspects of a computer forensics analysis, although several come close. These programs provide a broad range of forensics functions (Figure 12).

(a) Guidance Software's EnCase

(b) AccessData's Ultimate Toolkit

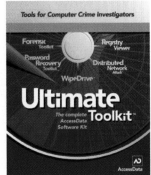

FIGURE 11 Popular computer forensics software.

1. Create disk images
2. Recover passwords
3. Perform file access, modification, and creation time analysis
4. Create file catalogs
5. View system and application logs
6. Determine the activity of users and/or applications on a system
7. Recover "deleted" files and examine unallocated file space
8. Obtain network information such as IP addresses and host names, network routes, and Web site information
9. Track forensics activity and aid in documentation and report writing

FIGURE 12 Common tasks handled by computer forensics software.

COMPUTER FORENSICS AT WORK

A computer forensics specialist needs to have a working knowledge of a wide range of topics related to computers and networks. The most essential bit of knowledge concerns how files are stored on disk drives and the various file systems that will be found. The following sections illustrate some of the tasks computer forensic specialists use to search for clues in an investigation.

Analyzing Deleted Files

Consider the scenario shown in Figure 13. Figure 13a shows the suspect displaying the names of the files involved in the criminal activity. Figure 13b shows the suspect deleting the files. Figure 13c shows the computer forensics specialist using special programs to retrieve the deleted files.

(a) The display shown is from the Windows Command Prompt instruction dir performed on a floppy disk. The floppy disk contains 18 files and its volume name is TEST_FLOPPY.

Suspect Manipulates Files

directory listing of floppy disk

delete all the files on the floppy...

...and confirm that they are no longer there

(b) In an attempt to destroy evidence, the suspect deletes all the files from the floppy disk using the Windows Command Prompt del *.*.

Computer Forensics Examiner Retrieves Deleted Files

first character in the name of a deleted file is overwritten with a "a" character (0xE5)

this symbol indicates that the image was found in a "deleted file

(c) Programs, such as WinHex (left) and EnCase (above), are used to review the file names and contents of the files deleted from the floppy disk by the suspect.

FIGURE 13 The top portion of this figure shows the suspect (a) listing the files involved in criminal activity, (b) later deleting the files in an attempt to cover-up the illegal activity, and then the lower portion of the figure shows (c) the computer forensics specialist retrieving the deleted files using special programs.

Tracing Nodes

Knowledge of the Internet is another essential skill. Figure 14a shows the output from McAfee's Visual Trace, listing the intermediate nodes between a local host computer (altamont) and a Web server (www.garykessler.net). Visual Trace is a graphical version of the tracert (DOS) and traceroute (Linux) command line utilities and lists the IP address of all hops along the path between the two computers. This display also shows the round-trip delay and can be used to show whois information about each node in the path. Visual Trace also can show a geographical map of the path (Figure 14b).

Analyzing Network Traffic

The ability to analyze network traffic also is an essential skill for a computer forensics specialist. E-mail headers are particularly important, as they provide many clues as to the origin and authenticity of e-mail messages. By now you should be familiar with the standard e-mail headers, such as To:, From:, and Subject:. But e-mail headers contain more information than what you see at the top of an e-mail. In addition, e-mail headers can reveal the name and version of the e-mail program you use, the operating system, the name and version of your mail server, internal IP addresses, and the type of firewall you are using.

(a) Route between two hosts, round-trip delay, and whois information.

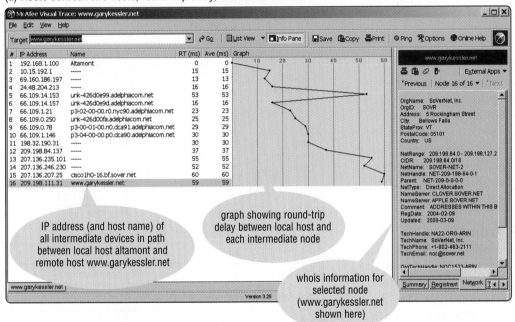

(b) Geographic map display of the route between two hosts.

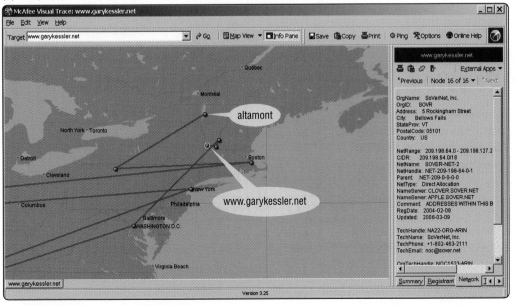

FIGURE 14 Tracing nodes between a local host computer (altamont) and a Web server using McAfee's Visual Trace.

Analyzing ISP Logs

During a computer forensics investigation, the specialist might request logs from an Internet access provider. The Internet access provider will deliver the logs, but they will be in the raw format in which they are saved.

While SMTP is used to forward e-mail across the Internet, other protocols are used to download e-mail by the client. One such protocol is the Post Office Protocol version 3 (POP3). Figure 1a on page 607 shows a set of three records from a POP3 server log showing a user logging on to check and download e-mail messages. All records show a date (March 13) and time stamp on a host named watson running the POP service (ipop3d) and access by a user on the host with IP address 192.168.187.35.

Analyzing Chat Logs

Analysis of chat logs is another important aspect of network analysis. The log shown in Figure 1c on page 607 is a conversation between BettyF, billy89, and other members of the Internet Relay Chat (IRC) Strong&40 channel. Although this conversation is relatively innocuous, analysis of logs such as these can turn up evidence of cyberstalking, criminal conspiracy, economic espionage, harassment, or other items of interest.

Analyzing a Packet Trace

Packet sniffers are an important software tool in the understanding of network traffic. A **packet sniffer** monitors all of the traffic seen on the network port of a computer and keeps a copy for later analysis. One of the most commonly used packet sniffers is tcpdump, a command line utility for UNIX/Linux; WinDump is the Windows version.

LEARNING MORE ABOUT COMPUTER FORENSICS

Every action a user takes on a computer leaves a trail. Deleting files really does not erase information. Evidence of computer activity is stored in many places on the hard disk, some obvious and some very obscure. Information about network access potentially is logged on many computers throughout the local network and global Internet. Digital tracks are everywhere.

Computer forensics specialists must possess an array of skills to uncover these tracks and recreate the activities

under investigation. They certainly must be technically knowledgeable and enjoy troubleshooting and solving puzzles. They must be aware of the legal constraints and organizational polices that guide what they can and cannot do. They must be able to communicate the process and results of their analysis in both written and oral form. Finally, they also must possess and demonstrate a high degree of honesty and integrity.

Many sources for news and information about computer forensics are available online. Using the popular Web portals such as Google, Yahoo!, and others, you will find links to hundreds of computer forensics sites. Figure 15 lists sources for information about computer forensics and their Web addresses.

	WEB SITE	WEB ADDRESS
Computer Forensics Hardware Companies	Digital Intelligence, Inc.	digitalintelligence.com
	Intelligent Computer Solutions, Inc.	ics-iq.com
	WiebeTech	wiebetech.com
Computer Forensics Software	AccessData Corp. Ultimate Toolkit	accessdata.com
	Guidance Software EnCase	guidancesoftware.com
	Knoppix STD	knoppix-std.org
	SleuthKit and Autopsy	sleuthkit.org
	Symantec Ghost	symantec.com/ghost
	WinHex	winhex.com
Network Analysis Web Sites	DNSstuff.com	dnsstuff.com
	SamSpade.org	samspade.org
Network Analysis Software	McAfee Visual Trace	downloadsuperstore.com/ mcafee_visual_trace.htm
	tcpdump	tcpdump.org
	WinDump	windump.polito.it
Additional Information	Gary Kessler's Cybercrime and Cyberforensics-related URLs	www.garykessler.net/ library/forensicsurl.html
	High Technology Crime Investigation Association (HTCIA)	htcia.org
	International Association of Computer Investigative Specialists (IACIS)	cops.org
	National White Collar Crime Center (NW3C)	nw3c.org

For an updated list, visit scsite.com/dc2006/ch11/computerforensics.

FIGURE 15 Online sources for information about computer forensics.

APPENDIX A
Coding Schemes and Number Systems

CODING SCHEMES

As discussed in Chapter 4, a computer uses a coding scheme to represent characters. This section of the appendix presents the ASCII, EBCDIC, and Unicode coding schemes and discusses parity.

ASCII and EBCDIC

Two popular coding schemes that represent characters in a computer are ASCII and EBCDIC. The **American Standard Code for Information Interchange**, or ASCII (pronounced ASK-ee), coding scheme is the most widely used coding scheme to represent data. Many personal computers and midrange servers use ASCII. The **Extended Binary Coded Decimal Interchange Code**, or EBCDIC (pronounced EB-see-dik), coding scheme is used primarily on mainframe computers and high-end servers. As shown in Figure A-1, the combination of bits (0s and 1s) is unique for each character in the ASCII and EBCDIC coding schemes.

When a computer uses the ASCII or EBCDIC coding scheme, it stores each represented character in one byte of memory. Other binary formats exist, however, that the computer sometimes uses to represent numeric data. For example, a computer may store, or pack, two numeric characters in one byte of memory. The computer uses these binary formats to increase storage and processing efficiency.

Unicode

The 256 characters and symbols that are represented by ASCII and EBCDIC codes are sufficient for English and western European languages but are not large enough for Asian and other languages that use different alphabets. Further compounding the problem is that many of these languages use symbols, called **ideograms**, to represent multiple words and ideas. One solution to this situation is Unicode. **Unicode** is a 16-bit coding scheme that has the capacity of representing all the world's current languages, as well as classic and historical languages, in more than 65,000 characters and symbols.

ASCII	SYMBOL	EBCDIC
00110000	0	11110000
00110001	1	11110001
00110010	2	11110010
00110011	3	11110011
00110100	4	11110100
00110101	5	11110101
00110110	6	11110110
00110111	7	11110111
00111000	8	11111000
00111001	9	11111001
01000001	A	11000001
01000010	B	11000010
01000011	C	11000011
01000100	D	11000100
01000101	E	11000101
01000110	F	11000110
01000111	G	11000111
01001000	H	11001000
01001001	I	11001001
01001010	J	11010001
01001011	K	11010010
01001100	L	11010011
01001101	M	11010100
01001110	N	11010101
01001111	O	11010110
01010000	P	11010111
01010001	Q	11011000
01010010	R	11011001
01010011	S	11100010
01010100	T	11100011
01010101	U	11100100
01010110	V	11100101
01010111	W	11100110
01011000	X	11100111
01011001	Y	11101000
01011010	Z	11101001
00100001	!	01011010
00100010	"	01111111
00100011	#	01111011
00100100	$	01011011
00100101	%	01101100
00100110	&	01010000
00101000	(	01001101
00101001	)	01011101
00101010	*	01011100
00101011	+	01001110

FIGURE A-1

A Unicode code for a symbol, as shown in Figure A-2, is obtained by appending the symbol's corresponding digit in the left-most column to the end of the symbol's corresponding three-digit code in the column heading. For

	003	004	005	006	007
0	0 0030	@ 0040	P 0050	` 0060	p 0070
1	1 0031	A 0041	Q 0051	a 0061	q 0071
2	2 0032	B 0042	R 0052	b 0062	r 0072
3	3 0033	C 0043	S 0053	c 0063	s 0073
4	4 0034	D 0044	T 0054	d 0064	t 0074
5	5 0035	E 0045	U 0055	e 0065	u 0075
6	6 0036	F 0046	V 0056	f 0066	v 0076
7	7 0037	G 0047	W 0057	g 0067	w 0077
8	8 0038	H 0048	X 0058	h 0068	x 0078
9	9 0039	I 0049	Y 0059	i 0069	y 0079
A	: 003A	J 004A	Z 005A	j 006A	z 007A
B	; 003B	K 004B	[005B	k 006B	{ 007B
C	< 003C	L 004C	\ 005C	l 006C	| 007C
D	= 003D	M 004D	] 005D	m 006D	} 007D
E	> 003E	N 004E	^ 005E	n 006E	~ 007E
F	? 003F	O 004F	_ 005F	o 006F	DEL 007F

FIGURE A-2

example, the Unicode for the capital letter C is 0043. In Unicode, 30,000 codes are reserved for future use, such as ancient languages, and 6,000 codes are reserved for private use. Existing ASCII coded data is fully compatible with Unicode because the first 256 codes are the same. Unicode is implemented in several operating systems, including Windows XP, Mac OS X, and Linux. Unicode-enabled programming languages and software include Java, XML, Microsoft Office, and Oracle. Some experts believe that Unicode eventually will replace all other coding schemes.

Parity

Regardless of the coding scheme used to represent characters in memory, it is important that the computer store characters accurately. For each byte of memory, most computers have at least one extra bit, called a **parity bit**, that the computer uses for error checking. A parity bit can detect if one of the bits in a byte has been changed inadvertently. While such errors are extremely rare (most computers never have a parity error during their lifetime), they can occur because of voltage fluctuations, static electricity, or a memory failure.

Computers are either odd- or even-parity machines. In computers with odd-parity, the total number of on bits in the byte (including the parity bit) must be an odd number (Figure A-3). In computers with even parity, the total number of on bits must be an even number. The computer checks parity each time it uses a memory location. When the computer moves data from one location to another in memory, it compares the parity bits of both the sending and receiving locations to see if they are the same. If the computer detects a difference or if the wrong number of bits is on (e.g., an odd number in a computer with even parity), an error message is displayed. Many computers use multiple parity bits that enable them to detect and correct a single-bit error and detect multiple-bit errors.

FIGURE A-3

NUMBER SYSTEMS

This section of the appendix describes the number systems used with computers. Technical computer personnel require a thorough knowledge of this subject, but most users need only a general understanding of number systems and how they relate to computers.

The binary (base 2) number system is used to represent the electronic status of the bits in memory. It also is used for other purposes such as addressing the memory locations. Another number system commonly used with computers is **hexadecimal** (base 16). The computer uses the hexadecimal number system to communicate with a programmer when a problem with a program exists, because it would be difficult for the programmer to understand the 0s and 1s of binary code. Figure A-4 shows how the decimal values 0 through 15 are represented in binary and hexadecimal number systems.

The mathematical principles that apply to the binary and hexadecimal number systems are the same as those that apply to the decimal number system. To help you better understand these principles, this section starts with the familiar decimal system, then progresses to the binary and hexadecimal number systems.

The Decimal Number System

The decimal number system is a base 10 number system (deci means ten). The base of a number system indicates how many symbols it uses. The decimal number system uses 10 symbols: 0 through 9. Each of the symbols in the number system has a value associated with it. For example, 3 represents a quantity of three and 5 represents a quantity of five.

The decimal number system also is a positional number system. This means that in a number such as 143, each position in the number has a value associated with it. When you look at the decimal number 143, the 3 is in the ones, or units, position and represents three ones (3×1); the 4 is in the tens position and represents four tens (4×10); and the 1 is in the hundreds position and represents one hundred (1×100). The number 143 is the sum of the values in each position of the number ($100 + 40 + 3 = 143$). The chart in Figure A-5 shows how you can calculate the positional values (hundreds, tens, and units) for a number system. Starting on the right and working to the left, the base of the number system, in this case 10, is raised to consecutive powers (10^0, 10^1, 10^2). These calculations are a mathematical way of determining the place values in a number system.

When you use number systems other than decimal, the same principles apply. The base of the number system indicates the number of symbols that it uses, and each position in a number system has a value associated with it. By raising the base of the number system to consecutive powers beginning with zero, you can calculate the positional value.

DECIMAL	BINARY	HEXADECIMAL
0	0000	0
1	0001	1
2	0010	2
3	0011	3
4	0100	4
5	0101	5
6	0110	6
7	0111	7
8	1000	8
9	1001	9
10	1010	A
11	1011	B
12	1100	C
13	1101	D
14	1110	E
15	1111	F

FIGURE A-4

power of 10	10^2	10^1	10^0	**1**	**4**	**3**	**=**
positional value	100	10	1	**(1 x 10^2)** +	**(4 x 10^1)** +	**(3 x 10^0)**	**=**
				(1 x 100) +	**(4 x 10)** +	**(3 x 1)**	**=**
number	1	4	3	**100** +	**40** +	**3**	**= 143**

FIGURE A-5

The Binary Number System

As previously discussed, binary is a base 2 number system (bi means two), and the symbols it uses are 0 and 1. Just as each position in a decimal number has a place value associated with it, so does each position in a binary number. In binary, the place values, moving from right to left, are successive powers of two (2^0, 2^1, 2^2, 2^3 or 1, 2, 4, 8). To construct a binary number, place ones in the positions where the corresponding values add up to the quantity you want to represent and place zeros in the other positions. For example, in a four-digit binary number, the binary place values are (from right to left) 1, 2, 4, and 8. The binary number 1001 has ones in the positions for the values 1 and 8 and zeros in the positions for 2 and 4. Therefore, as shown in Figure A-6, the quantity represented by binary 1001 is 9 (8 + 0 + 0 + 1).

The Hexadecimal Number System

The hexadecimal number system uses 16 symbols to represent values (hex means six). These include the symbols 0 through 9 and A through F (Figure A-4 on the previous page). The mathematical principles previously discussed also apply to hexadecimal (Figure A-7).

The primary reasons the hexadecimal number system is used with computers are (1) it can represent binary values in a more compact and readable form, and (2) the conversion between the binary and the hexadecimal number systems is very efficient.

An eight-digit binary number (a byte) can be represented by a two-digit hexadecimal number. For example, in the ASCII code, the character M is represented as 01001101. This value can be represented in the hexadecimal number system as 4D. One way to convert this binary number (4D) to a hexadecimal number is to divide the binary number (from right to left) into groups of four digits, calculate the value of each group, and then change any two-digit values (10 through 15) to the symbols A through F that are used in the hexadecimal number system (Figure A-8).

power of 2	2^3	2^2	2^1	2^0
positional value	8	4	2	1
binary	1	0	0	1

$$1 \quad 0 \quad 0 \quad 1 \ =$$
$$(1 \times 2^3) + (0 \times 2^2) + (0 \times 2^1) + (1 \times 2^0) =$$
$$(1 \times 8) + (0 \times 4) + (0 \times 2) + (1 \times 1) =$$
$$8 + 0 + 0 + 1 = 9$$

FIGURE A-6

power of 16	16^1	16^0
positional value	16	1
hexadecimal	A	5

$$A \quad 5 \quad =$$
$$(10 \times 16^1) + (5 \times 16^0) =$$
$$(10 \times 16) + (5 \times 1) =$$
$$160 + 5 = 165$$

FIGURE A-7

positional value	8421	8421
binary	0100	1101
decimal	4	13
hexadecimal	4	D

FIGURE A-8

APPENDIX B

Quiz Yourself Answers

Following are possible answers to the Quiz Yourself boxes throughout the book.

Quiz Yourself 1-1

1. A computer is ~~a motorized~~an electronic device that processes ~~output~~input into ~~input~~output.
2. A storage device records (~~reads~~writes) and/or retrieves (~~writes~~reads) items to and from storage media.
3. An ~~output~~input device is any hardware component that allows you to enter data and instructions into a computer.
4. True Statement
5. Computers have the ~~dis~~advantages of fast speeds, ~~high~~low failure rates, producing consistent results, storing ~~small~~enormous amounts of data, and communicating with others.
6. Three commonly used ~~input~~output devices are a printer, a monitor, and speakers.

Quiz Yourself 1-2

1. A ~~resource~~network is a collection of computers and devices connected together via communications devices and transmission media.
2. True Statement
3. Popular ~~system~~application software includes Web browsers, word processing software, spreadsheet software, database software, and presentation graphics software.
4. The ~~Internet~~Web is one of the more popular services on the ~~Web~~Internet.
5. Two types of ~~application~~system software are the operating system and utility programs.

Quiz Yourself 1-3

1. A ~~desktop computer~~notebook computer (or laptop computer) is a portable, personal computer designed to fit on your lap.
2. True Statement
3. Each ~~large business~~home user spends time on the computer for different reasons that include budgeting and personal financial management, Web access, communications, and entertainment.
4. A ~~home~~power user requires the capabilities of a workstation or other powerful computer.
5. ~~Mainframes~~Supercomputers are the fastest, most powerful computers — and the most expensive.
6. The elements of an information system are hardware, ~~e-mail~~software, data, people, and ~~the Internet~~procedures.
7. With ~~embedded computers~~online banking, users access account balances, pay bills, and copy monthly

transactions from the bank's computer right into their personal computers.

Quiz Yourself 2-1

1. True Statement
2. ~~A WISP~~An IP address (or Internet Protocol address) is a number that uniquely identifies each computer or device connected to the Internet.
3. ~~An IP address~~A domain name, such as www.google.com, is the text version of ~~a domain name~~an IP address.
4. Dial-up access takes place when the modem in your computer uses ~~the cable television network~~a standard telephone line to connect to the Internet.
5. The World Wide Web Consortium (W3C) oversees research and ~~owns~~sets standards and guidelines for many areas of the Internet.

Quiz Yourself 2-2

1. True Statement
2. A ~~Web browser~~subject directory classifies Web pages in an organized set of categories, such as sports or shopping, and related subcategories.
3. Audio and video files are ~~downloaded~~compressed to reduce their file sizes.
4. Popular ~~portals~~players include iTunes, RealOne Player, and Windows Media Player.
5. The more widely used ~~search engines~~Web browsers for personal computers are Internet Explorer, Netscape, Mozilla, Opera, and Safari.
6. To develop a Web page, you do not have to be a computer programmer.
7. To improve your Web searches, use ~~general~~specific nouns and put the ~~least~~most important terms first in the search text.

Quiz Yourself 2-3

1. True Statement
2. An e-mail address is a combination of a user name and ~~an e-mail program~~a domain name that identifies a user so he or she can receive Internet e-mail.
3. ~~Business~~Consumer-to-consumer e-commerce occurs when one consumer sells directly to another, such as in an online auction.
4. FTP is an Internet standard that permits file ~~reading~~uploading and ~~writing~~downloading with other computers on the Internet.
5. ~~Spam~~Internet telephony uses the Internet (instead of the public switched telephone network) to connect a calling party to one or more called parties.
6. Netiquette is the code of ~~un~~acceptable behaviors while on the Internet.
7. On a newsgroup, a ~~subscription~~thread (or threaded discussion) consists of the original article and all subsequent related replies.

Quiz Yourself 3-1

1. True Statement
2. ~~Public domain~~Packaged software is mass produced, copyrighted retail software that meets the needs of a wide variety of users, not just a single user or company.
3. To use ~~system~~application software, your computer must be running ~~application~~system software.
4. When an application is started, the program's instructions load from ~~memory~~a storage medium into ~~a storage medium~~memory.

Quiz Yourself 3-2

1. ~~Audio~~Video editing software typically includes ~~video~~audio editing capabilities.
2. ~~Enterprise computing~~Image editing software provides the capabilities of paint software and also includes the ability to modify existing images.
3. Millions of people use ~~spreadsheet~~word processing software every day to develop documents such as letters, memos, reports, fax cover sheets, mailing labels, newsletters, and Web pages.
4. Professional ~~accounting~~DTP (or desktop publishing) software is ideal for the production of high-quality color documents such as textbooks, corporate newsletters, marketing literature, product catalogs, and annual reports.
5. ~~Spreadsheet~~Presentation graphics software is application software that allows users to create visual aids for presentations to communicate ideas, messages, and other information to a group.
6. Two of the more widely used ~~CAD programs~~software suites are Microsoft Office and Sun StarOffice.
7. True Statement

Quiz Yourself 3-3

1. An ~~anti-spam~~antivirus program protects a computer against viruses by identifying and removing any computer viruses found in memory, on storage media, or in incoming files.
2. ~~Computer~~Web-based training is a type of ~~Web~~computer-based training that uses Internet technology and consists of application software on the Web.
3. True Statement
4. ~~Legal~~Personal finance software is a simplified accounting program that helps home users and small office/home office users balance their checkbooks, pay bills, track investments, and evaluate financial plans.
5. ~~Personal DTP~~Photo editing software is a popular type of image editing software that allows users to edit digital photographs.

Quiz Yourself 4-1

1. True Statement
2. Four basic operations in a machine cycle are: (1) ~~comparing~~fetching, (2) decoding, (3) executing, and, if necessary, (4) ~~pipelining~~storing.
3. Processors contain a ~~motherboard~~control unit and an arithmetic logic unit (ALU).
4. The ~~central processing unit~~motherboard, sometimes called a system board, is the main circuit board of the system unit.
5. The leading processor chip manufacturers for personal computers are ~~Microsoft~~Intel, AMD, IBM, Motorola, and Transmeta.
6. The pace of the system clock, called the clock speed, is measured by the number of ticks per ~~minute~~second.
7. The system unit is a case that contains ~~mechanical~~electronic components of the computer used to process data.

Quiz Yourself 4-2

1. True Statement
2. A gigabyte (GB) equals approximately 1 ~~trillion~~billion bytes.
3. Memory cache helps speed the processes of the computer because it stores ~~seldom~~frequently used instructions and data.
4. Most computers are ~~analog~~digital, which means they recognize only two discrete states: on and off.
5. Most RAM ~~retains~~loses its contents when the power is removed from the computer.
6. Read-only memory (ROM) refers to memory chips storing ~~temporary~~permanent data and instructions.

Quiz Yourself 4-3

1. A ~~bus~~port is the point at which a peripheral attaches to a system unit so the peripheral can send data to or receive information from the computer.
2. An ~~AC adapter~~expansion slot is a socket on the motherboard that can hold an adapter card.
3. Near the power supply is a ~~heater~~fan that keeps components of the system unit ~~warm~~cool.
4. ~~Serial~~USB ports can connect up to 127 different peripherals together with a single connector type.
5. The higher the bus clock speed, the ~~slower~~faster the transmission of data.
6. True Statement

Quiz Yourself 5-1

1. A keyboard is an ~~output~~input device that contains keys users press to enter data in a computer.
2. A ~~light pen~~graphics tablet is a flat, rectangular, electronic plastic board.
3. A ~~trackball~~touch pad is a small, flat, rectangular pointing device commonly found on notebook computers.

4. True Statement
5. Operations you can perform with a ~~wheel~~ mouse include point, click, right-click, double-click, triple-click, drag, right-drag, rotate wheel, press wheel button, and tilt wheel.
6. ~~PDAs~~ Tablet PCs use a pressure-sensitive digital pen, and ~~Tablet PCs~~ PDAs use a stylus.

Quiz Yourself 5-2

1. True Statement
2. DV cameras record video as ~~analog~~ digital signals.
3. ~~Instant messaging~~ Voice recognition (or speech recognition) is the computer's capability of distinguishing spoken words.
4. Many smart phones today have a built-in or attachable camera so users easily can send ~~text~~ picture messages.
5. The ~~lower~~ higher the resolution of a digital camera, the better the image quality, but the more expensive the camera.

Quiz Yourself 5-3

1. A fingerprint scanner captures curves and indentations of a ~~signature~~ fingerprint.
2. After swiping a credit card through ~~an MICR~~ a magstripe (or magnetic stripe card) reader, a POS terminal connects to a system that authenticates the purchase.
3. ATMs ask you to enter a password, called a ~~biometric identifier~~ PIN (or personal identification number), which verifies that you are the holder of the bankcard.
4. Four types of ~~source documents~~ scanners are flatbed, pen, sheet-fed, and drum.
5. Retail and grocery stores use the ~~POSTNET~~ UPC (Universal Product Code) bar code.
6. RFID is a technology that uses ~~laser~~ radio signals to communicate with a tag placed in an object, an animal, or a person.
7. True Statement

Quiz Yourself 6-1

1. A ~~lower~~ higher resolution uses a greater number of pixels and thus provides a smoother image.
2. An output device is any type of ~~software~~ hardware component that conveys information to one or more people.
3. Documents often include ~~text~~ graphics to enhance their visual appeal and convey information.
4. ~~LCD~~ CRT monitors have a larger footprint than ~~CRT~~ LCD monitors.
5. Types of ~~CRTs~~ flat-panel displays include LCD monitors, LCD screens, plasma monitors, and many HDTVs.
6. True Statement

Quiz Yourself 6-2

1. A ~~laser~~ thermal printer generates images by pushing electrically heated pins against heat-sensitive paper.
2. A ~~photo~~ laser printer creates images using a laser beam and powdered ink, called toner.
3. An ink-jet printer is a type of impact printer that forms characters and graphics by spraying tiny drops of liquid ~~nitrogen~~ ink onto a piece of paper.
4. Printed information is called ~~soft~~ hard copy.
5. Two commonly used types of impact printers are ~~ink-jet~~ dot-matrix printers and line printers.
6. True Statement

Quiz Yourself 6-3

1. A digital light processing (DLP) projector uses tiny ~~lightbulbs~~ mirrors to reflect light.
2. True Statement
3. Many personal computer users add surround sound ~~printer systems~~ speakers to their computers to generate a higher-quality sound.
4. Multifunction peripherals require ~~more~~ less space than having a separate printer, scanner, copy machine, and fax machine.
5. Some joysticks and wheels include ~~real-time action~~ force feedback, which is a technology that sends resistance to the device in response to actions of the user.

Quiz Yourself 7-1

1. Floppy disks are a type of ~~optical disc~~ magnetic disk.
2. True Statement
3. SATA is a hard disk interface that uses ~~parallel~~ serial signals to transfer data, instructions, and information.
4. ~~Storage media~~ A storage device is the computer hardware that records and/or retrieves items to and from ~~a storage device~~ storage media.
5. Three types of ~~manual~~ magnetic disks are floppy disks, Zip disks, and hard disks.
6. Users can move an ~~internal~~ external Zip drive from computer to computer as needed by connecting the drive to a USB port or FireWire port on the system unit.

Quiz Yourself 7-2

1. A ~~CD-RW~~ CD-ROM is a type of optical disc on which users can read but not write (record) or erase.
2. A ~~DVD-RAM~~ Picture CD is a single-session disc that stores digital versions of a single roll of film using a jpg file format.
3. DVDs have the ~~same~~ much greater storage capacities ~~as~~ than CDs.
4. Optical discs are written and read by ~~mirrors~~ a laser.
5. ~~Single session~~ Multisession means you can write on part of the disc at one time and another part at a later time.
6. True Statement

Quiz Yourself 7-3

1. A smart card stores data on a thin ~~magnetic stripe~~microprocessor embedded in the card.
2. A USB flash drive is a flash memory storage device that plugs in a ~~parallel~~USB port on a computer or mobile device.
3. Flash memory cards are a type of ~~magnetic~~solid-state media, which means they consist entirely of electronic components and contain no moving parts.
4. Microfilm and microfiche have the ~~shortest~~longest life of any storage media.
5. Tape storage requires ~~direct~~sequential access, which refers to reading or writing data consecutively.
6. True Statement

Quiz Yourself 8-1

1. A ~~buffer~~driver is a small program that tells the operating system how to communicate with a specific device.
2. A ~~cold~~warm boot is the process of using the operating system to restart a computer.
3. A password is a ~~public~~private combination of characters associated with the user name that allows access to certain computer resources.
4. Firmware that contains the computer's startup instructions is called the ~~kernel~~BIOS.
5. The program you currently are using is in the ~~background~~foreground, and the other programs running but not in use are in the ~~foreground~~background.
6. Two types of system software are operating systems and ~~application~~utility programs.
7. True Statement

Quiz Yourself 8-2

1. A ~~file manager~~firewall is a utility that detects and protects a personal computer from unauthorized intrusions.
2. ~~Fragmenting~~Defragmenting a disk is the process of reorganizing it so the files are stored in contiguous sectors.
3. ~~Linux~~Windows XP is available in five editions: Home Edition, Professional, Media Center Edition, Tablet PC Edition, and 64-bit Edition.
4. True Statement
5. ~~Windows XP~~Linux is a UNIX-type operating system that is open source software.
6. You should ~~uninstall~~back up files and disks regularly in the event your originals are lost, damaged, or destroyed.

Quiz Yourself 8-3

1. A ~~pop-up blocker~~file compression utility shrinks the size of a file(s).
2. An ~~anti-spam~~antivirus program protects a computer against viruses by identifying and removing any computer viruses found in memory, on storage media, or on incoming files.
3. True Statement
4. Pocket PCs use ~~Palm OS~~Windows Mobile as their operating system.
5. ~~Web filtering~~CD/DVD burning software writes text, graphics, audio, and video files to a recordable or rewritable CD or DVD.

Quiz Yourself 9-1

1. A ~~cybercafé~~hot spot is a wireless network that provides Internet connections to mobile computers and other devices.
2. A ~~Web folder~~GPS (global positioning system) is a navigation system that consists of one or more earth-based receivers that accept and analyze signals sent by satellites in order to determine the receiver's geographic location.
3. True Statement
4. ~~Receiving~~Sending devices initiate an instruction to transmit data, instructions, or information.
5. Users can send graphics, pictures, video clips, and sound files, as well as short text messages with ~~text~~picture messaging.

Quiz Yourself 9-2

1. A wireless LAN is a LAN that uses no physical wires.
2. An intranet is an internal network that uses ~~video conferencing~~Internet technologies.
3. Four popular types of digital ~~dial-up~~dedicated lines are ISDN lines, DSL, T-carrier lines, and ATM.
4. In a client/server network, ~~servers~~clients on the network access resources on the ~~client~~server.
5. In a networked environment, any ~~un~~authorized computer user can access data and information stored on other computers on the network.
6. True Statement

Quiz Yourself 9-3

1. A ~~cable~~dial-up modem converts a computer's digital signals to analog signals before they are transmitted over standard telephone lines.
2. A ~~hardware firewall~~wireless access point is a communications device that allows computers and devices to transfer data wirelessly among themselves or to transfer data wirelessly to a wired network.
3. True Statement
4. ~~Analog~~Digital signals consist of individual electrical pulses that represent bits grouped together into bytes.

5. ~~Physical~~Wireless transmission media send communications signals through the air or space using radio, microwave, and infrared signals.
6. The ~~lower~~higher the bandwidth, the more data, instructions, and information the channel transmits.
7. Two types of wireless home networks are HomeRF and ~~powerline cable~~Wi-Fi.

Quiz Yourself 10-1

1. A ~~coding scheme~~check digit is a number(s) or character(s) that is appended to or inserted in a primary key value.
2. A ~~database~~field is a combination of one or more related characters or bytes and is the smallest unit of data a user accesses.
3. A ~~record~~database is a collection of data organized in a manner that allows access, retrieval, and use of that data.
4. ~~Data~~Information is processed ~~information~~data.
5. ~~Hierarchy of data~~File maintenance procedures include adding records to, changing records in, and deleting records from a file.
6. True Statement

Quiz Yourself 10-2

1. A DBMS is ~~hardware~~software that allows you to create, access, and manage ~~an operating system~~a database.
2. A ~~query~~data dictionary contains data about files and fields in the database.
3. ~~Backup and recovery procedures~~Access privileges for data involve establishing who can enter new data, change existing data, delete unwanted data, and view data.
4. Strengths of the database approach include ~~increased~~reduced data redundancy, ~~reduced~~improved data integrity, shared data, easier access, and ~~increased~~reduced development time.
5. To reduce data entry errors, well-designed forms should ~~rollback~~validate data as it is entered.
6. True Statement

Quiz Yourself 10-3

1. Data warehouses often use a process called ~~OQL~~data mining to find patterns and relationships among data.
2. ~~Object-oriented~~Relational databases store data in tables.
3. True Statement
4. Relational database users refer to a file as a table, a record as a ~~column~~row, and a field as a ~~row~~column.
5. SQL is a ~~data modeling~~query language that allows users to manage, update, and retrieve data.
6. The database ~~analyst~~administrator requires a more technical inside view of the data than does the ~~database administrator~~data analyst.

Quiz Yourself 11-1

1. A ~~back door~~denial of service (DoS) attack is an assault whose purpose is to disrupt computer access to an Internet service such as the Web or e-mail.
2. True Statement
3. A biometric device translates a personal characteristic into ~~an analog~~a digital code that then is compared with a digital code stored in the computer.
4. Computer viruses, worms, and Trojan horses are malicious-logic programs that act with~~out~~ a user's knowledge.
5. Perpetrators of cybercrime and other intrusions fall into seven basic categories: hacker, cracker, ~~CERT/CC~~script kiddie, corporate spy, unethical employee, ~~trusted source~~cyberextortionist, and cyberterrorist.
6. ~~Shorter~~Longer passwords provide greater security than ~~longer~~shorter ones.
7. Updating an antivirus program's ~~quarantine~~signature file protects a computer against viruses written since the antivirus program was released.

Quiz Yourself 11-2

1. An end-user license agreement (EULA) ~~permits~~does not permit users to give copies to friends and colleagues, while continuing to use the software.
2. Encryption is a process of converting ~~ciphertext~~plaintext into ~~plaintext~~ciphertext to prevent authorized access.
3. Mobile users are ~~not~~susceptible to hardware theft.
4. True Statement
5. Three ~~backup~~wireless security standards are Wired Equivalent Privacy, Wi-Fi Protected Access, and 802.11i.
6. To prevent against data loss caused by a system failure, computer users should ~~restore~~back up files regularly.

Quiz Yourself 11-3

1. A ~~code of conduct~~copyright gives authors and artists exclusive rights to duplicate, publish, and sell their materials.
2. Factors that cause ~~CVS~~tendonitis or CTS (carpal tunnel syndrome) include prolonged typing, prolonged mouse usage, or continual shifting between the mouse and the keyboard.
3. ~~Phishing~~Computer forensics is the discovery, collection, and analysis of evidence found on computers and networks.
4. True Statement
5. Users should not store obsolete computers and devices in their basement or attic.
6. Web sites use ~~electronic profiles~~cookies to track user preferences, store users' passwords, keep track of items in a user's shopping cart, and track Web site browsing habits.
7. You can~~not~~ assume that information on the Web is correct.

APPENDIX C
Computer Acronyms

Acronym	Description	Page
0NF	zero normal form	540
1NF	first normal form	540
2NF	second normal form	540
3NF	third normal form	540
AA	Audible Audio	87
AAC	Advanced Audio Coding	87
AC adapter	alternating current adapter	213
ADA	Americans with Disabilities Act	266
ADC	analog-to-digital converter	38
ADSL	asymmetric digital subscriber line	482
AES	advanced encryption standard	592
AGP	Accelerated Graphics Port	212
AIFF	Audio Interchange File Format	87
ALU	arithmetic logic unit	188
AMD	Advanced Micro Devices	219
AOL	America Online	72, 82
ARPA	Advanced Research Projects Agency	69
ARPANET	Advanced Research Projects Agency network	69
ASCII	American Standard Code for Information Interchange	195, 518
ASF	Advanced Streaming (or Systems) Format	87
ASP	application service provider	164
ATC	advanced transfer cache	201
ATM	Asynchronous Transfer Mode	482, 483
ATM	automated teller machine	262
AUP	acceptable use policy	565
B2B	business-to-business	92
B2C	business-to-consumer	92
BIOS	basic input/output system	400
Bit	binary digit	195, 518
BLOB	binary large object	518
BMP	bit map	85
BSA	Business Software Alliance	571
BTW	by the way	100
C2C	consumer-to-consumer	92
CA	certificate authority	573
CAD	computer-aided design	327
CAD database	computer-aided design database	534
CAD software	computer-aided design software	150, 151
CAI	computer-aided instruction	160
Caller ID	caller identification	581
CAM	computer-aided manufacturing	36
CATV	cable television	482
CBT	computer-based training	160
CCD	charge-coupled device	251
CD	compact disc	8, 9, 17, 27, 89, 357
CD drive	compact disc drive	27
CD/DVD burner	compact disc/digital versatile disc burner	162
CD recorder	compact disc recorder	371
CDMA	Code Division Multiple Access	494, 499

Acronym	Description	Page
CD-R	compact disc-recordable	371
CD-R drive	compact disc-recordable drive	371
CD-ROM	compact disc read-only memory	369-70
CD-ROM drive	compact disc read-only memory drive	369
CD-RW	compact disc-rewritable	371, 576
CD-RW drive	compact disc-rewritable drive	371
CERT/CC	Computer Emergency Response Team Coordination Center	558
CF	CompactFlash	376
CGI script	Common Gateway Interface script	537
CIPA	Children's Internet Protection Act	480, 585
CMOS	complementary metal-oxide semiconductor	203
CMOS battery	complementary metal-oxide semiconductor battery	203
CMOS chip	complementary metal-oxide semiconductor chip	400
Coax	coaxial cable	493
COBOL	COmmon Business-Oriented Language	53
COM port	communications port	207
COPPA	Children's Online Privacy Protection Act	585
CPU	central processing unit	8, 187
CRT	cathode-ray tube	307
CRT monitor	cathode-ray tube monitor	307-8
CST	Computer Service Technician	381
CTS	carpal tunnel syndrome	588
CVS	computer vision syndrome	588
DA	database analyst	538
DAC	digital-to-analog converter	38
DBA	database administrator	538
DBMS	database management system	515
DDoS attack	distributed denial of service attack	562
DDR SDRAM	double data rate synchronous dynamic random access memory	199
DHCP	Dynamic Host Configuration Protocol	102
DIMM	dual inline memory module	199
DL	distance learning	166
DLP projector	digital light processing projector	324
DMCA	Digital Millennium Copyright Act	585
DNS	domain name system	74
DNS server	domain name system server	74, 102
DOS	Disk Operating System	417
DoS attack	denial of service attack	562
Dpi	dots per inch	252, 313
DRAM	dynamic random access memory	199
DSL	Digital Subscriber Line	70, 449, 482, 486
DSL modem	Digital Subscriber Line modem	485
DSP	digital signal processor	38
DTP	desktop publishing	152
DTP software	desktop publishing software	152
DTV	digital television	306
DV camera	digital video camera	253
DVD	digital versatile disc or digital video disc	8, 17, 59, 89, 357

Acronym	Description	Page
DVD/CD-RW	digital video disc/compact disc-rewritable drive	368, 372
DVD drive	digital versatile disc or digital video disc drive	9, 27, 212
DVD recorder	digital versatile disc or digital video disc recorder	373
DVD+R	digital versatile disc or digital video disc recordable	373
DVD-R	digital versatile disc or digital video disc recordable	373
DVD+RAM	digital versatile disc or digital video disc + random access memory	373
DVD-ROM drive	digital versatile disc or digital video disc read-only memory drive	372
DVD-ROM	digital versatile disc or digital video disc read-only memory	9, 372
DVD+RW	digital versatile disc or digital video disc + rewritable	373
DVD-RW	digital versatile disc or digital video disc + rewritable	373
DVD+RW drive	digital versatile disc or digital video disc + rewritable drive	373
DVD-RW drive	digital versatile disc or digital video disc + rewritable drive	373
DVI	Digital Video Interface	305
DVI port	Digital Video Interface port	305
Dynamic IP address	dynamic Internet Protocol address	102
EB	exabyte	356
EBCDIC	Extended Binary Coded Decimal Interchange Code	195, 518
E-book	electronic book	61, 303
E-commerce	electronic commerce	28, 30, 60, 61, 91-92
ECPA	Electronic Communications Privacy Act	585
EDI	electronic data interchange	470
EEPROM	electrically erasable programmable read-only memory	202
E-file	electronic filing	157
E-form	electronic form	530
EFS	Encryption File System	592
EFT	electronic funds transfer	470
EIDE	Enhanced Integrated Drive Electronics	365
E-mail	electronic mail	12, 31, 69, 92-95, 101, 161, 462
E-mail address	electronic mail address	94
E-mail filtering	electronic mail filtering	584
E-mail program	electronic mail program	93, 161
EMR	electromagnetic radiation	308
ENIAC	Electronic Numerical Integrator and Computer	52
Enterprise ASP	enterprise application service provider	164
EP	Enterprise Portal	541
EULA	end-user license agreement	571
FAQ	frequently asked questions	6, 100
Fax	facsimile	322-23
Fax machine	facsimile machine	322-23
Fax modem	facsimile modem	322, 323
Fortran	FORmula TRANslator	53

Acronym	Description	Page
FRED	Forensic Recovery of Digital Evidence	612
FTP	File Transfer Protocol	68, 96, 134, 161, 462
FTP server	File Transfer Protocol server	96
FWIW	for what it's worth	100
FYI	for your information	100
GB	gigabyte	197, 356
Gbps	giga [billion] bits per second	476
GHz	gigahertz	189
GIF	Graphics Interchange Format	85
GIGO	garbage in, garbage out	10, 516
GLBA	Graham-Leach-Bliley Act	585
GPRS	General Packet Radio Service	494
GPS	global positioning system	466, 513
GPS receiver	global positioning system receiver	466-67
GPU	graphics processing unit	305
GSM	Global System for Mobile Communications	494
GUI	graphical user interface	15, 137, 402, 420, 421
HD	high density	358
HDTV	high-definition television	306-7
HIPAA	Health Insurance Portability and Accountability Act	379, 585
Hi-Speed USB	high speed universal serial bus	365
HomeRF network	home radio frequency network	490
HP	Hewlett-Packard	329
http	Hypertext Transfer Protocol	76, 477
Hz	hertz	189
I-4	International Information Integrity Institute	593
IBM	International Business Machines	53, 54, 55, 138
IBM processor	International Business Machines processor	190
IC	integrated circuit	186
ICANN	Internet Corporation for Assigned Names and Numbers	74
ICRA	Internet Content Rating Association	587
IEEE 1394 port	Institute of Electrical and Electronics Engineers 1394 port	209
IM	instant messaging	98
IMDb	Internet Movie Database	536
IMHO	in my humble opinion	100
Interactive TV	interactive television	307
IP	intellectual property	579
IP address	Internet Protocol address	73, 102
IPng	Internet Protocol Next Generation	102
IPv6	Internet Protocol version 6	102
IR	infrared	494
IrDA	Infrared Data Association	210, 478
IrDA port	Infrared Data Association port	210
IRQ	interrupt request	409
IS	information system	25
ISDN	Integrated Services Digital Network	482
ISDN modem	Integrated Services Digital Network modem	485
ISP	Internet service provider	72
IT	information technology	25
IT department	information technology department	30
JPEG	Joint Photographic Experts Group	85, 345
JPEG 2000	Joint Photographic Experts Group 2000	324
K	kilobyte	197

INDEX

PHOTO CREDITS

Chapter 1: PY1-01, study hall, ©Bill Aron/PhotoEdit Inc.; PY1-02, laptop user, © Jose Luis Pelaez, Inc./CORBIS; PY1-03, computer store, ©Spencer Grant/PhotoEdit Inc.; PY1-04, people in coffee shop, ©Gary Conner/PhotoEdit Inc.; PY1-05, Camera, Courtesy of Sony Electronics Inc.; PY1-06, wireless bluetooth card, Courtesy of 3Com Corporation; PY1-07, USB flash drive, Courtesy of SimpleTech, Inc.; PY1-08, instructor, Photodisc Collection/Getty Images; Figure 1-01a, Person using PDA, © Thierry Dosogne/Getty Images Figure 1-01b, Person using notebook computer, © Roy Morsch/CORBIS; Figure 1-01c, Person using desktop computer, © Jose Luis Pelaez, Inc./CORBIS; Figure 1-01d, Person using Tablet PC, Courtesy of Motion Computing, Inc.; Figure 1-01e, Person using smartphone, Siemens AG Press Picture; Figure 1-02, payroll check, © C Squared Studios/Getty Images; Figure 1-03a, Computer with CD drive, DVD drive, Zip® drive, and floppy drive, keyboard, flat panel monitor, mouse, speakers, Courtesy of Acer America Corp.; Figure 1-03b, PC video camera (input device), Courtesy of Logitech, Inc.; Figure 1-03c, Microphone, Courtesy of Logitech, Inc.; Figure 1-03d, Open flatbed scanner, Courtesy of Umax Systems GmbH; Figure 1-03e, External card reader, Courtesy of Sandisk Corporation; Figure 1-03f, USB flash drive, Courtesy of Sandisk Corporation; Figure 1-03g, External cable modem, Courtesy of Linksys, a Division of Cisco Systems Inc.; Figure 1-03h, digital camera, Courtesy of Umax Systems GmbH; Figure 1-03i, Ink-jet printer, Courtesy of Epson America, Inc.; Figure 1-04, Hard disk, Courtesy of Seagate Technology; Figure 1-05, DVD disc in the DVD tray, ©Rachel Epstein/Photo Edit; Looking Ahead 1-1, Implant and/or robotics (Bionics), © AP/WIDE WORLD PHOTOS; Figure 1-06a,b,c, desktop computers, Courtesy of Sony Electronics Inc.; Figure 1-07a, desktop computer, Courtesy of Acer America Corp.; Figure 1-07b, desktop computer, Courtesy of Sony Electronics Inc.; Figure 1-07c, desktop computer, © Gateway, Inc.; Figure 1-07d, desktop computer, Courtesy of Acer America Corp.; Figure 1-07e, smartphone, Courtesy of Nokia; Figure 1-07f, PDA, Courtesy of Sony Electronics Inc.; Figure 1-11, person standing in the software aisle at a computer store, ©Bonnie Kamin/Photo Edit; Figure 1-12, notebook computers, Courtesy of Acer America Corp.; Figure 1-15, IBM ThinkCentre Computer, Courtesy of IBM Corporation; Figure 1-16, Latest iMac with 20" monitor, Courtesy of Apple Computer, Inc.; Figure 1-17, Notebook computer, Courtesy of Sony Electronics Inc.; Figure 1-18, Tablet PC, Courtesy of Motion Computing, Inc.; Figure 1-19, WORLD'S SMALLEST AND LIGHTEST WINDOWS XP PC, VAIO TYPE U, © ISSEI KATO/Reuters/Corbis; Figure 1-20a, PDA with keyboard, Courtesy of palmOne, Inc. palmOne, Zire, Tungsten, Treo, logos, stylizations and design marks associated with all the preceding, and trade dress associated with palmOne, Inc.'s products, are among the trademarks or registered trademarks owned by or exclusively licensed to palmOne, Inc.; Figure 1-20b, PDA without keyboard, Courtesy of Sony Electronics Inc.; Figure 1-20c, stylus, Courtesy of Belkin Corporation; Figure 1-21, Smartphone in a person's hand (close-up), Courtesy of Nokia; Figure 1-22, Smart watch, Courtesy of Fossil, Inc. ; Figure 1-23, Midrange server, Copyright 2005 Sun Microsystems, Inc. All Rights Reserved. Used by permission.; Figure 1-24, Mainframe computer, Courtesy of IBM Corporation; Figure 1-25, Earth Simulator computer, COPYRIGHT: JAMSTEC/ESC; Figure 1-26a, car with an onboard navigation system, Toyota photo; Figure 1-26b, Deplyed airbag, © Patti McConville/Imagestate; Figure 1-26c, on-board navigation system, Toyota photo; Figure 1-26d, Gas pedal/brake pedal in car, Toyota photo; Figure 1-26e, Wheel in motion, © DiMaggio/Kalish/CORBIS; Figure 1-26f, Cruise control on a steering wheel, Toyota photo; Figure 1-27, Step 3, Midrange server, Courtesy of Fujitsu Siemens Computers; Figure 1-27, Step 4, Corporate Printer System, Courtesy of IBM Corporation; Figure 1-28, Home user, © Jose Luis Pelaez, Inc./CORBIS; Figure 1-29, couple looking at digital camera, Courtesy of Sony Electronics Inc.; Figure 1-30, home office/small business user, © Britt Erlanson/Getty Images; Figure 1-31a, Mobile user with a notebook computer, © Andersen-Ross/Brand X Pictures; Figure 1-31b, Mobile user with PDA, © David Pollack/CORBIS; Figure 1-31c, tablet PC user, Courtesy of Motion Computing, Inc; Figure 1-31d, Mobile user with smart phone, © Edward Bock/CORBIS; Figure 1-32, Power user, © Richard T. Nowitz/CORBIS; Figure 1-33, Many users in large business, © Comstock Images; Figure 1-34, Customer using a kiosk, Courtesy of IBM Corporation; Figure 1-35a, telecommuter working at home, © Jose Luis Pelaez, Inc./CORBIS; Figure 1-35b, home office, © Britt Erlanson/Getty Images; Figure 1-35c, laptop user, © Andersen-Ross/Brand X Pictures; Figure 1-35d, Power user, © Richard T. Nowitz/CORBIS; Figure 1-35e, users in a large office, © Comstock Images; Looking Ahead 1-2, QRIO robot, Courtesy of Sony Electronics Inc.; Figure 1-36, red-head girl using laptop at school, © David Roth/Getty Images; Figure 1-38, Police officer in police car that has a notebook computer and shows officer using a PDA, Courtesy of IBM Corporation; Figure 1-39, medical professional and computer, © Peter Beck/CORBIS; Figure 1-40a, How a Camera Pill Works — hand holding camera pill, © AP/WIDE WORLD PHOTOS; Figure 1-40c, How a Camera Pill Works — Doctor looking at x-rays in front of a computer, © Gabe Palmer/CORBIS; Figure 1-42, person using notebook computer, © EPA/Ulrich Perrey/Landov; Figure 1-43, Robot in a CAM (computer aided manufacturing) environment, © Charles O'Rear/CORBIS; Career Corner, Personal computer salesperson, © Jana Birchum/Getty Images; Technology Trailblazer 1, Bill Gates, © Justin Sullivan/Getty Images; Technology Trailblazer 2, Carly Fiorina, © Justin Sullivan/Getty Images; **Special Feature: Timeline** 1937, COLLAGE: Clifford Berry, Courtesy of Iowa State University; 1937, Atanasoff-Berry-Computer (ABC), Courtesy of Iowa State University; 1937, Dr. John V. Atanasoff, Courtesy of Iowa State University; 1943, Alan Turing, Photo courtesy of Computer History Museum; 1943, Colossus computer, Photo courtesy of Computer History Museum; 1945, Dr. John von Neumann, Courtesy of the Archives of the Institute for Advanced Study; 1945, Dr. Von Neumann with computer, Courtesy of the Archives of the Institute for Advanced Study; 1946, The ENIAC (Electronic Numerical Integrator And Computer) created by Dr. John W. Mauchly and J. Presper Eckert, Jr., From the Collections of the University of Pennsylvania Archives; 1947, transfer resistence device (transistor); © IBM Corporate Archives; 1947, close-up of transistor with pencil, © IBM Corporate Archives; 1951, Univac I (UNIVersal Automatic Computer), Courtesy Unisys Corporation; 1952, Dr. Grace Hopper, Courtesy of Hagley Museum and Library; 1953, IBM model 650 (hands holding magnifying glass), © IBM Corporate Archives; 1957, Fortran (FORmula TRANslation) is introduced by John Backus, © IBM Corporate Archives; 1957, IBM 305 RAMAC system uses magnetic disk for external storage, © IBM Corporate Archives; 1957, close-up of magnetic disks for storage, Courtesy of the Department of the Navy; 1958, Jack Kilby, Courtesy of Texas Instruments; 1958, integrated circuit, Courtesy of Texas Instruments; 1959, IBM 1602 CADET, © IBM Corporate Archives; 1960, Dr. Grace Hopper invents COBOL, Courtesy of Hagley Museum and Library; 1964, computer chip on finger, © IBM Corporate Archives; 1964, TYPEWRITER, © IBM Corporate Archives; 1964, IBM System/360, © IBM Corporate Archives; 1965, Dr. John Kenney of Dartmouth, Courtesy of Dartmouth College; 1965, Digital Equipment Corp. (DEC) introduces the first mini-computer the PDP-8, Courtesy of Digital Equipment Corporation; 1970, LSI chip (large-scale integration), © IBM Corporate Archives; 1971, Dr. Ted Hoff, Courtesy of Intel Corporation; 1971, Intel 4004 - microprogrammable computer chip, Courtesy of Intel Corporation; 1975, Bob Metcalfe (develops Ethernet), Courtesy of InfoWorld; 1975, Altair - one of the first microcoputers., Photo courtesy of Computer History Museum; 1976, Image of first Apple Computer, Courtesy of Apple Computer, Inc.; 1976, Steve Wozniak and Steve Jobs, © Bettmann/CORBIS; 1979, Bob Frankston and Dan Bricklin, writers of VisiCalc, Photo courtesy of Computer History Museum; 1980, Alan Shugart introduces Winchester hard drive, © IBM Corporate Archives; 1980, Bill Gates, Courtesy of Microsoft Corporation; 1981, IBM PC is introduced, © IBM Corporate Archives; 1982, Hayes 300 bps smart modem, Courtesy of Zoom Telephonics, Inc. ; 1983, Box shot of Lotus 1-2-3, © IBM Corporate Archives; 1983, Cover of mag. Announces computer as "Machine of the Year", © Time Life Pictures/Getty Images; 1984, Hewlett-Packard introduces laser-jet printer, Courtesy of Hewlett-Packard Company; 1984, Macintosh computer introduced, Courtesy of Apple Computer, Inc.; 1989, Intel 486 transistor microprocessor, Courtesy of Intel Corporation; 1989, Tim Berners-Lee, © 1997-1998W3C (MIT, INRIA, Keio); 1992, Screen shot of Windows 3.1, Courtesy of Microsoft Corporation; 1993, Intel Pentium processor chip, Courtesy of Intel Corporation; 1993, photo of the White House, © Costa Cruise Lines/Getty Images; 1994, Screen shot of Netscape Navigator 1.0, Courtesy of Netscape Communications Corporation; 1995, box shot of Windows 95, Box shot reprinted with permission from Microsoft Corporation; 1995, Java logo, Copyright 2005 Sun Microsystems, Inc. All Rights Reserved. Used by permission; 1996, box shot Microsoft Windows NT 4.0 Server, Box shot reprinted with permission from Microsoft Corporation; 1996, PalmPilot, Courtesy of palmOne, Inc. palmOne, Zire, Tungsten, Treo, logos, stylizations and design marks associated with all the preceding, and trade dress associated with palmOne, Inc.'s products, are the trademarks or registered trademarks owned by or exclusively licensed to palmOne, Inc.; 1997, Intel Pentium II, Courtesy of Intel Corporation; 1997, Teminator CD, Motion Picture & Television Archives; 1997, DVD player, Courtesy of Denon Electronics; 1998, Box shot Windows 98, Box shot reprinted with permission from Microsoft Corporation; 1998, telecommuting, © Andersen Ross/Getty Images; 1998, Apple introduces iMac, Courtesy of Apple Computer, Inc.; 1999, box shot, Microsoft Office 2000, Box shot reprinted with permission from Microsoft Corporation; 2000, Microsoft Windows Me, Box shot reprinted with permission from Microsoft Corporation; 2000, Micrsoft's Windows 2000 Professional, Box shot reprinted with permission from Microsoft Corporation; 2000, telemedicine, © B Busco/Getty Images; 2001, Intel Pentium 4 chip, Courtesy of Intel Corporation; 2001, box shot, Box shot reprinted with permission from Microsoft Corporation; 2001, e-book, Courtesy of RCA/Thomson Consumer Electronics; 2002, Open DVD drive, © Scott Goodwin Photography; 2002, digital video camera, Courtesy of Sharp Electronics; 2002, web cam, Courtesy of Intel Corporation; 2002, Tablet PC, Courtesy of ViewSonic® Corporation; 2002, Handspring TREO, Courtesy of Handspring, Inc.; 2002, Pentium 4 with .13 micron processor, Courtesy of Intel Corporation; 2002, judge with gavel, © Getty Images; 2003, PC with open cd TRAY, Courtesy of Sony Electronics Inc.; 2003, Palm VIIx, Courtesy of palmOne, Inc. palmOne, Zire, Tungsten, Treo, logos, stylizations and design marks associated with all the preceeding, and trade dress assocated with palmOne, Inc.'s products, are among the trademarks or registered trademarks owned by or exclusively licensed to palmOne, Inc.; 2003, man with notebook computer, ©LWA- JDC/CORBIS; 2003, girl with notebook computer, © Royalty-Free/CORBIS; 2003, child with a PDA, © Jim Cummins/CORBIS; 2003, Man using desktop computer, © Ed Bock/CORBIS; 2003, woman watching plasma tv, © Koichi Kamoshida/Getty Images; 2003, Computer with bugs, © Jeff Nishinaka/Getty Images; 2003, downloading graphic, © Nick Koudis/Getty Images; 2003, Recording Industry Association of America (RIAA), © REUTERS/Mannie Garcia; 2003, box shot, Box shot reprinted with permission from Microsoft Corporation; 2004, lcd monitor, Courtesy of Sony Electronics Inc.; 2004, crt monitor, Courtesy of ViewSonic® Corporation. All rights reserved.; 2004, USB flash drive #1, © Transcend Information Inc. All rights reserved.; 2004, USB flash drive #2, Courtesy of Sandisk Corporation; 2004, RFID tags, Siemens press picture; 2004, front view photo of iMacG5, Courtesy of Apple Computer, Inc.; 2005, FireFox logo, Courtesy of The Mozilla Foundation; 2005, OQO handheld computer, Courtesy of OQO, Inc.; 2005, smart phone, Courtesy of palmOne, Inc. palmOne, Zire, Tungsten, Treo, logos, stylizations and design marks associated with all the preceeding, and trade dress assocated with palmOne, Inc.'s products, are among the trademarks or registered trademarks owned by or exclusively licensed to palmOne, Inc.; **Chapter 2:** PY2-1, movie theater, © Ryan McVay/Getty Images; Py2-2, movie theater 2, © Tom

Courtesy of Oki Data Amercas, Inc.; Figure 6-25, line printer, Courtesy of Printronix, Inc.; Figure 6-26, PC with 5:1 stereo speakers and a woofer, Courtesy of Mind Computer Products; Figure 6-27, people wearing headsets at computer, ©Jeff Greenberg/PhotoEdit Inc.; figure 6-29, person using fax machine, © John A Rizzo/Getty Images; Figure 6-30a, laptop, Courtesy of MPC Computers, LLC.; Figure 6-30b, PC card fax modem, Courtesy of U.S. Robotics Corporation; Figure 6-30c, fax machine, ©Spencer Grant/Photo Edit Inc.; Figure 6-30d, PC, Courtesy of MPC Computers, LLC.; Figure 6-31, multifunction peripheral — fax, copier, printer, scanner, Courtesy of Xerox Corporation; Figure 6-32, data projector, Courtesy of InFocus® Corporation; Looking Ahead 6-2, Digital Cinema Just the Right Picture, © Nick Koudis/Getty Images; Figure 6-33a, Forcefeed joystick, Courtesy of Logitech; Figure 6-33b, Forcefeedback wheel, Courtesy of Microsoft Corporation; Figure 6-34a, home user, © Jose Luis Pelaez, Inc./CORBIS; Figure 6-34b, home office, © Britt Erlanson/Getty Images; Figure 6-34c, laptop user, © Andersen-Ross/Brand X Pictures; Figure 6-34d, Power user, © Richard T. Nowitz/CORBIS; Figure 6-34e, users in a large office, © Comstock Images; Figure 6-36A, braille printer, Courtesy of Enabling Technologies; Figure 6-36b, close-up of finger reading braille, © Don Farrall/Getty Images; Figure 6-37, Intel pentium 4, Courtesy of Intel Corporation; Career Corner, graphic designer, © Robert Llewellyn/Imagestate; Technology Trailblazer 1, Steve Jobs, ©Fujifotos/The Image Works; Technology Trailblazer 2, Donna Dubinsky, © AP/WIDE WORLD PHOTOS; **Special Feature: Digital Imaging and Video Technology:** Intro 1, family at beach, © Comstock Images; Intro 2, graduation, © Comstock Images; Intro 3, Asian girls getting picture taken, © Tim Pannell/CORBIS; Figure 01a, Digital camera, Courtesy of Nikon USA; Figure 01b, Digital video camera, Courtesy of Sony Electronics Inc.; Figure 01c, Television, Courtesy of BenQ America Corp.; Figure 01d, Personal computer, Courtesy of Sony Electronics Inc.; Figure 01e, Photographic-quality printer, Courtesy of Canon USA Inc.; Figure 01f, DVD recorder, Courtesy of Sony Electronics Inc.; Figure01f2, DVD, © Spike Mafford/Getty Images; Figure 01g, VCR, Courtesy of JVC Company of America; Figure 01h, action shot, © Getty Images; Figure 01i, Person using digital camera, © Tim Kiusalaas/Masterfile; Figure 01j, Person using digital video camera, © J. Fisher/Zefa/Masterfile; Figure 02a, Point and shoot camera, Courtesy of Sony Electronics Inc.; Figure 02b, field digital camera, Courtesy of Canon U.S.A, Inc.; Figure 02c, studio digital camera, Courtesy of Canon U.S.A, Inc.; Figure 05a, microdrive, Courtesy of Hitachi Global Storage Technologies; Figure 05b, Compact Flash, Courtesy of Lexar Media, Inc.; Figure 05c, memory stick 1 GB, Courtesy of Sony Electronics Inc.; Figure 06, FireWire Compact Flash Card Reader, Courtesy of SanDisk Corporation; Figure 08, photo kiosk, Courtesy of Pixel Magic Imaging™, Inc.; Figure 09, photo slide show software, Courtesy of Ulead Systems, Inc.; Figure 10a, high-end consumer digital video camera, Courtesy of Sony Electronics Inc.; figure 10b, consumer digital video camera, Courtesy of Sony Electronics Inc.; Figure 10c, webcasting and monitoring digital video camera, Courtesy of Logitech; Figure 11a, PC, Courtesy of Sony Electronics Inc.; Figure 11b, screen photos, © Royalty-Free/CORBIS ; Figure 11c, Digital video camera, Courtesy of Sony Electronics Inc.; Figure 12a, S-VCR, Courtesy of JVC Company of America; Figure 12b, video capture card (PCi card), Courtesy of Pinnacle Systems, Inc.; Figure 12c, analog camera, Courtesy of Matsushita Electric Corporation of America; Figure 12d, screen image, © Chase Jarvis/Getty Images; Figure 12e, PC, Courtesy of Sony Electronics Inc.; Figure 15, DivX codec, Courtesy of DivXNetworks, Inc.; Figure 16, Color correction for video editing (screen), Screenshot reprinted by permission from Apple Computer, Inc.; Figure 17, video editing "sequencing" screen-shot — Windows Movie Maker, Courtesy of Microsoft Corporation; Figure 18a, Video editing "transitions", Courtesy of Microsoft Corporation; Figure 19, screen-shot, Courtesy of Pinnacle Systems, Inc.; **Chapter 7:** PY7-01, job interview, © Noel Hendrickson/Masterfile; PY7-02, photojournalists, © Photodisc Collection; PY7-03, mini storage media, Courtesy of SanDisk Corporation; PY7-04, card reader, Courtesy of Delkin Devices, Inc.; PY7-05, compact flash, Courtesy of Lexar Media, Inc.; PY7-06, Sandisk 2GB, Courtesy of SanDisk Corporation; PY7-07, keychain USB, Courtesy of Kingston Technology, Inc.; PY7-08, photo station in store, Courtesy of Sony Electronics Inc.; PY7-09, print photos on HP printer, © RICK MAIMAN/Bloomberg News/Landov; PY7-10, newspaper printing, Copyright ©NOVASTOCK/Photo Edit — All rights reserved.; Figure 7-1a, Inserting a floppy disk, © Masterfile; Figure 7-1b, Zip disk sticking out of drive, Photo Courtesy of Iomega Corporation. Copyright © 2003 Iomega Corporation. All Rights Reserved. Zip is a registered trademark in the United States and/or other countries. Iomega, the stylized "i" logo and product images are property of Iomega Corporation in the United States and/or other countries.; Figure 7-01c, SATA (serial ATA) hard disk, Courtesy of Western Digital; Figure 7-01d, miniature hard disk, Courtesy of Toshiba America Information Systems, Inc.; Figure 7-1e, external hard drive, Courtesy of Seagate Technology; Figure 7-1f, CD-ROM/DVD-ROM, Courtesy of Fujitsu Siemens Computers; Figure 7-1g, tape cassette and tape drive, Courtesy of Quantum Corp.; Figure 7-1h, PC card product shot, Courtesy of SimpleTech, Inc.; Figure 7-1i, media card in PDA, Courtesy of ASUSTEK Computer, Inc.; Figure 7-1j, USB flash drive, Courtesy of M-Systems Flash Disk Pioneers Ltd.; Figure 7-1k, microfiche, Copyright ©Bill Aron/Photo Edit — All rights reserved.; Figure 7-05, internal hard disk, Courtesy of Western Digital; Figure 7-06a, person inserting floppy disk into PC, Courtesy of Quantum Corp.; Figure 7-06b, external floppy disk drive, Photo Courtesy of Iomega Corporation. Copyright © 2003 Iomega Corporation. All Rights Reserved. Zip is a registered trademark in the United States and/or other countries. Iomega, the stylized "i" logo and product images are property of Iomega Corporation in the United States and/or other countries.; Figure 7-09a, Iomega 750 MB Zip disk and drive, Photo Courtesy of Iomega Corporation. Copyright © 2003 Iomega Corporation. All Rights Reserved. Zip is a registered trademark in the United States and/or other countries. Iomega, the stylized "i" logo and product images are property of Iomega Corporation in the United States and/or other countries.; Figure 7-10a, system unit opened with SATA hard disk, © 2004 Tim Gilman; Figure 7-10b, SATA hard disk, Courtesy of Western Digital; Looking Ahead 7-1, Heat Increases Disk Capacity, Courtesy of IBM Corporation; Figure 7-12, SATA hard disk, Courtesy of Maxtor Corporation. © 2004 Maxtor Corporation. All rights reserved.; Figure 7-15a, processor chip, Coutesy of Intel Corporation; Figure 7-16, Mini hard disk, Courtesy of Toshiba America Information Systems, Inc.; Figure 7-17a, external hard disk drive plugged into a computer, Courtesy of Fujitsu Siemens Computers; Figure 7-17b, removable hard disk drive, Photo Courtesy of Iomega Corporation. Copyright © 2003 Iomega Corporation. All Rights Reserved. Zip is a registered trademark in the United States and/or other countries. Iomega, the stylized "i" logo and product images are property of Iomega Corporation in the United States and/or other countries.; Figure 7-23a, Dictionary CD-ROM, Courtesy of Merriam-Webster; Figure 7-23b, CD-R (box shot), Courtesy of Memorex Products, Inc.; Figure 7-23c, CD-RW box shot, Courtesy of Memorex Products, Inc.; Figure 7-23d1, TopoUSA DVD-ROM, © 2004 DeLorme (www.delorme.com) Topo USA®; Figure 7-23d2, DVD-ROM (disk), © 2004 DeLorme (www.delorme.com) Topo USA®; Figure 7-23e1, DVD-R (box shot), Courtesy of Memorex Products, Inc.; Figure 7-23e2, DVD+R (box shot), Courtesy of Memorex Products, Inc.; Figure 7-23f1, DVD-RW (box shot), Courtesy of Memorex Products, Inc.; Figure 7-23f2, DVD+RW (box shot), Courtesy of Memorex Products, Inc.; Figure 7-23f3, DVD-RAM (box shot), Courtesy of Memorex Products, Inc.; Figure 7-24c, stack of CD Roms, © Gary Herrington Photography; Figure 7-25a, photo processing envelope with Photo CD check box, Courtesy of AR Photo Research; Figure 7-25b, picture CD with envelope of processed pictures, Courtesy of AR Photo Research; Figure 7-25c, Kodak picture kiosk, © Steven Brahms/Bloomberg News/Landov; Figure 7-25d1, flat panel monitor with photo editing software, Courtesy of NEC Solutions (America), Inc.; Figure 7-25d2, photo editing software, Courtesy of Ulead Systems, Inc.; Figure 7-25d, photo editing software, © Steven Brahms/Bloomberg News/Landov; Figure 7-26a, TopoUSA screen shot for LCD monitor, © 2004 DeLorme (www.delorme.com) Topo USA®; Figure 7-26b, TopoUSA DVD software disc, © 2004 DeLorme (www.delorme.com) Topo USA®; Looking Ahead 7-2, Paper Disks Offer Increased Capacity, © YOSHIKAZU TSUNO/AFP/Getty Images); Figure 7-28, tape cartridge and tape drive, Courtesy of Sony Electronics Inc.; Figure 7-29a, PC card sticking out of laptop computer, Courtesy of Toshiba America Information Systems, Inc.; Figure 7-31a, USB flash drive in desktop computer, Courtesy of Fujitsu Siemens Computers; Figure 7-31b, card reader in notebook computer, Courtesy of SanDisk Corporation; Figure 7-31c, miniature storage media sticking out of PDA, Courtesy of Sandisk Corporation; Figure 7-31c2, miniature storage media sticking out of PDA, Courtesy of palmOne, Inc. palmOne, Zire, Tungsten, Treo, logos, stylizations and design marks associated with all the preceeding, and trade dress assocated with palmOne, Inc.'s products, are among the trademarks or registered trademarks owned by or exclusively licensed to palmOne, Inc.; Figure 7-31d, smartcard for access control, Siemens press picture; Figure 7-31e1, digital photo viewer with a card sticking out, Courtesy of Delkin Devices, Inc.; Figure 7-31e2, TV, Courtesy of JVC Company of America; Figure 7-32a, CompactFlash 4.0 Sandisk, Courtesy of Sandisk Corporation; Figure 7-32b, SmartMedia 32MB to 128MB, Courtesy of Sandisk Corporation; Figure 7-32c, SecureDigital card 64MB to 1 GB, Courtesy of Sandisk Corporation; Figure 7-32d, 1G xD-Picture Card 64 MB to 512 MB, Courtesy of Lexar Media, Inc.; Figure 7-32e, memory stick 256MB to 2GB, Courtesy of Sandisk Corporation; Figure 7-33, SD card reader, Courtesy of Delkin Devices, Inc.; Figure 7-33b, SD card 1GB, Courtesy of Delkin Devices, Inc.; Figure 7-34, USB flash drive, Photo courtesy of Iomega Corporation. Copyright © 2003 Iomega Corporation. All Rights Reserved. Zip is a registered trademark in the United States and/or other countries. Iomega, the stylized "i" logo and product images are property of Iomega Corporation in the United States and/or other countries; Figure 7-35, smart card in use, © Jean-Yves Bruel/Masterfile; Figure 7-36a, microfilm in microfilm reader, Copyright ©Bill Aron/Photo Edit — All rights reserved.; Figure 7-36b, microfilm in roll, Copyright ©Bill Aron/Photo Edit — All rights reserved.; Figure 7-38a, home user, © Jose Luis Pelaez, Inc./CORBIS; Figure 7-38b, home office, © Britt Erlanson/Getty Images; Figure 7-38c, laptop user, © Andersen-Ross/Brand X Pictures; Figure 7-38d, Power user, © Richard T. Nowitz/CORBIS; Figure 7-38e, users in a large office, © Comstock Images; Career Corner, Computer Technician, © Noel Hendrickson/Masterfile; Technology Trailblazer 1, Al Shugart, Courtesy of Al Shugart International; Technology Trailblazer 2, Mark Dean, Courtesy of IBM Research; **Chapter 8:** PY8-01, college students talking outside, © Mark Scott/Getty Images; PY8-02, new mail message screen, © VCL/Spencer Rowell/Getty Images; PY8-03, distraught female looking at screen, © Paul Thomas/Getty Images; PY8-04, female hand holding a phone, © Masterfile Royalty-free; PY8-05, distraught male on phone, Lawrence Lawry/PhotoDisc/Getty Images; PY8-07, Norton Internet Security boxshot, Courtesy of Symantec; PY8-08, Windows XP boxshot, Courtesy of Microsoft Coporation; PY8-09, technical support center, Manchan/PHotoDisc/Getty Images; PY8-10, Windows XP installation screen, Courtesy of Microsoft Corporation; PY8-11, Windows splash screen, Courtesy of Microsoft Coporation; Figure 8-01a, hand switching on computer, © Gary Herrington Photography; Figure 8-01b, memory module, Courtesy of Kingston Technology; Figure 8-01c, laser printer, Courtesy of Lexmark; Figure 8-01d, CPU, monitor, keyboard,speakers, Courtesy of Acer; Figure 8-01e, system unit, Courtesy of Acer; Figure 8-03, monitor, keyboard and mouse, Courtesy of Motion Computing; Figure 8-07a, memory module, Courtesy of Kingston Technology; Figure 8-07b, hard disk, Courtesy of Seagate Technology; Figure 8-08a, server, Courtesy of IBM Corporation; Figure 8-08b, hard disk, Courtesy of Seagate Technology; Figure 8-08c, laser printer, Courtesy of Lexmark; Looking Ahead 8-1, longhorn, © PhotoDisc Collection/Getty Images; Figure 8-26, Media Center PC, © Getty Images; Figure 8-26b, Windows XPscreenshot, Courtesy of Microsoft Corporation; Figure 8-27, Mac OSX screenshot, Screenshot reprinted by permission from Apple Computer, Inc.; Figure 8-28, UNIX screenshot, Courtesy of the K Destop Environment; Figure 8-29, RedHat Linux screenshot, Courtesy of RedHat; Looking Ahead 8-2, Linux Penguin, Courtesy of The Gimp, lewing@isc.tamu.edu; Figure 8-30, Vonage softphone, Courtesy of Vonage; Figure 8-31a, Pocket PC using Windows Mobile, Courtesy of Fujitsu Siemens; Figure 8-31b, smart phone using Windows Mobile, Courtesy of Microsoft Coporation; Figure 8-32a, Palm powered PDA, Courtesy of palmOne, Inc. palmOne, Zire, Tungsten, Treo, logos, stylizations and design marks associated with all the preceding, and trade dress associated with palmOne, Inc.'s products, are among the trademarks or registered trademarks owned by or exclusively licensed to palmOne, Inc.; Figure 8-32b, Palm powered smartphone, Courtesy of Kyocera; Figure 8-33, Sharp Zaurus, Courtesy of Sharp Electronics; Figure 8-34, Symbian Operating system smartphone, Courtesy of Symbian; Figure 8-38, Roxio Easy Media Creator 7, Courtesy of Roxio; Figure 8-39, Norton System Works, Courtesy of Symantec; Career Corner, systems programmer, © MTPA Stock/Masterfile; Technology Trailblazer, Alan Kay, © AP/Wide World Photos; Technology Trailblazer, Linus Torvalds, © Kim Kulish/CORBIS; **Special Feature: Buyer's Guide:**, Intro 1, desktop computer, Courtesy of Acer America Corp.; Intro 2, iMac, Courtesy of Apple Computer, Inc.; 8SF, Intro 3, notebook, Courtesy of Acer America Corp.; Intro 4, background art, © Jason Reed/Photodisc/Getty Images; Figure 01a, desktop computer, Courtesy of IBM Corporation; Figure 8-01b1, mobile computer, Courtesy of Sony Electronics, Inc.; Figure 01b2, notebook computer\ tablet PC, Courtesy of Motion Computing; Figure 01c1, personal mobile device, Courtesy of palmOne, Inc. palmOne, Zire, Tungsten, Treo, logos, stylizations and design marks associated with all the preceding, and trade dress associated with palmOne, Inc.'s products, are among the trademarks or registered trademarks owned by or exclusively licensed to palmOne, Inc.; Figure 01c2, smartphone or PDA, Siemens press picture; Figure 01d, African-American female, Digital Vision/Getty Images; Figure 04a, CD\ DVD drives, Courtesy of JVC; Figure 04b, Card Reader\ Writer, Courtesy of Sandisk; Figure 04c, Digital Camera, Courtesy of UMAX; Figure 04d, Digital Video Capture Device, Courtesy of Pinnacle Systems, Inc.; Figure 04f, Hard Disk, Courtesy of Seagate; Figure 04g, Joystick\ Wheel, Courtesy of Logitech; Figure 04h, Keyboard, Courtesy of Microsoft; Figure 04j, Modem, Courtesy of US Robotics; Figure 04k, Monitor, Courtesy of ViewSonic Corporation; Figure 04l, Mouse, Courtesy of Microsoft; Figure 04m, Network Card, Courtesy of 3Com Corporation; Figure 04n, Printer, Courtesy of EPSON America, Inc.; Figure 04o, Processer, Courtesy of Intel Corporation; Figure 04p, RAM, Courtesy of Kingston Technology; Figure 04q, Scanner, Courtesy of UMAX; Figure 04s, Speakers, Courtesy of Logitech; Figure 04t, PC Video Camera, Courtesy of Logitech; Figure 04u, USB Flash Drive, Courtesy of Sandisk; Figure 04v, Video Graphics Card, Courtesy of 3Com Corporation; Figure 04x, Zip Drive, Photo Courtesy of Iomega Corporation. Copyright © 2003 Iomega Corporation. All Rights Reserved. Zip is a registered trademark in the United States and/or other countries. Iomega, the stylized "i" logo and product images are property of Iomega Corporation in the United States and/or other countries.; Figure 12, notebook computer converts to a Tablet PC, Courtesy of Toshiba America Information Systems, Inc.;, Figure 13, notebook computer carrying case, Courtesy of Toshiba America Information Systems, Inc.; Figure 14, a notebook computer connected to a video projector, Britt Erlanson/Getty Images; Figure 16, Tablet PC with handwriting, Thomas Barwick/PhotoDisc Collection/Getty Images; Figure 19, Tablet PC with handwriting, Courtesy of ViewSonic Corporation; Figure 21, A Tablet PC docked, Courtesy of Fujitsu Siemens Computers; **Chapter 9:** PY9-1, car driving on autumn road, © Getty Images; PY9-2, T-mobile sign in Starbucks, © James Leynse/CORBIS; PY9-3, Centrino logo from Intel, Courtesy of Intel Corporation; PY9-4, wireless PC card modem, Courtesy of Sierra Wireless Inc.; PY9-5, laptop on table at Starbucks, ©LWA-Stephen Welstead/CORBIS; PY9-6, antique store exterior, © Hubert Stadler/CORBIS; PY9-7, Couple taking pictures with smartphone, Siemens press picture; PY9-8, suitcase with electronic devices, © Nick Koudis/Getty Images; PY9-9, GPS device for PDA, Courtesy of Socket Communications, Inc.; Figure 9-1a, Mainframe computer, Courtesy of Fujitsu Siemens Computers; Figure 9-1b, mid-range server, Courtesy of Acer America Corp.; Figure 9-1c, desktop computer, Courtesy of IBM Corporation; Figure 9-1d, notebook computer, Courtesy of Acer America Corp.; Figure 9-1e, TabletPC, Courtesy of Motion Computing; Figure 9-1f, smart phone, Courtesy of Motorola, Inc.; Figure 9-1g, Internet-enabled PDA with Internet screen, Courtesy of Fujitsu Siemens Computers; Figure 9-1h, car that has built-in GPS capability, Toyota photo; Figure 9-03a, teens using smart phone, © Kaz Mori/Getty Images; Figure 9-03b, home user, ©LWA-Dann Tardif/CORBIS; Figure 9-03c, adult male using smart phone, © Digital Vision; Figure 9-04a, people in a coffee shop, © Justin Sullivan/Getty Images; Figure 9-04b, Centrino Logo, Courtesy of Intel Corporation; Figure 9-04c, wireless network PC card, Courtesy of Linksys, a Division of Cisco Systems Inc.; Figure 9-04d, T-Mobile "hotspot" sign in Starbucks, © James Leynse/Corbis; Figure 9-05, people in Cybercafe, © Ryan McVay/Getty Images; Figure 9-06a1, GPS device that goes in dash of car, Courtesy of Garmin Ltd.; Figure 9-06a2, car, © George Simhoni/Masterfile; Figure 9-06b1, Child's GPS locator watch, Courtesy of Wherify Wireless, Inc.; Figure 9-06b2, child in playground, Courtesy of Wherify Wireless, Inc.; Figure 9-06c1, smartphone with GPS, © Siemens AG Press Pictures; Figure 9-06c2, person using GPS device, © Jasper James/Getty Images; Figure 9-06d1, handheld GPS device, Courtesy of Garmin Ltd.; Figure 9-06d2, Person hiking, using GPS device, © Ron Chapple/Getty Images; Figure 9-06e1, Pet collar with GPS, Courtesy of GPS Tracks, Inc.; Figure 9-06e2, dog, © Dante Burn-Forti/Getty Images; Figure 9-07, female headshot, © Jose Luis Pelaez, Inc./CORBIS; Figure 9-08a, person using smart phone, © Javier Pierini/Getty Images; Figure 9-08b, person using PDA, © Jon Feingersh/CORBIS; Figure 9-08c, person using desktop computer in business office setting, © Andersen Ross/Brand X Pictures; Figure 9-08d, web-server, Copyright 2005 Sun Microsystems, Inc. All Rights Reserved. Used by permission.; Figure 9-08d2, another web-server, Copyright 2005 Sun Microsystems, Inc. All Rights Reserved. Used by permission.; Figure 9-10, multi-story office building, © Image Source/Imagestate; Figure 9-11, wireless access point, Courtesy of 3Com Corporation; Figure 9-11b, desktop PC, Courtesy of Acer America Corp.; Figure 9-11c, notebook computer, Courtesy of Courtesy of Toshiba America Information Systems, Inc.; Figure 9-18a, network hub, Courtesy of SMC Networks Inc.; Figure 9-18b, desktop PC, Courtesy of Acer America Corp.; Figure 9-18c, desktop PC, Courtesy of Sony Electronics Inc.; Figure 9-19a, female using desktop computer, © Jose Luis Pelaez, Inc./CORBIS; Figure 9-19b, web-server, Courtesy of Fujitsu Siemens Computers; Figure 9-21 Step 1, E-Z pass RFID reader, © E-ZPass/Getty Images; Figure 9-21 Step 1, transponder in windshield, © James Leynse/CORBIS; Figure 9-21 Step 2, electronic collection tollbooths, © James Leynse/CORBIS; Figure 9-21 Step 3, desktop PC, Courtesy of Acer America Corp.; Figure 9-25a, desktop PC, Courtesy of Sony Electronics Inc.; Figure 9-25b, ADSL modem, Courtesy of Zoom Technologies, Inc.; Figure 9-26a, digital modem, Courtesy of Toshiba America Information Systems, Inc.; Figure 9-26b, internal dial-up modem card (v.90/v.92 - 56K), Courtesy of Cnet USA, Inc.; Figure 9-26c, computer, Courtesy of Acer America Corp.; Figure 9-26d, computer, Courtesy of Sony Electronics Inc.; Figure 9-27, internal dial-up modem card, Courtesy of U.S. Robotics Corporation; Figure 9-28a, computer, Courtesy of Saenix Technology Inc.; Figure 9-28b, external cable modem, Courtesy of Motorola, Inc.; Figure 9-28c, modern looking television, Courtesy of Panasonic; Figure 9-28d, cable company, © Erik S. Lesser/Bloomberg News/Landov; Figure 9-29a, notebook computer, Courtesy of Toshiba America Information Systems, Inc.; Figure 9-29b, wireless modem PC card with antenna up, Courtesy of Sierra Wireless Inc.; Figure 9-30a, Internal network card for desktop computer, Courtesy of Linksys, a Division of Cisco Systems Inc.; Figure 9-30b, Network 10/100 PC card (for notebook), Courtesy of Linksys, a Division of Cisco Systems Inc.; Figure 9-31a, Wireless access point (802.11g), Courtesy of Linksys, a Division of Cisco Systems Inc.; Figure 9-31b, map of college grounds, Copyright ©Bonnie Kamin/Photo Edit — All rights reserved.; Figure 9-31c, student using laptop in classroom, Copyright ©CLEO PHOTOGRAPHY/Photo Edit — All rights reserved.; Figure 9-31d, student using laptop in school library, © F64/Getty Images; Figure 9-31e, students using laptop in dorm, Copyright ©Michael Newman/Photo Edit — All rights reserved.; Figure 9-32a, cable or dsl modem, Courtesy of Zoom Technologies, Inc.; Figure 9-32b, broadband router, Courtesy of SMC Networks Inc.; Figure 9-32c, printer, Courtesy of Epson America, Inc.; Figure 9-32d, PC, Courtesy of Acer America Corp.; Figure 9-32e, PC, Courtesy of Sony Electronics Inc.; Figure 9-33, hub, Courtesy of 3Com Corporation; Figure 9-34a, PDA with wireless network card, Courtesy of Sony Electronics Inc.; Figure 9-34b, notebook with Centrino technology, Courtesy of Seanix Technology Inc.; Figure 9-34c, cable/dsl modem, Courtesy of Toshiba America Information Systems, Inc.; Figure 9-34d, COMBINATION router/wireless access point, Courtesy of U.S. Robotics Corporation; FAQ 9-10, Chart, Reprinted with permission of WebSiteOptimization.com; Looking Ahead 9-1, Broadband Sparks Portal Services, © Sanford/Agliolo/CORBIS; Figure 9-42, Microwave ground station, © Vince Streano/CORBIS; Figure 9-43, communications satellite showing earth-based stations, © Antonio M Rosario/Getty Images; Looking Ahead 9-2, Hear the Music on a Smart Phone, courtesy of Mobile Broadcasting Corporation (MBCO); Career Corner, Network administrator (specialist), © Dana Hursey/Masterfile; Technology Trailblazer 1, Robert Metcalfe, inventor of Ethernet, © Kim Kulish/Corbis; Technology Trailblazer, Patricia Russo, Lucent Technologies, © WOLFGANG VON BRAUCHITSCH/BLOOMBERG NEWS;/Landov; Chapter Review, tablet PC user, © Comstock Images; **Chapter 10:** PY10-01, businesswoman thinking, © Larry Williams/CORBIS; PY10-02, businesswoman at home, © Larry Williams/CORBIS; PY10-03, On-line grocery delivery, © UPI/Landov; PY10-04, On-line shopping cart icon, © Rob Atkins/Getty Images; PY10-05, businesswoman at bank, © Keith Brofsky/Getty Images; PY10-06, on-line banking, "Credit", © Antonio M Rosario/Getty Images; PY10-07, document folder stamped "Approved", © Dennie Cody/Getty Images; PY10-08, businesswoman greeting friend outdoors, © Emily Shur/Getty Images; Figure 10-01 Step 1, headshot sideways, © Chabruken/Getty Images; Figure 10-01 Step 1, digital camera, Courtesy of Umax Systems GmbH; Figure 10-01 Step 1, tripod, Copyright ©Tony Freeman/Photo Edit — All rights reserved.; Figure 10-01 Step 1, headshot forward, © Chabruken/Getty Images; Figure 10-01 Step 1, keyboard/monitor/mouse set, Courtesy of Fujitsu Siemens Computers; Figure 10-01 Step 3, PC, Courtesy of Fujitsu Siemens Computers; Figure 10-01 Step 4, color laser printer, Courtesy of Epson America, Inc.; Figure 10-01 Step 5, Handing photo ID card or hand holding ID card, © Carlos Alvarez/Getty Images; Figure 10-01 Step 5, color ID printer, Courtesy of Fargo Electronics, Inc.; Figure 10-1, discount warehouse, © RICHARD SHEINWALD/Bloomberg News/Landov; Figure 10-02, shopping warehouse, Copyright ©Robert W. Ginn/Photo Edit — All rights reserved.; Figure 10-5, headshot, © Chabruken/Getty Images; Figure 10-6, headshot, © Chabruken/Getty Images; Figure 10-7, headshot of female, © Mitch Diamond/Imagestate; Figure 10-9a, employee working on a computer, Copyright ©Spencer Grant/Photo Edit — All rights reserved.; Figure 10-9b, customer in a checkout line, © THOMAS ENGLAND/BLOOMBERG NEWS/Landov; Looking Ahead 10-1, Having a Voice with Web Databases, ©LWA-JDC/CORBIS; Figure 10-17, headshot, © Chabruken/Getty Images; Figure 10-25, PDA/smart phone accessing a database, Courtesy of Symbol Technologies; Looking Ahead 10-2, Preserving Electronic Files for Future Generations, © Lester Lefkowitz/CORBIS; Career Corner Box, Database Administrator, © Yang Liu/CORBIS; Technology Trailblazer 1, E.F. Codd, Courtesy of the National Academy of Engineering; Technology Trailblazer 2, Larry Ellison, © Justin Sullivan/Getty Images; **Chapter 11:** PY11-01, security screen, © Don Farrall/Getty Images; PY11-02, new email screen, © Daisuke Morita/PhotoDisc/Getty Images; PY11-03, woman at laptop with credit card, ©Peter Scholey/Getty Images; PY11-04, password screen, © Comstock Images/Getty Images; PY11-05, surge protector, Courtesy of American Power Conversion Corp.; PY11-06, hotel computer work area, © Rob Melnychuk/Getty Images; PY11-08, lightning strike, Martial Trezzini/EPA/Landov; PY11-09, doctor pointing to woman's wrist, © Digital Vision/Getty Images; PY11-10, hand holding wrist, © Michael Keller/CORBIS; PY11-11, hand on mouse, © Thinkstock/Getty Images; Figure 11-01a, distraught person at computer, © Royalty-Free/CORBIS; Figure 11-01b1, Hardware theft: empty computer case, © Thinkstock; Figure 11-01b2, Hardware theft: public area, © Zoran Milich/Masterfile; Figure 11-01c, Illegal Copying: CDs, Copyright ©David Young-Wolff/Photo Edit — All rights reserved.; Figure 11-01d, Information Theft: hands using computer with screen visible, © Paul Eekhoff/Masterfile; Figure 11-01e, System Failure: monitor with black screen, Courtesy of Sony Electronics Inc.; Figure 11-01e, Internet and network attacks: system unit/monitor, Courtesy of Acer America Corp.; Figure 11-01f, Unauthorized access and use: